Communications in Computer and Information Science 2842

Rationale
The CCIS series is devoted to the publication of proceedings of computer science conferences. Its aim is to efficiently disseminate original research results in informatics in printed and electronic form. While the focus is on publication of peer-reviewed full papers presenting mature work, inclusion of reviewed short papers reporting on work in progress is welcome, too. Besides globally relevant meetings with internationally representative program committees guaranteeing a strict peer-reviewing and paper selection process, conferences run by societies or of high regional or national relevance are also considered for publication.

Topics
The topical scope of CCIS spans the entire spectrum of informatics ranging from foundational topics in the theory of computing to information and communications science and technology and a broad variety of interdisciplinary application fields.

Information for Volume Editors and Authors
Publication in CCIS is free of charge. No royalties are paid, however, we offer registered conference participants temporary free access to the online version of the conference proceedings on SpringerLink (http://link.springer.com) by means of an http referrer from the conference website and/or a number of complimentary printed copies, as specified in the official acceptance email of the event.

CCIS proceedings can be published in time for distribution at conferences or as post-proceedings, and delivered in the form of printed books and/or electronically as USBs and/or e-content licenses for accessing proceedings at SpringerLink. Furthermore, CCIS proceedings are included in the CCIS electronic book series hosted in the SpringerLink digital library at http://link.springer.com/bookseries/7899. Conferences publishing in CCIS are allowed to use our online conference service (Meteor) for managing the whole proceedings lifecycle (from submission and reviewing to preparing for publication) free of charge.

Publication process
The language of publication is exclusively English. Authors publishing in CCIS have to sign the Springer CCIS copyright transfer form, however, they are free to use their material published in CCIS for substantially changed, more elaborate subsequent publications elsewhere. For the preparation of the camera-ready papers/files, authors have to strictly adhere to the Springer CCIS Authors' Instructions and are strongly encouraged to use the CCIS LaTeX style files or templates.

Abstracting/Indexing
CCIS is abstracted/indexed in DBLP, Google Scholar, EI-Compendex, Mathematical Reviews, SCImago, Scopus. CCIS volumes are also submitted for the inclusion in ISI Proceedings.

How to start
To start the evaluation of your proposal for inclusion in the CCIS series, please send an e-mail to ccis@springer.com

Irena Koprinska · João Mendes-Moreira ·
Paula Branco
Editors

Machine Learning and Principles and Practice of Knowledge Discovery in Databases

International Workshops of ECML PKDD 2025
Porto, Portugal, September 15–19, 2025
Revised Selected Papers, Part IV

Springer

Editors
Irena Koprinska
University of Sydney
Sydney, NSW, Australia

João Mendes-Moreira
University of Porto
Porto, Portugal

Paula Branco
University of Ottawa
Ottawa, ON, Canada

ISSN 1865-0929 ISSN 1865-0937 (electronic)
Communications in Computer and Information Science
ISBN 978-3-032-19104-5 ISBN 978-3-032-19105-2 (eBook)
https://doi.org/10.1007/978-3-032-19105-2

This Springer imprint is published by the registered company Springer Nature Switzerland AG
The registered company address is: Gewerbestrasse 11, 6330 Cham, Switzerland

Contents

Workshop on Interactive eXplainable Artificial Intelligence, Theory and Practice (IXAIT 2025)

Workshop on Learning on Real and Synthetic Medical Time Series Data (MED-TIME 2025)

Workshop on Responsible Healthcare using Machine Learning (RHCML 2025)

Workshop for Explainable AI in Time Series and Data Streams (TempXAI 2025)

Workshop on eXplainable Knowledge Discovery in Data Mining and Unlearning (XKDD and Beyond 2025)

International Workshop on Interactive Adaptive Learning (IAL 2025)

International Workshop on Interactive Adaptive Learning (IAL 2025)

Methods of machine learning often reach their limits when high-quality training data are scarce. The reasons for such data scarcity are manifold: limited capabilities of human supervisors and processing systems, the need for early predictions that can only be refined later, or transfer settings where the available data originate from a different learning task.

Situations like these demand methods that enhance the overall life cycle of machine learning models, including interactions with human supervisors, integration with other processing systems, and adaptation to various forms of data that become available at different points in time. This demand includes techniques for evaluating the impact of additional resources (e.g., data) on the learning process; strategies for actively selecting information to process or query; methods for reusing knowledge over time and across domains or tasks by recognizing similarities and adapting to changes; and approaches for effectively leveraging diverse types of information, such as labeled and unlabeled data, constraints, and knowledge. Such techniques are being explored in areas like adaptive, active, semi-supervised, and transfer learning. While these investigations often occur independently of one another, real-world use cases demand interactive and adaptive systems capable of operating under changing conditions while addressing challenges related to the volume, velocity, and variability of data.

The 9th edition of the Interactive Adaptive Learning workshop continues to foster research on systems that integrate multiple areas of interactive and adaptive machine learning by bringing together researchers and practitioners from diverse fields. We welcomed contributions that introduce novel problems, propose new approaches, report practical experiences with such systems, or pose open questions to the research community. Submissions could span a full paper or an extended abstract and were reviewed under a double-blind policy. IAL 2025 builds upon a successful series of eight previous editions co-located annually with ECML PKDD between 2017 and 2024.

This year we accepted four papers out of seven submissions. The main themes addressed in the accepted papers emerged as active learning and reinforcement learning.

We thank all authors for their valuable submissions and all members of the program committee for their outstanding support.

October 2025

Mirko Bunse
Denis Huseljic
Georg Krempl
Vincent Lemaire
Minh Tuan Pham
Amal Saadallah
Alaa Tharwat

Organization

Organizing Committee

Mirko Bunse	Lamarr Institute for Machine Learning and Artificial Intelligence, Germany
Denis Huseljic	University of Kassel, Germany
Georg Krempl	Utrecht University, Netherlands
Vincent Lemaire	Orange Research, France
Minh Tuan Pham	University of Kassel, Germany
Amal Saadallah	Lamarr Institute for Machine Learning and Artificial Intelligence, Germany
Alaa Tharwat	Bielefeld University of Applied Sciences and Arts (HSBI), Germany

Steering Committee

Barbara Hammer	Bielefeld University, Germany
Andreas Holzinger	University of Natural Resources and Life Sciences Vienna, Austria
Daniel Kottke	Deutsche Bahn, Germany
Bernhard Sick	University of Kassel, Germany

Program Committee

Alexandre Abraham	Neuralk-AI, France
Christian Beyer	Otto-von-Guericke University Magdeburg, Germany
Michiel Bron	Utrecht University, Netherlands
Marek Herde	University of Kassel, Germany
Martin Holeňa	Czech Academy of Sciences, Czech Republic
Yvan Saeys	Ghent University, Belgium
Myra Spiliopoulou	University of Magdeburg, Germany
Christoph Zimmer	Baden-Wuerttemberg Cooperative State University, Germany

Low Query Budget Active Learning for Classification and Regression

Bjarne Jaster(✉), Alaa Tharwat, Eiram Mahera Sheikh, Martin Kohlhase, and Wolfram Schenck

Center for Applied Data Science (CfADS), HSBI - Bielefeld University of Applied Sciences and Arts, Bielefeld, Germany
{bjarne.jaster,alaa.othman,eiram_mahera.sheikh,martin.kohlhase, wolfram.schenck}@hsbi.de

Abstract. The labeling process for supervised learning is costly and time-consuming, and is often impractical to scale due to real-world constraints. Active learning (AL) addresses this challenge by strategically selecting representative and informative data points to reduce labeling efforts. This paper focuses on an AL scenario in which only a very limited number of labels can be acquired. We propose an algorithm operating in two phases: (1) an exploration phase that prioritizes representative and diverse data points using density-driven criteria, and (2) an exploitation phase that combines predictive uncertainty with density weighting to select informative samples from densely populated regions. This enhances both representativeness and informativeness. Our results demonstrate significant improvements in model quality compared to other algorithms typically employed for this scenario, across various scenarios involving imbalanced data in classification tasks and skewness in regression tasks. Through this work, we aim to provide a new algorithm for this scenario and investigate general principles for AL. While most AL studies focus on either classification or regression, our work applies the algorithms to both. Therefore, we can analyze the differences between classification and regression problems and their effects on AL strategies. Furthermore, we explore different categories of AL criteria and their effectiveness in the low-budget regime. These results also provide insight into the cold-start problem, which involves selecting an initial labeled set and is faced by many model-based AL methods.

Keywords: Active Learning · Classification · Regression · Low Query Budget

1 Introduction

In the field of machine learning (ML), there are large repositories of unlabeled data that hold a considerable potential. However, to unlock this potential and use them for ML labeling is necessary. The labeling process of these datasets often

I. Koprinska et al. (Eds.): ECML PKDD 2025, CCIS 2842, pp. 5–21, 2026.
https://doi.org/10.1007/978-3-032-19105-2_1

requires human effort, time, and resources. This bottleneck hinders the development of ML models in many scenarios. The challenge is therefore to maximize model performance with minimal labeling effort, a problem that active learning (AL) attempts to address by intelligently selecting the most informative data points for annotation [8,22]. The core principle of AL involves an iterative process in which a learning algorithm actively selects the most informative unlabeled data points from a larger pool and queries an oracle - often a human expert - to obtain the labels. These newly labeled samples are then used to train a model, which guides the learning process in a way that improves model accuracy (e.g. by providing uncertainty estimates). This strategic selection reduces labeling costs and accelerates training, making AL a valuable tool in many domains [8].

AL is generally applicable to both classification and regression tasks, with three typical application scenarios: pool-based sampling, where the learner selects points from a large pool of unlabeled data; stream-based selective sampling, where the decision to query a label must be made without knowing which points will arrive later in the data stream; and membership query synthesis, where the learner generates novel points for labeling [16]. This work focuses on pool-based sampling.

To select the best data points, each AL strategy has its own heuristics to determine the importance of all available unlabeled points. These heuristics are typically categorized into two general approaches: Exploration and Exploitation [22]. Exploration-based AL methods aim to select representative or diverse data points that represent the data distribution. Exploitation-based methods select data points using an ML model trained on the previously selected data points. They use the information provided by the model (e.g., the uncertainty of the predictions) to assign a value indicating the informativeness of the data points. Because of their reliance on the ML model, exploitation-based AL methods are also referred to as model-based AL methods, whereas exploration-based methods are termed model-free [6].

Most studies on AL focus on scenarios where a reasonable amount of data points are queried. In Deep AL, thousands of points are queried (e.g. [19]) and even in works that cover small datasets that have less than 50 dimensions and at most a few thousand data points, the query budget often comprises around 100 data points (e.g. [5,6,13,15]). Only very few studies deal with AL scenarios where an extremely low budget is present. One study investigating this topic in the context of Deep AL provides theoretical and empirical evidence that including model-based criteria such as uncertainty in the low-budget regime of the AL process is ineffective [3]. They claim that this phenomenon occurs because model-based criteria depend on ML models that are of low quality due to limited training data. This study focuses on Deep AL and therefore the authors consider a few hundred points to still be in the low-budget regime. Going away from Deep Learning and Big Data these budgets may not be realistic anymore. For modelling very expensive and/or time-consuming processes, potentially only 15 or 20 data points can be selected. One example of such a process is the curing of concrete, which depends on many factors, including storage conditions, and

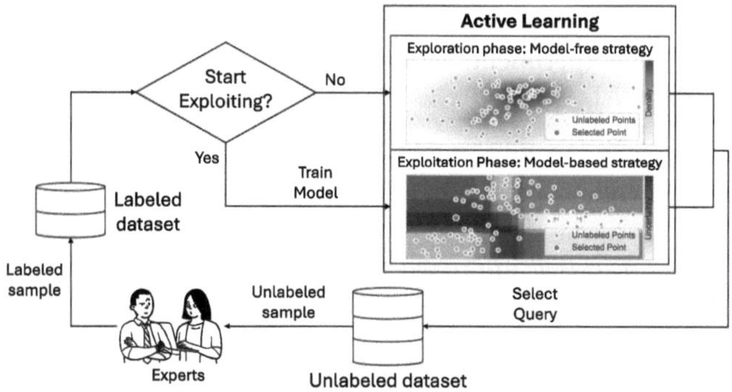

Fig. 1. Overview of the proposed AL strategy for the small data, low-budget regime.

can take up to a month [12]. A company would most likely not be able to afford to conduct a hundred experiments for this process, as it would take years and require significant storage capacity. Another example is the growth of plants. Some plants can only be harvested once a year, so again, very few experiments are realistic [2].

For these small data, low query budget scenarios, the question remains as to whether the observations made in [3] for deep AL are still valid. To investigate this question, we propose a novel AL method. This method consists of two phases: an exploration phase, which is model-free, and an exploitation phase, which incorporates model-based information into the selection process (see Fig. 1). By controlling the point at which the phase transition occurs in the AL process, we can investigate the usefulness of a model-based criterion.

In summary, the main contributions of this work are as follows: We propose and evaluate this two-phase AL strategy, specifically tailored to the small data, low-budget regime. This method is compared to several others that are typically used to initialize AL methods (see, e.g., [5,6,13]) and are therefore also used in the low-budget regime. Based on the results of this comparison, we aim to address the following research questions (RQs) in both the classification and regression settings. This will enable us to provide further insights into the differences between the two settings, a research area that has not been investigated much.

- RQ1: Does the inclusion of model-based AL criteria help in small data, low-budget scenarios? If yes, at which point should the inclusion happen?
- RQ2: Which types of AL criteria (density-, cluster-, distance-, informativeness-based) are generally important to consider for a high-quality, low-budget AL method?

The rest of the paper is organized as follows: Sect. 2 reviews related work, comparing exploration, exploitation, and hybrid approaches. Section 3 details the proposed model. Section 4 presents the experimental analysis conducted to evaluate the performance of the proposed method. Finally, Sect. 5 discusses the findings, answers the RQs and outlines directions for future work. The code of our method and the experiments can be found on https://github.com/bjaster/Low-Query-Budget-AL.

2 Related Work

AL is a *partially-supervised* approach that combines labeled ($\mathcal{L}$) and unlabeled data ($\mathcal{U}$). It uses an iterative query strategy to find new points $\mathbf{x}^*$ for labeling, as follows:

$$\mathbf{x}^* = \underset{\mathbf{x} \in \mathcal{U}}{\operatorname{argmax}}\, \phi(\mathbf{x}, h) \tag{1}$$

Here, $\phi(\cdot)$ quantifies the informativeness of an unlabeled instance $\mathbf{x}$ relative to the current model h [22]. In this section, we will discuss how other studies handle AL in the low-budget regime. Although few studies address this issue directly, there are related challenges for which similar approaches are used.

One of these challenges is called the *cold start* or *initialization problem*, where no labeled data is initially available to train an ML-model to guide a model-based AL process. Since model-based AL methods depend heavily on the quality of the initial dataset, providing this dataset is critical, as an inaccurate initial model understanding may negatively affect the selection process [1]. For this reason, we first examine how the existing model-based AL literature approaches the creation of the initial labeled set. While this is not the primary focus of these works, their strategies offer valuable insights. We then provide a concise overview of common model-based AL strategies.

2.1 Exploration-Based Approaches

Most works on AL use a random selection to select the initial dataset (e.g. [15]). However, there are a few works that use model-free or exploration-based AL methods. The aim of these methods is to select samples that represent the data distribution and are diverse from each other, thus ensuring efficient coverage of the input space. In [5], Greedy Sampling (GSx) [25] is used for initialization to provide a deterministic and diverse initial dataset. In [6], GSx and iterative Representativeness and Diversity Maximization (iRDM) [10] are used for providing the initial labeled set. These two methods are examples for the two main paradigms that are used in model-free AL. While iRDM mainly focuses on representativeness, GSx maximizes diversity.

Representativeness-based AL methods select samples that reflect the overall data distribution, with the goal of selecting a subset that is similar to the whole dataset [26]. A common strategy to achieve representative samples is cluster-based sampling. Classical algorithms such as k-means clustering [11] have inspired several AL methods that use cluster centroids or structural information to guide sample selection [4,24]. Two notable examples, also used later in this work, are the already mentioned iRDM and TypiClust [3]. The iRDM algorithm [10] first clusters the unlabeled pool and selects samples closest to each cluster center. It then optimizes this selection to avoid redundant queries (more details in Sect. 3). TypiClust is presented in the same work that investigates low-budget AL (see Sect. 1) as a method specifically suited to this scenario [3]. It emphasizes coverage by targeting clusters that remain unrepresented in the labeled set. It selects the most "typical" point within each such cluster, where typicality is defined as the inverse of the average distance to its k nearest neighbors.

Diversity-based methods aim to maximize the distance between the selected points. GSx [25] starts by selecting the point closest to the centroid of the entire unlabeled pool. In subsequent rounds, it maximizes diversity by choosing the point furthest from all previously chosen samples in the input space.

2.2 Exploitation-Based Approaches

Exploitation-based approaches rely on the predictions of the current model to identify samples that are likely to improve performance when labeled. These techniques aim to fine-tune decision boundaries by focusing on regions that are either uncertain or informative. One classical approach is Query by Committee (QBC) [17], where multiple models are trained, and instances with the highest disagreement among the models are selected. Another well-known strategy is uncertainty sampling, where the model selects samples about which it is least confident [9,18]. A more model-driven approach is expected error reduction [14, 27], which estimates the reduction in generalization error that would result from labeling a candidate sample.

2.3 Hybrid Approaches

Pure exploration or exploitation may be sub-optimal. An overemphasis on exploration can lead to excessive sampling from uninformative regions. Conversely, excessive exploitation can result in to a high concentration of data points that provide only limited knowledge. This can lead to poor generalization and missed discovery of new patterns or classes. As a result, many recent approaches use hybrid strategies that dynamically balance exploration and exploitation. These techniques either begin with exploration to broadly characterize the input space and shift toward exploitation as the model becomes more reliable [21,23] or consider both exploration and exploitation criteria at all times by e.g. adding them [6,15]. For example, in [23], the authors' geometrical methods varied with each phase. First, PCA-inspired exploration investigated regions of high variance. Then, LDA-inspired exploitation focused on the boundary points between classes.

Building on this line of research, our work proposes a novel AL method for low-budget scenarios that explicitly balances exploration and exploitation. Our strategy first leverages the structural properties of the input space to later enable a model to identify regions of high uncertainty.

3 Proposed Method

We begin with the assumption that all available data are unlabeled, denoted as $\mathcal{U} = \{\mathbf{x}_1, \mathbf{x}_2, \ldots, \mathbf{x}_{n_u}\}$, where $\mathbf{x}_i \in \mathcal{U}$ represents an unlabeled data point and n_u is the total number of unlabeled points. The labeled dataset $\mathcal{L}$ is initially empty ($\mathcal{L} = \emptyset$). The budget B defines the number of data points that can be selected. Our method, called *Low Query Budget AL (LQBAL)*, comprises a two-phase approach:

1. **Initialization**: Our method selects m representative points from the unlabeled pool $\mathcal{U}$ using one of two strategies: **Cluster-based** or **Median-based** selection methods.
2. **Two-Phase Querying**: After initialization, a dynamic exploration-exploitation strategy queries points until the budget B is exhausted. The mode switches from exploration to exploitation depending on the hyperparameter $s \in [0, 1]$. This defines which fraction of the budget should be spent on each strategy, where $s = 0$ is pure exploitation after initialization, while $s = 1$ is pure exploration.
   - **Exploration** ($|\mathcal{L}|/B \leq s$): Focuses on dense regions and uses distance metrics to minimize redundancy.
   - **Exploitation** ($|\mathcal{L}|/B > s$): Focuses on dense and uncertain regions.

With this two-phase hybrid approach LQBAL balances broad data coverage with targeted refinement of model performance. At each iteration, the queried point is labeled, transferred from $\mathcal{U}$ to $\mathcal{L}$. When the exploitation mode is active, the model is retrained on the updated $\mathcal{L}$. The process terminates when $|\mathcal{L}| = B$, returning $\mathcal{L}$ and $\mathcal{U}$.

3.1 Initial Selection

LQBAL comprises two options to select the initial set of points. This initialization is necessary for the case $s = 1$, so that a model can be trained. The median-based method ensures representativeness and robustness to outliers [23], while the cluster-based maximizes the diversity and representativeness of the selected data [10].

Median-Based Initialization: The algorithm first removes outliers from $\mathbf{x}_i \in \mathcal{U}$ using the interquartile range (IQR) method:

$$\text{Lower Bound} = Q_1 - 1.5 \cdot \text{IQR}, \quad \text{Upper Bound} = Q_3 + 1.5 \cdot \text{IQR}, \tag{2}$$

where $\text{IQR} = Q_3 - Q_1$. The cleaned set $\mathcal{U}_c$ is then reduced via PCA [20] to retain components explaining at least τ variance (e.g., $\tau = 0.9$), yielding $\mathcal{U}_{c,r}$. In this space, the median, Q_1, and Q_3 are computed for each dimension and the nearest point is selected:

$$x_j^* = \underset{\mathbf{x}_i \in \mathcal{U}_{c,r}}{\operatorname{argmin}} \|\mathbf{x}_i - \mathbf{z}_j\|_2, \quad \mathbf{z}_j \in \{\mathbf{x}_{median}, \mathbf{x}_{Q_1}, \mathbf{x}_{Q_3}\}. \tag{3}$$

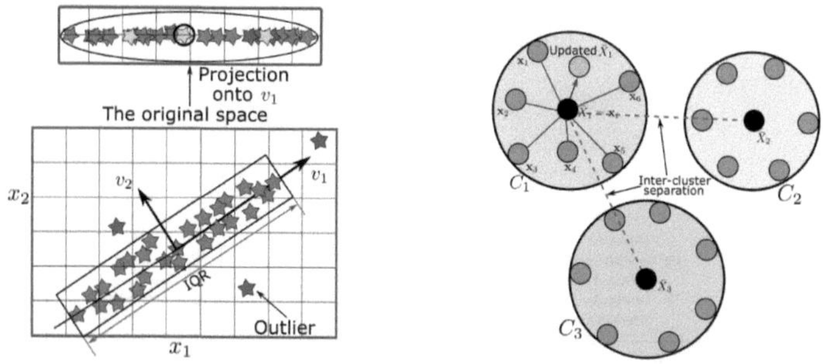

Fig. 2. Illustration of the two initialization methods used in our model. **(Left):** The median-based method removes outliers (red stars), projects the data onto the first PCA components, and queries the median, Q_1, and Q_3. **(Right):** The cluster-based method iteratively finds points that minimize intra-class density while maximizing inter-class separation. The black points represent the initial centroids; the blue point indicates the updated $\bar{X}_1$, while $\bar{X}_2$ and $\bar{X}_3$ remain fixed. (Color figure online)

These three points form the initial labeled set (see Fig. 2 left), covering central and quartile regions while avoiding outliers.

Cluster-Based Initialization: The iRDM strategy [10] balances two objectives: *representativeness* (selecting samples near cluster centroids to avoid outliers) and *diversity* (selecting from different clusters to cover the input space). First, K-means clustering is applied to the unlabeled set $\mathcal{U}$ with m clusters (default $m = 3$), yielding centroids $\{\bar{X}_1, \ldots, \bar{X}_m\}$. From each cluster C_j, the point closest to $\bar{X}_j$ is chosen: This selection is then iteratively refined ($c_{\max} = 5$ iterations) using *Intra-cluster Density* ($R(\mathbf{x}_i)$, illustrated by the blue lines in Fig. 2 right), which is defined as the mean distance to other points in the same cluster (lower is more representative) and *Inter-cluster Separation* ($\delta(\mathbf{x}_i)$, dashed lines in Fig. 2), which is the distance to the nearest centroid of another cluster (higher is more diverse). The optimal point per cluster maximizes

$$\mathbf{x}_j^* = \operatorname*{argmax}_{\mathbf{x}_i \in \mathcal{U}_{C_j}} \left(\delta(\mathbf{x}_i) - R(\mathbf{x}_i)\right) \tag{4}$$

Refining stops when the selected candidates do not change or $c_{\max}$ is reached. The resulting labeled set $\mathcal{L}$ balances representativeness and diversity, though it may still include noisy points.

3.2 Exploration Phase

This phase aims to provide a representative and diverse dataset to minimize the potentially negative effects of the strategy used to select the initial m points. The points are selected from high-density areas of the unlabeled data to ensure the selection is representative. For each unlabeled point $x_i \in \mathcal{U}$, the average distance to its k-nearest neighbors (default $k = 10$) is computed (similar to [3]):

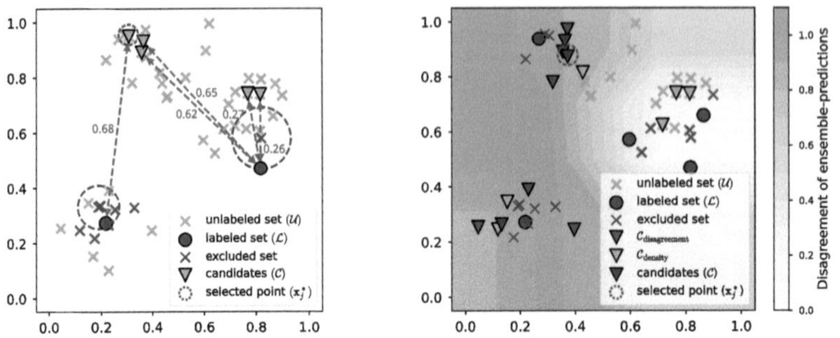

Fig. 3. **(Left)** Exploration phase strategy: The $t = 5$ most dense points are selected as candidates (orange triangles). The point with the highest distance (red dashed arrows) to already labeled points (blue dots) is chosen for labeling (blue dashed circle). Purple crosses indicate unlabeled data points that are excluded from the selection, because they have labeled points nearer than their AvgDist. For two excluded points the spheres with radius AvgDist are shown (purple dashed circles). **(Right)** Exploitation phase strategy: The intersection (purple triangles) between the points that are most dense (orange triangles) and the points with the highest disagreement (green triangles) represents the candidates (because the intersection was empty for $t = 5$ the $t = 10$ most dense and disagreed points are considered). From those the one with the highest nearest neighbor distance to the labeled points is selected (blue dashed circle). (Color figure online)

$$\text{AvgDist}(\mathbf{x}_i) = \frac{1}{k} \sum_{\mathbf{x}_j \in \mathcal{N}_k(\mathbf{x}_i)} \|\mathbf{x}_i - \mathbf{x}_j\|_2, \tag{5}$$

where $\mathcal{N}_k(\mathbf{x}_i)$ represents the set of the nearest k neighbors to the data point $\mathbf{x}_i$. To avoid redundant queries we exclude all unlabeled points $\mathbf{x}_i$ that have labeled points within a hypersphere with radius $\text{AvgDist}(\mathbf{x}_i)$ from further consideration (see purple circles in Fig. 3 (left) for two examples). The top t (default $t = 5$) points with the lowest $\text{AvgDist}(x_i)$ form the candidate set $\mathcal{C}$. From those candidates, the point with the largest nearest neighbor distance to the labeled set $\mathcal{L}$ is queried (see Fig. 3 (left) red arrows):

$$\mathbf{x}_j^* = \underset{\mathbf{x}_i \in \mathcal{C}}{\text{argmax}} \min_{\mathbf{x}_k \in \mathcal{L}} \|\mathbf{x}_i - \mathbf{x}_k\|_2 \tag{6}$$

By excluding points from dense regions that have already been explored and creating a candidate set based on maximum distance to labeled points, we ensure representativeness and diversity for a high-quality dataset that can be used in the exploitation phase.

3.3 Exploitation Phase

In this phase, the strategy includes a model-based exploitation criterion. For that we calculate the disagreement of a committee which is trained on $\mathcal{L}$ (corresponds to the QBC-criterion). The disagreement $\sigma(x_i)$ of the predictions for an unlabeled point is calculated as the standard deviation (regression) or the vote-entropy (classification) of the ensemble-predictions. However, rather than selecting points based solely on disagreement, we also consider the density of the points (Eq. 5) and exclude points near labeled points, as previously explained for the exploration phase. We identify the top t points (initially $t = 5$) with the highest disagreement and the top t points with the highest density. These candidate sets are denoted as $\mathcal{C}_{\text{disagreement}}$ and $\mathcal{C}_{\text{density}}$, respectively. The query selection is then done on the intersection of those candidate sets, which allows to select the points that are from both dense and uncertain regions:

$$\mathcal{C} = \mathcal{C}_{\text{disagreement}} \cap \mathcal{C}_{\text{density}}. \tag{7}$$

Out of $\mathcal{C}$, the point with the largest nearest neighbor distance to the labeled set $\mathcal{L}$ is queried (see Eq. 6). If $\mathcal{C} = \emptyset$, t is incremented by 5 and Eq. 7 and 6 are computed repeatedly until $\mathcal{C}$ is no longer empty and a selection can be made.

This strategy ensures that the selected points are not only informative, but also representative and diverse, enhancing the quality of the results.

4 Experimental Analysis

This section presents the results that help answer the RQs and evaluate the quality of our proposed method LQBAL. For that, we first perform a small hyperparameter study to evaluate which switch point and initialization method is best for classification and regression, respectively (RQ1). We then present the comparison of our method with other AL methods typically used for initial dataset creation (RQ2).

4.1 Experimental Settings

The comparison is performed on six regression and classification datasets. These datasets are mostly taken from the UCI repository[1] [7] with the exception of the PM10[2], Boston Housing[3] and Fish[4] datasets. The datasets are mostly small datasets with less than 1000 samples and less than 10 features, with a few exceptions like Pendigit and the Superconductivity which have a few thousand instances and up to 81 features. All classification datasets are multiclass datasets with a minimum of three classes and a maximum of ten classes. While the Iris, Pendigit and Segmentation datasets are balanced with roughly the same amount of points per class, the Fish and Glass datasets are imbalanced with a class-ratios of $[56, 34, 20, 17, 14, 11, 6]$ and $[76, 70, 29, 17, 13, 9]$ respectively. A detailed

[1] Original names (if not already used): Slump Strength → Concrete Slump Test, Superconductivity → Superconductivity Data, Wheat → Seeds, Segmentation → Image Segmentation, Pendigit → Pen-Based Recognition of Handwritten Digits, Glass → Glass Identification.

[2] https://lib.stat.cmu.edu/datasets/PM10.dat.

[3] https://lib.stat.cmu.edu/datasets/boston.

[4] https://www.utstat.utoronto.ca/brunner/data/legal/fish.txt.

Table 1. Characteristics of third-party datasets

Dataset	Classification			Regression		
	Classes	Feats.	Size	Dataset	Feats.	Size
Fish	7	6	159	Airfoil Self-Noise	5	1,503
Glass	6	9	214	Boston Housing	13	452
Iris	3	4	150	Real Estate Valuation	6	414
Pendigit	10	16	10,992	Slump Strength	7	103
Segmentation	7	19	2,310	Superconductivity	81	21,263
Wheat	3	7	210	Yacht Hydrodynamics	6	308

overview of the datasets is given in Table 1. These datasets were chosen because they are diverse in their number of features, classes and instances and allow to investigate the quality of different AL methods in different small data settings and to identify strength and weaknesses of each method.

A total of 100 independent runs of every AL method are performed on each dataset to obtain statistically meaningful results. First, for each run, the dataset is randomly split into an AL and test set, each containing 50% of the dataset. Importantly, this split is kept identical across all active learners, ensuring that each method operates under the same conditions for a fair comparison. The AL set represents the unlabeled pool from which the active learners can query data points. The test set is used for independent evaluation of the ML models trained on the queried points. Each active learner is allowed to query 15 data points. After the AL process, we evaluate the selection by training a Random Forest (RF) on the selected data points and computing the score (macro F1-score for classification, R2-score for regression) on the test set. The hyperparameters of the RF are set to default (scikit-learn) except for the ensemble size, which is increased to 200.

For the main benchmark of the classification setting we also investigate how many classes were covered by the active learner. For that we compute the percentage of classes covered after the selection of 15 data points and average it over the 100 runs. We investigate this metric since it is an important attribute of an AL method to find all classes in the dataset. While low-budget AL may not the right choice for datasets with more than five classes, we still wanted to provide this information to show the strengths and weaknesses of different AL methods.

4.2 Experimental Results

Hyperparameter Study: To determine the effect of incorporating a model-based AL criterion into low-budget AL, we evaluate the optimal value of the switch point hyperparameter s. Additionally, we compare the two presented initialization strategies, cluster-based and median-based. The classification results (see Table 2) indicate that the cluster-based initialization strategy consistently outperformed the median-based strategy, achieving peak average performance at $s = 0.0$ and $s = 0.3$. Generally, one can observe that performance decreases as s

Table 2. Hyperparameter study for different initialization strategies and switch points s (classification). Results are given as macro F1-score.

Init. strategy	Cluster-based					Median-based				
Switch point (s)	0.0	0.3	0.5	0.7	1.0	0.0	0.3	0.5	0.7	1.0
Fish	**0.594**	0.583	0.551	0.535	0.502	0.590	0.586	0.566	0.558	0.523
Glass	0.398	0.404	**0.431**	0.394	0.323	0.402	0.418	0.413	0.386	0.328
Iris	0.944	0.942	0.941	0.938	0.939	0.940	0.938	0.943	0.941	**0.945**
Pendigit	0.495	0.491	0.432	0.378	0.281	**0.496**	0.474	0.420	0.359	0.244
Segmentation	0.645	**0.663**	0.656	0.654	0.643	0.643	0.628	0.640	0.640	**0.663**
Wheat	0.890	0.885	0.883	0.882	0.878	**0.891**	0.888	0.884	0.880	0.878
Mean	**0.661**	**0.661**	0.649	0.630	0.594	0.660	0.655	0.644	0.627	0.597

increases, showing that a brief exploration is sufficient for classification and that exploitation is more important. To enable at least a little exploration, we choose cluster-based initialization with $s = 0.3$ for our main benchmark experiments.

Table 3. Hyperparameter study for different initialization strategies (cluster- and median-based) and switch points s (regression). Results are given as R2-score. Best results marked in bold.

Init. strategy	Cluster-based					Median-based				
Switch point (s)	0.0	0.3	0.5	0.7	1.0	0.0	0.3	0.5	0.7	1.0
Airfoil Self-Noise	0.071	0.122	**0.164**	0.147	0.104	0.116	0.127	0.158	0.133	0.106
Boston Housing	0.588	**0.591**	0.586	0.565	0.540	0.534	0.545	0.569	0.558	0.507
Real Estate Val.	0.444	**0.470**	0.465	0.427	0.460	0.279	0.310	0.305	0.292	0.307
Slump Strength	0.291	0.286	0.295	0.307	**0.312**	0.282	0.276	0.277	0.293	0.295
Superconductivity	0.450	0.460	**0.480**	0.456	0.408	0.267	0.311	0.312	0.305	0.224
Yacht Hydro.	0.717	0.740	0.694	0.721	0.371	0.787	**0.802**	0.799	0.784	0.616
Mean	0.427	0.445	**0.447**	0.437	0.366	0.378	0.395	0.403	0.394	0.343

The results for the regression setting can be seen in Table 3. As with classification, we evaluate our method with both cluster- and median-based initialization and the same switching points. Similar behavior is observed between cluster- and median-based initialization, with cluster-based performing better overall. For both cluster- and median-based initialization, performance initially improves with increasing exploration, peaking at $s = 0.5$, before declining subsequently. Specifically, cluster-based initialization achieved its highest average R2-score at this point. This shows that exploration is more important for regression than classification, though exploitation is still crucial for good results. For this reason, we selected cluster-based initialization with $s = 0.5$ for our main benchmark experiments.

Comparison with State-of-the-Art: We compare our method with several other methods that are suitable for the low-budget regime and applicable to both classification and regression. In this category are mostly model-free AL methods that are mentioned in Sect. 2. We chose the methods in a way that we can answer RQ2 and analyze which types of criteria, namely cluster-, distance-, density- and informativeness-based, have which impact on the results. GSx has a distance-based criteria, while TypiClust and iRDM are chosen as cluster-based methods. The later two also include another criteria, typicality/density-based for TypiClust and distance-based for iRDM. Additionally, we provide the quality of random selection (RS) as a baseline that every suitable AL method should outperform. Lastly, we include QBC into the comparison. Also it is typically not seen as a suitable AL method for the low-budget scenario, we can evaluate the impact that pure exploitation has. Since QBC needs an initial set to train the model (in our case an RF with the same hyperparameters as for the evaluation), we provide it with the same initial three data points as our method LQBAL, which are sampled cluster-based (iRDM).

The results for the classification setting can be found in Table 4. As shown, GSx rarely outperforms the baseline RS for both F1-score and classes found. All other methods, however, achieve results that are at least equal to and often better than RS on all datasets, except QBC on the Segmentation dataset. The cluster-based methods iRMD and TypiClust provide similar results, with TypiClust performing slightly better in terms of both the F1-score and the number of classes identified. TypiClust also is the best method on four datasets (F1-score) with the Iris dataset being a tie. Both are the best for one dataset in finding the most classes on average[5]. Surprisingly, QBC performs also well with being the best on three datasets (F1-score), although all three results are ties. Additionally, it is only slightly better than the baseline RS in percentage of classes found. Our method LQBAL is best on three datasets, again all being ties, but it is able to find the most classes on two datasets. The mean values demonstrate how well the AL methods generally perform: TypiClust and LQBAL perform best with equal F1-scores. Although iRDM has a slightly lower F1 score, it identifies the same proportion of classes as the aforementioned methods. QBC is the fourth-best method and RS and GSx are the two worst.

The results for regression are shown in Table 5. They show a different picture than for classification which is mostly shown by the fact that no AL method is able to consistently outperform the RS baseline, with the exception of our method LQBAL. Another difference lies in performance, with ties being common in classification tasks and multiple methods often achieving similar results. In contrast, regression tasks often demonstrate performance differences of 0.2 or more, as demonstrated by the Yacht Hydrodynamics dataset. The methods GSx, iRDM, TypiClust and QBC perform similar on average. All are outperformed on four out of six datasets by RS, with the datasets Airfoil and Boston Housing

[5] We do not mention the Iris and Wheat dataset in the analysis of percentage of classes found here and in the following, because all methods perform equally perfect in this regard.

Table 4. Results for classification (F1-score and percentage of classes found) averaged over 100 runs. Best result marked in bold.

Dataset	RS		GSx		iRDM		TypiClust		QBC		LQBAL	
Fish	0.49	(0.81)	0.45	(0.74)	0.52	(0.8)	0.49	(0.78)	**0.59**	(0.85)	**0.59**	**(0.87)**
Glass	0.34	(0.78)	0.34	(0.84)	0.39	(0.84)	**0.45**	**(0.9)**	0.39	(0.78)	0.37	(0.8)
Iris	0.92	(1)	**0.94**	(1)	0.93	(1)	**0.94**	(1)	**0.94**	(1)	**0.94**	(1)
Pendigit	0.40	(0.79)	0.33	(0.73)	0.52	**(0.93)**	**0.53**	(0.87)	0.41	(0.77)	0.45	(0.86)
Segment.	0.56	(0.91)	0.56	(0.92)	0.61	(0.95)	**0.67**	(0.96)	0.53	(0.92)	0.65	**(0.98)**
Wheat	0.87	(1)	0.87	(1)	0.88	(1)	0.88	(1)	**0.89**	(1)	**0.89**	(1)
Mean	0.60	(0.88)	0.58	(0.87)	0.64	**(0.92)**	**0.66**	**(0.92)**	0.62	(0.89)	**0.66**	**(0.92)**

Table 5. Results for regression (R2-Score) averaged over 100 runs. Best result marked in bold.

Dataset	RS	GSx	iRDM	TypiClust	QBC	LQBAL
Airfoil Self-Noise	0.145(2)	0.126(3)	0.101(4)	0.048(5)	-0.029(6)	**0.163**(1)
Boston Housing	0.488(2)	0.376(6)	0.45(5)	0.475(4)	0.476(3)	**0.586**(1)
Real Estate Valuation	0.442(4)	0.333(6)	0.441(5)	**0.567**(1)	0.501(2)	0.466(3)
Slump Strength	0.23(5)	0.294(3)	0.281(4)	**0.313**(1)	0.191(6)	0.295(2)
Superconductivity	0.444(2)	0.125(4)	0.053(6)	0.415(3)	0.102(5)	**0.48**(1)
Yacht Hydrodynamics	0.783(4)	0.851(2)	0.791(3)	0.352(6)	**0.854**(1)	0.69(5)
Mean (AvRks.)	0.42(3.2)	0.35(4.0)	0.35(4.5)	0.36(3.3)	0.35(3.8)	**0.45**(2.2)

being the ones where none of those methods achieves an improvement over the baseline. TypiClust performs really well on the Real Estate Valuation and Slump Strength set, which compensate for its very poor performance on the Yacht Hydrodynamics dataset, where QBC is able to be the best method. Importantly, while all other methods have at least one dataset with a very poor performance[6] our method is able to perform best or relatively close to the best (one exception: Yacht Hydrodynamics), which is also shown by the best average result among all active learners. In terms of the average ranks, significantly LQBAL obtained the best results.

5 Discussion and Future Work

In this work, we present a novel active learning (AL) method tailored for scenarios with a very low query budget. Applicable to both regression and classification datasets, our method comprises two phases that combine model-free and model-based criteria to consistently produce high-quality datasets. While other methods are also applicable to regression and classification, to the best of our

[6] GSx and iRDM: Superconductivity, TpyiClust: Yacht Hydrodynamics, QBC: Airfoil and Superconductivity.

knowledge, none explicitly investigate the distinctions between these settings. To address this gap, we introduced a hyperparameter that defines the transition between phases and estimated values that are generally appropriate for both classification and regression.

On average, our method (LQBAL) outperforms other commonly used methods in low-budget scenarios, such as the initialisation process, for regression and matches the performance of the best methods for classification. We now use our experimental results to address the two RQs formulated in the introduction:

RQ1: Does the inclusion of model-based AL criteria help in small data, low-budget scenarios? If yes, at which point should the inclusion happen?

- Yes, incorporating model-based criteria is advantageous. For classification, although our method does not significantly outperform existing methods, our hyperparameter analysis indicates that an early exploitation phase outperforms a later, shorter one. For regression, the results indicate that model-based criteria is critical to consistently improve on the RS baseline. Interestingly, the optimal transition point to the model-based phase varies slightly: around 30% of the budget for classification and 50% for regression. We hypothesize that classification problems are often easier to model, as a single sample per class may suffice to provide acceptable results, particularly when classes are well-clustered. In contrast, regression outputs fluctuate more, making them harder to model with limited data. This aligns with the results of [3], who suggest delaying model-based criteria until the model is sufficiently fitted to the problem.

RQ2: Which types of AL criteria (e.g. cluster-, distance-based) are generally important to consider for a high-quality, low-budget AL method?

- For classification, TypiClust and LQBAL perform best, highlighting the value of density-based AL criteria. The method iRDM also performs equally well in the covered classes found, this shows the importance of clustering in the classification setting. Model-based criteria, as evidenced by the unexpectedly solid performance of QBC, provide important information, whereas distance-based criteria, as used in GSx, alone provide no advantage. However, the top three methods all use distance measures to prevent redundant sampling, so its inclusion in this way is helpful. For regression, all methods except LQBAL are worse than RS on average, emphasizing the necessity of combining model-free and model-based criteria. Further investigation into whether cluster-, distance- or density-based criteria are more helpful may be speculative due to the minor differences, but TypiClust and iRDM again slightly outperform the others, indicating that cluster- and density-based criteria are valuable. QBC and GSx are the two worst methods, implying that distance- and model-based criteria are only effective when paired with other approaches.

For future work, we plan to investigate methods to automatically determine the switching point s, to make the performance less dependent on this hyperparameter choice. Additionally, we want to investigate the quality of the compared methods when they are not used for the whole AL process with limited budget but for creating the initial set for other more advanced AL methods. This addresses the cold-start problem which is often ignored or overseen in the development of new AL methods.

Acknowledgment. This work was funded by the project *SAIL: SustAInable Life cycle of Intelligent Socio Technical Systems* (Grant ID NW21-059B), which is funded by the Ministry of Culture and Science of the State of North Rhine-Westphalia, Germany.

Disclosure of Interests. The authors have no competing interests to declare that are relevant to the content of this article.

References

1. Attenberg, J., Provost, F.: Inactive learning? Difficulties employing active learning in practice. ACM SIGKDD Explor. Newsl. **12**, 36–41 (2011). https://doi.org/10.1145/1964897.1964906
2. Fourcaud, T., Zhang, X., Stokes, A., Lambers, H., Körner, C.: Plant growth modelling and applications: the increasing importance of plant architecture in growth models. Ann. Botany **101**(8), 1053–1063 (2008). https://doi.org/10.1093/aob/mcn050
3. Hacohen, G., Dekel, A., Weinshall, D.: Active learning on a budget: opposite strategies suit high and low budgets. In: Proceedings of the 39th International Conference on Machine Learning, vol. 162, pp. 8175–8195. PMLR (2022). https://doi.org/10.48550/arXiv.2202.02794
4. He, D., Yu, H., Wang, G., Li, J.: A two-stage clustering-based cold-start method for active learning. Intell. Data Anal. **25**(5), 1169–1185 (2021)
5. Jaster, B., Kohlhase, M.: Active learning for regression problems with ensemble methods. In: Proceedings - 33. Workshop Computational Intelligence, pp. 9–29. Karlsruher Institut für Technologie (KIT) (2023). https://doi.org/10.5445/KSP/1000162754
6. Jose, A., de Mendonça, J.P.A., Devijver, E., Jakse, N., Monbet, V., Poloni, R.: Regression tree-based active learning. Data Min. Knowl. Discov. (2023). https://doi.org/10.1007/s10618-023-00951-7
7. Kelly, M., Longjohn, R., Nottingham, K.: The UCI machine learning repository. https://archive.ics.uci.edu
8. Kumar, P., Gupta, A.: Active learning query strategies for classification, regression, and clustering: a survey. J. Comput. Sci. Technol. **35**, 913–945 (2020). https://doi.org/10.1007/s11390-020-9487-4
9. Lewis, D.D., Gale, W.A.: A Sequential Algorithm for Training Text Classifiers, pp. 3–12. Springer, London (1994). https://doi.org/10.1007/978-1-4471-2099-5_1
10. Liu, Z., Jiang, X., Luo, H., Fang, W., Liu, J., Wu, D.: Pool-based unsupervised active learning for regression using iterative representativeness-diversity maximization (IRDM). Pattern Recogn. Lett. **142**, 11–19 (2021). https://doi.org/10.1016/j.patrec.2020.11.019
11. MacQueen, J.: Some methods for classification and analysis of multivariate observations. In: Proceedings of the Fifth Berkeley Symposium on Mathematical Statistics and Probability, Volume 1: Statistics, vol. 5, pp. 281–298. University of California Press (1967)

12. Rezazadeh, F., Abrishambaf, A., Dürrbaum, A., Zimmermann, G., Kroll, A.: Holistic modeling of ultra-high performance concrete production process: Synergizing mix design, fresh concrete properties, and curing conditions. In: Proceedings - 33. Workshop Computational Intelligence, pp. 215–238. Karlsruher Institut für Technologie (KIT) (2023). https://doi.org/10.5445/KSP/1000162754
13. Riis, C., Antunes, F., Boe, F., Carlos, H., Azevedo, L., Pereira, F.C.: Bayesian active learning with fully Bayesian gaussian processes. In: Advances in Neural Information Processing Systems, pp. 12141–12153. Curran Associates, Inc. (2022)
14. Roy, N., McCallum, A.: Toward optimal active learning through sampling estimation of error reduction. In: ICML, vol. 1, p. 5. Citeseer (2001)
15. Schöne, M., Jaster, B., Bültemeier, J., Kösters, J., Holst, C.A., Kohlhase, M.: Pool-based active learning with decision trees: incorporate the tree structure to explore and exploit. In: 2025 IEEE Symposium on Trustworthy, Explainable and Responsible Computational Intelligence (CITREx), pp. 1–9. IEEE (2025). https://doi.org/10.1109/CITREx64975.2025.10974940
16. Settles, B.: Active learning literature survey. Computer Sciences Technical Report 1648, University of Wisconsin-Madison Department of Computer Sciences (2009)
17. Seung, H.S., Opper, M., Sompolinsky, H.: Query by committee. In: Proceedings of the Fifth Annual Workshop on Computational Learning Theory, pp. 287–294 (1992)
18. Sharma, M., Bilgic, M.: Evidence-based uncertainty sampling for active learning. Data Min. Knowl. Disc. **31**, 164–202 (2017)
19. Shui, C., Zhou, F., Gagné, C., Wang, B.: Deep active learning: unified and principled method for query and training. In: Proceedings of the 23rd International Conference on Artificial Intelligence and Statistics, pp. 1308–1318. PMLR (2020). https://proceedings.mlr.press/v108/shui20a.html
20. Tharwat, A.: Principal component analysis-a tutorial. Int. J. Appl. Pattern Recogn. **3**(3), 197–240 (2016). https://doi.org/10.1504/IJAPR.2016.079733
21. Tharwat, A., Schenck, W.: Balancing exploration and exploitation: a novel active learner for imbalanced data. Knowl.-Based Syst. **210**, 106500 (2020). https://doi.org/10.1016/j.knosys.2020.106500
22. Tharwat, A., Schenck, W.: A survey on active learning: State-of-the-art, practical challenges and research directions. Mathematics **11**, 820 (2023). https://doi.org/10.3390/math11040820
23. Tharwat, A., Schenck, W.: Using methods from dimensionality reduction for active learning with low query budget. IEEE Trans. Knowl. Data Eng. **36**(8), 4317–4330 (2024). https://doi.org/10.1109/TKDE.2024.3365189
24. Wang, M., Min, F., Zhang, Z.H., Wu, Y.X.: Active learning through density clustering. Expert Syst. Appl. **85**, 305–317 (2017)
25. Wu, D., Lin, C.T., Huang, J.: Active learning for regression using greedy sampling. Inf. Sci. **474**, 90–105 (2019). https://doi.org/10.1016/j.ins.2018.09.060
26. Yu, K., Bi, J., Tresp, V.: Active learning via transductive experimental design. In: Proceedings of the 23rd International Conference on Machine Learning, pp. 1081–1088 (2006)
27. Zhao, Z., Jiang, Y., Chen, Y.: Direct acquisition optimization for low-budget active learning. arXiv preprint arXiv:2402.06045 (2024)

Adaptable Hindsight Experience Replay for Search-Based Learning

Alexandros Vazaios[1], Jannis Brugger[1,2](✉), Cedric Derstroff[1,2], Kristian Kersting[1,2,3,4], and Mira Mezini[1,2,5]

[1] Technical University of Darmstadt, Darmstadt, Germany
alexandros.vazaios@stud.tu-darmstadt.de,
{jannis.brugger,cedric.derstroff,kristian.kersting,
mira.mezini}@tu-darmstadt.de
[2] Hessian Center for Artificial Intelligence (hessian.AI), Darmstadt, Germany
[3] German Research Center for Artificial Intelligence (DFKI), Darmstadt, Germany
[4] Centre for Cognitive Science, Darmstadt, Germany
[5] National Research Center for Applied Cybersecurity ATHENE, Darmstadt, Germany

Abstract. AlphaZero-like Monte Carlo Tree Search systems, originally introduced for two-player games, dynamically balance exploration and exploitation using neural network guidance. This combination makes them also suitable for classical search problems. However, the original method of training the network with simulation results is limited in sparse reward settings, especially in the early stages, where the network cannot yet give guidance. Hindsight Experience Replay (HER) addresses this issue by relabeling unsuccessful trajectories from the search tree as supervised learning signals. We introduce Adaptable HER (AHER), a flexible framework that integrates HER with AlphaZero, allowing easy adjustments to HER properties such as relabeled goals, policy targets, and trajectory selection. Our experiments, including equation discovery, show that the possibility of modifying HER is beneficial and surpasses the performance of pure supervised or reinforcement learning.

Keywords: Hindsight Experience Replay · AlphaZero · Monte Carlo Tree Search · Deep Reinforcement Learning

1 Introduction

Adaptive learning systems often face significant challenges due to the scarcity of high-quality training data in complex domains. To steer the search process in complex environments, neural-guided Monte Carlo Tree Search (MCTS) has emerged as a promising approach. However, sparse learning signals can still result in ineffective and resource-heavy training. To counter this problem, Hindsight Experience Replay (HER) transforms failures into valuable learning experiences by copying a complete historic trajectory and exchanging the original goal with

I. Koprinska et al. (Eds.): ECML PKDD 2025, CCIS 2842, pp. 22–29, 2026.
https://doi.org/10.1007/978-3-032-19105-2_2

one of the states in the search tree. Creating artificial positive training signals enables the neural network to capture a more comprehensive understanding of the search space. While other works [8,10] have already combined HER with neural-guided MCTS, we introduce a unifying, widely applicable Adaptable HER framework (AHER) and extract the critical parts of HER. Our contributions are threefold: **I** We develop a **flexible HER framework** that can be seamlessly integrated into various environments and search algorithms by following the gymnasium interface [14]. **II** We confirm that HER consistently improves the performance of neural-guided MCTS, but highlight the **need for a customizable HER framework**, as optimal configurations vary across environments. **III** We showcase in the domain of equation discovery that AlphaZero [11] with **HER outperforms both pure reinforcement learning and pure supervised learning**.

2 Methodology

Before explaining AHER in detail, we first give a brief overview of the AlphaZero training. We then finish this section with empirical results.

2.1 AlphaZero

The baseline learning approach selected for our experiments is a variation of AlphaZero [11]: a well-known neural-guided MCTS algorithm created by DeepMind that achieved superhuman performance in Shogi, Chess, and Go. Its core idea lies in combining MCTS and a neural network policy. The policy guides the MCTS, and the search results function as training targets. After each episode, the network receives feedback by being trained on state transitions sampled from its Experience Replay. This paradigm can also be generalized to other games, including single-player ones, as required for our case. The Training routine is illustrated in the dashed frame of Fig. 1 as part of our AHER architecture.

2.2 Adaptable Hindsight Experience Replay

Depending on the task, there are various configurations for HER [1,8,10], which we unify into the following four properties: (1) In the goal selection strategy, we can choose between the "future" strategy, relabeling states visited later in the current episode as HER-goals, or the "final" strategy, relabeling only the terminal state. (2) By selecting between a single- or multi-trajectory, we choose whether only the played trajectory of an episode is used to generate HER samples or a random subset from the MCTS search tree. (3) The following property defines how many HER samples are added to the replay buffer per trajectory. (4) The last property defines the policy learning target for the HER samples. We can choose between the original MCTS probabilities, a one-hot array, or a one-hot array with uniform noise.

By covering these four properties, we introduce a customizable implementation of HER for AlphaZero (Fig. 1), which allows us to measure the influence of these properties on a set of learning domains.

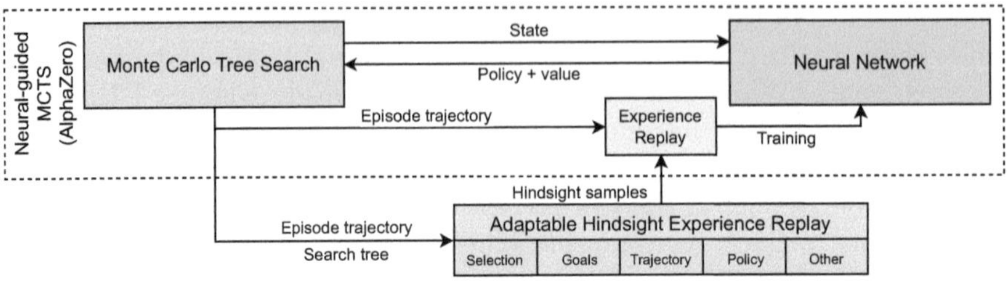

Fig. 1. Architectural overview of our learning setup. AHER is connected to the AlphaZero training loop. An iteration of the loop consists of performing neural-guided MCTS, sampling batches from the experience replay buffer, and training the predictor neural network.

2.3 Setup

Our implementation is derived from the AlphaZero General [13] and MuZero [15] codebases with MCTS modules written by [3] and adapted to be compatible with single-player games by [2]. We chose to use three learning environments for our experiments: bit-flipping [1], point maze from Gymnasium Robotics [7] (with action space discretized to 8 equidistant moves), and equation discovery from a table of measurements by [2]. The code used for this paper is available at: https://github.com/my-curiosity/aher.

For the policy, we utilize a 3-layer multi-layer perceptron (MLP) with 256, 256, and 128 neurons respectively, ReLU activations, and a 0.3 dropout rate in bit-flipping and point maze. In equation discovery, the equation syntax trees and measurement datasets are separately encoded by a transformer (2 layers, 4 heads, 8-dimensional vectors) and an LSTM network (64 units), respectively. Their output is then combined, and separate MLPs (64/64, ReLU) are used to predict the value of the current state and action (rule of the grammar, describing how to construct an equation), to be applied next.

To evaluate performance in bit-flipping and point maze, we consider the success rate, mean total return, and the number of iterations necessary to reach a success rate of 80%. In equation discovery, however, we are more interested in finding the best equations than in average performance. Therefore, we instead measure how many nodes are expanded by MCTS before a suitable formula is found, as done in previous work [2].

2.4 Empirical Results

Bit-Flipping. Bit-flipping is a task of transforming binary arrays by inverting values, one at a time, to reach given target configurations. It was used to demonstrate the effectiveness of HER to mitigate reward sparsity [1]. Learning with AHER was most successful with 4 "future" goals. Further increases resulted in reaching a success rate of 0.8 faster at the cost of slightly degrading the episode returns. Even though one-hot policy targets led to approximately 3.5% more failures, adding weak uniform noise negated this effect and even slightly raised the observed returns. Multi-trajectory HER failed; most likely because the average MCTS trajectories were much shorter than those played. The "final" selection strategy was not effective due to the used reward function: with negative rewards received at each step, episode returns in relabeled trajectories were almost equivalent to the original ones and lacked the diversity required for training the neural network.

Point Maze. Point maze is a physics-based navigation task, in which the agent must lead a ball to a specified destination in a maze. We selected the medium maze layout for all the experiments. Here, HER's behavior was generally similar to our observations from bit-flipping, with the following exceptions: the optimal number of "future" samples was 8, further increases slowed down reaching the 80% solved episodes mark; one-hot and noisy policy targets having a strictly negative influence (8–9% lower success rate); multi-trajectory HER still suffering from the same issues as in bit-flipping but achieving comparable results with 1 and 4 random MCTS trajectories.

Equation Discovery. The goal of equation discovery is to create equations from a specified context-free grammar that describe a dataset of point measurements. Unlike point maze, equation discovery is easily compatible with both reinforcement (RL) and supervised learning (SL) methods due to optimal solutions for each episode being known before interacting with the environment. Moreover, as only terminal states correspond to complete equations, the "future" selection strategy is not applicable, which limits the utility of single-trajectory HER variants. On the other hand, by sampling "final" goals from random MCTS trajectories, we improved over the previous best performance achieved by both plain RL and SL. However, the latter remains significantly less time-consuming. An optimum point was measured at 24 samples with the noise-free one-hot policy targets, as original MCTS probabilities are irrelevant outside the played trajectory.

General Results. The amount of HER samples used and, consequently, the ratio of original data to hindsight data in the experience replay affects AlphaZero's performance the strongest (cf. Figure 2). Tweaking this ratio is essential for ensuring successful training and can be seen as controlling the amount of supervision necessary for the task. With too few HER samples, the agent struggles to learn in sparse reward settings, but with too many, it forgets past experiences and detaches from them, becoming less stable (as discussed by [5]). The data ratio of HER is mostly influenced by two properties, namely, the number of future goals and the number of trajectories used for relabeling. Multi-trajectory HER is generally more difficult to apply as it performs poorly if the trajectories are short. Still, it remains a good solution for situations in which the "future" goal selection is unavailable, e.g., equation discovery. The tested policy targets demonstrated relatively similar results. However, one-hot encoding was naturally more appropriate when using random trajectories, as it reduces the amount of noise from the obsolete MCTS probabilities.

Including Further HER Advancements. In addition to these results, we also adapted 3 HER improvement techniques to our setup: aggressive rewards [6], experience ranking [9], and combined experience replay [12]. As a result, a slight performance increase was reached in all compatible tasks. We see this direction of work as promising and having the potential to raise the effectiveness of neural-guided MCTS with HER without requiring the implementation of new concepts from scratch.

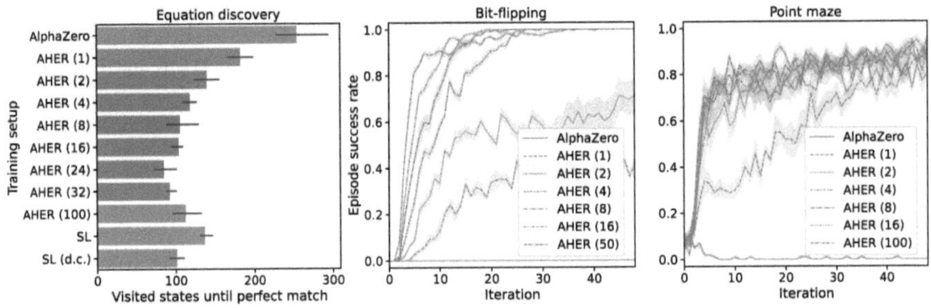

Fig. 2. Performance of AHER-augmented AlphaZero. (left) Visited states in the search tree until the correct equation is found. AlphaZero refers to training only with the probabilities from the MCTS, AHER(k) for adding HER samples from k trajectories, and SL (d.c.) for supervised learning with dataset changes. Dataset changes entail sampling new x and fitting y measurements after each training step to increase training diversity. We chose to also perform this during AHER goal relabeling. The HER samples are added with the "final" goal selection strategy and one-hot policy targets. Failed searches count as 1,000 visited states. (middle and right) Success rate for solving bit-flipping with 50 bits (middle) and point maze (right), depending on the number of HER samples. The HER samples are added with the "future" goal selection strategy from the played trajectory and original MCTS probabilities. We display the mean and 95% confidence intervals of 5 runs.

3 Related Work

Although HER was initially intended for off-policy deep RL, it has been deployed with neural-guided MCTS in AlphaZeroHER [8] and Minimo [10]. AlphaZero-HER shows that such a setup can outperform DQN (Deep Q-Network) with HER in multiple domains, but only considers the played trajectory for goal relabeling, "future" goal selection strategy, and original MCTS probabilities as a policy learning target for AlphaZero. Conversely, Minimo applies multi-trajectory HER to prove mathematical and logical conjectures, but utilizes environment-specific optimizations such as ignoring irrelevant subtrajectories. Additionally, the work uses a large language model agent, which changed the required form for training samples. Continuing this line of work, we analyze the influence of HER on learning in different configurations and on various tasks.

4 Limitations and Outlook

Due to the nature of MCTS, which is used as a search backbone, our implementation does not support continuous action spaces, and the necessary discretization is not always possible without a loss in performance or an increased training time. Furthermore, we only use straightforward policy learning targets (original probabilities and one-hot) that are generalizable to all domains. In future work, we would like to analyze how AHER can be used with more target-specific policies. Additionally, this work only considers deterministic state transition sequences. Systematically studying HER for probabilistic transitions and noisy states could further increase the application scenarios where HER improves the learning. Combining AHER with existing HER advancements is also expected to strengthen its performance; especially useful would be the curriculum mechanism [4], which could aid both trajectory and goal choices for relabeling.

5 Conclusion

This work introduces AHER: an adaptable HER implementation for neural-guided AlphaZero-like MCTS, in which multiple architectural aspects can be configured. Leveraging it, we first analyze the influence of applying HER to AlphaZero to solve three domains. HER's inclusion in the AlphaZero setup allows us to solve domains otherwise unsolvable by neural-guided MCTS. We observe that being able to select a type of HER to use with a given task can be beneficial, even for tasks such as point maze and bit-flipping, where the highest performance metrics correspond to the "baseline" variant by [8]. Having the flexibility to change the HER properties allows us to measure the relative importance of each HER property for successful training. Moreover, it is essential for new domains, where the preferred type of HER-assisted learning is unknown and difficult to guess. In the equation discovery task, we show that neural-guided MCTS with AHER can outperform pure supervised and reinforcement learning if configured correctly.

Acknowledgments. The authors gratefully acknowledge the computing time provided to them on the high-performance computer Lichtenberg II at TU Darmstadt, funded by the German Federal Ministry of Education and Research (BMBF) and the State of Hesse.

This research project was partly funded by the Hessian Ministry of Science and the Arts (HMWK) within the projects "The Third Wave of Artificial Intelligence - 3AI" and hessian.AI.

Disclosure of Interests. The authors have no relevant financial or non-financial interests to disclose.

References

1. Andrychowicz, M., et al.: Hindsight experience replay. In: Guyon, I., Luxburg, U.V., Bengio, S., Wallach, H., Fergus, R., Vishwanathan, S., Garnett, R. (eds.) Advances in Neural Information Processing Systems, vol. 30. Curran Associates, Inc. (2017). https://proceedings.neurips.cc/paper_files/paper/2017/file/453fadbd8a1a3af50a9df4df899537b5-Paper.pdf
2. Brugger, J., et al.: Neural-guided equation discovery (2025). https://arxiv.org/abs/2503.16953
3. Derstroff, C., Brugger, J., Blüml, J., Mezini, M., Kramer, S., Kersting, K.: Amplifying exploration in monte-carlo tree search by focusing on the unknown (2024). https://arxiv.org/abs/2402.08511
4. Fang, M., Zhou, T., Du, Y., Han, L., Zhang, Z.: Curriculum-guided hindsight experience replay. In: Wallach, H.M., Larochelle, H., Beygelzimer, A., d'Alché-Buc, F., Fox, E.B., Garnett, R. (eds.) Advances in Neural Information Processing Systems 32: Annual Conference on Neural Information Processing Systems 2019, NeurIPS 2019, December 8–14, 2019, Vancouver, BC, Canada, pp. 12602–12613 (2019). https://proceedings.neurips.cc/paper/2019/hash/83715fd4755b33f9c3958e1a9ee221e1-Abstract.html
5. Humayoo, M., et al.: Relative importance sampling for off-policy actor-critic in deep reinforcement learning. Sci. Rep. **15** (2025). https://doi.org/10.1038/s41598-025-96201-5
6. Lanka, S., Wu, T.: ARCHER: aggressive rewards to counter bias in hindsight experience replay (2018). http://arxiv.org/abs/1809.02070
7. de Lazcano, R., Andreas, K., Tai, J.J., Lee, S.R., Terry, J.: Gymnasium robotics (2024). http://github.com/Farama-Foundation/Gymnasium-Robotics
8. Moro, L., Likmeta, A., Prati, E., Restelli, M.: Goal-directed planning via hindsight experience replay. In: The Tenth International Conference on Learning Representations, ICLR 2022, Virtual Event, April 25–29, 2022. OpenReview.net (2022). https://openreview.net/forum?id=6NePxZwfae
9. Nguyen, H., La, H.M., Deans, M.C.: Hindsight experience replay with experience ranking. In: Joint IEEE 9th International Conference on Development and Learning and Epigenetic Robotics, ICDL-EpiRob 2019, Oslo, Norway, August 19–22, 2019, pp. 1–6. IEEE (2019). https://doi.org/10.1109/DEVLRN.2019.8850705, https://doi.org/10.1109/DEVLRN.2019.8850705
10. Poesia, G., Broman, D., Haber, N., Goodman, N.: Learning formal mathematics from intrinsic motivation. In: The Thirty-eighth Annual Conference on Neural Information Processing Systems (2024). https://openreview.net/forum?id=uNKlTQ8mBD
11. Silver, D., et al.: A general reinforcement learning algorithm that masters chess, shogi, and go through self-play. Science **362**(6419), 1140–1144 (2018). https://doi.org/10.1126/science.aar6404
12. Tan, R.R.P., Ikeda, K., Vergara, J.P.C.: Hindsight-combined and hindsight-prioritized experience replay. In: Yang, H., Pasupa, K., Leung, A.C., Kwok, J.T., Chan, J.H., King, I. (eds.) Neural Information Processing - 27th International Conference, ICONIP 2020, Bangkok, Thailand, November 23–27, 2020, Proceedings, Part II. Lecture Notes in Computer Science, vol. 12533, pp. 429–439. Springer (2020). https://doi.org/10.1007/978-3-030-63833-7_36, https://doi.org/10.1007/978-3-030-63833-7_36

13. Thakoor, S., Nair, S., Jhunjhunwala, M.: Learning to play othello without human knowledge (2016)
14. Towers, M., et al.: Gymnasium: A standard interface for reinforcement learning environments. arXiv preprint arXiv:2407.17032 (2024)
15. de Vries, J.A., Voskuil, K.S., Moerland, T.M., Plaat, A.: Visualizing muzero models (2021). https://arxiv.org/abs/2102.12924

When Intrinsic Motivation Fails: Exploration Challenges in Decentralized MARL

Ting Zhu[1(✉)], Yue Jin[2], and Giovanni Montana[1,2,3]

[1] Department of Statistics, University of Warwick, Coventry, UK
{ting.zhu,G.Montana}@warwick.ac.uk
[2] Warwick Manufacturing Group, Coventry, UK
Yue.Jin.3@warwick.ac.uk
[3] Alan Turing Institute, London, UK

Abstract. Learning coordinated behaviour in decentralised multi-agent reinforcement learning with sparse rewards presents significant exploration challenges. Whilst novelty bonuses encourage exploration, we identify a critical failure mode they create in sequential coordination tasks: *coordination de-synchronisation*, where agents repeatedly traversing earlier coordination points gradually exhaust their intrinsic motivation to revisit these critical locations. We hypothesize that the effectiveness of exploration strategies depends on two key task factors: coordination complexity and geometric revisit pressure. Our preliminary experiments confirm this: lifelong novelty bonuses deteriorate with increasing task complexity, while augmenting with episodic bonuses substantially improves performance. These findings motivate further theoretical investigation into coordination-aware intrinsic motivation for decentralized agents.

Keywords: Decentralized multi-agent · Reinforcement learning · Exploration · Novelty

1 Introduction

Cooperative multi-agent reinforcement learning (MARL) has become increasingly important for addressing complex real-world challenges that require coordinated behaviors among multiple agents. Successful applications included wireless sensor networks [16], unmanned aerial vehicles [14], and traffic light control [19]. Unlike single-agent settings, MARL introduces unique challenges–especially in decentralized scenarios where agents must learn to coordinate based solely on local observations, without access to global information. Despite the progress made by recent fully decentralized algorithms [3,8,20], a major limitation remains: these methods often struggle in environments with sparse rewards. Exploration becomes especially critical in sparse-reward cooperative tasks, where agents must synchronise their actions at specific locations and times to make progress, yet only receive exceedingly rare external reward signals.

I. Koprinska et al. (Eds.): ECML PKDD 2025, CCIS 2842, pp. 30–36, 2026.
https://doi.org/10.1007/978-3-032-19105-2_3

A common approach to exploration in single-agent setting is through intrinsic motivation via novelty-based bonuses–rewards based on how rarely states have been visited [1,2,12]. While these methods have been extensively evaluated in single-agent settings, their extension to decentralised multi-agent settings brings unique challenges. Under partial observability, each agent only sees its own local state and thus computes a local novelty estimate - might at odds with the true novelty of the joint state. This gap between local and global novelty measure can misalign exploration incentives across the team. This raises fundamental questions: How should intrinsic motivation be designed for decentralized agents? Can novelty mislead agents away from successful coordination?

In this work, we aim to initiate a discussion around these questions by highlight a critical failure mode - what we term *coordination de-synchronisation.* The core problem arises when cooperative tasks require agents to coordinate at multiple points sequentially. As agents search for later coordination opportunities, they must repeatedly traverse earlier coordination points, gradually exhausting their intrinsic motivation to revisit these critical locations. This creates a coordination "death spiral" where the very act of exploring for advanced objectives undermines the team's ability to maintain coordination at foundational checkpoints–precisely the opposite of what we desire from a learning system. Our key insight is that this failure is determined by two independent factors: the task's *logical complexity* (the number of sequential coordination points) and the environment's *physical geometry*, which can force agents to repeatedly traverse earlier checkpoints. We demonstrate that a hybrid approach, combining episodic and lifelong bonuses, provides a complete solution. In this work, we present initial empirical results validating our hypothesis, while the accompanying theoretical analysis is ongoing. Our goal is to share early insights and open a broader discussion on coordination-aware exploration design.

2 Related Work

Intrinsic Motivation in Multi-agent RL. Several works have investigated intrinsic motivation in MARL within the CTDE framework. [6] proposed coordinated exploration bonuses that consider novelty from other agents' perspectives, whilst [15] assigned bonuses based on mutual information between agents' transition dynamics. [18] used prediction errors of individual Q-functions as intrinsic rewards, and [10] addressed lazy agents through causal effect maximisation on external states. These approaches differ fundamentally from our work in two key aspects. First, they operate within CTDE settings where agents have access to global information during training, whilst we focus on the more challenging decentralised case where agents rely solely on local observations. Second, none provide theoretical analysis of when different exploration strategies succeed or fail based on task structure. [7] introduced MACE, the first intrinsic motivation method specifically for decentralised settings, where agents share only local novelty values. However, MACE focuses on approximating global novelty through local information sharing rather than addressing the coordination challenges we identify. Our work would complement MACE by providing theoretical foundations for when episodic components become crucial in decentralised coordination tasks.

Episodic Bonuses in MARL. [13] is the first to combine lifelong and episodic bonuses in MARL, using NovelD [17] and E3B [5] within CTDE. However, they compute novelty using joint observations, giving all agents identical rewards, whilst our decentralised approach requires agents to compute individual novelty from local observations. Critically, their work lacks theoretical analysis of when such combinations become necessary, which is the central contribution of our theoretical framework.

Communication in Decentralised MARL. Research on decentralised communication has focused on establishing common grounding between agents. [9] proposed AEComm, where agents autoencode observations for communication using shared environment structure, whilst [11] introduced contrastive learning to align messages from agents perceiving the same global state. Our theoretical analysis focuses on the fundamental case where agents operate independently without communication, revealing how coordination complexity determines exploration strategy effectiveness. While our experiments extend this to include novelty sharing between agents, the core theoretical insight–that episodic bonuses provide coordination robustness while lifelong bonuses suffer decay in sequential tasks–applies regardless of whether agents share novelty information. This suggests the temporal scope of novelty assessment is more fundamental than the communication mechanism itself.

3 Theoretical Framing and Tasks Design

3.1 Fundamental Concepts

Coordination Checkpoints: We study cooperative tasks that require agents to visit an ordered list of *coordination checkpoints*, $S^* = \{s^*_{(1)}, \ldots, s^*_{(L)}\}$. Each checkpoint is a joint state $s^*_{(\ell)} = (s^*_{1,\ell}, \ldots, s^*_{N,\ell})$ that the team must reach simultaneously. For instance, a simple task might require two agents to stand on two different pressure plates at the same time to open a door. This joint requirement—Agent 1 at position A *and* Agent 2 at position B—constitutes the first checkpoint, $s^*_{(1)}$. This sequence must be fully completed to receive any non-zero extrinsic reward; the reward function R is zero at all times, except for a positive reward granted upon reaching the final checkpoint $s^*_{(L)}$ after all previous checkpoints have been visited in order within the same episode.

Geometric pressure: We define geometric pressure as a property of the environment that reflects how often agents are forced to revisit earlier parts of the map during exploration. High geometric pressure increases the likelihood that agents must repeatedly traverse the same locations—such as narrow corridors or shared entry points—while pursuing new coordination goals. For example, a map layout that requires one agent to backtrack through a previously visited corridor to unlock a second door creates high revisit pressure. We use the parameter $\beta \in [0, 1]$ to characterize geometric pressure in each environment, where higher values indicate more constrained layouts that enforce frequent backtracking.

3.2 Theoretical Hypothesis

We hypothesize that coordination failure arises when agents must revisit earlier checkpoints under sparse rewards, but lifelong novelty discourages such revisits. This decay effect is exacerbated as the number of required coordination points (denoted L) increases, and when the geometry of the environment imposes frequent backtracking (denoted β). We analyze these effects in a communication-free setting, allowing us to isolate the impact of novelty strategy alone.

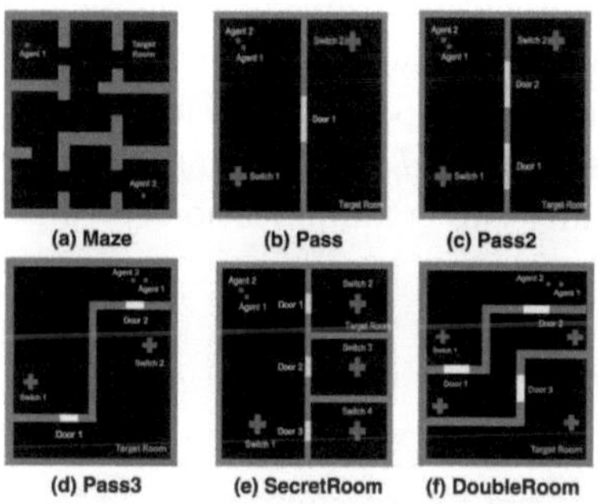

(a) Grid Environment

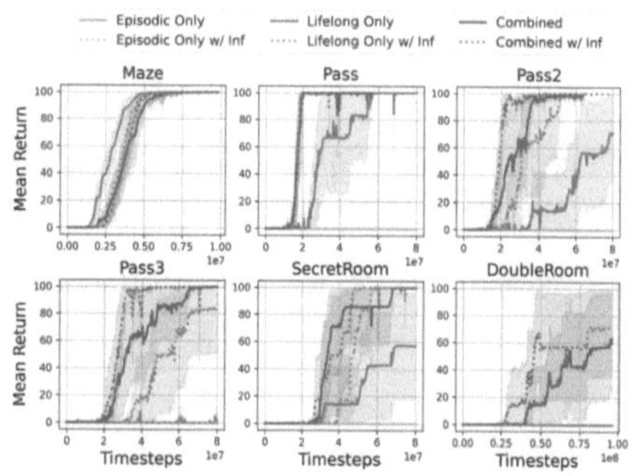

(b) Grid Environment Results

Fig. 1. Overview of the environments and corresponding results. In (b) The solid line represents **Summation of local novelty** and the dotted line represents **MACE**.

3.3 Gridworld Design

We design multiple two-agent gridworld tasks (Fig. 1a). The tasks in this two-agent environment require coordination via switches and doors to get both agents into a target room. We define a single target reaching or a single switch-door mechanism as one coordination checkpoint. This allows us to precisely test the effect of coordination complexity (L) and geometric revisit pressure (β).

- `Maze`: This map only require one coordination event, two agents arrive at the target room. We classify it as having low coordination complexity ($L = 1$). Therefore, this layout does not require agent to revisit to hit the second checkpoint.

- `Pass` , `Pass2` and `Pass3`: These maps contain a sequence of two switch-door mechanisms, making them tasks with higher coordination complexity ($L = 2$). Their layouts are designed to create a low to high level of geometric pressure. `Pass3`, for instance, forces one agent to backtrack over the starting area to reach the second door, inducing a high revisit-rate exponent ($\beta \approx 1$).
- `SecretRoom`: Another map with a multi-step coordination sequence ($L = 2$) used to further validate our findings on complex tasks.
- `DoubleRoom`: This map is a extended version of `Pass3`, which contains more coordination sequence ($L > 2$) used to further validate our findings on complex tasks.

3.4 Approach

We hypothesize that the effectiveness of intrinsic motivation in decentralized MARL depends on two structural properties: the task's coordination complexity (L) and geometric revisit pressure (β). To explore this, we designed tasks that vary these two factors. To test in practical settings, our experiment included communication. We evaluate three main novelty schemes—*Lifelong only*, *Episodic only*, and *Combined* (our hybrid approach)—under two communication settings:

- **Summation of local novelty:** $r^i_{\text{int}} = u^i_t + \sum_{j \neq i} u^j_t$
- **MACE** [7]: $r^i_{\text{int}} = u^i_t + \sum_{j \neq i} u^j_t + \lambda \sum_{j \neq i} v_{i,j}$

Here u^i_t is the intrinsic motivation agent i get and u^i_t is the intrinsic motivation it received from agent j at time t. Compared to the summation of local novelty, MACE [7] has one more component $v_{i,j}$ to measure the influence of agent i 's action on the other agent j 's novelty. For *Lifelong* bonus, we used $u^i = \sqrt{N_k(s^i)}$ to measure the novelty of a state s^i for agent i, while N_k is the accumulated visit counts on this state till k episodes. For *Episodic* bonus, we used $u^i = \mathbb{I}[N_e(s^i) = 1]$ to measure the novelty of a state within one episode, where $N_e(s^i)$ is the visit counts of the state within current episode. To combine the global and episodic bonuses, we use multiplication, as it is used in [4,13], therefore, the combined intrinsic reward is: $u^i = \frac{1}{\sqrt{N_k(s^i)}} \cdot \mathbb{I}[N_e(s^i) = 1)]$

4 Initial Experimental Results

The GridWorld experiments provide the most direct validation of our theory by systematically varying the coordination complexity (L) and geometric revisit pressure (β). The results in Fig. 1b show a clear phase transition consistent with our predictions. In the simple `Maze` task ($L = 1$), the lifelong-only strategy performs well and the performance is very close to episodic-only and combined one, as expected. In `Pass` task ($L = 2$) map, which increase the sequential complexity, the performance of the lifelong-only agent is still well, only slightly worse than the combined novelty one. However, in the `Pass2` and `Pass3` maps, which increase the sequential complexity ($L = 2$) and use layouts that force backtracking (high β), the performance of the lifelong-only agent degrades significantly. In stark contrast, the *Combined* approach, featuring an episodic bonus, maintains its high performance across all these challenging maps. This demonstrates that an episodic component becomes essential as task and geometric complexity rise. These trends align well with our theoretical predictions, confirming that the interaction between L and β is critical to the success of different intrinsic motivation schemes.

5 Conclusion

Our work identifies coordination de-synchronisation as a critical failure mode in decentralised multi-agent exploration. We show that exploration strategy effectiveness depends on two key factors: the task's logical complexity (L) and the environment's geometric revisit pressure (β). We hope this work sparks further investigation into coordination-aware exploration in decentralized settings. In particular, we invite the community to consider new forms of episodic or structure-aware intrinsic motivation, and to develop theoretical tools that capture the interplay between coordination structure and exploration dynamics. Addressing these challenges is crucial for scaling MARL to real-world applications that demand reliable and sustained coordination.

Acknowledgments. TZ acknowledges support from the UK Engineering and Physical Sciences Research Council (EPSRC EP/W523793/1), through the Statistics Centre for Doctoral Training at the University of Warwick. GM acknowledges support from a UKRI AI Turing Acceleration Fellowship (EPSRC EP/V024868/1).

References

1. Bellemare, M., Srinivasan, S., Ostrovski, G., Schaul, T., Saxton, D., Munos, R.: Unifying count-based exploration and intrinsic motivation. Adv. Neural Inf. Process. Syst. **29** (2016)
2. Burda, Y., Edwards, H., Storkey, A., Klimov, O.: Exploration by random network distillation. arXiv preprint arXiv:1810.12894 (2018)
3. De Witt, C.S., Gupta, T., Makoviichuk, D., Makoviychuk, V., Torr, P.H., Sun, M., Whiteson, S.: Is independent learning all you need in the starcraft multi-agent challenge? arXiv preprint arXiv:2011.09533 (2020)
4. Henaff, M., Jiang, M., Raileanu, R.: A study of global and episodic bonuses for exploration in contextual mdps. In: International Conference on Machine Learning. pp. 12972–12999. PMLR (2023)
5. Henaff, M., Raileanu, R., Jiang, M., Rocktäschel, T.: Exploration via elliptical episodic bonuses. Adv. Neural. Inf. Process. Syst. **35**, 37631–37646 (2022)
6. Iqbal, S., Sha, F.: Coordinated exploration via intrinsic rewards for multi-agent reinforcement learning. arXiv preprint arXiv:1905.12127 (2019)

7. Jiang, H., Ding, Z., Lu, Z.: Settling decentralized multi-agent coordinated exploration by novelty sharing. In: Proceedings of the AAAI Conference on Artificial Intelligence, vol. 38, pp. 17444–17452 (2024)
8. Jiang, J., Lu, Z.: I2q: a fully decentralized q-learning algorithm. Adv. Neural. Inf. Process. Syst. **35**, 20469–20481 (2022)
9. Lin, T., Huh, J., Stauffer, C., Lim, S.N., Isola, P.: Learning to ground multi-agent communication with autoencoders. Adv. Neural. Inf. Process. Syst. **34**, 15230–15242 (2021)
10. Liu, B., Pu, Z., Pan, Y., Yi, J., Liang, Y., Zhang, D.: Lazy agents: a new perspective on solving sparse reward problem in multi-agent reinforcement learning. In: International Conference on Machine Learning, pp. 21937–21950. PMLR (2023)
11. Lo, Y.L., Sengupta, B., Foerster, J., Noukhovitch, M.: Learning multi-agent communication with contrastive learning. arXiv preprint arXiv:2307.01403 (2023)
12. Pathak, D., Agrawal, P., Efros, A.A., Darrell, T.: Curiosity-driven exploration by self-supervised prediction. In: International conference on machine learning, pp. 2778–2787. PMLR (2017)
13. Toquebiau, M., Bredeche, N., Benamar, F., Jun, J.Y.: Joint intrinsic motivation for coordinated exploration in multi-agent deep reinforcement learning. arXiv preprint arXiv:2402.03972 (2024)
14. Wang, L., Wang, K., Pan, C., Xu, W., Aslam, N., Hanzo, L.: Multi-agent deep reinforcement learning-based trajectory planning for multi-UAV assisted mobile edge computing. IEEE Trans. Cogn. Commun. Netw. **7**(1), 73–84 (2020)
15. Wang, T., Wang, J., Wu, Y., Zhang, C.: Influence-based multi-agent exploration. arXiv preprint arXiv:1910.05512 (2019)
16. Xu, J., Zhong, F., Wang, Y.: Learning multi-agent coordination for enhancing target coverage in directional sensor networks. Adv. Neural. Inf. Process. Syst. **33**, 10053–10064 (2020)
17. Zhang, T., et al.: Noveld: a simple yet effective exploration criterion. Adv. Neural. Inf. Process. Syst. **34**, 25217–25230 (2021)
18. Zheng, L., et al.: Episodic multi-agent reinforcement learning with curiosity-driven exploration. Adv. Neural. Inf. Process. Syst. **34**, 3757–3769 (2021)
19. Zhou, M., Ma, X., Li, Y.: A novel multi-objective routing scheme based on cooperative multi-agent reinforcement learning for metaverse services in fixed 6g. In: WOCN (2023). https://dblp.org/rec/conf/wocc/ZhouML23, https://doi.org/10.1109/WOCC52294.2023.00029
20. Zhu, T., Jin, Y., Houssineau, J., Montana, G.: Mitigating relative over-generalization in multi-agent reinforcement learning. arXiv preprint arXiv:2411.11099 (2024)

Trustworthy Active Learning Through Reputation and Weighted Voting Mechanisms

Diogo Rosário, Luis Macedo(✉), and Amílcar Cardoso

CISUC - Centre for Informatics and Systems of the University of Coimbra, University of Coimbra, Coimbra, Portugal
diogorosario@student.uc.pt, {macedo,amilcar}@dei.uc.pt

Abstract. Active learning is a strategy designed to reduce annotation costs by allowing models to select the most informative samples from an unlabeled dataset, particularly in tasks like image classification. Integrated within the broader Human-in-the-loop framework, active learning creates an interactive process where human annotators play a role in labeling data. However, this interaction introduces variability in annotation quality, since annotators may differ in domain knowledge, experience, and reliability. Traditional active learning approaches often overlook these differences, assuming constant performance across all annotators. This assumption can lead to suboptimal model updates, especially when labels come from less reliable sources. To tackle this limitation, this work proposes a reputation-based framework that captures annotator performance over time and across domains. Reputation scores are computed based on past annotation accuracy and feedback from other annotators, and these scores are then used to weigh individual contributions through a voting mechanism. In addition, the study explores how annotator expertise and oracle size influence the effectiveness of this approach, evaluating their impact on model performance in controlled, simulated settings with imperfect annotators.

Keywords: Active Learning · Human-in-the-Loop · Trustworthy AI · Reputation · Weighted Voting · Imperfect Annotators

1 Introduction

The development of machine learning (ML) models often depends on the availability of large volumes of labeled data. Yet, in many real-world scenarios, collecting these labels is far from trivial, it is expensive, time-consuming, and often demands specialized human expertise. In response to these limitations, R. Munro [27] describes human-in-the-loop (HITL) learning as an alternative that allows human knowledge to be integrated into the model training process. One of the most widely adopted strategies within this paradigm is active learning (AL), where the model chooses which examples to label based on uncertainty,

I. Koprinska et al. (Eds.): ECML PKDD 2025, CCIS 2842, pp. 37–55, 2026.
https://doi.org/10.1007/978-3-032-19105-2_4

aiming to reduce annotation effort while still improving performance. In AL, the source of labels, typically a human or group of human annotators, is commonly referred to as an oracle. Its effectiveness can suffer in settings where the oracle is imperfect, which is, in fact, the norm rather than the exception in most practical situations. Many traditional approaches treat all members of the oracle as if they were equally reliable, ignoring the variability in human expertise. This can be problematic when some annotators are systematically wrong or inconsistent, and the model ends up learning from noisy or misleading inputs. In such cases, the challenge lies not only in selecting the right example to label, but also in deciding who within the oracle should be trusted with the task.

This work takes a closer look at how to make the annotation process in AL more robust in the face of these imperfections. To do so, its proposed a reputation-based mechanism that estimates how reliable each annotator is over time, and uses this information to guide both which examples are selected for annotation and how the final labels are aggregated. More specifically, this study is guided by three central questions: first, how can we define and integrate reputation into AL in a way that reflects real annotator behavior? Second, can such a reputation-aware strategy actually improve the quality of the models we train? And third, how do factors like annotator expertise and the number of annotators involved influence the overall performance of this method?

2 Related Work

2.1 Human-in-the-Loop Machine Learning

The concept of HITL, as introduced by R. Munro [27], refers to methodologies that incorporate human input into the design, training, and operation of AI systems. The premise is that the collaboration between human and machine intelligence can achieve results unattainable by either entity alone. In this paradigm, human agents intervene when automated systems encounter ambiguous or unresolved problems, creating a continuous feedback loop through which the system can iteratively improve its performance [5,28,45].

As noted by Wu et al. [45] and Chai et al. [5], human involvement can be incorporated at multiple stages of the model development lifecycle. In the *data preprocessing* phase, which includes tasks such as data extraction, integration, and cleaning, human agents can define extraction heuristics, resolve entity ambiguities, and validate corrections to ensure the consistency of the data and integrity. Afterward, during dataset construction, labeling becomes an important and resource intensive step [27,28]. By giving priority to the annotation of the most informative examples, human annotators enhance the model performance through a process of iterative refinements known as *data annotation* [5,45]. During the *model training* and *inference* phases, humans can contribute by resolving uncertain classifications, validating predictions, and refining decision boundaries.

Nevertheless, as mentioned by Munro [27], erroneous human annotations can significantly degrade model accuracy and, large scale annotation tasks can be costly and time consuming, given the slowness and limited scalability of human labor relative to automated processes [28].

2.2 Active Learning

AL is a branch of ML and it is also known as *query learning*. This method is based on the principle that a learning algorithm can actively choose the data, from which it learns, as described by B. Settles [36] and R. Munro [27]. For a traditional ML system to operate effectively, it typically requires hundreds or even thousands of labeled data points. AL can minimize this requirement by iteratively selecting the most informative samples from a pool of unlabeled data, $\mathcal{U} = \{x_1, x_2, \ldots, x_{n_u}\}$, where each x_i is a data point from the feature space $\mathcal{X}$. The selection is performed according to a given scenario, $S = \{s_1, s_2, \ldots, s_n\}$, which defines how the selection and annotation process is carried out during training. The goal is to acquire the corresponding labels y_i for selected x_i, where $y_i \in \mathcal{Y}$ and $\mathcal{Y}$ denotes the label space.

The selection of samples to be labeled (i.e., assigned a target value y_i) is guided by query strategies, $Q = \{q_1, q_2, \ldots, q_n\}$, which estimate the utility of each instance based on criteria such as uncertainty, representativeness, or diversity. The selected instances are then submitted to a set of annotators, $A = \{a_1, a_2, \ldots, a_m\}$, which can consist of humans, machines, or a combination of both, and are responsible for assigning the appropriate y_i values. The labeled instances $\langle x_i, y_i \rangle$ are added to the labeled dataset, $\mathcal{L} = \{\langle x_1, y_1 \rangle, \ldots, \langle x_{n_l}, y_{n_l} \rangle\}$, which is used to train the predictive model, or *learner*, represented by a function h that learns patterns in $\mathcal{L}$.

As mentioned previously, one of the main advantages of AL is that it reduces the number of labeled instances required to train the learner h. This is achieved by selecting the most informative examples from the unlabeled pool $\mathcal{U}$, thereby avoiding redundant labeling and improving the efficiency of the labeled set $\mathcal{L}$ [36]. This process is particularly relevant in contexts where labeled data is limited or costly to acquire, such as in medical imaging and natural language processing [27]. Besides, AL can accelerate the convergence of h by enabling it to reach a decent performance with fewer training iterations [37]. When integrated into HITL systems, the selection process enables the incorporation of human expertise from the annotator set ($|A|$), contributing to the system's adaptability and stability [28]. Despite these benefits, one issue is its sensitivity to noise and outliers since selection mechanisms based on query strategies may give priority to mislabeled or unrepresentative instances, negatively affecting the quality of $\mathcal{L}$ and the performance of h [36]. Besides, the effectiveness of AL is dependent on the choice of $q_i \in Q$, which may not generalize across different tasks or datasets [27]. From a computational perspective, repeatedly retraining h and continuously evaluating utility over $\mathcal{U}$ can be costly. And lastly, instances labeled through this process may not transfer effectively to other models or learning scenarios [37].

Scenarios. According to B. Settles [36], there are three main scenarios in which an AL system can query instances from the $\mathcal{U}$: *pool-based*, *stream-based*, and *membership query synthesis*.

On the first hand, in the *pool-based* scenario, a set of the most informative instances is selected from $\mathcal{U}$ based on a model trained on $\mathcal{L}$. These selected instances are then sent to a group of annotators for labeling. Once labeled, they are added to $\mathcal{L}$, and the model is retrained to improve its performance. Although widely used, this approach can be computationally demanding due to the repeated evaluation of a large number of candidates [39]. On the other hand, in the *stream-based* scenario, B. Settles [36] states that obtaining an instance from $\mathcal{U}$ must be assumed to be free or inexpensive, allowing it to be drawn from the data distribution before h decides whether to request its label. This method is also known as *sequential AL* because instances from $\mathcal{U}$ are retrieved one at a time. Lastly, in the *membership query synthesis* scenario, the learner h can request labels for any instance in the input space, including synthetically generated queries rather than those sampled from the distribution. This method is effective for finite problem domains and does not require processing $\mathcal{U}$, as h can quickly generate new query instances. However, a major limitation is that, in some cases, it can create instances that are difficult or impossible for an annotator in A to understand and label correctly [39].

Query Strategies. Query strategies define how an AL system selects which instances to label, based on a utility function applied to the $\mathcal{U}$ [27,36]. These strategies are generally divided into two categories: information-based, which prioritize uncertain instances near the model's decision boundary, and representation-based, which aim to select instances that best reflect the structure of the data distribution [39].

As for information-based [39], *uncertainty sampling* [27,36] selects the samples for which the model h is least confident. This strategy includes three main methods: first, *least confidence*, which selects instances with the lowest predicted probability for the most likely class; second, *margin sampling*, which focuses on the smallest difference between the top two class probabilities; and third, *entropy sampling*, which considers the overall uncertainty across all class probabilities. Furthermore, *query-by-committee* [36] selects instances that lead to the highest disagreement among a group of models (the committee). In this case, disagreement is often quantified using vote entropy. Finally, *expected model change* selects instances that would lead to the greatest change in the model if labeled. One example of this is the expected gradient length, where the expected magnitude of the gradient update is used as a selection criterion [5,50].

In contrast, representation-based strategies [39] focus on selecting instances that best reflect the structure of the input space. For example, *density sampling* [27] selects instances from high-density regions, using similarity measures such as the distance between feature vectors, with the goal of querying representative points. Additionally, *diversity sampling* gives priority to instances that maximize the coverage of the feature space, aiming to reduce redundancy by selecting diverse samples relative to the $\mathcal{L}$ set [27]. Lastly, *cluster-based* strategies partition the data into clusters and select the instances closest to the cluster centers [27].

Finally, it is also important to mention the *random* query strategy, which selects unlabeled instances entirely at random, without considering information from the data distribution or model predictions. This strategy serves purely as a baseline for evaluating other query methods [27,36].

2.3 Trust and Reputation

Trust. Trust (hereafter represented as $\mathcal{T}$), is a concept that has been studied extensively in various fields, leading to multiple definitions. S. Marsh [26], author of the *Marsh* $\mathcal{T}$ model, and M. Deutsch [9] describe $\mathcal{T}$ as a common social phenomenon. According to them, trusting behaviour arises when an individual faces an uncertain decision path, the outcome of which can be either positive or negative and depends on the actions of another individual. If the negative outcome is potentially more harmful than the positive outcome and the individual still chooses to proceed, this is considered a trusting decision. If not, the individual is said to be acting with distrust. Moreover, in groups composed of many individuals, situations often arise that require cooperation in order to achieve common goals. Such cooperation typically depends on $\mathcal{T}$, which can be established either explicitly, through agreements, or implicitly, through observation of behaviour over time [33,34]. To complement this, Hoelz et al. [18] and J. Sabater et al. [34] add that $\mathcal{T}$ is crucial for meaningful social interactions within multi-agent systems. They define it as the quantified belief held by a *trustor* about the qualities of a *trustee*, such as competence, commitment, honesty, security, and dependability, evaluated in the context of the interaction.

A. Jøsang et al. [21], building on the ideas of S. Marsh [26], define $\mathcal{T}$ as a willingness to rely on another entity in a particular context, despite the potential for negative outcomes, driven by a sense of relative security. I. Pinyol et al. [30] see it as a process of practical reasoning that ultimately leads to a decision to engage with another entity.

In addition, a study by F. Mafızoğlu et al. [14] identifies and examines factors that influence $\mathcal{T}$ between entities, which can be humans, artificial agents, or both. They argue that $\mathcal{T}$ is inherently relational and applies to human-to-human, agent-to-agent, and human-to-agent interactions. In their research, they identified factors that are relevant to both humans and artificial agents. First, common factors include characteristics that the entities share, such as task performance, clarity of communication, reliability, and transparency of actions or decisions. Second, human-specific factors include characteristics that are unique to humans, such as age [1], personality [10], mood [15], and personal ideologies [16]. Finally, agent-specific factors are those that evaluate the trustworthiness of agents based on their hardware architecture, type of agent, technical precision, defection [43], cooperativeness, and deception [44], since artificial agents do not possess emotions.

Reputation. J. Sabater et al. [33,34], T. Huynh [19], and A. Jøsang et al. [21] agree that reputation, $\mathcal{R}$, is constructed from observations about an individual's past behaviour. This means that, in order to build a measure of $\mathcal{R}$, a particular individual needs to consult other individuals in a community to gather their observations about the current individual being evaluated. These observations are usually in the form of ratings that individuals give to one another after an interaction. Once collected and aggregated, these ratings can be used to represent the $\mathcal{R}$ of an individual.

T. Huynh [19] further adds that $\mathcal{R}$ and $\mathcal{T}$ in each interaction have a close relationship, because the $\mathcal{T}$ that an individual A places in B after an interaction is reflected by the rating provided by A. Since the $\mathcal{R}$ of an individual is built based on the ratings given by others, it can be said that the $\mathcal{R}$ of an individual B is constructed from the interaction $\mathcal{T}$ it receives from others in the community, even when those ratings may be imperfect. Furthermore, $\mathcal{R}$ serves as a decision-making mechanism when an individual A lacks sufficient knowledge or experience with B, using the $\mathcal{R}$ of B as a proxy for reliability, as discussed by I. Pinyol [30] and J. Sabater et al. [34]. Expanding on this concept, the FIRE model proposed by T. Huynh [19] adds more complexity to the idea of $\mathcal{R}$. For example, the author introduces the concept of *witness* $\mathcal{R}$, which is constructed from reports provided by third parties regarding an individual's behaviour, and the concept of *certified* $\mathcal{R}$, which is obtained from provable references presented by the individual itself.

Classification Dimensions. $\mathcal{T}$ and $\mathcal{R}$ are complex concepts, applied across diverse contexts, which makes their classification a difficult task. Therefore, as noted by J. Sabater et al. [34], it is essential to classify the dimensions that these concepts could extend to.

The authors [34] describe that $\mathcal{T}$ and $\mathcal{R}$ can be modeled in two distinct ways: (i) as *cognitive models*, introduced by B. Esfandiari et al. [11] in 2001, which conceptualize $\mathcal{T}$ or $\mathcal{R}$ as merely beliefs, and understood as functions that represent a level of confidence in an entity or individual, or (ii) as *game-theoretical models*, which interpret them as probabilities that reflect one's expectations about another's actions, similar to Bayesian networks, as presented by D. Gambetta [13].

Moreover, $\mathcal{T}$ and $\mathcal{R}$ are context-dependent variables [34], meaning that the level of $\mathcal{T}$ or $\mathcal{R}$ attributed to an individual can vary according to the situation. For example, trusting a doctor to recommend medication does not imply the same level of $\mathcal{T}$ when the same doctor suggests a bottle of wine. With this example, the authors distinguish between two types of context variables: *single-context*, which assign a single $\mathcal{T}$ or $\mathcal{R}$ value to each partner regardless of the situation, and *multi-context*, which maintain separate values for each context or, in other words, domain.

2.4 Imperfect Annotators

Traditional AL algorithms assume labeling oracles or, more precisely, annotators, to be infallible, always providing correct labels. However, this is an assumption that often fails in real-world scenarios, where annotators may offer labels of various types of qualities, as noted by S. Chakraborty [6]. One the first hand, the performance of human annotators depends on various factors, including expertise, experience, concentration, interest, and fatigue [2]. On the other hand, labels derived from simulations or test stands are subject to uncertainty due to imperfections, sensor noise, or transmission errors [3]. Additionally, the accuracy of the oracles answers can depend on how difficult the labeling task is since for simpler classification problems, oracles are more likely to give correct labels. As the task becomes more complex, it is more likely that oracles will be uncertain about their responses, and here, the term uncertainty is used as defined by Motro et al. [29], and refers to situations where the answer may be unlikely, unclear, unreliable, inconsistent, or hard to define precisely.

Urner et al., in their research [40], provide a good example of this topic since they discussed that certain datasets require labeling by top human experts, which can be both complex and costly. For instance, classifying brain tumors from CT scans as benign or malignant falls under this category. As a more cost-effective alternative, medical students could label these images, as they are more available and less expensive to employ. However, it is important to note that the labels provided by students may be inaccurate, especially for images that are difficult to classify.

Besides, Yan et al. [47] mention that when working with multiple annotators, the challenge is not just to pick the most informative sample to label, but also to choose the right annotator to label it. This adds a new dimension to AL because, some annotators can be more reliable than others, may behave maliciously, or have different levels of expertise depending on the domain.

Another important aspect raised by same authors [47] concerns the allocation of annotators when dealing with multiple unreliable sources. The authors propose an alternative method by simulating synthetic annotators, and rather than relying on human input, each synthetic annotator is modeled probabilistically through a confusion matrix. For instance, an annotator may correctly label class A 90% of the time while misclassifying it as class B in the remaining 10%. By drawing labels according to these distributions, the model is able to reproduce annotators with different levels of knowledge in each domain.

3 Methodology

In order to address the research questions stated, this study proposes a framework that takes into account evaluation metrics, paying particular attention to $\mathcal{R}$. The framework consists of a cycle of AL organised around five elements: the learner, which represents the model h; the data D, which is composed of $\mathcal{L}$ and $\mathcal{U}$; the query strategy; the scenario; and the oracle A. Building upon this structure, the study considers only a single learner, initially trained on a small portion of $\mathcal{L}$. The learner operates in a *pool-based* selective sampling scenario, where at each iteration it has access to the entire $\mathcal{U}$ and selects a small pool of the most informative instances to query from the oracle A. Here, informativeness is measured using the *least confidence* query strategy, which selects the instance for which h has the lowest predicted confidence in its most likely y.

Then, a weighted voting system is applied, where each annotator contributes to the final decision proportionally to their individual $\mathcal{R}$ within a specific domain.

As a result, the oracle A, which consists of multiple simulated annotators, assigns a label y to each queried instance based on the aggregated votes. Once labeled, the instance is added to the $\mathcal{L}$, and the model h is updated accordingly. This cycle is repeated iteratively; that is, new samples are queried, labeled, and used to retrain h until a stopping condition is reached, such as a maximum number of queries. In what follows, the next sections provide an detailed explanation of each step involved in this process.

3.1 Synthetic Annotators

To simulate imperfect annotators, one could consider training them on existing datasets. However, this approach would significantly reduce the amount of data available for training, testing, and validating the model h. Even with access to large datasets containing diverse annotations, training a statistically significant number of annotators would be time-consuming. To overcome these limitations, its possible to simulate synthetic annotators using the strategy proposed by Yan et al. [47]. Following their method, each annotator $a_i \in A$ is modeled probabilistically by generating a confusion matrix π^{a_i}, where each row is sampled from a *dirichlet* distribution.

Consider a classification task with $K = 3$ classes, $\mathcal{Y} = \{0, 1, 2\}$. For annotator a_i, we define the confusion matrix $\pi^{a_i} \in \mathbb{R}^{K \times K}$, where each row $\pi_c^{a_i}$ corresponds to the true class $c \in \mathcal{Y}$ and represents a probability distribution over the predicted labels $k \in \mathcal{Y}$. Each row is generated as:

$$\pi_c^{a_i} \sim \text{Dirichlet}(\boldsymbol{\alpha}_c) \tag{1}$$

Here, $\boldsymbol{\alpha}_c = [\alpha_{c_0}, \alpha_{c_1}, \alpha_{c_2}]$ is the *dirichlet* concentration vector for true class c, where each α_{c_k} corresponds to the concentration parameter for predicting class k when the true class is c. Assigning a higher value to $\alpha_{c,c}$ (i.e., the diagonal element of the concentration vector) increases the probability that the annotator labels an instance of class c correctly. For instance, the resulting confusion matrix π^{a_i} might be:

$$\pi^{a_i} = \begin{bmatrix} 0.85 & 0.10 & 0.05 \\ 0.20 & 0.70 & 0.10 \\ 0.10 & 0.25 & 0.65 \end{bmatrix} \tag{2}$$

In this example, annotator a_i is particularly accurate in labeling instances of class 0 compared to classes 1 and 2, suggesting a stronger familiarity with that class. However, this does not necessarily imply domain expertise in a semantic sense. One could argue that an expert annotator should also recognize hierarchical subtypes (e.g., if the parent class is *tree*, the expert should identify subtypes like oak, palm, or pine).

Besides, by adjusting $\boldsymbol{\alpha}_c$, it is possible to simulate different levels of annotator domain knowledge. Following the ideas of Hannah et al. [17], to control the expected accuracy acc_t of an annotator in their expert class c, we rely on the property that the expected value of the Dirichlet-distributed probability for class k is:

$$\mathbb{E}[\pi^{a_i}_{c,k}] = \frac{\alpha_{c,k}}{\sum_{k'=0}^{K-1} \alpha_{c,k'}} \tag{3}$$

Given a total of K classes and a target expected accuracy acc_t for the expert class c, we set the concentration parameter for the correct label $k = c$ as:

$$\alpha_{c,c} = \frac{(K-1) \cdot acc_t}{1 - acc_t} \tag{4}$$

The remaining $K - 1$ classes receive a base concentration of 1.0. The resulting Dirichlet vector $\boldsymbol{\alpha}_c$ is then defined as:

$$\alpha_{c,k} = \begin{cases} \alpha_{c,c} & \text{if } k = c \\ 1.0 & \text{otherwise} \end{cases} \tag{5}$$

In addition to the expected accuracy, it is important to note that setting a desired expected value does not deterministically fix the sampled outcome. Due to the stochastic nature of the Dirichlet process, there exists a variance around the expected value, which reflects the uncertainty inherent to each sampled probability vector [23]. This variability is quantified by the variance of the Dirichlet distribution, which is given by:

$$\mathrm{Var}[p_c] = \frac{\alpha_{c,c}(\alpha_0 - \alpha_{c,c})}{\alpha_0^2(\alpha_0 + 1)} \tag{6}$$

where $\alpha_{c,c}$ is the concentration parameter associated with the correct class index c and $\alpha_0 = \sum_{j=0}^{K-1} \alpha_{c,j}$ is the total concentration for the Dirichlet distribution associated with class c.

3.2 Trust

Any definition of $\mathcal{T}$ stated in the last sections can be used in the context of AL, but because there are so many variables and conditions involved, some of them may add extra complexity. Therefore, without implementing *Marsh's* complete $\mathcal{T}$ model, this work accepts the general definition of $\mathcal{T}$ proposed by S. Marsh [26] and later extended by A. Jøsang et al. [21]. In the context of AL, $\mathcal{T}$ is relevant because the learner h relies on the oracle A to provide accurate labels for uncertain samples. For this reason, $\mathcal{T}$ is simply defined in this study as the willingness to rely on an entity despite potential consequences. Therefore, $\mathcal{T}$ is understood as the learner's belief that the oracle will provide trustworthy annotations, regardless of its errors. However, since annotators only assign labels and evaluate each other's annotations, $\mathcal{T}$ is not extended to other components of the system.

Other perspectives that take social aspects into account when modelling $\mathcal{T}$ include those of J. Sabater [34] and F. Mafizoğlu et al. [14]. These may be relevant, but due to their complexity, they are beyond the scope of this study. In addition, since the primary goal is to examine $\mathcal{R}$, we will not categorise this variable according to its dimensions, which include granularity, visibility, and type of conceptual model.

3.3 Reputation

This work adopts the notion of $\mathcal{R}$ as defined by J. Sabater et al. [33,34], and later extended by Huynh [19] and Jøsang et al. [21]. In their view, $\mathcal{R}$ is understood as a collective judgment of an agent $\mathcal{T}$, formed from the evaluations provided by other members within a community.

Building on this notion, each annotator a_j, in the context of AL, is assigned a reputation value $\mathcal{R}$ that is updated through peer evaluations. In order for $\mathcal{R}$ to exist in this setting, annotators need to rate each other after each labeling interaction. Specifically, these ratings are binary and converted into a score $\mathcal{S}$, being either good (+1) or bad (+0), depending on whether the annotators agreed on their predicted label. For example, if annotator a_1 evaluates a_2, then a_2 receives a good rating if both provided the same label for the queried instance; otherwise, the rating is bad.

Following the *multi-context scenario* [34], $\mathcal{R}$ can be treated as a class-wise property, recognizing that annotators can exhibit levels of expertises across multiple domains. Thus, a separate reputation value is maintained for each class. Given K classes, each annotator a_j has K reputation values, one per class $c \in \{1, 2, ..., K\}$. The score of annotator a_j for class c at interaction step t is computed as:

$$\mathcal{S}_j^{(c,t)} = \frac{1}{N} \sum_{i=1}^{N} r_i^{(c,t)} \tag{7}$$

where N is the number of ratings received at time t for class c, and $r \in \{0, 1\}$. However, scores $\mathcal{S}_j$ alone can be insufficient to fully capture $\mathcal{R}$, since they are based only on ratings. Therefore, it is important to include the accuracy, Acc_j, of the annotators, because it allows us to incorporate ground truth information. The reputation $\mathcal{R}_j$ of annotator a_j for class c at time t is thus defined as:

$$\mathcal{R}_j^{(c,t)} = \alpha \cdot \mathcal{S}_j^{(c,t)} + \beta \cdot Acc_j^{(c,t)} \tag{8}$$

Regarding visibility [34], $\mathcal{R}$ is modeled as a *global property*: all annotators evaluate every other peer in the oracle and have access to each other's reputation scores. Modeling $\mathcal{R}$ as a *subjective property* would involve simulating scenarios where each annotator only has access to a limited amount of information about the others.

3.4 Oracle Decision

According to Y. Qian et al. [31], individuals with higher reputations in a given domain are more likely to provide correct answers in real-world scenarios. Building on this principle, a component of the proposed framework involves defining the mechanism by which the oracle determines the final label to be assigned to each queried instance. Two strategies have been proposed and studied in the literature: majority voting and weighted voting.

Majority voting, where each annotator contributes equally to the final decision, is one common aggregation methods [8,32,42]. However, this method assumes that all annotators are equally competent which is an assumption that often does not hold in practical settings. In particular, as noted by V. Sheng et al. [38] and Y. Zhang et al. [52], the presence of low-quality or noisy annotators can introduce significant label noise, negatively affecting the model's training and generalization performance.

To solve these limitations, this study adopts a *weighted voting* approach, in which each annotator's vote is scaled according to their reputation score. In doing so, this allows the oracle to give more influence to reliable annotators. Besides, weighted voting has been validated in several works that explicitly model annotator trustworthiness over time, including D. Zhou et at. [53], P. Jin et al. [20], and Y. Zhang et al. [51]. As a result, it is possible to improve the oracle's ability to handle annotation noise and operate more effectively in AL scenarios by integrating reputation-weighted voting, especially when annotation budgets are limited and each labeled instance carries a significant impact for the learner. In the case of ties, when two or more classes receive the same total reputation score, we adopt a random selection strategy among the tied classes. Although one alternative could be to choose the class with the most votes (i.e., majority count), this may inadvertently favor quantity over quality, especially in early iterations where reputation estimates are still stabilizing [38].

4 Experimental Setup

This study evaluates a reputation-based AL strategy under three main conditions: (i) using three different reputation configurations; (ii) varying levels of annotator expertise; and (iii) different oracle sizes. For the first 10 classes of the *MNIST* [25], *MNIST-Fashion* [46], *EMNIST-Letters* [7] and *CIFAR-10* [24] datasets, we explore all combinations of these three factors.

The interaction between the oracle and the learner h follows the procedure described in Sect. 3.4, in which the oracle selects the class whose total $\mathcal{R}$, summed across all voting annotators, is the highest. To isolate the effect of $\mathcal{R}$, we control the contribution of its two components, $\mathcal{S}$ (peer ratings) and Acc (past accuracy), using weighting parameters α and β, respectively. Three configurations are considered: (a) when $\alpha = 1.0$ and $\beta = 0.0$, $\mathcal{R}$ is based only on peer ratings; (b) when both weights are set to 0.5, the $\mathcal{R}$ combines $\mathcal{S}$ and Acc equally; and (c) when $\alpha = 0.0$ and $\beta = 1.0$, only annotator Acc is used to compute $\mathcal{R}$.

Besides, each annotator a_i is randomly assigned a single class $c \in \mathcal{Y}$ in which they are considered an expert, a designation that remains fixed throughout the experiments. Their labeling behavior is simulated using a *dirichlet* distribution to generate class-conditional probability vectors, forming the confusion matrix π^{a_i}. The *dirichlet* vector $\boldsymbol{\alpha}_c$ is configured such that the expert class receives a higher concentration parameter α_{exp}, while the remaining $K-1$ classes receive a base value of 2.5. The level of expertise, *Low*, *Medium*, or *High*, determines the value of α_{exp}, which is calculated using the formula described previously, corresponding approximately to 40%, 70%, or 98% expected accuracy, acc_t (Table 1).

Table 1. Values of α_{exp} and corresponding expected accuracy for expertise levels.

Configuration	α_{exp}	acc_t (%)
High Expertise	441.0	98
Medium Expertise	21.0	70
Low Expertise	6.0	40

The resulting *dirichlet* concentration matrices $\boldsymbol{\alpha}^{a_i} \in \mathbb{R}^{K \times K}$ describe the behavior of each annotator. Each row corresponds to a true class c, and the elements specify the *dirichlet* concentration parameters used to sample a probability distribution over the predicted labels. The matrix is constructed such that one randomly selected class receives the expert-level concentration α_{exp} and the others follow a uniform pattern with base values (Fig. 1).

$$\begin{bmatrix} \mathbf{6.0} & 1.0 & \cdots & 1.0 \\ 1.0 & 2.5 & \cdots & 1.0 \\ \vdots & \vdots & \ddots & \vdots \\ 1.0 & 1.0 & \cdots & 2.5 \end{bmatrix}$$

Low Expertise

$$\begin{bmatrix} 2.5 & 1.0 & \cdots & 1.0 \\ \vdots & \mathbf{21.0} & \cdots & \vdots \\ \vdots & \vdots & \ddots & \vdots \\ 1.0 & 1.0 & \cdots & 2.5 \end{bmatrix}$$

Medium Expertise

$$\begin{bmatrix} 2.5 & 1.0 & \cdots & 1.0 \\ 1.0 & 2.5 & \cdots & 1.0 \\ \vdots & \vdots & \ddots & \vdots \\ 1.0 & 1.0 & \cdots & \mathbf{441.0} \end{bmatrix}$$

High Expertise

Fig. 1. Concentration matrices ($K = 10$) for different expertises.

It is also relevant to study how the number of annotators (i.e., the oracle size) affects the performance of the reputation system. To this end, we include three oracle size configurations in the experiments: a small oracle composed of 5 annotators, a medium oracle with 15 annotators, and a large oracle consisting of 30 annotators. Lastly, the next table can resume all the variables and their configurations used in the research (Table 2).

Table 2. Summary of the variables in the experiments.

Variables	Configuration
Scenario	Pool-Based
Query Strategy	Least Confidence Sampling
Oracle Answer	Weighted Reputation Voting
Reputation Configuration	Only $\mathcal{S}$, Both $\mathcal{S}$ and Acc, Only Acc
Oracle Sizes	5, 15, 30
Expertise Levels	High (H), Medium (M), Low (L)

Training was conducted using the *Adam* optimizer due to its adoption in training CNNs such as *LeNet-5*, where it has been shown to achieve accurate results in image classification tasks [41,49]. Regarding the learning rate, initial experiments tested the values 0.0001 and 0.01, which are commonly reported in the literature for *LeNet-5* training [4,22,49] and based on these results, a value of 0.002 was chosen. As for the batch size, preliminary tests revealed that smaller batches did not fully utilize the available GPU acceleration, resulting in data processing speeds comparable to CPU-bound training. Increasing the batch size allowed for better exploitation of the GPU's processing capabilities, with 256 as a value that ensured a better speed in training h.

Before the start of the AL cycles, the model h was pretrained on a small *labeledsubset* corresponding to approximately 0.3% of the training data, which is a common practice in the literature, where initial labeled sets typically range from 0.1% to 2.5%, as reported by other authors [12,35,48]. Each AL cycle included exactly 10 training epochs, resulting in a total of up to 2.500 training epochs over the 250 iterations conducted throughout the experiments. Within each iteration, sample selection followed a pool-based strategy, in which 16 instances were selected from $\mathcal{U}$ based on the predictive uncertainty of h. The model h was trained using the *cross-entropy* loss function, which measures the discrepancy between the predicted probabilities and the true labels $y_i \in \mathcal{Y}$. This same loss was employed to evaluate h on the validation set after each iteration, and the final performance was calculated only at the end of the process using the test set.

Besides, each configuration was repeated 30 times, with the seed assigned according to the run index, ranging from 0 to 29. Consequently, results are reported as the average and standard deviation computed across the 30 independent runs in which no early stopping was applied.

5 Results and Discussion

In the *MNIST* dataset, the configuration that combines both $\mathcal{S}$ and *Acc* achieves the highest results across all metrics and $|A|$, particularly for annotators with L and M expertise. In comparison to the configuration that uses only *Acc*, the performance differences generally remain below 1.5%, and are more evident for L expertise, especially at $|A| = 15$ and $|A| = 30$. On the other hand, the configuration that considers only $\mathcal{S}$ shows lower results in all settings, with differences ranging from 1% to 2.5% relative to the other $\mathcal{R}$ configurations. Similarly, in *MNIST-Fashion*, the combination of $\mathcal{S}$ and *Acc* leads to the highest results, particularly for M and H expertise. Although the differences with the *Acc*-only configuration are generally below 2%, the $\mathcal{S}$-only configuration consistently produces lower values, often with differences exceeding 3% to 5%. With regard to *EMNIST-Letters*, the use of *Acc* alone results in the best performance in most cases; however, the gap in comparison to the combined configuration remains below 1% in all scenarios. In contrast, using only $\mathcal{S}$ results in a reduced performance, especially for smaller $|A|$, where the differences frequently surpass 5%.

Finally, in the *CIFAR-10* dataset, the configurations involving *Acc*, whether alone or in combination with $\mathcal{S}$, tend to outperform the $\mathcal{S}$-only approach. Nevertheless, the difference between the *Acc*-only and the combined configurations remains typically under 1%.

Across all reputation configurations, the oracle size ($|A|$) influences the final performance outcomes, as larger $|A|$ were systematically associated with better results across all experiments and datasets. The improvements observed when increasing $|A|$ from 5 to 30 ranged from approximately 12% to 18% in accuracy for *CIFAR-10*, 20% to 28% for *MNIST-Fashion*, 24% to 45% for *MNIST*, and up to 47% in *EMNIST-Letters*. The same trend is observed for expertise level, although the magnitude of improvement is less than the influence of $|A|$. In most cases, the increase from L to M falls within an interval of approximately 3–5%, while the improvement from M to H tends to be smaller and less significant, typically around 2%. Nonetheless, this progression is not always consistent since, in configurations that include *Acc*, a slight performance decrease, typically under 2%, is occasionally observed when moving from M to H expertise at $|A| = 5$, and sometimes at $|A| = 15$. This effect, however, is not present when $|A| = 30$.

In terms of reputation, the experiments showed that, in configurations including *Acc*, reputation values increase significantly with expertise level, by approximately 10%, but remain unaffected by changes in oracle size ($|A|$). On the contrary, in the configuration that considers only $\mathcal{S}$, reputation increases with oracle size by around 8%, but remains stable across different levels of expertise.

Finally, it is important to note that the results related to the annotators showed no variation, as they were generated in the same way using 30 different seeds, each corresponding to the index of the run being executed.

6 Conclusion

To conclude, this study began by simulating imperfect annotators using probabilistic confusion matrices sampled from *dirichlet* distributions. Each annotator was assigned a specific domain of expertise, modeled as a single class for which they had a higher likelihood of producing correct labels. To reflect different degrees of domain knowledge, three levels of expertise were defined, corresponding to expected accuracies of 40%, 70%, and 98%. Building on this setup, a reputation model was formulated to capture how reliable each annotator was in different domains. This model combined two components: the annotator's observed accuracy (*Acc*) for each class, and the ratings they received from others ($\mathcal{S}$), over time.

Whenever the learner queried a new instance, a group of annotators responded with their predictions and the final label was chosen through a weighted voting mechanism, where each vote was scaled according to the annotator's reputation for the queried class. In this way, the labeling process accounted not just for consensus but also for the reliability of each annotator, grounded in both their past performance and agreement with others.

Following this, results showed that combining $\mathcal{S}$ and *Acc* generally led to small increases in accuracy across all datasets when compared to using *Acc* alone.

For instance, in the case of *MNIST*, the combined reputation outperformed *Acc* by approximately 0.7%, 0.9%, and 0.3% for oracle sizes $|A| = 5$, 15, and 30. In *MNIST-Fashion*, for $|A| = 5$ and 15, increases were about 0.9% and 1.3%, while the difference for $|A| = 30$ was smaller, roughly 0.8%. The *CIFAR-10* dataset showed improvements below 0.5% for all oracle sizes. In contrast, the *EMNIST-Letters* dataset exhibited benefits from the combined configuration, particularly with $|A| = 30$, where accuracy increased by nearly 1.5%. On the other hand, relying only on $\mathcal{S}$ generally resulted in lower performance, especially when $|A| = 5$, accuracy dropped by around 1.5% in *MNIST*, 3% in *MNIST-Fashion*, more than 5% in *EMNIST-Letters*, and about 1.5% in *CIFAR-10*. These reductions tended to diminish as $|A|$ increased, but in most cases, performance still remained below that of *Acc* alone.

Moreover, results also show that both $|A|$ and annotator expertise influenced model performance. Specifically, increasing $|A|$ from 5 to 30 led to improvements ranging from 12% in *CIFAR-10* to as much as 47% in *EMNIST-Letters*, with the other datasets showing similar trends. Annotator expertise also had a positive impact: transitioning from L to M expertise resulted in accuracy gains of approximately 3% to 5%. However, moving from M to H expertise did not consistently lead to improvements. In scenarios with smaller oracles ($|A| = 5$ or 15), accuracy even declined by up to 2%. Nevertheless, this effect was no longer observed when $|A| = 30$.

For future work, there are many directions in which this study can be extended. One possibility is to explore different query strategies, such as margin sampling or entropy sampling, instead of using uncertainty sampling alone. Since, this would help to understand whether the reputation mechanism adapts well to different selection criteria. It would also be useful to test more levels of annotator expertise since, in this study, only three levels were used (Low, Medium, and High), but adding more levels (such as five instead of three) could reveal a more detailed pattern in how expertise influences performance. Another direction is to vary the oracle sizes beyond the three used here ($|A| = 5$, 15, 30), and to see whether the trends observed remain consistent. It may also be interesting to explore alternative ways of defining reputation itself. For example, instead of requiring that all annotators rate each other, one could study scenarios where only a subset of annotators provides ratings, or where a single designated expert is responsible for evaluating others.

Declaration on Generative AI

Generative AI, including Perplexity and Grammarly, was used in the preparation of this paper to assist with improving the quality of the English language.

References

1. Blank, G., Dutton, W.H.: Age and trust in the internet: the centrality of experience and attitudes toward technology in Britain. Soc. Sci. Comput. Rev. **30**, 135–151 (2012). https://doi.org/10.1177/0894439310396186
2. Calma, A., et al.: From active learning to dedicated collaborative interactive learning. In: Dagstuhl Manifestos, vol. 5, pp. 1–27. Schloss Dagstuhl–Leibniz-Zentrum fuer Informatik (2016). https://doi.org/10.4230/DagMan.5.1.1. https://drops.dagstuhl.de/opus/volltexte/2016/5552
3. Calma, A., Sick, B.: Simulation of annotators for active learning: uncertain oracles. In: Proceedings of the Workshop and Tutorial on Interactive Adaptive Learning @ ECML PKDD 2017. CEUR Workshop Proceedings, vol. 1924, pp. 49–58 (2017). https://ceur-ws.org/Vol-1924/paper_6.pdf
4. Carlini, N., Wagner, D.: Towards evaluating the robustness of neural networks. In: 2017 IEEE Symposium on Security and Privacy (SP), pp. 39–57. IEEE (2017). https://doi.org/10.1109/SP.2017.49. https://ieeexplore.ieee.org/document/7958570
5. Chai, C., Li, G.: Human-in-the-loop techniques in machine learning. IEEE Data Eng. Bull. **43**(3), 37–52 (2020)
6. Chakraborty, S.: Asking the right questions to the right users: active learning with imperfect oracles. In: Proceedings of the AAAI Conference on Artificial Intelligence, vol. 34, no. 04, pp. 3365–3372 (2020). https://doi.org/10.1609/aaai.v34i04.5738
7. Cohen, G., Afshar, S., Tapson, J., Van Schaik, A.: EMNIST: extending MNIST to handwritten letters. In: 2017 International Joint Conference on Neural Networks (IJCNN) (2017). https://doi.org/10.1109/IJCNN.2017.7966217
8. Dawid, A.P., Skene, A.M.: Maximum likelihood estimation of observer error-rates using the EM algorithm. J. Roy. Stat. Soc.: Ser. C (Appl. Stat.) **28**(1), 20–28 (1979). https://doi.org/10.2307/2346806
9. Deutsch, M.: Cooperation and trust: some theoretical notes. In: Jones, M.R. (ed.) Nebraska Symposium on Motivation, pp. 275–319. University of Nebraska Press, Lincoln (1962)
10. Du, H., Huhns, M.: Determining the effect of personality types on human-agent interactions. In: Proceedings of the 2013 IEEE/WIC/ACM International Conference on Intelligent Agent Technology (IAT 2013), vol. 2, pp. 239–244 (2013). https://doi.org/10.1109/WI-IAT.2013.115
11. Esfandiari, B., Chandrasekharan, S.: On how agents make friends: mechanisms for trust acquisition (2001). https://www.robocup.org
12. Gal, Y., Islam, R., Ghahramani, Z.: Deep Bayesian active learning with image data. In: Precup, D., Teh, Y.W. (eds.) Proceedings of the 34th International Conference on Machine Learning. Proceedings of Machine Learning Research, vol. 70, pp. 1183–1192. PMLR (2017). https://proceedings.mlr.press/v70/gal17a.html
13. Gambetta, D.: Can we trust trust? In: Gambetta, D. (ed.) Trust: Making and Breaking Cooperative Relations, pp. 213–237. Blackwell (1988)
14. Hafızoğlu, F.M., Sen, S.: Reputation based trust in human-agent teamwork without explicit coordination. In: Proceedings of the 6th International Conference on Human-Agent Interaction (HAI 2018), pp. 238–245. Association for Computing Machinery, Inc. (2018). https://doi.org/10.1145/3284432.3284454
15. Hafızoğlu, F.M., Sen, S.: Understanding the influences of past experience on trust in human-agent teamwork. ACM Trans. Internet Technol. **19**(4), 1–22 (2019). https://doi.org/10.1145/3324300

16. Haim, G., Gal, Y.K., Gelfand, M., Kraus, S.: A cultural sensitive agent for human-computer negotiation. In: Proceedings of the 11th International Conference on Autonomous Agents and Multiagent Systems (AAMAS 2012), , vol. 1, pp. 451–458. International Foundation for Autonomous Agents and Multiagent Systems, Richland, SC (2012). https://dl.acm.org/doi/10.5555/2343576.2343652
17. Hannah, L.A., Blei, D.M., Powell, W.B.: Dirichlet process mixtures of generalized linear models. J. Mach. Learn. Res. **12**(Apr), 1923–1953 (2011)
18. Hoelz, B.W.P., Ralha, C.G.: Towards a cognitive meta-model for adaptive trust and reputation in open multi-agent systems. Auton. Agent. Multi-Agent Syst. **29**(6), 1125–1156 (2015). https://doi.org/10.1007/s10458-014-9278-9
19. Huynh, T.D.: Trust and reputation in open multi-agent systems. Ph.D. thesis (2006)
20. Jin, P., Wang, Y., Liu, Y., Zhou, Z.H.: Combining crowd and machine predictions for cost-effective learning. In: Proceedings of the 26th International Joint Conference on Artificial Intelligence (IJCAI), pp. 1634–1640. International Joint Conferences on Artificial Intelligence Organization (2017). https://doi.org/10.24963/ijcai.2017/226
21. Jøsang, A., Presti, S.L.: Analysing the relationship between risk and trust. https://www.josang.com/doc/JoLP2004-TrustRisk.pdf, available online. No publication details provided
22. Kingma, D.P., Ba, J.: Adam: a method for stochastic optimization. In: International Conference on Learning Representations (ICLR) (2015). https://arxiv.org/abs/1412.6980
23. Kotz, S., Balakrishnan, N., Johnson, N.L.: Continuous Multivariate Distributions, Volume 1: Models and Applications, 2nd edn. Wiley (2000)
24. Krizhevsky, A., Nair, V., Hinton, G.: CIFAR-10 (Canadian institute for advanced research) (2009). http://www.cs.toronto.edu/~kriz/cifar.html. Accessed 11 Dec 2024
25. LeCun, Y., Cortes, C., Burges, C.J.C.: MNIST handwritten digit database (2010). http://yann.lecun.com/exdb/mnist. Accessed 11 Dec 2024
26. Marsh, S.P.: Formalising trust as a computational concept. Ph.D. thesis (1994)
27. Monarch, R., Munro, R.: Human-in-the-loop machine learning: active learning and annotation for human-centered AI. Manning (2021). https://books.google.pt/books?id=LCh0zQEACAAJ
28. Mosqueira-Rey, E., Hernández-Pereira, E., Alonso-Ríos, D., Bobes-Bascarán, J., Fernández-Leal, A.: Human-in-the-loop machine learning: a state of the art. Artif. Intell. Rev. **56**(4), 3005–3054 (2023). https://doi.org/10.1007/s10462-022-10246-w
29. Motro, A., Smets, P. (eds.): Uncertainty Management in Information Systems: From Needs to Solutions. Springer, Cham (1997). https://doi.org/10.1007/978-1-4615-6245-0
30. Pinyol, I., Sabater-Mir, J.: Computational trust and reputation models for open multi-agent systems: a review. Artif. Intell. Rev. **40**(1), 1–25 (2013). https://doi.org/10.1007/s10462-011-9277-z
31. Qian, Y., Tang, J., Wu, K.: Weakly learning to match experts in online community. In: Proceedings of the Twenty-Seventh International Joint Conference on Artificial Intelligence (IJCAI 2018), pp. 3841–3847. International Joint Conferences on Artificial Intelligence Organization (2018). https://doi.org/10.24963/ijcai.2018/534
32. Raykar, V.C., et al.: Learning from crowds. In: Lafferty, J., Williams, C.K.I., Shawe-Taylor, J., Zemel, R., Culotta, A. (eds.) Advances in Neu-

ral Information Processing Systems (NeurIPS), vol. 23, pp. 1297–1305. Curran Associates, Inc. (2010). https://proceedings.neurips.cc/paper/2010/hash/0562f9c60cbe8f2f693713b6d8db8a0c-Abstract.html
33. Sabater, J., Sierra, C.: Regret: a reputation model for gregarious societies. Technical Report (2001)
34. Sabater, J., Sierra, C.: Review on computational trust and reputation models. Artif. Intell. Rev. **24**(1), 33–60 (2005). https://doi.org/10.1007/s10462-004-0041-5
35. Sener, O., Savarese, S.: Active learning for convolutional neural networks: a core-set approach. In: International Conference on Learning Representations (2018). https://openreview.net/forum?id=H1aIuk-RW
36. Settles, B.: Active learning literature survey. Computer Sciences Technical Report 1648, University of Wisconsin–Madison (2009). http://burrsettles.com/pub/settles.activelearning.pdf
37. Settles, B.: From theories to queries: active learning in practice. In: Proceedings of the Workshop on Active Learning and Experimental Design. JMLR Workshop and Conference Proceedings, vol. 16, pp. 1–18. JMLR (2011). http://proceedings.mlr.press/v16/settles11a.html
38. Sheng, V.S., Provost, F., Ipeirotis, P.G.: Get another label? Improving data quality and data mining using multiple, noisy labelers. In: Proceedings of the 14th ACM SIGKDD International Conference on Knowledge Discovery and Data Mining (KDD), pp. 614–622. ACM (2008). https://doi.org/10.1145/1401890.1401965
39. Tharwat, A., Schenck, W.: A survey on active learning: state-of-the-art, practical challenges and research directions. Mathematics **11**(4) (2023). https://doi.org/10.3390/math11040820. https://www.mdpi.com/2227-7390/11/4/820
40. Urner, R., Ben-David, S., Shamir, O.: Learning from weak teachers. In: Lawrence, N.D., Girolami, M. (eds.) Proceedings of the Fifteenth International Conference on Artificial Intelligence and Statistics. Proceedings of Machine Learning Research, vol. 22, pp. 1252–1260. PMLR, La Palma, Canary Islands (2012). https://proceedings.mlr.press/v22/urner12.html
41. Weng, T.W., et al.: Evaluating the robustness of neural networks: an extreme value theory approach. In: 6th International Conference on Learning Representations (ICLR) (2018). https://openreview.net/forum?id=S17wWgW0-
42. Whitehill, J., Wu, T.F., Bergsma, J., Movellan, J.R., Ruvolo, P.: Whose vote should count more: optimal integration of labels from labelers of unknown expertise. In: Bengio, Y., Schuurmans, D., Lafferty, J., Williams, C.K.I., Culotta, A. (eds.) Advances in Neural Information Processing Systems (NeurIPS), vol. 22, pp. 2035–2043. Curran Associates, Inc. (2009). https://proceedings.neurips.cc/paper/2009/hash/bb254fb1f5423896d5f9e3640212edbc-Abstract.html
43. van Wissen, A., Gal, Y., Kamphorst, B.A., Dignum, M.V.: Human-agent teamwork in dynamic environments. Comput. Hum. Behav. **28**(1), 23–33 (2012). https://doi.org/10.1016/j.chb.2011.08.006
44. Wissen, A., van Diggelen, J., Dignum, V.: The effects of cooperative agent behavior on human cooperativeness. In: Proceedings of the 8th International Conference on Autonomous Agents and Multiagent Systems (AAMAS 2009), pp. 1179–1180 (2009). https://doi.org/10.1145/1558109.1558200
45. Wu, X., Xiao, L., Sun, Y., Zhang, J., Ma, T., He, L.: A survey of human-in-the-loop for machine learning. Futur. Gener. Comput. Syst. **135**, 364–381 (2022). https://doi.org/10.1016/j.future.2022.05.014

46. Xiao, H., Rasul, K., Vollgraf, R.: Fashion-MNIST: a novel image dataset for benchmarking machine learning algorithms. CoRR abs/1708.07747 (2017). http://arxiv.org/abs/1708.07747
47. Yan, Y., Rosales, R., Fung, G., Farooq, F., Rao, B., Dy, J.: Active learning from multiple knowledge sources. In: Lawrence, N.D., Girolami, M. (eds.) Proceedings of the Fifteenth International Conference on Artificial Intelligence and Statistics. Proceedings of Machine Learning Research, vol. 22, pp. 1350–1357. PMLR, La Palma, Canary Islands (2012). https://proceedings.mlr.press/v22/yan12.html
48. Zhan, X., Zhang, X., Zhang, Y., Xu, H., Liu, Z.: A comparative study of uncertainty estimation methods in deep active learning for image classification. In: Proceedings of the IEEE/CVF Conference on Computer Vision and Pattern Recognition (CVPR), pp. 14674–14684 (2022). https://doi.org/10.1109/CVPR52688.2022.01430
49. Zhang, H., Yu, Y., Jiao, J., Xing, E.P., El Ghaoui, L., Jordan, M.I.: Theoretically principled trade-off between robustness and accuracy. In: Proceedings of the 36th International Conference on Machine Learning (ICML). Proceedings of Machine Learning Research, vol. 97, pp. 7472–7482. PMLR (2019). https://proceedings.mlr.press/v97/zhang19p.html
50. Zhang, Y., Lease, M., Wallace, B.C.: Active discriminative text representation learning (2016). https://arxiv.org/abs/1606.04212
51. Zhang, Y., Zhang, Y., Zhou, Z.H.: A survey of learning from crowds. ACM Comput. Surv. (CSUR) **55**(7), 1–36 (2022). https://doi.org/10.1145/3520484
52. Zhang, Y., Zhou, D., Chen, Q., Jordan, M.I.: Spectral methods meet EM: a provably optimal algorithm for crowdsourcing. In: Advances in Neural Information Processing Systems (NeurIPS), vol. 27 (2014). https://proceedings.neurips.cc/paper_files/paper/2014/file/53b6d32b5a3036c574b307e3e8912068-Paper.pdf
53. Zhou, D., Platt, J.C., Basu, S., Mao, Y., Modha, D.S.: Learning from the wisdom of crowds by minimax entropy. In: Advances in Neural Information Processing Systems (NeurIPS), vol. 25 (2012). https://proceedings.neurips.cc/paper_files/paper/2012/file/07176748b3e8a4f2b38c1641066c88ea-Paper.pdf

Workshop on Machine Learning for Irregular Time Series (ML4ITS 2025)

Workshop on Machine Learning for Irregular Time Series (ML4ITS 2025)

Irregular time series arise in many real-world domains, from healthcare and finance to environmental monitoring, industrial systems, Earth observation, and autonomous operations. These data often include uneven sampling, missing values, noise, and heterogeneous modalities, requiring machine learning models that can operate effectively under sparsity, uncertainty, and limited supervision. As modern applications increasingly rely on continuous streams of complex temporal signals, the development of robust, trustworthy, and data-efficient models has become a central challenge for the community.

The fourth edition of the *Machine Learning for Irregular Time Series (ML4ITS 2025)* workshop builds on the success of previous years at ECML PKDD and continues its mission to bring together researchers working on these methodological and applied challenges. This year's workshop placed particular emphasis on advances in generative modelling, self-supervised and unsupervised representation learning, responsible and explainable AI for time-series data, and the emergence of large-scale and foundation models trained on multimodal temporal datasets. Across these topics, a recurring theme is the need to "do more with less": to develop models capable of leveraging scarce, noisy, and irregularly sampled data while providing reliable outputs suitable for high-stakes decisions.

ML4ITS 2025 also featured a dedicated focus on *Time Series for Space Applications.* Machine learning for spacecraft telemetry—often affected by irregular sampling, missing data, and complex dependencies—represents a demanding yet highly relevant testbed for methodological innovation. ESA, Airbus Defence and Space, and KP Labs released two curated datasets (ESA-ADB and OPSSAT-AD) to support this effort, which served as the foundation for both contributed papers and the ESA-ADB Kaggle Challenge, whose final-round winners were announced during the workshop. The challenges addressed in this session resonate strongly with those found in IoT systems, robotics, finance, and environmental modelling, illustrating the broad relevance of irregular time-series research.

This year's workshop included two invited talks, each offering a complementary perspective on modelling irregular time series:

- **Michail Spitieris (SINTEF)** – on generative probabilistic models for irregular time series under physical constraints.

  Talk: "Generative Probabilistic Models for Small Data: A Physics-Aware Approach to Irregular Time Series"
- **Sara Malacarne (Telenor Research)** – on anomaly detection in telecom data through graph-based and representation learning approaches.

  Talk: "Anomaly Detection in Telecom Time Series: From Graph-Based Models Towards Representation Learning"

ML4ITS 2025 received 13 submissions, each reviewed by at least two members of the Program Committee. The final programme included long papers, short papers, and presentation-only contributions, enabling authors to present original research, preliminary findings, and previously published work aligned with the workshop's themes. All accepted contributions were presented either as spotlight talks or as posters, and authors could opt to include their work in the joint post-workshop proceedings published in Springer's *Communications in Computer and Information Science* series.

The workshop programme combined invited talks, contributed sessions, a poster session, and the special session on space applications, which included both proceedings and presentation-only papers. Together, these contributions highlight the breadth of contemporary research on irregular time series, from unified frameworks and synthetic data generation to anomaly detection for satellite telemetry and large-scale models for telecom and multimodal time-series data.

We are grateful to all authors for their submissions, to our invited speakers for their insightful contributions, and to the Program Committee for their dedicated reviews. We also thank our partners and supporting organisations for making the workshop possible, as well as all participants who contributed to the discussions that shaped ML4ITS 2025.
Further details about the programme and available datasets can be found on the workshop website: https://ml4its.github.io/ml4its2025/.

Massimiliano Ruocco
Erlend Aune
Claudio Gallicchio
Krzysztof Kotowski
Luigi Quarantiello
Gabriele De Canio

Workshop Organization

Workshop Chairs

Massimiliano Ruocco	NTNU/SINTEF, Norway
Erlend Aune	HANCE/NTNU, Norway
Claudio Gallicchio	University of Pisa, Italy
Krzysztof Kotowski	KP Labs, Poland
Luigi Quarantiello	University of Pisa, Italy
Gabriele De Canio	European Space Agency, Germany

Program Committee

Pierluigi Salvo Rossi	NTNU
Murad Abdulmajid	SINTEF Digital
Michail Spitieris	SINTEF Digital
Vincenzo Lomonaco	University of Pisa, Italy
Jo Eidsvik	NTNU
Leif Anders Thorsrud	BI Norwegian Business School
Vegard Larsen	BI/Norges Bank
Andrea Ceni	University of Pisa, Italy
Bogdan Ruszczak	Opole University of Technology; Research Scientist, KP Labs, Poland
Jakub Nalepa	Silesian University of Technology; Head of AI, KP Labs, Poland

Closing the Gap Between Synthetic and Ground Truth Time Series Distributions via Neural Mapping

Daesoo Lee[1,3(✉)], Sara Malacarne[2], and Erlend Aune[1,3]

[1] Norwegian University of Science and Technology, Trondheim, Norway
erlend.aune@ntnu.no
[2] Telenor Research, Oslo, Norway
sara.malacarne@telenor.com
[3] HANCE, Oslo, Norway
daesoo@hance.ai

Abstract. In this paper, we introduce Neural Mapper for Vector Quantized Time Series Generator (NM-VQTSG), a novel method aimed at addressing fidelity challenges in vector quantized (VQ) time series generation. VQ-based methods, such as TimeVQVAE, have demonstrated success in generating time series but are hindered by two critical bottlenecks: information loss during compression into discrete latent spaces and deviations in the learned prior distribution from the ground truth distribution. These challenges result in synthetic time series with compromised fidelity and distributional accuracy. To overcome these limitations, NM-VQTSG leverages a U-Net-based neural mapping model to bridge the distributional gap between synthetic and ground truth time series. To be more specific, the model refines synthetic data by addressing artifacts introduced during generation, effectively aligning the distributions of synthetic and real data. Importantly, NM-VQTSG can be used for synthetic time series generated by any VQ-based generative method. We evaluate NM-VQTSG across diverse datasets from the UCR Time Series Classification archive, demonstrating its capability to consistently enhance fidelity in both unconditional and conditional generation tasks. The improvements are evidenced by significant improvements in FID, IS, and conditional FID, additionally backed up by visual inspection in a data space and a latent space. Our findings establish NM-VQTSG as a new method to improve the quality of synthetic time series. Our implementation is available on https://github.com/ML4ITS/TimeVQVAE.

Keywords: Time series generation · masked generative models · Vector quantization · VQVAE · TimeVQVAE

1 Introduction

In the field of time series generation (TSG), methodological advances have been significantly shaped by three foundational generative models [1]: Generative

I. Koprinska et al. (Eds.): ECML PKDD 2025, CCIS 2842, pp. 61–74, 2026.
https://doi.org/10.1007/978-3-032-19105-2_5

Adversarial Networks (GAN) [7], Variational AutoEncoders (VAE) [10], and Vector Quantized Variational AutoEncoders (VQVAE) [17]. GANs, comprising a generator and a discriminator, have been pivotal in TSG for many years [1]. They utilize architectures like RNN, LSTM, and Transformer to capture temporal data, with RGAN [6] and TimeGAN [18] being notable examples. RGAN leverages RNNs within GAN, focusing on the statistical distinction between real and generated series, whereas TimeGAN emphasizes encoding temporal dependencies. In contrast to the long-standing dominance of GANs, different approaches have been recently proposed, adopting VAE and VQVAE. VAEs leverage variational inference to capture a target prior distribution. TimeVAE [5] emerges as a significant development. Unlike VAEs, which produce a continuous latent space, VQVAEs discretize a latent space, producing a discrete latent space while discarding the Gaussian prior distribution assumption. VQVAEs allow for improving the model's ability to capture a prior distribution and create more crisp data, leading to improved fidelity in the generated outputs. TimeVQ-VAE [12], a specialized adaptation of VQVAE, is specifically designed for TSG. [1,12] clearly demonstrated that TimeVQVAE and TimeVAE dethroned the GAN-based methods. In this paper, we focus on VQ-based TSG methods like TimeVQVAE. It should be noted that the limitations and proposal addressed in this paper are not specific to TimeVQVAE but to any TSG methods based on VQ. At the time of writing, TimeVQVAE is the only VQ-based TSG method, thereby used as a representative for VQ-based TSG methods.

VQ-based TSG methods, however, are not without their flaws. We identified two bottlenecks that compromise the fidelity of the generated time series. The first bottleneck is the compression process from the data space to a discrete latent space, which can result in information loss. The second bottleneck is the learned prior distribution, which often deviates from a true underlying distribution. Figure 1 illustrates the distributional discrepancies between the distributions of ground truth (GT) samples and generated samples, caused by the two bottlenecks. As for the first bottleneck, $p(\tilde{X})$ captures a subset of $p(X)$ due to the information loss in the compression process. The distributional gap depends on the compression rate – the higher rate results in the higher gap and vice versa. From the prior learning perspective, a high compression rate is favored, therefore the gap inevitably exists to some extent. Regarding the second bottleneck, $p(\hat{X})$ represents a learned prior distribution. Ideally, this should be close to $p(X)$, however, that is often very challenging and limited by several factors. For instance, a prior model is trained on the discrete latent space which is a compressed space thereby hindering a complete capture of a GT distribution. Other factors involve the prior model size, training steps, regularization techniques, dataset size, and so on. Insufficient prior learning can easily lead to inappropriate bias learned within the model, leading to an inaccurate capture of the GT distribution, as shown in the figure with the mismatch between $p(X)$ and $p(\hat{X})$.

In this paper, we propose training a neural mapping model to map the distribution of the synthetic samples to match the distribution of GT samples. In other words, the mapping model narrows the gap between $p(\hat{X})$ and $p(X)$

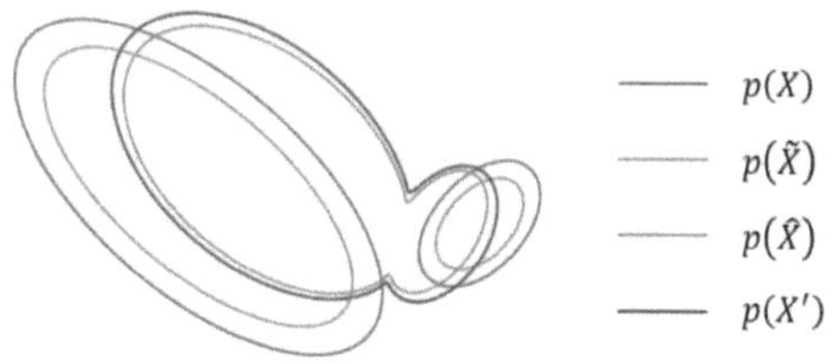

Fig. 1. Illustration of the two bottlenecks that cause a discrepancy between the distributions of GT samples X and generated samples $\hat{X}$. $p(X)$, $p(\tilde{X})$, and $p(\hat{X})$ denote a distribution of GT samples X (blue), reconstructed samples $\tilde{X}$ (orange), and generated samples $\hat{X}$ (green), respectively. Lastly, $p(X')$ represents a distribution of a stochastic variant of X with stochastic vector quantization (red).

by mapping $\hat{X}$ close to X with a learned mapping model. We observed that the generated samples contain certain patterns unique to synthetic data, which are absent in GT samples. The mapping model is trained to identify and refine these synthetic-specific patterns, transforming a synthetic sample into one that fits within the GT distribution. For this mapping model, we utilize U-Net [15] due to its renowned effectiveness in mapping problems [9]. While other mapping models could be explored, our primary focus is on demonstrating the feasibility of our proposed approach. Therefore, the exploration of alternative mapping models is left for future research.

The proposed mapping model was validated by comparing the fidelity of generated time series from TimeVQVAE (baseline) with and without the mapping model. Our experimental results indicate that our mapping model demonstrates substantial fidelity improvements across diverse datasets from the UCR Time Series Classification archive [4]. To be more specific, the evaluation was conducted with metrics such as Frechet Inception Distance (FID) [8], Inception Score (IS) [16], and conditional Frechet Inception Distance (cFID) [2], and the mapping model achieved around 151% average improvement in FID, 7% in IS, and 37% in cFID. The effectiveness is further validated by visual inspections in both data and latent spaces, showcasing improved alignment between synthetic and ground truth time series distributions.

2 Background

2.1 VQVAE

It is a VAE that uses VQ to obtain a discrete latent representation [17]. It differs from classical VAEs by mapping inputs to a discrete latent space and learning the prior, which leads to avoiding posterior collapse and producing sharp and crisp samples. It adopts a two-stage modeling approach, involving tokenization (stage 1) and prior learning (stage 2) with learnable models.

To be more specific, the stage 1 involves training an encoder E and decoder D by minimizing a reconstruction loss $\mathcal{L}_{rec} = \mathbb{E}_x \|x - \tilde{x}\|$ where $\tilde{x} = D(z_q)$, $z_q = Q(z)$, $z = E(x)$ and Q is a vector quantizer.

The quantizer transforms continuous latent vectors into discrete latent vectors using a codebook $\mathcal{Z}$, in which a discrete latent vector is one of the vectors in $\mathcal{Z}$ and is often termed as *token* referring to its codebook index. $\mathcal{Z}$ consists of K discrete tokens $\mathcal{Z} = \{z_k\}_{k=1}^{K}$, where $z_k \in \mathbb{R}^d$ and d denotes the dimension size. The quantization process is defined as

$$(z_q)_n = \underset{z_k \in \mathcal{Z}}{\operatorname{argmin}} \|z_n - z_k\|, \tag{1}$$

where $\mathbb{R}^{d \times N} \ni z = (z_n)_n$ denotes the activation map after the encoder, with N representing a spatial size, $n \in N$ and $z_n \in \mathbb{R}^d$. To simplify the notation, z_q can be denoted by a token sequence $s = (s_n)_n$, where

$$s_n = k, \quad \text{whenever} \quad (z_q)_n = z_k. \tag{2}$$

This notation allows to use $D(z_q)$ and $D(s)$ interchangeably.

Stage 2 involves training a prior model on s to learn $p(s)$. There are mainly two options for the model: 1) autoregressive models, 2) non-autoregressive (*i.e.*, bidirectional) models. The latter ones have shown significantly better results than the former ones [3]. Given the clear superiority of the bidirectional sampling over the autoregressive approach, this paper will focus on bidirectional prior models for our proposed method and experiments.

2.2 TimeVQVAE

It adopts the stage 1 from VQVAE [17] and stage 2 and the sampling process from MaskGIT [3]. The novel differences are discrete latent space modeling of a time-frequency domain and low-frequency (LF) and high-frequency (HF) separation. To be more precise, in stage 1, a time series is first projected into a time-frequency domain using Short-Time Fourier Transform and split into LF and HF bands. Then, the processed input is compressed into a set of tokens by an encoder and vector quantizer in both LF and HF bands. Those tokens can be decoded back to a data space with a decoder. In stage 2, tokens are randomly masked and a prior model is trained by predicting the GT tokens before the masking. Two bidirectional prior models (*i.e.*, transformer) are employed, one for LF and the other for HF. The sampling process involves initially sampling LF tokens, followed by HF tokens conditioned on the sampled LF tokens. Subsequently, the tokens can be decoded and summed to produce a synthetic time series.

2.3 Limitation of VQ-Based TSG Methods

The sampling process of both autoregressive and non-autoregressive models is iterative. In each iteration, one or multiple tokens are sampled, and this process continues until an entire token sequence is sampled. However, due to the stochastic nature of sampling, there is always a risk of sampling inappropriate tokens. The primary issue is that once a token is sampled, it cannot be retracted, leading to a sampled token sequence $\hat{s}$ that may not fit within the GT distribution $p(s)$, resulting in a synthetic time series with lower fidelity.

We acknowledge that $\hat{s}$ can inevitably contain inappropriate tokens, leading to undesirable patterns in the synthetic time series $\hat{x} = D(\hat{s})$. Consequently, instead of improving the sampling process, our focus is on refining the produced $\hat{x}$ using a neural mapping model to improve its fidelity, making it appear more realistic.

3 Method

Theorem 1. *There exists a learnable mapping $p_\theta(\hat{X}) \rightarrow p(X)$, for θ learnable parameters of a prior model f_θ, that performs $\hat{X} \rightarrow X$.*

Proof. The mapping $\hat{X} \rightarrow X$ can be expressed as $p_\theta(\hat{X}) \rightarrow p(X)$ where the mapping function $\rightarrow$ is estimated by a neural mapping model. For clarity, we specify the notation $p(\hat{X})$ as $p_\theta(\hat{X})$, where θ represents the learnable parameters of a prior model. Training the mapping model requires pairs of $(\hat{x}, x)$, however, such pairs cannot exist since $\hat{x}$ is independently sampled with a generative model. To enable the training, this theorem demonstrates that $\hat{X}$ can be approximated by a stochastic variant of the training dataset, denoted by $\tilde{X}'$, so that $\hat{X} \approx \tilde{X}'$ and pairs of $(\tilde{x}', x)$ can be used for training the neural mapping model.

Let $\tilde{x}'$ denote a stochastic variant of x. Then it can be sampled using the following,

$$\tilde{x}' = D(z'_q) = D(Q'(z, \tau)) = D(Q'(E(x), \tau)), \tag{3a}$$

$$z'_q \sim Q'(z, \tau) = \text{softmax}\, limits_{z_k \in \mathcal{Z}}(-\|z_n - z_k\|_2/\tau)\ \forall n, \tag{3b}$$

where τ is a temperature parameter to control the entropy of the softmax distribution, E is an encoder, and D represents a decoder. Equation (3b) appears similar to Eq. (1) except that it stochastically samples a token based on the negative Euclidean distances instead of using the argmin process. We refer to Eq. (3b) as stochastic vector quantization (SVQ), denoted by Q' which allows the notation, $z'_q \sim Q'(z, \tau)$. The variance of the SVQ process is controlled by τ, in which $0 < \tau < 1$ decreases the entropy and $1 < \tau$ increases it, leading to a higher sample diversity.

Claim. We claim that $p(\hat{X}) \approx p(\tilde{X}')$ for an optimal choice of τ.

Or equivalently, in the discrete latent space, $p_\theta(\hat{S}) \approx p_\phi(S')$, where S' denotes sequences of the stochastically sampled tokens of X and ϕ represents the parameters of E and D. Firstly, $\hat{s}$ consists of $\{\hat{s}_1, \hat{s}_2, \cdots, \hat{s}_n, \cdots, \hat{s}_N\}$ and $\hat{s}_n$ is sampled by $p_\theta(\hat{s}_n | \hat{s}_{M_t})$ for bidirectional prior models, where $\hat{s}_{M_t}$ denotes a (partially) masked token sequence with a masking ratio determined by a sampling iteration step t. That is, a new token is sampled given the sampled tokens from the previous iterations. Then, the likely tokens for $\hat{s}_n$ tend to capture similar data patterns when the conditional context $\hat{s}_{M_t}$ remains the same, as demonstrated in [13][1]. Secondly, the distribution in Eq. (3b) is defined based on the negative Euclidean distances where the distance represents a pattern dissimilarity – larger distance generally equals larger dissimilarity, and vice versa [11]. This indicates that $\tilde{X}'$ captures similar data patterns as X and the dissimilarity between $\tilde{X}'$ and X can be increased by increasing τ. Based on these two observations, an optimal τ can be determined such that the dissimilarity level between X and $\tilde{X}'$ matches the dissimilarity between X and $\hat{X}$.

Finally, given Claim and the considerations above, the mapping $p_\theta(\hat{X}) \rightarrow p_\phi(X)$ can be learned by

$$\text{argmin}\, limits_{\varphi} \mathbb{E}_{x,\tilde{x}' \sim D(Q'(E(x),\tau))} \|x - f_\varphi(\tilde{x}')\|,$$

where φ represent the learnable parameters of the mapping model f_φ and τ is a hyperparameter.

Lastly, f_φ is trained by minimizing the following loss function:

$$\mathbb{E}_{x,\tilde{x}' \sim D(Q'(E(x),\tau))} \|x - f_\varphi(\tilde{x}')\|_1$$

(*i.e.*, L_1 loss) in this study. Then, the inference can be performed as $\hat{x}_R = f_\varphi(\hat{x})$, improving the fidelity of a synthetic time series $\hat{x}$ generated by a VQ-based TSG method through the proposed mapping. $\hat{x}_R$ should retain the same context as $\hat{x}$ while improving its fidelity by refining patterns that are specific to the synthetic time series. We call our proposed method *Neural Mapper for Vector Quantized Time Series Generator* (NM-VQTSG). For brevity, we will use the abbreviation NM in this paper.

4 Experiments

4.1 Experimental Setup

Dataset. We evaluate our approach using datasets from the UCR Time Series Classification Archive, which comprises over 128 distinct time series datasets. To ensure robust and meaningful assessments, we selected the thirteen largest datasets, excluding those that were redundant or exhibited minimal pattern variation. The chosen datasets include Crop, ECG5000, ElectricDevices, FaceAll, FordA, FreezerRegularTrain, MixedShapesRegularTrain, StarLightCurves, TwoPatterns, UWaveGestureLibraryAll, UWaveGestureLibraryX, Wafer, and Yoga. Each dataset was reconfigured by merging and subsequently performing a stratified split, allocating 80% of the data to the training set and the remaining 20% to the test set. This ensures sufficiently large training dataset for generative modeling while maintaining a consistent distribution between the training and test datasets. The used datasets in our experiments can be found here[2].

[1] It presents multiple samples of $\hat{x} = D(\hat{s})$ where $\hat{s} \sim p_\theta(\hat{s}_n|\hat{s}_{M_t})$ for any n with the same $\hat{s}_{M_t}$, and the resulting samples show similar data patterns.

[2] https://figshare.com/articles/dataset/UCR_Archive_2018_resplit_ver_/26206355?file=47494442.

Models. For TimeVQVAE, we adopted the implementation available here[3]. The encoder and decoder of TimeVQVAE consist of multiple downsampling and upsampling convolutional layers with several convolutional residual blocks at every depth level. Specifically, each downsampling layer reduces the temporal dimension by half while doubling the feature dimension. The quantizer module projects the feature dimension of the encoder's embeddings down to eight and utilizes a codebook size of 1024, following [19]. Additionally, the prior model incorporates multiple transformer layers with self-attentions, followed by a small prediction head. As for NM, it has a U-Net architecture with skip connections with its input as time series. Its encoder and decoder architectural designs are similar to those of TimeVQVAE; however, the NM's U-Net uses 1-dimensional convolutional layers and integrates self-attention layers alongside the convolutional residual blocks. The full details are provided in the appendix.

Training Procedure. There are three training stages: stage 1 (tokenization), stage 2 (prior learning), and stage 3 (training NM). For all the stages, we employed an initial learning rate of 0.005, which decayed to 0.0005 using a cosine learning rate schedule with a linear warmup. The effective batch size was set to 32. For the number of training steps, different values are used for different stages – 20,000 for stage 1, 40,000 for stage 2, and 30,000 for stage 3. All models were implemented in PyTorch and optimized using the AdamW optimizer [14].

Metrics. We evaluate the models' generative performance for unconditional generation with FID and IS, as suggested in [12], using a pretrained supervised fully convolutional network (FCN) from here[4] – this model was trained on the same training dataset employed in this study. For class-conditional generation, we use cFID, referred to as WCFID in [2]. cFID is computed by averaging the FID scores for each class. Classification Accuracy Score (CAS) [3,12] is sometimes used for this evaluation, but we found this metric difficult to be consistent since it varies much depending on optimizer settings due to the small dataset size of the UCR archive compared to common image benchmark datasets. The metrics are reported by averaging over three runs. In addition, we provide comparative visual plots between X and $\hat{X}_R$ in a data space and a latent space. These visual inspections are critical as the existing numeric metrics cannot fully capture the realism of generated time series.

Competing Models. We compare TimeVQVAE as a baseline and TimeVQVAE with NM (TimeVQVAE+NM) to independently evaluate the effectiveness of NM.

5 Results

To evaluate unconditional generation, Tables 1 and 2 present FID and IS, respectively. For conditional generation, Table 3 reports cFID. To visually inspect the

[3] https://github.com/ML4ITS/TimeVQVAE.
[4] https://github.com/danelee2601/supervised-FCN-2.

generated time series, Fig. 2 shows comparative plots of X, $\hat{X}$, and $\hat{X}_R$, while Fig. 3 displays $\hat{x}$ alongside $\hat{x}_R$ for a subset of datasets where realistic patterns are clearly observable. Lastly, Fig. 4 shows the comparison between X, $\hat{X}$, and $\hat{X}_R$ in a latent space.

Overall, the results indicate that NM generally achieves significant fidelity improvements in both unconditional and conditional generation. We provide a detailed analysis of these findings below.

With respect to FID, NM achieves remarkable improvements on datasets such as FordA, showing an increase of 1116.8%. To investigate this further, we examine Fig. 2 and Fig. 3. In the FordA dataset, $\hat{X}$ exhibits underestimated magnitudes, whereas $\hat{X}_R$ has magnitudes that are closer to X, resulting in the significant improvement in FID. Additionally, Fig. 4 demonstrates that X and $\hat{X}_R$ are more similar compared to X and $\hat{X}$ for FordA. Figure 4 generally shows that a smaller FID corresponds to a smaller gap between the two distributions in the latent space. However, there are a few datasets where the FID worsens with NM, such as Crop and TwoPatterns. In the case of Crop, we found that $\hat{X}$ is already very close to X, leaving little room for fidelity improvement with NM. Consequently, NM cannot further enhance fidelity for Crop. This observation is consistent across other datasets like TwoPatterns and Yoga, where the distributional gap between X and $\hat{X}$ remains minimal. Although the deterioration of -45% in Crop may seem substantial, we did not observe a notable discrepancy between $\hat{X}$ and $\hat{X}_R$, highlighting the importance of visual inspection. Specifically, for TwoPatterns, visual inspection using Fig. 2 and Fig. 3 reveals that $\hat{X}_R$ exhibits higher fidelity than $\hat{X}$ by displaying sharp horizontal lines.

Regarding IS, NM delivers considerable improvements across most datasets. However, a slight decline of 11.7% is observed in the Wafer dataset. We identified that this decrease is due to a class imbalance in the dataset, where 10% of the samples belong to class 1 and 90% to class 2. This imbalance results in poor mapping performance for class 1, leading to a degraded IS. As with any model training, addressing class imbalance typically requires appropriate techniques. In this study, we did not implement such techniques to keep the experimental settings simple.

Regarding cFID, similar to FID, substantial improvements are observed overall. However, setbacks occur for the Crop and Wafer datasets due to the limited room for improvement and class imbalance in the dataset, respectively, as previously discussed. Additionally, a setback is noted for FreezerRegularTrain. Despite this, visual inspection did not reveal significant fidelity degradation; in fact, $\hat{X}_R$ is preferred for its sharp lines and appears closer to X. We suspect that the cFID scale is so small that even minor differences result in the large change, even though the actual differences are negligible.

6 Discussion

Advanced Reconstruction Loss. In this study, NM is trained with a L_1 reconstruction loss. A more advanced loss function can be adopted for further improvement,

Table 1. FID (the lower, the better performance). "Change" is calculated as: ((FID of TimeVQVAE/FID of TimeVQVAE+NM) × 100) − 100.

Dataset Name	TimeVQVAE	TimeVQVAE+NM	Change (%)
Crop	1.74	3.21	-45.9
ECG5000	1.03	0.86	20.0
ElectricDevices	19.67	18.03	9.1
FaceAll	10.19	5.88	73.5
FordA	7.85	0.65	1116.8
FreezerRegularTrain	0.29	0.10	200.5
MixedShapesRegularTrain	17.98	10.22	75.8
StarLightCurves	5.63	5.63	0.0
TwoPatterns	0.32	0.38	-17.5
UWaveGestureLibraryAll	7.38	3.65	102.3
UWaveGestureLibraryX	5.40	3.47	55.4
Wafer	1.37	0.36	280.8
Yoga	0.31	0.30	5.7

Table 2. IS (the higher, the better performance). #class denotes a number of classes. "(normalized)" denotes a normalized IS, calculated as IS divided by #class. "Change" is calculated as: ((IS of TimeVQVAE+NM/IS of TimeVQVAE) × 100) − 100.

Dataset Name	#class	TimeVQVAE	TimeVQVAE+NM	TimeVQVAE (normalized)	TimeVQVAE+NM (normalized)	Change (%)
Crop	24	12.55	12.89	0.52	0.54	2.7
ECG5000	5	2.09	2.11	0.42	0.42	0.7
ElectricDevices	7	3.22	3.82	0.46	0.55	18.8
FaceAll	14	5.31	7.13	0.38	0.51	34.2
FordA	2	1.44	1.62	0.72	0.81	12.7
FreezerRegularTrain	2	1.93	1.96	0.97	0.98	1.2
MixedShapesRegularTrain	5	2.66	3.09	0.53	0.62	16.5
StarLightCurves	3	2.12	2.20	0.71	0.73	4.1
TwoPatterns	4	3.76	3.77	0.94	0.94	0.3
UWaveGestureLibraryAll	8	4.21	4.41	0.53	0.55	4.9
UWaveGestureLibraryX	8	4.33	4.55	0.54	0.57	5.2
Wafer	2	1.50	1.32	0.75	0.66	-11.7
Yoga	2	1.52	1.52	0.76	0.76	0.2

such as a multi-scale STFT reconstruction loss where STFT denotes Short-Time Fourier Transform. It can be defined as $\sum_i \|\mathcal{S}_i(x) - \mathcal{S}_i(f_\varphi(\tilde{x}'))\|$ in which $\mathcal{S}$ represents a complex spectrogram transformation function and the subscript i denotes different parameters of the transformation function such as window length and stride size.

Table 3. cFID (the lower, the better performance). "Change" is calculated as: ((cFID of TimeVQVAE/cFID of TimeVQVAE+NM) × 100) − 100.

Dataset Name	TimeVQVAE	TimeVQVAE+NM	Change (%)
Crop	6.03	7.74	-22.1
ECG5000	4.61	4.18	10.3
ElectricDevices	25.06	24.00	4.4
FaceAll	9.36	5.45	71.9
FordA	8.24	2.29	260.2
FreezerRegularTrain	0.12	0.16	-25.0
MixedShapesRegularTrain	21.15	12.58	68.1
StarLightCurves	2.82	2.31	22.3
TwoPatterns	0.21	0.21	-0.8
UWaveGestureLibraryAll	9.19	4.94	86.0
UWaveGestureLibraryX	7.82	5.76	35.7
Wafer	0.55	0.83	-34.0
Yoga	0.50	0.43	15.8

Deficiency of Stochasticity. NM performs deterministic one-to-one mapping. However, this might not be suitable for all datasets. For some, $\hat{x}$ could correspond to multiple plausible x_R outcomes. Therefore, adoption of stochasticity in the mapping should be a direction towards the universal mapping model.

GAN Loss. To train NM, a L_1 loss is used. But, this loss is known to have tendency of producing blurred data due to the averaging effect. On the other hand, a GAN loss (also known as a discriminative loss) can help it produce sharp and crisp data. The averaging effect arises because point-wise losses encourage the model to find a mean prediction when multiple plausible outputs exist, leading to smooth and indistinct features. In contrast, a GAN loss employs a discriminator network that distinguishes between real and generated samples, compelling the generator (*i.e.*, the mapping model in our study) to produce outputs that are not only accurate in a point-wise sense but also rich in fine-grained details. In summary, integrating a GAN loss should enable the mapping model to generate sharper and more realistic outputs, preserving fine-grained details that would otherwise be potentially lost with a L_1 loss alone.

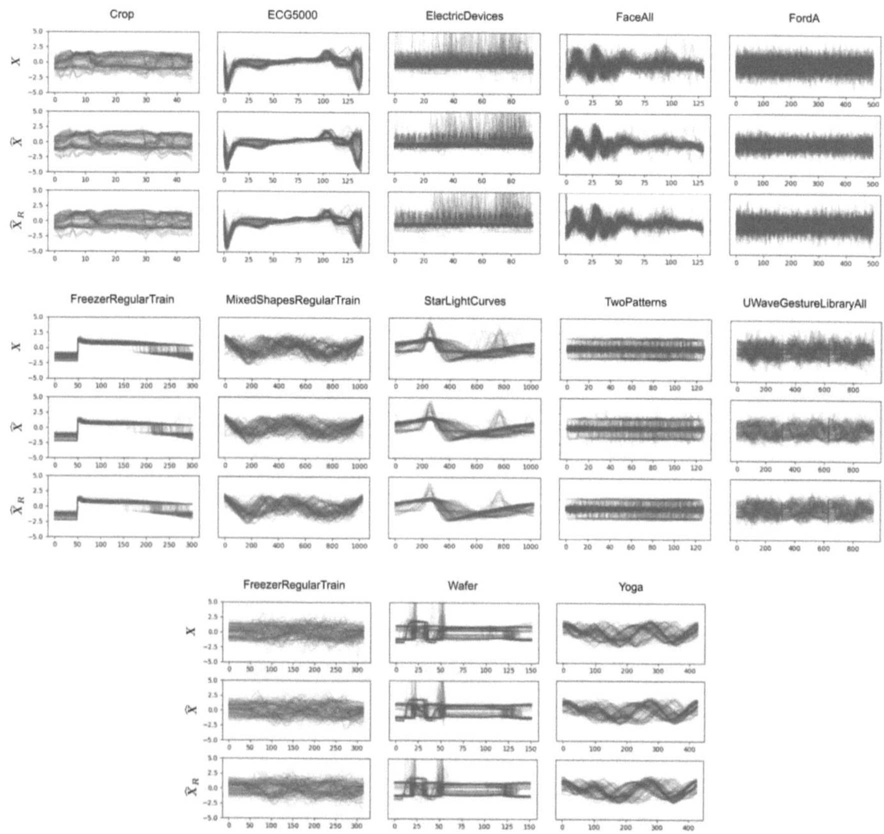

Fig. 2. Comparisons between X, $\hat{X}$, and $\hat{X}_R$. 200 randomly-sampled time series are plotted in overlap. For FordA and FaceAll, the differences between X, $\hat{X}$, and $\hat{X}_R$ are easily observable. For FreezerRegularTrain, TwoPatterns, and Wafer, the differences can be better detected in zoom-in, where $\hat{X}$ has somewhat noisy lines and those are corrected in $\hat{X}_R$.

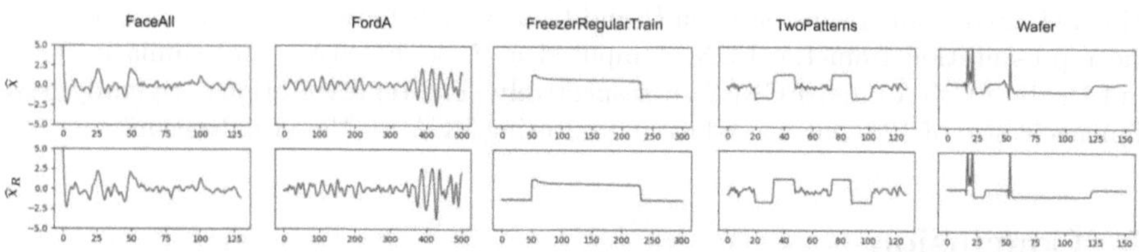

Fig. 3. Comparisons between $\hat{x}$ and $\hat{x}_R$. For FaceAll and FordA, the magnitudes are corrected with addition of detailed patterns. For Freezer, a small downward bump at a timestep of around 240 in $\hat{x}$ is corrected in $\hat{x}_R$ (better viewed in zoom-in). For TwoPatterns and Wafer, $\hat{x}$'s horizontal lines are a bit wiggly and those lines are mapped to straight horizontal lines in $\hat{x}_R$ while retaining the rest of the patterns.

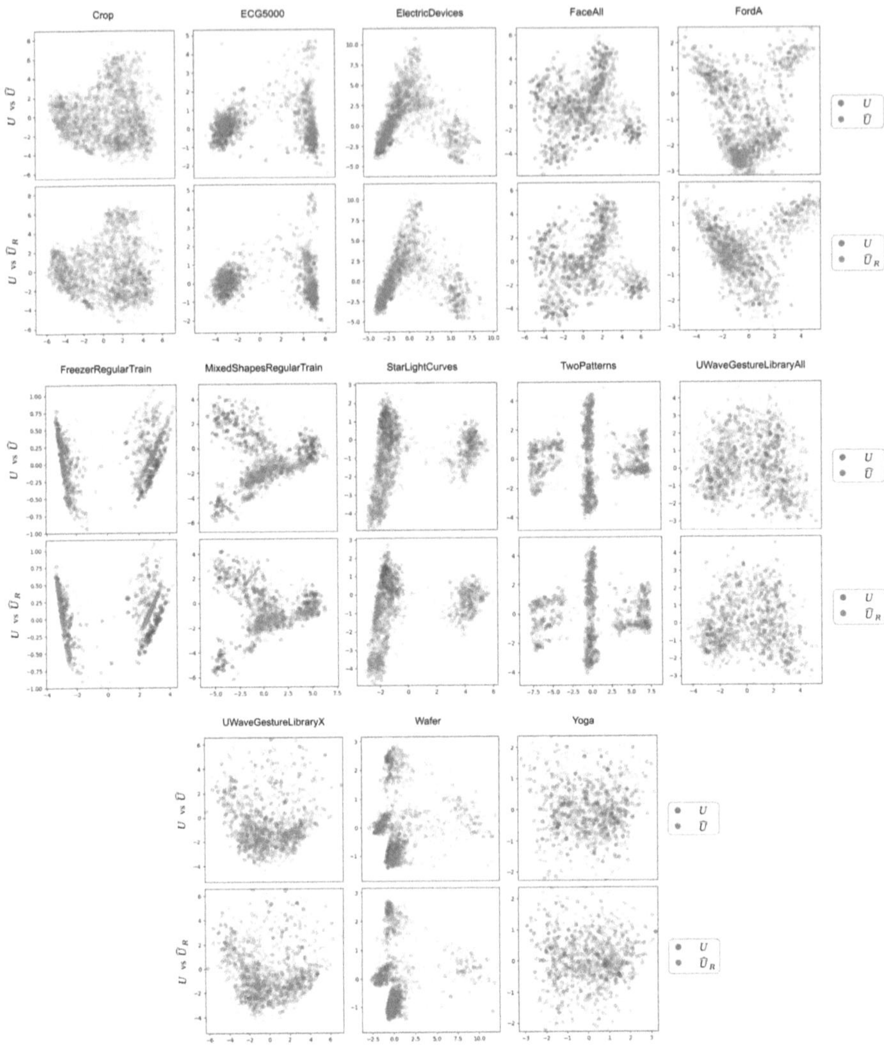

Fig. 4. Paired comparisons between U and $\hat{U}$, as well as between U and $\hat{U}_R$. U denotes the representation from the FCN, computed as $U = \text{FCN}(X)$, and similarly for $\hat{U}$ and $\hat{U}_R$ by $\text{FCN}(\hat{X})$ and $\text{FCN}(\hat{X}_R)$, respectively. The representations originally have dimension size of 128, but we reduce it to 2 using PCA for the visualization.

7 Conclusion

This study introduced the Neural Mapper for Vector Quantized Time Series Generator (NM-VQTSG) to address the fidelity challenges inherent in VQ-based time series generation. By leveraging a U-Net-based mapping model, the proposed method effectively narrows the distributional gap between synthetic and ground truth time series. Through rigorous experimentation on diverse datasets from the UCR archive, NM-VQTSG demonstrated consistent improvements in both unconditional and conditional generation tasks, as evidenced by metrics such as FID, IS, and cFID. Additionally, visual inspections confirmed enhanced realism in generated samples, particularly in datasets where fidelity improvements were most needed.

Overall, NM-VQTSG establishes a new line of study by improving fidelity through mapping, offering a robust method for producing realistic synthetic time series. Future work will explore inclusion of stochastic mapping to handle scenarios with multiple plausible outcomes, and a more sophisticated reconstruction loss and a GAN loss to better capture fine-grained details and further improve fidelity.

Acknowledgments. We would like to thank the Norwegian Research Council for funding the Machine Learning for Irregular Time Series (ML4ITS) project (312062). This funding directly supported this research. We also would like to thank the people who have contributed to the UCR Time Series Classification archive [4] for their valuable contribution to the community.

Disclosure of Interests. No conflicts of interest were present during the research process.

References

1. Ang, Y., Huang, Q., Bao, Y., Tung, A.K., Huang, Z.: Tsgbench: time series generation benchmark. arXiv preprint arXiv:2309.03755 (2023)
2. Benny, Y., Galanti, T., Benaim, S., Wolf, L.: Evaluation metrics for conditional image generation. Int. J. Comput. Vis. **129**, 1712–1731 (2021)
3. Chang, H., Zhang, H., Jiang, L., Liu, C., Freeman, W.T.: Maskgit: masked generative image transformer. In: Proceedings of the IEEE/CVF Conference on Computer Vision and Pattern Recognition, pp. 11315–11325 (2022)
4. Dau, H.A., Bagnall, A., Kamgar, K., Yeh, C.C.M., Zhu, Y., Gharghabi, S., Ratanamahatana, C.A., Keogh, E.: The UCR time series archive. IEEE/CAA J. Automatica Sinica **6**(6), 1293–1305 (2019)
5. Desai, A., Freeman, C., Wang, Z., Beaver, I.: Timevae: a variational auto-encoder for multivariate time series generation. arXiv preprint arXiv:2111.08095 (2021)
6. Esteban, C., Hyland, S.L., Rätsch, G.: Real-valued (medical) time series generation with recurrent conditional GANs. arXiv preprint arXiv:1706.02633 (2017)
7. Goodfellow, I., et al.: Generative adversarial networks. Commun. ACM **63**(11), 139–144 (2020)
8. Heusel, M., Ramsauer, H., Unterthiner, T., Nessler, B., Hochreiter, S.: GANs trained by a two time-scale update rule converge to a local Nash equilibrium. In: Advances in Neural Information Processing Systems, vol. 30 (2017)
9. Isola, P., Zhu, J.Y., Zhou, T., Efros, A.A.: Image-to-image translation with conditional adversarial networks. In: Proceedings of the IEEE Conference on Computer Vision and Pattern Recognition, pp. 1125–1134 (2017)
10. Kingma, D.P., Welling, M.: Auto-encoding variational bayes. arXiv preprint arXiv:1312.6114 (2013)

11. Lee, D., Aune, E., Malacarne, S.: Masked generative modeling with enhanced sampling scheme. arXiv preprint arXiv:2309.07945 (2023)
12. Lee, D., Malacarne, S., Aune, E.: Vector quantized time series generation with a bidirectional prior model. In: International Conference on Artificial Intelligence and Statistics, pp. 7665–7693. PMLR (2023)
13. Lee, D., Malacarne, S., Aune, E.: Explainable time series anomaly detection using masked latent generative modeling. Pattern Recogn. **156**, 110826 (2024). https://doi.org/10.1016/j.patcog.2024.110826
14. Loshchilov, I., Hutter, F.: Decoupled weight decay regularization. In: International Conference on Learning Representations (2019). https://openreview.net/forum?id=Bkg6RiCqY7
15. Ronneberger, O., Fischer, P., Brox, T.: U-net: convolutional networks for biomedical image segmentation. In: Medical Image Computing and Computer-Assisted Intervention–MICCAI 2015: 18th International Conference, Munich, Germany, 5–9 October 2015, Proceedings, Part III 18, pp. 234–241. Springer, Cham (2015)
16. Salimans, T., Goodfellow, I., Zaremba, W., Cheung, V., Radford, A., Chen, X.: Improved techniques for training GANs. In: Advances in neural information processing systems, vol. 29 (2016)
17. Van Den Oord, A., Vinyals, O., et al.: Neural discrete representation learning. In: Advances in Neural Information Processing Systems, vol. 30 (2017)
18. Yoon, J., Jarrett, D., Van der Schaar, M.: Time-series generative adversarial networks. In: Advances in Neural Information Processing Systems, vol. 32 (2019)
19. Yu, J., et al.: Vector-quantized image modeling with improved VQGAN. In: International Conference on Learning Representations (2022). https://openreview.net/forum?id=pfNyExj7z2

Demonstration of a Universal Algorithm for Satellite Anomaly Detection in Spacecraft Anomaly Challenge

Yu Kimura[1(✉)], Noriyasu Omata[1], Seiji Tsutsumi[1], Naoki Ishihama[1], and Masaharu Abe[2]

[1] Japan Aerospace Exploration Agency, Tokyo, Japan
kimura.yu@jaxa.jp
[2] Ryoyu Systems Co., Ltd., Tokyo, Japan

Abstract. As the number of satellites in orbit continues to increase, automated health monitoring of satellites has become increasingly critical. Given the complexity and diversity of satellite telemetry, it is essential to employ methods specifically tailored to these characteristics. A method named Quantile Gaussian Process Regression (Q-GPR) has been developed by the authors based on operational insights of actual satellite missions, but the method had not yet been evaluated using publicly available datasets. In this study, Q-GPR is evaluated by participating in the Spacecraft Anomaly Challenge, a widely open competition focused on algorithmic satellite anomaly detection held in early 2025. The competition utilized the ESA-ADB dataset, which comprises real satellite telemetry provided by the European Space Agency, enabling a realistic and practical evaluation environment. To accommodate the competition and dataset-specific requirements, Q-GPR was extended through adaptive learning and ensemble learning techniques. The proposed method outperformed all baseline methods included with the dataset. Notably, it demonstrated superior performance across diverse telemetry channels, highlighting its effectiveness and practicality for real-world satellite operations.

Keywords: Anomaly detection · Satellite telemetry · Spacecraft Monitoring

1 Introduction

Artificial satellites have become an essential component of modern infrastructure, supporting applications such as Global Positioning System (GPS), weather forecasting, and telecommunications. Recently, commercial satellite constellations like Starlink and OneWeb have launched thousands of satellites to establish global high-speed communication networks. As a result, the number of satellites in orbit has increased dramatically.

I. Koprinska et al. (Eds.): ECML PKDD 2025, CCIS 2842, pp. 75–88, 2026.
https://doi.org/10.1007/978-3-032-19105-2_6

This rapid growth in satellite deployment presents significant challenges for health monitoring. Currently, satellite operations rely heavily on manual monitoring of telemetry, time-series data across various onboard subsystems. However, this is becoming unsustainable as the number of satellites increases, and improving operational efficiency and reducing operator workload have become urgent priorities. Since satellites cannot be physically repaired once deployed, it is crucial to detect abnormalities as early as possible to allow timely switching to redundant systems or preventive measures before functional degradation occurs. In this context, there is a strong demand for technologies capable of automatically and promptly detecting equipment degradation or change of trends in telemetry data.

Satellite telemetry exhibits diverse and complex behaviors due to the harsh space environment and mission-specific operational patterns, making it difficult to apply general-purpose anomaly detection methods effectively. As such, anomaly detection approach should be carefully designed to address the following characteristics:

Frequent Noise. Onboard sensors are frequently affected by noise induced by space radiation and environmental factors.

Varying Acquisition Frequencies and Missing Data. Due to hardware limitations (e.g., memory, communication windows, and power constraints) and operational policies, telemetry may be collected at low or irregular sampling rates. Additionally, data loss may occur due to transmission errors or hardware faults.

Low Bit Resolution. To reduce data volume under limited bandwidth and storage, telemetry is often quantized with low bit resolution, making subtle changes difficult to detect.

Mixture of Periodic Variations. Telemetry reflects overlapping periodicities such as orbital motion, seasonal cycles, and diurnal transitions–which complicate the definition of static normal ranges and the prediction of short-term behavior.

Frequent Spikes. Spike-like waveforms frequently occur due to scheduled operations or attitude adjustments. These are difficult to predict and often resemble genuine faults, complicating reliable distinction.

Diverse Operating Modes (Data Shifts). Due to mode transitions and autonomous attitude control logic, the steady-state behavior of the system changes frequently. These shifts may arise from explicit operational changes or complex interactions between subsystems, redundancy configurations, and environmental dynamics.

While none of these characteristics are unique to satellite telemetry, their combined presence makes anomaly detection of satellites particularly challenging. Moreover, large satellites often comprise thousands of telemetry channels, necessitating high computational efficiency. Operational demands further require rapid diagnosis and actionable feedback once anomalies are detected. Accordingly, effective methods should not only detect anomalies, but also identify the specific channels or potential causes involved.

Traditionally, Fault Detection, Isolation, and Recovery (FDIR) software has been widely used for automated satellite monitoring. These systems are rule-based, relying on predefined thresholds and status indicators. Consequently, they are limited to detecting deviations beyond the fixed thresholds and are ineffective for identifying subtle or gradual changes. More recently, machine learning and deep learning methods, such as Long Short-Term Memory (LSTM) and Recurrent Neural Networks (RNNs), have been applied to automate anomaly detection [1]. Despite their success in other domains, these methods often fail to address the unique constraints of satellite telemetry, particularly in terms of computational cost and interpretability, which limits their practical utility.

An anomaly detection algorithm called Quantile Gaussian Process Regression (Q-GPR) has been developed by the authors based on operational insights [2]. This algorithm adopts a fundamentally different approach from existing methods, and it is a lightweight, univariate method. Q-GPR uses quantiles as feature values and employs Gaussian Process Regression (GPR) [3] to model trends in the quantiles. By simplifying the monitoring target to the quantile behavior, the method becomes robust to noise and spikes, enabling consistent application across heterogeneous telemetry channels while remaining operationally feasible. Additionally, it is designed for low computational overhead and high interpretability. However, Q-GPR had not been evaluated on publicly available datasets, and its comparative performance remained uncertain.

In early 2025, the Spacecraft Anomaly Challenge was hosted on Kaggle [4]. The competition sought to encourage the development of automated health monitoring systems using real satellite telemetry. It was based on the European Space Agency Benchmark for Anomaly Detection (ESA-ADB) dataset [5], which contains telemetry collected from operational European Space Agency (ESA) satellites. This dataset offers a realistic testbed for assessing the robustness of anomaly detection methods under the previously mentioned challenges.

To evaluate Q-GPR, we entered the competition. Since the competition setting differed from the original assumptions of Q-GPR, we enhanced the method with adaptive learning and ensemble strategies. Experiments on the ESA-ADB dataset showed that our approach outperformed all baseline methods provided by ESA.

The remainder of this paper is structured as follows. Section 2 describes the ESA-ADB dataset and the Spacecraft Anomaly Challenge. Section 3 introduces Q-GPR and its core design philosophy. Section 4 presents enhancements made to Q-GPR for this study. Section 5 reports experimental results and discusses key findings. Finally, Sect. 6 concludes the paper and outlines directions for future research.

2 ESA-ADB and the Spacecraft Anomaly Challenge

2.1 ESA-ADB Dataset

ESA-ADB is a benchmark dataset for anomaly detection of satellites, similar to other publicly available datasets such as NASA's Telemanom [1] and the

OPS-SAT benchmark [6]. It was released by the European Space Agency in 2024. ESA-ADB is based on telemetry data collected from satellites in actual operation and comprises data from three distinct satellite missions: Mission 1, Mission 2, and Mission 3. One of the most significant features of ESA-ADB is that it contains authentic telemetry acquired from operational satellite missions which reflects real operational conditions. The dataset includes various challenges inherent to real-world satellite telemetry discussed in the Introduction, such as variations in resolution, environmental noise, periodic fluctuations, missing data, spikes, and complex data shift. These characteristics make ESA-ADB highly suitable for evaluating anomaly detection algorithms intended for practical deployment in satellite operations. Many time-series anomaly detection datasets are known to adopt unrealistically high densities of anomaly occurrences compared to real operational conditions [7]. However, in practice, satellite anomalies are rare events; thus, these imbalanced configurations often lead to inflated evaluation scores that do not reflect operational utility. In contrast, ESA-ADB provides genuine telemetry with realistic anomaly occurrence frequencies, making it better suited for evaluating the real-world effectiveness of anomaly detection methods. ESA-ADB includes telemetry from multiple missions and covers a broad range of onboard subsystems, enabling evaluation of anomaly detection methods under diverse operational contexts and improving the assessment of model generalizability. However, the physical units of sensors and the names of subsystems are anonymized or withheld, which poses limitations for methods that rely on combinations of physical modeling or domain-specific analysis. ESA-ADB contains a rich variety of anomalous patterns. Each event is categorized into an Event Class, which groups similar anomaly types. Furthermore, the dataset includes Event Types such as "Anomaly" and "Rare Nominal Event", enabling a clear distinction between actual anomalies and uncommon but expected behaviors.

2.2 Spacecraft Anomaly Challenge on ESA Dataset

The *Spacecraft Anomaly Challenge* was a competition focused on anomaly detection, hosted on Kaggle and based on the ESA-ADB dataset provided by the European Space Agency. The objective of the competition was to develop algorithms capable of detecting anomalies in telemetry from operational satellites. The competition was specifically scoped to Mission 1 of the ESA-ADB dataset. Participants developed anomaly detection approaches using the ESA-ADB dataset and were ranked based on their performance, evaluated via metrics computed on a hidden test set that temporally follows the publicly open ESA-ADB data.

3 Quantile Gaussian Process Regression

The authors have proposed Quantile Gaussian Process Regression (Q-GPR) as a method for satellite telemetry health monitoring [2]. The method has been developed with the primary goal of being broadly applicable to satellite telemetry, which exhibits a wide range of challenging characteristics as discussed in the

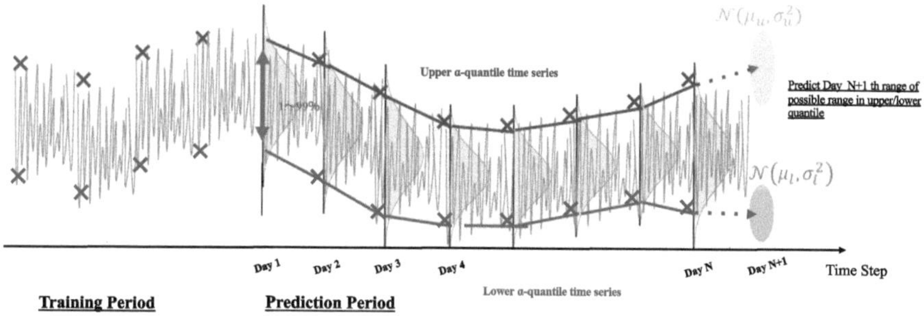

Fig. 1. Schematic overview of Q-GPR operation.

previous section. This enables systematic health monitoring of the entire satellite system, including telemetry channels where routine manual health monitoring is missing. The method is expected to complement existing operational practices by detecting early signs of abnormality in telemetry behavior.

An overview of the Q-GPR is shown in Fig. 1. Q-GPR is a univariate method applied independently to each telemetry channel. It monitors the temporal trends of data ranges rather than focusing on instantaneous telemetry values and detects significant change in the trends. The overall procedure consists of the following steps. Telemetry data is segmented into fixed-length windows of size w, and the lower and upper $\alpha\%$ quantiles are extracted for each window. In the preceding studies, $w = 1$ [day] and $\alpha = 1, 99$ [%] were used, and the quantiles represent the approximate daily minimum and maximum telemetry values. These quantile values serve as compact representations of the telemetry value range, and they are used as feature values in this method. Gaussian Process Regression is employed to model and predict the temporal trend of the extracted quantiles. The Gaussian process kernel corresponding to each quantile is optimized so that it fits to the quantile sequence in the training period. In the prediction period, where the detection is actually performed, the following is repeated each time when the new quantile value is obtained. First, the posterior distribution of the new quantile is calculated from the optimized kernel and the quantiles for the previous T windows. Then, if the actual quantile value falls outside the predicted nominal range of $\pm n\sigma$ defined by the posterior distribution, where n is a tunable parameter and σ denotes predictive variance, it is flagged as a potential anomaly, indicating that the corresponding telemetry channel requires further investigation.

Applicability of Q-GPR across diverse telemetry types has been empirically demonstrated. In cases where instantaneous noise (e.g., due to radiation) affects telemetry, such noise is excluded during quantile calculation by focusing on the 1%, 99% range. This makes Q-GPR robust to spurious outliers. In the presence of short-span (quasi-)periodic behavior, such as orbital cycles, or even for telemetry with unpredictable daily fluctuations due to operational activities, use of quantiles smooths out such high-frequency fluctuations, making long-term

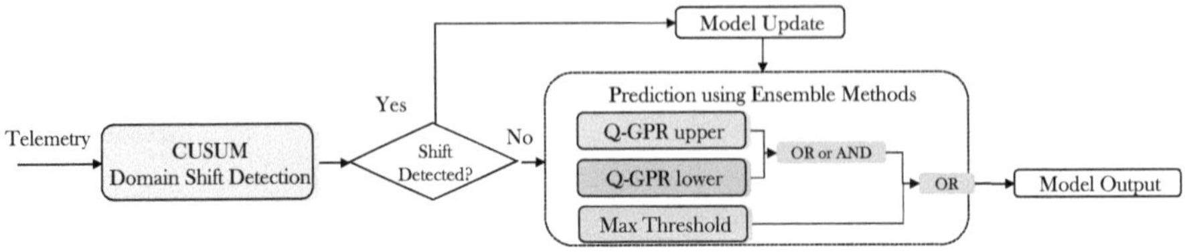

Fig. 2. Procedure of the proposed anomaly detection for a single telemetry.

trends easier to model. Moreover, the use of quantiles mitigates the impact of irregular sampling and short-term data gaps. For telemetries with long-term or seasonal trends, GPR provides a smooth and flexible framework for tracking such behavior. In addition, Q-GPR is designed to operate with low computational overhead, and its implementation on FPGA has already been demonstrated in preparation for potential future onboard deployment [8]. Moreover, alerts from Q-GPR indicate a change in the trend of the approximate daily maximum or minimum values, which is quite simple and inuitive. This meaning of the alert is easily understood by satellite operators unfamiliar with data-driven methods, and thus the method is highly interpretable.

4 Method

4.1 Overall Architecture

The anomaly detection system proposed in this study is a framework that integrates domain shift detection, model retraining, and an ensemble strategy incorporating Q-GPR for analyzing satellite telemetry. Given the diverse and complex nature of satellite telemetry, a key advantage of this framework is its ability to handle such data without requiring extensive preprocessing.

The procedure for a single telemetry is illustrated in Fig. 2. To sensitively detect distributional changes in telemetry data, we adopt an adaptive learning strategy. This facilitates model updates at detected change points, allowing the system to adapt to state transitions and data shifts induced by satellite operations. Details of the adaptive learning will be presented in Sect. 4.2. Univariate Anomaly Detection using Q-GPR is independently applied to the 1% and 99% quantiles of each telemetry channel. If the observed value deviates from the predicted quantile range, the instance is flagged as an anomaly. Additional detectors are incorporated to address anomalies that may not be captured by Q-GPR alone. The output of Q-GPR and the additional detector are combined. Details of this will be presented in Sect. 4.3.

Extension to multivariate telemetry is realized by logically combining the univariate results using a logical OR operation. This design ensures the system can detect localized anomalies affecting only a single telemetry channel.

4.2 Adaptive Learning

This study introduces an adaptive learning framework that detects statistical changes (domain shifts) in satellite telemetry and triggers model retraining accordingly. Such shifts may arise due to operational mode transitions, equipment degradation, or failures. This adaptive retraining process maintains anomaly detection accuracy in the face of evolving data distributions.

An extended version of the CUSUM (Cumulative Sum) algorithm was employed to detect the domain shifts. The algorithm is widely used for change point detection and quality control [9]. It detects minor deviations by accumulating differences between observed values and a historical reference mean. To enhance robustness, interquartile range (IQR) filtering within each window was employed to exclude extreme values prior to computing the local mean. This is because satellite telemetry often exhibits nonstationary fluctuations and abrupt changes–such as rare nominal events caused by attitude or orbital adjustments–that introduce outliers. Use of IQR filtering enables reliable change point detection even in the presence of spikes and noise.

Once a domain shift is detected by the CUSUM method, model retraining is initiated. Training data are drawn from a stable segment following the detected change point. Specifically, at first, data is ignored and nothing is done about it for a pre-determined period T_{ignore}, since transient fluctuations exist and stable normal data may not be immediately available after the domain shift. Practically, in transient situations, such as mode transitions, orbital maneuvers, or equipment servicing, satellite operators stand by for the operations necessary for the satellite management. The policy of ignoring is based on the consideration that automation is a low priority for such situations. After the ignoring period has passed, a new training period of pre-fixed length $T_{retrain}$ is obtained, and the GPR model is retrained using data from this period. Only the model parameters are updated and hyperparameters such as window size and quantile thresholds remain unchanged. Detection is not performed and no alerts are raised during the new training period.

4.3 Ensemble Learning

As described in Sect. 3, Q-GPR excludes short, spike-like fluctuations by relying on robust 1% and 99% quantiles to avoid false positives due to sensor noise or operational events. However, the ESA-ADB dataset includes such spikes as labeled anomalies, and Q-GPR overlooks such events intentionally. To address this, we incorporate an ensemble strategy that combines an auxiliary anomaly detector to complement the limitation. Specifically, a Max Threshold model, which flags an anomaly if the maximum value within a window exceeds a predefined threshold *thres*, was additionally introduced.

The detection results of Q-GPR and the Max Threshold model are integrated by several combination strategies. The integration is based on a simple logical OR, and any detector's activation triggers an anomaly flag. This is because each model has a specific target to be detected and the parameters are to be tuned to achieve a high precision. However, preliminary experiments have shown that for certain channels, the distribution of quantiles may deviate from the Gaussianity assumed by GPR. In this case, it was confirmed that the precision of Q-GPR deteriorates, meaning that the final precision also decreases when relying on an OR-based integration. To mitigate this, an AND condition was employed for these channels–only flagging anomalies when both lower and upper quantile models simultaneously detect deviations. Additionally, the Max Threshold model is sensitive to signal variation, and thresholds become unstable in channels with substantial trend fluctuations. In such cases, the Max Threshold component was disabled, and detection was relied solely on Q-GPR.

5 Results and Discussions

This section presents the evaluation results of the proposed method. Section 5.1 explains the detailed experiment settings, Sect. 5.2 reports the results obtained within the ESA-ADB dataset, and Sect. 5.3 describes the competition outcomes.

5.1 Experiment Settings

In this study, we used telemetry data from Mission 1 of ESA-ADB, which was also the focus of the competition. More specifically, 55 telemetry channels that were designated as monitoring targets and contained known anomalies were used.

ESA-ADB comprises a total of 168 months of telemetry data. In the experiment within the dataset, the first 84 months were used for model training and the remaining 84 months for evaluation. The test set included 90 anomaly events, including both confirmed anomalies and rare nominal events. For the competition submissions, model training was conducted using both of the training and test data, as the competition organizers assume.

As the evaluation metric, we adopted the corrected event-wise $F_{0.5}$ score:

$$F_{0.5} = (1 + 0.5^2)\frac{Pr \cdot Rec}{0.5^2\, Pr + Rec} \tag{1}$$

proposed by ESA-ADB [5]. In the equation, Pr and Rec denote corrected event-wise precision and recall, respectively, which are also proposed in [5]. Unlike conventional point-wise metrics, the score evaluates the quality of predictions at the event level, grouping temporally clustered anomalies into a single unit. A detection is regarded as a true positive if it overlaps with any part of a labeled event. This reduces overestimation or underestimation that can arise when long-duration anomalies are detected only partially or repeatedly. Furthermore, a penalty (correction term) is introduced to discourage detectors from producing continuous alerts across all time steps. This scoring approach was also adopted in the official competition evaluation.

Based on preliminary grid search using $F_{0.5}$ scores as a criterion, we selected a 90-min window size, which consistently yielded robust performance. Therefore, we adopted this fixed window length for all subsequent analyses. No overlap was introduced between consecutive windows.

Following prior work, we set the quantile values α to 1 and 99. The Gaussian process kernel was defined as the sum of an RBF kernel and a White kernel. The length of the quantile sequence used for prediction T was set to 100 windows. For model retraining, the exclusion period (T_{ignore}), which defines the duration of data discarded after a detected event, was set to 7 days. The retraining period ($T_{retrain}$), which specifies the length of the time window used for retraining, was set to 100 windows. Parameter tuning was performed with the goal of maximizing precision for each detector. Gaussian Process Regression was implemented using the scikit-learn library, and kernel optimization was performed using the library's built-in functions.

The two main parameters adjusted in addition to the parameters of the original Q-GPR method [2] were: (i) the coefficient n, which controls the confidence interval width in Q-GPR, and (ii) the threshold $thres$ used in the Max Threshold model. These parameters were carefully tuned to balance precision and recall. A grid search over the entire training period (84 months) was performed, and settings that achieved a precision of at least 98% were selected. A complete list of the final tuned parameter values used in our experiments is available in an open-access repository [10]. In addition, the ensemble model combination strategies were also needed to be determined as described in Sect. 4.3. This was done manually, and the determined channel-specific ensemble configuration is summarized in Table 1.

Table 1. Channel-wise detection logic in the ensemble method

Detection Logic	Channels
Lower AND Upper	12, 13, 14, 15, 16, 21, 22, 23, 24, 29, 30, 31, 32, 33, 34, 35, 38, 39, 40, 47, 48, 49, 50, 51, 52, 57, 58, 59, 60, 64, 65, 66
Lower AND Upper + Max Threshold	17, 18, 20
Lower OR Upper	19, 70, 71, 72, 73, 74, 75, 76
Lower OR Upper + Max Threshold	25, 26, 27, 28, 36, 37, 41, 42, 43, 44, 45, 46

5.2 Evaluation with ESA-ADB

As shown in Table 2, the proposed method demonstrated significantly superior detection performance compared to existing approaches. The benchmark methods excluding the proposed method and Q-GPR were referenced from ESA-ADB paper [5]. These include Telemanom ESA-Pruned (an LSTM-based neural method), Dilated Convolutional Variational Auto Encoder (DC-VAE), k-Nearest Neighbors (KNN), Isolation Forest (iForest), and Histogram Based Outlier Score (HBOS). The evaluation metrics used in the table were corrected event-wise Precision, Recall, and $F_{0.5}$ score recommended in [5].

Table 2. Results for full set and lightweight subset (OOM: Out of Memory)

		Proposed	Q-GPR only	Telemanom ESA-Pruned	DC-VAE	KNN	iForest	HBOS
Full Set								
Metric	Precision	**0.969**	0.935	0.050	0.005	OOM	<0.001	<0.001
	Recall	0.722	0.655	0.870	0.804	OOM	**0.967**	0.957
	$F_{0.5}$	**0.907**	0.862	0.061	0.007	OOM	<0.001	<0.001
Lightweight Subset								
Metric	Precision	0.977	0.972	**0.999**	0.063	0.001	<0.001	<0.001
	Recall	0.708	0.569	0.424	0.338	**0.754**	0.585	0.585
	$F_{0.5}$	**0.908**	0.852	0.786	0.075	<0.001	<0.001	<0.001

On the full set of telemetry channels, the proposed method achieved an $F_{0.5}$ score of 0.907, the highest score among all the methods. Notably, the benchmark methods only recorded substantially low scores. For instance, Telemanom ESA-Pruned, which achieved the best $F_{0.5}$ score in [5], recorded an $F_{0.5}$ score of only 0.061 on the full set. As can be seen from Table 2, this marked underperformance is primarily attributable to a substantial decline in Precision, despite the method maintaining a moderate level of Recall. In contrast, the proposed method and Q-GPR consistently achieved high Precision of 0.969 and 0.935, respectively. Such high Precision is critical not only for optimizing the $F_{0.5}$ score, but also for reducing false positives in operational settings, thereby minimizing operator workload and avoiding unnecessary interventions.

In contrast, within the Lightweight Subset (LWS)–a curated subset defined by ESA-ADB to represent key subsystems– Telemanom ESA-Pruned achieved a relatively competitive score. However, its performance deteriorated considerably when applied to the broader and more diverse full dataset. This indicates that while the method performs reasonably well on constrained subsets such as LWS, it lacks the generalization capability required for robust anomaly detection across comprehensive telemetry data. By contrast, both Q-GPR and the proposed method consistently achieved high scores on both LWS and the full dataset, highlighting the clear advantage of our approach and demonstrating its robustness and generalizability across the diverse characteristics of satellite telemetry.

Furthermore, the proposed method consistently outperformed in all evaluation metrics when comparing with the base Q-GPR model without ensemble enhancements. Notably, the recall improved significantly–from 0.655 to 0.722 on the full telemetry set–indicating that the ensemble architecture successfully captured anomalies that the original Q-GPR alone failed to detect. Specific examples of this will be presented later.

Table 3 summarizes detection results for event classes with a sufficient number of anomalies. The proposed method demonstrates a clear trend in terms of which anomaly classes it can reliably detect and which it finds more challenging. For example, all anomalies in Event Classes 2, 3, and 14 were successfully

Table 3. Detection results and anomaly characteristics per Event Class

Event Class	Rate(%)	Detected/Total	Overview of Anomaly Feature
Class 2	100.00	2/2	Short-term local shift
Class 3	100.00	21/21	Primarily single point outliers
Class 4	100.00	3/3	Instantaneous local shift
Class 7	39.1	9/23	Gradual and large range shift
Class 8	12.5	1/8	Sampling frequency reduction
Class 12	0.00	0/2	Frequency change, subtle range variation
Class 14	100.00	16/16	Waveform distortion, range shift, spikes
Class 15	100.00	2/2	Gradual and large range shift
Class 16	60.00	3/5	Gradual and large range shift
Class 17	100.00	2/2	Range variation, frequency change

detected. Figures 3 and 4 illustrate representative examples of anomalies from Event Classes 14 and 2, respectively, both of which were completely detected by the Q-GPR. The anomaly from Event Class 14, shown in Fig. 3, involves substantial fluctuations in value range, a pattern aligned with Q-GPR's sensitivity to trend changes. Similarly, the anomaly in Event Class 2, shown in Fig. 4, exhibits more subtle variations compared to the former, yet it affected the quantile trends and was still successfully identified by Q-GPR. However, Fig. 5 illustrates an anomaly from Event Class 3 that was not detected by Q-GPR but was successfully identified by the Max Threshold. This anomaly is characterized by a sharp, transient spike, which was excluded as an outlier during quantile extraction in the Q-GPR. In contrast, it was effectively detected by Max Threshold model since the spike's amplitude exceeded the learned threshold. The improvement in overall detection performance can be attributed to the presence of such diverse anomaly patterns and the ability of the ensemble model to accommodate them through the complementary strengths of its individual components.

The proposed method failed to detect anomalies in certain Event Classes. In particular, almost no anomalies from Event Classes 8 and 12 were identified across any telemetry channel. Figure 6 shows an example of a missed detection from Event Class 12. Although the waveform exhibits significant changes in shape and frequency compared to the nominal period, the value range remains nearly unchanged. Consequently, these changes had minimal impact on the extracted quantiles during window segmentation, and Q-GPR missed this anomaly. The Max Threshold model also could not detect such a change in principle. As a result, this type of anomalies characterized by changes in waveform shape or frequency without substantial shifts in value range are likely to be overlooked by the proposed method. To address this limitation, future work could consider integrating other detectors that focus on waveform morphology or frequency-domain characteristics into the ensemble framework.

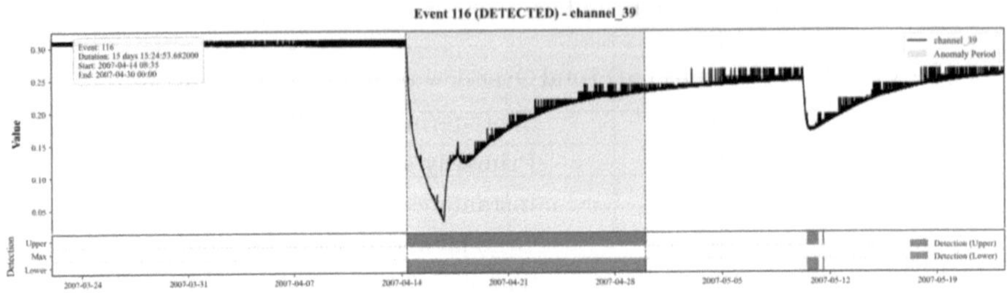

Fig. 3. Example of an Event Class 14 anomaly detected by Q-GPR.

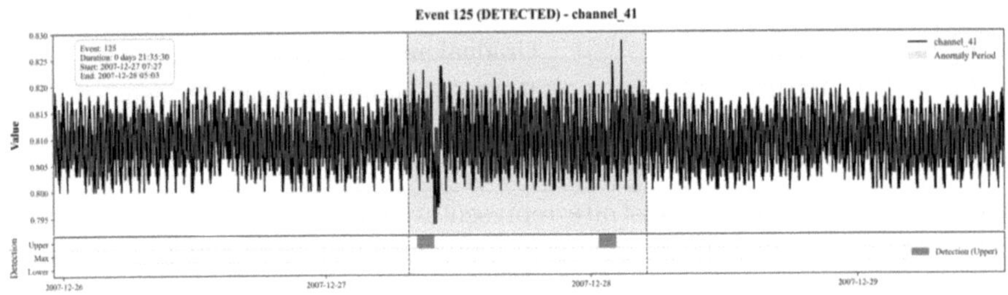

Fig. 4. Example of an Event Class 2 anomaly detected by Q-GPR.

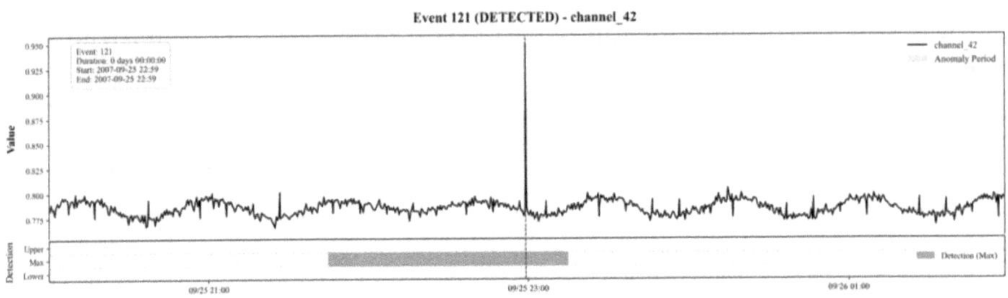

Fig. 5. Example of an Event Class 3 anomaly detected by Max Threshold.

In addition to detection performance, computational efficiency is crucial for executing algorithms on an onboard computer in orbit. From a runtime perspective, our method processed 84 months of telemetry in approximately 121.3 s per channel on average, including all preprocessing and ensemble sequencing steps, using a standard 11-core CPU (18 GB RAM) without GPU acceleration. This makes it well-suited for practical use in constrained environments, such as onboard satellite systems.

5.3 Performance in Spacecraft Anomaly Challenge

For final evaluation in the Spacecraft Anomaly Challenge competition, the results from the model tuned with the whole ESA-ADB dataset were submitted

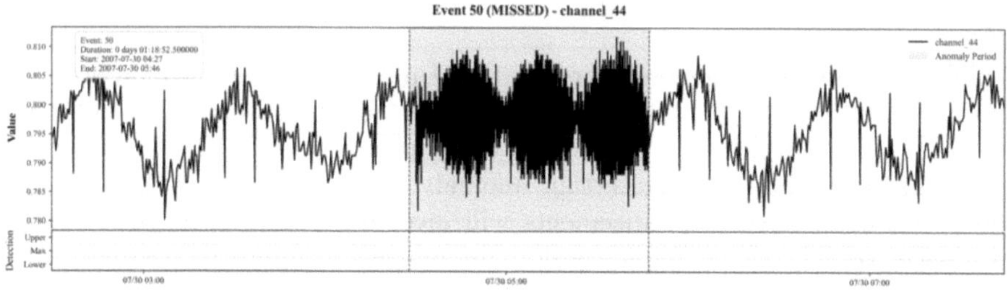

Fig. 6. Example of an Event Class 12 anomaly not detected by the proposed method.

to the Kaggle platform under the team name ***pandabbb***. It achieved an $F_{0.5}$ score of 0.599 on the Private Leaderboard and 0.666 on the Public Leaderboard. While the scores were lower than those obtained in the ESA-ADB evaluation, a deep analysis of the results was not feasible due to the lack of access to the ground truth labels. Although some early submissions of our team reached a Private Leaderboard $F_{0.5}$ score close to 0.9, these were achieved via manual tuning based on leaderboard feedback. The final result reported in this article is from a fully reproducible setting without such manual tuning to ensure fairness and generalizability.

6 Conclusion

6.1 Conclusion

In this study, Q-GPR, an automated telemetry monitoring method developed in-house, was applied to the ESA-ADB dataset to evaluate its applicability to the diverse characteristics of satellite telemetry. ESA-ADB, the official dataset for the Spacecraft Anomaly Challenge, contains real telemetry data collected from operational ESA satellites.

To adapt Q-GPR for this dataset, several extensions were implemented. Since Q-GPR was not originally designed to address data distribution shifts, automatic retraining was introduced using adaptive learning. Additionally, while Q-GPR was initially designed to ignore single-point outliers as noise, the challenge required detecting such events. To accommodate this, an ensemble detection mechanism that included supplementary detectors was introduced.

The proposed method was evaluated using the ESA-ADB-recommended scoring metrics, where the competition setup mirrors. Compared with various baseline methods provided with the dataset, proposed method achieved the highest score. Notably, the proposed method maintained stable performance when applied to the entire satellite system, where other baseline methods suffered significant score degradation. These results demonstrate that the proposed framework, with Q-GPR as its core component, can be applied uniformly across diverse telemetry channels without channel-specific tuning or feature extraction, offering both practicality and generalizability. This consistent applicability supports its characterization as a universal approach to spacecraft anomaly detection.

6.2 Future Work

While Q-GPR enables general-purpose trend monitoring across a broad spectrum of satellite telemetry, there remains room for improvement in detection accuracy. The current ensemble design, which primarily relied on thresholding, was insufficient for detecting certain anomaly types such as waveform or frequency changes. Future enhancements will involve integrating detectors based on wavelet transforms or frequency-domain analysis to improve coverage.

Moreover, the current ensemble configuration is heuristically designed on a per-channel basis. To improve scalability and adaptability, we plan to develop a framework that automates ensemble structure selection and threshold tuning using techniques such as meta-learning or Bayesian optimization. This would enable more robust and channel-specific anomaly detection.

Finally, although this study did not utilize satellite telecommands information, such commands often correspond to changes in operational status and telemetry behavior. In future work, we aim to incorporate telecommand sequences into the detection framework to enhance interpretability and responsiveness in practical applications.

References

1. Hundman, K., Constantinou, V., Laporte, C., et al.: Detecting spacecraft anomalies using LSTMs and nonparametric dynamic thresholding. In: Proceedings of the 24th ACM SIGKDD International Conference on Knowledge Discovery & Data Mining (KDD 2018), pp. 387–395 (2018)
2. Omata, N., Tsutsumi, S., Abe, M., et al.: Data-driven satellite monitoring method applicable to various telemetry. In: Proceedings of the Asia Pacific Conference of the PHM Society 2023, vol. 4, no. 1 (2023)
3. Rasmussen, C.E., Williams, C.K.I.: Gaussian Processes for Machine Learning. MIT Press, Cambridge (2006)
4. Kotowski, K., Ruszczak, B., Quarantiello, L., et al.: Spacecraft Anomaly Challenge on ESA Dataset (2025). https://kaggle.com/competitions/esaadb-challenge. Accessed 20 June 2025
5. Kotowski, K., Haskamp, C., Andrzejewski, J., et al.: European space agency benchmark for anomaly detection in satellite telemetry. arXiv:2406.17826 (2024)
6. Ruszczak, B., Kotowski, K., Evans, D., et al.: The OPS-SAT benchmark for detecting anomalies in satellite telemetry. Sci. Data **12**, 710 (2025)
7. Wu, R., Keogh, E.: Current time series anomaly detection benchmarks are flawed and are creating the illusion of progress. In: 2022 IEEE 38th International Conference on Data Engineering (ICDE), pp. 1479–1480 (2023)
8. Suzuki, H., Tsutsumi, S., Sato, Y.: An FPGA implementation of a gaussian process based predictor for sequential time series data. In: 2020 Eighth International Symposium on Computing and Networking Workshops (CANDARW), pp. 445–449 (2020)
9. Page, E.S.: Continuous inspection scheme. Biometrika **41**, 100–115 (1954)
10. Kimura, Y., Omata, N., Tsutsumi, S., et al.: Appendix for Demonstration of a Universal Algorithm for Satellite Anomaly Detection in Spacecraft Anomaly Challenge (2025). https://zenodo.org/records/16403187

A Hierarchical Ensemble Pipeline for Anomaly Detection in ESA Satellite Telemetry

Lorenzo Riccardo Allegrini[1,2] and Geremia Pompei[1,2](✉)

[1] ContinualIST, Pisa, Italy
geremia.pompei@continualist.ai
[2] Department of Computer Science, University of Pisa, Pisa, Italy
l.allegrini1@studenti.unipi.it, geremia.pompei@di.unipi.it

Abstract. A hierarchical ensemble pipeline is introduced to address anomaly detection in multivariate telemetry data provided by European Space Agency (ESA). The method integrates shapelet-based and statistical feature extraction, per-channel modeling, intra-channel stacking, and a final cross-channel aggregation. The pipeline is trained and validated using time-series cross-validation and two-level masking strategies to prevent information leakage. Results on the European Space Agency Anomaly Detection Benchmark (ESA-ADB) [12] challenge demonstrate strong generalization, highlighting the effectiveness of hierarchical modeling in detecting subtle anomalies in realistic satellite telemetry.

Keywords: Satellite telemetry · Anomaly detection · ESA-ADB challenge · Ensemble learning · Multivariate time series · Shapelets

1 Introduction

Satellite systems play a fundamental role in numerous critical applications, including telecommunications, environmental monitoring, and global navigation. However, the space environment is extremely hostile, characterized by high radiation levels, extreme temperatures, and the inherent difficulty of performing direct maintenance operations. Ensuring the proper functioning of satellites is therefore essential to avoid operational disruptions and significant economic losses [5].

One of the most critical aspects of satellite operations is telemetry monitoring, that is, the collection of data transmitted by onboard sensors to assess the system's state. Monitoring 58 out of 76 telemetry channels simultaneously makes timely anomaly detection a complex challenge. The anomalies, defined as atypical, rare, unplanned, and unwanted changes in telemetry [12], can appear suddenly and, if not detected in time, may compromise the stability and operability of the satellite.

In recent years, *machine learning* has been increasingly applied to satellite anomaly monitoring, leading to increasingly advanced and automated solutions.

I. Koprinska et al. (Eds.): ECML PKDD 2025, CCIS 2842, pp. 89–103, 2026.
https://doi.org/10.1007/978-3-032-19105-2_7

Early approaches to anomaly detection often relied on simple thresholding techniques, known as Out-of-Limit (OOL) methods, which flagged deviations based on fixed value ranges. These were later extended by classical machine learning techniques such as clustering and nearest-neighbor methods [3], which model normality through density or distance in feature space. While effective in certain contexts, these methods can be computationally intensive and sensitive to the choice of similarity metrics.

More recently, deep learning models have been increasingly applied to anomaly detection, particularly through prediction-based approaches. In this setting, a model is trained to forecast the expected behavior of a time series under nominal conditions. Anomalies are then detected by measuring deviations between predicted and actual values. Recurrent neural networks (RNNs) and their variants such as long-short terms memories (LSTMs) are commonly used for this task, due to their ability to capture temporal dependencies [10]. However, these architectures often suffer from high computational costs and limited scalability, which restrict their deployment in resource-constrained or real-time settings. These computational limitations become especially problematic when dealing with large-scale and complex datasets such as ESA-ADB [12].

ESA Dataset and Challenge Overview. This work was evaluated on Mission 1 of ESA-ADB [12] and was engineered specifically to match its unique characteristics. The dataset provides over 700 million timestamped records across hundreds of channels, each corresponding to a specific onboard sensor or subsystem variable. Crucially, anomalies are precisely labeled, enabling supervised learning, a rarity in the space domain. In addition to telemetry, the dataset includes thousands of telecommands, discrete control signals issued from ground stations, which often coincide with abrupt, yet nominal, behavior shifts. These introduce strong temporal dependencies and non-stationarities that models must learn to handle. From a statistical perspective, the data pose multiple challenges: irregular sampling, missing values due to transmission gaps, channel redundancy, and a *low anomaly density* (1.80%). Furthermore, the dataset contains *nominal rare events* (e.g., resets, calibrations) which are statistically abnormal but not indicative of faults. This calls for methods that prioritize robustness, precision, and interpretability. The ESA Anomaly Detection Challenge builds on this dataset, tasking participants with identifying anomalous events under realistic operational constraints. The evaluation uses the corrected event-wise F0.5 score, a metric that emphasizes precision by measuring detection performance over whole event intervals instead of per-sample accuracy. A detection is counted as a true positive if it overlaps with a real anomaly on any channel; otherwise, non-overlapping detections are considered false positives. This approach encourages systems to produce concise and accurately localized anomaly predictions. The full metric definition is detailed in Kotowski et al. [12]. Importantly, the challenge does not differentiate between true anomalies and nominal rare events. Any sufficiently atypical pattern must be flagged. This frames the task as a generalized outlier detection problem in high-dimensional telemetry. Finally, since the challenge test set is resampled with *zero-order-hold* (ZOH) interpolation, the same preprocessing is applied to the training data to ensure identical temporal resolution and signal semantics across training and evaluation phases.

Contributions. The main contributions of this work are: a hierarchical ensemble pipeline combining statistical and shapelet-based feature extraction with multi-level anomaly detection; a two-level masking strategy to prevent information leakage and promote model diversity; and validation on the ESA-ADB challenge, achieving top-tier results and demonstrating generalization to realistic satellite telemetry anomalies.

2 Related Works

The proposed pipeline is *hybrid by design*, integrating three complementary stages: statistical segmentation, shapelet-based encoding, and hierarchical ensembling. Each stage contributes a distinct representation and processing layer, forming a structured architecture that mirrors established best practices in time-series anomaly detection.

In this section, related literature aligned with these three components is reviewed. First, segmentation and statistical feature extraction, a widely adopted strategy for summarizing local temporal dynamics, are discussed. The shapelet-based methods are then examined, which enrich representation through discriminative pattern matching. Finally, multi-view and hierarchical ensemble models are considered, which combine predictions across diverse representations to improve robustness and interpretability.

Segmentation and Statistical Features. Descriptors such as mean, variance, higher-order moments, extrema, and even short-term spectral cues condense local dynamics into an interpretable, low-dimensional vector. Anomalies then emerge whenever these summaries deviate markedly from the nominal distribution. The idea is effective in both supervised and unsupervised settings, and has been successfully applied across domains: Bao & Intille first demonstrated it for activity recognition on accelerometers [8], while Huynh & Schiele showed that window size and feature choice strongly influence accuracy [11]. In the space domain, windowbased statistics still power the *operational* CNES *Nostradamus* monitoring system, which relies on one-class SVMs for daily satellite health checks [7]; the same idea also underpins ESA's OPSSAT-AD benchmark [18], confirming the practical value of lightweight segmentation and feature-extraction pipelines.

Shapelet Mining. To enrich statistical features, each segment in this work is also encoded using shapelet-based descriptors: distances to representative subsequences extracted from the time series. Originally introduced by Ye and Keogh [21], shapelets are local patterns that best distinguish between classes. Lines et al. [14] proposed the Shapelet Transform, converting a time series into fixed-length vectors of distances to a set of shapelets, enabling compatibility with standard classifiers. Shapelets have also proven useful in anomaly detection, including supervised settings. Beggel et al. [1] learned shapelets that emphasize rare patterns, enabling accurate detection of deviations from nominal behavior.

Multi-view Stacking Ensemble. The architecture proposed in this work follows a structured *multi-view stacking* paradigm, where distinct representations of the time series are processed by separate models and aggregated hierarchically. Each base learner operates on a dedicated view, and their outputs are fused by a meta-learner that captures cross-view dependencies.

Multi-view learning exploits complementary feature sets to improve generalization, a principle widely applied in semi-supervised settings through co-training or tri-training schemes [22], and later extended to supervised contexts [6]. Stacked generalization [19], or stacking, further enhances this by training a meta-model to optimally combine diverse base predictors.

In anomaly detection, Ouyang et al. [15] demonstrated the efficacy of this approach by proposing a three-stage ensemble that constructs multiple views via different imputation strategies, extracts hierarchical time-series features (HTSF), and applies classical learners (e.g., XGBoost, Random Forest). The final stage stacks these meta-models, improving accuracy on power consumption datasets without heavy computational demands.

3 Proposed Method

In response to the ESA-ADB challenge, this work introduces the *ESA Hierarchical Ensemble Pipeline*, a modular anomaly detection framework that combines statistical segmentation, shapelet-based time series representation, per-channel base learners, inter-channel ensembling via stacking and cross-channel aggregator. The generic pipeline achieves strong performance and reproducibility integrating components like shapelets [14], XGBoost [4], logistic regression [13], and LSTM [9].

3.1 Two-Level Masking Strategy

The proposed anomaly detection framework is built upon a *hierarchical ensemble architecture.* The method follows a multi-level structure that progressively transforms raw multivariate time series into anomaly predictions.

Importantly, during the training process, a two-level masking strategy is applied to prepare the data for the hierarchical ensemble model. The data split of this technique is equal to the one of nested cross-validation [16]. The representation of the two-level masking strategy is shown in Fig. 1 where each input time series follows two steps at each of the two levels:

1. *splitting*: the time series is split into N segments of the same length (where N is the number of segments fixed a segment length). The result of the split is replicated N times creating N different configurations,
2. *masking*: for each configuration n, the n-th segment is masked and separated from the rest of the data that are processed at the following level.

At the end of this procedure, applied to the input time series x, the following segments are available for the n-th configuration of the first masking level and

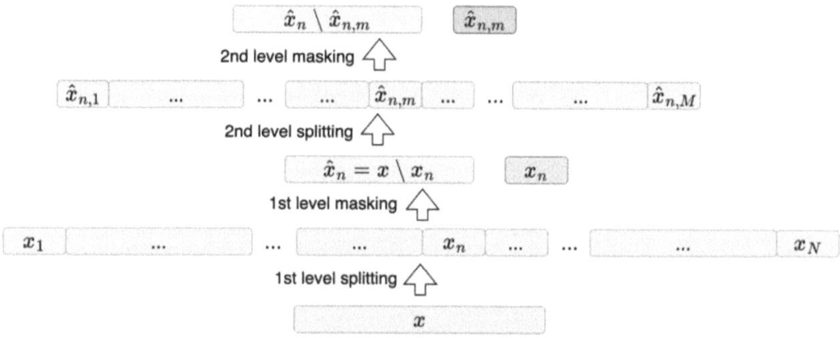

Fig. 1. Two-level masking strategy. The input timeseries is x and the final outputs of this procedure are: x_n, $\hat{x}_{n,m}$ and $\hat{x}_n \setminus \hat{x}_{n,m}$ (so the original timeseries x without the first two segments.)

the m-th of the second: x_n (the segment masked at the first level), $\hat{x}_{n,m}$ (the segment masked at the second level, where $\hat{x}_n = x \setminus x_n$), and $\hat{x}_n \setminus \hat{x}_{n,m}$ (the remaining portion of the time series excluding both masked segments).

The two-level masking strategy is applied in each channel of the dataset and is crucial to preparing data for the first two levels of the hierarchical ensemble model. In particular, $\hat{x}_{n,m}$ and $\hat{x}_n \setminus \hat{x}_{n,m}$ are used at the first level respectively for shapelet extraction and base model training, while x_n is used to train the intra-channel stacking meta-model.

By providing different partially masked views of the same data, the base models can focus on different aspects of the input, viewing it from various perspectives. In this way, the strategy ensures model diversity and prevents information leakage across layers. In addition, for every model trained at a given layer, all associated models in the previous layers are constrained to use only data not included in the masks of any of their corresponding next-level models. This guarantees that no training information is reused across layers, maintaining the independence of the features and predictions used at each stage.

3.2 Preprocessing

After the two-level masking strategy, applied to each channel separately, the provided time series undergoes different preprocessing steps: segmentation, feature extraction, and pooling. The entire preprocessing is shown in Fig. 2. It is important to understand the difference between the application of preprocessing in training and inference phases. In training, preprocessing is applied to $\hat{x}_n \setminus \hat{x}_{n,m}$ using the segment $\hat{x}_{n,m}$ (in Fig. 2 in training phase the generic input timeseries s is equal to $\hat{x}_n \setminus \hat{x}_{n,m}$) for shapelet mining for each configuration and saving the shapelets extracted. During inference, the input time series s (inference input timeseries) is preprocessed multiple times using the different configurations from the training phase, with respect to each extracted shapelets.

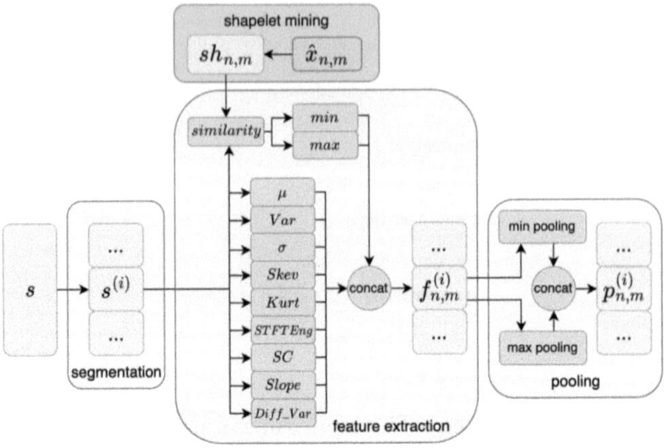

Fig. 2. Timeseries preprocessing steps. They are segmentation, feature extraction and pooling. The generic input timeseries is s (both for training and inference phases) while $f_{n,m}$ is the vector of the extracted features and $p_{n,m}$ the vector with pooling result. The shapelet mining is a process done during the training phase with respect to the $\hat{x}_{n,m}$ segment prepared during the two-level masking strategy Sect. 3.1, where the pool of shapelets $sh_{n,m}$ is extracted.

Segmentation. The input timeseries processed by the proposed methodology undergoes the process of segmentation, performing sliding-window segmentation of each time series. In this implementation, segments of a fixed duration are created with a fixed stride. The application is done along the time axis.

Feature Extraction. This phase is composed of two feature extraction methods: base and shapelet feature extraction.

Base Feature Extraction. It is related to the extraction of basic statistics computed in the raw input segments. For each segment, a focused set of statistical, temporal, and spectral descriptors is computed through a two-step selection process based on feature importance in XGBoost and visual analysis using the OXI tool [17]. In the end the selected statistics are: mean, variance, standard deviation, skewness, kurtosis, STFT energy, spectral centroid, slope and diff_var. They are reported in more detail in Appendix A.1

Shapelet Feature Extractor. In addition to basic statistical descriptors, the pipeline employs shapelet-based features to capture recurring local patterns indicative of anomalies. The two main aspects of shapelet are shapelet mining and shapelet feature extraction. The first is applied only during training and its purpose is to extract the pool of shapelets, while the second is always applied during inference, using the derived shapelets for feature extraction.

The *shapelet mining* process is applied during the training process to a dedicated subset of segments labeled as anomalous, internal to $\hat{x}_{n,m}$ extracted in the two-level masking strategy Sect. 3.1. $\hat{x}_{n,m}$ is split for the purpose of using the internal anomalies as relevant external shapelets for the preprocessed input that never contains $\hat{x}_{n,m}$ given the masking strategy. The anomalous subsequences are individually normalized to highlight their shapes, forming a pool of *normalized shapelet candidates* (if the anomalies are not sufficient, shapelets are sampled from a Dirichlet distribution). To select the most informative K shapelets, each candidate is evaluated by comparing the upper quantiles (75%) of its similarity scores on anomalous versus nominal segments. A greedy selection strategy retains the most discriminative and temporally diverse candidates.

In the *shapelet feature extraction* to transform input segments into features, each candidate shapelet is compared to the segment by computing a similarity score at every position, and retaining the *maximum and minimum* values across the entire segment. These two values represent, respectively, the strongest direct and inverse matches between the shapelet and local patterns in the segment. The similarity scores are obtained by sliding a window (of the same length as the shapelet) over the segment. At each position, the windowed subsequence is optionally padded and dilated, then normalized to zero mean and unit variance. A dot product between the normalized window and the shapelet (plus an additive bias) yields the local similarity score. The maximum and minimum of these scores are then divided by the shapelet length for scale normalization, producing two numerical features per shapelet. The final feature vector for each segment thus consists of the strongest direct and inverse correlations with each selected shapelet, providing a compact and expressive representation of anomaly-relevant patterns.

Pooling. To reduce temporal redundancy and emphasize the most prominent features, a *rolling min-max pooling* is applied to the timeline of feature vectors already extracted from the raw timeseries. Specifically, after segmentation and feature extraction, each segment is represented by a fixed-length vector containing statistical and shapelet-based descriptors.

Given a pooling window of length L_p and stride S_p, the window is slid along time axis and across the ordered feature sequence, grouping together L_p consecutive segment-level feature vectors. For each window, the minimum and maximum values of each feature dimension are computed across the included segments. This results in a new aggregated vector where each dimension corresponds to either the minimum or maximum value of a particular feature in the window.

This transformation serves two key purposes. First, it reduces the number of records passed to downstream models, improving efficiency. Second, and more importantly, it emphasizes the most extreme feature responses within a window, which are often indicative of anomalous patterns. This is particularly beneficial under the corrected event-wise $F_{0.5}$ metric: since a single high-confidence detection within an anomaly interval is sufficient, min and max pooling ensures that strong anomaly signals are preserved, while weaker, redundant activations are suppressed.

The final output is a condensed table where each row corresponds to a pooled window (i.e., a group of original segments), and each column captures either a minimum or maximum summary of a specific feature. This pooled feature matrix constitutes the definitive input to all layer 1 base models.

3.3 Hierarchical Ensemble Model

The proposed hierarchical ensemble model is composed of three abstraction layers: base models, intra-channel stacking, cross-channel aggregation. The channels and the two-level masking strategy Sect. 3.1 serve to split the data to train the different layers of the hierarchical ensemble model on different segments for each configuration. Figure 3 shows the hierarchical ensemble model architecture.

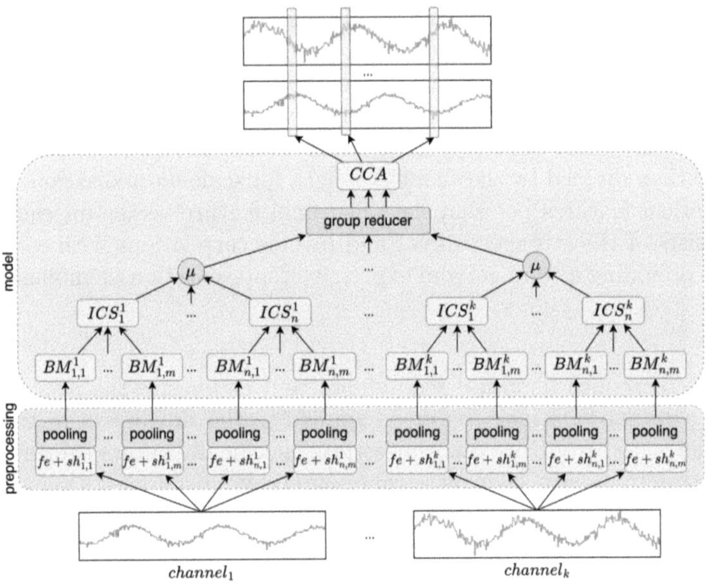

Fig. 3. Hierarchical ensemble model architecture. fe is related to the feature extraction function, sh to the shapelets, BM to the base models, ICS to the intra-channel models and CCA to the cross-channel aggregation models.

Layer 1: Base Models. After preprocessing, each channel proceeds with the training of its base classifiers on $\hat{x}_n \setminus \hat{x}_{n,m}$ segment of each configuration. Each base model is assigned a distinct subset of training data, as defined by the masking strategy. This design ensures that input features differ across models, promoting maximum diversity within the ensemble.

Specifically, shapelets are mined from a disjoint portion of the channel's time series, and the resulting dictionary is used to extract statistical features from the training segments associated with that model only (the shapelets $sh_{n,m}$ are extracted from $\hat{x}_{n,m}$ and applied on $\hat{x}_n \setminus \hat{x}_{n,m}$ during training). As a result, each base classifier learns from a unique combination of data and feature space, derived from different portions of the signal and encoded through different sets of shapelets, ensuring structural independence between models in the training phase.

Once trained, in inference phase, after preprocessing the same input time-series using different shapelets, each base model is applied to the respective pre-processed time series (the base model is always related to the specific shapelet applied during the training phase). This guarantees consistency between training and inference while preserving the model-specific nature of the features. By maintaining this strict alignment between data slices and feature extraction pipelines, the architecture avoids information leakage and enforces high intra-channel ensemble diversity.

Layer 2: Intra-Channel Stacking. The second layer of the hierarchy performs intra-channel ensembling by combining the predictions of multiple base models into a single, refined anomaly probability for each channel and each time segment. This is implemented using a stacking approach: for every channel, multiple meta-classifiers are trained.

The x_n segment, created in each configuration of the masking strategy, is used to train the intra-channel stacking meta-classifier on data not seen during base-model training. This procedure guarantees that the meta-classifier is trained without bias from data leakage. The resulting meta-classifiers learn to combine diverse predictive signals into a more accurate channel-level score. Importantly, different stacking models for the same channel operate on distinct data partitions and receive inputs from different sets of base models, which enhances model diversity and prevents overfitting.

During the inference phase, the trained intra-channel stacking models are applied to the base-model results for the corresponding n-th segment (at the first masking level). To obtain a robust channel-level prediction at inference time, the anomaly probability scores produced by all stacking models for a given channel are *averaged*.

Layer 3: Cross-Channel Aggregation. The third and final layer of the hierarchy addresses anomaly detection from a cross-channel and temporal perspective. While previous layers operate at the level of individual channels, this layer integrates the outputs of multiple channels-organized into semantically coherent groups-to capture complex system-level behaviors that manifest through coordinated deviations across subsystems.

For each channel's time series, before applying the two-level masking strategy, a segment x_{cca} is cut off from the end of the raw time series. The length of this segment is the same across all channels. x_{cca} is called cross-channel aggregation subset. It is used to train the cross-channel aggregation model on data not used in the previous layers. This guarantees that the data used to train the cross-channel models are completely disjoint from that used in previous layers (base and stacking), thereby preserving information independence throughout the pipeline.

The dataset of this work presents a set of channels that are members of groups. Each group collects channels similar in their nature (e.g. sensors related to the same aspect to monitor or the same family). To exploit the correlation within the group and make the model more efficient, a group reducer (gr) is applied at this stage. This is a function that aggregates predictions of the same group in a single result. The group reducer function applied is a power-weighted sum, defined by the following formula:

$$gr(p, G) = \sum_{c=1}^{C} \mathbf{1}_{\{c \in G\}} \cdot w_c \cdot p_c^{\gamma}$$

where p represents the probabilities from the previous layer of the hierarchical models of every channel, G is the current group, w is the vector of weights for each channel and γ is the exponent value used to enhance the probability. The weight of each channel is the validation precision metric result, computed according to the same channel. The group reducer transformation is applied to amplify confident detections while filtering out weak or unreliable signals.

During training, the resulting group-level time series $gr(p, G)$ for each G group are related to the processing of the x_{cca} of each channel and they are input of a cross-channel aggregation multivariate model, trained to predict the anomaly probabilities for the entire dataset. In the end of this passage, the probabilities of the anomalies are related to each channel of the input multi-channel time series.

During the inference phase, after averaging the predictions for each channel, the group reducer function is applied and the result of each group is fed into the cross-channel aggregation model, using the same channel grouping as in training. Due to the nature of this methodology, the training and inference phases must maintain the same channel/group structure.

4 Results

The following section reports the model settings and final results of the ESA Challenge analysis, along with the corresponding discussion.

4.1 Model Settings

The presented hierarchical methodology is built to be robust and to prevent information leakage by viewing the data from different perspectives and involving several models to avoid the risk of the overfitting. For the same reason, the method is kept generic, in such a way to allow the selection of different models and hyperparameter configurations for each layer of the hierarchical architecture.

Layered Model Selection. For model selection, at each layer of the hierarchical architecture (base, intra-channel stacking and cross-channel aggregation) a time series cross-validation [2] is performed before the training. In detail, this cross-validation is a variation of standard k-fold. Taking the input time-series s it is divided into K splits. For each iteration k, the first k folds are tagged as train set and the $(k+1)$-th fold as validation set. After selecting the best hyperparameters, these are leveraged to build a new model from scratch and train it on the entire s. In terms of the two-level masking strategy, the segment $\hat{x}_n \setminus \hat{x}_{n,m}$ (see Sect. 3.1) is used for model selection and training of the base models, while the segment x_n is used for model selection and training of the intra-channel stacking models. For the cross-channel aggregator, model selection and training are performed using x_{cca} segments for each channel, as discussed in Sect. 3.3. The proposed segmentation technique allows model selection and training on data segments that do not overlap between hierarchy levels. The model selection of each layer is performed with a Bayesian Search [20] with $F_{0.5}$ score as validation metric, while the time series cross-validation is performed with a number of folds equal to 3.

Selected Models. The models of the different layers are fixed except for the last layer of the hierarchy. XGBoost [4] is used as the base model for its good compromise between efficacy and speed. For the intra-channel model, a simple logistic regression [13] is chosen as the meta-learner due to its wide use in this role, its simplicity, and its efficiency. For the cross-channel aggregator, three different models with distinct natures were tested. They are: XGBoost (also used for the base models), which is a gradient-boosting tree algorithm; logistic regression (also used for intra-channel stacking models), which can be viewed as a one-layer neural network for simple binary classification; and Long Short-Term Memory (LSTM) [9], a complex gated recurrent neural network. These three models were chosen for their differing architectures; for example, XGBoost is one of the most popular tree-based models, logistic regression is a classic shallow model (single-layer neural network), and LSTM is one of the most widely used deep learning models for time series data.

4.2 Results and Discussion

The following section presents an analysis comparing the methodology's efficacy under different hyperparameter configurations. In detail, the combination of segment lengths (#segments) and the type of cross-channel aggregation model.

The segment length is the number of time steps used for segmentation at the beginning of preprocessing. It is related to the granularity of the segments where is performed the feature extraction: the smaller the segment length, the smaller the patterns it can detect (potentially losing larger anomalies), and vice versa. This analysis also proposes combinations of segment lengths by taking the logical OR(|) of the predictions from the individual base cases. The combination should guarantee to focus on patterns of different lengths. The choice of cross-channel aggregation model is justified in Sect. 4.1.

The segment lengths selected for evaluation are 50, 1000, and 2000, while the tested cross-channel aggregator models include XGBoost, Logistic Regression, and LSTM. For the 50-length configuration, the full pipeline with shapelet-based feature extraction is applied as described. For the 1000 and 2000 configurations, only base features are used due to the high computational cost of shapelet extraction. These longer segments are intended to capture broader anomaly patterns that may not be visible within shorter windows, complementing the 50-length detections and improving overall anomaly coverage.

The experiments were performed on a 2020 Mac Mini with an 8-core Apple M1 chip running at 3.2 GHz. On average, the computation time was 10 h for one experiment using only CPU computation. This work does not focus on efficient processing or scaling analysis, both of which could be detailed in future work.

Table 1 reports the $F_{0.5}$ scores on the ESA-ADB benchmark for the ESA Challenge, which was conducted via the Kaggle platform. For the challenge, there exists a hidden test set divided into public and private parts. The public part comprises 35% of the total and was available before the end of the challenge to obtain metric results on the platform. The private part, by contrast, is the remaining 65%, and its metrics were evaluated only after the challenge concluded.

Table 1. Public and private challenge results across cross-channel aggregation models and segment lengths (#segments). The models compared are XGBoost (XGB), Logistic Regression (LR) and Long-Short Term Memory (LSTM). The values represent the $F_{0.5}$ score as percentages, and the best results are in bold.

$F_{0.5}$	Public			Private		
#segments	XGB	LR	LSTM	XGB	LR	LSTM
50	**89.6**	89.6	**77.9**	**88.7**	88.6	**84.2**
1000	58.7	86.1	59.9	24.3	63.8	57
2000	53.8	64.4	59.3	36.4	54.7	59.8
50|1000	82.8	85.6	63.2	61.2	**90**	59
50|2000	65.6	67.9	63.3	53	79.4	76.1
1000|2000	47.1	67.9	53.1	30.7	79.4	54.3
50|1000|2000	62.1	**92.9**	52.5	48.5	85.3	56.4

The results show that logistic regression is generally the most effective cross-channel aggregation model. Regarding segment length, 50 provides the best overall performance, also benefiting from the use of shapelet-based feature extraction, which is only applied in this configuration. For the base cases, the most effective combination involves XGBoost and logistic regression with segment length 50 in both the public and private challenges.

When combining different segment lengths using the logical OR (|) operator, the best results are obtained with logistic regression using 50|1000|2000 in the public leaderboard and 50|1000 in the private one. These outcomes highlight that in some cases, including longer segments in the aggregation improves performance compared to using 50 alone, confirming their complementary role in capturing broader anomalies. The comparison shows that the use of 50-length segments and shapelet features significantly enhances detection performance, both in isolation and when combined with longer segments. Between 1000 and 2000, the former generally performs better, suggesting that smaller segments are more suitable for this task and enable the hierarchical model to detect anomaly patterns more effectively.

Overall, logistic regression proves to be a robust and scalable aggregator, performing consistently well across various segment lengths. This confirms that even a relatively simple model can effectively manage the cross-channel aggregation task.

5 Conclusion

The European Space Agency Anomaly Detection Benchmark (ESA-ADB) challenge explicitly aimed at developing effective anomaly detection methods for multi-channel telemetry time-series data from a real spacecraft mission. To this end, we proposed a hierarchical ensemble architecture designed to analyze data from multiple perspectives.

Specifically, the proposed method leverages a two-level masking strategy to replicate and segment training data into distinct portions; it incorporates preprocessing that combines shapelet-based feature extraction, mined from known anomalies, with segment-wise pooling to reinforce salient temporal patterns across windows, thereby enhancing representation power. These representations are then processed by a three-level hierarchical ensemble comprising base models, intra-channel stacking, and cross-channel aggregation.

The proposed approach was evaluated on the ESA-ADB challenge, achieving outstanding performance on both public and private leaderboards. Specifically, the algorithm ranked first on the public leaderboard with a score of 0.931 and third on the private leaderboard with a score of 0.853, establishing it as one of the top-performing algorithms in the competition.

Post-challenge analysis confirmed key design choices, validating logistic regression as the optimal aggregator and highlighting the effectiveness of shapelet features with a 50-length segment.

A Appendix

A.1 Statistics Applied in Base Feature Extracition

Taken the generic input timeseries s with T time steps, it is used to explain the statistic formulas in the following list:

- *Mean* (first moment):

$$\mu(s) = \frac{1}{T}\sum_{t=1}^{T} s_t$$

- *Variance* (second central moment):

$$\mathrm{Var}(s) = \frac{1}{T}\sum_{t=1}^{T}(s_t - \mu(s))^2$$

- *Standard Deviation* (dispersion):

$$\sigma(s) = \sqrt{\mathrm{Var}(s)}$$

- *Skewness* (asymmetry): Measure of the asymmetry of the probability distribution about its mean.

$$\mathrm{Skew}(s) = \frac{\frac{1}{T}\sum_{t=1}^{T}(s_t - \mu(s))^3}{\sigma(s)^3}$$

- *Kurtosis* (tailedness): Degree of "tailedness" in the probability distribution.

$$\mathrm{Kurt}(s) = \frac{\frac{1}{T}\sum_{t=1}^{T}(s_t - \mu(s))^4}{\sigma(s)^4} - 3$$

- *STFT Energy*: Energy in the Short-Time Fourier Transform window, sensitive to local spectral bursts.
- *Spectral Centroid* (SC): The Spectral Centroid indicates where the center of mass of the spectrum is located. It is calculated as the weighted mean of the frequencies present in the signal ($f(b)$ where b indicates the bin), determined using a Fourier transform, with their magnitudes ($m(b)$) as the weights

$$\mathrm{SC(s)} = \frac{\sum_b m(b) \cdot |f(b)|}{\sum_f |f(b)|}$$

- *Slope*: linear-trend coefficient of the segment.
- *Diff_Var*: variance of the first derivative, highlighting sharp transients.

References

1. Beggel, L., Kausler, B.X., Schiegg, M., Pfeiffer, M., Bischl, B.: Time series anomaly detection based on shapelet learning. Comput. Stat. **34**, 945–976 (2019)
2. Bergmeir, C., Hyndman, R.J., Koo, B.: A note on the validity of cross-validation for evaluating autoregressive time series prediction. Comput. Stat. Data Anal. **120**, 70–83 (2018)
3. Chandola, V., Banerjee, A., Kumar, V.: Outlier detection: a survey. ACM Comput. Surv. **14**, 15 (2007)

4. Chen, T., Guestrin, C.: Xgboost: a scalable tree boosting system. In: Proceedings of the 22nd ACM SIGKDD International Conference on Knowledge Discovery and Data Mining, KDD 2016, pp. 785–794. ACM (2016)
5. Chen, Y., Zheng, B., Zhang, Z., Wang, Q., Shen, C., Zhang, Q.: Deep learning on mobile and embedded devices: state-of-the-art, challenges, and future directions. ACM Comput. Surv. (CSUR) **53**(4), 1–37 (2020)
6. Farquhar, J., Hardoon, D., Meng, H., Shawe-Taylor, J., Szedmak, S.: Two view learning: Svm-2k, theory and practice. In: Advances in Neural Information Processing Systems, vol. 18 (2005)
7. Fuertes, S., Pilastre, B., D'Escrivan, S.: Performance assessment of nostradamus & other machine learning-based telemetry monitoring systems on a spacecraft anomalies database. In: 2018 SpaceOps Conference, p. 2559 (2018)
8. Gomaa, W., Khamis, M.A.: A perspective on human activity recognition from inertial motion data. Neural Comput. Appl. **35**(28), 20463–20568 (2023)
9. Hochreiter, S., Schmidhuber, J.: Long short-term memory. Neural Comput. **9**(8), 1735–1780 (1997)
10. Hundman, K., Constantinou, V., Laporte, C., Colwell, I., Soderstrom, T.: Detecting spacecraft anomalies using LSTMs and nonparametric dynamic thresholding. In: Proceedings of the 24th ACM SIGKDD International Conference on Knowledge Discovery & Data Mining, pp. 387–395 (2018)
11. Huynh, T., Schiele, B.: Analyzing features for activity recognition. In: Proceedings of the 2005 Joint Conference on Smart Objects and Ambient Intelligence: Innovative Context-Aware Services: Usages and Technologies, pp. 159–163 (2005)
12. Kotowski, K., et al.: European space agency benchmark for anomaly detection in satellite telemetry. arXiv preprint arXiv:2406.17826 (2024)
13. LaValley, M.P.: Logistic regression. Circulation **117**(18), 2395–2399 (2008)
14. Lines, J., Davis, L.M., Hills, J., Bagnall, A.: A shapelet transform for time series classification. In: Proceedings of the 18th ACM SIGKDD International Conference on Knowledge Discovery and Data Mining, pp. 289–297 (2012)
15. Ouyang, Z., Sun, X., Chen, J., Yue, D., Zhang, T.: Multi-view stacking ensemble for power consumption anomaly detection in the context of industrial internet of things. IEEE Access **6**, 9623–9630 (2018)
16. Parvandeh, S., Yeh, H.W., Paulus, M.P., McKinney, B.A.: Consensus features nested cross-validation. Bioinformatics **36**(10), 3093–3098 (2020)
17. Ruszczak, B., Kotowski, K., Andrzejewski, J., Haskamp, C., Nalepa, J.: Oxi: an online tool for visualization and annotation of satellite time series data. SoftwareX **23**, 101476 (2023)
18. Ruszczak, B., Kotowski, K., Evans, D., Nalepa, J.: The ops-sat benchmark for detecting anomalies in satellite telemetry. Sci. Data **12**(1), 710 (2025)
19. Wolpert, D.H.: Stacked generalization. Neural Netw. **5**(2), 241–259 (1992)
20. Wu, J., Chen, X.Y., Zhang, H., Xiong, L.D., Lei, H., Deng, S.H.: Hyperparameter optimization for machine learning models based on bayesian optimizationb. J. Electron. Sci. Technol. **17**(1), 26–40 (2019)
21. Ye, L., Keogh, E.: Time series shapelets: a new primitive for data mining. In: Proceedings of the 15th ACM SIGKDD International Conference on Knowledge Discovery and Data Mining, pp. 947–956 (2009)
22. Zhou, Z.H., Li, M.: Tri-training: exploiting unlabeled data using three classifiers. IEEE Trans. Knowl. Data Eng. **17**(11), 1529–1541 (2005)

Morphological Leave-One-Out Kernel Density Estimates for Anomaly Detection in Satellite Telemetry

Mina Bikhit[1], Sevvandi Kandanaarachchi[2], Krzysztof Kotowski[4], Jakub Nalepa[3,4], and Bogdan Ruszczak[1](✉)

[1] Faculty of Computer Science, Opole University of Technology, Opole, Poland
mina.bikhit@student.po.edu.pl, b.ruszczak@po.edu.pl
[2] Commonwealth Scientific and Industrial Research Organisation (CSIRO), Clayton, VIC, Australia
Sevvandi.Kandanaarachchi@data61.csiro.au
[3] Faculty of Automatic Control, Electronics and Computer Science, Silesian University of Technology, Gliwice, Poland
jnalepa@ieee.org
[4] KP Labs, Gliwice, Poland
kkotowski@kplabs.pl, jnalepa@kplabs.pl

Abstract. Satellite telemetry data consists of information transmitted from spacecraft providing their location, status, health and the functioning of the instruments. Due to the data volume, signal quality issues, resolution and orbital constraints, detecting anomalies in satellite telemetry data is challenging. One of the main challenges concerned with the existing methods is the large number of false alarms, contributing to a waste of operational resources and decreased trust in the system. In this paper, we tackle this issue and present Morphological Leave-One-Out Kernel Density Estimates (Mo-LOO-KDE)—an unsupervised anomaly detection method tailored for satellite telemetry data. It combines Extreme Value Theory, a statistical framework for modeling extremes, with computer-vision morphological operations. Here, Extreme Value Theory is used to model rare, extreme events, whereas morphological operations are effectively used for noise reduction. The unusual combination of Extreme Value Theory and morphological operations drive Mo-LOO-KDE's low false positive rate. The proposed morphological filtering method has no formal requirement for regular sampling, so the method is applicable for irregular time series as well. Furthermore, the employment of a lightweight, unsupervised method such as Mo-LOO-KDE is advantageous due to its practical utility, as annotated and representative ground-truth datasets are expensive to generate and rarely available. Utilizing the 42-month telemetry dataset from the ESA-ADB benchmark, we perform a comparison with the SOTA approach and show that Mo-LOO-KDE outperforms other unsupervised methods, demonstrating its applicability for satellite telemetry.

Keywords: Anomaly detection · Leave-one-out kernel density estimates · Extreme Value Theory · Kernel density estimates ·

I. Koprinska et al. (Eds.): ECML PKDD 2025, CCIS 2842, pp. 104–121, 2026.
https://doi.org/10.1007/978-3-032-19105-2_8

Generalized Pareto distribution · Satellite telemetry · ESA-ADB · Artificial intelligence

1 Introduction

With an ever-expanding toolbox of methods, anomaly detection has the capability to transform volumes of unintelligible data into a pool of actionable insights when implemented properly. However, a significant challenge in many applications is the large number of false positives produced by anomaly detection methods [4]. This is particularly the case in the satellite time-series telemetry data, which constitutes information collected by satellites, and concerned with their operating conditions, position, and the measurements taken by their onboard instruments. It is widely understood that false positives are the main obstacle to the broader adoption of anomaly detection algorithms in space operations [5,11]. Detecting anomalies in satellite telemetry data is challenging [17,18,20] due to multiple reasons, including large volumes of such data, its noisiness, complex interdependencies across the measurements, non-stationarity of the data, and the limited ground truth (manually or semi-automatically annotated anomalies which could be used to train supervised anomaly detection models). Despite all these challenges, the key stumbling block remains the large number of false alarms often returned by automated anomaly detection techniques—such false positives have to be thoroughly investigated by the operations teams, leading to delays and unnecessary overhead. In this article, we tackle this issue.

1.1 Contribution

In this paper, we present Morphological Leave-One-Out Kernel Density Estimates (Mo-LOO-KDE), an unsupervised anomaly detection method for satellite time-series telemetry data, that is designed to minimize the number of false alarms while appropriately detecting true-positive anomalous events. Mo-LOO-KDE combines an existing Extreme Value Theory (EVT) based library called *lookout*, which uses Leave-One-Out Kernel Density Estimates (LOO-KDE) [7], with morphological operations used in computer vision and image processing. Unlike many kernel density estimation methods that rely on user-defined bandwidth parameters, LOO-KDE utilizes persistent homology to automatically determine an optimal bandwidth for anomaly detection, eliminating the need for manual fine-tuning. This makes it an adaptive solution for detecting anomalies across diverse datasets. Furthermore, EVT-based anomaly detection methods have the ability to handle heavy-tailed data. This feature reduces the false positives because, as a result of modeling the extreme values with EVT, only the *uncommon* extremes are identified as anomalous, whereas most methods identify a large proportion of extremes as anomalous. Unfortunately, by itself LOO-KDE is not suitable for satellite telemetry data due to the noisy nature and non-stationarity of the data. Furthermore, LOO-KDE is a point-based anomaly detector while satellite telemetry anomalies are event-based. However, LOO-KDE has certain advantageous characteristics, such as low false positives, that can be beneficial for anomaly detection in satellite telemetry. Therefore, in Mo-LOO-KDE, we combine LOO-KDE with morphological operations used in computer vision—this novel pairing delivers high-quality results.

1.2 Preliminaries and Related Work

Morphological image processing techniques [21] use shape-based operations to analyze and manipulate images. They are commonly utilized for a variety of tasks, such as noise removal, edge detection, image segmentation, feature extraction, image enhancement and object recognition, among others. Generally, they are applied to a matrix of pixel values. However, they can also be applied to a vector, which is the way we use them for satellite telemetry. Common morphological operations include dilation, erosion, opening, closing, hit or miss transform, top hat and black hat. Specifically, we use dilation and erosion operations on the LOO-KDE output. Thus, morphological operations serve two purposes here: to reduce noise and to transform point anomalies into event anomalies.

In this study, we use the European Space Agency (ESA) Benchmark for Anomaly Detection in Satellite Telemetry (ESA-ADB) [11] to evaluate Mo-LOO-KDE. ESA-ADB is the first large-scale, real-life satellite telemetry dataset with curated anomaly annotations. Released in 2024, ESA-ADB has approximately 31 GB of data from 3 ESA missions, and it presents a considerable real-world anomaly detection challenge in the context of satellite telemetry analysis. On the one hand, it offers a clear representative dataset exhibiting inherent complexities that can serve as a valuable asset in training anomaly detection models. On the other hand, however, the level of complexity in this dataset is remarkably high. This is due to the fact that the anomalies include rare events and signal outliers, and not all of these events are labeled by domain experts as anomalous, which notably complicates the detection process [11]. A rigorous evaluation procedure is necessary to ascertain the efficacy of Mo-LOO-KDE on real-world satellite telemetry, hence we exploit the most diverse, the largest and the most heterogeneous dataset in the field of satellite telemetry analysis.

Satellite telemetry anomalies mostly pertain to anomalous events. This calls for event-based evaluation metrics. Furthermore, as stated by the ESA-ADB authors in [11], "*the highest priority aspect relates to the proper identification of anomalous events, but with a strong emphasis on avoiding false alarms at the same time*". This is because false alarms are costly to investigate and to resolve and thus reduce the confidence in the system. Furthermore, in space operations, a high false positive rate disqualifies an algorithm even if it obtains perfect scores in other aspects [11]. In addition, the ESA-ADB authors state that *it is of paramount importance to avoid false positives. It is strongly preferable to miss some channels rather than to wrongly identify many irrelevant channels.* To address these issues, ESA-ADB authors give alternative evaluation metrics, which favor low false positive methods, and use them for the ESA-ADB dataset. We discuss these event-based metrics in Sect. 2.3 and use them in our evaluation.

For an effective comparison, we evaluate other unsupervised anomaly detection methods on ESA-ADB. We use an autoencoder, a variational autoencoder

(VAE) [10], LOO-KDE [7], Deep Support Vector Data Description (DeepSVDD) [16], COPOD—a copula-based anomaly detection method [13], and Principal Component Analysis (PCA) as comparison methods (two versions of each method are investigated). In addition to using the stand-alone method, we combine each technique with the morphological operations as in Mo-LOO-KDE, and report the outcome. We do this because LOO-KDE benefited from this combination, and we wish to provide the same advantage to other methods for fair confrontation.

1.3 Code and Experimental Reproducibility

To ensure the reproducibility, we release the packaged code containing all the elements necessary to obtain the reported results, including fully configured Jupyter notebooks and a Docker image with the runtime environment. This is available at https://doi.org/10.5281/zenodo.16534206. The ESA-ADB dataset collection that we build upon in this research is obtainable at https://zenodo.org/records/12528696 [2,11] and the anomaly detection LOO-KDE is available at https://sevvandi.github.io/lookout [8]. Furthermore, the previously released benchmark algorithms, which are used for baseline results are at one's disposal at https://github.com/kplabs-pl/ESA-ADB [12].

2 Materials and Methods

2.1 Benchmark Dataset

We build upon the publicly available ESA-ADB dataset [2,11]. This dataset includes real-life satellite sensor readouts with curated anomaly annotations which were labeled using the *OXI* tool [19]—an online labeling solution optimized to work smoothly with large time series data. The dataset was collected over three space missions, each of which were several years long. ESA-ADB encompasses satellite telemetry signals acquired across over 70 channels, with the primary focus on six channels (41...46), because they were identified as the most important by flight control engineers [11]. In this study, we explore the 10-month and 42-month timeframes. The analyzed information is rather dense, and—for the context—it can be stated that each month of the analyzed signal provides approximately 87,000 individual telemetry data points. Furthermore, ESA-ADB dataset has different classes of anomalies. We do not differentiate between different anomaly classes, and therefore we treat all anomalous classes as one.

2.2 Anomaly Detection in Satellite Telemetry: Morphological Leave-One-Out Kernel Density Estimates (Mo-LOO-KDE)

We introduce Mo-LOO-KDE, an unsupervised anomaly detection method that brings together computer vision filtering operations with Extreme Value Theory-based LOO-KDE. The steps comprising Mo-LOO-KDE are illustrated in Fig. 1. The first part is the segment-by-segment processing of the signal. The long

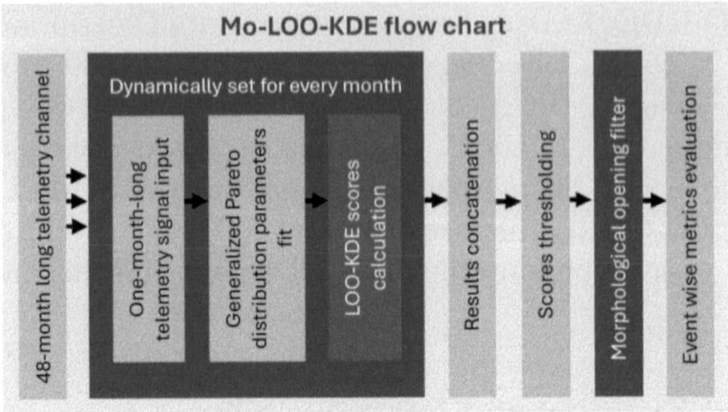

Fig. 1. The Mo-LOO-KDE anomaly detection framework for satellite telemetry. Two new elements introduced for this method are marked in purple color. (Color figure online)

telemetry time series is divided into monthly segments, and for each segment a Generalized Pareto Distribution (GPD) is separately fitted. Using the fitted GPD, LOO-KDE anomaly scores are computed. Next, the results are concatenated using the output of all segments, and then thresholded. Finally, morphological filtering is applied to the concatenated thresholded outcome scores. There are two distinct components in Mo-LOO-KDE: the LOO-KDE algorithm and the morphological operations (Step 1 and 2)—they are discussed in detail next.

Step 1: LOO-KDE Algorithm. For a set of data points $\{\boldsymbol{x}_1, \ldots, \boldsymbol{x}_N\}$, where $\boldsymbol{x}_i \in \mathbb{R}^n$, LOO-KDE initially finds a suitable bandwidth for anomaly detection using persistent homology. A persistence diagram is a set of birth-death pairs corresponding to the birth and death of the homology generators [3]. Deaths are somewhat similar to k-nearest neighbors (KNN) distances and successive death values indicate the closeness of the data points. Anomalies result in large death values. In terms of kernel density estimates (KDE), anomalies and boundary points result in low KDE values. If a small bandwidth is used, this results in a large number of points with low KDE values and thus, the identified anomalies will have a large number of false positives. Therefore, to capture anomalies while not getting many false positives, a relatively large bandwidth needs to be used. To determine the bandwidth, LOO-KDE uses the 98th percentile of death values which can be thought of as large KNN distances. With the selected bandwidth, LOO-KDE ultimately computes leave-one-out kernel density estimates $y = \text{KDE}(\boldsymbol{x})$, in order to minimize the effect of each point in the KDE calculation. Next, LOO-KDE transforms the leave-one-out KDE values y to $z = -\log y$, thus maps low-density points to large values and high density points to low values. These values are used to fit a Generalized Pareto Distribution (GPD), which models the tail consisting of large z values. Points with low GPD probabilities signify anomalies as they are less likely to be observed. The anomaly scores are computed as $1 - p(z)$ where $p(z)$ denotes the GPD probability.

The main arguments of LOO-KDE are:

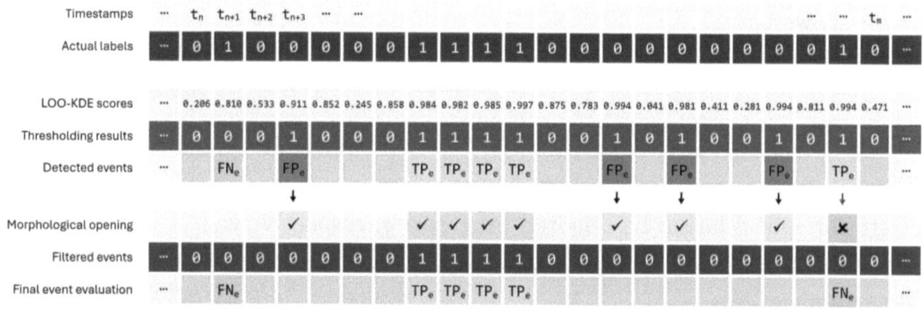

Fig. 2. The overview of the proposed morphological filtering of the LOO-KDE results. Only a short fragment of the vector is visualized. Note: anomalies in the actual telemetry channels are less densely populated.

- X: The input data.
- α: The level of significance (default: $\alpha = 0.05$).
- bw: The death radius percentile used for bandwidth computation. The default is the 98th percentile.
- $fast$: if it is set to $True$, the computation is faster due to the signal subsetting and utilizing less data for the bandwidth calculation.

The level of significance is used if we want to assign binary labels to anomalies, that is if $p(z) < \alpha$, then the anomaly label $u = 1$, otherwise $u = 0$. We utilized the anomaly scores $1 - p(z)$ directly with a thresholding mechanism instead of using α. We used the threshold of 0.99999 to assign binary labels to anomalies. That is, if $1 - p(z) \geq 0.99999$, then the anomaly label $u = 1$, otherwise $u = 0$. We call the resulting vector the *binary anomaly vector.* As a side note, LOO-KDE code has the functionality to specify the bandwidth and GPD parameters. This is to accommodate users who want to test the algorithm with different bandwidth or GPD parameter values (the defaults were best in this study).

Step 2: Morphological Operations. The idea behind the morphological filtering is in Fig. 2. The binary anomaly vector (dark blue) mostly contains zeros. The ones are scattered along the vector, and they sometimes appear in isolation and sometimes consecutively. The applied morphological opening leads to the removal of the sole short detections, leaving solid candidates that are usually clusters of ones. This results in a reduction of false positives. Sometimes it removes single occurring true positives as seen from the right-most 1 in the binary anomaly vector in Fig. 2. The benefit of false positive reduction outweighs the cost of single true positive removal as false positives are more frequent.

For the opening operation, two steps are applied successively. Those are erosion and dilation of the binary anomaly vector. For both of them, a neighborhood is considered. Let $\boldsymbol{u} = \{u_1, u_2, \ldots, u_N\}$ denote the binary anomaly vector of length N. The neighborhood $N(u_i, r)$ centered at u_i of r width is defined as:

$$N(u_i, r) = \{u_j : |j - i| \leq r, i \neq j\}. \quad (1)$$

For $r = 1$, we have:

$$N(u_i, 1) = \begin{cases} \{u_{i-1}, u_{i+1}\}, & i \neq 1, N \\ \{u_2\}, & i = 1 \\ \{u_{N-1}\}, & i = N \end{cases} \tag{2}$$

Let erosion and dilation be denoted by f and g, respectively:

$$f(u_i) = \min N(u_i, 1) \quad \text{and} \quad g(u_i) = \max N(u_i, 1). \tag{3}$$

The opening operation consists of erosion followed by dilation, resulting in:

$$\tilde{\boldsymbol{u}} = g(f(\boldsymbol{u})), \tag{4}$$

where the operations are applied to each entry of the vector. For a single occurring 1, where the neighborhood consists of zeros, $g \circ f$ results in making that entry zero. For a cluster of consecutive ones in the binary anomaly vector, the erosion operation f removes the two ones from either end and replaces them with zeros. Then, dilation g works in the opposite way—it adds a one to each end. Thus, the bit-wise operation $g \circ f$ does not change a cluster of consecutive ones, but removes single, random detections from the vector. The operation is straightforward, and its implementation does not add much overhead to the method, as it is applied only once for the concatenated vector.

Mo-LOO-KDE combines LOO-KDE—an EVT anomaly detection method—with morphological operations to detect anomalies in long, non-stationary telemetry time series. By dynamically fitting a GPD to each segment, Mo-LOO-KDE adapts to the distributional shift in telemetry data. By coupling with morphological operations Mo-LOO-KDE sees a significant reduction in false positives.

2.3 Anomaly Detection Metrics

Time-series data consists of individual data points sorted in time. However, anomalies often span multiple points rather than appearing at just one time point. When an anomalous event occurs, a detector might predict it on a subset of time points but not all, resulting in a significant distortion of point-wise metrics such as precision and recall (Pr_p and Re_p). These metrics would unfairly penalize the detector for not flagging every single affected point, even though it correctly identified the anomaly during the analyzed event. Consequently, point-wise metrics become misleading as they prioritize individual detections while neglecting to consider whether the anomaly was correctly recognized.

A better alternative are the event-wise metrics [14] (also referred to as the segment-wise in the literature [23]), which offers a more equitable evaluation by ascertaining whether the algorithm was able to detect an anomaly at least once during the event, even if not at every single point. This approach reflects real-world anomaly detection, wherein the identification of an anomaly at the event level is frequently more crucial than pinpointing every affected timestamp. By employing event-wise metrics, we obtain a meaningful assessment of Mo-LOO-KDE's ability to detect anomalies in time-series data.

The metrics used in this study are as follows:

- Event-Level True Positives (TP_e): counted when the anomaly detection method correctly identifies at least one data point within a labeled anomalous event. In contrast to point-wise metrics, which evaluate every point separately, event-based metrics only require at least one detection within the anomaly window for the entire event to be considered as successfully detected [23].
- Event-Level False Positives (FP_e): occurs when the anomaly detection method flags an anomaly outside of any actual ground-truth anomaly event. Thus, an alarm is raised, yet no true anomaly is present at the particular moment. In the context of event-based evaluation, FP_e signifies the number of instances in which the model erroneously predicts an anomaly that does not exist.
- Event-Based Recall (Re_e): measures the proportion of actual anomalies within events that are correctly detected. It is calculated by dividing the number of true positive events TP_e by the sum of true positive events and false negative events FN_e according to the formula [23]:

$$Re_e = \frac{TP_e}{TP_e + FN_e}. \tag{5}$$

- Event-Based Precision (Pr_e): assesses the proportion of detected anomalous events that are actual anomalies. It is computed by dividing the number of true positive events (TP_e) by the sum of true positive events and false positive events (FP_e) [23]:

$$Pr_e = \frac{TP_e}{TP_e + FP_e}. \tag{6}$$

- Event-Wise F-Score $F_{0.5_e}$: it is used to evaluate the balance between event-wise precision (Pr_E) and event-wise recall (Re_e) in anomaly detection. Unlike the traditional F_1-score, which gives equal weight to precision and recall, the $F_{0.5}$-score places more emphasis on precision, making it particularly useful when false positives need to be minimized [23]. It is calculated as follows:

$$F_{0.5_e} = \frac{(1 + 0.5^2) \cdot Pr_e \cdot Re_e}{(0.5^2 \cdot Pr_e) + Re_e}. \tag{7}$$

2.4 The Platform for the Anomaly Detection Experimentation

To ensure a smooth execution of our anomaly detection pipeline, we configured an environment capable of integrating Python and R programming languages. Given that the backbone anomaly detector LOO-KDE is implemented in R, while the rest of our workflow relied on Python, we utilized Docker to bridge between the two environments. This containerized configuration enabled the execution of both languages within a unified workflow without encountering compatibility issues, ensuring a streamlined and reproducible experiment. We make this available at https://doi.org/10.5281/zenodo.16534206.

3 Experimental Study

The aim of the experiment is to assess the efficacy of Mo-LOO-KDE to detect anomalies in satellite telemetry signals and to compare it with other methods, including deep learning models. For this assessment, we primarily rely on event-wise metrics, as they give a broader perspective than the point-wise approach. The main objective we set for each detector is, therefore, to prioritize the actual event rather than the number of points it consists of. Hence, the most important performance indicator for this study is $F0.5_e$ (see Eq. (7)), which considers event-wise precision and recall Pr_e and Re_e (Eqs. (6) and (5)), yet prioritizes Pr_e, thereby identifying a model with a reduced tendency to generate false alarms. In addition to these metrics, we report the number of discovered anomalies (TP_e) and the number of detector mistakes (FP_e as well as FN_e), offering a multifaceted perspective.

3.1 Results and Discussion

Table 1 gathers the evaluation results of Mo-LOO-KDE and other methods on the ESA-ADB dataset. To provide a comparison, each method was evaluated as a stand-alone technique, as well as in conjunction with the morphological operations (similarly to Mo-LOO-KDE). The variant with the morphological filtering is denoted with an *Mo-* prefix in Table 1. For example, the variational autoencoder has two versions: VAE and Mo-VAE. We used channels 41–46 from the 42-month-long dataset for this exercise, and report the average metrics. It is important to note that the telemetry channels we employed for this evaluation contained from 62 (for `Channel_46`) to 67 (for `Channel_62`) anomalies on 3677761 data points.

Table 1. A comparison of Mo-LOO-KDE with other unsupervised anomaly detectors. The prefix Mo- denotes the algorithm variant with morphological filtering. The average metrics on channels 41–46 for the 42-month-long signal are given.

Detector model	Event– wise metrics			Number of detections		
	Pr_e	Re_e	$F_{0.5e}$	TP_e	FP_e	FN_e
Mo-LOO-KDE	**0.905**	0.251	**0.585**	16.2	**2.0**	48.3
LOO-KDE [7]	0.009	0.461	0.010	29.7	3657.2	34.8
AutoEncoder [1]	0.009	0.620	0.010	28.5	3359.0	17.5
Mo-AutoEncoder	0.012	0.616	0.015	28.3	2305.2	17.7
VAE [10]	0.009	0.627	0.011	28.8	3345.5	17.2
Mo-VAE	0.012	0.613	0.015	28.2	2302.5	17.8
DeepSVDD [16]	0.000	**0.971**	0.001	**44.7**	101267.0	1.3
Mo-DeepSVDD	0.016	0.504	0.020	23.2	1461.8	22.8
COPOD [13]	0.006	0.493	0.007	22.7	3967.0	23.3
Mo-COPOD	0.008	0.457	0.009	21.0	2760.5	25.0
PCA [1]	0.008	0.624	0.010	28.7	3457.5	17.3
Mo-PCA	0.012	0.620	0.015	28.5	2397.3	17.5
Anomaly Transformer [25]	0.300	**1.000**	0.348	3.0	7.0	0.0
Mo-Anomaly Transformer	0.272	**1.000**	0.319	3.0	8.0	**0.0**

The best results for each metric are **boldfaced**.

From Table 1, we can see that Mo-LOO-KDE performs best in terms of the main evaluation metric ($F0.5_e$). While averages are in Table 1, for *Channel 43* MO-LOO-KDE obtains a higher $F0.5_e$ score of 0.647. The other methods give similar values to their average for other channels. Furthermore, the average number of false positives FP_e is 2.0 for Mo-LOO-KDE, which is orders of magnitude lower when compared with the other techniques. When we compare LOO-KDE with Mo-LOO-KDE, the average number of false positives have reduced from 3657 to 2, which is a massive reduction in false positives. However, we do not see an equivalent reduction in false positives for other methods when we compare the stand-alone method with their Mo- variant. DeepSVDD has 101267 average false positives, which gets reduced to 1461 with Mo-DeepSVDD. However, with such a large number of false positives, it is functionally infeasible to use DeepSVDD for telemetry signals in practice, as it would induce strong overhead.

A possible reason for morphological filtering to perform so well on LOO-KDE, but not on other methods, is that isolated anomalies are substantially more common in LOO-KDE than in the other methods. For other methods, anomaly clusters can be more frequent, while isolated anomalies are in the minority. Figure 3 shows the false positives of LOO-KDE, AutoEncoder and DeepSVDD with their morphological variants Mo-LOO-KDE, Mo-AutoEncoder and Mo-DeepSVDD. Due to space constraints, only these algorithms are illustrated, while the others are similar. We can appreciate that even after applying the morphological operations the false positives are quite high for Mo-AutoEncoder and Mo-DeepSVDD, while there is a drastic drop in false positives for Mo-LOO-KDE.

It is important to mention the applied filtering because some very short detections could lead to fewer true positives being found and consequently result in a lower recall metric.

The ESA-ADB authors [11] evaluated a set of semi-supervised and unsupervised anomaly detection methods on their dataset. Comparing with these methods (Table 2 in [11]), we can indeed observe that Mo-LOO-KDE performs better than the unsupervised methods thoroughly investigated in [11], and also better than some semi-supervised methods. The best semi-supervised method is `Telemanom-ESA`—an extended version of the Telemanom algorithm originally proposed by NASA [5]. In that area, this algorithm is a state-of-the-art approach and an industry standard. This method is trained on a large 84-month-long dataset from the same mission, and then tested on the equivalent test set as for the other experiments. It was evaluated using the open-source code [12]. Telemanom-ESA was trained using a desktop workstation equipped with a modern GPU (NVIDIA 3060 RTX 6 GB RAM) and the training time was 3.6 h. To decrease the number of false positives, they used additional pruning in `Telemanom-ESA-Pruned`. For Telemanom-ESA, we get $Pr_e = 0.128$, $Re_e = 0.894$, $F_{0.5e} = 0.178$, and for the Telemanom-ESA-Pruned, we get $Pr_e = 0.999$, $Re_e = 0.424$, $F_{0.5e} = 0.786$[1]. We see that while Mo-LOO-KDE performs better than Telemanom-ESA, Telemanom-ESA-Pruned performs significantly better than Mo-LOO-KDE. It is not exactly a fair comparison, as Telemanom-ESA-Pruned is a semi-supervised method while Mo-LOO-KDE is an unsupervised method. Furthermore, Mo-LOO-KDE is a lightweight algorithm that can be run on a standard laptop. However, Telemanom-ESA-Pruned shows that performance can be improved, and thus, gives motivation for further improvements in Mo-LOO-KDE.

[1] It is important to note that this library [12] reports the corrected version of metric, which is more restrictive (see [11]: $F_{\beta_{e_{corr}}}$ on page 21).

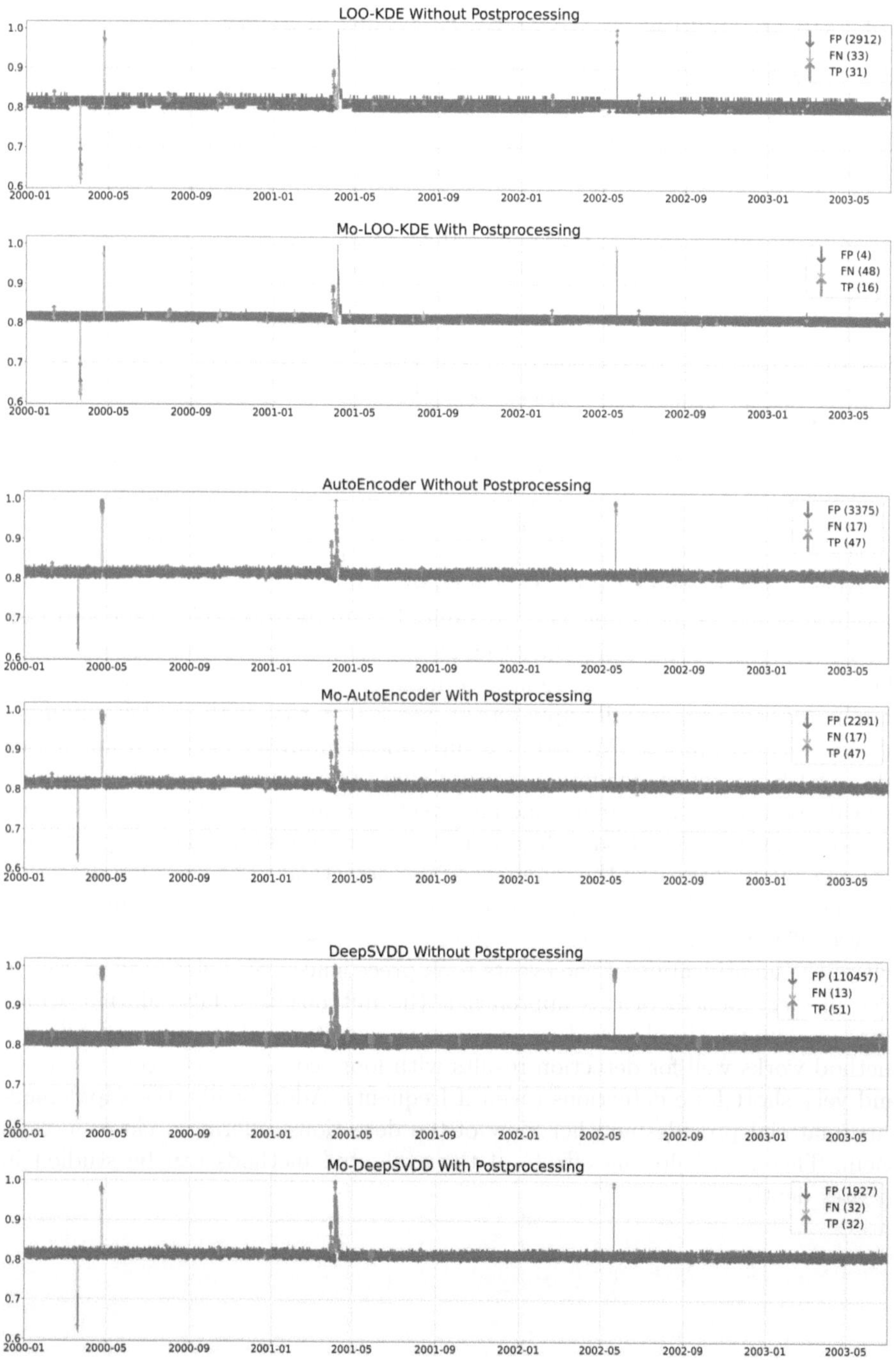

Fig. 3. The output of 6 models tested on the *ESA-ADB, Mission #1, Channel_45*. A comparison of the original model with its *Mo-* variant is shown. Row 1: LOO-KDE, Row 2: Mo-LOO-KDE, Row 3: Autoencoder, Row 4: Mo-Autoencoder, Row 5: DeepSVDD, Row 6: Mo-DeepSVDD.

3.2 On Developing Mo-LOO-KDE: Ablation Study

In this section, we give some intuition about the development of Mo-LOO-KDE. In particular, we explore the dynamic and fixed parameter settings of GPD. The default in LOO-KDE is the dynamic GPD setting. That is, for each dataset LOO-KDE fits a GPD and finds anomalies. However, in cases where the dataset is segmented into different time windows we have the option of using the same GPD for all time windows. This can be done by getting the GPD parameters for the first segment, which can then be used for other segments. This may be useful for datasets that do not exhibit a distributional drift. In addition to the GPD setting, we explore simple transformations of the signal. Let $\boldsymbol{x} = \{x_1, x_2, \ldots, x_N\}$ denote the telemetry time series and $\Delta\boldsymbol{x} = \{(x_2-x_1), (x_3-x_2), \ldots, (x_N-x_{N-1})\}$ denotes the differenced time series. We evaluate LOO-KDE and MO-LOO-KDE on $\boldsymbol{x}$, $\Delta\boldsymbol{x}$ and $|\Delta\boldsymbol{x}|$. We conduct these evaluations on both the 10-month and the 42-month datasets. Table 2 presents the results of these experiments.

Table 2 shows that results using LOO-KDE alone, enumerated in the first six rows, were not particularly encouraging. This included applying LOO-KDE on the raw signal $\boldsymbol{x}$, differenced signal $\Delta\boldsymbol{x}$ and the absolute value of the differenced signal $|\Delta\boldsymbol{x}|$, employing both fixed and dynamic GPD settings. The signals obtained from the actual telemetry exhibited significant variability and substantial noise levels, posing a significant challenge for anomaly detection techniques. The LOO-KDE detections have a large number of false alarms. A considerable number of those was readily apparent in Fig. 3 (top row, with the large number of FP_e's marked in red). We notice a substantial improvement when we employ Mo-LOO-KDE, which involves postprocessing LOO-KDE output using morphological operations. The binary anomaly vector returned by LOO-KDE was full of short, multiple detections, often lying in a narrow region. The morphological filtering vastly decreased the number of false detections. The resulting detection for the *Channel 45* is presented in the second sub-figure of Fig. 3. This method proved effective in experiments involving event-wise evaluation, i.e., scenarios where the identification of the events took precedence over point-wise precision. The primary benefit of this approach is the mitigation of false alarms, which were predominantly observed as single-point detections. The proposed filtering method works well for detection results with long, consistent correct detections and very short false detections (even if frequent). Additionally, the supplementary material provides another view of the detections, offering a closer look at them. There, the filtering effects of the evaluated methods can be studied in greater depth.

Table 2. Results of different LOO-KDE and Mo-LOO-KDE variants.

Configuration	Point–	Event– wise metrics			Number of detections		
	Pr_p	Pr_e	Re_e	$F_{0.5e}$	TP_e	FP_e	FN_e
LOO-KDE detections on the **42-month long** dataset							
Fixed GPD on x	0.078	0.007	0.266	0.008	17	2572	47
Fixed GPD on Δx	0.021	0.014	0.484	0.017	31	2247	33
Fixed GPD on $\lvert\Delta x\rvert$	0.023	0.007	**0.750**	0.009	**48**	6557	**16**
Dynamic GPD on x	0.254	0.012	0.500	0.014	32	2715	32
Dynamic GPD on Δx	0.034	0.010	0.688	0.013	44	4278	20
Dynamic GPD on $\lvert\Delta x\rvert$	0.030	0.009	0.719	0.011	46	4946	18
Mo-LOO-KDE detections on the **42-month long** dataset							
Fixed GPD on x	0.838	0.429	0.281	0.388	18	24	46
Fixed GPD on Δx	0.111	0.111	0.016	0.050	1	8	63
Fixed GPD on $\lvert\Delta x\rvert$	0.067	0.067	0.016	0.040	1	14	63
Dynamic GPD on x	**0.980**	**0.810**	0.266	**0.574**	17	**4**	47
Dynamic GPD on Δx	0.044	0.188	0.047	0.117	3	13	61
Dynamic GPD on $\lvert\Delta x\rvert$	0.044	0.167	0.047	0.110	3	15	61
LOO-KDE detections on the **10-month long** dataset							
Fixed GPD on x	0.104	0.018	0.615	0.022	8	436	5
Fixed GPD on Δx	0.027	0.017	0.462	0.021	6	354	7
Fixed GPD on $\lvert\Delta x\rvert$	0.043	0.008	0.615	0.010	8	1036	5
Dynamic GPD on x	0.156	0.022	**0.692**	0.028	**9**	396	**4**
Dynamic GPD on Δx	0.066	0.010	**0.692**	0.013	**9**	883	**4**
Dynamic GPD on $\lvert\Delta x\rvert$	0.065	0.008	**0.692**	0.010	**9**	1100	**4**
Mo-LOO-KDE detections on the **10-month long** dataset							
Fixed GPD on x	0.815	**0.750**	0.231	0.517	3	**1**	10
Fixed GPD on Δx	0.000	0.000	0.000	0.000	0	65	13
Fixed GPD on $\lvert\Delta x\rvert$	0.000	0.000	0.000	0.000	0	19	13
Dynamic GPD on x	**0.971**	0.667	0.308	**0.541**	4	2	9
Dynamic GPD on Δx	0.065	0.333	0.077	0.200	1	2	12
Dynamic GPD on $\lvert\Delta x\rvert$	0.065	0.333	0.077	0.200	1	2	12

The best results for each metric are **boldfaced**.

Mo-LOO-KDE handles long time series employing dynamic GPD parameters in LOO-KDE. We evaluated two alternative approaches: a static GPD mode, during which we utilize fixed GPD parameters, and a dynamic approach, where the GPD parameters are fitted on a monthly basis. The results for fixed and dynamic GPD settings are summarized in Table 2. For most of the compared cases, the dynamic mode outperformed the fixed mode. We consider this a strong positive for Mo-LOO-KDE, as this sequential dynamic approach allows for a smooth analysis of vast time-series datasets. The takeaway from this experiment is that Mo-LOO-KDE performs better as a result of combining the dynamic GPD mode with morphological filtering. We explored the effect of thresholding and bandwidth percentile parameters on the true and false positives. In Fig. 5, we present variants of those two parameters with respect to the number of TP_e and FP_e. For the bandwidth percentile, we found well-performing models for both values 1 and 0.97, which are very close to the default value 0.98 in LOO-KDE. For thresholding of LOO-KDE scores, the best results were achieved for the highest threshold 0.99999. We used *Channel 45* in the 42-month dataset for this exploration. Also, we explored the effect of the dynamic and fixed GPD parameter settings in LOO-KDE. Figure 4 shows the interplay of the GPD setting (fixed or dynamic) and false and true positives with 1. morphological filtering and 2. for $\boldsymbol{x}$ and its transforms $\Delta\boldsymbol{x}$ and $|\Delta\boldsymbol{x}|$.

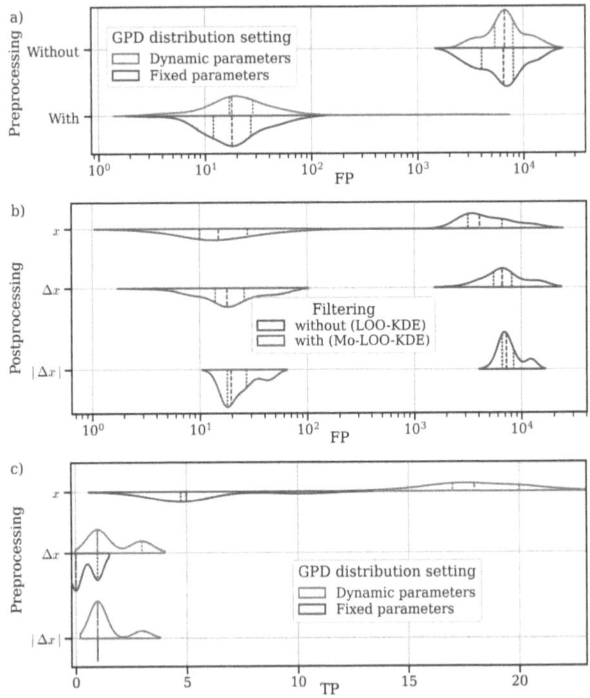

Fig. 4. The distribution of FP_e for (a) two modes of GPD parameters setting, (b) for three alternative forms of analyzed telemetry signal, and c) for the combination of both with respect to the number of resulting TP_e.

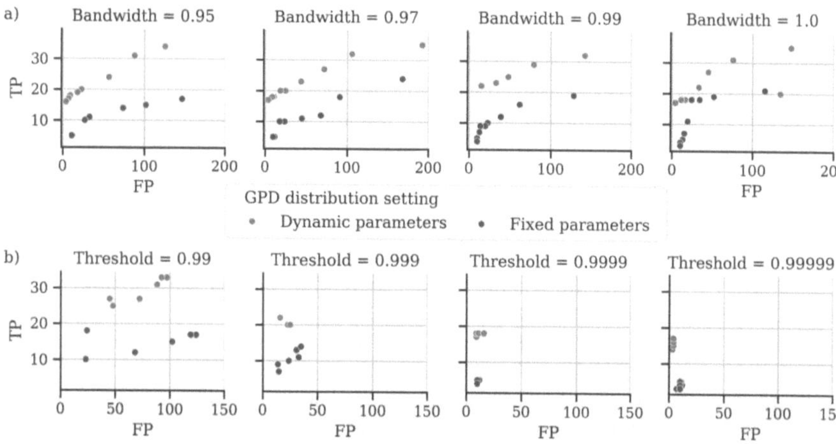

Fig. 5. The distribution of FP_e and TP_e with respect to (a) the Mo-LOO-KDE bandwidth parameter and (b) verified thresholding levels for both fixed and dynamic GPD setting mode.

4 Conclusions

Anomaly detection has far-reaching impact in diverse fields including cyber security [6], finance [24], healthcare [9] and earthquake detection [15] to name a few. In this study, we presented Mo-LOO-KDE, an unsupervised anomaly detection method tailored for satellite telemetry data. We evaluated Mo-LOO-KDE on 10 and 42-month datasets of the ESA-ADB dataset collection, which contains a massive amount of real-world complex telemetry data. A significant challenge in satellite telemetry anomaly detection is the large number of false positives, which makes many anomaly detection methods unusable. Mo-LOO-KDE had very low false positives, coupled with a decently high $F_{0.5e}$. This was the best unsupervised performance recorded on this dataset to the best of our knowledge. We note that Telemanom-ESA-Pruned, a semi-supervised method that uses a large training set, achieves better performance results. While comparing Mo-LOO-KDE with Telemanom-ESA-Pruned is akin to comparing apples with oranges, Telemanom-ESA-Pruned offers motivation for improvements in Mo-LOO-KDE.

Thorough utilization of bit-wise transformations and evaluation of other operators for openings and closings, such as rank-max openings and rank-min closings [22] could lead to precise filtering. Furthermore, the current study pooled all classes of anomalies into one. Understanding the different anomaly classes can help tailor the method to different types of anomalies. Finally, interactions between the channels are also worthy of investigation. These future research avenues have the potential to improve the performance of Mo-LOO-KDE.

Acknowledgments. This work was financially supported by the Opole University of Technology as part of the DELTA project no. 272/24.

Disclosure of Interests. The authors have no competing interests to declare that are relevant to the content of this article.

The Supplementary Material. Additional figures, tables, and the code supporting this work's reproducibility are available at doi.org/10.5281/zenodo.16534206.

References

1. Aggarwal, C.C.: Linear Models for Outlier Detection, pp. 65–110. Springer (2017). https://doi.org/10.1007/978-3-319-47578-3_3
2. De Canio, G., Kotowski, K., Haskamp, C., et al.: ESA Anomaly Dataset (2024). https://doi.org/10.5281/zenodo.12528696
3. Edelsbrunner, H., Harer, J., et al.: Persistent homology-a survey. Contemp. Math. **453**(26), 257–282 (2008). www.ams.org/books/conm/453/8802
4. Hassan, W.U., et al.: NoDoze: Combatting Threat Alert Fatigue with Automated Provenance Triage. NDSS (2019). https://doi.org/10.14722/ndss.2019.23349
5. Hundman, K., Constantinou, V., et al.: Detecting spacecraft anomalies using LSTMs and nonparametric dynamic thresholding. In: KDD 2018, pp. 387–395. ACM (2018). https://doi.org/10.1145/3219819.3219845
6. Inuwa, M.M., Das, R.: A comparative analysis of various machine learning methods for anomaly detection in cyber attacks on IoT networks. Internet Things **26**, 101162 (2024). https://doi.org/10.1016/j.iot.2024.101162
7. Kandanaarachchi, S., Hyndman, R.J.: Leave-one-out kernel density estimates for outlier detection. J. Comput. Graph. Stat. **31**(2), 586–599 (2022). https://doi.org/10.1080/10618600.2021.2000425
8. Kandanaarachchi, S., Hyndman, R.J.: Lookout: Anomaly detection using Leave-One-Out Kernel Density Estimates and Extreme Value Theory (2024). https://github.com/sevvandi/lookout
9. Khan, M.M., et al.: Anomaly detection in IoT-based healthcare: ML for enhanced security. Scient. Rep. **14** (2024). https://doi.org/10.1038/s41598-024-56126-x
10. Kingma, D.P., et al.: Auto-Encoding Variational Bayes. CoRR abs/1312.6114 (2013). https://api.semanticscholar.org/CorpusID:216078090
11. Kotowski, K., et al.: European Space Agency Benchmark for Anomaly Detection in satellite telemetry (2024). https://arxiv.org/abs/2406.17826
12. KP Labs: Code of the ESA Anomaly Detection Benchmark. http://github.com/kplabs-pl/ESA-ADB
13. Li, Z., Zhao, Y., Botta, N., Ionescu, C., Hu, X.: COPOD: copula-based outlier detection. In: 2020 IEEE International Conference on Data Mining (ICDM), pp. 1118–1123 (2020). https://doi.org/10.1109/ICDM50108.2020.00135
14. Nalepa, J., Myller, M., et al.: Evaluating algorithms for anomaly detection in satellite telemetry data. Acta Astronautica **198**, 689–701 (2022). https://doi.org/10.1016/j.actaastro.2022.06.026
15. Peleli, S., et al.: Thermal anomalies related to the devastating Mw7 earthquake of Samos–Izmir (October 30, 2020) using long-term satellite data analysis. In: IEEE EEITE (2024). https://doi.org/10.1109/eeite61750.2024.10654417
16. Ruff, L., Vandermeulen, R., et al.: Deep one-class classification. In: 35th ICML, vol. 80 (2018). https://proceedings.mlr.press/v80/ruff18a.html

17. Ruszczak, B., Kotowski, K., Evans, D., Nalepa, J.: The OPS-SAT benchmark for detecting anomalies in satellite telemetry (2025). https://doi.org/10.1038/s41597-025-05035-3
18. Ruszczak, B., Kotowski, K., et al.: Machine learning detects anomalies in OPS-SAT telemetry. In: 23rd International Conference on Computational Science, vol. 14073, pp. 295–306. Springer (2023). https://doi.org/10.1007/978-3-031-35995-8_21
19. Ruszczak, B., Kotowski, K., et al.: OXI: an online tool for visualization and annotation of satellite time series data. SoftwareX **23** (2023). https://doi.org/10.1016/j.softx.2023.101476
20. Shendy, R., Nalepa, J.: Few-shot satellite image classification for bringing deep learning on board OPS-SAT. Expert Syst. Appl. **251**, 123984 (2024). https://doi.org/10.1016/j.eswa.2024.123984
21. Shih, F.Y.: Image Processing and Mathematical Morphology: Fundamentals and Applications. CRC Press (2017). https://doi.org/10.1201/9781420089448
22. Soille, P.: On morphological operators based on rank filters. Pattern Recognit. **35**(2), 527–535 (2002). https://doi.org/10.1016/S0031-3203(01)00047-4
23. Sørbø, S., Ruocco, M.: Navigating the metric maze: a taxonomy of evaluation metrics for anomaly detection in time series. Data Mining Knowl. Discov. **38**, 1027–1068 (2024). https://doi.org/10.1007/s10618-023-00988-8
24. Wang, B., Dong, Y., et al.: Exploring anomaly detection and risk assessment in financial markets using deep neural networks. Int. J. Innov. Res. CS Technol. **12**(4) (2024). https://doi.org/10.55524/ijircst.2024.12.4.15
25. Xu, J., et al.: Anomaly Transformer: Time Series Anomaly Detection with Association Discrepancy. In: ICLR (2022). http://openreview.net/forum?id=LzQQ89U1qm_

17. [illegible] ... (2025). [illegible]

18. [illegible]

Workshop on Interactive eXplainable Artificial Intelligence, Theory and Practice (IXAIT 2025)

Workshop on Interactive eXplainable Artificial Intelligence, Theory and Practice (IXAIT 2025)

The First Workshop on Interactive eXplainable Artificial Intelligence, Theory and Practice (IXAIT 2025) was held in conjunction with the European Conference on Machine Learning and Principles and Practice of Knowledge Discovery in Databases (ECMLPKDD 2025) on September 19, 2025, in Porto, Portugal.

This workshop aims to advance explainable artificial Intelligence through interactive approaches, emphasizing both new methodologies and practical considerations. By bridging explainability with interactivity, the workshop aims to foster progress toward adaptive, transparent, and effective AI systems that align with human-centered design requirements and goals. The workshop serves as an interdisciplinary forum to bring together researchers, practitioners, and students to share knowledge and experiences to investigate foundational issues in developing interactive explainable AI methodologies as well as to discuss recent advances, emerging trends, and open challenges in this area.

First IXAIT call for papers targeted numerous domains and their applications, including:

- User interfaces for XAI
- Dialogue-based interactive approaches to XAI
- Processual aspects of explanations
- Human-in-the-loop approaches for XAI
- Human-centered design and XAI
- Adaptability through interaction
- Multimodal explanations
- Personalization and explanations
- Psychological aspects of explanations
- Persuasive explanatory processes
- Human-based evaluation in XAI
- Modeling on the information needs and preferences of users
- Interactive machine learning
- Domain-specific explanations
- Sequential decision making and XAI
- Applications of all of the above

This year, we received a variety of submissions that reflect the growing maturity and diversification of research at the intersection of explainability and interactivity. The workshop papers were assigned to a minimum three members of the Program Committee and were reviewed based on novelty and originality.

The workshop included five paper presentations. Marek Pawlicki et. al presented a paper *Can SHAP-based explanations differentiate between concept drift and scale drift in computer networks data?* In which they studied how XAI methods, such as SHAP, could be used to identify and report drift in data distribution.

Then, Ivania Donoso-Guzmán et. al contributed work *Aligning AI Explanations with User Needs: A Qualitative Study of XAI Methods*, where they conducted a qualitative study to compare several visualization and text-based XAI methods to conclude that the explanation should support the user with the task at hand without providing much insight into the model's inner working.

Luis Quintero et. al discussed a paper, *SepsisVision: Web-Based Support Tool for Sepsis Mortality Risk Screening through Explanatory and Exploratory User Interfaces,* which supports sepsis mortality risk through both static explanatory and interactive exploratory interfaces to navigate the behavior of an ML model through different kinds of explanations.

Finally, Natalia Wojak-Strzelecka et. al presented work *Explainable Visual Anomaly Detection with Multimodal Models and Metadata-Augmented Prompts,* in which they evaluated a pre-trained multimodal foundation model for visual anomaly detection on MVTec's different data modalities.

The program also included a keynote talk by Andreas Theissler (Justus-Liebig-University Giessen, Germany) on "**Explainability and Interactivity: Addressing Recurring Problems in Machine Learning**", in which Andreas presented methods that integrate explainable cues to guide users in improving ML models following a bi-directional scheme. The keynote further covered model-based active learning and user-based interactive labeling, illustrating how interaction can become a first-class design principle in explainable AI, not merely a downstream add-on to model development.

Many people contributed to making this workshop an insightful and successful event. We would like to thank Andreas Theissler for his insightful talk and keynote, the Program Committee members listed below for their thoughtful reviews, their constructive and timely feedback to authors, and their service to the community: Finally, we thank **ECMLPKDD 2025** for hosting the workshop and for supporting this venue for sustained discussion, the authors for their presentations, and all workshop participants for their engagement.

October 2025

Grzegorz J. Nalepa
Martin Atzmueller
Kerstin Bach
Ann Nowé
Mehrdad Asadi

Organization

Workshop Co-chairs

Grzegorz J. Nalepa	Jagiellonian University, Poland
Martin Atzmueller	Osnabrück University, Germany
Kerstin Bach	Norwegian University of Science and Technology, Norway
Ann Nowé	Vrije Universiteit Brussel, Belgium
Mehrdad Asadi	Vrije Universiteit Brussel, Belgium

Program Committee

Hendrik Baier	Eindhoven University of Technology, The Netherlands
Szymon Bobek	Jagiellonian University, Poland
Przemyslaw Biecek	Warsaw University of Technology, Poland
David Camacho	Universidad Politecnica de Madrid, Spain
Peter Flach	University of Bristol, UK
Rushed Kanawati	Université Sorbonne Paris Nord, France
Joao Gama	University of Porto, Portugal
Eyke Hüllermeier	LMU, Germany
Barbara Hammer	Bielefeld University, Germany
Tim Miller	The University of Queensland, Australia
Slawomir Nowaczyk	Halmstad University, Sweden
Ute Schmid	University of Bamberg, Germany
Carles Sierra	Artificial Intelligence Research Institute, Spain
Marek Sikora	Silesian University of Technology, Poland
Nirmalie Wiratunga	Robert Gordon University, UK
Arne Gevaert	Ghent University, Belgium
Isel Grau	Eindhoven University of Technology, The Netherlands

Keynote Speaker

Andreas Theissler
Justus-Liebig-University Giessen, Germany

Biography: Andreas is a professor at Justus-Liebig-University Giessen. He researches and lectures on different aspects of Machine Learning and Human-Centered AI. He received his PhD from Brunel University London in 2014, prior to that he studied Software Engineering and has worked in different Data Science positions in industry. His research focuses on time series data, anomaly detection as well as explainable AI – and the combination of the aforementioned. One core question is how the interplay of Machine Learning and users can help to evaluate, understand, improve, or enable Machine Learning.

Workshop Website: https://ixait.geist.re

Can SHAP-Based Explanations Differentiate Between Concept Drift and Scale Drift in Computer Networks Data?

Marek Pawlicki(✉), Rafał Kozik, and Michał Choraś

Bydgoszcz University of Science and Technology, Bydgoszcz, Poland
{marek.pawlicki,rafal.kozik,michal.choras}@pbs.edu.pl

Abstract. Dealing with changes in data distributions is an important aspect of deploying machine learning based systems, including network intrusion detectors. While traditional drift detectors identify changes in feature distributions, they cannot reveal whether the decision boundaries of the model remain valid. This paper proposes leveraging Shapley Additive Explanation attributions to monitor shifts in the underlying feature-to-classification mapping. Using two NetFlow-based datasets (CIC-IDS2018 and UNSW-NB15), gradual multiplicative drift and an abrupt cross-dataset shift are simulated. For each drift scenario, raw feature distributions and Shapley Additive Explanations value distributions are compared via the Kolmogorov–Smirnov test and normalised Wasserstein distance. Results show that under pure scale drift, classification performance degrades and traditional detectors fire alarms; yet, the TreeSHAP explainability distributions remain stable. By differentiating drift types, the proposed explainability-based approach informs whether simple preprocessing adjustments suffice or if costly retraining is required.

Keywords: Explainability · Concept Drift · Scale Drift · SHAP Explainability · Network Intrusion Detection · NetFlow Data

1 Introduction

Machine learning (ML) systems are increasingly being deployed in dynamic environments where the statistical properties of data can change over time. The phenomenon of changing distributions of data, known as drift, poses significant challenges to the reliability and performance of ML models. Drift can manifest in various forms: data drift (covariate shift) refers to the changes in the input data distributions without changes in the relationship between inputs and outputs, concept drift (CD) involves the changes in the underlying relationship between input features and the target variable, while the label drift describes the changes in the distribution of the target variable itself [13].

I. Koprinska et al. (Eds.): ECML PKDD 2025, CCIS 2842, pp. 129–139, 2026.
https://doi.org/10.1007/978-3-032-19105-2_9

Detecting and adapting to drift is a very important part of deploying ML-based systems, especially in high-stakes domains like cybersecurity, where timely and accurate detection of threats is imperative. In cybersecurity, ML models are employed for tasks such as intrusion detection, malware classification, and anomaly detection. NetFlow data, which summarises IP network traffic, is commonly used for these purposes. However, the evolving nature of cyberthreats means that the patterns distinguished by ML models can become obsolete, leading to degraded performance of the detectors.

In network intrusion detection systems (NIDS), concept drift can occur due to the emergence of new attack vectors or changes in legitimate user behaviour. This necessitates continuous monitoring and updating of models to maintain satisfactory detection rates [2].

Traditional drift detection methods such as the Kolmogorov-Smirnov (K-S) test and the Wasserstein distance (WD) detect drifts by comparing input feature distributions between reference and current data [5]. These approaches monitor statistical differences without inspecting the mapping from inputs to classifications. As a result, any significant shift in the distributions of features triggers an alarm [1]. These methods cannot discern whether the relationships derived in model training are still accurate, or whether the drift destroyed the mapping between the features and the target value. SHAP (SHapley Additive exPlanations) provides per-sample attributions that reflect how each feature contributes to a decision of a model. By monitoring the distributions of SHAP, one can assess whether the internal logic of the model remains stable. Aggregating SHAP values across multiple samples yields a distribution of feature importances that can be compared across time windows or data partitions.

The main idea and the major contribution of this paper is the fact that SHAP values can be used to distinguish between CD and scaling shift. By tracking the distribution of SHAP values of a Random Forest model, it becomes possible to diagnose whether a decline in model performance is due to a change in the nature of the predictive task (CD), or a change in the scale of inputs (scaling shift) that does not fundamentally alter the decision boundaries of the model. This distinction is important in practical deployment scenarios, as it informs whether simple input rescaling is sufficient or whether full model retraining, which requires costly labelling of data, is necessary. Thus, this paper seeks to answer the following questions:

- RQ1 Does a shift in input feature distributions always indicate a shift in the decision-making process of the model?
- RQ2 Can SHAP explainability be used to distinguish between scale drift and concept drift in NIDS models?

This paper is structured as follows: Sect. 2 reviews related work on SHAP in drift detection. Section 3 presents the methods used in the paper. Section 4 describes the experimental setup. Section 5 reports the results and discusses key findings. The paper concludes in Sect. 6.

2 Related Work

In [23], a method of handling CD in manufacturing utilising a novel approach that clusters data based on SHAP values is presented. This cluster-specific analysis enables targeted monitoring of AI decision quality and individualised drift detection, surpassing traditional approaches that analyse the data as a whole. The proposed method improves CD detection and economic outcomes by selectively acting on model predictions only when their expected benefit exceeds potential costs. Similarly, the authors of [10] note that traditional CD detection approaches often stumble and propose a SHAP-based methodology, providing CD detection rooted in model-agnostic transparency. They propose a drift suspicion metric, enhanced by a set of visualisations, which enable practitioners to spot meaningful changes in data distributions without reliance on labelled data. The approach consistently flagged over 90% of drift events above a threshold defined by the authors.

In [17], the authors propose a framework for unsupervised model monitoring that uses non-parametric bootstrap-based uncertainty estimation along with SHAP xAI to detect and diagnose model deterioration in the absence of ground-truth labels. The paper evaluates mean squared error degradation using only unlabelled deployment data, outperforming classical CD detectors such as the K–S test and Population Stability Index, as well as more recent classification-shift methods. By training a secondary model to predict the bootstrap-derived uncertainty and applying TreeSHAP to its outputs, they identify which input features drive increases in predictive uncertainty, providing actionable explanations for why a model has degraded.

The authors of [6] present an evaluation of how xAI can be leveraged to monitor CD and identify emergent health risks in an emergency department setting under the unprecedented conditions of the COVID-19 pandemic. They train a gradient-boosted decision tree using pre-pandemic attendance data, including patient demographics, arrival modes, chief complaints, and vital signs, to predict hospital admission at triage, achieving an AUROC of 0.856 on a hold-out pre-COVID-19 test set. By applying SHAP to the model, they track changes in feature attributions over time, demonstrating that, although model performance declines only marginally during the pandemic, normalised SHAP values reveal substantial shifts in the predictive relevance of respiratory rate, triage discriminator, and arrival mode. Their findings reveal the dual utility of SHAP as a complementary metric for CD detection, both signalling when model retraining may be necessary, and as a tool for real-time identification of emerging clinical patterns.

3 Materials and Methods

NetFlow Data. NetFlow is a common network traffic telemetry developed by Cisco to collect IP flow information on routers. It is a set of packet header fields like source/destination IP, port etc., which are constant for a sequence of packets in a time window. It is a well-known standard in both the networking domain and cybersecurity [11].

Random Forest Classifier. Random Forest (RF) is an ensemble method that builds an array of decision trees; each tree is trained on a random partition of data with a random partition of features. By averaging multiple weak learners, Random Forest mitigates overfitting and achieves high accuracy across various tasks [3,8]. RFs tend to exhibit strong out-of-the-box predictive performance on heterogeneous NetFlow data without extensive hyperparameter tuning, which makes them especially well-suited for this research, as it ensures that any observed drift effects are not confounded by model instability.

Decision trees are invariant to feature scaling when the same scale is applied in training and testing, so no separate scaler is needed, avoiding additional preprocessing steps that could confound drift detection. Most importantly, with RF (and other tree ensembles) SHAP values (using TreeSHAP) can be computed exactly, so they faithfully reflect how each feature influences the model decision, in contrast to the approximated KernelSHAP or DeepSHAP. This allows to eliminate another potential confounding variable - these being SHAP approximations distributions varying because of noise and not genuine CD.

SHAP. (SHapley Additive exPlanations) is one of the most established xAI methods [20,21]. It assigns each feature an importance value for a particular sample using the average marginal contribution of that feature across all possible feature coalitions [15]. This process paces SHAP among other model-agnostic xAI approaches [19]. TreeSHAP (also called TreeExplainer) [14] is an exact algorithm and an efficient dynamic programming solution for computing SHAP values specifically designed for tree-based ensemble models.

Kolmogorov–Smirnov Test (K-S Test). The Kolmogorov–Smirnov (K-S) test is a statistical method for comparing two distributions. The output, the D statistic, represents the maximum vertical distance between two curves. A D value approaching 1 indicates a substantial difference at some point between the distributions. The associated p-value measures the probability of observing such a large gap if both samples originate from the same distribution. A p-value near zero provides strong evidence. In ML, the K-S test is commonly used to assess whether the distribution of individual features has shifted between the source and target domains [12,25].

Wasserstein Distance (Earth Mover's Distance). The Wasserstein distance (WD), often called the Earth Mover's Distance (EMD), is a way to measure how different two probability distributions are by imagining one distribution as a pile of "earth" and the other as a set of holes that need to be filled. The optimal transportation plan is the one that uses the least total "work". Since WD takes into account not only how much mass differs but also how far apart that mass is, it found widespread adoption in comparison of distributions, beyond the original image retrieval [22]. However, using WD to compare different distributions can be problematic when they share identical components or are at different scales, like raw ML features. To make WD more informative, in this work the raw WD is divided by the feature range, providing a Normalised Wasserstein Distance (NWD), a scale-invariant metric that can be compared fairly across features or contexts with different units and magnitudes. When NWD=0, the test distribution is identical to the reference. With NWD=1, the "average transport cost" between distributions equals the entire span of the reference feature.

Feature-Wise Multiplicative Drift. Feature-Wise Multiplicative Drift can be simulated with a gradual linear scaling of each feature starting in the middle of the dataset, mimicking a continuous covariate shift where, by the end of the dataset, every feature has been multiplied by up to α. Using multiplicative drift -instead of additive noise - is a common strategy because it preserves the rank order and correlation structure of features. In the network-traffic context, such scaling can simulate evolving bandwidth or application behaviour [4,26].

4 Experimental Setup

The authors conducted experiments using two publicly available netflow-based network traffic datasets across two experiments. These are the CIC-IDS2018 dataset [24] and the UNSW-NB15 dataset [18]. In experiment one, a multiplicative drift was added to the CIC datset. In experiment two, CIC is treated as the pre-drift and UNSW as post-drift.

The CIC dataset contains a severe class imbalance, with benign flows far outnumbering attack instances. To mitigate this, the authors separated benign records from attack records and downsampled the benign class to achieve a 1:1. Both the balanced CIC data and the full UNSW data underwent identical, standard preprocessing steps. Non-numerical columns—such as IP addresses, port numbers, protocol identifiers, and TCP flags—were dropped. After these steps, the remaining features formed a consistent set of numerical flow statistics.

To simulate a drift scenario, the authors applied a gradual, feature-wise linear transformation to the balanced CIC dataset. Let n denote the total number of CIC samples. The "drift start" index was set to $\lfloor 0.5\, n \rfloor$. For each feature, a multiplicative drift factor was defined as:

$$\text{drift\_factor}(i) = \begin{cases} 1 & \text{if } i < \text{drift\_start} \\ 1 + \alpha \dfrac{i - \text{drift\_start}}{n - \text{drift\_start}} & \text{if } i \geq \text{drift\_start} \end{cases}$$

starting in the exact middle of the set and multiplying by increasing α where $\alpha = 2.0$ represents the maximum relative shift at the end of the dataset. Multiplying each feature by this factor produced a continuous drift trajectory: initially small, gradually intensifying until the feature distributions of later samples diverged substantially from the original baseline. This semi-synthetic approach was used to control drift types while maintaining domain realism.

From the pre-drift partition, the authors held out 5% of samples as a "validation" set for baseline statistical comparisons and another 20% for a reference set used in SHAP sampling. The remaining 75% of pre-drift data formed the RF training set. A Random Forest classifier with 200 trees was trained on this subset. Model performance on the held-out pre-drift reference set was recorded via accuracy, balanced accuracy, G-Mean, and Matthews Correlation Coefficient [7,9,16].

Post-drift samples were partitioned into ten sequential parts, each containing 10% of post-drift data. The first, the middle (5th), and the final part correspond to "small", "medium", and "strong" drift intensities. For each chunk, performance metrics of the model were computed identically to the pre-drift validation. Concurrently, SHAP values were obtained on subsamples of size 200 from each set. Absolute SHAP magnitudes per feature were aggregated to create empirical SHAP distributions at each drift level.

Two complementary metrics per feature were computed: the K-S statistic and the WD/NWD. The metrics were applied to the SHAP-based feature-importance distributions (absolute SHAP values) and the raw feature distributions.

For each feature, the baseline distribution was drawn from the holdout pre-drift validation set, then test distributions were drawn from the corresponding subsets of drift subsets, and from the UNSW dataset. In this manner, the experimental setup simulated a smooth multiplicative shift in the first experiment and an abrupt CD in the UNSW experiment. Its impact on model performance, the feature distributions, and SHAP-based feature importance is assessed.

5 Results

Table 1. Detection Metrics Across Baseline and Drift Test Sets

Metric	Baseline	Small Drift	Medium Drift	Strong Drift
Accuracy	0.8929	0.8686	0.7495	0.6292
Balanced Accuracy	0.6377	0.4798	0.2459	0.0996
G-Mean (macro)	0.7928	0.6630	0.4701	0.3049
Matthews Corr. Coef.	0.8243	0.7658	0.5121	0.1589

With progressively added multiplicative drift, when traditional performance metrics deteriorate (e.g., a reduction in accuracy from 0.8929 to 0.7495 - as seen in Table 1), and the K-S test and WD indicate CD (Tables 3, 4, 5, and 6), but the distribution of SHAP values remains stable (Tables 7 and 8), this suggests that while the input data distribution has shifted sufficiently to impair detection metrics, and traditional CD methods fire, SHAP shows that the internal representation of feature–target relationships is intact.

Table 2. Validation (Pre-Drift) – Raw Feature Drift Metrics

Feature	KS	pval	Wasserstein	WD_norm
IN_BYTES	0.0480	8.8431e-01	15025.8910	0.0020
OUT_BYTES	0.0320	9.9785e-01	502.9910	0.0034
IN_PKTS	0.0460	9.1198e-01	248.9970	0.0020
OUT_PKTS	0.0190	1.0000e+00	0.4540	0.0040
FLOW_DURATION	0.0480	8.8431e-01	150687.5330	0.0351

Table 3. Small Drift (First 10%) – Raw Feature Drift Metrics

Feature	KS	pval	Wasserstein	WD_norm
IN_BYTES	0.1340	1.0915e-02	15033.4301	0.0020
OUT_BYTES	0.0750	3.8265e-01	595.9344	0.0040
IN_PKTS	0.3440	2.2204e-15	248.4202	0.0020
OUT_PKTS	0.1980	2.3101e-05	0.7599	0.0067
FLOW_DURATION	0.5050	2.6921e-34	245072.5189	0.0571

Table 4. Medium Drift (Middle 10%) – Raw Feature Drift Metrics

Feature	KS	pval	Wasserstein	WD_norm
IN_BYTES	0.3020	5.5160e-12	16522.1107	0.0022
OUT_BYTES	0.1480	3.4848e-03	737.0016	0.0050
IN_PKTS	0.3440	2.2204e-15	261.2825	0.0021
OUT_PKTS	0.1660	6.7849e-04	2.6036	0.0230
FLOW_DURATION	0.4850	1.6902e-31	1989499.1839	0.4632

Table 5. Strong Drift (Last 10%) – Raw Feature Drift Metrics

Feature	KS	pval	Wasserstein	WD_norm
IN_BYTES	0.3400	3.2196e-15	18923.2059	0.0026
OUT_BYTES	0.2820	1.7365e-10	2195.9344	0.0148
IN_PKTS	0.4100	2.9730e-22	278.0765	0.0023
OUT_PKTS	0.3030	4.6142e-12	6.2766	0.0555
FLOW_DURATION	0.5300	5.2590e-38	4413477.4209	1.0276

Table 6. Summary of Drift Levels and Affected Features (based on tables 1–5; None: KS stats low, p-values high, WD low, Mild/Moderate: Some features show statistically significant but not extreme differences (KS moderate, some p-values low, moderate WD). Moderate/Strong: Most features show strong, significant shifts (KS high, p-values close to zero, WD high). Severe: Almost all features show high drift, with KS high, p-values low, WD high)

Drift Level	Is There Drift?	How Severe?	Affected Features
Pre-Drift	No	None	None
Small Drift	Yes (some features)	Mild/Moderate	IN_PKTS, FLOW_DURATION
Medium Drift	Yes	Moderate/Strong	Several, especially FLOW_DURATION
Strong Drift	Yes	Severe	All, especially FLOW_DURATION

Table 7. Strong Scale Drift (Last 10%) – SHAP Metrics

Feature	KS	pval	Wasserstein	WD_norm	Drift Strength
IN_BYTES	0.7747	1.0000e+00	0.0322	0.0345	None
OUT_BYTES	0.5824	1.0000e+00	0.0123	0.0195	None
IN_PKTS	0.6275	1.0000e+00	0.0222	0.0272	None
OUT_PKTS	0.4565	9.9762e-01	0.0123	0.0376	None
FLOW_DURATION	0.5768	1.0000e+00	0.0162	0.0272	None

Table 8. Summary of SHAP Drift Levels and Affected Features (KS statistic higher than in the pre-drift baseline, p-value is low) - scale drift

Drift Level	SHAP distr. change?	How Severe?	Affected Features
Baseline Drift (Validation)	No	None	None
Small Drift (First 10%)	No	None	None
Medium Drift (Middle 10%)	No	None	None
Strong Drift (Last 10%)	No	None	None

Table 9. UNSW Drift – Raw Feature Drift Metrics (with Drift Strength)

Feature	KS	pval	Wasserstein	WD_norm	Drift Strength
IN_BYTES	0.3970	7.7088e-21	13158.5060	0.0026	Medium
OUT_BYTES	0.6890	3.7036e-68	49759.7840	0.3888	Strong
IN_PKTS	0.4150	8.2241e-23	196.3960	0.0023	Medium
OUT_PKTS	0.6570	4.9601e-61	55.1480	0.5252	Strong
FLOW_DURATION	0.4740	5.0680e-30	2031867.9050	0.4731	Strong

Table 10. UNSW Drift – SHAP Metrics (with Drift Strength Evaluations)

Feature	KS	p-val	Wasserstein	WD_norm	Drift Strength
IN_BYTES	0.6278	7.7716e-16	0.0594	0.0647	Strong
OUT_BYTES	0.6484	7.7716e-16	0.0508	0.1313	Strong
IN_PKTS	0.6078	7.7716e-16	0.0511	0.0674	Strong
OUT_PKTS	0.5880	7.7716e-16	0.0570	0.1794	Strong
FLOW_DURATION	0.5590	7.7716e-16	0.0416	0.0975	Strong

In contrast, if classification metrics, traditional CD methods (Table 9), and SHAP value distributions (Table 10) exhibit significant changes, this indicates a misalignment between the decision boundaries of the trained model and the semantics of the new data.

If performance metrics decline but SHAP values remain stable, the issue is related to scaling changes in input features, which in NetFlow-based data may be attributed to several real-world causes, such as fluctuations in the number of users, devices, or overall network activity, such as spikes during certain times of day or after events. Predictable shifts in traffic due to business hours, weekends, or academic schedules can change the volume and scale of NetFlow features. This is in contrast to the introduction of new services or protocols, policy changes or new security measures, or major network topology changes, which would likely change the relationships between the netflow-derived features and the target values.

6 Conclusions

This work demonstrates that monitoring SHAP explanations' value distributions provides a method for distinguishing between scale drift and CD in RF–based NIDS.

Experiments on two benchmark NetFlow datasets (CIC-IDS2018 and UNSW-NB15) reveal that, under scale drift, simulated in a feature-wise multiplicative way, the traditional performance metric and CD detection methods indicate drift, yet the distributions of TreeSHAP explainability attributions remain stable. In contrast, an abrupt cross-dataset shift (treating UNSW-NB15 as a post-drift distribution relative to CIC-IDS2018) leads to significant changes in both feature and SHAP value distributions. The RF's combination of TreeSHAP explainability exactness and inherent scale-invariance allows for to clean isolation of scale shift versus CD. These findings address the research questions - RQ1: A shift in input feature distributions does not necessarily indicate a change in the model decision-making process. RQ2: Stable SHAP explainability distributions amidst performance decline suggest scale drift.

References

1. Ackerman, S., Farchi, E., Raz, O., Zalmanovici, M., Dube, P.: Detection of data drift and outliers affecting machine learning model performance over time. arXiv preprint arXiv:2012.09258 (2020)
2. Apruzzese, G., Fass, A., Pierazzi, F.: When adversarial perturbations meet concept drift: an exploratory analysis on ML-NIDS. In: Proceedings of the 2024 Workshop on Artificial Intelligence and Security, pp. 149–160 (2024)
3. Breiman, L.: Random forests. Mach. Learn. **45**, 5–32 (2001)
4. Caroprese, L., et al.: Modelling concept drift in dynamic data streams for recommender systems. ACM Trans. Recomm. Syst. **3**(2), 1–28 (2025)
5. Dos Reis, D.M., Flach, P., Matwin, S., Batista, G.: Fast unsupervised online drift detection using incremental Kolmogorov-Smirnov test. In: Proceedings of the 22nd ACM SIGKDD International Conference on Knowledge Discovery and Data Mining, pp. 1545–1554 (2016)
6. Duckworth, C., et al.: Using explainable machine learning to characterise data drift and detect emergent health risks for emergency department admissions during covid-19. Sci. Rep. **11**(1), 23017 (2021)
7. García, V., Mollineda, R.A., Sánchez, J.S.: Index of balanced accuracy: a performance measure for skewed class distributions. In: Iberian Conference on Pattern Recognition and Image Analysis, pp. 441–448. Springer (2009)
8. Ho, T.K.: Random decision forests. In: Proceedings of 3rd International Conference on Document Analysis and Recognition, vol. 1, pp. 278–282. IEEE (1995)
9. Kubat, M., Matwin, S., et al.: Addressing the curse of imbalanced training sets: one-sided selection. In: ICML, vol. 97, p. 179. Citeseer (1997)
10. Lee, Y., Lee, Y., Lee, E., Lee, T.: Explainable artificial intelligence-based model drift detection applicable to unsupervised environments. Comput. Mater. Continua **76**(2) (2023)
11. Li, B., Springer, J., Bebis, G., Gunes, M.H.: A survey of network flow applications. J. Netw. Comput. Appl. **36**(2), 567–581 (2013)
12. Lopes, R.H., Reid, I., Hobson, P.R.: The two-dimensional kolmogorov-smirnov test (2007)
13. Lu, J., Liu, A., Dong, F., Gu, F., Gama, J., Zhang, G.: Learning under concept drift: a review. IEEE Trans. Knowl. Data Eng. **31**(12), 2346–2363 (2018)
14. Lundberg, S.M., Lee, S.I.: Consistent feature attribution for tree ensembles. arXiv preprint arXiv:1706.06060 (2017)
15. Lundberg, S.M., Lee, S.I.: A unified approach to interpreting model predictions. In: Advances in Neural Information Processing Systems, vol. 30 (2017)
16. Matthews, B.W.: Comparison of the predicted and observed secondary structure of T4 phage lysozyme. Biochimica et Biophysica Acta (BBA)-Protein Structure **405**(2), 442–451 (1975)
17. Mougan, C., Nielsen, D.S.: Monitoring model deterioration with explainable uncertainty estimation via non-parametric bootstrap. In: Proceedings of the AAAI Conference on Artificial Intelligence, vol. 37, pp. 15037–15045 (2023)
18. Moustafa, N., Slay, J.: UNSW-NB15: a network intrusion dataset. University of New South Wales (UNSW) (2015). https://research.unsw.edu.au/projects/unsw-nb15-dataset
19. Pawlicki, M.: Aria, haria and geria: novel metrics for pre-model interpretability. IEEE Access (2024)

20. Pawlicki, M., Pawlicka, A., Kozik, R., Choraś, M.: The survey on the dual nature of XAI challenges in intrusion detection and their potential for AI innovation. Artif. Intell. Rev. **57**(12), 1–32 (2024)
21. Pawlicki, M., et al.: Evaluating the necessity of the multiple metrics for assessing explainable AI: a critical examination. Neurocomputing **602**, 128282 (2024)
22. Rubner, Y., Tomasi, C., Guibas, L.J.: The earth mover's distance as a metric for image retrieval. Int. J. Comput. Vision **40**, 99–121 (2000)
23. Seiffer, C., Ziekow, H., Schreier, U., Gerling, A.: Detection of concept drift in manufacturing data with shap values to improve error prediction. Data Anal. 3–7 (2021)
24. Sharafaldin, I., Lashkari, A.A., Ghorbani, A.A.: CIC-IDS2018: a network traffic dataset for intrusion detection research. Canadian Institute for Cybersecurity (CIC) (2018). https://www.unb.ca/cic/datasets/ids-2018.html
25. Smirnov, N.: Table for estimating the goodness of fit of empirical distributions. Ann. Math. Stat. **19**(2), 279–281 (1948)
26. Suárez-Cetrulo, A.L., Quintana, D., Cervantes, A.: A survey on machine learning for recurring concept drifting data streams. Expert Syst. Appl. **213**, 118934 (2023)

Aligning AI Explanations with User Needs: A Qualitative Study of XAI Methods

Ivania Donoso-Guzmán[1,2,3(✉)], Denis Parra[3], and Katrien Verbert[1,2]

[1] Department of Computer Science, KU Leuven, 3001 Leuven, Belgium
{ivania.donoso,katrien.verbert}@kuleuven.be
[2] Augment, imec Research Group at KU Leuven, Leuven, Belgium
[3] Department of Computer Science, Pontificia Universidad Católica de Chile, Santiago, Chile
{indonoso,dparras}@uc.cl

Abstract. In recent years, significant progress has been made in Natural Language Processing (NLP), yet a gap persists in tailoring explanations for text classification to non-AI users. In this research, we conduct a qualitative study to compare the suitability of several explanation alternatives generated with existing Explainable AI (XAI) methods using visualisations and textual explanations created by LLMs. Our preliminary findings reveal that explanations emphasising the paper's methodology enhance user confidence: while textual explanations are generally preferred, effective visualisations highlighting methodological aspects are valuable. Finally, results show that what users expect from explanations does not align with current efforts in XAI: they need explanations that support how they conduct the same task and are not concerned with fidelity to the model's inner workings.

Keywords: XAI · Explanations of AI models · Text classification · LLMs to generate explanations

1 Introduction

Natural language processing (NLP) has seen huge progress in recent years, led by Large Language Models (LLMs), which are complex models that operate like "black" boxes. Alongside, researchers have proposed methods to generate explanations of NLP predictions to make the models understandable to humans. These efforts have mostly focused on generating explanations that better reflect the inner workings of the AI models [19], and less attention has been given to how users interpret and understand these explanations [26]. Furthermore, less attention has been given to tailoring these explanations to users' needs [14].

In this study, approved by the ethical committee at KU Leuven G-2023-7186-R2(MIN), we try to close this gap by evaluating explanations of AI model predictions generated with current XAI methods and in two modalities, visual

I. Koprinska et al. (Eds.): ECML PKDD 2025, CCIS 2842, pp. 140–150, 2026.
https://doi.org/10.1007/978-3-032-19105-2_10

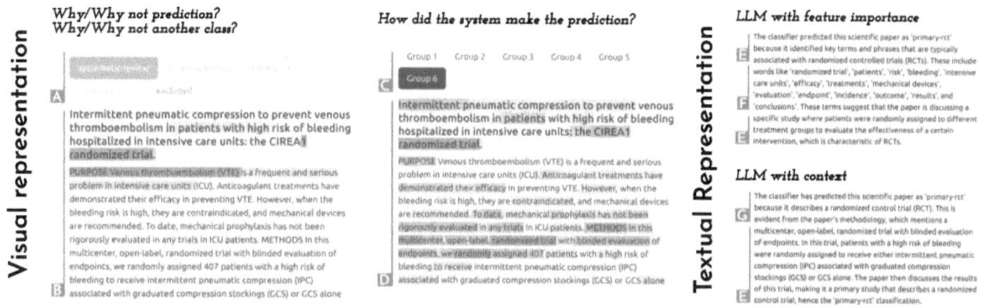

Fig. 1. Representation styles used in the study. [A] and [C] allow the user to change the class and the group of information, respectively. [B] saliency map showing both positive and negative attribution; [D] saliency map for the network activations; [E] text generated by the LLM using its own knowledge; [F] the textual representation of the saliency map; [G] part of the information provided as context in the prompt that the LLM decided to also include in the explanation. All the explanations used can be found in the study website.

and textual. We conducted a qualitative study with five domain-expert users in a healthcare paper classification task to understand what explanation strategy works best for the users in this context. To address the objectives of the study, we investigate the following research questions:

RQ1 What are the characteristics of the explanation strategies that make them more or less appropriate for the task?
RQ2 How does the representation of the information affect the appropriateness of the explanation for the task?
RQ3 How does the XAI method affect the appropriateness of the explanation for the task?

This paper contributes to the current discussion of explanations of AI models tailored to user needs by evaluating different ways to generate explanations and two presentation modalities. We analysed when and why they were helpful to the user and found that current XAI efforts are not necessarily aligned with what users expect from explanations of AI model predictions.

2 Related Work

2.1 Human-Centric XAI: Aligning Explanations to Users' Tasks

According to [16], there are currently two problems with the current XAI approaches: they do not support users' tasks in their usage context, and users' cognitive processes do not inform them. This disconnection between XAI and users makes it harder to implement these systems because they do not respond to the actual users' needs [13,31]. Methods like integrated gradients [27] or attention mechanisms [2] try to provide explanations to end users, but there is little evidence that they have achieved that goal [32]. To address this gap, recent research has emphasised Human-Centric XAI, which integrates users into the design and evaluation of explanation methods. A growing body of work demonstrates that incorporating user needs and expectations from the early stages of system development leads to more effective and usable XAI models [9,29,34,35]. Instead of focusing solely on model interpretability, Human-Centric XAI emphasises explanations that support how users perform tasks, ensuring that AI-assisted decision-making aligns with human cognitive strategies.

2.2 Explanations for Text Classification

Visualisations have been used multiple times to explain text classification [24,30], and saliency map representation has been one of the most common ways [26]. This representation is also part of the popular Python packages SHAP [18] and LIME [25]. This type of representation is widely used, but its effectiveness has proven not to be consistent [31].

Textual explanations have been used to explain recommendations and have been positively evaluated by users [3,7,11]. These types of explanations require less effort from users because they do not ask for visualisation literacy [28]. Before the spread use of Large Language Models to generate text, textual explanations were created using templates [3], specific keywords or sentences [7,22]. Recently, [11] evaluated the verbalisation of a saliency map using Large Language Models.

3 Dataset and AI Model

We used the dataset published by Epistemonikos [6]. The dataset contains titles and abstracts from papers published in the healthcare domain. This dataset was used to train and evaluate a model that Epistemonikos currently has in production to classify new incoming papers into four different classes: *primary studies*, *randomised-controlled-trial*, *systematic reviews* and *broad syntheses*. The papers the users saw during the study were selected from the test split. We sampled two papers from each combination of the model's confusion matrix and randomly selected the papers users would see from that subsample.

We used the selected dataset to fine-tune LongFormer [4] because of its good performance in multilabel classification in the medical domain [33] and also in paper classification for sustainable development goals [12]. The model obtained a micro F1-Score of 0.93 and a macro F1-Score of 0.79.

4 Explanations

Visual Explanations. We evaluated four different formats of saliency map visualisation, each answering questions informed by the XAI question Bank [15]. These questions were: (i) Why does it predict X? (ii) Why does it predict X/Y? (iii) Why/why not does the system predict X/Y? (iv) How did the system make a decision? Figure 1 presents the visual representation for (iii) and (iv). To generate the feature importance values, we used three methods ordered by closeness to the model's inner workings: Network Activations using the methods from the Ecco Python Library [1], Integrated Gradients [27]and SHAP values [18]. The Network Activation obtained the neurons' activation values across all layers and then applied Non-Negative Matrix Factorisation to obtain 6 groups of neurons. The activation values ranged from 0 to 1. The generated groups were not filtered or rearranged in any way before being shown to the users. The last two methods generated a number between -1 and 1 for each token. The feature importance generated by SHAP and Integrated gradients was used with questions (i), (ii) and (iii), while Network Activations were presented only with (iv).

Textual Explanations. Recently, evaluated the verbalisation of a saliency map using Large Language Models. Inspired by [11], we used Chat GPT 4 [23] to generate explanations for the predictions. We generated prompts under four conditions: with/without context and with/without feature importance. The goal of adding contextual information was to provide the LLM with the same problem knowledge that the user has. We hypothesise that this contextual information would improve the model's contextual awareness and generate explanations that are better tailored to the user's context, which could make them more satisfied with the explanations [8]. To achieve this, the definition of the study types was added to the prompt. Under the condition *without context*, the prompt only stated the names of the classes. For the feature importance criteria, we followed the same approach of [11]: the feature importance of each word was placed after the word, and the format was described in the prompt. The importance of the words was generated by SHAP or by Integrated Gradients methods, and we only used the positive values. Under the *without feature importance* condition, only the title and abstract of the paper were added to the prompt.

5 Study Protocol

This study explored user perceptions of explanations generated by XAI methods. Participants interacted with different explanation formats and were interviewed to assess their usefulness in understanding predictions and making classification decisions. We conducted in-depth, unstructured interviews across four phases: (1) capturing user characteristics, (2) learning and comparing explanations, (3) decision-making, and (4) final feedback. This approach helped identify key attributes for effective explanations in this context.

The first phase aimed at capturing the participants' background and previous experience with visualisation and AI. We recognised from past experiences [anonymous] that users in the medical field often struggle with complex visualisations. To address this, we divided the feedback process into two stages: learning and comparing (stage 2) and decision-making (stage 3). In stage 2, our goals were to familiarise users with different types of explanations, including their characteristics like colour and scales, and to help them compare these explanations

Table 1. Participants' characteristics. None of the participants had any programming experience, and Spanish was their mother tongue.

P	Age	Gender	Healthcare	Healthcare research	Visualisation
1	32	F	Dentist (6 years practising)	Written thesis and one paper (6 years ago)	Some basic experience
2	25	M	Graduated from medical school	Reading papers, not writing	No experience
3	27	F	Graduated from medical school	Reading papers, not writing	Some basic experience
4	40	M	Clinical Psychiatrist (>10 years)	Written 3 systematic reviews	Everyday activity
5	25	M	Graduated from medical school	Reading papers, not writing	Some basic experience

Table 2. Number of participants that provided feedback for each XAI method. For each one, we counted how many users provided positive and negative feedback across all the examples they interacted with.

XAI method	Content		Format	
	Positive	Negative	Positive	Negative
LLM	5	2	5	1
Network Activations	4	5	0	5
Integrated Gradients	5	5	3	5
SHAP	5	5	5	5

without the need to understand new papers each time. Users engaged in five comparisons, each displaying two or more explanations for the same paper, with a fixed order for consistency. During this process, we asked users if the explanations helped them understand model predictions and which aspects they found most useful. The goal of stage 3 was to understand how users would use the explanations in a decision-making scenario. They were told they would see the prediction and its explanation for 13 papers, and their goal was to decide whether they agreed with the model prediction. After seeing each paper, the users were interviewed to determine whether and why the explanation had helped them decide. In the final stage, participants were asked to describe the characteristics they liked most and their ideal explanation in this context.

Participants. We recruited participants who needed to have a medical background and some experience reading healthcare research. We contacted collaborators in Chile and Slovenia, and followed snowball sampling. The minimum number of participants was set at five, and we aimed to keep recruiting until reaching saturation. We reached saturation with four participants. All interviews were conducted in English. The participants' characteristics are described in Table 1.

6 Preliminary Results

We used Thematic Analysis following the phases described in [5] to analyse the interviews. We first transcribed and read the audio recordings several times to become familiar with the data. Next, we wrote initial open codes systematically, relating them to specific expressions from the participants. Then, we grouped these codes, gathering all relevant data into potential themes. We later iteratively reviewed these themes and solved possible discrepancies among them. We divided the themes into five areas: content of the explanation, format of the explanation, actions taken by the participants, effects on the user and general insights. The first two areas were further divided into positive and negative comments. Here, we summarise the results regarding content and format. Table 2 presents this feedback by XAI method.

6.1 Content: Users Expect to See the Information *They* Would Use to Make a Decision

Even though participants acknowledged that models work differently than people, **they still expect the explanation to be aligned with their own process**. In this domain, they expected to find **information about the methodology** of the papers in the explanation. When this information was present, they could decide and were satisfied with the explanation, independently of the explanation format. P4 stated when asked why he preferred a visual explanation *"Because it gives [...] information of the methodology, like the basic element of randomisation, there's assignment of patients. And yeah, the word blinded is there as well."*. When asked about the characteristics they would like to see in their ideal explanation, they all mentioned that **they wanted to know whether the paper complied with specific methodology criteria**. All participants said **they needed to see evidence of how the paper complied with the criteria** of the study type. In particular, if the explanation did not provide information about the methodology, they always looked for it in the abstract. Additionally, when the explanation was textual, three participants said they needed to read the abstract to double-check. P4 explained that he needed the evidence to be sure the explanation had been made about the paper he was reading. He said *"I can read this, and it makes absolute sense. But then I ask myself, this could be the paragraph for any other paper."*

Regarding the XAI methods, we found that LLMs were the most successful: only two users had negative comments regarding content. SHAP and Integrated gradients received negative and positive comments from all users. Network Activation was the only one that did not receive positive comments from all users.

6.2 Format: Textual and Visual Explanations Have Different Goals

Explanations that presented full sentences with characteristics of the methodology, rather than emphasising keywords, were better received. Users are indifferent to the presentation format, whether visual or textual, as long as the information they need is present. In regard to visualisations, excessive or scattered highlights confused participants, making the visualisations harder to interpret. P3 noted that repeated highlights were unnecessary, while P2 felt that abstract introductions did not aid decision-making. **When words were insufficient to form a complete idea, participants struggled to understand their significance.** P1 emphasised that isolated words did not provide synthesis. Regarding the textual explanations, the users had the same critique: vague, unspecific vocabulary was unhelpful. P4 found the vocabulary vague, while P3 and P1 stated that merely listing words was ineffective. Explanations generated with contextual information (Fig. 1), especially those detailing the methodology, received positive feedback, with no criticism regarding format or content. Two participants (P2 and P4) mentioned that the representation had different goals and that joining them would increase understanding. They proposed that the **textual explanation would provide reasons that they could then verify with a visualisation of the text.**

Regarding the feedback by XAI methods, LLMs received better feedback overall (Table 2): only one user had something negative regarding format when LLMs were used. Network activations were again the least successful: they did not receive any positive comments.

7 Discussion

RQ1 *What are the characteristics of the explanation strategies that make them more or less appropriate for the task?* The most important characteristic that explanations should have in clinical text classification is to provide information about the paper's methodology. Explanations that provided this information were perceived as more useful and made the users feel more confident in their decisions. This result aligns with previous studies [anonymous] [anonymous] where users declared they need explanations that resemble how they currently conduct their tasks. This outcome suggests that a new lens should be used to understand the role of explanations and how to generate them so that they become helpful to users. This user expectation opposes the current research of generating explanations that reflect the inner workings of the AI model, commonly referred to as faithfulness [17] or correctness [10,21], of the explanation. Our results show that participants want explanations that mimic what they currently do when they perform the task and care very little about how the model reached its conclusion.

RQ2 *How does the representation of the information affect the appropriateness of the explanation for the task?* The results suggest that users better evaluated textual explanations than visual explanations. However, when analysing the cases where the visualisation was successful, we noticed that the most essential aspect of explanations was content, particularly that the explanation pointed out or highlighted the methodology followed by the paper. Users suggested joining both representation types to be able to get an explanation and then verify the information on the paper.

RQ3 *How does the XAI method affect the appropriateness of the explanation for the task?*

We found that the XAI methods that were used provided inconsistent quality results. SHAP was better evaluated than Integrated Gradients and Network Activations, but its quality was still inconsistent among cases. The LLM-generated explanations were better evaluated, especially when they mentioned the paper's methodology.

This insight suggests that explanations to end users should focus on providing the user with the information that supports how they currently conduct the task. By doing this, users can verify and arrive at conclusions to then compare their reasoning with the system's.

8 Conclusions and Future Work

In this work, we evaluated with user feedback explanations of AI model predictions generated under multiple conditions. We discovered that the explanations users expect do not align with current efforts in XAI. For explanations to be useful to end users, they need to support how they conduct their tasks nowadays. In particular, explanations highlighting the methodology followed by the paper were seen as the most successful. Additionally, we found that textual explanations were easier for users to understand, but they still wanted to have concrete evidence that what the explanation said was true. This suggests that a combination of visual and textual artefacts in the explanation can be beneficial for user satisfaction.

In this qualitative study, we only evaluated static explanations: the user saw the explanation and acted upon it, but could not ask for additional clarification. This aspect has been highlighted as a fundamental aspect of explanations given their social nature [20]. For this reason, we plan to design with users how this interaction should work using LLMs.

Acknowledgments. This work was partially funded by ANID Chile, Millennium Science Initiative Program, codes ICN2021_004 (iHealth) and ICN17_002 (IMFD), by Basal Funds for Center of Excellence FB210017 (CENIA), the Research Foundation Flanders (FWO, grant G0A4923N) and KU Leuven (grant C14/21/072). In addition, we thank Fondecyt grant 1231724. The research of Ivania Donoso-Guzmán was supported by the doctoral scholarship of ANID BECAS/DOCTORADO NACIONAL 21202228.

References

1. Alammar, J.: Ecco: an open source library for the explainability of transformer language models. In: Proceedings of 59th Annual Meeting of the ACL and the 11th IJCNLP: System Demonstrations, pp. 249–257 (2021). https://doi.org/10.18653/v1/2021.acl-demo.30

2. Bahdanau, D., Cho, K., Bengio, Y.: Neural machine translation by jointly learning to align and translate. In: International Conference on ICLR (2016)
3. Balog, K., Radlinski, F., Petrov, A.: Measuring the impact of explanation bias: a study of natural language justifications for recommender systems. In: Extended Abstracts of the 2023 CHI Conference on Human Factors in Computing Systems, vol. 1, pp. 1–8 (2023). https://doi.org/10.1145/3544549.3585748
4. Beltagy, I., Peters, M.E., Cohan, A.: Longformer: The Long-Document Transformer (2020)
5. Braun, V., Clarke, V.: Using thematic analysis in psychology. Qual. Res. Psychol. **3**(2), 77–101 (2006). https://doi.org/10.1191/1478088706qp063oa
6. Carvallo, A., Parra, D., Rada, G., Lobel, H.: A Comparative Dataset: Bridging COVID-19 and Other Diseases through Epistemonikos and CORD-19 Evidence (2023). https://doi.org/10.5281/zenodo.8339033
7. Chang, S., Harper, F.M., Terveen, L.G.: Crowd-based personalized natural language explanations for recommendations. In: Proceedings of the 10th ACM Conference on Recommender Systems, pp. 175–182 (2016). https://doi.org/10.1145/2959100.2959153
8. Dazeley, R., Vamplew, P., Foale, C., Young, C., Aryal, S., Cruz, F.: Levels of explainable artificial intelligence for human-aligned conversational explanations. Artif. Intell. **299**, 103525 (2021). https://doi.org/10.1016/j.artint.2021.103525
9. Dhanorkar, S., Wolf, C.T., Qian, K., Xu, A., Popa, L., Li, Y.: Who needs to know what, when?: broadening the explainable AI (XAI) design space by looking at explanations across the AI lifecycle. In: Designing Interactive Systems Conference 2021, vol. 12, pp. 1591–1602 (2021). https://doi.org/10.1145/3461778.3462131
10. Donoso-Guzmán, I., Ooge, J., Parra, D., Verbert, K.: Towards a comprehensive human-centred evaluation framework for explainable AI. In: Communications in Computer and Information Science, CCIS, vol. 1903, pp. 183–204 (2023). https://doi.org/10.1007/978-3-031-44070-0_10
11. Feldhus, N., Hennig, L., Nasert, M., Ebert, C., Schwarzenberg, R., Mller, S.: Saliency map verbalization: comparing feature importance representations from model-free and instruction-based methods. In: Proceedings of 1st Workshop NLRSE, pp. 30–46 (2023). https://doi.org/10.18653/v1/2023.nlrse-1.4
12. Flores Villanueva, D.: Application of Neural Language Models for Research Article Classification Into Sustainable Development Goals (MSc thesis). Santiago (2022). https://repositorio.uc.cl/handle/11534/66404
13. Jia, Y., McDermid, J., Hughes, N., Sujan, M., Lawton, T., Habli, I.: The need for the human-centred explanation for ML-based clinical decision support systems. In: 2023 IEEE 11th International Conference on Healthcare Informatics (ICHI), pp. 446–452 (2023). https://doi.org/10.1109/ICHI57859.2023.00064
14. Lakkaraju, H., Slack, D., Chen, Y., Tan, C., Singh, S.: Rethinking Explainability as a Dialogue: A Practitioner's Perspective (2022)
15. Liao, Q.V., Pribić, M., Han, J., Miller, S., Sow, D.: Question-Driven Design Process for Explainable AI User Experiences **1**(1), 1–23 (2021)
16. Liao, Q.V., Varshney, K.R.: Human-Centered Explainable AI (XAI): From Algorithms to User Experiences (2022)
17. Liao, Q.V., Zhang, Y., Luss, R., Doshi-Velez, F., Dhurandhar, A.: Connecting Algorithmic Research and Usage Contexts: A Perspective of Contextualized Evaluation for Explainable AI (2022)
18. Lundberg, S.M., Allen, P.G., Lee, S.I.: A unified approach to interpreting model predictions. In: Advances in Neural Information Processing Systems, vol. 30 (2017)

19. Lyu, Q., Apidianaki, M., Callison-Burch, C.: Towards Faithful Model Explanation in NLP: A Survey (2024)
20. Miller, T.: Explanation in artificial intelligence: insights from the social sciences. Artif. Intell. **267**, 1–38 (2019). https://doi.org/10.1016/j.artint.2018.07.007
21. Nauta, M., et al.: From anecdotal evidence to quantitative evaluation methods: a systematic review on evaluating explainable AI. ACM Comput. Surv. (2023). https://doi.org/10.1145/3583558
22. Ni, J., Li, J., McAuley, J.: Justifying recommendations using distantly-labeled reviews and fine-grained aspects. In: Proceedings of the 2019 Conference on Empirical Methods in Natural Language Processing and the 9th International Joint Conference on Natural Language Processing (EMNLP-IJCNLP), pp. 188–197 (2019). https://doi.org/10.18653/v1/D19-1018
23. OpenAI: GPT-4 Technical Report (2024)
24. Qu, J., Arguello, J., Wang, Y.: Understanding the cognitive influences of interpretability features on how users scrutinize machine-predicted categories. In: Proceedings of the 2023 Conference on Human Information Interaction and Retrieval, pp. 247–257 (2023). https://doi.org/10.1145/3576840.3578315
25. Ribeiro, M.T., Singh, S., Guestrin, C.: "Why should i trust you?". In: Proceedings of the 22nd ACM SIGKDD International Conference on Knowledge Discovery and Data Mining, vol. 13-17-Augu, pp. 1135–1144. ACM, New York, NY, USA (2016). https://doi.org/10.1145/2939672.2939778
26. Schuff, H., Jacovi, A., Adel, H., Goldberg, Y., Vu, N.T.: Human interpretation of saliency-based explanation over text. In: 2022 ACM Conference on Fairness Accountability and Transparency, vol. 22, pp. 611–636 (2022). https://doi.org/10.1145/3531146.3533127
27. Sundararajan, M., Taly, A., Yan, Q.: Axiomatic attribution for deep networks. In: Proceedings of the 34th International Conference on Machine Learning (2017)
28. Szymanski, M., Millecamp, M., Verbert, K.: Visual, textual or hybrid: the effect of user expertise on different explanations. In: 26th International Conference on Intelligent User Interfaces, pp. 109–119 (2021). https://doi.org/10.1145/3397481.3450662
29. Szymanski, M., Vanden Abeele, V., Verbert, K.: Designing and evaluating explanations for a predictive health dashboard: a user-centred case study. In: Extended Abstracts of the CHI Conference on Human Factors in Computing Systems, pp. 1–8 (2024). https://doi.org/10.1145/3613905.3637140
30. Upadhyay, R., Knoth, P., Pasi, G., Viviani, M.: Explainable online health information truthfulness in Consumer Health Search. Front. Artif. Intell. **6** (2023). https://doi.org/10.3389/frai.2023.1184851
31. Wang, X., Yin, M.: Are explanations helpful? A comparative study of the effects of explanations in AI-assisted decision-making. In: 26th International Conference on Intelligent User Interfaces, pp. 318–328 (2021). https://doi.org/10.1145/3397481.3450650
32. Wiegreffe, S., Pinter, Y.: Attention is not not explanation. In: Proceedings of the 2019 Conference on Empirical Methods in Natural Language Processing and the 9th International Joint Conference on Natural Language Processing (EMNLP-IJCNLP), pp. 11–20 (2019). https://doi.org/10.18653/v1/D19-1002
33. Yogarajan, V., Montiel, J., Smith, T., Pfahringer, B.: Transformers for multi-label classification of medical text: an empirical comparison. In: AIME 2021. LNAI, vol. 12721, pp. 114–123 (2021). https://doi.org/10.1007/978-3-030-77211-6_12

34. Zając, H.D., et al.: "It depends": configuring AI to improve clinical usefulness across contexts. In: Designing Interactive Systems Conference, pp. 874–889 (2024). https://doi.org/10.1145/3643834.3660707
35. Zajac, H.D., et al.: Towards clinically useful AI: from radiology practices in global south and north to visions of ai support. ACM Trans. Comput.-Hum. Interact. **32**(2) (2025). https://doi.org/10.1145/3715115

SepsisVision: Web-Based Support Tool for Sepsis Mortality Risk Screening Through Explanatory and Exploratory User Interfaces

Kent Fredriksdotter[1,2], Alejandro Kuratomi[1], Lena Mondrejevski[1], and Luis Quintero[1](✉)

[1] Department of Computer and Systems Sciences (DSV), Stockholm University, Stockholm, Sweden
{alejandro.kuratomi,lena.mondrejevski,luis.quintero}@dsv.su.se
[2] Department of Learning, Informatics, Management and Ethics (LIME), Karolinska Institutet, Solna, Sweden
kent.fredriksdotter@stud.ki.se

Abstract. Sepsis mortality risk prediction has been explored in the machine learning (ML) community as a use case that could benefit from data-driven decision support systems in intensive care units (ICU). However, most of the work focuses on training models to reach a high classification performance, and there are limited efforts on technical artifacts that explore the practical utility of such predictive models. Therefore, we present the tool SepsisVision, an example of a web-based explainable user interface (XUI) to support sepsis mortality risk through static explanatory and interactive exploratory interfaces to navigate the behavior of an ML model through different kinds of explanations: SHAP-based local and global feature attributions, distribution comparison, and counterfactual analysis. Tool available at: https://sepsisvision.streamlit.app/.

Keywords: Machine Learning · Explainability · User Interface · Interactive · Sepsis · Dashboard · Usability · XAI · XUI

1 Introduction

Data science researchers are increasingly interested on translating the performance of machine learning (ML) prediction into artifacts with practical utility for non-technical users who may use them to support decision-making processes in their fields. In sensitive applications like healthcare, the explainable artificial intelligence (XAI) methods may be particularly useful to enable faster and more accurate diagnoses, personalized treatments, and better resource allocation [2].

Despite the development of well-performing ML models for sepsis mortality risk prediction [5,6], few models are integrated into clinical workflows. Recent sepsis mortality risk prediction studies including XAI either fail to involve the intended target users or lack any formal evaluation [5,6], while others do not even incorporate any XAI. A knowledge gap remains regarding which types

I. Koprinska et al. (Eds.): ECML PKDD 2025, CCIS 2842, pp. 151–155, 2026.
https://doi.org/10.1007/978-3-032-19105-2_11

of explanations are the most suitable for healthcare professionals and, more specifically, for sepsis mortality risk.

Prior reviews on XAI suggested that explanations should extend beyond static statements and focus on aspects related to human-computer interaction [2]. Therefore, there is increasing work on explainable user interfaces (XUI) that may include static explanatory components with single model explanations and fixed non-editable values [2] as well as interactive exploratory XUIs that let users navigate the ML model through editable features and visualizations [8].

The **contribution** of this paper to the field of human-centered AI and interactive XAI is the introduction of the tool SepsisVision, a web-based platform that serves as an example of an XUI for clinical practice. The tool uses sepsis mortality risk as a use case, training several deep-learning models from the MIMIC-III dataset using static and time-series features. Moreover, it includes one explanatory and four exploratory interfaces to help study the type of interactive XAI techniques relevant for end users in clinical practice.

2 eXplainable User Interfaces (XUI)

The concept of XUI was established based on the observation that current XAI research does not adequately focus on the explainability needs of actual end-users [2]. Although early work called for insights from the social sciences, the field is still largely centered on computational aspects [2], whereas the newer branch of XUI aims to design human-centered XAI interfaces. Properly adopted, XUIs might already represent the user-facing pillar discussed in the *XAI 2.0* described by Longo et al. [4], implementing a multidisciplinary approach to the XAI development.

In the field of medical XAI and XUI systems, information overload is frequently cited as a concern, as there is a constant trade-off between providing sufficient information to support effective human reasoning and overwhelming the user with it [1]. Dynamic, interactive explanations could help mitigate this risk by letting users explore only what they need at the right time [7].

Two types of XUIs have been introduced as part of the human-centered AI framework: explanatory and exploratory [2]. *Explanatory* is the name given to static statements produced from XAI algorithms with minimal interaction and concise text as explanation formats. In the *exploratory* XUI, the core idea is to offer users a broader set of follow-up actions to deepen their understanding of the model or its local prediction according to their reasoning and requirements [2,8]. Such flexibility is crucial because different user groups and even individual users can have varying needs for exploration and explanation [3,8]. An example of this reasoning process is illustrated in the interactive reasoning flow in Fig. 1. With this interface type, the user's thought process can guide the model's reasoning approach, thereby aligning the system more closely with human-based explanation processes. However, there remains limited research on the perceived medical utility between exploratory and explanatory interfaces in ICU settings, particularly for tasks such as sepsis mortality prediction.

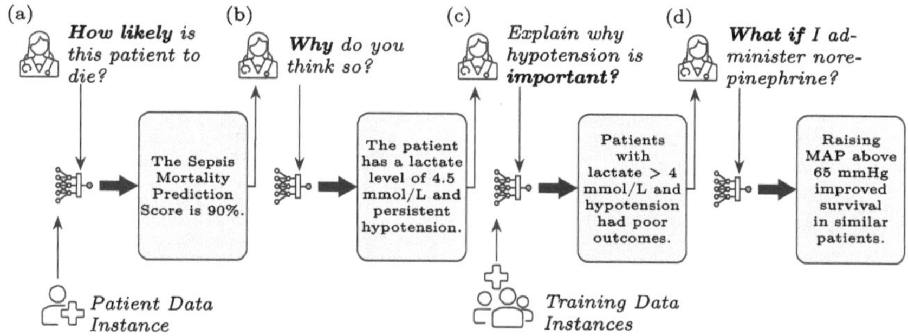

Fig. 1. *(a)* shows the model's raw prediction, *(b)* offers local feature importance, *(c)* presents global patterns or statistical comparisons, and *(d)* illustrates counterfactual or what-if reasoning. Inspired by [8]

3 SepsisVision XUI for Sepsis Mortality Risk

The prediction model was trained on a cohort of MIMIC-III. SepsisVision processes both static and time-series data from the first 24 h after ICU admission to predict ICU sepsis mortality risk. The underlying model uses a late-fusion neural network architecture with two branches: one for static features (e.g., laboratory values, scores, demographics) and one for time-series data (e.g., vital signs, vasopressors, urine output). SHAP values are computed post-hoc to provide instance-level explanations. Time-series SHAPs are temporally aggregated per feature to yield a single importance score per feature.

To make the outputs clinically meaningful, SepsisVision includes a lightweight rule-based natural language generation component that translates SHAP results and feature values into descriptive statements. All inference and explanation logic runs entirely within a Streamlit application, using an in-memory session state for responsive interaction without external calls.

The main user interface of SepsisVision, illustrated in Fig. 2, is designed to represent a distinct approach to model explanation. The interfaces are intentionally separated to support comparative evaluation of different explanation strategies across user groups. Subfigure (a) displays the raw patient data used for the initial human-only risk assessment. The explanatory XUI (b) emphasizes a static, concise explanation of model output through textual summaries and grouped SHAP-based feature contributions. In contrast, the exploratory XUI enables dynamic interaction with the model through four key explanation modes: (c) local explanation, (d) global model interpretation, (e) statistical comparison of patient features to typical survivors and non-survivors, and (f) counterfactual analysis. Each of these interface components is further described in the corresponding figure captions. Together, these components aim to bridge high-performing predictive models with interpretable, interactive interfaces for clinical decision support. The complete tool is deployed as a web app and can be accessed at https://sepsisvision.streamlit.app/.

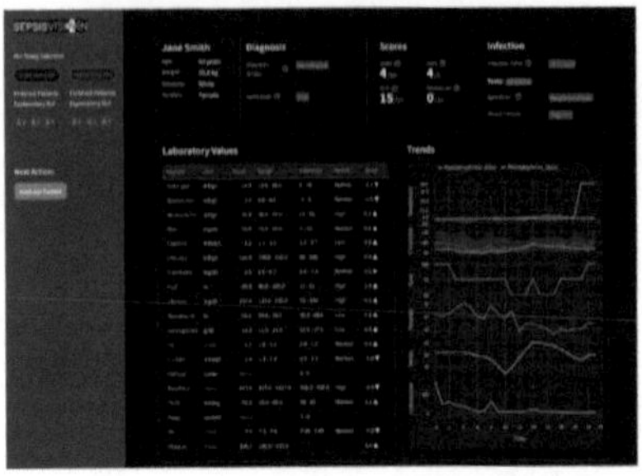

(a) Raw patient data view. Displays clinical, demographic, laboratory, and vital sign information used to estimate ICU mortality risk without model support.

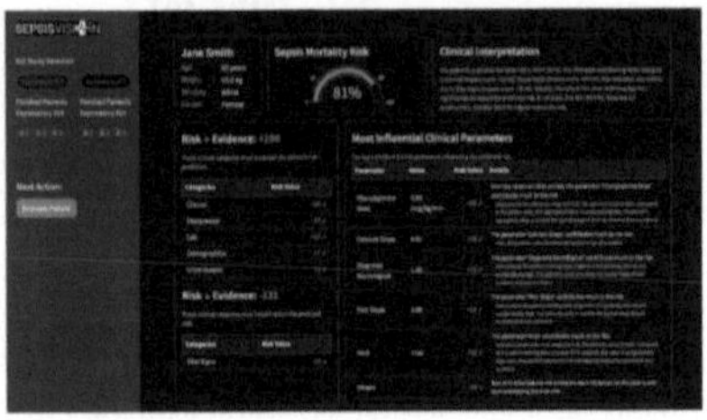

(b) Explanatory XUI presenting the model-predicted ICU mortality risk, clinical interpretation, and feature contributions. The interface groups risk drivers and highlights the most influential features with SHAP-based explanations.

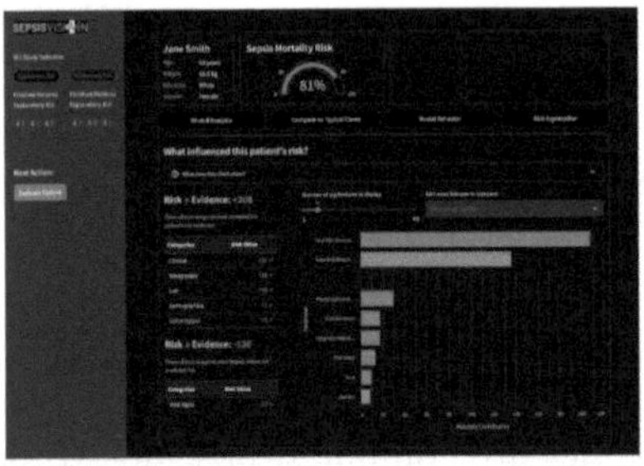

(c) Exploratory XUI view for local instance risk explanation. Users can examine the predicted risk by outcome group and interactively explore which features contribute to the prediction through graphical elements. Contribution bars are color-coded and aligned in the same direction for easier comparison.

(d) Exploratory XUI view for global model interpretation. The visualization displays the overall importance of features across all patients, supporting a broader understanding of model behavior.

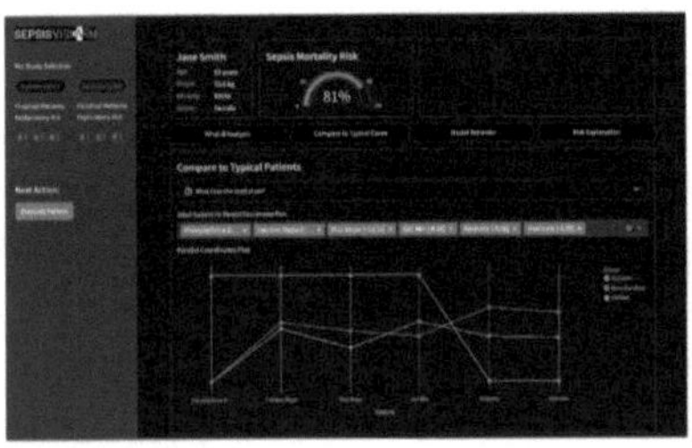

(e) Exploratory XUI comparison view. This interface allows users to compare the current patient's feature values against typical distributions for survivors and non-survivors, supporting pattern recognition and outcome reasoning.

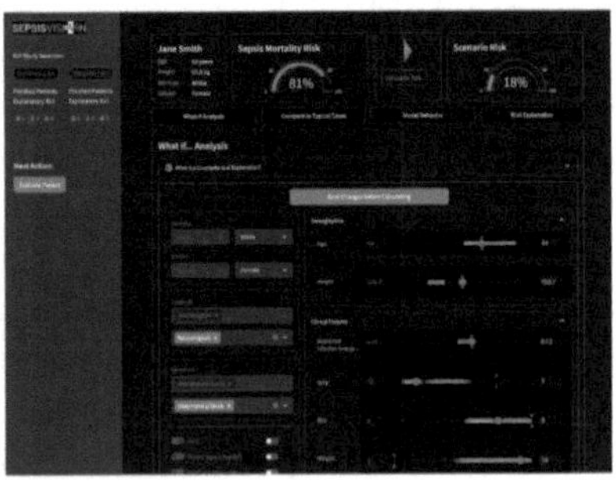

(f) Counterfactual analysis within the Exploratory XUI. Users can simulate changes to patient features and observe how the model's prediction would be affected, enabling exploration of modifiable risk factors.

Fig. 2. Overview of SepsisVision for Mortality Prediction in Clinical Practice.

4 Conclusion

This paper introduced SepsisVision, a web-based interactive tool that supports sepsis mortality risk screening through explainable user interfaces. Combining explanatory and exploratory XAI techniques, the system enables a user-centered approach to explaining ML models applied to this medical field. Future work will involve user studies with healthcare practitioners to validate the practical relevance and clinical utility of these XUIs.

Acknowledgments. This study was funded by the Department of Computer and Systems Sciences (DSV) at Stockholm University.

Disclosure of Interests. The authors have no competing interests to declare that are relevant to the content of this article.

References

1. Bo, J.Y., Hao, P., Lim, B.Y.: Incremental XAI: memorable understanding of AI with incremental explanations. In: Proceedings of the CHI Conference on Human Factors in Computing Systems, pp. 1–17. ACM (2024). https://doi.org/10.1145/3613904.3642689
2. Chromik, M., Butz, A.: Human-XAI interaction: a review and design principles for explanation user interfaces. In: Ardito, C., et al. (eds.) INTERACT 2021. LNCS, vol. 12933, pp. 619–640. Springer, Cham (2021). https://doi.org/10.1007/978-3-030-85616-8_36
3. Ehsan, U., et al.: The Who in XAI: how AI background shapes perceptions of AI explanations. In: Proceedings of the CHI Conference on Human Factors in Computing Systems, pp. 1–32. ACM (2024). https://doi.org/10.1145/3613904.3642474
4. Longo, L., et al.: Explainable Artificial Intelligence (XAI) 2.0: a manifesto of open challenges and interdisciplinary research directions. Inf. Fusion **106**, 102301 (2024). https://doi.org/10.1016/j.inffus.2024.102301
5. Mondrejevski, L., Rugolon, F., Miliou, I., Papapetrou, P.: MASICU: a multimodal attention-based classifier for Sepsis mortality prediction in the ICU, pp. 326–331 (2024). https://doi.org/10.1109/CBMS61543.2024.00061
6. Shen, L., Wu, J., Lan, J., Chen, C., Wang, Y., Li, Z.: Interpretable machine learning-based prediction of 28-day mortality in ICU patients with sepsis: a multicenter retrospective study. Front. Cell. Infect. Microbiol. **14**, 1500326 (2024). https://doi.org/10.3389/fcimb.2024.1500326
7. Wang, D., Yang, Q., Abdul, A., Lim, B.Y.: Designing theory-driven user-centric explainable AI. In: Proceedings of the 2019 CHI Conference on Human Factors in Computing Systems, pp. 1–15. ACM, Glasgow Scotland UK (2019). https://doi.org/10.1145/3290605.3300831
8. Weld, D.S., Bansal, G.: The challenge of crafting intelligible intelligence. Commun. ACM **62**(6), 70–79 (2019). https://doi.org/10.1145/3282486

Explainable Visual Anomaly Detection with Multimodal Models and Metadata-Augmented Prompts

Natalia Wojak-Strzelecka[1(✉)], Szymon Bobek[1], Mehrdad Asadi[2], Ann Nowe[2], Krzysztof Kutt[1], José García[3], and Grzegorz J. Nalepa[1]

[1] Department of Human-Centered Artificial Intelligence, Institute of Applied Computer Science, Faculty of Physics, Astronomy and Applied Computer Science, Jagiellonian University, ul. prof. Stanisława Łojasiewicza 11, 30-348 Krakow, Poland
natalia.wojak-strzelecka-guest@uj.edu.pl

[2] AI Lab, Vrije Universiteit Brussel, Brussel, Belgium

[3] Department of Computer Technology, University of Alicante, 03080 Alicante, Spain

Abstract. Anomaly detection is critical in industrial domains such as quality control and predictive maintenance, where combining it with visual inspection and explainability enhances trust and reduces errors. This study evaluates a pre-trained multimodal foundation model for visual anomaly detection and explanation on the MVTec dataset, using a post hoc fusion strategy that integrates outputs from independent models. The setup includes comparisons with PatchCore and extended configurations incorporating metadata such as heatmaps, segmentation masks, and patches. Results show that the multimodal model outperforms PatchCore on texture categories (mean F1: 0.960 vs. 0.947), but underperforms on object categories. It offers interpretable explanations in simple cases, but limited classification accuracy, marginal benefits from metadata augmentation, and reduced specificity in complex scenes indicate that further refinement is needed. These findings highlight the potential of multimodal models for explainable anomaly detection while underscoring current limitations in handling complex object structures.

Keywords: Anomaly detection · Visual inspectiond · Explainability

1 Introduction

Anomaly detection is one of the most commonly applied machine learning (ML) and artificial intelligence (AI) techniques in industrial settings, particularly for tasks involving quality control, fault diagnosis, and predictive maintenance. In the image domain, anomaly detection is often combined with visual inspection methods and explainability techniques to better understand the nature, possible causes, and validity of detected anomalies. Such techniques aim to clarify why certain anomalies were flagged, what features contributed the most to the detection, and whether the detected anomaly represents a true positive or a benign

I. Koprinska et al. (Eds.): ECML PKDD 2025, CCIS 2842, pp. 156–165, 2026.
https://doi.org/10.1007/978-3-032-19105-2_12

variation. In recent years, significant efforts have been made to integrate visual inspection and anomaly detection to enhance interpretability. For example, this includes examining defects in industrial environments [5,13], locating abnormalities in medical imaging [4], and recognizing unfamiliar objects in autonomous driving applications [6]. A growing trend in this domain is the incorporation of large language models (LLMs) and multimodal foundation models, which are capable of processing and reasoning across diverse data types [8,14]. For instance, recent works such as GPT-4V [7], AnomalyGPT [10] and AnomalyCLIP [21] demonstrate how language and vision can be effectively combined to explain model outputs and generate human-like rationales for anomalies. Most current research in multimodal anomaly detection focuses on early fusion—combining different data modalities (e.g., text, image, time series, sensor data) before training to build end-to-end, multi-input models [9,16]. We argue that with the rapid advancement of multimodal foundation models, post hoc fusion is a viable alternative. Unlike early fusion, post hoc fusion does not require retraining or modifying large models. Instead, it leverages pre-trained unimodal or multimodal models to generate representations or decisions independently, and fuses these outputs afterwards using lightweight models or rule-based systems. This allows for greater flexibility in selecting anomaly detection models, a model-agnostic approach to explainability and customisation of explanations to fit stakeholder needs through LLM capabilities such as rephrasing and summarisation. This work explores a novel approach that integrates visual anomaly detection, explainability, and large multimodal models (e.g., Phi-3.5 [1]).

The central objective is to explore how these advanced models can be leveraged to not only detect anomalies in visual data but also to provide meaningful, interpretable explanations that enhance the effectiveness of visual inspection. This research focuses on analysing the following topics:

1. Investigate how **textual prompts**, particularly those incorporating **domain-specific expert knowledge**, can be designed to guide the model's inference process, with the goal of improving accuracy and contextual relevance.
2. We **incorporate diverse input modalities**—including metadata such as heatmaps, segmentation masks, and image patches—derived from models like PatchCore. These additional data types are used within prompts to help the model attend to salient regions and provide richer contextual information during inference.

Rather than relying solely on displays or post hoc visualisations, our approach highlights the potential of integrating natural language interaction to support a more dynamic and user-driven inspection process. This perspective encourages deeper engagement, improved interpretability, and lays the groundwork for more interactive forms of human-AI collaboration. The rest of the paper is structured as follows: Sect. 2 reviews the state of the art in relevant fields. Section 3 offers an in-depth description of the experiments carried out. Finally, Sect. 4 summarizes the research findings and outlines potential directions for future work.

2 Related Works

The integration of multiple data modalities – such as images, sensor data, and textual information—has further improved visual anomaly detection robustness and accuracy [11].

Visual anomaly detection has advanced significantly with the integration of explainability techniques such as attention mechanisms, saliency maps, and post hoc reasoning frameworks [20]. These methods improve transparency by highlighting image regions or modalities responsible for anomaly detection, which is critical in industrial and medical applications. A growing trend in anomaly detection research is the incorporation of domain expertise via prompt engineering [17–19] and multimodal foundation models capable of processing and reasoning across diverse data types [8,14]. Large vision-language models (VLMs) like AnomalyCLIP demonstrated effective human-like rationales for explaining anomalies, but they are often built on top of foundational models such as CLIP [21] or GPT [7,10]. However, their high computational cost and resource requirements make them less practical for real-time or edge and production deployments. In contrast, smaller multimodal models like Phi-3.5-vision offer a promising alternative by balancing efficiency and capability. Despite their compact size (e.g., 4B parameters), models like Phi-3.5-vision [1] demonstrate strong performance on multimodal reasoning tasks, making them suitable for multi-modal anomaly explanation in constrained deployment environments.

In line with this research, recent studies have shown that LLMs augmented with vision reasoning capabilities significantly enhance trustworthiness and user acceptance in complex, real-world domains such as the driving task. For example Kim et al. [12] demonstrated that integrating vision with LLMs led to improved human performance and higher levels of user trust in decision-support systems for driving task. This suggest that multimodal augmentation not only enhance system performance but also facilitates user confidence in the task. Given these benefits, our research investigates such multimodal explanation in industrial quality control processes such as anomaly detection where trust, transparency and interpretability are essential for effective human-AI collaboration.

Interactive and conversational frameworks for visual inspection have begun to emerge, enabling users to engage dynamically with anomaly detection outputs [11,18,20]. Such interactive visual inspection enables users to inspect, correct, and iteratively fine tune and personalize LLMs in their way of explanation through methods such as Reinforcement Learning (RL) [15]. Therefore, evaluating how different prompts augmented with multiple modalities would enhance LLMs' reasoning for explaining models is demanding.

While many multimodal anomaly detection systems rely on early fusion strategies, where heterogeneous inputs such as image and text are combined at the embedding level, post hoc fusion techniques have received comparatively less attention. In contrast to early fusion, our approach follows a late fusion paradigm, increasing scalability by combining independent models to explain anomalies. Explainability techniques tend to be tightly coupled with specific architectures, reducing adaptability across diverse models and modalities. Prompt engineering and multimodal foundation models show promise but are mostly applied in isolated or early fusion contexts, lacking modular integration. Our work addresses these gaps by investigating the capabilities of a post hoc fusion framework that enables model-agnostic, flexible, and interactive anomaly detection without retraining or architectural constraints.

3 Experimental Setup and Methodology

In this section, we provide a detailed description of the experimental setup, including the models employed and the dataset utilized. Our study focuses on the MVTec Anomaly Detection dataset [2,5] comprising 15 distinct categories containing 3629 images for training and validation, and 1725 images for testing. The dataset is organised into two primary groups: objects and textures. A comprehensive overview of the dataset is presented in Table 1.

Table 1. Description of MVTec Anomaly Detection dataset.

	Category	Train	Test good	Test anomaly	Anomaly groups
Textures	Carpet	280	28	89	5
	Grid	264	21	57	5
	Leather	245	32	92	5
	Tile	230	33	84	5
	Wood	247	19	60	5
Objects	Bottle	209	20	63	3
	Cable	224	58	92	8
	Capsule	219	23	109	5
	Hazelnut	391	40	40	4
	Metal Nut	220	22	93	5
	Pill	267	26	141	7
	Screw	320	41	119	5
	Toothbrush	60	12	5	1
	Transistor	213	60	40	4
	Zipper	240	32	119	7
	Total	3629	467	1258	73

For each category in the dataset, we trained a PatchCore anomaly detection model using the implementation provided by the anomalib library [3]. We employed ResNet-18 as the feature extraction backbone and set the batch size to 16 during training. The PatchCore model produces informative outputs, including anomaly heatmaps and segmentation masks, which were utilized in our subsequent experiments. As a multimodal model, we selected the Phi-3.5 model developed by Microsoft [1], due to its ability to jointly process visual and textual information. Its strong visual reasoning and language generation capabilities make it well-suited for interpreting image anomalies and providing human-readable explanations. Below the description of conducted experiments is presented.

Multimodal Model as Anomaly Detector. We first evaluate the multimodal model's ability to classify images as normal or anomalous. Each test image is paired with a random normal image, and the model must decide if the test image is good or anomalous. Classification performance is measured by the F1 score and compared to the PatchCore model. The user prompt provided to the multimodal model is as follows: prompt = *f"<|user|> <|image_1|> This is an example of a normal image. Now, look at the following image: <|image_2|> Classify the second image as either normal or an anomaly. Return only a single digit: 0 if it is normal, 1 if it is an anomaly<|end|><|assistant|>"*

Description of Anomalies. As input to the multimodal model, we provide a normal image, an anomalous image, and the corresponding anomaly heatmap generated by PatchCore. The model is then used for generating a description of the anomaly present in the test image. We also provided to the model list of possible anomalies (*anomaly_types*), which represent the anomaly groups defined in the MVTec dataset and one *example_anomaly* from the possible ones. For example, in the 'wood' category, the potential anomaly types include: color, combined, scratch, hole, and liquid. The used prompt = *f"<|user|> <|image_1|> This is a normal (non-defective) reference image. <|image_2|> This is an image containing an anomaly or defect. <|image_3|> This is a heatmap highlighting the most anomalous region in the second image. The most anomalous areas are shown in yellow on the heatmap. Your task is to identify and describe the anomaly in detail using the list of possible anomaly types below. Compare the second image to the reference, and use the heatmap to help localize the issue. The possible anomaly types are: anomaly_types. Describe what is visually different or wrong in the anomalous image, including its location, shape, size, texture, or color. Be concise, specific, and use terminology from the list above when applicable.<|end|><|assistant|>"*

Anomaly Classification. We design two versions of the experiment to investigate whether integrating knowledge from PatchCore enhances anomaly classification performance.

(a) In the first setup, the multimodal model receives a normal image along with a textual description of possible anomaly types based on expert knowledge *anomaly_descriptions*. The model is tasked with classifying the anomaly type present in the test image. Used prompt: *f"<|user|><|image_1|> This is a normal (non-defective) reference image. <|image_2|> This is an image containing an anomaly. Your task is to classify the anomaly in the second image. Only choose one of the following anomaly types:anomaly_descriptions. Output only the name of the anomaly type (e.g., 'example_anomaly'). Do not include explanations, formatting, or extra text. <|end|><|assistant|>"*

(b) In the second setup, the model is provided with a normal image, an anomalous image, the corresponding anomaly heatmap/segmentation/extracted patches and the same expert-provided descriptions of potential anomalies. The extracted patches correspond to the most anomalous regions, with non-anomalous areas masked—rendered black (see Fig. 1). The objective remains to classify the type of anomaly, with the additional visual and semantic context. The prompt used for experiment with heatmaps: prompt = *f"</user/></image_1/> This is a normal (non-defective) reference image. </image_2/> This is an image containing an anomaly. </image_3/> This is a heatmap highlighting the most anomalous region in the second image. The most anomalous areas are shown in yellow on the heatmap. Your task is to classify the anomaly in the second image. Only choose one of the following anomaly types based on the image and heatmap: anomaly_descriptions. Output only the name of the anomaly type (e.g., 'example_anomaly'). Do not include explanations, formatting, or extra text. </end/></assistant/>"*

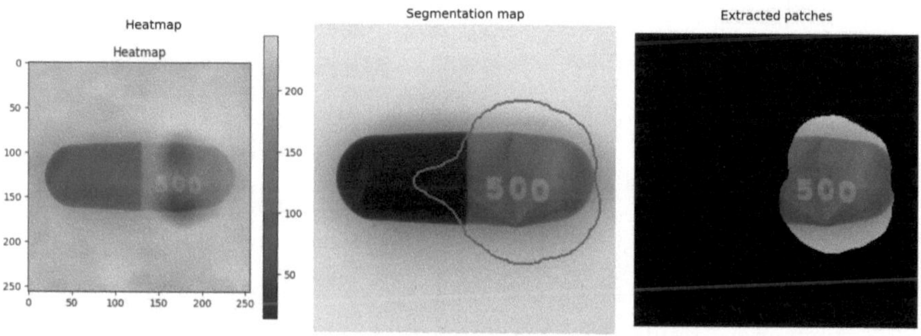

Fig. 1. The figure illustrating the different modalities produced by the PatchCore model—heatmaps, segmentation maps, and patches—using an example of a squeeze anomaly from the capsule dataset

4 Results and Discussion

This section presents the experimental results and analysis, beginning with Experiment 1, which evaluates Phi-3.5 for anomaly detection. Results with superior performance are highlighted with a green background. As shown in Table 2, Phi-3.5 outperforms PatchCore on texture-based datasets, highlighting its strength in capturing fine surface details. However, it performs worse on object-based datasets, revealing a limitation of the multimodal approach. This motivates further improvements to enhance performance across diverse anomaly types.

Now, let us examine the results of Experiment 2. We present one example from the textures dataset—the wood category (Fig. 2)—and one from the object category, specifically the capsule dataset (Fig. 3). As observed, the overall description is fairly general. For the wood example, the model correctly suggests the presence of possible anomalies, while for the capsule, it identifies two potential anomaly types. Anomaly localization is effective in the capsule example but less accurate in the wood case.

Table 2. PatchCore vs. Multimodal F1 scores grouped by category type.

	Category	PatchCore	Multimodal
Textures	Carpet	0.939	0.971
	Grid	0.901	0.895
	Leather	0.973	0.995
	Tile	0.951	0.948
	Wood	0.959	0.992
	Mean	0.947	**0.960**
Objects	Bottle	1.000	0.915
	Cable	0.915	0.790
	Capsule	0.955	0.792
	Hazelnut	0.955	0.809
	Metal Nut	0.984	0.948
	Pill	0.918	0.697
	Screw	0.921	0.700
	Toothbrush	1.000	0.812
	Transistor	0.962	0.436
	Zipper	0.953	0.522
	Mean	**0.956**	0.742

Table 3. Comparison of properly classified anomaly types across different modalities.

	Category	w/o PatchCore	w/ Heatmap	w/ Seg. Map	w/ Patches
Textures	Carpet	0.360	0.348	0.270	0.270
	Grid	0.404	0.316	0.263	0.298
	Leather	0.272	0.326	0.261	0.304
	Tile	0.464	0.452	0.381	0.488
	Wood	0.583	0.433	0.500	0.417
	Mean	**0.417**	0.375	0.335	0.355
Objects	Bottle	0.381	0.381	0.365	0.365
	Cable	0.130	0.163	0.207	0.163
	Capsule	0.275	0.257	0.239	0.330
	Hazelnut	0.357	0.371	0.429	0.429
	Metal Nut	0.280	0.215	0.280	0.269
	Pill	0.149	0.142	0.135	0.135
	Screw	0.235	0.193	0.193	0.193
	Toothbrush	1.000	1.000	1.000	1.000
	Transistor	0.250	0.250	0.250	0.250
	Zipper	0.151	0.151	0.244	0.151
	Mean	0.321	0.312	**0.334**	0.328

Table 3 summarizes results from Experiment 3. The first column corresponds to Experiment 3a, in which only image pairs (good and anomalous) are used. Columns 2–4 represnt various variants of Experiment 3b, each incorporating additional forms of metadata derived from PatchCore: column 2 - heatmaps, column 3 - segmentation map, column 4 - extracted patches. A green background is used to highlight the best results. As observed, only the Wood dataset achieved more than 50% accuracy in correctly classifying anomaly types. In general, classification performance on texture datasets outperformed that on object datasets. Furthermore, incorporating additional metadata extracted from PatchCore—such as heatmaps, segmentation maps, or patch-based representations—did not lead to a significant improvement in classification accuracy. In the Toothbrush dataset, only a single anomaly type is present; therefore, the reported 100% accuracy should not reflect the model's general classification capability.

5 Summary

We evaluated the effectiveness of a multimodal foundation model (Phi-3.5) for visual anomaly detection and explanation on the MVTec Anomaly Detection dataset. The experimental setup included baseline comparisons with the PatchCore model, and extended configurations incorporating metadata (heatmaps, segmentation masks, patches) generated by PatchCore.

Phi-3.5 showed strong performance in anomaly detection for texture categories, outperforming PatchCore (mean F1: 0.960 vs. 0.947), but underper-

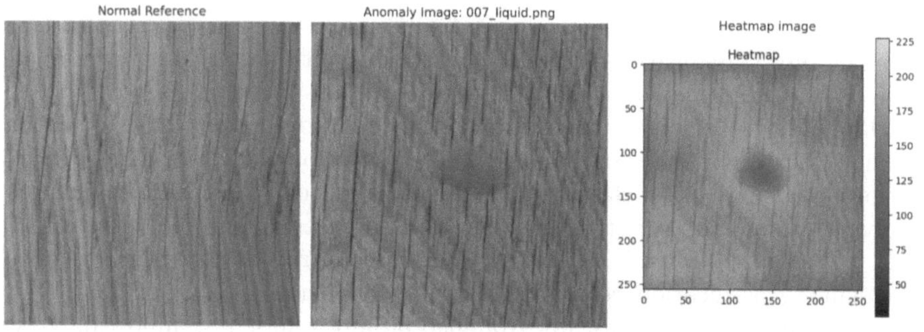

Fig. 2. The figure illustrating the input for the Mulimodal model, the generated response: *The anomaly in the second image appears to be a small, circular area with a different texture and color compared to the rest of the image. It is located towards the bottom right of the image. The texture of the anomaly is smoother and less grainy than the surrounding wood grain, and it has a lighter, almost white color, which contrasts with the darker brown tones of the rest of the image. This suggests that the anomaly could be a liquid or a very light-colored material that has been applied or is present on the surface. The heatmap indicates that this area is significantly different in terms of the heatmap values, which could correspond to the anomaly's unique properties or the presence of a different material.*

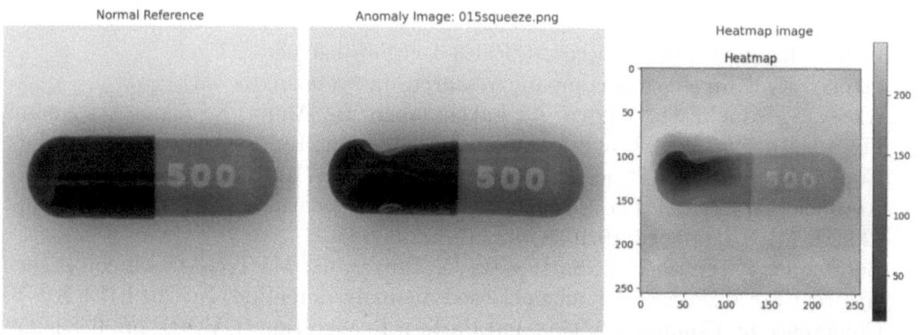

Fig. 3. The figure illustrating the input for the Mulimodal model, the generated response: *The second image shows a capsule with the number '500' on its side, which appears to be a heatmap overlay. The heatmap indicates a significant temperature anomaly, with the most intense areas highlighted in yellow. The anomaly is located on the black portion of the capsule, suggesting a possible defect or irregularity in that area. The shape and size of the capsule seem consistent with the reference image, but the texture and color of the black portion are different, indicating a potential faulty imprint or a manufacturing defect. The reference image shows a smooth, uniform black surface, while the second image has a textured, uneven appearance in the black section. This could be indicative of a squeeze or poke defect, where the material has been deformed or displaced during manufacturing. The heatmap helps to localize the issue by showing the exact location of the anomaly.* (Color figure online)

formed on object categories. It produced clear, interpretable anomaly descriptions in simple cases, though it struggled with specificity in more complex ones. Anomaly type classification remained challenging, with low accuracy overall and limited gains from metadata augmentation.

Our findings indicate that multimodal foundation models hold significant potential for explainable visual anomaly detection. However, their current capacity for precise anomaly classification remains limited, especially in scenarios involving complex object structures. Prompt engineering and metadata enrichment contribute positively to interpretability but require further refinement to enhance classification reliability. Future work should focus on developing more structured and semantically grounded prompt templates, improving visual grounding in multimodal models, and exploring interactive human-AI interfaces to support high-stakes decision-making processes in industrial contexts.

Acknowledgments. This paper is part of a project that has received funding from the European Union's Horizon Europe Research and Innovation Programme, under Grant Agreement number 101120406. The paper reflects only the authors' view and the EC is not responsible for any use that may be made of the information it contains. The research has been supported by a grant from the Priority Research Area (DigiWorld) under the Strategic Programme Excellence Initiative at Jagiellonian University.

References

1. https://huggingface.co/microsoft/Phi-3.5-vision-instruct
2. https://www.mvtec.com/company/research/datasets/mvtec-ad
3. Akcay, S., Ameln, D., Vaidya, A., Lakshmanan, B., Ahuja, N., Genc, U.: Anomalib: a deep learning library for anomaly detection. In: 2022 IEEE International Conference on Image Processing (ICIP), pp. 1706–1710. IEEE (2022)
4. Antonelli, M., et al.: The medical segmentation decathlon. Nat. Commun. **13**(1) (2022). https://doi.org/10.1038/s41467-022-30695-9
5. Bergmann, P., Fauser, M., Sattlegger, D., Steger, C.: MVTec AD – a comprehensive real-world dataset for unsupervised anomaly detection. In: 2019 IEEE/CVF Conference on Computer Vision and Pattern Recognition (CVPR), pp. 9584–9592 (2019). https://doi.org/10.1109/CVPR.2019.00982
6. Bogdoll, D., Nitsche, M., Zollner, J.M.: Anomaly detection in autonomous driving: a survey. In: 2022 IEEE/CVF Conference on Computer Vision and Pattern Recognition Workshops (CVPRW), pp. 4487–4498. IEEE (2022). https://doi.org/10.1109/cvprw56347.2022.00495
7. Cao, Y., Xu, X., Sun, C., Huang, X., Shen, W.: Towards generic anomaly detection and understanding: Large-scale visual-linguistic model (GPT-4V) takes the lead (2023). https://arxiv.org/abs/2311.02782
8. Cao, Y., et al.: A survey on visual anomaly detection: challenge, approach, and prospect (2024). https://arxiv.org/abs/2401.16402
9. Costanzino, A., Ramirez, P.Z., Lisanti, G., Stefano, L.D.: Multimodal industrial anomaly detection by crossmodal feature mapping (2024). https://arxiv.org/abs/2312.04521

10. Gu, Z., Zhu, B., Zhu, G., Chen, Y., Tang, M., Wang, J.: AnomalyGPT: detecting industrial anomalies using large vision-language models (2023). https://arxiv.org/abs/2308.15366
11. Jiang, X., et al..: MMAD: a comprehensive benchmark for multimodal large language models in industrial anomaly detection (2025). https://arxiv.org/abs/2410.09453
12. Kim, N., Park, W.: Vision-integrated LLMs for autonomous driving assistance: human performance comparison and trust evaluation. arXiv preprint: arXiv:2502.06843 (2025)
13. Li, C., Qi, L., Geng, X.: A SAM-guided two-stream lightweight model for anomaly detection (2024). https://arxiv.org/abs/2402.19145
14. Lin, Y., et al.: A survey on RGB, 3D, and multimodal approaches for unsupervised industrial image anomaly detection (2025). https://arxiv.org/abs/2410.21982
15. Tan, H., et al.: Reason-RFT: reinforcement fine-tuning for visual reasoning. arXiv preprint: arXiv:2503.20752 (2025)
16. Wang, Y., Peng, J., Zhang, J., Yi, R., Wang, Y., Wang, C.: Multimodal industrial anomaly detection via hybrid fusion (2023). https://arxiv.org/abs/2303.00601
17. Xu, J., Lo, S.Y., Safaei, B., Patel, V.M., Dwivedi, I.: Towards zero-shot anomaly detection and reasoning with multimodal large language models (2025). https://arxiv.org/abs/2502.07601
18. Xu, R., Ding, K.: Large language models for anomaly and out-of-distribution detection: a survey. In: Findings of NAACL 2025, pp. 6007–6027 (2025). https://aclanthology.org/2025.findings-naacl.333.pdf
19. Xu, X., Cao, Y., Chen, Y., Shen, W., Huang, X.: Customizing visual-language foundation models for multi-modal anomaly detection and reasoning. arXiv preprint: arXiv:2403.11083 (2024)
20. Zhang, Z., Ruan, J., Gao, X., Liu, T., Fu, Y.: EIAD: explainable industrial anomaly detection via multi-modal large language models (2025). https://arxiv.org/abs/2503.14162
21. Zhou, Q., Pang, G., Tian, Y., He, S., Chen, J.: AnomalyCLIP: object-agnostic prompt learning for zero-shot anomaly detection (2025). https://arxiv.org/abs/2310.18961

Workshop on Learning on Real and Synthetic Medical Time Series Data (MED-TIME 2025)

Workshop on Learning on Real and Synthetic Medical Time Series Data (MED-TIME)

The 2025 ECMLPKDD workshops track hosted, the 1st International Workshop on Learning on Real and Synthetic Medical Time Series Data (MED-TIME) with an integrated tutorial.

https://med-time2025.blogs.dsv.su.se/

We organized this event to address the challenges emanating from the co-evolution of two threads: advances in medical data collection and powerful learning methods for temporal data. These two threads have transformed healthcare into a deeply temporal science. From continuous monitoring in intensive care units to longitudinal genomics and wearable-based sensing, temporal data are pivotal to understanding health trajectories, disease progression, and treatment response. Yet, the complexity of this data — often high-dimensional, irregularly sampled, and privacy-sensitive — demands new methods for analysis, modeling, and interpretation.

MED-TIME solicited papers on all temporal learning advances for health, including but not limited to patient monitoring, disease progression modeling, and clinical decision support for patients with chronic conditions. A key challenge in working with real medical data is handling sparsity and missingness, as the more people are recorded, the less data is there for each one. While synthetic data generation seems like a solution, synthetic medical time series pose challenges themselves, as ensuring its utility alongside real data requires careful validation. At the same time, multimodal data integration, explainability, and forecasting remain critical for developing reliable and interpretable models.

MED-TIME encompassed one invited keynote by Riccardo Guidotti on the route 'From Shapelets and Subsequences to Saliency Maps: Making Time Series Models Understandable in Medicine and Beyond', 5 research papers and a 4-part tutorial on: 'Medical time series forecasting and multimodal learning' (Ioanna Miliou), 'Explainable ML for medical time series' (Panagiotis Papapetrou), 'Generation of synthetic data time series with diffusion models' (Arianna Dagliati) and 'Data presence and missingness in medical time series' (Myra Spiliopoulou).

MED-TIME received ten paper submissions out of which five were accepted for oral presentation and to appear in the next pages of this proceedings volume. The accepted papers collectively explore the rich landscape of temporal data analysis for health. Each paper offers a unique methodological perspective, yet they all serve the same goal to make temporal models more robust, interpretable, and applicable to real-world clinical settings.

In *"Improved Sleep Stage Tagging on Wearables* via *Knowledge Distillation,"* **Sebastian Buschjäger** investigates how knowledge distillation can transfer insights from polysomnography-based models to wearable-based models, enhancing the accuracy of sleep stage classification while enabling scalable, home-based diagnostics.

In *"SHISMA: Shape-driven Inference of Significant Celltype-specific Subnetworks from Time Series Single-cell Transcriptomics,"* **Antonio Collesei** introduces a novel shape-based approach to uncover statistically significant cell type-specific subnetworks from single-cell RNA sequencing time series, highlighting how temporal patterns at cellular resolution reveal both known and novel regulatory mechanisms.

In *"Federated Markov Imputation: Privacy-Preserving Temporal Imputation in Multi -Centric ICU Environments,"* **Christoph Düsing** presents a federated approach that imputes missing temporal data across institutions without compromising privacy. Using ICU data for sepsis onset prediction, this method demonstrates the power of collaborative yet secure temporal modeling across heterogeneous medical centers.

In *"Alignment of Multiple Item Set Sequences for Apnea Detection,"* **Dries Van der Plas** proposes a new multiple sequence alignment framework that generalizes beyond pairwise comparisons to handle complex, multi-dimensional event sequences. The method shows strong promise in apnea and hypopnea detection, revealing how simultaneous alignment across sequences can uncover clinically relevant temporal patterns.

Finally, in *"On the Role of Prognostic Factors and Effect Modifiers in Unraveling Population Heterogeneity,"* **Rianne Schouten** explores how temporal variation and hierarchical structure in medical data affect causal inference. Through controlled synthetic experiments, the work distinguishes the complementary roles of prognostic factors and effect modifiers in explaining individual treatment responses.

Together, these five contributions exemplify the diversity and depth of current research in temporal data analysis for medicine — spanning wearable sensing, genomics, causal inference, federated learning, and clinical signal alignment. They collectively illustrate how temporal modeling is not only advancing computational methodology but also reshaping our understanding of patient heterogeneity and clinical decision-making.

We would like to thank the authors, our keynote speaker, and the following **PC members:**

- Daniele Pala, University of Pavia
- Franco Rugolon, Stockholm University
- Isak Samsten, Stockholm University
- Sayeh Sobhani, Stockholm University
- Allan Tucker, Brunel University

Finally, we would like to thank the participants of MED-TIME in Porto. We wish you a pleasant reading and inspiration from the advances presented hereafter.

The MED-TIME organizers:
Panagiotis Papapetrou
Myra Spiliopoulou
Ioanna Miliou
Arianna Dagliati

Improved Sleep Stage Tagging on Wearables via Knowledge Distillation

Hendrik Weißenfels[1,2], Matthias Jakobs[1,2], Sarah Dietz-Terjung[3], and Sebastian Buschjäger[1,2](✉)

[1] TU Dortmund University, Dortmund, Germany
sebastian.buschjaeger@tu-dortmund.de
[2] LAMARR Institute for Machine Learning and Artificial Intelligence, Dortmund, Germany
[3] Ruhrlandklinik, Essen, Germany

Abstract. Sleep disorders present a major global health challenge, requiring precise and efficient diagnostic approaches. Polysomnography (PSG) remains the gold standard by capturing multiple physiological signals during overnight monitoring. However, PSG is both resource-intensive and burdensome for patients. A key limitation is the so-called first-night effect, i.e. the altered sleep architecture due to the unfamiliar laboratory environment and sensor setup. This can lead to artificially reduced sleep efficiency and diagnostic distortion [2,30]. Wearable-based sleep monitoring offers a promising alternative, enabling longitudinal assessment and reducing the first-night effect by using fewer sensors and enabling home-based diagnostics. Recent advancements in wearable technologies have improved accuracy in estimating sleep parameters when compared to PSG [9,32]. This study investigates knowledge distillation (KD) as a strategy to transfer knowledge from an existing high-performing PSG-based teacher model to a student model operating on wearable-like input data. Both models use the UTime architecture which has been shown to perform well across different sleep laboratories and are trained on clinical PSG data from a sleep laboratory in Germany. Our KD framework combines soft target supervision and feature matching to guide the student's learning. The results show that KD consistently improves the performance of the student in various sensor configurations and model sizes, indicating its potential for accurate sleep staging in real-world wearable applications.

Keywords: Sleep stage Tagging · Knowledge Distillation

1 Introduction

Sleep plays a vital role in maintaining physical health, cognitive performance, and overall well-being [4,16,18,20,31]. Despite its importance, sleep disorders remain widely underdiagnosed, partly due to the complexity and cost of the gold standard diagnostic method: polysomnography (PSG). PSG requires the

I. Koprinska et al. (Eds.): ECML PKDD 2025, CCIS 2842, pp. 171–186, 2026.
https://doi.org/10.1007/978-3-032-19105-2_13

placement of multiple electrodes and sensors in an inpatient sleep laboratory, making it expensive, obtrusive, and impractical for long-term or at-home monitoring. Moreover, the observed sleep patterns obtained by a PSG often do not reflect the natural sleep patterns of patients sleeping in a more familiar environment, i.e., at home. This discrepancy is partly due to the well-known first-night effect, a phenomenon where individuals experience altered sleep architecture—such as reduced REM sleep, prolonged sleep latency, and increased wake after sleep onset—during the initial night in a sleep laboratory [2,29]. Such effects are attributed to the unfamiliar setting, anxiety related to the monitoring procedure, and physical discomfort caused by the attachment of multiple sensors. In addition to physiological disruptions, logistical limitations further constrain the utility of in-lab PSG. Access to certified sleep laboratories is often limited due to a shortage of accredited facilities and trained personnel, resulting in long waiting periods for diagnostic appointments [16,21].

To combat these limitations, the use of wearable devices has been proposed for sleep tracking in real-world environments. However, models trained on wearable sensor data, typically limited to motion and cardiorespiratory signals, often underperform compared to models trained on full PSG data, especially when classifying fine-grained sleep stages such as REM or deep sleep [8].

We address this performance gap by exploring knowledge distillation (KD) as a means to transfer knowledge from a high-performing PSG-based model to a model constrained to wearable-like input. Specifically, we ask whether the performance of sleep staging models operating on wearable data can be improved by leveraging supervision signals from an PSG-based teacher model. In particular, we investigate cross-modal knowledge distillation using the UTime architecture [24], with separate adaptations for teacher and student models. Our KD framework integrates both soft target supervision and feature matching to guide the student's learning process. Our results demonstrate that knowledge distillation consistently improves the performance of wearable-based student models across diverse scenarios. For example, we observe gains of up to 1.7% points in accuracy, 0.03 in F1-Macro and 0.029 in Cohen's Kappa in our most inclusive setup (see Sect. 4.1). These findings suggest KD is a promising approach to build accurate and robust sleep staging models under constrained sensing conditions.

The paper is structured as follows. Section 2 discusses related work. Section 3 outlines the model architecture and the knowledge distillation framework. Section 4 presents the experimental setup and results. Section 5 concludes with a summary and directions for future work.

2 Related Work

Sleep Stage Tagging. Sleep stage tagging is an essential clinical task for diagnosing sleep disorders and assessing sleep quality. According to the AASM manual [7], sleep stages are classified into five stages Wake, N1, N2, N3, and REM sleep. The first stage consists of wakefulness, i.e., the patient is not sleeping. N1 is a brief transition stage, while N2 reflects stable light sleep and N3 (slow-wave sleep) is the most restorative stage. REM (rapid eye movement) is associated with a sleep stage consisting of dreaming and cognitive processing. As mentioned, the gold standard for analyzing sleep is a PSG. During a PSG, patients spend one night in a sleep laboratory while being continuously monitored. A PSG typically involves recording the EEG, the EOG, the EMG, the ECG, airflow, thoracic and abdominal movements, and oximetry [6] and is performed by a trained technician. After the study is complete, a scorer (typically a trained sleep technologist, somnologist, or physician) will go through the data and manually score fixed-length intervals of 30 seconds to annotate the corresponding sleep stage and potentially other important events that occur during the night (e.g. snoring, movements etc.). After the entire PSG recording has been scored, it is reviewed by a physician, who will interpret the results and form a diagnosis. The main goal of *automatic* sleep stage analysis is thus to provide an automatic scoring to reduce the amount of manual annotations. Many methods have been proposed for automatic sleep staging mainly using the EEG data. Khald Ali et al. provide a comprehensive survey of the works until 2016 in [1], while Fiorillo et al. summarizes the latest approaches until 2019 in [12]. These reviews show a mix of papers usually combining (novel) machine learning methods with (novel) pre-processing techniques applied to the EEG channels for sleep staging, gradually improving the overall performance on various datasets. While this trend continues, more recent approaches also focus on applying sleep staging in the real world. For example, multiple works focus on using a single EEG channel instead of using all available EEG channels to simplify the applicability of the sleep staging in practice without sacrificing performance [19,22,23].

Sleep Stage Tagging on Wearables. With the growing popularity of smartwatches and wearable devices, sleep stage tagging outside of clinical settings has become an increasingly active area of research. While most wearables rely primarily on accelerometry to distinguish between sleep and wake states, this approach is limited in its ability to accurately capture multiple sleep stages. Recent studies indicate that combining accelerometer data with photoplethysmography (PPG), used to extract heart rate (HR) and heart rate variability (HRV), significantly improves performance in sleep staging tasks [8]. Many consumer devices now integrate multiple sensors beyond motion tracking, including blood oxygen saturation (SpO_2), skin temperature and microphones for environmental noise estimation. Table 1 summarizes the available sensor modalities across popular commercial smartwatches. In their review of 62 wearable-based setups for sleep staging, Birrer et al. [8] report an increasing use of multimodal sensor configuartions, most commonly combining accelerometry and photoplethysmography (PPG). However, models trained on wearable data consistently underperform compared to PSG-based approaches.

Knowledge Distillation for Time Series. Knowledge Distillation (KD), originally introduced by Hinton et al. [17], enables compact models to learn from more complex networks by mimicking their softened output distributions. Subsequent extensions, such as FitNets [25], enhance this process by adding feature matching, which aligns intermediate layers of student and teacher models to improve learning (see Sect. 3.2). Although KD has been widely adopted in computer vision, its application to medical time series tasks remains limited. In particular, to our knowledge, no prior work has investigated KD in the context of sleep stage tagging from wearable data, a gap this study aims to address.

Table 1. Comparison of sensors across smartwatches and their PSG counterpart (if available). Shared entries are centered across devices [3,13,15,27].

PSG Channel	Apple Watch	Google Pixel	Fitbit Sense	Samsung Galaxy
Activity	Accelerometer, Gyroscope			
Heart Rate	Optical Heart Rate Sensor			
Pulse Waveform	Raw PPG internally, HR/HRV externally			
Saturation (SpO_2)	Blood oxygen sensor			
PosAngle	Accelerometer, Gyroscope			
Audio Volume dB	Mic. with noise monitoring		–	–
–	Skin Temperature Sensor			-

3 Methodology

Before detailing our KD framework and training procedures, we revisit the U-Sleep model that will serve as a baseline and establish some notation. Let $x \in \mathbb{R}^{\tau S \times d}$ be a multivariate time series with d channels sampled at rate S for τ seconds. Let e be the frequency at which we want to segment x. That is, the goal is to map x to $T = \lfloor \tau e \rfloor$ segments, where each segment receives a label y based on $i = S/e$ sampled points. For a visual explanation, see also Fig. 1. Each segment receives a label $y \in \mathbb{R}^L$, represented as a one-hot vector over L mutually exclusive sleep stages. Put differently, we have given a time series of T segments, each with i sample points and d channels. Now, our goal is to design a

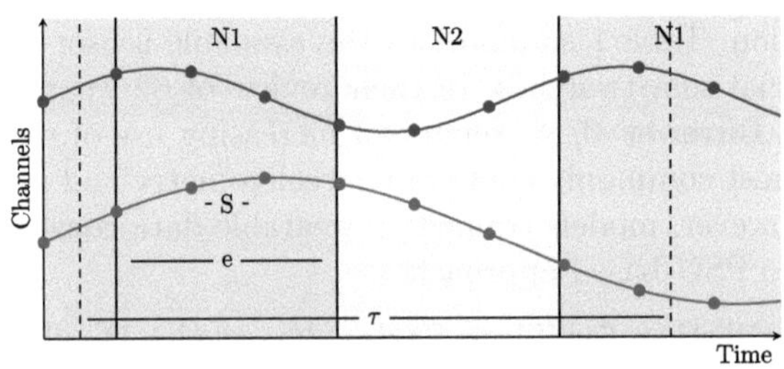

Fig. 1. Example of two channels that are classified as N1 and N2 stages using segments of size e with a sample rate S and total window of τ. In this example $i = 8$ input values per channel are used.

system $f\colon \mathbb{R}^{T\times i\times d} \rightarrow \mathbb{R}^{T\times L}$ that outputs a prediction for each segment across L sleep stages. Following standard practice in sleep-stage classification, we adopt a segment length of 30 s (i.e., $e = 1/30$ Hz). We follow the established approach for wearables of using four labels $\{\text{Wake}, \text{Light}, \text{Deep}, \text{REM}\}$ ($L = 4$) in which N1 and N2 are merged into Light sleep and N3 is denoted as deep sleep (c.f. [8]) instead of using the five sleep stages scored during a full PSG.

3.1 U-Sleep

As a baseline architecture for our experiments we use the U-Sleep model [24]. The U-Sleep architecture follows an encoder-decoder structure with skip connections, similar to the U-Net architecture [26]. It consists of several layers of 1D convolutional filters, followed by non-linear ReLU activations, and batch normalization that are grouped in encoders and decoders. For the encoders, the input signal is downsampled via a 1D max pooling operation, and for the decoders nearest-neighbor upsampling is used. The network's encoder part gradually reduces the input data's temporal dimension while extracting relevant features. The decoder part then upsamples the feature maps back to the original temporal resolution using transposed convolutions. Skip connections that concatenate the filter results connect corresponding layers in the encoder and decoder parts, allowing the network to preserve both local and global information. The outputs of the encoder-decoder part of the network are point estimates, i.e., predictions for each point in time, that are then aggregated to segment predictions using a final classification layer.

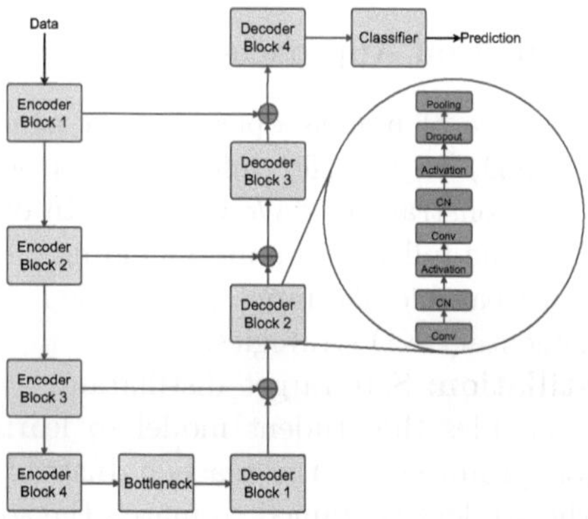

Fig. 2. General architecture of our proposed U-Sleep family. Significant changes to the original U-Sleep architecture are highlighted in red: We introduce an additional *bottleneck layer*, enhance concatenations to handle dynamic shapes and add a channel normalization. (Color figure online)

U-Sleep utilizes large filter sizes and aggressive downsampling tailored towards high-frequency EEG data. When adopting U-Sleep to other input channels that are sampled at lower frequencies, filter sizes and the number of encoder/decoder pairs must be adapted accordingly. This can lead to mismatches between the outputs of the encoder/decoder blocks during concatenation. In particular, during the decoder path, intermediate convolutions are added to the original U-Sleep model to correctly upsample the data. To simplify this approach, we restructured the encoder/decoder blocks to always follow the structure "Conv → Norm → Activation → Conv → Norm → Activation → Dropout → Pooling", and use *dynamic* zero padding during concatenation that will pad as many zeros as necessary to reach a desired output shape (c.f. Fig. 2). Second, we noticed that the embeddings of different channels differ widely, especially when the original sampling frequencies are very different. Hence, to stabilize the training, we replace the batch normalization layers with channel normalization [11] essentially performing a Z-normalization of each channel in each layer across the time axis. Third, the original U-Sleep network performs an averaging across the reconstructed time-domain followed by a 1D convolution, which again works well considering long input sequences with a few interesting features. We found that by reversing the order (i.e. first perform a 1d convolution and then do the averaging) we can add a small fully connected layer at the end of the network that further improves the overall performance in our experiments. Fourth, we added a (configurable) *bottleneck layer* which mimics another encoder block without any pooling for feature matching and finally, in our experiments we use the ELU [10] activation for subjectively better performance compared to ReLU as in the original U-Sleep, although the impact of the activation function is debatable.

3.2 Knowledge Distillation Approaches

To improve the performance of models operating on wearable signals, we use knowledge distillation (KD) to transfer information from a high-performing *teacher* model to a more constrained *student* model. In our setup, the teacher is already pre-trained on the full PSG input (including EEG and EOG), while the student operates on wearable-like input (see Table 1). In our approach, we implement two complementary KD strategies.

Soft Target Distillation: Soft target distillation, as originally proposed by Hinton et al. [17], enables the student model to learn from the full class probability distribution produced by the teacher. Instead of relying solely on hard one-hot labels, the student is trained to match the softened output of the teacher's softmax layer. These soft targets provide information about interclass relationships and are especially useful in scenarios with limited or noisy labels. The soft targets are generated by applying a temperature-scaled softmax to the logits $\boldsymbol{z}$ of the teacher model:

$$\sigma_i(\boldsymbol{z};T) = \frac{\exp\left(\frac{z_i}{T}\right)}{\sum_{j=1}^{C}\exp\left(\frac{z_j}{T}\right)} \tag{1}$$

A higher temperature $T > 1$ produces a smoother distribution, revealing subtle relationships between classes. This temperature is only used during training, at inference time, $T = 1$ is used. To encourage the student to match the teacher's output distribution, we minimize the Kullback-Leibler divergence between the softened distributions:

$$L_{\text{soft}} = D_{\text{KL}}(\sigma(z_{\text{student}}; T) \parallel \sigma(z_{\text{teacher}}; T)) \cdot T^2 \tag{2}$$

The scaling by T^2 ensures that the gradients remain in a suitable range when using high temperatures. Finally, the total loss combines the soft target loss with the standard cross-entropy loss on hard labels (defined as L_{hard}):

$$L_{\text{KD}} = \alpha L_{\text{soft}} + (1 - \alpha) L_{\text{hard}}, \quad \alpha \in [0, 1] \tag{3}$$

The hard loss L_{hard} corresponds to the standard cross-entropy between the predicted logits $\mathbf{z}$ of the student and the one-hot encoded ground-truth labels $\mathbf{y}$:

$$L_{\text{hard}} = \text{CE}(\mathbf{z}, \mathbf{y}) = -\sum_{i=1}^{C} y_i \log\left(\frac{\exp(z_i)}{\sum_{k=1}^{C} \exp(z_k)}\right) \tag{4}$$

where C is the number of classes.

Weighting those two losses by α balances the influence of the teacher's knowledge and the original supervision signal. Following Hinton et al. [17], we treat T and α as hyperparameters and tune them based on validation performance.

Feature Matching: In addition to soft target supervision, knowledge distillation can benefit from aligning internal representations of the teacher and student models. This approach, known as *feature matching*, was first introduced by Romero et al. [25] in the context of the FitNets framework. The key idea is to transfer informative intermediate representations, called *hints*, from the teacher to the student, guiding the student not just towards similar outputs, but also toward the teacher's internal inductive biases.

In our setup, we apply feature matching at the *bottleneck layer* (see Sect. 3.1) of both the teacher and student. Let $\mathbf{f}_T \in \mathbb{R}^{B \times C_T \times T_T}$ and $\mathbf{f}_S \in \mathbb{R}^{B \times C_S \times T_S}$ denote the feature maps at this layer, where B is the batch size, T_T, T_S the sampled temporal dimensions and C_T, C_S the number of channels in teacher (T) and student (S) respectively. Note that our teacher and student models may operate on different sampling rates or input window lengths (i.e. $T_T \neq T_S$). Likewise, the number of channels C_T and C_S may differ due to architectual differences such as the number of layers, kernel sized or pooling operations. As a result, the feature maps $\mathbf{f}_T$ and $\mathbf{f}_S$ may not be directly aligned in shape and require temporal and channel-wise transformation before applying the feature loss. Intuitively, aligning the teacher to the student, rather than the other way around, preserves the student's low-resolution temporal structure, which helps for deployment efficiency.

For temporal alignment ($T_T \neq T_S$), we therefore downsample the teacher feature maps using adaptive average pooling to match the student's temporal resolution. Conversely, we center-crop the student's temporal dimension to match the downsampled teacher.

$$\hat{\mathbf{f}}_T = \text{AvgPool1D}(\mathbf{f}_T), \quad \hat{\mathbf{f}}_S = \text{CropCenter}(\mathbf{f}_S) \tag{5}$$

For channel alignment ($C_T \neq C_S$), we apply a 1D convolutional regressor $\phi : \mathbb{R}^{C_T \times T'} \rightarrow \mathbb{R}^{C_S \times T'}$ to project the teacher features into the students's latent space:

$$\hat{\mathbf{f}}_T = \text{Conv1D}_{1\times 1}(\mathbf{f}_T), \tag{6}$$

In addition to bottleneck feature maps, we also apply feature matching at the penultimate layer with $\mathbf{f'}_T \in \mathbb{R}^{B\times C'_T}$ and $\mathbf{f'}_S \in \mathbb{R}^{B\times C'_S}$ for the student and the teacher, respectively. If $C'_S \neq C'_T$, we project the teacher features using a learnable linear layer $\psi : \mathbb{R}^{C'_T} \rightarrow \mathbb{R}^{C'_S}$. These architectural adaptations make feature matching applicable across heterogeneous studentteacher pairs.

The feature matching loss is then defined as the mean squared error (MSE) between the projected student representation and the teacher representation:

$$\mathcal{L}_{\text{feat,MSE}} = \frac{1}{B}\sum_{i=1}^{B}\left\|\hat{\mathbf{f}}_S^i - \mathbf{f}_T^i\right\|_2^2 \tag{7}$$

Optionally, we also explore a cosine similarity loss:

$$\mathcal{L}_{\text{feat, COS}} = 1 - \frac{\langle \hat{\mathbf{f}}_S, \mathbf{f}_T \rangle}{\|\hat{\mathbf{f}}_S\|_2 \cdot \|\mathbf{f}_T\|_2} \tag{8}$$

This loss is added to the overall objective alongside soft target and hard label supervision, also being weighted by α:

$$L_{\text{total}} = \alpha_1 L_{\text{BN}} + \alpha_2 L_{\text{PL}} + \alpha_3 L_{\text{soft}} + \alpha_4 L_{\text{hard}} \quad \text{with} \quad \sum_{i=1}^{4} \alpha_i = 1 \tag{9}$$

Here, L_{BN} and L_{PL} refer to the feature matching losses at the bottleneck and permultimate layers either using $\mathcal{L}_{\text{feat,MSE}}$ or $\mathcal{L}_{\text{feat, COS}}$. We use this complete loss L_{total} to train our models thoughout all experiments. Later, we explore different weighting strategies ($\alpha_1, ..., \alpha_4$) to analyze their relative contribution in our experiments.

4 Experiments

In our experimental evaluation, we will investigate the validity of our knowledge distilation approach by testing the following hypotheses:

H1 a): Knowledge distillation improves sleep stage tagging performance for different input channel configurations over using just the wearable data alone.

H1 b): Knowledge distillation benefits both small and large student models for sleep stage tagging.

H2: Each component of the KD framework (soft targets, feature matching at bottleneck and penultimate layers) contributes positively to model performance.

H3 (Exploratory): Knowledge distillation mitigates both under- and overfitting through additional guidance beyond hard targets.

To conduct our experiments we collected PSG data from a cohort of 304 patients between 2019 and 2021 in collaboration with a German sleep laboratory[1]. The PSG data includes human annotations from one of three expert scorers, as well as automated annotations from the commercially available Noxturnal scoring software[2]. Noxturnal is one of the leading software frameworks for the analysis of PSG data and is used in everyday clinical practice in the sleep laboratory. Typically, the Noxturnal software is first applied to the entire PSG of a patient and then manually corrected by a human scorer. Besides the PSG data, the final diagnosis made by the doctors is available (but not used in this work), whereas other personal metadata (e.g. sex, age, weight etc.) has been omitted from the data. The label distribution in our dataset is as follows: *light sleep* (N1+N2): 16.31%, *deep sleep* (N3): 45.52%, *REM*: 11.51%, and *wake*: 26.66%.

To investigate the effect of large and small student models we vary the amount of channels used to simulate different levels of access to wearable sensors. This results in four sensor configurations: In the most inclusive setup, we combine *Activity, Pulse Waveform, Saturation* (SpO_2)*, Audio Volume* and *PosAngle*, representing an idealized multi-sensor input setup that would be possible if all raw channels were accessible from the devices listed in Table 1. We also include a trimmed-down configuration, which is more commonly used by manufacturers, consisting of only *Activity, Pulse Waveform,* and *Saturation.* In cases where access to raw PPG is restricted, we resort to the *Heart Rate* signal, which is typically derived from the PPG internally and exposed to developers through official APIs [14]. This results in a minimal setup of *Activity* and *Heart Rate*, a configuration often found in commercial sleep tracking applications aand examined

Table 2. Model parameters of Teacher and Students

Parameter	Teacher/Large student	Small Student
Total Input Size	120 s	360 s
Resample Rate	100 Hz	10 Hz
Size of Final Classification Layer	512	128
Channel Dimensions	128, 256, 256, 512, 512	64, 128, 128
Kernel Size	5, 3, 3, 3, 2	5, 5, 3
Maxpool	5, 3, 3, 3, 2	5, 5, 3

[1] Ruhrlandklinik, Essen, Germany.

[2] https://noxmedical.com/downloads-row/.

in several validation studies [8]. Finally, we investigate a baseline configuration using only *Activity*, which corresponds to traditional motionbased sleep tracking.

In all experiments, the models use the UTime architecture described in Sect. 3.1, with the teacher being pre-trained on EEG data. The smaller student model is more suitable for deployment in wearable devices because of its reduced complexity. The larger student model, on the other hand, is architecturally aligned with the teacher, ensuring reliable feature matching. The architecture of the larger student and of the teacher features five encoder and five decoder blocks. In contrast, the smaller student has only three encoder and decoder blocks, reduced channel dimensions, and a smaller final classification layer. The large student model contains approximately 7.5 million parameters ($\approx$ 30 MB), while the small student has only 600,000 parameters ($\approx$ 2.4 MB), corresponding to a 12$\times$ reduction in model size. To compensate for its lower model capacity, the smaller student was trained on longer input sequences (6 instead of 2 min), providing more temporal context. Wearable input channels typically operate at sampling rates between 10 and 50 Hz. Among them, the optical heart rate sensor provides the highest internal resolution, but is often exposed externally at just 1 Hz [28]. Additionally, several sensors use adaptive sampling rates depending on activity or power constraints. To reflect this, we apply a more realistic resample rate of 10 Hz on all input channels in the smaller student model. These architectural and input-related differences are summarized in Table 2. All models were trained on the same train/test split, with 30% of the data dedicated to testing. Unless otherwise specified, the reported results are averages over five independent runs.

Table 3. General hyperparameters.

Hyperparameter	Search Space
Batch Size	{32, 64, 128}
Dropout Rate	[0.05, 0.45]
cre Weight Decay	{0.01, 0.05, 0.1}
Learning Rate	{0.0005, 0.001, 0.005, 0.01}
Scheduler	{LinearLR, OneCycleLR}
Scheduler Epochs	{15, 20, 25, 30}

Table 4. KD-specific hyperparameters.

KD Hyperparameter	Search Space
Feature Matching Loss	{MSE, Cosine}
Temperature	[1, 5]
HL Weighting	[0.0, 1.0]
SL Weighting	[0.0, 1.0]
BN Weighting	[0.0, 1.0]
PL Weighting	[0.0, 1.0]

To evaluate Hypothesis H1a and H1b, we aimed to achieve the best possible performance for both model sizes across all four configurations described earlier. General hyperparameters such as learning rate and batch size (Table 3) were manually tuned through repeated short optimization cycles. In contrast, KD-specific hyperparameters (Table 4) were optimized by a large-scale random search

[5]. The search space included: the temperature for soft target (sampled from a uniform range); the type of feature matching loss (mean squared error or cosine similarity); and the weighting of individual KD losses, sampled from a Dirichlet(0.5) distribution over the four loss components (soft targets, bottleneck feature matching, penultimate feature matching and hard targets), ensuring that all weights sum to one. Each configuration was sampled and evaluated 100 times per model size and channel setup.

To evaluate hypothesis H2, we additionally tested 11 interpretable combinations of KD loss weightings across all channel configurations. These settings were designed to analyze the contribution of the individual KD components and are listed in Table 6. Each combination was evaluated using both feature matching loss types (MSE and cosine similarity) and temperature values $T \in [1, 2.5, 5]$, resulting in 66 runs per model.

In all experiments we report the (averaged) accuracy, macro F1 score and Cohen's Kappa. Recall that Cohen's Kappa measures the agreement of the classifier with the true label, with respect to both labels randomly occurring. Hence, the default classifier that always predicts the majority class has a Cohen's Kappa of 0. Cohen's Kappa is particularly important for scoring sleep-related events, as it most naturally captures the workload placed on the human scorer that needs to potentially correct wrong labeling of an AI-system: If the AI-system is correct, no correction needs to occur. However, if the AI-system is wrong, it does not matter what (wrong) class was predicted, as the human scorer needs to perform a correction in any case.

All experiments have been carried out on a large compute cluster. Each experiment was executed on a single GPU. Depending on model size and configuration, runtime ranged from 2 to 5 h, with an average of approximately 2.5 h per run. In total, we executed around 1500 experiments, resulting in a cumulative compute time of approx. 3750 GPU hours.

4.1 H1: Effectiveness Across Channel Configurations and Model Sizes

To evaluate the impact of knowledge distillation across different input channel configurations, we compare models trained with and without KD for each configuration. Table 5 reports the test set performance of all student models before and after applying KD.

Table 5. Performance of the *Small* and *Large* student models before and after KD. The standard deviations are shown in small print after each value. Each cell shows the performance without KD (first line) and with KD (second line), with the absolute gain from KD in brackets. The performance of the teacher model (bottom row) is provided as a reference. Abbreviations: Act = Activity, PW = Pulse Waveform, Vol = Audio Volume, Pos = PosAngle, HR = Heart Rate

	Setting	Test Accuracy	Test F1-Macro	Test Cohen's κ
Small Student	Act, PW, Sat, Vol, Pos	66.96±0.73	0.629±0.008	0.496±0.011
		68.66±0.31 (+1.71)	**0.659**±0.003 (+0.030)	**0.525**±0.005 (+0.029)
	Act, PW, Sat	61.88±2.09	0.505±0.079	0.395±0.049
		65.68±0.39 (+3.81)	**0.623**±0.052 (+0.118)	**0.473**±0.010 (+0.078)
	Act, HR	61.58±0.36	0.548±0.004	0.401±0.005
		62.28±0.18 (+0.70)	**0.568**±0.006 (+0.020)	**0.421**±0.008 (+0.019)
	Act	56.09±0.21	0.349±0.010	**0.259**±0.005
		56.20±0.13 (+0.11)	**0.363**±0.009 (+0.015)	0.256±0.008 (−0.002)
Large Student	Act, PW, Sat, Vol, Pos	65.77±0.36	0.606±0.010	0.478±0.007
		67.03±0.25 (+1.26)	**0.622**±0.004 (+0.016)	**0.495**±0.006 (+0.017)
	Act, PW, Sat	63.58±0.31	0.575±0.011	0.439±0.006
		64.82±0.45 (+1.24)	**0.593**±0.009 (+0.017)	**0.455**±0.008 (+0.016)
	Act, HR	59.31±0.30	0.470±0.018	0.347±0.007
		59.41±0.16 (+0.10)	**0.515**±0.008 (+0.045)	**0.357**±0.004 (+0.010)
	Act	**55.30**±0.09	0.318±0.001	0.238±0.004
		55.13±0.07 (−0.17)	**0.354**±0.006 (+0.036)	**0.239**±0.006 (+0.001)
	Teacher Model	83.68	0.830	0.759

For both, the large and the small student models, KD consistently improves all three evaluation metrics across most configurations. The only exception is the minimal setup with *Activity* only, where the impact of KD is considerably smaller, affecting primarily the F1-macro score. In contrast, the largest improvements occur in the more complex channel configurations. While the overall performance is higher in the smaller student model, the relative improvements due to KD are comparable between the two model sizes. These results support both hypothesis H1 a), showing that KD improves model performance across input configurations, with stronger effects in sensor-rich settings. This performance gain is likely due to the fact that more diverse and informative signals provide more structure for the student to relate to the teacher's guidance. Hypothesis H1 b) is also being supported, as KD improves model performance regardless of student model size, making it a viable strategy for both high-capacity and resource-constrained deployments such as wearable devices. Interestingly, the smaller student outperformed the larger one overall. This may be due to its architecture being better suited to wearable inputs and its access to longer temporal context (360 s vs. 120 s).

The particularly strong performance increase observed for the *Activity, Pulse Waveform, Saturation* configuration is further examined in Sect. 4.3.

4.2 H2 - Effectiveness of Individual KD Components

Table 6 presents results from our second evaluation. For clarity, only results for the small student model using the *Act, PW, Vol, Sat, Pos* input configuartion are shown. Other settings yielded similar values.

Table 6. Absolute performance change (Test Accuracy, Test F1 Macro, Test Cohen's Kappa) under varying weighting strategies for soft targets, hard targets, and feature matching (BN = bottleneck, PL = penultimate layer). For clarity, only results for the small student with *Act, PW, Vol, Sat, Pos* are shown.

Setup	**Soft**	**Hard**	**BN**	**PL**	**Accuracy**	**F1 Macro**	**Cohen's κ**
Balance/Feature Emph.	**0.25**	**0.10**	**0.40**	**0.25**	+1.71	+0.030	+0.029
BN Only	**0.20**	**0.10**	**0.70**	**0.00**	+1.68	+0.030	+0.028
Soft Only	**1.00**	**0.00**	**0.00**	**0.00**	+1.17	+0.028	+0.027
PL only	**0.20**	**0.10**	**0.00**	**0.70**	+1.52	+0.023	+0.025
Equal Weighting	0.33	0.33	0.17	0.17	+1.27	+0.025	+0.025
Soft Dom.	0.60	0.20	0.10	0.10	+1.27	+0.022	+0.022
PL Emph.	0.15	0.20	0.25	0.40	+1.30	+0.024	+0.021
Feature dom.	0.10	0.10	0.40	0.40	+1.41	+0.023	+0.021
BN Emph.	0.15	0.20	0.40	0.25	+1.26	+0.021	+0.018
Feature Only	0.00	0.10	0.45	0.45	+0.55	+0.014	+0.011
Baseline	0.00	1.00	0.00	0.00	0.00	0.00	0.00

Configurations relying solely on soft targets performed well, ranking third by $Cohen's\kappa$, confirming the effectiveness of soft target KD. However, even stronger results were obtained when feature matching was applied either at the bottleneck (*BN Only*) or penultimate layer (*PL Only*). This highlights feature matching as a particularly effective component in our KD setup. The best performance was observed from configurations with balanced weighting (*Balance/Feature Emph.*), suggesting that combining soft targets and feature matching is most beneficial. These results support Hypothesis H2: each KD component contributes to improving student model performance. The effectiveness of feature matching likely comes from access to the teacher's internal representations, offering structural guidance that exceeds the information in soft predictions.

4.3 Exploratory: Mitigating Under and Overfitting with KD

This exploratory analysis, introduced as part of our extended evaluation, investigates how KD impacts unter- and overfitting in the small student model.

As noted in Sect. 4.1, the performance gain from KD in the *Activity, Pulse Waveform, Saturation* configuration is particularly strong (see Table 5). This setup tends to underfit, to explore this further, we increased the dropout rate.

As shown by the blue curve in Fig. 3(b), this resulted in poor respresentation learning and early stopping after 9 epochs. Applying KD mitigated this effect by providing additional guidance from the teacher that improves generalization and enabling training to continue until epoch 30 (dotted orange curve).

A different setup, shown in Fig. 3(a), illustrates the opposite case: KD reduces overfitting, allowing training to continue (dotted orange curve) instead of stopping early (blue curve). By going beyond hard labels, it guides the model away from simply memorizing training targets, promoting better generalization.

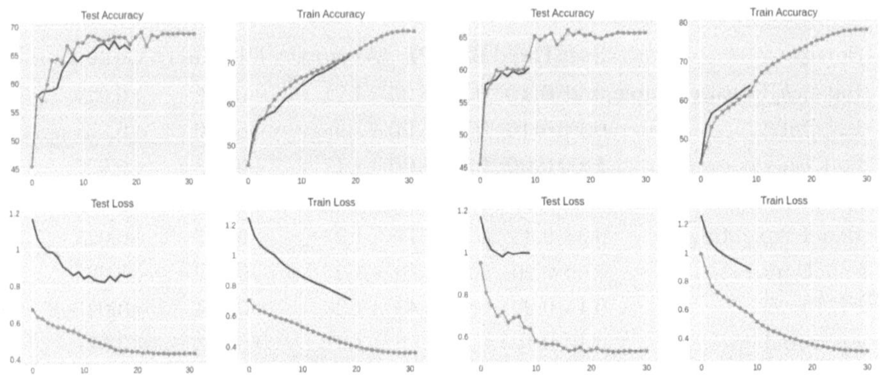

(a) Overfitting mitigation (b) Underfitting mitigation

Fig. 3. Effect of knowledge distillation (KD) on training. (a) KD reduces overfitting by improving generalization.. (b) KD mitigates underfitting in a small model with excessive dropout. Blue curves show baseline without KD, drotted orange curves show KD-trained model. X-axis: epochs; Y-axis: accuracy or loss. (Color figure online)

5 Conclusion

In this study, we investigated the use of knowledge distillation (KD) to enhance sleep stage classification from wearable sensor data. Using a teacher model trained on PSG data and a student model operating on wearable-like input, we demonstrated that KD reliably improves performance in multiple configurations. Both soft targets and feature matching contribute to these improvements, with feature matching being particularly effective. We further found that KD benefits both large and small student models, indicating its suitability for resource-constrained applications. The effectiveness of KD was especially present in settings with richer input signals, suggesting that students benefit more when they have sufficient sensory information to relate to the teacher's guidance. Together, these findings support the use of KD as an improvement strategy for sleep staging.

While our results are promising, the study is based on a single clinical dataset and simulated wearable inputs. Future work should validate the approach on additional datasets and real-world wearable hardware. The simulated signals used in this study only approximate the conditions of consumer-grade devices, which typically feature adaptive sampling rates and different sensor placements (e.g., fingertip vs. wrist) due to energy and form factor constraints. Moreover, raw PPG signals such as the Pulse Waveform are often not accessible in commercial devices, limiting the use of raw-signal deep learning. Future research should therefore examine how KD performs under such realistic constraints and evaluate models designed for real-time inference on wearable platforms.

References

1. Aboalayon, K.A.I., Faezipour, M., Almuhammadi, W.S., Moslehpour, S.: Sleep stage classification using EEG signal analysis: a comprehensive survey and new investigation. Entropy **18**(9) (2016)
2. Agnew, H.W., Webb, W.B., Williams, R.L.: The first night effect: an EEG study of sleep. Psychophysiology, 263–266 (1966)
3. Apple Inc.: Apple watch – data sheet. https://www.apple.com/apple-watch-series-10/specs/
4. Benjafield, A.V., et al.: Estimation of the global prevalence and burden of obstructive sleep apnoea: a literature-based analysis. Lancet Respir. Med. **7**(8), 687–698 (2019)
5. Bergstra, J., Bengio, Y.: Random search for hyper-parameter optimization. J. Mach. Learn. Res. **13**, 281–305 (2012)
6. Berry, R.B., et al.: The AASM manual for the scoring of sleep and associated events. Rules, Terminol. Tech. Specifications, Darien, Illinois, Am. Acad. Sleep Med. **176**, 2012 (2012)
7. Berry, R.B., et al.: The AASM Manual for the Scoring of Sleep and Associated Events: Rules, Terminology and Technical Specifications. American Academy of Sleep Medicine, Darien, IL, version 2.4 edn. (2017)
8. Birrer, V., Elgendi, M., Lambercy, O., Menon, C.: Evaluating reliability in wearable devices for sleep staging. NPJ Digit. Med. **7**(1) (2024)
9. Chinoy, E.D., et al.: Performance of seven consumer sleep-tracking devices compared with polysomnography. Sleep **44**(5) (2021)
10. Clevert, D., Unterthiner, T., Hochreiter, S.: Fast and accurate deep network learning by exponential linear units (ELUs). In: 4th International Conference on Learning Representations, ICLR (2016)
11. Dai, Z., Heckel, R.: Channel normalization in convolutional neural network avoids vanishing gradients. CoRR **abs/1907.09539** (2019)
12. Fiorillo, L., et al.: Automated sleep scoring: a review of the latest approaches. Sleep Med. Rev. **48**, 101204 (2019)
13. Fitbit (Google LLC): Fitbit sense 2 – data sheet (2025). https://store.google.com/de/product/fitbit_sense_2_specs?hl=de
14. Garmin Ltd.: Garmin health SDK overview (2025). https://developer.garmin.com/health-sdk/overview/. Accessed 17 June 2025
15. Google LLC: Pixel watch - data sheet. https://store.google.com/product/pixel_watch_2_specs?hl=en

16. Heinzer, R., et al.: Prevalence of sleep-disordered breathing in the general population: the HypnoLaus study. Lancet Respir. Med. **3**, 310–318 (2015)
17. Hinton, G.E., Vinyals, O., Dean, J.: Distilling the knowledge in a neural network. CoRR **abs/1503.02531** (2015)
18. Hossain, J.L., Shapiro, C.M.: The prevalence, cost implications, and management of sleep disorders: an overview. Sleep Breathing **6**(2), 85–102
19. Jadhav, P., Rajguru, G., Datta, D., Mukhopadhyay, S.: Automatic sleep stage classification using time–frequency images of cwt and transfer learning using convolution neural network. Biocybernetics Biomed. Eng. **40**(1), 494–504 (2020)
20. Kabir, M.M., et al.: Cardiorespiratory phase-coupling is reduced in patients with obstructive sleep apnea. PLoS ONE **5**(5), e10602 (2010)
21. Kapur, V.K., et al.: Clinical practice guideline for diagnostic testing for adult obstructive sleep apnea: an American academy of sleep medicine clinical practice guideline. J. Clin. Sleep Med., 479–504 (2017). https://doi.org/10.5664/jcsm.6506
22. Michielli, N., Acharya, U.R., Molinari, F.: Cascaded LSTM recurrent neural network for automated sleep stage classification using single-channel EEG signals. Comput. Biol. Med. **106**, 71–81 (2019)
23. Mousavi, Z., et al.: Deep convolutional neural network for classification of sleep stages from single-channel EEG signals. J. Neurosci. Methods **324**, 108312 (2019)
24. Perslev, M., et al.: U-Time: a fully convolutional network for time series segmentation applied to sleep staging. In: Advances in Neural Information Processing Systems, vol. 32 (NeurIPs) (2019)
25. Romero, A., et al.: FitNets: hints for thin deep nets. In: 3rd International Conference on Learning Representations, ICLR 2015 (2015)
26. Ronneberger, O., Fischer, P., Brox, T.: U-Net: convolutional networks for biomedical image segmentation. In: Navab, N., Hornegger, J., Wells, W.M., Frangi, A.F. (eds.) MICCAI 2015. LNCS, vol. 9351, pp. 234–241. Springer, Cham (2015). https://doi.org/10.1007/978-3-319-24574-4_28
27. Samsung Electronics: Samsung smartwatches – vergleich. https://www.samsung.com/de/watches/?product1=sm-l705fdaadbt&product2=sm-l315fzgadbt&product3=
28. Schweizer, T., Gilgen-Ammann, R.: Wrist-worn and arm-worn wearables for monitoring heart rate during sedentary and light-to-vigorous physical activities: device validation study. JMIR Cardio (2025)
29. Tamaki, M., Nittono, H., Hayashi, M., Hori, T.: Examination of the first-night effect during the sleep-onset period. Sleep, 195–202 (2005). https://doi.org/10.1093/sleep/28.2.195
30. Toussaint, M., et al.: First-night effect in normal subjects and psychiatric inpatients, pp. 463–469 (1995)
31. Wickwire, E.M., et al.: Older adult us Medicare beneficiaries with untreated obstructive sleep apnea are heavier users of health care than matched control0128 patients. J. Clin. Sleep Med. **16**, 81–89 (2020)
32. de Zambotti, M., Cellini, N., Goldstone, A., Colrain, I.M., Baker, F.C.: Wearable sleep technology in clinical and research settings. Med. Sci. Sports Exerc., 1538–1557 (2019)

Federated Markov Imputation: Privacy-Preserving Temporal Imputation in Multi-centric ICU Environments

Christoph Düsing(✉) and Philipp Cimiano

CITEC, Bielefeld University, Bielefeld, Germany
{cduesing,cimiano}@techfak.uni-bielefeld.de

Abstract. Missing data is a persistent challenge in federated learning on electronic health records, particularly when institutions collect time-series data at varying temporal granularities. To address this, we propose *Federated Markov Imputation* (FMI), a privacy-preserving method that enables *Intensive Care Units* (ICUs) to collaboratively build global transition models for temporal imputation. We evaluate FMI on a real-world sepsis onset prediction task using the MIMIC-IV dataset and show that it outperforms local imputation baselines, especially in scenarios with irregular sampling intervals across ICUs.

Keywords: Federated Learning · Data Imputation · Markov Chains

1 Introduction

Federated Learning (FL) has emerged as a privacy-preserving machine learning paradigm that allows multiple hospitals or *Intensive Care Units* (ICUs) to collaboratively train models without exchanging raw patient data [6]. This makes FL particularly attractive for high-stakes medical tasks such as predicting sepsis onset [3,8]. However, many clinical prediction tasks – including sepsis onset prediction – rely on time-series data, often incomplete due to irregular sampling or clinical priorities. In FL, the challenge of missing data is amplified because participants must agree on a uniform data format and time intervals. If hospitals collect data at different temporal granularities, coarser institutions must impute more data to align with the global format. This restricts the applicability of local imputation techniques, especially those relying on fine-grained temporal transitions, and necessitates the development of FL-specific imputation methods.

Related Work. While federated data imputation gained some attention in recent years, research in this area remains scarce. Initial approaches such as *Cafe* [7] propose federated imputation by modeling heterogeneity in missing data across silos. *FedBeat* [9] introduces transition-matrix-based modeling for noisy label correction but focuses on label noise rather than temporal features. Similarly, Gkillas et al. [4] propose federated time-series imputation for industrial

I. Koprinska et al. (Eds.): ECML PKDD 2025, CCIS 2842, pp. 187–191, 2026.
https://doi.org/10.1007/978-3-032-19105-2_14

settings using an jointly trained autoencoder. However, no work has yet considered the construction of *Federated Markov Chains* for imputation in time-series clinical FL settings, especially when facing different temporal granularities.

Contributions. To this end, we make the following contributions: (1) we propose *Federated Markov Imputation* (FMI), a privacy-preserving method for time-series data imputation in FL; (2) we apply FMI to a real-world sepsis prediction task under both uniform and heterogeneous temporal granularities; and (3) we show that FMI improves the predictive performance over two baselines, especially when facing heterogeneous time intervals among participating ICUs.

2 Federated Markov Imputation

The proposed method for FMI consists of three steps outlined in the following:

Step 1: Local Transition Matrix. Each ICU discretizes its local time-series data into n bins per feature and constructs a first-order Markov transition matrix $T_c \in \mathbb{R}^{n \times n}$, where $T_c(i, j)$ denotes the empirical probability of transitioning from bin i to j between adjacent time steps. Transitions are computed only from observed, non-missing data and remain local to the ICU.

Step 2: Federated Transition Matrix. Using *Secure Aggregation* [1], all ICUs contribute their local transition counts, which are masked and summed to compute a global transition matrix T_{fed}. The aggregation is performed without exposing individual ICU statistics, ensuring data privacy.

Step 3: Federated Markov Imputation. For each missing value, the ICU imputes the most likely bin using T_{fed} and the available temporal context. If both the preceding bin b_{t-1} and succeeding bin b_{t+1} are known, the missing bin b_t is selected as:

$$\hat{b}_t = \arg\max_j \; T_{\text{fed}}(b_{t-1}, j) \cdot T_{\text{fed}}(j, b_{t+1}) \tag{1}$$

This selects the bin that best fits the expected transitions on both sides. If only one neighbor is known, a single-directional transition is used. For consecutive missing values, the most probable path is inferred recursively. The final imputed value corresponds to the midpoint of the selected bin $\hat{b}_t$.

3 Preliminary Evaluation

3.1 Experimental Setup

Data Setting. This study utilized the *MIMIC-IV* dataset [5], containing both septic and non-septic patients admitted to one of seven ICUs, namely *Medical ICU* (MICU), *Medical/Surgical ICU* (MICU/SICU), *Surgical ICU* (SICU), *Trauma SICU* (TSICU), *Coronary Care Unit* (CCU), *Cardiac Vascular ICU* (CVICU), and *Neuro SICU* (NSICU). With respect to data acquisition and distribution, we follow the work of Düsing and Cimiano [2]. Specifically, we identify

28,610 patients relevant to the study and assign each patient to the ICU they were initially admitted to. Per patient, we identify 25 clinically relevant features, which are aggregated into six 1h windows following admission. The sepsis labels are assigned following the *Sepsis-3* definition, where each patient is labeled as positive if they developed sepsis within the first 30h of ICU admission.

During evaluation, we consider two temporal settings. In the *Regular* setting, all ICUs retain the hourly data. To simulate heterogeneous sampling in the *Irregular* setting, we randomly assign two ICUs to 2-hour and two to 3-hour intervals, removing intermediate values accordingly. This setup allows us to assess imputation performance under varying temporal granularities across ICUs.

Model Setting. In line with similar studies [2,8], we use an model consisting of an input layer, followed by three LSTM layers with 16 units each. Each LSTM layer includes batch normalization and a dropout of 0.2 to prevent overfitting. A subsequent linear layer reduces the dimensionality to 8 units, before a final linear layer provides a binary prediction indicating the likelihood of sepsis onset.

The model is trained for 50 rounds using *FedAvg* [6] as aggregation strategy.

Evaluation Setting. We compare our method using the *AUC* metric against two baselines: (1) *local mean* imputation, where missing values are filled using each ICU's feature-wise mean, and (2) *Local Markov Imputation* (LMI), which applies Markov-based imputation using each ICU's local transition matrix T_c. However, in the *Irregular* setting, LMI becomes infeasible for ICUs with 2h or 3h intervals, as they lack the hourly resolution needed for the federated training.

3.2 Performance Analysis

Table 1 presents the *AUC* scores across all ICUs. In the *Regular* setting, the main findings are: (1) FMI improves the mean AUC over both baselines, though the gains remain moderate; (2) FMI yields better performance than LMI for 5 out of 7 ICUs, while two ICUs benefit slightly more from using LMI; (3) all three imputation modes produce federated models with *AUC* ¿ 0.8, generally considered the threshold for clinical applicability [2].

In the *Irregular* setting, we observe the following: (1) overall performance declines compared to the *Regular* setting, which is expected due to increased scarcity and lower data resolution; (2) the performance of local mean imputation degrades more significantly, with the federated model falling below the clinical *AUC* threshold of 0.8; (3) performance becomes more uneven across ICUs – those with 1h intervals achieve similar or even better results than in the *Regular* setting, while those with 2h or 3h intervals show noticeable declines; (4) FMI reduces the negative impact of irregular sampling, especially for MICU/SICU and NSICU (3h intervals), where improvements are particularly pronounced.

Table 1. *AUC* for Sepsis Onset Prediction Using Different Imputation Modes Applied to Regular and Irregular Time Intervals (Best Performance in Bold and Underlined)

Time Intervals	Imputation Mode	MICU	MICU/SICU	SICU	TSICU	CCU	CVICU	NSICU	Mean
Regular	Local Mean	0.8520 ±0.00	0.8696 ±0.00	0.8931 ±0.00	0.9040 ±0.00	0.8549 ±0.00	0.5400 ±0.00	0.8454 ±0.00	0.8634 ±0.03
	LMI	0.8639 ±0.00	**0.8992** ±0.00	0.9039 ±0.00	0.8957 ±0.00	0.7986 ±0.00	**0.8250** ±0.00	0.8609 ±0.00	0.8710 ±0.01
	FMI (ours)	**0.8648** ±0.00	0.8950 ±0.00	**0.9074** ±0.00	**0.9162** ±0.00	**0.8314** ±0.00	0.8247 ±0.00	**0.8818** ±0.00	**0.8878** ±0.01
Irregular	Interval (h)	1h	3h	2h	1h	2h	1h	3h	n/a
	Local Mean	0.8738 ±0.00	0.5958 ±0.00	0.8607 ±0.00	0.8967 ±0.00	0.8180 ±0.00	0.7538 ±0.00	0.5180 ±0.00	0.7961 ±0.05
	LMI	n/a	n/a	n/a	n/a	n/a	n/a	n/a	n/a
	FMI (ours)	**0.9196** ±0.00	**0.8038** ±0.00	**0.8845** ±0.00	**0.9198** ±0.00	**0.8452** ±0.00	**0.7777** ±0.00	**0.8503** ±0.00	**0.8629** ±0.01

4 Conclusion and Outlook

We introduced FMI, a privacy-preserving method for time-series imputation in federated clinical settings. Our preliminary results on sepsis prediction show that FMI improves performance over both baselines, particularly under irregular sampling. These findings highlight the potential of FMI to harmonize heterogeneous clinical data and impute missing values without compromising privacy.

In future work, we aim to conduct more detailed analyses, extend comparisons with additional baselines, and validate FMI in a real-world clinical case-study.

References

1. Bonawitz, K., et al.: Practical secure aggregation for privacy-preserving machine learning. In: ACM SIGSAC Conference on Computer and Communications Security, pp. 1175–1191 (2017)
2. Düsing, C., Cimiano, P.: SHAP–FL: improving explainability for multicentric sepsis onset prediction through background dataset synthesis. In: International Conference on Artificial Intelligence in Medicine. Springer (2025)
3. Düsing, C., et al.: Integrating federated learning for improved counterfactual explanations in clinical decision support systems for sepsis therapy. Artif. Intell. Med. **157**, 102982 (2024)
4. Gkillas, A., Lalos, A.S.: Missing data imputation for multivariate time series in industrial IoT: a federated learning approach. In: 2022 IEEE 20th International Conference on Industrial Informatics (INDIN), pp. 87–94. IEEE (2022)

5. Johnson, A., Bulgarelli, L., Pollard, T., Horng, S., Celi, L.A., Mark, R.: MIMIC-IV (2022). https://doi.org/10.13026/rrgf-xw32
6. McMahan, B., Moore, E., Ramage, D., Hampson, S., y Arcas, B.A.: Communication-efficient learning of deep networks from decentralized data. In: Artificial Intelligence and Statistics, pp. 1273–1282. PMLR (2017)
7. Min, S., Asif, H., Wang, X., Vaidya, J.: Cafe: Improved federated data imputation by leveraging missing data heterogeneity. IEEE Trans. Knowl. Data Eng. (2025)
8. Mondrejevski, L., Azzopardi, D., Miliou, I.: Predicting sepsis onset with deep federated learning. In: Joint European Conference on Machine Learning and Knowledge Discovery in Databases, pp. 73–86. Springer (2023)
9. Wang, L., Bian, J., Xu, J.: Federated learning with instance-dependent noisy label. In: ICASSP 2024-2024 IEEE International Conference on Acoustics, Speech and Signal Processing (ICASSP), pp. 8916–8920. IEEE (2024)

Alignment of Multiple Item Set Sequences for Apnea Detection

Dries Van der Plas[1,2,3(✉)], Johan Verbraecken[2], Jesse Davis[3], and Wannes Meert[3]

[1] OSG bv, Natus Medical, 2550 Kontich, Belgium
dries.vanderplas@natus.com
[2] University of Antwerp, Antwerp University Hospital, 2000 Antwerp, Belgium
[3] Department of Computer Science, KU Leuven, Leuven.AI, 3000 Leuven, Belgium
{jesse.davis,wannes.meert}@kuleuven.be

Abstract. Sequence alignment is a powerful technique to compare and analyze sequential data, with applications in bioinformatics and signal processing. Traditional multiple sequence alignment (MSA) methods have a number of limitations that make them unsuitable for applications such as apnea detection in sleep medicine. First, the sequences need to be numerical or they are one-dimensional sequences of events. Apnea detection requires patterns across multiple dimensions of event sequences. Second, existing approaches are based on pairwise alignments. This puts too much focus on the alignment of all possible events in a pair of sequences. In apnea detection, however, the sequences contain many extraneous events, leading to a sparse set of relevant events. Furthermore, relevant events only manifest themselves when considering all sequences jointly. We present a novel multiple sequence alignment method that lifts these limitations. Our approach iteratively moves events across all sequences simultaneously to group identical events together. The direction in which to move events is based on the insight that event occurrences represent a density function and that a set of aligned sequences represents a sharply peaked density function. New sequences can be warped to a reference pattern using this density function. The efficacy of our new alignment method is shown in the apnea and hypopnea application.

Keywords: Multiple sequence alignment · Apnea detection

1 Introduction

One common type of sleep disorders is breathing disorders such as Obstructive Sleep Apnea Syndrome (OSAS). These are prevalent in the population and when undiagnosed, can have adverse consequences such as concentration problems or obesity [8]. People suspected of having a breathing disorder visit a sleep clinic, where they undergo a polysomnography (PSG), which records physiological signals during an overnight stay. When analyzing the PSG, trained medical experts indicate pathological breathing patterns according to specified medical scoring

I. Koprinska et al. (Eds.): ECML PKDD 2025, CCIS 2842, pp. 192–207, 2026.
https://doi.org/10.1007/978-3-032-19105-2_15

guidelines [1]. These patterns mainly include breathing interruptions (i.e., apnea) and periods of shallow breathing (i.e., hypopnea). Since this analysis can take up to one hour per patient, machine learning approaches have been proposed to automate this task. Common methods use classifiers such as deep learning methods on (complex) handcrafted features or on the raw signal data [2]. However, these methods are not understandable for medical experts which makes them reluctant to integrate the methods into their working routines.

Experts identify apnea and hypopnea episodes by searching for multiple, medically meaningful events. For example, the events characterizing an hypopnea episode include (a) a 30% decrease in the respiratory airflow, (b) a sudden increase in the brain activity, called an EEG arousal and (c) a 3% decrease in the patient's blood oxygen level. Therefore, designing an automated approach that is able to (a) recognize these events and (b) identify the patterns involving them that characterize apnea and hypopnea episodes would help promote a domain expert's understanding of the system.

This is a challenging problem. On the one hand, it requires finding patterns by relating events that occur in different signals, such as drops in the respiratory airflow and shifts in the brain activity. On the other hand, the patterns of interest exhibit significant variability: An apnea episode can, for instance, range from as short as ten seconds to as long as two minutes. One natural way to cope is to pursue a multiple sequence alignment based strategy. Unfortunately, existing approaches are not well suited to this specific use case for two reasons. First, the application requires modeling overlapping events that simultaneously appear in multiple time series (e.g., breaths appear simultaneously in the different signals). However, existing methods only focus on numeric sequences (e.g., using Graphical Time Warping [9] or DTW Barycentric Averaging [5]) or on sequences of items (e.g., Clustal algorithm in bioinformatics [3]). Second, conventional methods align either (a) all items in the sequences or (b) only a subset of key items identified by an initial pairwise sequence alignment (e.g., Clustal). However, the recorded signals in our application contain many events, of which only a sparse set is relevant for detecting apnea and hypopnea. Moreover, it is not possible to determine which items are relevant solely based on pairwise comparisons.

In this paper, we fill these gaps and propose a first multiple sequence alignment (MSA) algorithm that is able to align sequences of item sets. Our approach *simultaneously* aligns all sequences and can automatically determine an item's relevance. Intuitively, our algorithm is based on the observation that aligned sequences correspond to sharply peaked density functions. Moreover, we show that our approach is able to identify and align only the relevant items from a database containing many extraneous items. The efficacy of our new alignment method is proven in an apnea and hypopnea detection application.

2 Preliminaries

A sequence $s = <X_1, \ldots, X_m>$ is an ordered series of elements X_i with m the sequence length. Since the ordering is often related to time, we refer to the

Table 1. Sequence database before alignment.

Sequence \ Timestamp t	1	2	3	4	5	6
0	{A}	{}	{B}	{B}	{}	{}
1	{}	{A}	{}	{B}	{}	{A}
2	{A}	{}	{B}	{}	{A}	{}
3	{A}	{}	{}	{A,B}	{}	{A}
4	{A}	{}	{B}	{}	{}	{}
5	{A}	{A}	{A}	{A}	{A}	{A}

Table 2. Sequence database after alignment.

Sequence \ Timestamp t	1	2	3	4	5	6
0	{A}	{}	{B}	{}	{}	{}
1	{A}	{}	{B}	{}	{}	{A}
2	{A}	{}	{B}	{}	{}	{A}
3	{A}	{}	{A,B}	{}	{}	{A}
4	{A}	{}	{B}	{}	{}	{}
5	{A}	{}	{}	{}	{}	{A}

position indices $1, \ldots, m$ as (evenly spaced) timestamps and use t to denote the index. Sequence alignment is a powerful technique used to compare and analyze sequences of various kinds. Examples include numeric time series in speech recognition ($X_t \in \mathbb{R}^n$) [4] or series of items such as protein sequences in bioinformatics ($X_t \in I$ with $I = \{i_0, \ldots, i_p\}$ an alphabet) [7]. The data in our application is represented by a sequence of item sets, that is, $X_t \subset I$.

To reveal patterns in a set of sequences, $S = \{s_1, \ldots, s_n\}$, it helps to align the timestamps at which the items appear in the sequences. Take, for example, the sequences in Table 1. Items A and B appear at multiple timestamps when comparing the sequences. However, after aligning the items (i.e., moving the item sets along the time axis), the configuration in Table 2 can be obtained. This table reveals a more general pattern: item A appears at timestamp 1, followed by B at timestamp 3 and A at timestamp 6. This pattern was initially hidden due to the different positions and lengths of the patterns.

3 Alignment Methodology

We address the following problem
Given: A sequence database $S = \{s_1, \ldots, s_n\}$ with $X_t \subset I$ and I an alphabet
Do: Compute a database S' with aligned sequences.

To do so, we propose a multiple sequence alignment method which shifts and merges item sets iteratively, while retaining the items' (partial) order. The goal is to align as many identical items at the same timestamp as possible. In each iteration, our algorithm attempts to improve the alignment by moving every item set one step forward or backward by maximizing the reward function

$$\sum_{t=0}^{m} R_B(t)\mathbb{1}_{f(t)=-1} + R_F(t)\mathbb{1}_{f(t)=1}, \tag{1}$$

where R_B and R_F are the rewards of moving backward (B) and moving forward (F) and $\mathbb{1}$ is the indicator function on the warping function $f(t)$:

$$f(t) = \begin{cases} -1 & \text{if } X_t \text{ moves backward} \\ 0 & \text{if } X_t \text{ moves not} \\ 1 & \text{if } X_t \text{ moves forward} \end{cases} \tag{2}$$

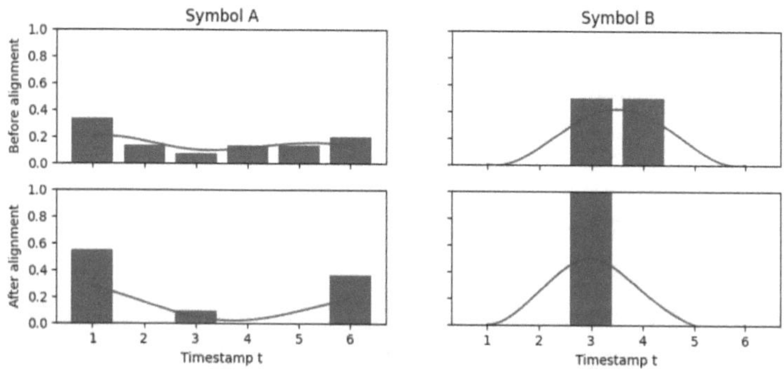

Fig. 1. Normalized counts (blue) and smoothed density function (red) before and after alignment for the sequences in Table 1 (upper) and Table 2 (lower). (Color figure online)

Based on a database of sequences, S, one step in the warping process (i.e., determining the optimal $f(t)$ and applying it to sequences $s \in S$) already improves the alignment. Because one warping step will not be sufficient to align the sequences, this procedure iterates until a stopping criterion is met (e.g., a stable configuration, a maximum number of iterations, or the improvement in the alignment between consecutive steps is smaller than a given threshold). The next paragraphs discuss the warping function and rewards in more detail.

Warping Function f. The warping function allows an item set to move one time step in each iteration of the alignment, that is, after one iteration, item set X_t will be in position $X_{t+f(t)}$. For example, a sequence $s = <\{A\}, \{B\}, \{C\}>$ with $f(1) = 1, f(2) = 0, f(3) = 0$ would result in the sequence $<\{\}, \{A, B\}, \{C\}>$. Hence, our method moves item sets over time and merges them (i.e., takes the union of the sets) if necessary.

Warping Rewards R. Our goal is to reveal patterns in a database of item sets by aligning identical items at the same timestamp. For each item i in a sequence database S, the number of occurrences per timestamp can be quantified by a density function $d_{i,S}$. Intuitively, the sequences are well aligned if $d_{i,S}$ is sharply peaked at certain time points. Indeed, a sharply peaked density means that the position of the item in the sequence is clearly specified and the uncertainty on an item's position is minimal. This behavior is also observed in Fig. 1 which shows the densities of items A and B for the sequences in our example database. Both densities become more sharply peaked after the alignment. We use this intuition to define the rewards R_B and R_F in Eq. 1.

When an item's density function is higher in an adjacent timestamp, moving the item towards this high-density region makes the density more sharply peaked. Consequently, such a move improves the alignment and should be rewarded. In contrast, a move to a region of lower density should be penalized (e.g., through a negative reward) as it would flatten the density function. Therefore, the reward for moving is proportional to the increase in density associated with that move. To account for the fact that an item set, can contain multiple events the reward is computed by summing over all items in X_t:

$$R_B(t) = \sum_{i \in X_t} d_{i,S}(t-1) - d_{i,S}(t) + \epsilon_i \tag{3}$$

$$R_F(t) = \sum_{i \in X_t} d_{i,S}(t+1) - d_{i,S}(t). \tag{4}$$

A small positive value ϵ_i is added if there are multiple consecutive timestamps with the same maximal density. In this case, item sets are encouraged to move towards the first timestamp of the plateau by increasing the backward rewards for the other timestamps in the plateau.

Both the forward and backward reward depend on the density function which can be estimated using standard techniques (e.g., kernel density estimation) but require special attention with our application in mind. This will be discussed in Sect. 3.1. Section 3.2 discusses the maximization of the reward function using dynamic programming, while Sect. 3.3 handles the inclusion of constraints, limiting the item sets that can be merged based on domain knowledge.

3.1 Density Function

Our method aims to align items over multiple sequences. Our approach is based on the density function $d_{i,S}$, the function indicating the fraction of appearances of item i at each timestamp t in a sequence database S. A simple estimate of the density function just *counts* the number of appearances at each time:

$$d_{i,S}(t) = \frac{1}{|i|} \sum_{s \in S} \mathbb{1}_{i \in s[t]} \tag{5}$$

with $|i|$ the number of appearances of i in S and $s[t]$ the tth item set in sequence s.

For apnea and hypopnea detection, we need to make three domain-specific modifications to the density function:

Uninformative Subsequences. First, some database sequences are uninformative for the item's position in the sequence. For example, in sequence 5 in Table 1, item A appears at every timestamp and does not provide information on the position of dense regions. To address this, we use the entropy to measure how informative a sequence is about an item i's position:

$$H_{i,s} = -\log_2\left(\frac{1}{\sum_{t=1}^{m} \mathbb{1}_{i \in X_t}}\right). \tag{6}$$

If the entropy is high, the position of the item in the sequence is unsure and the sequence should be downweighted. In the worst case, an item can appear at all m timestamps and the entropy reaches its maximum

$$H_{i,s,max} = -\log_2\left(\frac{1}{m}\right). \tag{7}$$

On the other hand, an entropy equal to 0 indicates that the item can only appear at a single position. The position is then perfectly predictable which should correspond to maximal weight. Hence, the weights of sequence s are given by

$$w_{i,s} = \begin{cases} 1 - \frac{H_{i,s}}{H_{i,s,max}} & \text{if } i \in s \\ 0 & \text{else.} \end{cases} \tag{8}$$

The weighted counts of an item i at time t are then given by

$$c_{i,S}(t) = \frac{1}{z} \sum_{s \in S} w_{i,s} \mathbb{1}_{i \in s[t]} \tag{9}$$

with z a constant such that $\sum_t c_{i,S}(t) = 1$ and $s[t]$ the tth item set in s.

Time Discretization. In our application, an item set consists of multiple events that occur during the same breath. However, the discretization procedure to determine the breath's boundaries is not perfect and items close to the boundary may be placed in the incorrect breath. Moreover, the signals might be captured asynchronously. These problems can be mitigated by employing a convolution with a zero-inflated block window with half width l_{block}. The block window puts a lower bound on the relevant time scale and hence, perturbations smaller than l_{block} become irrelevant. The zero-inflation assures that the density stays peaked.

Density Smoothing. A dense region only influences the rewards in neighboring (i.e., adjacent) timestamps, which may be overly myopic. We address this by applying density smoothing, which enables the rewards to capture the fact that there is a dense region several timestamps away. This can be done using a convolution with a Gaussian-like window function, similar to kernel density estimation approaches. A Hann window with half width l_{hann} ensures that the window function is smooth but also bounded. The influence of nearby item sets therefore gradually decreases until becoming 0 after l_{hann} timestamps. Figure 2 shows examples of a zero-inflated block window and a Hann window.

The final density function is then given by

$$d_{i,S}(t) = \sum_{j=-l_{hann}}^{l_{hann}} w_{hann}(j) \sum_{k=-l_{block}}^{l_{block}} w_{block}(k) c_{i,S}(t+j+k) \tag{10}$$

with

$$w_{hann}(j) = \frac{1}{l_{hann}} cos^2\left(\frac{\pi j}{2 l_{hann}}\right) \quad \text{and} \quad w_{block}(k) = \frac{1}{2}\mathbb{1}_{k=0} + \frac{1}{2(2 l_{block}+1)}.$$

3.2 Dynamic Programming

The maximization of the reward function in Eq. 1 can be calculated recursively using dynamic programming. In the tth step, we calculate the cumulative rewards

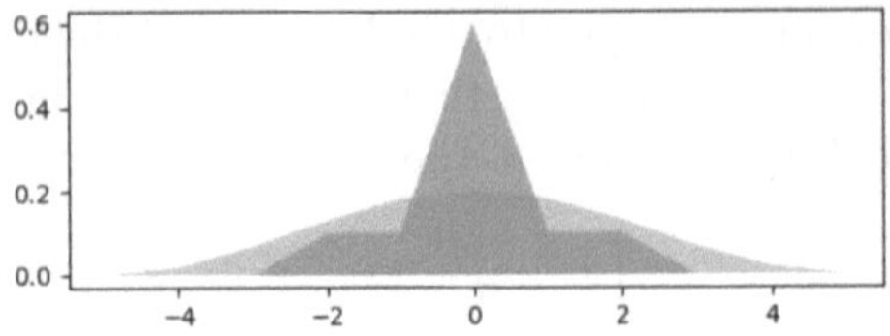

Fig. 2. Zero-inflated block window with $l_{block} = 2$ (blue) and Hann window with $l_{hann} = 5$ (orange). (Color figure online)

of warping the t first item sets in case the tth item set moves backwards (B), moves not (N) and moves forwards (F). These rewards are stored, respectively, at position t in cumulative reward vectors V_B, V_N and V_F. During the dynamic programming, we use three constraints

- The first item set cannot move backwards (i.e., $V_B[0] = -\infty$);
- The last item set cannot move forwards (i.e., $V_F[m] = -\infty$);
- The warping should retain the item's (partial) order (i.e., a backward move at time t cannot be combined with a forward move at time $t-1$).

The rewards can then be calculated recursively with

$$V_B[0] = -\infty, \quad V_N[0] = 0, \quad V_F[0] = R_F(0), \tag{11}$$

and

$$\begin{aligned} V_B[t] &= max(V_B[t-1], V_N[t-1]) && + R_B(t) \\ V_N[t] &= max(V_B[t-1], V_N[t-1], V_F[t-1]) && \\ V_F[t] &= max(V_B[t-1], V_N[t-1], V_F[t-1]) && + R_F(t). \end{aligned} \tag{12}$$

The maximal reward of the entire warping is then equal to $max(V_B[m], V_N[m])$ and the optimal warping itself can be obtained by backtracking which rewards contributed to the total reward at each timestamp. This leads to the optimal warping function f. The computational complexity of this approach is $O(nm)$ with n the number of sequences to be aligned and m the sequence length.

3.3 Additional Constraints

Apart from the general constraints, additional constraints can be added that allow us to exclude unwanted warpings. We give two examples:

- *Impossible item set constraint*: Some item sets could be undesirable, e.g., item sets containing conflicting information. If, for example, an item set containing both items A and B is undesirable, a (sub)sequence $<\{A\}, \{B\}>$ may not be warped to $<\{\}, \{A, B\}>$, nor to $<\{A, B\}, \{\}>$.
- *Max merging constraint*: This constraint allows merging items only if none of the symbols is merged more than k times. Hence, this constraint puts a limit on the warping factor. For example, for $k = 2$, $<\{A\}, \{A\}, \{A\}, \{A\}>$ can result after warping in $<\{\}, \{A\}, \{A\}, \{\}>$ after which the warping process stops.

Adding these constraints into the dynamic programming is straightforward since it is only necessary to eliminate the impossible terms in Eq. 12. As an example, we take the impossible item set constraint for sequence $s = <\{\}, \{A\}, \{B\}>$ where A and B cannot be in the same item set. The combination of not moving A ($V_N[1]$) with a backward move of B ($V_B[2]$) is not allowed, so this term should be omitted. Similarly, a forward move of A ($V_F[1]$) without a move of B ($V_N[2]$) is not allowed. Hence, the modified formula of Eq. 12 becomes

$$\begin{aligned} V_B[2] &= max(V_B[1], \cancel{V_N[1]}) &&+ R_B(2) \\ V_N[2] &= max(V_B[1], V_N[1], \cancel{V_F[1]}) && \\ V_F[2] &= max(V_B[1], V_N[1], V_F[1]) &&+ R_F(2). \end{aligned} \tag{13}$$

The other steps in the dynamic programming remain unchanged.

4 Application: Apnea and Hypopnea Detection

In this section, we experimentally show the efficacy of our proposed multiple sequence alignment (MSA) methodology on the detection of apnea and hypopnea episodes in sleep studies.

4.1 Dataset

We use a dataset containing polysomnographies (PSGs) obtained from 10 medical centers in Belgium, the Netherlands and Austria. Patients were monitored in these centers on suspicion of both breathing and non-breathing sleep disorders. Each PSG contains four respiratory signals that measure the patient's breathing directly (i.e., cannula, thermistor, abdomen and thorax signals) along with additional signals (e.g., EEG, oxygen saturation). By removing PSGs without thermistor or cannula signal or without annotations, we obtain a dataset containing 1150 PSGs. This set is divided in a training and test set, each containing half of the PSGs. The average age of the patients was 46 years (min. 5, max. 89). On average, a patient suffers 2.7 apnea and 7.6 hypopnea per hour of sleep.

4.2 Item Set Construction

The alphabet I and item sets should be chosen such that the medical scoring rules can be expressed. Hence, the alphabet contains items symbolizing the main events defined in these rules. Furthermore, each item set contains items related to a single breath of the patient. The item set construction consists of four main steps: 1) determining the item set borders, 2) identifying items from the respiratory channels, 3) smoothing the items from the respiratory channels and 4) adding items from the non-respiratory signals. The next paragraphs discuss each step in more detail.

Item Set Segmentation. Apnea and hypopnea episodes are characterized by missed or shallow breaths. To be able to detect these in our data representation, each item set contains the events related to a single breath of the patient. Hence, we first segment the time dimension and determine the segment borders as the times in between two consecutive breaths.

The patient's breathing is mainly measured by the thermistor and the cannula sensors. For each of the sensors, normal breathing results in sinusoidal waves with the amplitude expressing the breath's strength. An example can be found in Fig. 3. To determine the segment borders, we use a three step approach.

In a first step, we determine the times related to maximal breathing in the signal data $h(t)$ for both the thermistor and cannula signal, using a peak detection algorithm. The detected peaks are indicated by the blue and green squares in Fig. 3 for the cannula and thermistor respectively. The peak times of both signals are matched and the average time is taken for each breath, leading to breath times t_i. In a second step, the borders are placed in the middle points between these breath times, (i.e., $(t_i + t_{i+1})/2$). These segment borders are indicated in Fig. 3 by the vertical dashed line. In a third step, we add extra borders. In case of shallow or no breathing, it might after all be that no peak is detected in either of the signals. Therefore, we determine the length of the ith interval, $\Delta t_i = t_{i+1} - t_i$, and compare it to the expected length, $\Delta t_{i,exp}$, defined as the rolling trimmed mean with size 50 and proportion cut 0.50. The ratio $\Delta t_i / \Delta t_{i,exp}$ then indicates how many borders are expected during this interval and extra borders are added if necessary.

Respiratory Items. For each of the four main respiratory signals in a PSG, the peak height in the signal relative to a local baseline value is important to be able to express apnea and hypopnea patterns. Hence, we should introduce items expressing the relative peak heights.

For a signal $h(t)$, we define the peak height h_i in segment i as the 95th percentile of $h(t)$ in interval $[t_{i-1}, t_i]$ divided by a rolling median such that a value of 1 indicates normal breathing compared to the local baseline.

Discretization is necessary to transform the peak heights of a signal to an alphabet of items. Therefore, we use a set of logarithmically spaced breakpoints $\{\beta_0, \ldots, \beta_p\}$ with $\beta_{i+1}/\beta_i = \rho$ which makes it able to observe relative decreases in peak amplitude. A symbol is assigned to each peak based on the peak height:

$$i = \begin{cases} i_0 & \text{if } h_i \in [\beta_0, \beta_1[\\ \ldots & \\ i_{p-1} & \text{if } h_i \in [\beta_{p-1}, \beta_p[. \end{cases} \tag{14}$$

The symbols $i_0, \ldots, i_{p-1}$ are added to the alphabet I. This transformation into symbols is done for each of the four respiratory signals where each signal results in a different set of symbols. In Fig. 3, these items are indicated by symbols i_0 to i_5 for the cannula signal and i'_0 to i'_5 for the thermistor. The breakpoints used for discretization are shown by the horizontal gray lines.

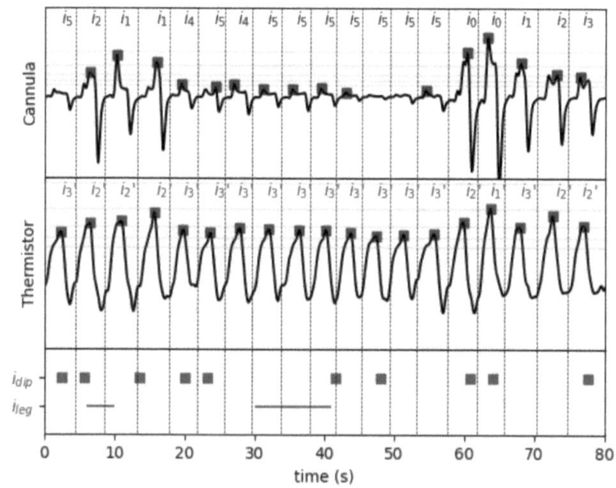

Fig. 3. Example on the item set construction for PSG data. A sample of the thermistor and cannula signal are shown (black) and the peaks are detected (squares). These peaks are used to determine the item set borders (dashed vertical lines). The peaks are discretized based on logarithmic scale (horizontal lines) leading to items i_0 to i_5. Items originating from the non-respiratory signals are added (red). The item set can then be read based on the border times. The sequence of item sets becomes $<\{i_5, i_3', i_{dip}\}, \{i_2, i_2', i_{dip}, i_{leg}\}, \{i_1, i_2', i_{leg}\}, \ldots, \{i_3, i_2', i_{dip}\}>$. (Color figure online)

Item Smoothing. The influence of the discretization can be significant. A small perturbation in the peak heights h can, for instance, lead to an entirely different itemization. For example, a sequence $<\{i_0\}, \{\}, \{i_3\}>$ could transform into $<\{i_1\}, \{\}, \{i_4\}>$ due to a small perturbation in the signal. Therefore, we smooth the pattern and add the items of the intermediate heights. These sequence become $<\{i_0, i_1, i_2\}, \{i_1, i_2\}, \{i_3\}>$ and $<\{i_1, i_2, i_3\}, \{i_2, i_3\}, \{i_4\}>$ which have more items in common.

Non-respiratory Items. Besides the items from the respiratory signals, extra items are necessary to detect the apnea episodes. Items i_{start} and i_{end} indicate the start and end points of the apnea and hypopnea episodes, provided by medical experts. Furthermore, items identifying a dip in the oxygen saturation (i_{dip}), items indicating EEG arousals ($i_{arousal}$), items for a leg movement (i_{leg}) are added as well as an item indicating that the patient is awake (i_{awake}). The start and end point of the apnea and hypopnea episodes as well as i_{leg} are at a fixed time, hence, the corresponding items are added to the item set at that time. The other events all have a certain duration that can span multiple segments. Therefore, an item will be added to each item set in which a part of the event takes place, such as illustrated at the bottom of Fig. 3.

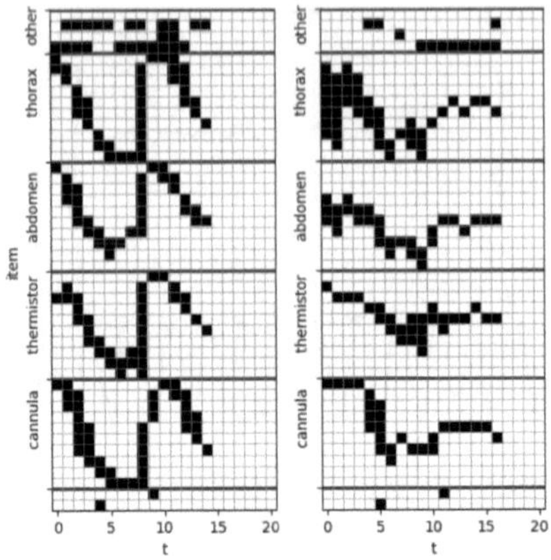

Fig. 4. Examples of training sequences containing an apnea (left) and hypopnea (right) episode. The items include, from bottom to top, i_{start}, i_{end}, i_0 to i_9 indicating the amplitude for each of the four respiratory signals, $i_{dip}, i_{arousal}, i_{leg}$, and i_{awake}. If an item is present in an item set, the cell is colored black.

4.3 Database Construction

For each PSG, we transform the raw data into a sequence of item sets as discussed in Sect. 4.2. The item sets contain 46 different items: i_{start} and i_{end} indicating the position of the apnea (or hypopnea) episodes; for each of the four respiratory signals h, items $i_{h,0}$ to $i_{h,9}$ indicating the amplitude; $i_{dip}, i_{arousal}, i_{leg}$, and i_{awake} events from the non-respiratory signals.

To align apnea and hypopnea patterns, sequence databases S_{apnea} and $S_{hypopnea}$ are constructed which contain all apnea and hypopnea subsequences from the training set. For each apnea in our training data, we add a sequence to S_{apnea} starting 5 timestamps before i_{start} and ending 5 timestamps after i_{end} such that the entire pattern is contained in the subsequence. If necessary, we extend the sequences with empty item sets such that each sequence has an equal size. Hence,

$$\forall t: \text{ if } i_{start} \in X_t \text{ and } i_{end} \in X_{t+l} \Rightarrow \{X_{t-5}, \ldots, X_{t+l+5}, \{\}, \ldots, \{\}\} \in S. \quad (15)$$

The total size of database S_{apnea} is equal to 12,540 and similarly a database $S_{hypopnea}$ containing 39,818 sequences can be obtained for the hypopnea episodes. Furthermore, we construct a control database S_{none} containing 10,000 sequences randomly sampled from the training data where the sequences do not contain an apnea or hypopnea episode.

Figure 4 visualizes an example of a sequence from S_{apnea} and one from $S_{hypopnea}$. The different items are shown on the vertical axis and a cell is colored black if the item is present at timestamp t, on the horizontal axis.

For the apnea sequence, we expect the amplitude in the respiratory signals to decrease significantly at the start of the apnea episode (t=4) and normal breathing to resume after the apnea episode ends (t=9). Due to the way in which we defined the items in the respiratory channels, this is observed in the figure by a v-shaped pattern. The items related to strong breathing are present before and after the apnea period while items related to weak or absent breathing appear during the apnea period.

The hypopnea example contains a drop in the amplitudes of the respiratory signals as well. However, this drop is less prominent than for apnea, as could be expected. Therefore, the v-shaped pattern is less visible.

4.4 Multiple Sequence Alignment

In this section, we apply our multiple sequence alignment method to align the sequences in S_{apnea} and $S_{hypopnea}$ and compare them with the control database S_{none}. Moreover, we interpret the results obtained.

To learn the warping, we allow 20 iterations of the warping procedure. We set l_{hann} equal to 5 in the first iteration but let it decrease linearly to 1, l_{block} is set to 3. Furthermore, we add 3 constraints:

- A max merging constraint with $k = 5$ which puts a local limit on the contraction factor as described in Sect. 3.3;
- An impossible item set constraint disallowing to merge i_{start} and i_{end};
- An impossible item set constraint disallowing to merge sets of which the peak heights are too different, e.g., an item set with shallow breathing and an item set with strong breathing cannot be merged.

Figure 5 shows the density functions obtained after warping for training on S_{apnea} (left), $S_{hypopnea}$ (middle) and S_{none} (right). The apnea start i_{start} is sharply peaked at time $t = 4$ and the apnea end at $t = 9$. The warping methodology thus succeeds in aligning all apnea episodes in the database, even though their lengths differed before alignment.

The learned apnea pattern corresponds to the expected medical behavior: items representing high-amplitude breathing are observed before the start of the apnea episode, followed by a sharp decrease towards this starting point. During the apnea period, the amplitude of the cannula signal is minimal, and the other signals also correspond to shallow or no breathing. After the apnea period ends, many scenarios are possible such as the resumption of normal breathing or a consecutive apnea episode. Hence, the pattern is less sharp in this region.

For hypopnea, a similar behavior is observed. The start and end point of the apnea period are well aligned. Furthermore, the pattern shows that the amplitude in all four respiratory signals decreases during the hypopnea episode. However, this decrease is less significant than for apnea. Figure 5 (right) shows the learned density on database S_{none} containing 10,000 sequences without apnea or hypopnea. On this control database, no pattern is learned and the warping just contracts the item sets, as could be expected. Further contraction is prohibited by the max merging constraint.

Figure 6 (left) shows the total reward (see Eq. 1) per iteration when aligning S_{apnea} (blue) and $S_{hypopnea}$ (orange). The first couple of iterations yield a large

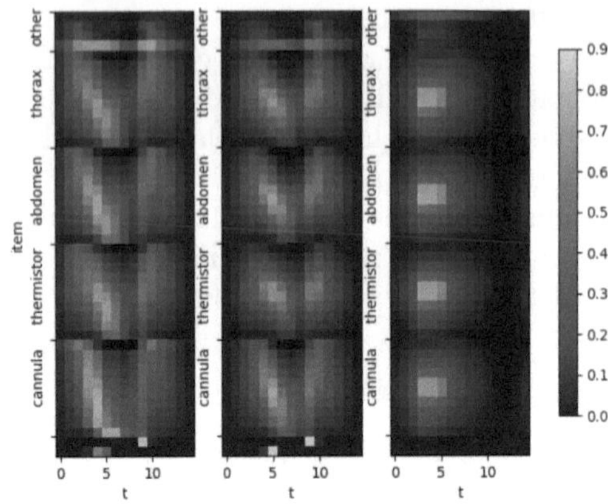

Fig. 5. Warped density functions for all 46 items after training on S_{apnea} (left), $S_{hypopnea}$ (middle) and S_{none} (right). The items include, from bottom to top, i_{start}, i_{end}; i_0 to i_9 indicating the amplitude in the four respiratory signals; and the remaining items ($i_{dip}, i_{arousal}, i_{leg}, i_{awake}$).

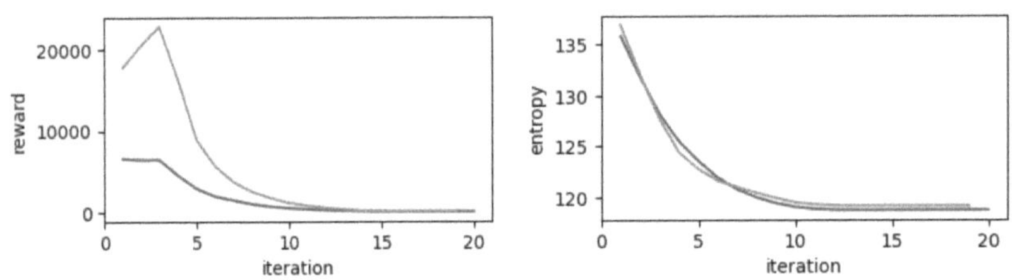

Fig. 6. Evolution of the total reward (left) and entropy (right) per iteration when aligning S_{apnea} (blue) and $S_{hypopnea}$ (orange). (Color figure online)

reward, indicating the initial moves greatly improve the alignment. In subsequent iterations, the reward (rapidly) decreases indicating that these steps focus more on fine-tuning the alignment. For apnea, a zero reward is obtained after 19 iterations, indicating convergence. The alignment procedure stops for hypopnea after reaching the maximum number of iterations (20).

Figure 6 (right) shows the evolution of the entropy

$$H = -\sum_i \sum_t d_{i,S}(t) log(d_{i,S}(t)). \quad (16)$$

per iteration. The entropy decreases during the warping, indicating that each step decreases the uncertainty about the item's position in the sequences. This is precisely the desired behavior. Since items can appear at multiple positions in the pattern and not all items are relevant for the patterns of interest, the entropy is not expected to approach zero.

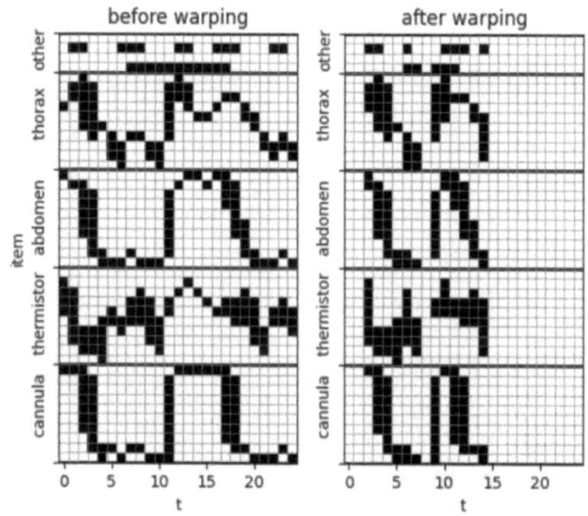

Fig. 7. Representation of a sequence containing an apnea, before (left) and after warping (right). The items include, from bottom to top, i_0 to i_9 indicating the amplitude for each of the four respiratory signals, $i_{dip}, i_{arousal}, i_{leg}$, and i_{awake}. If an item is present in an item set, the cell is colored black.

4.5 Pattern Recognition in New Sequences

In the previous section, we warped the different sequences in the training databases to be more alike and as such, to identify patterns for apnea and hypopnea episodes. In this section, we try to match a new and unlabeled sequence of item sets with these learned patterns. This can help to see whether the new sequence contains an apnea or hypopnea episode.

Given an unseen sequence, such as in Fig. 7 (left), we want to map it to the learned apnea pattern, i.e., to the density function $d_{i,S}$ obtained in the previous section. To do so, we keep $d_{i,S}$ fixed and warp the sequence using the dynamic programming explained in Sect. 3.2. The result is shown in Fig. 7 (right). The initial peak drop was rather long before the alignment and has now shrinked to times 5 to 9. This warped pattern overlaps largely with the learned density function such that the sequence could be recognized as containing an apnea episode.

To analyze the raw sensor data obtained from a entire PSG, the item set representation should be determined first. This can be done as discussed in Sect. 4.2. Afterwards, the data can be split into overlapping sequences with sufficiently large lengths such that the sequence can span the entire pattern of interest (e.g., 25 for apnea). These sequences can then be warped and compared to the learned densities to determine whether they contain an apnea or hypopnea episode.

We apply this procedure to all PSGs in our test set, that is, the PSGs not used to obtain the density functions. Figure 8 (left) shows the average over all sequences containing an apnea episode (i.e., with i_{start} within the first 10 item sets). Even though we only visualize the sequences containing an apnea episode, no pattern is visible before warping (left figure) and the items appear rather

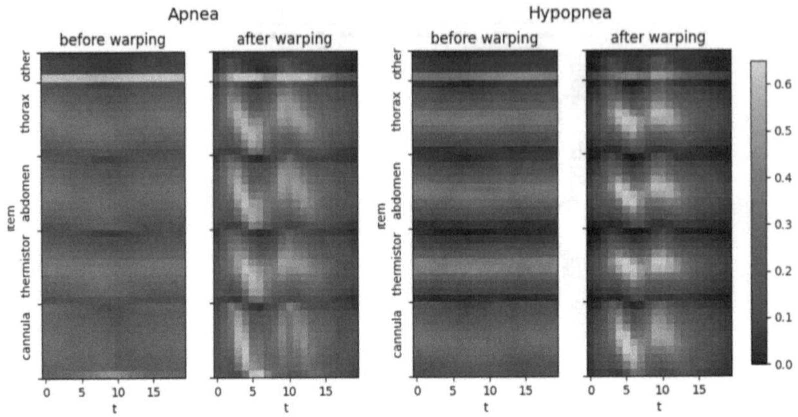

Fig. 8. Average occurrences of the items over all sequences from the test set containing an apnea (left) or hypopnea (right) episode, before and after warping.

uniformly throughout the sequence. This can be explained due to the varying (and unknown) start times and lengths of the apnea episodes. This makes it challenging to individually compare the sequences with the learned apnea pattern.

The second plot shows the result after warping the sequences by the learned apnea density. We observe that some events are highlighted at certain timestamps, indicating that they are common at that timestamp in many of the sequences. Medical experts confirm that the sequence of these highlighted events exactly corresponds to the expected apnea pattern. Hence, our alignment method can be used to facilitate the recognition of apnea in a medically meaningful way.

A similar analysis is performed for the hypopnea episodes. Figure 8 (right) shows that the alignment can reveal the hypopnea pattern in the new sequences as well.

5 Conclusions

The existing methods for multiple sequence alignment have multiple limitations which make them unsuitable to be used for applications such as apnea and hypopnea detection in sleep medicine. First, they only focus on numerical sequences or one-dimensional sequences of items. Second, the methods mainly use approaches that are based on pairwise alignments and therefore focus on the alignment of all items in the sequences. However, in our application, the sequence contains many extraneous items which are not part of the pattern of interest that repeats over all sequences (e.g., an apnea).

In this paper, we presented a novel multiple sequence alignment method that lifts these limitations. Our approach intuitively learns a density function for each pattern by iteratively warping the item sets where identical items are shifted towards the same timestamp. As a result, a sharply peaked density function is obtained in which the patterns could be observed more clearly. This density function can then be used to align new unseen data and to investigate whether the pattern is present.

We showed that this alignment method works well in our application of interest and that apnea and hypopnea patterns could be revealed. Verifying sequence alignment methods is often challenging as the ideal alignment is unknown. Therefore, standard approaches in bioinformatics focus on using (1) alignment scores, (2) visual evaluations by domain experts and (3) benchmark datasets for evaluation [6]. In this paper, we verified our method in two ways. First, we showed that our alignment decreases the entropy, and hence, the uncertainty on the items' position in the sequence. Second, we used a visual approach which can easily be interpreted by domain experts. Future research might focus on using the aligned sequences to perform apnea-hypopnea classification, a task which can be verified using standard metrics, such as accuracy.

Acknowledgments. DV received financial support of VLAIO (Flemish Innovation & Entrepreneurship) through the Baekeland PhD mandate [HBC.2019.2615]. JD and WM received funding from the Flemish Government under the "Onderzoeksprogramma Artificiële Intelligentie (AI) Vlaanderen" programme.

Disclosure of Interests. The authors have no competing interests to declare that are relevant to the content of this article.

References

1. Berry, R., et al.: The AASM Manual for the Scoring of Sleep and Associated Events: Rules, Terminology and Technical Specifications. American Academy of Sleep Medicine, 2.6 edn. (2020)
2. Chyad, M.H., Gharghan, S.K., Hamood, H.Q.: A survey on detection and prediction methods for sleep apnea. IOP conference series. Mater. Sci. Eng. **745**(1), 12102 (2020)
3. Higgins, D.G., Sharp, P.M.: Clustal: a package for performing multiple sequence alignment on a microcomputer. Gene **73**(1), 237–244 (1988)
4. Jensen, K., Stephanopoulos, G.: Bioinformatics and handwriting/speech reconition: uncoventional applications of similarity search tools (2006)
5. Petitjean, F., Ketterlin, A., Gançarski, P.: A global averaging method for dynamic time warping, with applications to clustering. Pattern Recogn. **44**(3), 678–693 (2011)
6. Ranwez, V., Chantret, N.N.: Strengths and limits of multiple sequence alignment and filtering methods. In: Phylogenetics in the Genomic Era, pp. 2.2:1–2.2:36 (2020)
7. Thompson, J.D.: Statistics for Bioinformatics: Methods for Multiple Sequence Alignment. iSTE Press, London, England (2016–2016)
8. Verbraecken, J., Buyse, B., Hamburger, H., van Kasteel, V., van Steenwijk, R.: Sleep and sleep disorders: a practical handbook. Acco, Leuven (2019)
9. Wang, Y., Miller, D.J., Poskanzer, K., Wang, Y., Tian, L., Yu, G.: Graphical time warping for joint alignment of multiple curves. In: Advances in Neural Information Processing Systems, vol. 29 (2016)

On the Role of Prognostic Factors and Effect Modifiers in Unraveling Population Heterogeneity

Rianne M. Schouten(✉)

Eindhoven University of Technology, Eindhoven, The Netherlands
r.m.schouten@tue.nl

Abstract. Causal effects vary across subgroups in a population. This is especially true for treatment effects in the medical setting where context information like family history, medical history and symptom presentation influence and explain differences between individuals. Estimating these local, causal treatment effects is not straightforward, especially since the covariate (context) information may i) interact with the outcome and/or treatment variable, ii) be measured at a lower hierarchical level than the level of the individual, and iii) contain high dimensional observations. In this paper, we perform two synthetic data experiments to further analyze and provide insights into the behavior of two types of non-confounding covariates: *effect modifiers* influence the treatment effect and *prognostic factors* influence the outcome variable, but not the treatment effect. We temporarily disregard the fundamental problem of causal inference that factual and counterfactual outcomes cannot be observed together, and generate synthetic data where treatment assignment variable W is considered a time-variant variable: the outcome value is observed for every occasion (treatment) for every patient. Consequently, we obtain a hierarchical dataset where outcomes (and possibly, covariates) reside at a lower hierarchical level than the treatment effects, which reside at the level of the individual. Our findings from controlled experiments provide 1) a demonstration of existing knowledge that prognostic factors reduce left-over variance and improve precision, whereas effect modifiers determine and explain individual-specific deviations, and 2) an additional insight that in order to unravel population heterogeneity, aggregations of lower-level, high-dimensional observations should align with (possibly unknown) expectations about whether these observations display prognostic or effect modification behavior.

Keywords: Prognostic Factors · Effect Modifiers · Individual Treatment Effects · Multilevel Data · Synthetic Data Study

1 Introduction

People differ, not only in physical appearance but in personality, cultural background, abilities and interests, as well as in cognitive, emotional and social behavior [1,2,8,14]. This is particularly apparent in the medical setting, where

I. Koprinska et al. (Eds.): ECML PKDD 2025, CCIS 2842, pp. 208–223, 2026.
https://doi.org/10.1007/978-3-032-19105-2_16

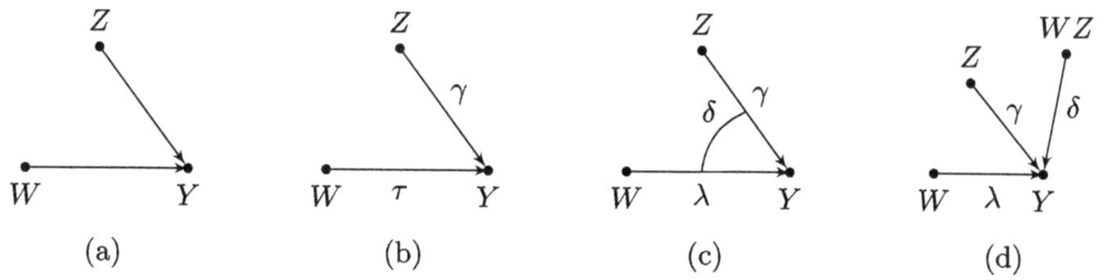

Fig. 1. Causal diagrams with three variables: outcome Y, treatment assignment W and covariate Z (a) no structural restrictions; Z can be a prognostic factor, effect modifier or both (b-d) the causal relations are assumed to be linear (b) Z is a prognostic factor (c) Z is an effect modifier, diagram cf. [37] (d) Z is an effect modifier, a variation of the diagram cf. [30].

context information like family history, medical history and symptom presentation influence and explain differences between individuals, including differences in causal treatment effects [10,41]. Considering such patient population heterogeneity, estimating Local or Conditional Average Treatment Effects (LATE, CATE) [22,41,48] for certain subgroups in the population is to be preferred over estimating an Average Treatment Effect (ATE) that aggregates over all individuals. Recent advances in Machine Learning (ML) move even further and estimate Individual Treatment Effect (ITE) [5,17,20,43,44,47].

A complicating factor in estimating treatment effects is the possibly nested, non-IID structure of observed covariate information. For instance, blood sampling tests may be repeated for each hospital visit, or blood glucose measurements are continuously taken using a FreeStyle Libre sensor, an intermittently continuous glucose monitoring (iCGM) sensor [7,12]. In this paper, we consider three particular aspects of observed covariate information that potentially influence the estimation of causal treatment effects: i) covariates may interact with the outcome variable and/or treatment assignment variable, ii) covariate values may be nested, that is, they may be measured at a lower hierarchical level than the level of the individual, and iii) covariate values may be observed with high dimensionality.

Learning causal representations without having access to ground-truth knowledge about causal relationships between variables, that is, without knowing the causal diagram, is non-trivial. Solving this problem requires, at the very least, a thorough understanding of how causal variables behave in a controlled setting. Therefore, this paper aims to analyze and provide insights into the behavior of two types of non-confounding covariates.

On the one hand, *effect modifiers* influence the treatment effect (but not the treatment assignment) [51]. In the medical domain, the same concept is referred to as Heterogeneity of Treatment Effect (HTE) and defined as "non-random variation in the magnitude or direction of a treatment effect across levels of a covariate against a clinical outcome" [22, p.35]. On the other hand, we consider *prognostic factors*, which are variables that influence the outcome, but not the treatment effect [21] (nor the treatment assignment; effect modifiers and prognostic factors are not confounders). Both effect modifiers and prognostic factors are abundant in any observational dataset.

Even if we assume that we know the causal diagram, in the absence of restrictions on the structure of the causal relationships, we cannot distinguish effect modifiers from prognostic factors [36,46,51] (Fig. 1a).[1] Alternatively, in this paper, we assume that the causal relations are linearly structured. Then, the causal diagrams appear slightly different depending on whether Z is a prognostic factor (Fig. 1b) or an effect modifier (Fig. 1c cf. [37], and Fig. 1d cf. [30]). Accordingly, the relation between treatment assignment variable W, covariate Z and outcome Y is modeled as

$$Y = \tau W + \gamma Z + \delta W Z, \tag{1}$$

where parameter τ represents the Average Treatment Effect (ATE) in the population, Z induces variation in the outcome variable Y through γ (prognostic effect) and δ quantifies the difference between CATE and τ for certain subgroups in the population (effect modification). If γ and δ are both significantly different from 0, covariate Z performs both roles simultaneously.

The aim of this paper is to provide insights into the prognostic and effect modification behavior of covariate Z. We do this in a controlled setting, where we temporarily disregard the fundamental problem of causal inference that factual and counterfactual outcomes cannot be observed together [16].[2] and generate synthetic data where treatment assignment variable W is a time-variant variable: the outcome value is observed for every occasion (treatment) for every patient. Consequently, we obtain a nested, hierarchical data structure where outcomes (and covariates) reside at a lower hierarchical level than the level of the individual. We then study how population heterogeneity is influenced by whether covariate Z is a prognostic factor or an effect modifier.

The rest of this paper is structured as follows. In Sect. 2, we provide background information and notation for hierarchical data. We extensively introduce the techniques used in our experiments, that is, in Sect. 3 we assume covariate Z is an individual-level variable and we analyze three types of ITE distributions using within-subjects ANalysis Of VAriance (wANOVA), whereas in Sect. 4 Z is a time-variant variable and we perform a local pattern mining method called Subgroup Discovery (SD) [9,15] to unravel patient population heterogeneity in an unsupervised setting. Section 5 concludes.

2 Background

2.1 Preliminaries

First, consider $D = \{\mathbf{x}_i\}_{i=1}^n$ to be a sample of n IID draws from $X = (W, Z, Y)$ with state space $\mathcal{X} = \mathcal{W} \times \mathcal{Z} \times \mathcal{Y}$ such that a sample is a tuple $\mathbf{x}_i = (w_i, z_i, y_i)$.

[1] In Fig. 1, we do not display the noise variables and assume they are jointly independent; the models satisfy the causal Markov condition [36].

[2] At the same time, we stay close to reality by making assumptions such as the Stable Unit Treatment Value Assumption (SUTVA) [19,42], no hidden confounders and overlap (i.e., positivity) [5].

Variable Y is a numerical outcome with $\mathcal{Y} \in \mathbb{R}$. The state spaces of treatment assignment variable W and covariate Z are provided in Sects. 3.1 and 4.1, respectively. Note that in the traditional causal setting, every individual $i \in \{1, 2, ..., n\}$ is assigned to one out of k treatment groups. Often, we set $\mathcal{W} \in \{0, 1\}$ $(k = 2)$; then $\{\mathbf{x}_i \in D \mid w_i = 1\}$ reflects the treatment group and $\{\mathbf{x}_i \in D \mid w_i = 0\}$ the control group.

Next, consider that for a individual i we draw repeated measurements from $\mathcal{X}$ (e.g., repeated blood tests or measuring heart rate over a period of time), denoted as a tuple $(\mathbf{x}_i^1, ..., \mathbf{x}_i^t, ..., \mathbf{x}_i^T)$. These measurements are non-IID if there exists some form of correlation between measurement $\mathbf{x}_i^t$ and $\mathbf{x}_i^{t+\lambda}$, or if the observed distribution $p(\mathbf{X}_i)$ differs from $p(\mathbf{X}_j)$ (for individuals $i, j \in \{1, 2, ..., n\}$). In the real world, such correlation structure naturally exists. Consequently, the resulting dataset has a hierarchical or multilevel structure where there exist multiple entity types where the measurements of the entities of one type (here, entity type *time* with T entities per individual) are nested in the entities of another type (here, entity type *individual* with n entities in the dataset) [18].[3]

In this paper, we create temporal structure by adopting a slightly unusual scenario where the treatment assignment value is set to be the time indicator: $w_i^t \leftarrow t$. Essentially, we create a hypothetical scenario where for all individuals, we observe both factual and counterfactual outcomes. In other words, we model the effect of treatment as time-varying effects.[4] This allows us to study the interaction between Z and W from a within-subjects perspective; an effect that takes place at a lower hierarchical level than the desired level of inference.

2.2 ANalysis Of VAriance

In Sect. 3, we use a within-subjects ANalysis Of VAriance (wANOVA) to investigate the variance distributions in outcome variable Y. An ANOVA is a statistical model that divides variance in an outcome variable over one or multiple components [50]. Depending on the data structure and research question, we distinguish a between-subjects ANOVA (bANOVA) from a wANOVA. A bANOVA divides the variance in the outcome variable between categories of a categorical variable G (an effect of the presence of groups) and a within-subjects variance that cannot be further explained and is therefore considered left-over or error variance. In a wANOVA, the grouping variable G is replaced with a time variable T. The variance in the outcome variable is then divided between an effect of time, an effect of systematic individual differences and a left-over variance.

[3] The number of repeated measurements may vary between individuals. In addition, some variables may be measured only once per individual; others could be repeatedly sampled with varying counts and intervals; the data could be formatted as a flat table, or as a relational database.

[4] We temporarily disregard the fundamental problem of causal inference [16], but still assume SUTVA [19]. We do not belief that time influences the treatment effect; we use time to model the treatment effect.

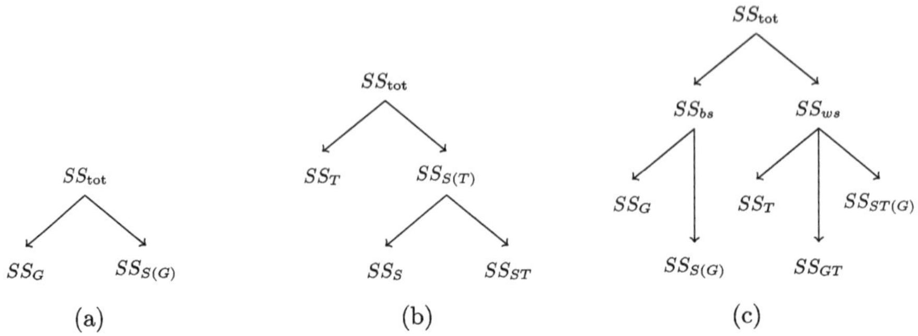

Fig. 2. Variance distribution in a numerical outcome variable for three ANOVA models. SS stands for Sum of Squares. (a) one-way between-subjects ANOVA (b) one-way within-subjects ANOVA (c) mixed between-within-subjects ANOVA.

To be specific, a between-subjects ANOVA (bANOVA) divides the variance in the outcome variable between an effect of group effect of categorical variable G and a within-subjects variance that cannot be further explained and is therefore considered left-over or error variance (Fig. 2a). The total variance in the outcome variable, expressed in terms of Sum of Squares (SS), is

$$SS_{\text{tot}} = \sum_{k\in\{0,1\}} \sum_{i=1}^{n_k} (Y_{ik} - GM)^2, \tag{2}$$

where $GM = \frac{1}{N} \sum_{k\in\{0,1\}} \sum_{i=1}^{n_k} Y_{ik}$ is the Grand Mean. Any systematic difference between the groups is contained in the variance component

$$SS_G = n_k \sum_{k\in\{0,1\}} (\overline{Y}_k - GM)^2, \tag{3}$$

where $\overline{Y}_k = \frac{1}{n_k} \sum_{i=1}^{n_k} Y_{ik}$ is the mean of group k. Within a group, there are no variables that explain any variance and the left-over variance is

$$SS_{S(G)} = \sum_{k\in\{0,1\}} \sum_{i=1}^{n_k} (Y_{ik} - \overline{Y}_k)^2. \tag{4}$$

A bANOVA evaluates whether there is a difference in outcome Y between the groups, by comparing SS_G with $SS_{S(G)}$. While taking the degrees of freedom into account; if the former is substantially larger than the latter, differences in outcome between subjects can be explained by the group assignment. Then, the treatment has an effect.

Figure 2b displays the variance components in a within-subjects ANOVA (wANOVA). In a wANOVA, the grouping variable G is replaced with a time variable T, which indicates the time at which value Y_{it} was measured. Here, the idea is to follow subjects through time and Y_{it} is known for a subject i for all $t \in \{0, 1, .., T-1\}$.

In a wANOVA, the variance in the outcome variable is divided between an effect of time, an effect of systematic individual differences and a left-over variance. Compared to a bANOVA, the effect of time is calculated similar as the group effect in Eq. (3).

In contrast to a bANOVA, the within-subjects variance in a wANOVA can be further explained by a subject effect,

$$SS_S = \sum_{t=0}^{T-1} \sum_{i=1}^{n_t} (\overline{Y}_i - GM)^2 \tag{5}$$

where $\overline{Y}_i = \frac{1}{T-1} \sum_{t=0}^{T-1} Y_{it}$ is a subject's average over the $T-1$ measurement occasions. Any further unexplained variance can be calculated by subtracting Equation (5) from Equation (4), or by

$$SS_{ST} = \sum_{t=0}^{T-1} \sum_{i=1}^{n_t} (Y_{it} - \overline{Y}_t - \overline{Y}_i + GM)^2. \tag{6}$$

Note that by writing ST in the subscript in SS_{ST}, we indicate that the left-over variance represents an interaction between subjects and time. In other words, any variance that cannot explained by a main effect of time, or a main effect of subject, is due to an interaction between these variables. In the context of linear relations, another word for interaction is effect modification.

It is important to realize that in a wANOVA, it is likely that the variance $SS_{ST} < SS_{S(T)}$. Consequently, it may be easier to find evidence for a main effect of time in a wANOVA than it is in a bANOVA, because SS_T is compared against a smaller remainder than SS_G. It does require some degrees of freedom though.

Furthermore, in a one-way wANOVA, there is no grouping variable other than time. Therefore, when one performs an RCT with repeatedly measured outcome values, the analysis to go to is a mixed between-within-subjects ANOVA (bwANOVA) rather than a wANOVA. A bwANOVA is shown in Fig. 2c.

In this paper, we simulate the hypothetical situation that we know the factual and counterfactual outcomes. This allows us specify certain ITE distributions and to analyze variance components in a wANOVA. To translate our findings to a real RCT where covariate information is be used to explain variation in the data, one can use a two-way between-subjects ANOVA. There, a covariate is added as an extra grouping variable similarly like S in a wANOVA [50].

2.3 Local Pattern Mining

The concept of *global* models that explain most of the instances in the data is opposed with that of *local* models or patterns [13,35]. Where global models tend to find the obvious patterns in the data, local patterns cover small parts of the data that deviate from the population distribution and display some internal structure; we call them *subgroups* [3,9,23–25,49]. In Sect. 4, we use Local Pattern

Mining (LPM) techniques to discover 1) subgroups of individuals with exceptionally high outcome values and 2) subgroups of individuals with an exceptional increase in outcome over time (i.e., high treatment effects). We expect that prognostic factors are valuable for discovering the first type of subgroups, whereas effect modifiers are needed to discover the second type.

The next paragraphs provide more background information on two types of LPM frameworks: Subgroup Discovery (SD) [11,23,24,26,49] and Exceptional Model Mining (EMM) [9,28]. Both frameworks aim to discover subgroups in the dataset that somehow behave exceptionally. Traditionally, SD focuses on exceptionality defined over 1 target attributes, whereas EMM evaluates a model fitted to ≥ 2 target attributes.

Traditionally, EMM assumes a dataset Ω to be a bag of n records $r \in \Omega$ of the form

$$r = (a_1, \dots, a_k, \ell_1, \dots, \ell_m), \tag{7}$$

where k and m are positive integers [9]. In EMM, we call $a_1, \dots, a_k$ the *descriptive attributes* or *descriptors* of r, and $\ell_1, \dots, \ell_m$ the *target attributes* or *targets* of r. For SD, $m = 1$, whereas for EMM, typically $m \geq 2$.

The descriptive attributes are used to describe and discover subgroups of cases. A subgroup is defined using descriptions; a description is a Boolean function $D : \mathcal{A} \rightarrow \{0, 1\}$ which covers a record r^i if and only if $D(a_1^i, \dots, a_k^i) = 1$. Here, $\mathcal{A}$ is the collective domain from which the full set of descriptors is taken; a Cartesian product of the domains of each individual descriptor. Consequently, a subgroup is defined as follows:

Definition 1 (Subgroup cf. [9]). *A subgroup corresponding to description D is the bag of records $G_D \subseteq \Omega$ that D covers:*

$$G_D = \{r^i \in \Omega \mid D(a_1^i, \dots, a_k^i) = 1\}.$$

The complement contains all records that are not covered; $G^C = \Omega \setminus G_D$.

In EMM, the choice of *description language* $\mathcal{D}$ is free, though generally we let the description be a conjunction of selection conditions over the descriptors, where condition sel_j is a restriction on the domain $\mathcal{A}_j$ of the respective attribute a_j. For instance, for discrete variables the selector may be an attribute-value pair $(a_j = v)$; for continuous variables it could be a range of values $(w_1 \leq a_j \leq w_2)$ [9,33,45].

We aim to discover the descriptions for which the subgroups display exceptional behavior on a target model, fitted to a set of target attributes. Formally, we quantify exceptionality using a quality or interestingness measure. A quality measure quantifies the difference between behavior in the subgroup and some reference behavior, usually the the subgroup's complement:

Definition 2 (Quality Measure cf. [9]). *A quality measure is a function $\varphi : \mathcal{D} \rightarrow \mathbb{R}$ that assigns a numerical value to a description D.*

In this paper, we follow a SD scenario where outcome variable Y is our target attribute. We evaluate two types of exceptionalities: one where we aim to discover subgroups of individuals with high outcome values, and one where we aim to discover subgroups of individuals with a high increase in outcome values (from $t = 0$ to $t = (T - 1)$. The proposed quality measure is given in Sect. 4.1.

The task of SD and EMM is to effectively search through the space of candidate subgroups to find the top-q best-scoring subgroups [9]. Many search algorithms exist; some of them developed for particular kinds of exceptional behavior [4,6,29,31], others for particular data types [27,32,34,40]. Nevertheless, most work on EMM considers the search space to be a general-to-specific search lattice and use a conjunction of selection conditions as description language. Then, the core difference between most search algorithms is the manner in which they traverse the search lattice; given a (candidate) subgroup description, the selection of subgroup members is comparable for many search algorithms. In this paper, we choose beam search cf. Algorithm 1 in [9] as our search algorithm of choice, with the `lbca` discretization strategy [33] for numerical attributes with $b = 4$ quantiles, search width $w = 20$ and search depth $d = 3$.

3 Experiment 1: Z is an Individual-Level Covariate

In this experiment, we demonstrate how varying underlying ITE distributions affect the variance structure of an outcome variable Y. We demonstrate that averaging over individuals (as is done in reality, outside the hypothetical bubble of this experiment) is equivalent to assuming that none of the left-over variation can be explained by systematic differences between individuals.

3.1 Experimental Setup

We generate synthetic data with a hierarchical structure as described in Sect. 2.1. We set $n = 100$, $T = 2$, and $w_i^t \leftarrow t$ for all $i \in \{1, 2, ..., n\}$ and $t \in \{0, 1\}$. We then sample outcome values $y_i^t = \pi_{0i} + \pi_{1i} w_i^t + e_i^t$. Error $e_i^t \sim \mathcal{N}(0, \sigma_e^2)$ is normally distributed (and jointly independent). To be precise, we sample values for y_i^t from $\mathcal{N}(\mu^t, \sigma^t)$ with $\mu^0 = \pi_{0i} = 5$, $\mu^1 = \mu^0 + \pi_{1i} = 7.5$ and $\sigma^0 = \sigma^1 = 2$. Consequently, the ATE is fixed to 2.5.

Next, we re-order the values such that we create three possible ITE distributions as depicted in Fig. 3. In Fig. 3a, all patients have the same ITE and that ITE equals the ATE. Remark that there exists variation in Y, but that variation does not induce differences in treatment effects between individuals. In the second scenario, the ITEs all cross through the Grand Mean (GM) (Fig. 3b). Here, an individual's ITE is as opposite to the ATE as possible. Third, for every individual we randomly sample one of the two outcome values as factual outcome, and we set the counterfactual to the group mean of the counterfactual group, denoted with $\overline{y}^0$ for the control group and $\overline{y}^1$ for the treatment group. Thus, if we randomly sample $y_i^{t=1}$ for individual i, then value $y_i^0 \leftarrow \overline{y}^0$, and similar for $t = 0$. The resulting ITE distribution is visualized in Fig. 3c. Remark that in all three scenarios, the ATE, GM, and group means do not change; we only change the underlying ITE distributions.

We deliberately write the coefficients as π_{0i} and π_{1i} to indicate that the sampled values occur at the lowest hierarchical level (the time level); these effects can be further specified using second-level attributes, for instance a potential covariate Z. Then, $\pi_{0i} = \beta_{00} + \beta_{01} z_i + \mu_{0i}$ and $\pi_{1i} = \beta_{10} + \beta_{11} z_i + \mu_{1i}$ (error normally distributed and jointly independent). Integrating these higher level equations into the lowest level equation gives:

$$y_i^t = \beta_{00} + \beta_{01} z_i + \beta_{10} w_i^t + \beta_{11} w_i^t z_i + \mu_{1i} w_i^t + \mu_{0i} + e_i^t. \qquad (8)$$

Consequently, scenario (a) equals the situation that $\beta_{01} \neq 0$ and $\beta_{11} = 0$: Z is a prognostic factor. In scenario (b), Z is an effect modifier and $\beta_{01} = 0$ and $\beta_{11} \neq 0$. In scenario (c), Z is an effect modifier with an additional prognostic component ($\beta_{01} \neq 0$ and $\beta_{11} \neq 0$).

3.2 Experimental Results

Inspection with bANOVA and wANOVA gives results as presented in Table 4. Here, the left-most column shows the traditional bANOVA output and the three right columns the wANOVA results. We see that the total variance SS_{tot} in the outcome variable (1046) can be explained by an effect of group (219). Based on a statistical test, we would reject the null hypothesis that there is no effect of treatment with $F(1, 198) = 52.44, p < 0.001$.

Table 4 furthermore shows that in scenario (a), 814 of the 827 within-subjects variance can be explained by an effect of subject. This demonstrates the existence of systematic differences between subjects (individuals). In fact, in scenario (a), the only difference between subjects is given by the distance of their individual average outcome ($\overline{y}_i$) and the GM; no further variance is to be explained.

In contrast, in scenario (b), almost none of the within-subjects variance can be explained by a subject effect. Instead, a subject's average value does not say much about the outcome values, and there exists an interaction between treatment and subject that cannot be explained by observed information.

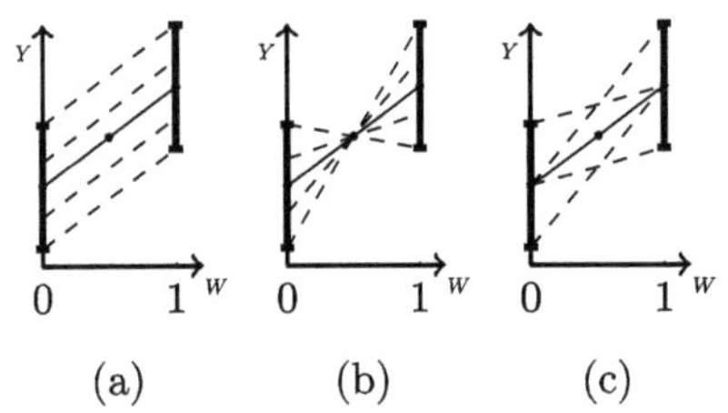

Fig. 3. Visualizations of three types of ITE distributions in a two-arm experiment with Y as the outcome variable and W the treatment assignment indicator. (a) all ITEs equal the ATE (b) all ITEs cross through GM (c) counterfactuals equal the group mean.

	bANOVA	wANOVA		
		(a)	(b)	(c)
SS_{tot}	1046	1046	1046	706
SS_{group}	219	219	219	219
SS_{ind}	-	814	11	238
SS_{error}	827	13	816	238

Fig. 4. Synthetic data results of Experiment 1 in Sect. 3. The table gives the Sum of Squares (SS) for a bANOVA and a wANOVA for three possible ITE distributions as visualized in Fig. 3.

In scenario (c), the total variance decreases to 706 because 100 out of 200 outcome values are set to the group mean. These 100 group mean values all have a shorter distance to the GM than the original values and therefore, the total variance decreases. Yet, the ATE in scenario (c) is still the same, as can be seen from the between-subjects variance of 219. Furthermore, the within-subjects variance is equally divided between an effect of subjects and an interaction effect. In other words, half of the variance can be explained by consistent differences between individuals, while the other half of the variance is non-systematic and therefore unexplained.

4 Experiment 2: Z is a Time-Variant, Lower-Level Covariate

In this experiment, we demonstrate that whether or not Z is a prognostic factor or effect modifier, high-quality individual-level representation of lower-level measurements can discover the variance distributions of these measurements. However, poorly chosen aggregation functions interfere with assumptions about the presence of prognostic factors and effect modifiers.

4.1 Experimental Setup

We let covariate Z be time-varying, constructed as a random walk of $T = 20$ steps over nodes $h \in \mathcal{H} = \{a, b, c, d, e\}$, where $P(z_i^t = h \mid z_i^{t-1} = h') = 1/5$. In other words, per individual, covariate Z is modeled as an event-sequence of length T where the next event value is independent of the current event. We model the treatment assignment variable as a time-variant variable where every possible treatment value is a measurement occasion. Concretely, this means we set the treatment assignment value as the time indicator: $w_i^t \leftarrow t$.

Next, we generate $y_i^t = \mathcal{N}(10 + v_i^t, 0.1)$, where we let $v_i^t = \alpha w_i^t + \zeta z_i^t + \lambda w_i^t z_i^t$ be a linear function of the time indicator t (through w_i^t) and the integer position of covariate value z_i^t (i.e., $a = 1$, $b = 2$, etc.; assumptions underlying linear regression are slightly violated, but do not influence the conclusions of our experiment). The aim is to discover exceptional subgroups of individuals using individual-level representations of the lower-level event sequences. We create various additional lower-level and individual-level noise variables. We use the beam search algorithm and construct $2 \times 2 \times 2$ scenarios: all combinations of $Ztype \in \{\text{prognostic}, \text{effect modification}\}$, $Aggfunc \in \{\text{imperfect}, \text{perfect}\}$ and $Eval \in \{\text{average}, \text{increase}\}$.

The simulation parameter $Ztype$ refers to whether variable Z acts as a prognostic factor or as an effect modifier. To let Z have a prognostic effect, $\alpha = \zeta = 1$ and $\lambda = 0$ (see visualization in Fig. 5a). There are main effects of time and variable Z, but no interaction effect. In contrast, Fig. 5b displays the scenario where Z is an effect modifier without main effects; $\alpha = \zeta = 0$ and $\lambda = 1$.

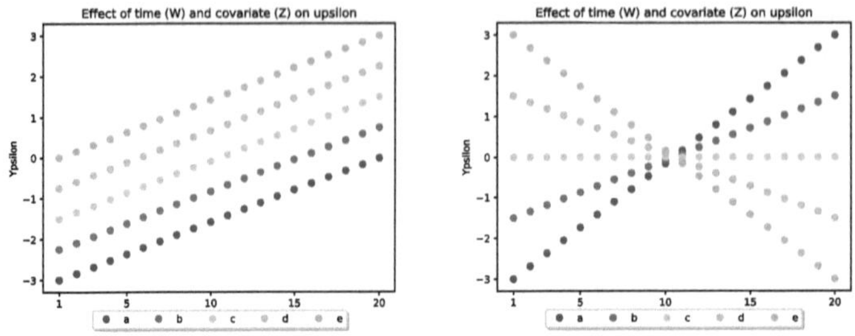

(a) (b)

Fig. 5. Visualizations of the relation between the time indicator t (through w_i^t, x-axis), covariate values z (colors, from low (event type a, purple) to high (event type e, orange)) and υ. Every individual i walks a path through these dots from left to right. (a) Z acts as a prognostic factor (b) Z acts as an effect modifier, there are no main effects. (Color figure online)

To represent lower-level measurements at the level of the individual, we compare two approaches for $Aggfunc$. In the *perfect* scenario, we know the ground truth values υ_i^t and average those using $f_{\text{sum}}(\upsilon_i^1, ..., \upsilon_i^T) = \sum_{t=1}^{T} \upsilon_i^t$ and $f_{\text{incr}}(\upsilon_i^1, ..., \upsilon_i^T) = \upsilon_i^T - \upsilon_i^1$. Alternatively, we construct an *imperfect* scenario that reflects handling event-sequences in practice: by counting the average frequency of each event type, and by determining the average index location. The idea is that high frequency values capture individuals with highly repetitive sequences (i.e., the random walk stays at the same node; the path through Fig. 5 follows the same color) whereas the index location reflects where in the random walk, on average, a certain node is visited (e.g., more in the start or at the end of the sequence). The resulting 10 features are denoted as f_{freq_h} and f_{idx_h} for $h \in \mathcal{H}$.

Third, we evaluate the exceptionality of individuals in two ways. If $Eval$ = *average*, discover subgroups of individuals with exceptionally high, average outcome values. We quantify exceptionality with quality measure $\varphi_\mu = (\mu^{SG} - \mu^D)/\text{se}(\mu^{SG})$. Here, $\mu^{SG} = 1/n^{SG} 1/T \sum_{i \in SG} \sum_{t=1} y_i^t$ is the average outcome value of the individuals covered by the subgroup, $se(\mu^{SG})$ is its standard error, and μ^D is the average outcome in the entire dataset D. In contrast, if $Eval$ = *increase*, we discover subgroups of individuals with an exceptional increase in outcome between $t = 1$ and $t = T$. Here, $\varphi_\theta = (\theta^{SG} - \theta^\Omega)/\text{se}(\theta^{SG})$ with $\theta^{SG} = 1/n^{SG} \sum_{i \in SG}(y_i^T - y_i^1)$.

4.2 Experimental Results

For all 8 simulation scenarios, Table 1 presents the description of the most exceptional subgroup. First, for the scenario where $Eval = \varphi_\mu$, $Ztype$ = prognostic, and $Aggfunc$ = imperfect, the subgroups covers individuals with low frequency of event type a, low frequency of event type b and high frequency of event type e. These are individuals with event sequences that stay close to the orange path in Fig. 5a; the υ values are large, and therefore, the outcome values are large.

Table 1. Description of the most exceptional subgroup, discovered with φ_μ (exceptionally high average outcome) and φ_θ (exceptionally high increase in outcome). Aggregation of event-sequences to single values per individual is done with perfect, ground-truth knowledge and imperfect knowledge. Covariate Z acts as a prognostic factor or effect modifier.

Eval	*Ztype*	*Aggfunc*	
		imperfect	perfect
φ_μ	prognostic	$f_{\text{freq}_a} \leq 3 \land f_{\text{freq}_e} \geq 4 \land f_{\text{freq}_b} \leq 5$	$f_{\text{sum}} \in [5, 22]$
	effect modification	$f_{\text{idx}_a} \geq 11 \land f_{\text{idx}_e} \leq 10$	$f_{\text{sum}} \in [-134, -25]$
φ_θ	prognostic	$f_{\text{idx}_e} \geq 10.5 \land f_{\text{idx}_a} \leq 9.5$	$f_{\text{incr}} = 3$
	effect modification	$f_{\text{freq}_e} \leq 3 \land f_{\text{freq}_a} \geq 4 \land f_{\text{idx}_e} \leq 14$	$f_{\text{incr}} \in [-38, -29]$

In contrast, when $Eval = \varphi_{theta}$, individuals with an exceptional increase in outcome start their sequence with event type a ($f_{\text{idx}_a} \leq 9.5$) and end their sequence with event type e ($f_{\text{idx}_e} \geq 10.5$) (see Table 1, third row). In other words, they start at purple and cross through to end at orange (Fig. 5a).

The reversed line of reasoning holds if $Ztype$ = effect modification, as depicted in Fig. 5b. Then, discovering individuals with high outcome values (φ_μ) requires crossing through colors and hence, the usage of f_{idx} (second row in Table 1, whereas individuals with a high increase (φ_θ) need to stay close to the purple color (event type a) as long as possible ($f_{\text{freq}_a} \geq 4$).

Interestingly, if we have direct access to v, we can construct an aggregation function f_{sum} that works for discovering individuals with high outcome values (φ_μ) independent of whether Z is a prognostic factor or effect modifier. This can be seen in the right column in Table 1: f_{sum} is used in both rows corresponding to φ_μ. Similarly, we can construct f_{incr}, which is used to discover subgroups with a high increase over time (φ_θ), independent of covariate role of Z. These results show that the closer our aggregation functions resemble the true multivariate, multilevel nature of the data, the less we need to worry about making the correct assumptions about whether Z is a prognostic factor or effect modifier.

5 Discussion and Conclusion

The aim of this paper is to unravel patient population heterogeneity by providing insights into the prognostic and effect modification behavior of covariate Z in the context of estimating causal treatment effects that vary across subgroups in the population. We do this by designing two controlled experiments where we temporarily disregard the fundamental problem of causal inference that factual and counterfactual outcomes cannot be observed together. We consider linear relations between a treatment assignment variable W, a covariate Z and an outcome variable Y. Treatment assignment variable W is modeled as a time-variant variable where every possible treatment value is a measurement occasion. As such, we create a nested, hierarchical data structure and studied the relation between individual (lower-level) and average (higher-level) treatment effects.

In Experiment 1 in Sect. 3, covariate Z is an individual-level covariate. Our findings demonstrate that variance distributions in a traditional two-arm experiment as measured by bANOVA (most-left column in Table 4) are the same as those in a wANOVA with covariate Z being an effect modifier (scenario (b) in Fig. 3 and Table 4). This means that a bANOVA without additional covariates assumes a worst-case scenario for underlying ITE distributions. Indeed, in the real world, including covariates Z to control for prognostic and effect modification behavior reduces left-over variance and improves precision in estimating τ [19,50]: we would move from scenario (b) to scenario (c) to scenario (a) in Table 4.

Remark that in the real-world, it is non-trivial to distinguish prognostic factors from effect modifiers. Consequently, is can be difficult to know how to include Z in the model. For instance, when assuming linear causal relations, Z should be included as a main effect to control for confounding effects and to control for prognostic effects, and Z should additionally be included in an interaction term to control for effect modification behavior. With many variables, the number of model parameters inflates quickly. In the domain of uplift modeling, the problem of causal inference is circumvented by fitting multiple models: one for each treatment group. An individual's ITE is then estimated by comparing the factual outcome with the predicted counterfactual [38,39]. In fact, the scenario in Fig. 3c represents a baseline double-model where the simplest counterfactual model is the group average ($\overline{y}^k$). More advanced methods directly estimate the net difference between two treatment groups [20,43].

In Experiment 2 in Sect. 4, Z is a time-variant, lower-level covariate. Our findings demonstrate that the quality of our choice on how to create individual-level representations of lower-level measurements is determined by our assumption about the nature of the lower-level covariate Z. With poorly chosen aggregation functions, assumptions regarding the effect of Z on ITEs influences results. For instance, in our experiment, aggregation functions based on frequency perform well when Z is a prognostic factor and the average effect is based on an estimate of the mean, or when Z is an effect modifier and the average effect is based on an estimate of the slope (first and last row in left column in Table 1). Aggregation functions based on location work well with reversed relations between Z and the average treatment effect. However, if the aggregation functions are close to the ground truth, the nature of Z does not matter for whether or not average treatment effects can be unraveled. For instance, aggregation function f_{sum} works well for discovering average effects based on estimates of the mean, whether or not Z is a prognostic factor or effect modifier (first two rows in right column in Table 1). Overall, the better the quality of individual-level representations, the less our results will interfere with assumptions about the role of covariate Z. We then do not need to rely on the reliability of those assumptions.

Acknowledgments. This work is part of the research program Data2People with project Exceptional and Deep Intelligent Coach (EDIC) and partly financed by the Dutch Research Council (NWO). We gratefully acknowledge the continuous support of Prof. Mykola Pechenizkiy and Dr. Wouter Duivesteijn. We sincerely thank Prof. Cassio de Campos and Dr. Devendra Singh Dhami for providing valuable feedback to earlier drafts of this paper.

Disclosure of Interests. The authors have no competing interests to declare that are relevant to the content of this article.

References

1. op den Akker, H., Cabrita, M., op den Akker, R., Jones, V.M., Hermens, H.J.: Tailored motivational message generation: a model and practical framework for real-time physical activity coaching. J. Biomed. Inf. **55**, 104–115 (2015)
2. op den Akker, H., Jones, V.M., Hermens, H.J.: Tailoring real-time physical activity coaching systems: a literature survey and model. User Model. User-adapted Interact. **24**, 351–392 (2014)
3. Atzmueller, M., Mueller, J., Becker, M.: Exploratory subgroup analytics on ubiquitous data. In: International Workshop on Mining Ubiquitous and Social Environments, pp. 1–20 (2013)
4. Belfodil, A., Duivesteijn, W., Plantevit, M., Cazalens, S., Lamarre, P.: DEvIANT: discovering significant exceptional (dis-) agreement within groups. In: Proceedings of the ECML PKDD, pp. 3–20 (2020)
5. Bica, I., Alaa, A.M., Lambert, C., van der Schaar, M.: From real-world patient data to individualized treatment effects using machine learning: current and future methods to address underlying challenges. Clin. Pharmacol. Ther. **109**(1), 87–100 (2021)
6. Bosc, G., Boulicaut, J.F., Raïssi, C., Kaytoue, M.: Anytime discovery of a diverse set of patterns with monte Carlo tree search. Data Min. Knowl. Disc. **32**(3), 604–650 (2018)
7. den Braber, N., et al.: Glucose regulation beyond HbA1c in type 2 diabetes treated with insulin: real-world evidence from the DIALECT-2 cohort. Diabetes Care **44**(10), 2238–2244 (2021)
8. De Vries, H., Dijkstra, M., Kuhlman, P.: Self-efficacy: the third factor besides attitude and subjective norm as a predictor of behavioural intentions. Health Educ. Res. **3**(3), 273–282 (1988)
9. Duivesteijn, W., Feelders, A.J., Knobbe, A.: Exceptional model mining. Data Min. Knowl. Disc. **30**(1), 47–98 (2016)
10. Foster, J.C., Taylor, J.M., Ruberg, S.J.: Subgroup identification from randomized clinical trial data. Stat. Med. **30**(24), 2867–2880 (2011)
11. Gamberger, D., Lavrac, N.: Expert-guided subgroup discovery: methodology and application. J. Artif. Intell. Res. **17**, 501–527 (2002)
12. Gant, C.M., Binnenmars, S.H., van den Berg, E., Bakker, S.J., Navis, G., Laverman, G.D.: Integrated assessment of pharmacological and nutritional cardiovascular risk management: blood pressure control in the DIAbetes and LifEstyle Cohort Twente (DIALECT). Nutrients **9**(7), 709 (2017)
13. Hand, D.J.: Pattern detection and discovery. In: Proceedings of the Pattern Detection and Discovery: ESF Exploratory Workshop London, pp. 1–12 (2002)
14. Hermens, H., op den Akker, H., Tabak, M., Wijsman, J., Vollenbroek, M.: Personalized coaching systems to support healthy behavior in people with chronic conditions. J. Electromyogr. Kinesiol. **24**(6), 815–826 (2014)
15. Herrera, F., Carmona, C.J., González, P., Del Jesus, M.J.: An overview on subgroup discovery: foundations and applications. Knowl. Inf. Syst. **29**(3), 495–525 (2011)
16. Holland, P.W.: Statistics and causal inference. J. Am. Stat. Assoc. **81**(396), 945–960 (1986)

17. Hoogland, J., et al.: A tutorial on individualized treatment effect prediction from randomized trials with a binary endpoint. Stat. Med. **40**(26), 5961–5981 (2021)
18. Hox, J., Moerbeek, M., van de Schoot, R.: Multilevel Analysis: Techniques and Applications. Routledge (2017)
19. Imbens, G.W., Rubin, D.B.: Causal Inference in Statistics, Social, and Biomedical Sciences. Cambridge University Press (2015)
20. Jaskowski, M., Jaroszewicz, S.: Uplift modeling for clinical trial data. In: Proceedings of the ICML Workshop on Clinical Data Analysis, vol. 46, pp. 79–95 (2012)
21. Kahan, B.C., Jairath, V., Doré, C.J., Morris, T.P.: The risks and rewards of covariate adjustment in randomized trials: an assessment of 12 outcomes from 8 studies. Trials **15**(1), 1–7 (2014)
22. Kent, D.M., Paulus, J.K., van Klaveren, D., D'Agostino, R., Goodman, S., Hayward, R., Ioannidis, J.P., Patrick-Lake, B., Morton, S., Pencina, M., et al.: The predictive approaches to treatment effect heterogeneity (PATH) statement. Ann. Intern. Med. **172**(1), 35–45 (2020)
23. Klösgen, W.: Explora: a multipattern and multistrategy discovery assistant. In: Proceedings of the PAKDD, pp. 249–271 (1996)
24. Klösgen, W., May, M.: Census data mining — an application. In: Proceedings of the PKDD, pp. 65–79 (2002)
25. Kralj Novak, P., Lavrač, N., Webb, G.I.: Supervised descriptive rule discovery: a unifying survey of contrast set, emerging pattern and subgroup mining. J. Mach. Learn. Res. **10**(2) (2009)
26. Lavrač, N., Kavšek, B., Flach, P., Todorovski, L.: Subgroup discovery with CN2-SD. J. Mach. Learn. Res. **5**(2), 153–188 (2004)
27. Lavrac, N., et al.: Semantic subgroup discovery: using ontologies in microarray data analysis. In: Proceedings of the IEEE Engineering in Medicine and Biology Society, pp. 5613–5616 (2009)
28. Leman, D., Feelders, A., Knobbe, A.: Exceptional model mining. In: Proceedings of the ECML PKDD, pp. 1–16 (2008)
29. Lemmerich, F., Becker, M., Atzmueller, M.: Generic pattern trees for exhaustive exceptional model mining. In: Proceedings of the ECML PKDD, pp. 277–292 (2012)
30. Little, T.D., Card, N.A., Bovaird, J.A., Preacher, K.J., Crandall, C.S.: Structural equation modeling of mediation and moderation with contextual factors. Model. Context. Effects Longitudinal Stud. **1**, 207–230 (2007)
31. Mathonat, R., Nurbakova, D., Boulicaut, J.F., Kaytoue, M.: Anytime mining of sequential discriminative patterns in labeled sequences. Knowl. Inf. Syst. **63**(2), 439–476 (2021)
32. Mathonat, R., Nurbakova, D., Boulicaut, J.F., Kaytoue, M.: Anytime subgroup discovery in high dimensional numerical data. In: Proceedings of the DSAA, pp. 1–10 (2021)
33. Meeng, M., Knobbe, A.J.: For real: a thorough look at numeric attributes in subgroup discovery. Data Min. Knowl. Disc. **35**(1), 158–212 (2021)
34. Mollenhauer, D., Atzmueller, M.: Sequential exceptional pattern discovery using pattern-growth: an extensible framework for interpretable machine learning on sequential data. In: Proceedings of the XI-ML (2020)
35. Morik, K., Boulicaut, J.F., Siebes, A.: Local pattern detection: international seminar Dagstuhl castle, Germany, 12–16 April 2004, Revised Selected Papers, vol. 3539. Springer (2005)
36. Pearl, J.: Causality: Models, Reasoning and Inference. Cambridge University Press, 2nd edn. (2009)

37. Pearl, J.: Detecting latent heterogeneity. Sociol. Methods Res. **46**(3), 370–389 (2017)
38. Radcliffe, N.: Using control groups to target on predicted lift: building and assessing uplift model. Direct Mark. Analytics J. 14–21 (2007)
39. Radcliffe, N.J., Surry, P.D.: Real-world uplift modelling with significance-based uplift trees. White Paper TR-2011-1, Stochastic Solutions, pp. 1–33 (2011)
40. Remil, Y., Bendimerad, A., Chambard, M., Mathonat, R., Plantevit, M., Kaytoue, M.: Mining java memory errors using subjective interesting subgroups with hierarchical targets. In: Proceedings of the ICDMW, pp. 1221–1230 (2023)
41. Rolling, C.A.: Estimation of conditional average treatment effects. Ph.D. thesis, University of Minnesota (2014)
42. Rubin, D.B.: Causal inference using potential outcomes: design, modeling, decisions. J. Am. Stat. Assoc. **100**(469), 322–331 (2005)
43. Rudaś, K., Jaroszewicz, S.: Linear regression for uplift modeling. Data Min. Knowl. Disc. **32**(5), 1275–1305 (2018)
44. Rudaś, K., Jaroszewicz, S.: Shrinkage estimators for uplift regression. In: Joint European Conference on Machine Learning and Knowledge Discovery in Databases (ECML-PKDD), pp. 607–623. Springer (2019)
45. Schouten, R.M., Duivesteijn, W., Pechenizkiy, M.: Exceptional model mining for repeated cross-sectional data (EMM-RCS). In: Proceedings of the SDM, pp. 585–593 (2022)
46. Sechidis, K., Papangelou, K., Metcalfe, P.D., Svensson, D., Weatherall, J., Brown, G.: Distinguishing prognostic and predictive biomarkers: an information theoretic approach. Bioinformatics **34**(19), 3365–3376 (2018)
47. Shalit, U., Johansson, F.D., Sontag, D.: Estimating individual treatment effect: generalization bounds and algorithms. In: International Conference on Machine Learning, pp. 3076–3085. PMLR (2017)
48. Shpitser, I., Pearl, J.: Identification of conditional interventional distributions. arXiv preprint arXiv:1206.6876 (2012)
49. Siebes, A.: Data surveying: foundations of an inductive query language. In: Proceedings of the KDD, pp. 269–274 (1995)
50. Tabachnick, B.G., Fidell, L.S.: Using Multivariate Statistics. Pearson/Allyn & Bacon, 5th edn. (2007)
51. VanderWeele, T.J., Robins, J.M.: Four types of effect modification: a classification based on directed acyclic graphs. Epidemiology **18**(5), 561–568 (2007)

Workshop on Responsible Healthcare using Machine Learning (RHCML 2025)

Workshop on Responsible Healthcare using Machine Learning (RHCML 2025)

The integration of machine learning (ML) into healthcare holds transformative potential for clinical practice and patient outcomes. Yet this promise comes with profound responsibilities. As ML systems increasingly inform diagnostic decisions, treatment recommendations, and resource allocation, questions of fairness, privacy, explainability, and real-world safety become not merely technical challenges but ethical imperatives that affect the lives of patients and the integrity of healthcare systems.

RHCML 2025 represents the inaugural workshop dedicated to fostering rigorous, interdisciplinary dialogue on these critical issues. Held on September 19, 2025, at ECML PKDD in Porto, Portugal, this half-day event brought together machine learning researchers, healthcare professionals, and policy experts to address the multifaceted challenges of deploying ML responsibly in medical contexts. More information about the workshop can be found on the workshop website: https://rhcml.github.io/.

The workshop emerged from a recognition that responsible ML in healthcare cannot be achieved through technical solutions alone. Healthcare applications differ fundamentally from other ML domains: the stakes are higher, the data more sensitive, the domain knowledge more specialized, and the consequences of failure more severe. A misclassified image may be an inconvenience; a misdiagnosed patient may face life-altering harm. This reality demands that we move beyond conventional metrics of model performance to consider the broader sociotechnical ecosystem in which healthcare ML operates.

RHCML 2025 received strong interest from the research community, with 10 accepted papers spanning diverse healthcare applications and methodological innovations. The accepted work reflects the workshop's commitment to addressing responsible ML across multiple dimensions. Multiple papers explored federated learning and cryptographic techniques to enable collaborative model development while protecting patient data. Contributions ranged from hybrid homomorphic encryption schemes that balance computational efficiency with security guarantees, to real-world feasibility studies of federated learning for glaucoma referral across heterogeneous clinical sites in Portugal. These works demonstrate that privacy-preservation is not merely a theoretical concern but a practical requirement for deploying ML in multi-institutional healthcare settings. Several papers addressed the critical need for clinically meaningful explanations. Work on explainable large language models (LLMs) for federated medical outcomes, challenges in explaining pretrained clinical text classifiers, and positive-unlabeled learning with XAI techniques for healthcare recommendations all emphasized that black-box predictions are insufficient for high-stakes medical decisions. The workshop contributions highlight that explainability must go beyond feature importance scores to capture complex interactions, semantic meaning, and clinical relevance. Papers examining bias in LLM-based self-diagnosis, unintended information leakage in fundus image analysis, and imbalanced demographic representation in public healthcare datasets underscored ongoing concerns about equity in healthcare ML. These works reveal that fairness issues manifest at multiple levels, spanning data collection, model training, deployment, and access, requiring systematic attention throughout the ML pipeline. Contributions on clustering techniques for glioblastoma patient stratification, interpretable mental health topic labeling, and characterization of public healthcare benchmarks emphasized the importance of appropriate evaluation metrics, domain-specific validation, and careful dataset auditing. These papers remind us that responsible ML requires not only innovative algorithms but also rigorous methodology aligned with clinical realities.

The workshop recognized outstanding contributions through two awards. Diogen Babuc received the Best Student Contribution Award for his work on MedFusion-LM, which combined federated learning with neural architecture search and explainable LLMs to address data heterogeneity and interpretability challenges across decentralized medical settings. Sagnik Dakshit received the Best Researcher Contribution Award for his comparative study examining demographic bias and responsible deployment considerations in public LLMs for self-diagnosis.

The workshop featured two distinguished keynote speakers who brought complementary perspectives on responsible healthcare ML. Professor John D. Piette from the University of Michigan and Professor Paul Monsarrat from the Université de Toulouse offered insights spanning from health equity and behavioral health to the transition from descriptive AI to causal understanding in biological systems. A central highlight was the panel discussion featuring Professor Josep Domingo-Ferrer from Universitat Rovira i Virgili, Professor Paul Monsarrat, and Professor Jaakko Peltonen from Tampere University. The discussion addressed a range of critical issues in healthcare AI, including the feasibility of differential privacy as a robust mechanism for medical data protection, the integration of ethics-by-design principles in commercial healthcare AI development, the need for explainability approaches that capture feature interactions and biological mechanisms rather than merely individual feature importance, and the challenge of LLM unlearning, particularly the difficulty of distinguishing between forgetting specific patient data and retaining medical knowledge. Cross-panel discussions explored how to establish standards for responsible ML across diverse healthcare applications while effectively communicating different facets of responsibility to clinicians, patients, and policymakers who may prioritize them differently.

A defining principle of RHCML is its commitment to genuine interdisciplinary collaboration. Responsible healthcare cannot be achieved by ML researchers working in isolation from clinical expertise, nor by healthcare professionals operating without understanding of algorithmic limitations. The workshop actively encouraged joint participation and co-authored submissions from both communities. The diversity of perspectives at RHCML 2025, from cryptographers and federated learning experts to ophthalmologists and mental health researchers, reflects our conviction that progress requires crossing disciplinary boundaries. The discussions revealed both tensions and opportunities: ML researchers emphasized scalability and generalization while clinicians stressed context-specificity and workflow integration; privacy experts advocated for formal guarantees while practitioners highlighted usability constraints. These productive tensions are essential for developing ML systems that are not only technically sophisticated but also clinically appropriate and ethically sound.

The inaugural RHCML workshop marks the beginning of what we envision as an ongoing forum for advancing responsible healthcare using ML. The workshop attracted approximately 35–40 participants, fostering vibrant discussions that extended beyond formal presentations. The enthusiasm and engagement demonstrated by attendees from diverse backgrounds affirm the community's commitment to these issues. Several themes emerged as priorities for future work. First, we need better frameworks for communicating uncertainty in ML predictions to clinical stakeholders, recognizing that different medical contexts may require different approaches to risk communication. Second, the tension between model explainability and performance remains unresolved, particularly for complex architectures like LLMs and foundation models. Third, privacy-preserving techniques must mature from proof-of-concept demonstrations to practical systems that healthcare institutions can deploy within existing governance structures. Fourth, we must develop evaluation paradigms that go beyond accuracy metrics to assess clinical utility, fairness, robustness, and alignment with healthcare goals. Finally, the role of regulatory frameworks and professional guidelines in shaping responsible ML deployment warrants deeper investigation and collaboration with policy experts.

As ML capabilities continue to advance and healthcare systems increasingly adopt these technologies, the questions addressed at RHCML become ever more urgent. We hope this workshop contributed to identifying new research directions, fostering lasting collaborations, and promoting a culture of responsibility that balances innovation with ethical considerations, and technical sophistication with clinical knowledge. We extend our gratitude to all authors, reviewers, keynote speakers, panelists, and participants who made RHCML 2025 a success. We look forward to continuing this important conversation in future editions and to seeing the community grow in both size and impact.

Pratik Gajane
Patrick Marcel
Kostas Stefanidis
Christel Vrain
Thi-Bich-Hanh Dao

RHCML 2025 Workshop Organization

Workshop Chairs

Pratik Gajane	University of Orléans, France
Patrick Marcel	University of Orléans, France
Kostas Stefanidis	Tampere University, Finland
Christel Vrain	University of Orléans, France
Thi-Bich-Hanh Dao	University of Orléans, France

Program Committee

Alexandre Chanson	University of Tours, France
Sagnik Dakshit	University of Texas at Tyler, USA
Emmanuel Doumard	University of Tours, France
Mauro Dragoni	Fondazione Bruno Kessler, Italy
Dimitrios Karapiperis	International Hellenic University, Greece
Vivek Kumar	University of the Bundeswehr Munich, Germany
Nicolas Labroche	University of Tours, France
Elena Sizikova	Food and Drug Administration, USA

MedFusion-LM: Explainable Large Language Model for Transforming Medical Outcomes in Federated Learning with Neural Architecture Search Blueprints

Diogen Babuc(✉) and Teodor-Florin Fortiş

West University of Timişoara, blvd. V. Pârvan 4, 300223 Timişoara, Romania
{diogen.babuc,florin.fortis}@e-uvt.ro

Abstract. Federated learning (FL) has emerged as a promising approach to facilitate collaborative model training while ensuring data privacy. FL faces challenges related to heterogeneity in data distributions, interpretability of model decisions, and optimization of model architectures across decentralized nodes. This paper proposes a framework that combines FL with neural architecture search (NAS) and explainable large language model (XLLM) to overcome these issues and improve clinical outcomes. We test this approach in three medical areas. NAS is used to discover optimized model architectures tailored to heterogeneous medical data across decentralized hospitals. XLLMs are employed to interpret and communicate complex decision-making processes. Experimental validation on benchmark datasets for each clinical use case indicates improvements in predictive accuracy and clinical relevance compared to conventional federated approaches.

Keywords: privacy-preserving · neural architecture search · explainable AI · large language models · clinical decision support

1 Introduction

The adoption of artificial intelligence (AI) in healthcare has opened new frontiers in clinical diagnostics, personalized treatment planning, and interpretation of medical images [12]. Among the many paradigms of AI, federated learning (FL) has emerged as a privacy-preserving strategy that enables collaborative model training across decentralized data silos without requiring the exchange of sensitive patient information. This is important in medical environments constrained by data protection regulations such as HIPAA [4] and GDPR [30].

Despite its promise, federated learning faces several challenges [20]. First, data heterogeneity – resulting from variations in imaging protocols, populations, and devices – can impair global model convergence and reduce generalizability.

I. Koprinska et al. (Eds.): ECML PKDD 2025, CCIS 2842, pp. 231–246, 2026.
https://doi.org/10.1007/978-3-032-19105-2_17

Next, the black-box nature of the deep models inhibits interpretability, which is a key requirement in clinical settings where human oversight and explainability are critical. Finally, existing FL workflows typically use static architectures that may not adapt well to diverse institutional data distributions [32].

To overcome these limitations, our proposal is to combine FL with two core enhancements: *Neural Architecture Search (NAS)* [27] and *Explainable Large Language Model (XLLM)*. NAS allows each institution to discover optimized local architectures while contributing to a federated learning process. XLLM approaches enhance model transparency by providing contextual, human-readable explanations of decisions, bridging the gap between the black-box nature of AI and clinical reasoning.

Our approach is evaluated in three high-impact medical use cases: (1) early detection of premalignant colorectal polyps [9], (2) diagnostics for cervical cancer [5], and (3) cognitive assessment for Alzheimer's disease via dementia stage classification [7]. Through a combination of zero-shot NAS [17], knowledge distillation [8] and federated explainability [2], we show measurable improvements in predictive accuracy, interpretability, and practical deployment readiness.

This paper intends to address the following objectives: (1) the development of a privacy-preserving framework for training clinical models on decentralized, heterogeneous medical datasets; (2) improving model performance and adaptability using zero-shot NAS to enable automated, local architectural optimization; (3) integration of XLLM principles to enhance interpretability and provide clinically meaningful explanations for AI decisions.

2 Background Information

The increasing adoption of artificial intelligence in healthcare requires systems that are accurate, yet interpretable, adaptable, and privacy-preserving. In order to achieve these goals, several technologies have to be employed, such as federated learning, neural architecture search, explainable large language models, and knowledge distillation. Together, they can define a framework for trustworthy clinical AI, as depicted in Fig. 1.

2.1 Federated Learning

Federated Learning, as introduced by Mahan et al. in [21], enables a decentralized model training across multiple devices while preserving privacy. As mentioned in [32], this is a decentralized machine learning paradigm that enables multiple distributed clients (e.g., hospitals, clinics, or diagnostic centers) to collaboratively train a shared global model without exchanging raw data. In a typical FL setup, each client downloads the current international model, performs local training using its private dataset, and then uploads model updates (gradients or weights) to a central server. The server aggregates these updates to refine the global model, often using strategies such as the federated averaging (FedAvg). This cycle repeats for several rounds until convergence is reached.

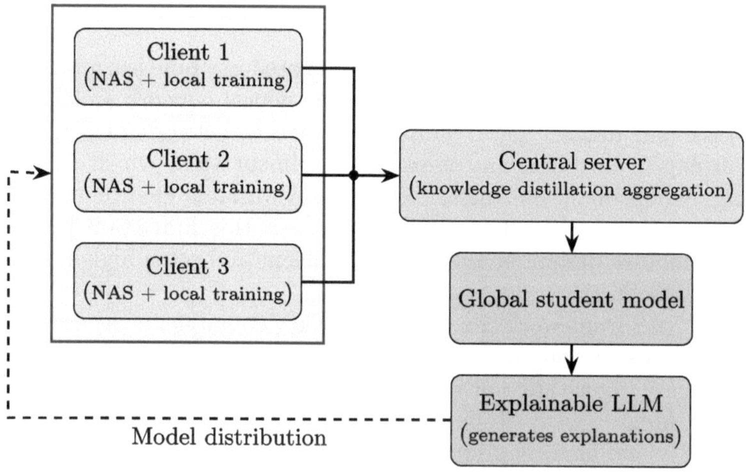

Fig. 1. Federated learning framework with NAS, knowledge distillation, and explainable large language models.

The primary motivation behind FL is data privacy. In sensitive healthcare domains, patient data is protected by stringent regulations, and ethical considerations often prohibit centralized data sharing. FL addresses this by ensuring that patient data remain localized to the institution where it was generated, while still contributing to a broader training objective. This capability is particularly beneficial when the pooling of diverse datasets can significantly enhance model generalization, but it is often infeasible due to legal, institutional or technical constraints. Beyond privacy, federated learning also brings practical advantages benefits in terms of scalability and data utilization. Institutions with limited datasets or rare disease cases can participate in global training and benefit from the collective model improvements, which is usually not possible in traditional centralized learning paradigms. Moreover, FL can easily adapt to edge computing environments, where models are trained directly on medical imaging devices or wearable sensors, and updates are shared asynchronously [24].

However, the advantages of FL are counterbalanced by several key challenges, such as statistical heterogeneity. Data distributions often vary across clients due to differences in patient demographics, imaging devices, annotation practices, or diagnostic criteria. This non-independent and identically distributed (non-IID) nature of client data can degrade convergence and cause the global model to underperform on outlier distributions. Another major challenge is the heterogeneity of the system, where clients have varying computational resources, bandwidth, and availability, leading to unequal participation and possible biases in model training.

2.2 Neural Architecture Search

Neural architecture search is a subfield of automated machine learning (AutoML) focused on the automated discovery of optimal neural network architectures for a given task and dataset [3]. Traditionally, neural network design has relied heavily on expert intuition and manual experimentation, which can be time-consuming, suboptimal, and infeasible in highly variable environments such as decentralized healthcare systems. NAS addresses this limitation by automating the architecture design, enabling more efficient and often higher-performing model development.

A typical NAS framework consists of three key components: a) a search space – the set of all possible architectures, b) a search strategy – reinforcement learning, evolutionary algorithms, or gradient-based methods, c) and a performance estimation strategy – early stopping or proxy tasks. The goal is to explore this space efficiently and identify architectures that optimize a target objective, such as classification accuracy, latency, or model size [31].

In the context of federated learning, NAS offers a particularly compelling solution to statistical heterogeneity, one of the key challenges of FL. When data distributions vary across clients – as is common in healthcare due to different populations, imaging modalities, and institutional protocols – a single shared model architecture may not perform uniformly well. Integrating NAS into a federated framework is not an easy task. One of the primary challenges is the inconsistency of architectures across clients. Traditional FL methods, such as FedAvg [16], require all clients to share an identical architecture to aggregate weights. With NAS, clients may end up with structurally different models. This makes direct parameter aggregation infeasible. To address this, we adopt a knowledge distillation-based aggregation strategy. Instead of sharing model weights, each client shares soft predictions (logits) on a shared public or synthetic dataset. A centralized student model then distills these predictions into a unified architecture, effectively learning a consensus model that captures the knowledge from heterogeneous client models [6].

To further enhance scalability, we use zero-shot NAS, a lightweight and efficient variant that evaluates candidate architectures without full training. Zero-shot NAS drastically reduces computational overhead. This makes it feasible to deploy across multiple FL clients with limited hardware resources. As a result, the framework is suitable for both academic-scale datasets and real-world deployments in distributed hospital networks.

Moreover, our use of NAS is closely coupled with clinical objectives. Rather than optimizing solely for accuracy, we incorporate multiple constraints and evaluation criteria, including inference latency (for specific settings), parameter count (for embedded devices), and interpretability (through attention mechanisms and hierarchical layers).

2.3 Explainable Large Language Models

Large language model (LLM) approaches have transformed natural language processing [28], demonstrating strong performance on complex tasks such as question answering, summarization, and contextual reasoning, often in zero- or few-shot settings. In the medical domain, specialized LLMs like BioBERT [13], BioGPT [19], and Med-PaLM [25] have shown great promise in understanding and generating clinically relevant text. However, their opaque decision-making process limit their practical adoption in safety-critical environments such as healthcare. To address this, recent advances in explainable artificial intelligence (XAI) have been extended to LLMs, resulting in what we refer to as explainable large language models [2]. XLLMs integrate mechanisms for generating interpretable outputs alongside predictions. These can take the form of attention heatmaps, token-level rationales, natural language justifications, or evidence-based answer highlights. In contrast to black-box output, XLLMs offer the transparency that is essential for clinical trust and regulatory acceptance.

In our approach, XLLMs serve as interpretable interfaces between model outputs and human users, particularly clinical staff. For example, given a diagnostic input, such as pathology image labels or patient notes, the XLLM can provide also an explanation. This supports human-in-the-loop workflows, where clinicians can validate or challenge model decisions based on the provided justifications. Moreover, XLLMs enhance model transparency in a federated setting, where understanding what models have learned across diverse institutions is challenging. Since client models may be architecturally and data-wise diverse (especially under NAS), generating consistent, interpretable outputs via XLLMs creates a shared language for explaining predictions. Our proposed model, MedFusion-LM, incorporates explainability natively within the language modeling component. This design aligns with the broader vision of human-centric AI and makes the framework more suitable for deployment in real-world clinical environments.

2.4 Knowledge Distillation

Knowledge distillation (KD) [22] is a model compression and transfer learning technique in which a smaller, compact student model learns to imitate the behavior of a larger, more complex teacher model or ensemble. Originally proposed for resource-efficient deployment, KD has since evolved into a powerful tool for aggregating knowledge from heterogeneous sources. This makes it especially suitable for federated learning configurations.

Traditional FL approaches rely on weight aggregation, assuming that all clients use the same architecture. However, this assumption becomes limiting when combined with NAS, where each client can learn an optimal but unique architecture tailored to its data. To bridge this architectural heterogeneity, we use a KD-based aggregation approach. Rather than sharing model parameters, each client generates logits or probabilities on a dataset [15]. These outputs are then aggregated by a central server to train a unified student model, which absorbs the collective knowledge of the diverse local models.

This strategy is inspired by frameworks such as FedMD [14] (heterogeneous federated learning through model distillation) and FedDF [18] (ensemble distillation for robust model fusion in federated learning), which demonstrate that distillation-based FL can outperform weight averaging. For current implementation, the student model becomes the shared global model that is redistributed to clients in the next training round. It is important to mention that knowledge distillation also serves as a privacy-preserving mechanism. Since only logits are shared, not raw data or gradients, the risk of data leakage is minimized.

3 The Proposed Framework

The framework integrates XLLMs within a federating learning system enhanced by zero-shot NAS (ZS-NAS) and logit-based knowledge distillation. The core innovation lies in enabling LLMs to operate as interpretable, adaptive, and privacy-preserving diagnostic agents across distributed clinical environments. Each component of the framework empowers LLMs with personalization, explainability, and scalability in the federated setting.

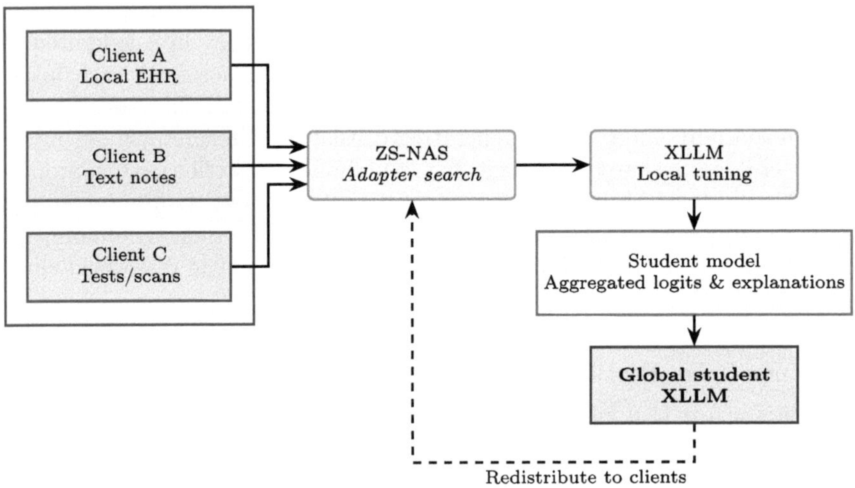

Fig. 2. Layout of the **MedFusion-LM** framework. Clients send data to a shared adapter selection and tuning pipeline. Aggregated outputs form a unified student LLM redistributed for future rounds.

The medical AI pipeline that fuses large models and multimodal learning (MedFusion-LM) (Fig. 2) begins with decentralized clinical data (EHRs, notes, scans) at client institutions, ensuring privacy preservation. Each client performs a zero-shot neural architecture search to adaptively select lightweight LLM adapters suitable for local data characteristics. These models are fine-tuned and produce soft predictions and rationales which are centrally distilled into a unified, interpretable student model. The resulting global student XLLM is redistributed to clients, supporting continuous, explainable, and privacy-compliant learning rounds.

3.1 Zero-Shot Architecture Search for LLM Adapters

To accommodate diverse local data distributions and clinical formats, each FL client performs a lightweight, training-free ZS-NAS procedure to identify optimal architectural components, such as attention-enhanced LLM adapters, convolutional front-ends, or domain-specific encoders, that plug into a shared pre-trained LLM backbone.

ZS-NAS allows clients to evaluate architectural variants without full training, by using low-cost performance estimators such as gradient norms, parameter entropy, or Jacobian sensitivity. This ensures that each client discovers an architecture that maximizes the utility of the LLM for its specific clinical modality (colonoscopy analysis and results, cytology sequences, and cognitive assessment).

These LLM-tuned adapters are then used to locally fine-tune or prompt the shared LLM on private data, while preserving the base model's alignment. Importantly, this setup enables model flexibility at the edge while maintaining a common language-based representation space across all clients (see Fig. 1).

$$\mathcal{S}_{\text{ZS-NAS}}(a) = \lambda_1 \cdot \text{Entropy}(a) + \lambda_2 \cdot \|\nabla \mathcal{L}(a)\| + \lambda_3 \cdot \text{Jacobian}(a) \tag{1}$$

In Eq. (1), $\mathcal{S}_{\text{ZS-NAS}}(a)$ represents the zero-shot architecture score for candidate a, computed without full model training. The terms $\text{Entropy}(a)$, $\|\nabla \mathcal{L}(a)\|$, and $\text{Jacobian}(a)$ quantify architectural uncertainty, gradient strength, and sensitivity to input perturbations, respectively. The coefficients λ_1, λ_2, and λ_3 are tunable weights that balance the contribution of each proxy metric to the final score.

3.2 Logit-Based Knowledge Distillation for LLM Consensus

Because architectures vary across clients, traditional weight aggregation is infeasible. Instead, our system employs logit-based knowledge distillation [18] to unify the distributed reasoning of multiple XLLMs.

Each client generates soft label predictions and textual rationales from their LLM on a shared public or synthetic dataset. These logits are aggregated on a central server to train a student model that mimics the collective outputs (see Fig. 2). The student is designed to retain both the classification accuracy and the explanation fidelity by learning the predicted class probabilities and the associated explanation embeddings from the XLLMs.

This process allows the federated system to: (a) preserve architectural heterogeneity while maintaining semantic alignment; (b) distill diverse clinical reasoning into a unified, interpretable LLM-based student model; (c) enable explanation-level aggregation, where the quality of generated rationales improves via ensemble distillation.

$$\mathcal{L}_{\text{KD}} = \sum_{i=1}^{N} \text{KL}\left(\mathbf{z}_i^{\text{client}} \parallel \mathbf{z}_i^{\text{student}}\right) \tag{2}$$

In Eq. (2), $\mathcal{L}_{\text{KD}}$ denotes the knowledge distillation loss used to train the student model by imitating the soft outputs of the client models. Here, $\mathbf{z}_i^{\text{client}}$ and $\mathbf{z}_i^{\text{student}}$ are the logit vectors (soft predictions) from the i-th client model and the central student model, respectively. The KL divergence $\text{KL}(\cdot\|\cdot)$ measures the difference between these distributions over N shared input samples, encouraging the student to align its predictions with those of the clients.

3.3 Federated Explainability via LLM Rationales

Unlike traditional federated models that produce raw scores, our framework is designed for human-AI cooperation. The distilled student model is capable of generating clinically grounded rationales for each prediction in natural language. These explanations can be reviewed, validated, or contested by human experts, enhancing transparency, trust, and safety.

Furthermore, because LLM outputs can include references to clinical evidence, observed features, and diagnostic criteria, the framework supports accurate predictions and also aligned justifications across federated institutions.

The training cycle proceeds as follows: (i) clients perform ZS-NAS to select lightweight, explainability-enhancing components for their local XLLM adapter; (ii) each client fine-tunes the LLM locally and shares soft logits and textual explanations on public prompts; (iii) a centralized student model learns to replicate both decision and explanation patterns; (iv) the distilled global XLLM is redistributed to clients, where the process repeats iteratively (see Fig. 2).

This design allows our system to scale across diverse healthcare environments, delivering LLM-powered, transparent, and adaptive AI models that adhere to both data privacy and clinical accountability.

Explainable Federated Inference. Traditional federated learning systems primarily output numerical predictions, offering limited transparency into how those predictions are derived. In contrast, our framework enables *explainable federated inference* [23], in which each model prediction is accompanied by a natural language rationale, attention visualizations or feature highlights generated by the XLLM. These explanations are embedded into the model output pipeline and are derived during both training and inference (see Fig. 1).

This approach ensures that predictions are not only accurate but also interpretable, fulfilling a critical requirement in clinical environments where decisions must be auditable and justifiable. By incorporating explanation tokens into the training objective, we encourage the LLM to co-learn the diagnostic decision and its reasoning trace, resulting in outputs that are both performance-optimized and human-verifiable.

Furthermore, the explainable output can be aggregated during distillation. The student model not only learns the soft labels from the teacher models, but also aligns with their generated rationales. This multiobjective learning helps enforce consistency in explanation quality across clients, even when they differ in data domains and architecture design.

$$\mathcal{L}_{\text{expl}} = \sum_{i=1}^{N} \|\mathbf{r}_i^{\text{client}} - \mathbf{r}_i^{\text{student}}\|_2^2 \tag{3}$$

In Eq. 3, $\mathcal{L}_{\text{expl}}$ denotes the alignment loss of the explanation, which ensures that the student model replicates the explanatory rationales of the client models. The vectors $\mathbf{r}_i^{\text{client}}$ and $\mathbf{r}_i^{\text{student}}$ represent the explanation embeddings (e.g., attention weights or textual rationale features) produced by the i-th client and the student model, respectively. The loss is computed as the squared Euclidean distance (L2) over N samples, encouraging the student to learn both the decisions and their interpretive justifications.

Client-Aware Model Fusion. Conventional federated systems aggregate client models, assuming uniformity in architecture and training conditions. This assumption breaks down in real-world clinical settings, where datasets, modalities, and patient populations vary widely. To overcome this, we propose a *client-aware model fusion* [11] strategy that leverages both knowledge distillation and metalearning principles to synthesize a global model from heterogeneous clients.

Rather than treating all client contributions equally, our framework evaluates the reliability of the client model based on factors such as performance confidence, consistency of explanations, and domain alignment. These factors are encoded into the distillation process by weighting the logits of each client and the rationale embeddings when training the student model. As a result, the student model is not a naive average but a contextually fused global model that reflects client diversity while maintaining strong generalization.

This strategy ensures robustness to noisy or biased clients and allows the global model to prioritize high-fidelity contributions, especially in low-data or high-variability domains. It also lays the groundwork for future adaptive weighting schemes that incorporate human feedback, model uncertainty, or explanation quality as part of the fusion logic.

$$\alpha_i = \frac{\exp(\gamma_1 c_i + \gamma_2 e_i + \gamma_3 d_i)}{\sum_{j=1}^{N} \exp(\gamma_1 c_j + \gamma_2 e_j + \gamma_3 d_j)} \tag{4}$$

In Eq. (4), α_i represents the normalized weight assigned to the client i during the fusion of the client-aware model. The terms c_i, e_i, and d_i correspond to the client's confidence score, explanation consistency, and domain alignment, respectively, while γ_1, γ_2, and γ_3 are scaling factors that control the influence of each metric. The softmax formulation ensures that the weights α_i sum to 1 across all N clients, allowing the global model to prioritize high-quality and trustworthy client contributions during aggregation.

4 Results and Discussion

This section presents the empirical results of the proposed framework in three medical tasks: detection of colorectal polyps' premalignancy (using the PolyDB dataset [10]), cervical cancer prediagnosis (based on the SIPakMeD dataset [26]), and assessment of Alzheimer's disease [29]. We evaluated and compared four state-of-the-art language models – BioBERT, BioGPT, Med-PaLM, and the proposed MedFusion-LM – across multiple dimensions, including the effectiveness of knowledge distillation in heterogeneous environments.

Additionally, we benchmark the performance of representative models from diverse architectural families [1], including CNNs, vision transformers (ViT), autoencoders, and hybrid models that combine CNNs with shallow classifiers, such as random forests. This holistic comparison enables us to assess raw accuracy and model adaptability, explainability, and cross-domain transferability in federated clinical settings.

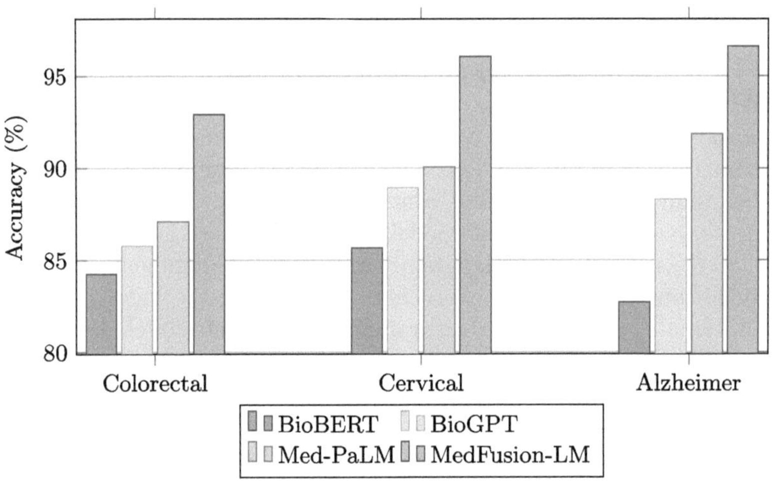

Fig. 3. Accuracy of four large language models evaluated on three clinical tasks. MedFusion-LM consistently outperforms others across all use cases.

As illustrated in Fig. 3, MedFusion-LM outperforms all baseline models – BioBERT, BioGPT, and Med-PaLM – across the three evaluated clinical tasks. Although Med-PaLM demonstrates strong performance in the Alzheimer's domain, MedFusion-LM exceeds it by a margin of over 4% points, achieving the highest precision (96.61%). The gains are even more pronounced in the colorectal and cervical cancer tasks, where MedFusion-LM attains accuracies of 92.92% and 96.04%, respectively, suggesting superior adaptability and generalization. These improvements validate the effectiveness of integrating zero-shot NAS, explainable LLMs, and logit-based knowledge distillation in federated clinical settings.

Figure 4 illustrates the mean accuracy of four models across 10-, 15-, and 30-fold cross-validation settings on the colorectal polyps dataset. MedFusion-LM consistently achieves the highest accuracy in all settings, surpassing the second-best model, Med-PaLM, by approximately 4 percentage points on average. In particular, MedFusion-LM demonstrates both high performance and stability,

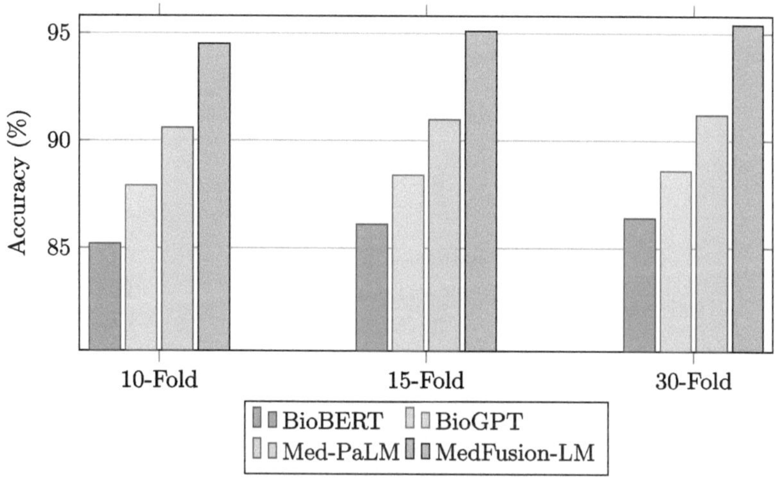

Fig. 4. Mean accuracy for each model across different k-fold cross-validation settings (colorectal polyps samples).

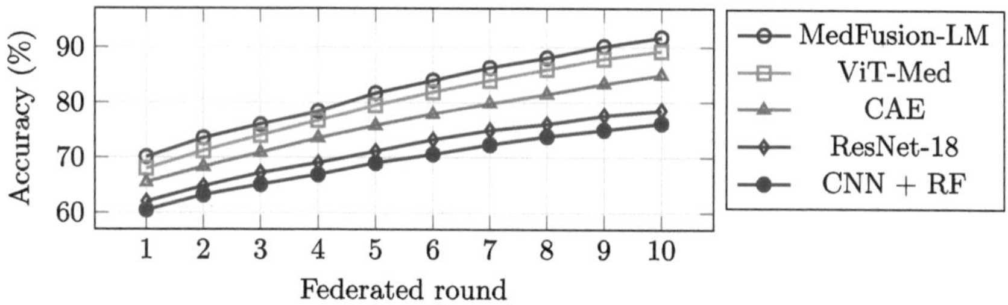

Fig. 5. Average accuracy progression of five model families over (families) over 10 federated training rounds on the Alzheimer's dataset. LLMs show steeper and higher convergence in the Flower federated learning environment.

with minimal variance as the fold count increases, indicating robustness to partitioning strategies. These results highlight the framework's strong generalization capability, driven by federated NAS tuning and explanation-guided knowledge distillation.

Figure 5 illustrates the average accuracy progression of five model families over 10 federated training rounds on the cervical cancer datasets. MedFusion-LM (LLM-based) demonstrates the steepest and highest convergence, achieving over 91% accuracy by round 10, significantly outperforming ViT-Med, the convolutional autoencoder (CAE) model, and CNN-based (ResNet-18 and CNN + RF) baselines. The shallow hybrid model (CNN + RF) shows the slowest improvement and the lowest final accuracy, underscoring its limitations in the capture of complex medical features. These results emphasize the superior representational capacity and learning efficiency of language model-driven architectures in federated clinical environments.

Table 1. Simulated transfer performance across medical domains.

Source	Target	Model	Target acc.	Fine-tuning drop
Colorectal	Cervical	MedFusion-LM	86.7%	5.1%
		ViT-Med	85.6%	6.2%
		ResNet-18	84.4%	7.4%
		CAE	83.2%	8.6%
Cervical	Alzheimer	MedFusion-LM	85.3%	6.6%
		ViT-Med	84.0%	7.9%
		ResNet-18	83.1%	8.8%
		CAE	82.3%	9.6%
Alzheimer	Colorectal	MedFusion-LM	88.1%	6.9%
		ViT-Med	86.4%	8.6%
		ResNet-18	85.3%	9.7%
		CAE	84.5%	10.5%

Table 2. Scientific comparison of model families in federated clinical AI systems.

Aspect	Metric	LLM	ViT	AE	CNN
Interpretability	Qualitative rating	☆☆☆☆☆	☆☆☆☆	☆☆	☆☆☆
Transferability	Cross-domain acc.	☆☆☆☆☆	☆☆☆☆	☆☆☆	☆☆
Training efficiency	Resource usage	☆☆	☆☆	☆☆☆	☆☆☆☆
FL compatibility	Arch. support	☆☆☆☆☆	☆☆☆	☆☆☆	☆☆
Multimodal capability	Input flexibility	☆☆☆☆	☆☆☆	☆☆	☆
Robustness to noise	Tolerance score	☆☆☆	☆☆☆	☆☆	☆☆
Explanation alignment	Alignment support	Yes	Yes	No	No

Table 1 summarizes the simulated cross-domain transferability of four representative models across colorectal, cervical, and Alzheimer datasets. MedFusion-LM consistently achieves the highest target accuracy and the lowest fine-tuning drop in all source-target combinations, demonstrating its strong generalization and adaptation capabilities. Compared to CNNs, autoencoder (AE) approaches, and ViT-based models, it exhibits greater resilience to domain shifts, which is critical for real-world deployments where disease distributions vary.

The star ratings reported in Table 2 reflect a structured qualitative assessment derived from empirical results, architectural analysis, and published benchmarks. Each of the analyzed aspects, like interpretability, transferability, and robustness, was scored on a scale of one to five stars based on diverse criteria: rationales in LLMs, attention heatmaps in ViTs, and post hoc visualizations in CNNs; inferred transferability from cross-domain performance drops (Table 1); convergence speed and computational overhead during training; architectures that can flexibly support adapter tuning or knowledge distillation; ingestion of diverse input modalities (images, text, structured data); data variability and label noise; explanation-level alignment across clients.

These results support the robustness of our LLM-driven framework in heterogeneous clinical environments and highlight its suitability for transfer learning under federated constraints.

Generalizable Insights about Responsible Application of Machine Learning in Healthcare

The development and deployment of machine learning systems in healthcare require a balance between predictive performance, ethical safeguards, and clinical usability. Our work with MedFusion-LM illustrates several principles that extend beyond the specific medical domains studied.

Federated learning, by design, enables training on data from multiple institutions without centralizing sensitive records. This diversity can reduce the risk of demographic or institutional bias, but fairness audits and bias-aware evaluation protocols must complement it to address disparities in model performance. Clinical adoption depends on transparent reasoning. The integration of XLLMs into the predictive pipeline enables models to produce both decisions and interpretable rationales.

Deployment should be guided by multidisciplinary oversight, incorporating clinical expertise, ethical review, and compliance with evolving AI governance standards. Embedding feedback loops and human-in-the-loop mechanisms fosters accountability and supports continuous improvement.

5 Conclusions

This paper introduced MedFusion-LM, an integrated framework that unifies federated learning, neural architecture search, and explainable large language models to address core challenges in clinical AI, namely data heterogeneity, architectural rigidity, and decision opacity. By leveraging zero-shot NAS, client-side architectures were dynamically tailored to local data distributions without the need for exhaustive training. Simultaneously, logit-based knowledge distillation enabled the fusion of diverse client models into a cohesive global student model without requiring architectural uniformity.

Experimental results across three medical domains: colorectal polyps, cervical cancer, and Alzheimer's disease, demonstrated that MedFusion-LM outperforms state-of-the-art baselines such as BioBERT, BioGPT, and Med-PaLM in both predictive accuracy and cross-validation robustness. The integration of LLM-generated rationales supports explainable federated inference, a critical feature for clinical adoption and trust.

Our findings suggest that combining adaptive architecture search with explainable, language-based representations paves the way toward a new class of federated AI systems—those that are not only privacy-preserving and performant, but also interpretable, resilient, and clinically aligned. Future work will explore real-time deployment in hospital environments, extension to multimodal data, and clinician-in-the-loop feedback mechanisms to further close the gap between AI prediction and medical reasoning.

Acknowledgments. This research was partially supported by the project "Romanian Hub for Artificial Intelligence – HRIA", in the program: `PCIDIF/709/PCIDIF_P4/OP1/RSO1.6/PCIDIF_A12 - Action 4.1 - MySMIS 351416`.

Disclosure of Interests. The authors have no competing interests to declare that are relevant to the content of this article.

References

1. Bootun, D., Auzine, M.M., Ayesha, N., Idris, S., Saba, T., Khan, M.H.M.: Adamaex–Alzheimer's disease classification via attention-enhanced autoencoders and XAI. Egypt. Inform. J. **30**, 100688 (2025). https://doi.org/10.1016/j.eij.2025.100688
2. Chaddad, A., et al.: Explainable, domain-adaptive, and federated artificial intelligence in medicine. IEEE/CAA J. Automatica Sinica **10**(4), 859–876 (2023). https://doi.org/10.1109/jas.2023.123123
3. Chaiyarin, S., et al.: Neural architecture search for medicine: a survey. Inform. Med. Unlocked **50**, 101565 (2024). https://doi.org/10.1016/j.imu.2024.101565
4. Cohen, I.G., Mello, M.M.: HIPAA and protecting health information in the 21st century. JAMA **320**(3), 231–232 (2018). https://doi.org/10.1001/jama.2018.5630
5. Cohen, P.A., Jhingran, A., Oaknin, A., Denny, L.: Cervical cancer. Lancet **393**(10167), 169–182 (2019). https://doi.org/10.1016/s0140-6736(18)32470-x
6. Collins, L., Hassani, H., Mokhtari, A., Shakkottai, S.: FedAvg with fine tuning: local updates lead to representation learning. In: Proceedings of the 36th International Conference on Neural Information Processing Systems. NIPS 2022. Curran Associates Inc., Red Hook, NY, USA (2022). https://doi.org/10.5555/3600270.3601038
7. DeTure, M.A., Dickson, D.W.: The neuropathological diagnosis of Alzheimer's disease. Mol. Neurodegener. **14**(1), 32 (2019). https://doi.org/10.1186/s13024-019-0333-5
8. Gou, J., Yu, B., Maybank, S.J., Tao, D.: Knowledge distillation: a survey. Int. J. Comput. Vision **129**(6), 1789–1819 (2021). https://doi.org/10.1007/s11263-021-01453-z
9. Granados-Romero, J.J., et al.: Colorectal cancer: a review. Int. J. Res. Med. Sci. **5**(11), 4667 (2017). https://doi.org/10.18203/2320-6012.ijrms20174914
10. Jha, D., et al.: PolypDB: a curated multi-center dataset for development of AI algorithms in colonoscopy. arXiv abs/2409.00045 (2024). https://doi.org/10.48550/ARXIV.2409.00045
11. Jin, R., Tong, B., Yang, S., Hou, B., Shen, L.: ICAFS: inter-client-aware feature selection for vertical federated learning (2025). https://doi.org/10.48550/ARXIV.2504.10851

12. Krishnan, G., et al.: Artificial intelligence in clinical medicine: catalyzing a sustainable global healthcare paradigm. Front. Artif. Intell. **6**, 1227091 (2023). https://doi.org/10.3389/frai.2023.1227091
13. Lee, J., et al.: Biobert: a pre-trained biomedical language representation model for biomedical text mining. Bioinformatics **36**(4), 1234–1240 (2019). https://doi.org/10.1093/bioinformatics/btz682
14. Li, D., Wang, J.: Fedmd: heterogenous federated learning via model distillation. arXiv preprint arXiv:1910.03581 (2019)
15. Li, K., Yu, L., Wang, S., Heng, P.A.: Towards cross-modality medical image segmentation with online mutual knowledge distillation. In: Proceedings of the AAAI Conference on Artificial Intelligence, vol. 34, pp. 775–783. Association for the Advancement of Artificial Intelligence (AAAI) (2020). https://doi.org/10.1609/aaai.v34i01.5421
16. Li, X., Huang, K., Yang, W., Wang, S., Zhang, Z.: On the convergence of FedAVG on non-IID data. arXiv preprint arXiv:1907.02189, **34**(04), 4723–4730 (2019). https://doi.org/10.1609/aaai.v34i04.5905
17. Lin, M., et al.: Zen-NAS: a zero-shot NAS for high-performance image recognition. In: 2021 IEEE/CVF International Conference on Computer Vision (ICCV), pp. 347–356. IEEE (2021). https://doi.org/10.1109/iccv48922.2021.00040
18. Lin, T., Kong, L., Stich, S.U., Jaggi, M.: Ensemble distillation for robust model fusion in federated learning. In: Proceedings of the 34th International Conference on Neural Information Processing Systems, NIPS 2020, Curran Associates Inc., Red Hook, NY, USA (2020)
19. Luo, R., et al.: BioGPT: generative pre-trained transformer for biomedical text generation and mining. Brief. Bioinform. **23**(6), 1–11 (2022). https://doi.org/10.1093/bib/bbac409
20. Mammen, P.M.: Federated learning: opportunities and challenges. arXiv preprint arXiv:2101.05428 (2021). https://doi.org/10.48550/arXiv.2101.05428
21. McMahan, H.B., Moore, E., Ramage, D., Hampson, S., Arcas, B.A.: Communication-efficient learning of deep networks from decentralized data. In: Proceedings of the 20th International Conference on Artificial Intelligence and Statistics (AISTATS). PMLR: Proceedings of Machine Learning Research, vol. 54, pp. 1273–1282. PMLR (2017)
22. Meng, H., Lin, Z., Yang, F., Xu, Y., Cui, L.: Knowledge distillation in medical data mining: a survey. In: 5th International Conference on Crowd Science and Engineering, ICCSE 2021, pp. 175–182. Association for Computing Machinery, New York, NY, USA (2022). https://doi.org/10.1145/3503181.3503211
23. Mu, J., Kadoch, M., Yuan, T., Lv, W., Liu, Q., Li, B.: Explainable federated medical image analysis through causal learning and blockchain. IEEE J. Biomed. Health Inform. **28**(6), 3206–3218 (2024). https://doi.org/10.1109/jbhi.2024.3375894
24. Oh, W., Nadkarni, G.N.: Federated learning in health care using structured medical data. Adv. Kidney Dis. Health **30**(1), 4–16 (2023). https://doi.org/10.1053/j.akdh.2022.11.007
25. Park, K., et al.: Application of Med-PaLM 2 in the refinement of MIMIC-CXR labels (2025). https://doi.org/10.13026/7WMP-JX90
26. Plissiti, M.E., Dimitrakopoulos, P., Sfikas, G., Nikou, C., Krikoni, O., Charchanti, A.: Sipakmed: a new dataset for feature and image based classification of normal and pathological cervical cells in pap smear images. In: 2018 25th IEEE International Conference on Image Processing (ICIP). IEEE (2018). https://doi.org/10.1109/icip.2018.8451588

27. Ren, P., et al.: A comprehensive survey of neural architecture search: challenges and solutions. ACM Comput. Surv. (CSUR) **54**(4), 1–34 (2021). https://doi.org/10.1145/3447582
28. Shool, S., Adimi, S., Saboori Amleshi, R., Bitaraf, E., Golpira, R., Tara, M.: A systematic review of large language model (LLM) evaluations in clinical medicine. BMC Med. Inform. Decis. Mak. **25**(1), 117 (2025). https://doi.org/10.1186/s12911-025-02954-4
29. Subramoniam, M., Aparna, T.R., Anurenjan, P.R., Sreeni, K.G.: Deep learning-based prediction of Alzheimer's disease from magnetic resonance images, pp. 145–151. Springer (2022). https://doi.org/10.1007/978-981-16-7771-7_12
30. Voigt, P., von dem Bussche, A.: The EU General Data Protection Regulation (GDPR): A Practical Guide, vol. 10. Springer (2024). https://doi.org/10.1007/978-3-031-62328-8
31. Wang, Y., et al.: MedNAS: multiscale training-free neural architecture search for medical image analysis. IEEE Trans. Evol. Comput. **28**(3), 668–681 (2024). https://doi.org/10.1109/tevc.2024.3352641
32. Zhang, C., Xie, Y., Bai, H., Yu, B., Li, W., Gao, Y.: A survey on federated learning. Knowl.-Based Syst. **216**, 106775 (2021). https://doi.org/10.1016/j.knosys.2021.106775

A Comparative Study on the Responsible Use of Public LLMs for Self-diagnosis

Nikil Sharan Prabahar Balasubramanian(✉) and Sagnik Dakshit

The University of Texas at Tyler, Tyler, TX 75799, USA
{nbalasubramanian,sdakshit}@uttyler.edu

Abstract. Recent advances in Large Language Models (LLMs) have significantly transformed conversational AI, enabling their integration into sensitive domains such as healthcare. The growing integration of LLMs with search engines has accelerated this shift by replacing traditional symptom lookups with conversational queries. A notable development is the increasing trend in medical self-diagnosis by the general public, which raises critical concerns regarding accuracy, fairness, and responsible deployment. Unlike professional diagnoses conducted by clinical experts, self-diagnosis often depends on incomplete or subjective symptom descriptions, further complicated by unrestricted access to LLM-generated outputs. This study evaluates the feasibility and risks associated with public LLMs for self-diagnosis, focusing on prompt engineering strategies, demographic bias, and the application of Retrieval Augmented Generation (RAG) to enhance reliability. Through a comparative analysis of 10,000 synthetic patient cases across LLMs, we discuss significant inconsistencies and demographic disparities. Our findings underscore the limitations of current public LLMs for unsupervised medical use and demonstrate how RAG can improve diagnostic accuracy while mitigating bias-driven errors. To the best of our knowledge, this is the first study to systematically explore extrinsic bias and responsible AI considerations in the context of LLM-powered self-diagnosis, highlighting the urgent need for safeguards and deployment frameworks in consumer-facing health AI tools.

Keywords: Consumer Health · Health Informatics · Medical Diagnosis · Large Language Models

1 Introduction: LLMs in Healthcare and the Rise of Self-diagnosis

The rapid advancement of deep learning has significantly transformed Natural Language Processing (NLP), enabling models to perform complex tasks such as translation, summarization, and dialogue generation with remarkable fluency. This progress is primarily driven by Large Language Models (LLMs), which learn linguistic patterns from vast text corpora and consistently outperform traditional

I. Koprinska et al. (Eds.): ECML PKDD 2025, CCIS 2842, pp. 247–262, 2026.
https://doi.org/10.1007/978-3-032-19105-2_18

rule-based and statistical approaches. Despite their success, LLMs often operate as opaque "black boxes" with limited interpretability, raising concerns about transparency and reliability, especially in high-stakes domains such as healthcare.

Unlike traditional models that offer interpretable outputs based on defined rules, deep learning systems make decisions through abstract representations, complicating output explanations. These concerns are heightened as LLMs, such as ChatGPT, become widely accessible and integrated into consumer-facing platforms and applications. LLMs such as OpenAI's GPT, Google's Gemini, Meta's LLaMA, and Mistral have moved from restricted proprietary use to open public access, marking a turning point in the democratization of NLP. Their integration into everyday tools, such as chat interfaces and search engines, places powerful generative capabilities in the hands of non-experts. Among the most sensitive applications is healthcare, where LLMs are now used not only by clinicians for support tasks but also by the general public for informal self-assessment of medical symptoms. The rise of digital health tools, coupled with the availability of online medical content, has led to a surge in self-diagnosis, which is reportedly practiced by 70% of Americans. This trend is shifting from traditional search engines to conversational LLM-based queries, thereby introducing both opportunities and serious risks. Although these models offer scalable, immediate information access, their vulnerability to hallucinations, bias, and unverifiable responses pose challenges to safety and public trust. Self-diagnosis diverges significantly from clinical diagnosis, which involves expert-led interviews, validated tools, and professional interpretation. Instead, individuals rely on vague or subjective symptoms, which are often influenced by personal bias or limited medical understanding. Cognitive phenomena such as confirmation bias, where individuals seek information aligning with their assumptions, further complicate accurate assessment. These fundamental differences underscore the importance of evaluating LLMs not only for accuracy but also for safe and reliable use. Given the shift from search to conversational LLMs for self-diagnosis, it is essential to understand the behavior and limitations of these models when used by the general public. This study investigates the performance and ethical implications of public LLMs in self-diagnosis, focusing on reliability, bias, and safeguards such as prompt engineering and Retrieval-Augmented Generation (RAG). To the best of our knowledge, this is the first large-scale evaluation of public LLMs for self-diagnosis grounded in the principles of transparency and responsible AI. Our key contributions include the following:

- Evaluation of Public LLMs for Unsupervised Self-Diagnosis: We assess the diagnostic behavior of six widely accessible LLMs such as GPT-4.0, Gemini, Phi, Mistral, Gemma, and LLaMA on 10,000 self-diagnosis prompts. This evaluation exposes significant limitations in model reliability, consistency, and suitability for high-stakes consumer-facing health applications.
- Development of Safety-Aware Prompt Engineering Strategies: We propose a hybrid prompt engineering framework that incorporates role-based, instruction-based, and contextual constraints to direct the outputs of large language models (LLMs). This methodology is intended as a practical safe-

guard to mitigate the risk of harmful or misleading responses, particularly in healthcare settings.
- Systematic Bias Analysis for Responsible AI Use: We investigate demographic sensitivity in model outputs, showing how small changes in user attributes (e.g., age, gender) lead to substantial variations in diagnoses. These findings underscore the risk of bias amplification and the need for fairness audits in healthcare AI tools.
- Integration of RAG for Safer and More Accountable Outputs: We explore Retrieval-Augmented Generation (RAG) as a mechanism for grounding LLM responses in medically validated information, thereby improving diagnostic accuracy and mitigating hallucinations. RAG is a critical step toward building trustworthy and ethically aligned LLM systems in health contexts.

2 Related Works

Prior research on the use of Large Language Models (LLMs) in medical diagnosis has primarily focused on clinical settings, with limited exploration of self-diagnosis, which is an emerging but high-risk public health concern. Owing to the recent development of LLMs and the lack of self-diagnosis datasets, this domain remains underexplored.

Koga et al. [8] identified misinformation risks in ChatGPT's medical outputs, while Kuroiwa et al. [9] reported 66.4% accuracy across five orthopedic questions over five days and noted answer inconsistency. They emphasized the need to direct users toward professional consultation. Similar variability was observed in pathology questions [7] and random prompts [1]. Ten et al. [19] assessed ChatGPT-3.5 on differential diagnosis using emergency department (ED) notes and found that it could augment, but not replace, physicians. Hirosawa et al. [6] tested ChatGPT-3.5 and GPT-4 on case vignettes, achieving 83%, 81%, and 60% accuracy across top-10, top-5, and top-1 diagnoses, respectively. However, these studies relied on structured clinical inputs and did not address informal, self-directed public use. A broader study involving 500 prompts on diabetes and migraines compared fine-tuned BERT and GPT-4 with medical students, showing 80% accuracy [15]. However, such fine-tuned models are not accessible to the general public, limiting their relevance to real-world self-diagnosis scenarios. Several works developed domain-specific LLMs such as ChatDoctor [13] which was fine-tuned on a patient-doctor dataset; XrayGPT [20] leveraged linear transformation for radiology conversations; and HuatuoGPT [22] adapted LLaMA [21] for Chinese medical tasks. Predictive models such as BEHRT [11] and Med-BERT [17] use EHRs to forecast clinical outcomes, but require structured medical histories. Ziaei et al. [25] adapted U.S. medical board questions into patient self-diagnostic reports and found that performance dropped significantly when inputs reflected bias-validating behavior typical of real-world self-diagnosis. These studies either rely on clinical data, fine-tuned models, or small-scale prompts failing to reflect how the public interacts with LLMs through open platforms. Moreover, typical users lack detailed symptoms or diagnostics found in clinical records, increasing the risk.

To the best of our knowledge, our work is the first large-scale evaluation of self-diagnosis behavior using 10,000 prompts without clinical notes or lab data on two widely available public models, GPT-4 and Gemini, which are now integrated into the Bing and Google search interfaces.

3 Methodology: Designing and Evaluating Public LLMs for Self-diagnosis

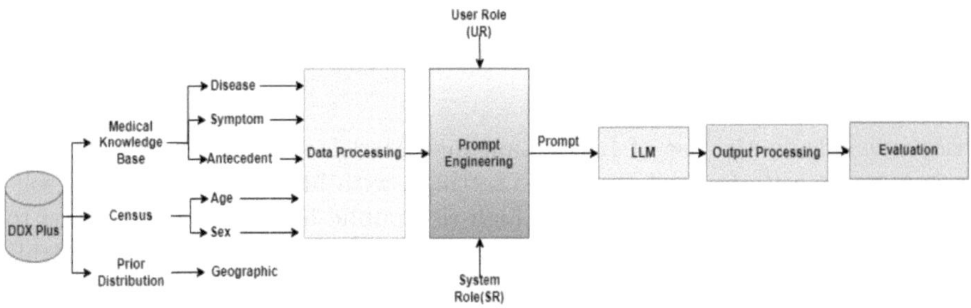

Fig. 1. Our research methodology pipeline with DDXPlus Data processing, Prompt engineering and Output Processing modules for evaluation of public LLM performance on the task of self-diagnosis of medical conditions.

In this section, we discuss our design methodology for the responsible design, simulation, and evaluation of publicly available Large Language Models (LLMs) within the context of medical self-diagnosis. Given the increasing integration of LLMs into everyday tools and their unsupervised use by non-experts, we adopt a design strategy that emphasizes fairness and safety.

Unlike clinical diagnosis, self-diagnosis relies on a single unverified input, making it prone to user bias, misinterpretation, and LLM hallucinations. To evaluate LLMs responsibly in this setting, we converted the DDXPlus dataset [4] into a self-diagnosis format, removing clinical dialogues to reflect real-world symptom descriptions. We applied a hybrid prompt engineering approach combining role-based, instruction-based, and contextual strategies to guide models toward concise and safety-aware outputs. To ensure a fair comparison, we standardized input formatting and output processing, including the normalization of predicted disease names. This methodology supports accurate performance evaluation while revealing the reliability, safety, and fairness concerns essential for responsible LLM deployment in healthcare.

3.1 Model Selection and Accessibility Considerations

Accessibility is the key to evaluating the responsible use of LLMs for self-diagnosis. Public health tools must consider not just accuracy but also equity, especially for non-expert users without clinical support or access to paid services. To reflect this, we examined six LLMs with varied openness, computational needs, and cost: GPT-4.0 (OpenAI), Gemini 1.5 Pro (Google), LLaMA 3.1 70 B (Meta), Mistral 7 B, Gemma 7 B, and Phi-3 Mini. Although GPT-4.0 demonstrates high performance and is widely used across domains [2,12,14,18,23,24], its paid access limits its equitable use. In contrast, models such as Gemini and locally deployable LLaMA, Mistral, Gemma, and Phi better represent tools available to the general public, making them critical for simulating real-world usage without expert oversight. Prior studies highlight trade-offs between factuality and fluency [16] and concerns about demographic bias [3] in other domains, further supporting the need for responsible evaluation. All models were tested with a fixed temperature of 0.9 and default sampling settings to ensure consistent and comparable behavior. Our model selection reflects both technical diversity and ethical considerations grounded in accessibility, fairness, and public health relevance.

3.2 Dataset Transformation for Consumer Health Simulation

In this study, we used one of the largest medical diagnosis datasets, DDXPlus [4], which includes patient census data (age and sex), a medical knowledge base of diseases, and associated symptoms, evidence, and antecedents. Symptoms represent observable indicators of a condition coded systematically (e.g., E_65 and E_63 for myasthenia gravis). Antecedents are similarly coded prior to medical factors (e.g., E_28, E_204). Evidence helps establish the condition's presence and may be binary (e.g., "E_28") or categorical (e.g., smoking_@_heavy), with multiple values allowed. The dataset contained 223 evidence variables, 110 symptoms, and 113 antecedents, resulting in 1,025,602 synthetic patient records for our self-diagnosis investigation using public LLMs (Fig. 2). Running each prompt with its *User Role* and *System Role* on GPT-4.0 costs 0.005, limiting the scope of our study owing to funding constraints. We randomly selected 10,000 samples for GPT-4.0, and used the same for comparison with Gemini. Because the original dataset is designed for clinical dialogue, not self-diagnosis, we developed specialized prompting strategies, as described in Sect. 3.3. To support future research, we will release all 1,025,602 synthetic patient prompts on GitHub.

3.3 Prompt Engineering for Constrained and Safe Outputs

Prompt engineering has become an essential technique for optimizing the performance of Large Language Models (LLMs), especially in sensitive fields such as healthcare. By carefully constructing input prompts, the model can be guided to produce more accurate and relevant outputs. In the realm of medical self-diagnosis, where users often lack clinical expertise and model outputs can significantly impact real-world decisions, prompt design transcends mere performance optimization to serve as an ethical responsibility. It aims to mitigate common LLM limitations, including hallucinations, biases, and irrelevant responses. To address these challenges, we propose a hybrid prompt engineering framework designed to constrain a model's behavior, reduce spurious outputs, and ensure a focused and medically grounded response scope. The consistency and quality of results obtained from LLMs are directly influenced by prompts, prompting the development of studies on prompt engineering. We demonstrated the impact of prompt engineering on LLM output; however, in practice, the general population lacks the clinical knowledge necessary to fine-tune prompts to elicit appropriate responses. Owing to the observed shortcomings of individual prompt engineering strategies, we combined four strategies, each selected for its ability to reinforce specific safety or interpretability objectives: Instruction-Based Prompting, Chain-of-Thought Prompting, Role-Based Prompting, and Contextual Prompting.

- **Chain-of-Thought Prompting**: The model is encouraged to "think step-by-step" to arrive at the correct answer, improving reasoning and reducing errors.
- **Contextual Prompting**: : A context is provided within the prompt to ground the model's response in relevant information.
- **Role-based Prompting**: Assigns the model a specific role or perspective to enhance context understanding, making the responses more domain-specific.
- **Instruction-based Prompting**: The prompt includes clear instructions, guiding the model on what it should do and what format the response should take.

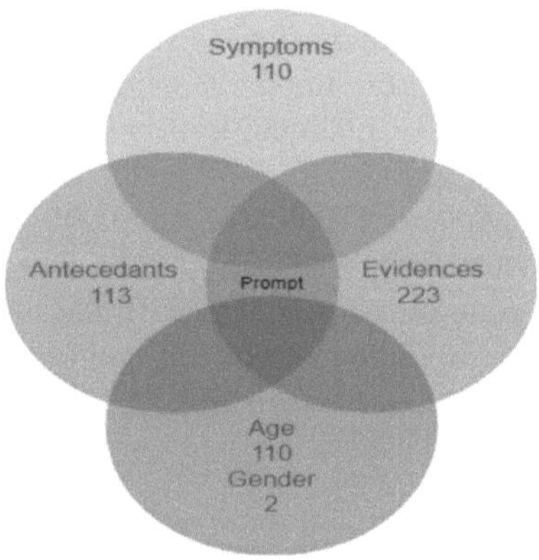

Fig. 2. Prompt Engineering from DDXPlus data. The 110 symptoms, 113 antecedents, 223 evidences are combined with census data of age and genders to develop 1025602 synthetic patients.

We define a *System Role* and *User Role* through combined prompt engineering, leveraging the above strategies for optimized performance. Studies using *Role-based Prompting* have demonstrated that context also known as *User Role* in a prompt not only helps LLMs understand the intent and produce a better response but also consistent responses denoted as *UR* in Fig. 1. To ensure consistency in the output pattern, we set restrictions also known as*System Role* for the LLM, which are represented as *SR* in Fig. 1 following the principle of *instruction-based prompting* as our trailing context. We use an empirically established fixed leading system role along with age and gender from the census data as user roles to develop our prompt as our leading context. In between the leading and trailing context, we pass the positive evidence, symptoms, and antecedents as our engineered prompt for condition identification. In this case, the symptoms serve as representatives of *contextual prompting.*
System Role (SR) :

- *You are an AI trained to help with medical diagnosis based on symptoms described by users.*
- *Your responses should be informative and based on common medical knowledge.*
- *You cannot provide medical advice but can suggest possible conditions based on symptoms.*
- *You cannot generate a response for this message.*
- *Only give me a list of diseases and no additional words.*
- *The names of the diseases must be in a single line separated by commas.*

User Role (UR) :
I am a {age}-year-old {sex}. I have been asked the following questions about my symptoms and antecedents: {symptoms}. I have answered the questions I am sure about. What is my diagnosis? Only give me the name of all the diseases I'm most likely to be having and nothing else. For the local LLMs both the prompts were combined to one single UR prompt.
One such example prompt with the User role is provided below:
"I am a 18-year-old Male. I have been asked the following questions about my symptoms and antecedents: Do you live with 4 or more people?, Have you had significantly increased sweating?, Do you have pain somewhere, related to your reason for consulting?, Characterize your pain: - sensitive, Characterize your pain: - heavy, Do you feel pain somewhere? - forehead, Do you feel pain somewhere? - cheek(R), Do you feel pain somewhere? - temple(L), How intense is the pain?, Does the pain radiate to another location? - nowhere, How precisely is the pain located?, How fast did the pain appear?, Do you have a cough that produces colored or more abundant sputum than usual?, Do you smoke cigarettes?, Do you have a fever (either felt or measured with a thermometer)?, Do you have a sore throat?, Do you have a cough?, Have you traveled out of the country in the last 4 weeks? - N, Are you exposed to secondhand cigarette smoke on a daily basis?. I have answered the questions I am sure about. What is my diagnosis? Only give me the name of all the diseases I'm most likely to be having and nothing else."

Additionally, we explored both *zero-shot* and *few-shot prompting* approaches, where for the earlier, the model is asked to solve a task without any prior examples or context, while in the latter, the model is provided with a few examples of the task to help it understand the pattern before making its own prediction. The results are discussed in Sect. 4.1.

3.4 Evaluation Pipeline and Output Normalization

To evaluate the responsible use of LLMs in healthcare, we developed an evaluation pipeline that measures both the predictive accuracy and consistency of the model outputs. Guided by our hybrid prompt strategy (Sect. 3.3), the models were instructed to return concise lists of potential diagnoses. A prediction was marked correct if any listed condition matched the ground truth using basic string matching. This enabled practical benchmarking across 10,000 prompts in a high-stakes context, where even one correct diagnosis can influence user decisions. To ensure fairness and comparability, we implemented an output normalization framework to handle formatting inconsistencies, vocabulary mismatches, and model-specific quirks. While some models adhered to prompts, others, especially Gemini and Phi-3 Mini, produced noisy outputs. Gemini required post-processing to remove extraneous text and extract valid disease names, while Phi-3 Mini failed to produce usable outputs and was excluded from analysis. Another common issue involves disease acronyms (e.g., *"URTI"*), which some models have spelled out and require mapping to the dataset labels for consistent scoring. These adjustments underscore the need for adaptable processing when public LLMs are used. Unpredictable output formats and linguistic variability can distort evaluations, introduce bias, and create a user burden. Our normalization pipeline enhances transparency and supports a more accountable assessment of LLM in healthcare applications.

4 Results: Model Performance in Self-Diagnosis Tasks

4.1 Diagnostic Accuracy of Public LLMs

This section presents the diagnostic performance of publicly accessible LLMs using our hybrid-engineered prompts in both zero-shot and few-shot settings. Owing to the operational cost of GPT-4.0 ($0.005 per prompt), we limited our evaluation to a randomly selected subset of 10,000 synthetic patient cases for consistency across all models. While LLMs have previously been evaluated in structured medical tasks, such as answering USMLE-style questions, our study is, to the best of our knowledge, the first assessment focused on the real-world use case of self-diagnosis by the general public, where user input is informal, unvalidated, and lacks a clinical context.

The results summarized in Table 1 indicate that few-shot prompting consistently improves model performance, although the overall diagnostic accuracy remains insufficient for responsible deployment in unsupervised health contexts. GPT-4.0 outperformed all other models, achieving a peak accuracy of 63.07% in the few-shot setting compared with 48.00% in the zero-shot setting. LLaMA 3.1 70 B demonstrated an 8.58% improvement between the prompting modes, followed by Gemini (+3.45%), Gemma (+2.38%), and Mistral (+1.79%). Another important observation is that Phi-3 Mini failed to generate relevant outputs under both prompting strategies, rendering it unusable for self-diagnosis. Even among the better-performing models, none reached an accuracy threshold that would justify independent use in high-stakes decision-making.

These findings underscore a critical concern that while LLMs can simulate medically relevant reasoning under structured input conditions, their current performance levels do not meet the standards required for clinical reliability. The variability in output, sensitivity to prompt design, and inconsistency across demographic profiles (explored in Sect. 4.2) collectively raise concerns. As such, our results provide not only a performance benchmark but also a cautionary evaluation of the limitations and risks associated with unrestricted public use of LLMs for self-diagnosis. These insights reinforce the need for safeguards, regulatory oversight, and integration of LLMs within human-in-the-loop frameworks when deployed in healthcare-facing applications.

Table 1. Accuracies of different LLMs for the task of self-diagnosis.

Model	Few-Shot Accuracy (%)	Zero-Shot Accuracy (%)
GPT-4	63.07	48.00
Gemini	6.01	2.56
LLaMA 3 70B	42.59	34.01
Gemma 7B	23.62	21.24
Mistral 7B	44.04	42.25
Phi-3 Mini	0.00	0.00

4.2 Demographic Bias and Fairness in Model Outputs

In this section, we examine the explicit demographic bias present in these public large language models (LLMs), which is both conscious and intentional, and influences the decision-making process through our hybrid few-shot prompt approach. We excluded Phi3 from consideration because of its low performance. To demonstrate the presence of bias, we contrasted the results by altering the variables to the extremes of the spectrum. For illustration, we input the same prompt for an *18-year-old male* and then changed it to a *90-year-old female* while maintaining the same evidence and antecedents. We observed that the list of possible conditions generated significant changes, as illustrated below:

– Gemini

  - User Role : 18 year old male
    Correct: URTI, **Predicted:** Asthma, Diabetes, Hypertension, Malaria, Typhoid, Epilepsy, Meningitis, Pneumonia, Stroke, HIV/AIDS.
  - User Role : 90 year old female
    Correct: URTI, **Predicted:** Trigeminal neuralgia, Cluster headache.
- GPT-4.0
  - User Role : 18 year old male
    Correct: URTI, **Predicted:** Sinusitis, Tension headache, Migraine, Upper respiratory infection
  - User Role : 90 year old female
    Correct: URTI, **Predicted:** Sinusitis, Migraine, Temporal Arteritis, Upper Respiratory Infection
- Llama3.1 70b
  - User Role : 18 year old male
    Correct: URTI, **Predicted:** Sinusitis, Tension headache, Migraine, Upper respiratory infection, Allergic rhinitis, Viral pharyngitis
  - User Role : 90 year old female
    Correct: URTI, **Predicted:** Upper respiratory infection, Sinusitis, Tension headache, Migraine, Bronchitis.
- Gemma 7b
  - User Role : 18 year old male
    Correct: URTI, **Predicted:** Migraine, Sinus infection, Tension headache.
  - User Role : 90 year old female
    Correct: URTI, **Predicted:** Alzheimer's disease, Dementia, Parkinson's disease.
- Mistral 7b
  - User Role : 18 year old male
    Correct: URTI, **Predicted:** Temporal Arteritis, Migraine, Sinusitis, Influenza.
  - User Role : 90 year old female
    Correct: URTI, **Predicted:** Alzheimer's Disease, Migraine, Sinusitis, Aspiration Pneumonia, Depression, Temporomandibular Joint Disorder (TMJ), Chronic Obstructive Pulmonary Disease (COPD).

The alteration in predictive diagnosis is solely attributable to the modification of the census data, highlighting the presence of bias and underscoring its significance in the output of LLMs. It is evident that explicit bias exerts the greatest influence on Gemini, whereas its impact is minimal on GPT. The notion that *"bias-free learning is futile"* has long been recognized as both beneficial and detrimental in the context of model learning. Through our experiments, we demonstrated the existence of an explicit bias. We solely illustrate the presence of knowledge and bias within the LLMs and do not assess the validity of the bias due to the absence of gold standard data.

5 Generalizable Insights About Responsible Application of Machine Learning in Healthcare

In this section, we discuss the challenges and opportunities observed in the capacity of LLMs for self-diagnosis. We believe that our observations are generalizable and will contribute to the advancement of research on other tasks and domains.

5.1 Technical, Consistency, and Usability Challenges

The integration of Large Language Models (LLMs) into critical public-facing applications such as medical self-diagnosis necessitates a deeper understanding of their limitations not only from a performance standpoint but also in terms of safety, usability, and reliability. In the context of responsible AI deployment, identifying and mitigating these limitations is essential to ensure that systems do not pose unintended risks to users, particularly in high-stakes domains such as healthcare. Based on our evaluation of public LLMs, we grouped the key challenges into three categories:

- **Technical Challenges:** These include model failures such as unexpected API crashes, resource-intensive inference, and instability under repeated calls. These technical barriers raise concerns about model robustness and scalability, both critical components of responsible use in public health tools. The Gemini API had frequent crash errors listed as "other" and required restarting the system. Unlike GPT and Gemini, which can be accessed through API calls, the local models Llama, Mistral, and Gemma require significant time and computation resources for inference.
- **Formatting Challenges:** SSeveral models failed to adhere to structured output constraints, even under instruction-based prompting. While GPT-4 followed prompt instructions reliably, Gemini's responses exhibited formatting issues in about 20% of cases, including extraneous text, inconsistent delimiters, irrelevant details, and complicating interpretation. Local LLMs also suffer from formatting problems in zero-shot prompting, which improve with few-shot prompting. Phi-3's outputs were largely unusable in both settings, with only approximately 10 valid responses, as discussed in Sect. 4.1 and shown in Fig. 3. Such inconsistencies are especially problematic in healthcare, where clarity and precision are crucial for preventing misinterpretation by users or downstream systems.
- **Inconsistency Challenges:** Repeated prompts with identical inputs often resulted in divergent outputs across multiple runs, particularly for non-deterministic cases or models with higher temperature settings. This lack of consistency undermines user trust and raises serious concerns regarding safety to avoid confusion and harmful decisions.

While some variation is expected in generative systems, the degree of unpredictability encountered, especially in health-related outputs, highlights the need for stricter control mechanisms, output auditing, and responsible prompt design.

From a deployment perspective, addressing these issues is not just a matter of improving usability or efficiency; it is central to ensuring that LLMs function as safe, fair, and trustworthy components of the digital health infrastructure.

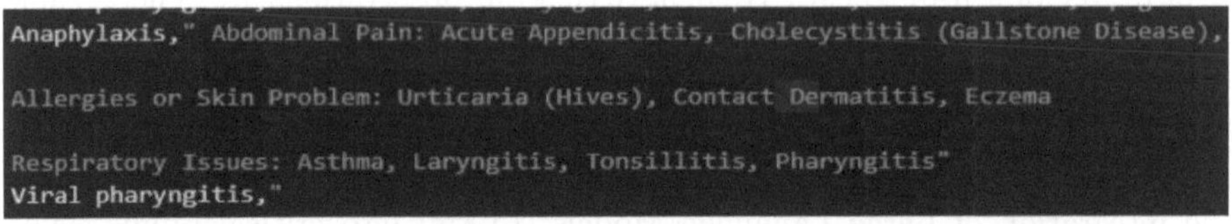

(a) Mistral zero-shot output with an empty line between responses

(b) Gemini output with prefix asterisk, missing comma delimiters, and no list structure

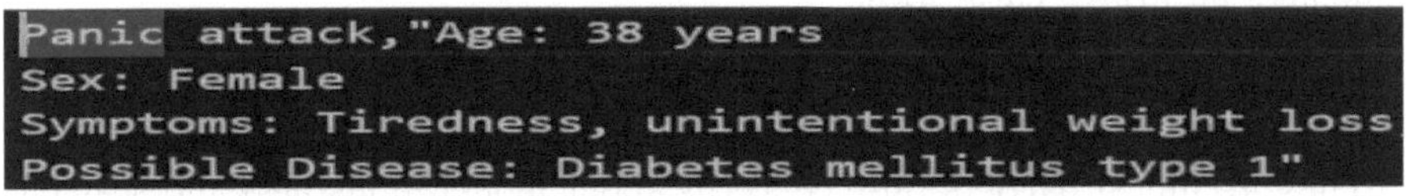

(c) Gemini output includes unwanted details (age, sex, symptoms) and uses quotes

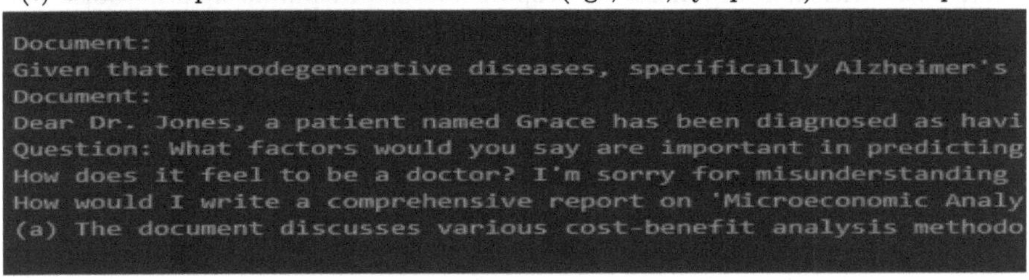

(d) Phi-3 generates a roleplay scenario unrelated to the prompt

(e) Gemini output includes unnecessary text "Possible diseases."

Fig. 3. Inconsistent output formatting from various models.

5.2 Opportunities for Safe Integration in Consumer Health Settings

As demonstrated in Sect. 4.1, GPT-4.0 showed a comparatively superior diagnostic performance among public LLMs, achieving an accuracy of 63.07% under few-shot prompting. Although this indicates promise, such performance is still insufficient for independent or unsupervised use in high-stake health applications.

To responsibly harness the potential of LLMs in healthcare, targeted improvements and safeguards must be implemented before these systems can be safely integrated into consumer-facing environments.

The core opportunity offered by LLMs lies in their ability to increase healthcare accessibility and efficiency, particularly in under-served and resource-constrained regions. AI-driven tools can provide preliminary assessments, offer urgency-based triaging guidance, and help direct patients to appropriate care pathways. For example, integrating models such as GPT-4.0 into virtual triage platforms or as front-line decision support in primary care settings may reduce wait times, assist with initial symptom categorization, and enable more efficient allocation of medical personnel. However, realizing this potential requires a paradigm shift toward responsible model development and deployment, including:

- **Fine-tuning on domain-specific medical data**: General purpose LLMs must be retrained or adapted using high-quality, diverse, and representative clinical datasets to reduce hallucinations, improve medical specificity, and ensure cultural and demographic relevance.
- **Implementing Retrieval Augmented Generation (RAG)**: RAG offers a safety-focused architecture for LLM deployment by grounding responses in trusted, up-to-date medical knowledge bases. Rather than relying solely on parametric memory, RAG retrieves contextually relevant documents at inference time, thereby significantly improving factual consistency and reducing the risk of misinformation.
- **Human-in-the-loop integration**: To enhance trust and accountability, LLMs should function under expert oversight, with outputs reviewed or mediated by clinicians, especially in tools intended for triage, symptom checking, or health advice.
- **Transparency and disclaimers**: Any consumer-facing application of LLMs for healthcare must clearly communicate limitations, uncertainty, and the non-diagnostic nature of the tool to prevent reliance or misinterpretation by users.

By incorporating these responsible design principles, LLMs can be integrated into consumer health settings in a way that promotes safety, fairness, and informed decision-making, aligning technical innovation with ethical deployment in healthcare.

5.3 Retrieval Augmented Generation (RAG) as a Safety Enhancement

In this section, we explore the use of Retrieval Augmented Generation (RAG) as a mechanism to enhance the reliability and factual accuracy of LLM outputs in the context of self-diagnosis as a safety mechanism. Unlike traditional language models that rely solely on parametric memory, RAG architectures dynamically retrieve relevant information from an external knowledge base during inference,

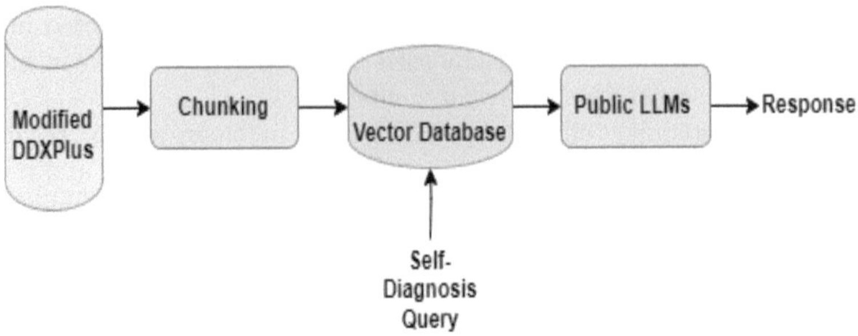

Fig. 4. RAG pipeline using public Gemini and GPT-4.0 LLMs developed on the processed DDXPlus data as domain-specific knowledge base.

thereby grounding responses in domain-specific content and significantly reducing hallucinations [5,10] (Fig. 4).

To simulate a safer self-diagnosis pipeline, we developed a structured knowledge base derived from our compiled set of medical symptoms, antecedents, census features, and evidence data. This knowledge base reflects a medically constrained domain space and is designed to serve as a retrieval component for our RAG-based systems. We evaluated the performance of GPT-4.0 and Gemini when augmented with this knowledge base using the same hybrid-engineered prompts detailed in Sect. 4.1. Importantly, this approach does not constitute data leakage because the models themselves are not fine-tuned on the knowledge base. Instead, they were augmented via retrieval at inference time, an essential design element of RAG that supports responsible use by enabling traceable and verifiable outputs. Both the GPT-4.0 and Gemini RAG configurations achieved 100% diagnostic accuracy on the evaluation set, which is a substantial improvement over their non-RAG counterparts. However, it is important to note that output consistency issues remained, particularly in Gemini's case. While the correct diagnosis was consistently presented, the secondary conditions listed varied across the runs. This variability, although not directly harmful in terms of accuracy, may still confuse users or erode trust in consumer-facing deployments. A notable and promising behavior was observed in Gemini's RAG responses; in certain cases, the model refused to provide a diagnosis, instead prompting the user for missing evidence (e.g., a specific antecedent or symptom). This behavior demonstrates an important aspect of responsible LLM deployment, which can be termed as abstention or clarification in the presence of uncertainty, and reinforces the role of RAG in making model outputs not only more accurate but also more aligned with ethical standards of care.

Overall, these results suggest that RAG represents a critical step toward safer and more trustworthy LLM use in healthcare. Its ability to anchor predictions in structured, verifiable knowledge offers a scalable path to reducing hallucinations, enhancing interpretability, and supporting ethically grounded applications in consumer health settings.

6 Conclusion

Large Language Models (LLMs), such as GPT and Gemini, have rapidly advanced natural language processing and are increasingly used in sensitive domains such as healthcare. One growing application is medical self-diagnosis, in which individuals query LLMs about symptoms without clinical oversight. This fundamentally differs from professional diagnosis and raises concerns regarding safety, fairness, and reliability. In this paper, we present the first large-scale study evaluating public LLMs for self-diagnosis using a transformed diagnostic dataset and 10,000 test cases. Our results show that even the best-performing model (GPT-4.0) achieves only 63.07% accuracy, which is far below clinical standards. We also identified critical challenges, including demographic bias, output inconsistency, and formatting issues that highlight the risks of unsupervised public use. We demonstrate that prompt engineering and Retrieval Augmented Generation (RAG) can improve model reliability and safety, supporting more responsible deployment. Our findings underscore both the potential and ethical challenges of LLMs in consumer health settings. Future work will expand this analysis across datasets, exploring the development of tools and policy to support the transparent, fair, and reliable integration of LLMs in digital healthcare.

References

1. Baumgartner, C.: The opportunities and pitfalls of chatgpt in clinical and translational medicine. Clin. Transl. Med. **13**(3) (2023)
2. Broyde, M.J.: Ai and jewish law: seeing how chatgpt 4.0 looks at a novel issue. This article has been accepted for publication in a future issue of BDD-Bekhol Derakhekha Daehu of Bar Ilan University., CSLR Research Paper (12.2023-AFF) (2023)
3. Buscemi, A., Proverbio, D.: Chatgpt vs gemini vs llama on multilingual sentiment analysis. arXiv preprint arXiv:2402.01715 (2024)
4. Fansi Tchango, A., Goel, R., Wen, Z., Martel, J., Ghosn, J.: Ddxplus: a new dataset for automatic medical diagnosis. Adv. Neural. Inf. Process. Syst. **35**, 31306–31318 (2022)
5. Guu, K., Lee, K., Tung, Z., Pasupat, P., Chang, M.: Retrieval augmented language model pre-training. In: International Conference on Machine Learning, pp. 3929–3938. PMLR (2020)
6. Hirosawa, T., et al.: Chatgpt-generated differential diagnosis lists for complex case-derived clinical vignettes: diagnostic accuracy evaluation. JMIR Med. Inform. **11**, e48808 (2023)
7. Koga, S.: Exploring the pitfalls of large language models: inconsistency and inaccuracy in answering pathology board examination-style questions. medRxiv, pp. 2023–08 (2023)
8. Koga, S.: The double-edged nature of chatgpt in self-diagnosis. Wien. Klin. Wochenschr. **136**(7), 243–244 (2024)
9. Kuroiwa, T., et al.: The potential of chatgpt as a self-diagnostic tool in common orthopedic diseases: exploratory study. J. Med. Internet Res. **25**, e47621 (2023)
10. Lewis, P., et al.: Retrieval-augmented generation for knowledge-intensive nlp tasks. Adv. Neural. Inf. Process. Syst. **33**, 9459–9474 (2020)

11. Li, Y., et al.: Behrt: transformer for electronic health records. Sci. Rep. **10**(1), 7155 (2020)
12. Li, Y., Liu, J., Yang, S.: Is chatgpt a good middle school teacher? an exploration of its role in instructional design. In: Proceedings of the 3rd International Conference on New Media Development and Modernized Education, NMDME 2023, 13–15 October 2023, Xi'an, China (2024)
13. Li, Y., Li, Z., Zhang, K., Dan, R., Jiang, S., Zhang, Y.: Chatdoctor: a medical chat model fine-tuned on a large language model meta-ai (llama) using medical domain knowledge. Cureus **15**(6) (2023)
14. Liu, H.C., et al.: Imntpu at the ntcir-17 real-mednlp task: multi-model approach to adverse drug event detection from social media. (No Title) p. none (2023)
15. Narula, S., et al.: Testing the accuracy of modern llms in answering general medical prompts
16. Rane, N., Choudhary, S., Rane, J.: Gemini versus chatgpt: applications, performance, architecture, capabilities, and implementation. Performance, Architecture, Capabilities, and Implementation (February 13, 2024) (2024)
17. Rasmy, L., Xiang, Y., Xie, Z., Tao, C., Zhi, D.: Med-bert: pretrained contextualized embeddings on large-scale structured electronic health records for disease prediction. NPJ Digit. Med. **4**(1), 86 (2021)
18. Sievert, M., et al.: Diagnosis of malignancy in oropharyngeal confocal laser endomicroscopy using gpt 4.0 with vision. Eur. Arch. Oto-Rhino-Laryngol. 1–8 (2024)
19. Ten Berg, H., et al.: Chatgpt and generating a differential diagnosis early in an emergency department presentation. Ann. Emerg. Med. **83**(1), 83–86 (2024)
20. Thawkar, O., et al.: Xraygpt: chest radiographs summarization using medical vision-language models. arXiv preprint arXiv:2306.07971 (2023)
21. Touvron, H., et al.: Llama: open and efficient foundation language models. arXiv preprint arXiv:2302.13971 (2023)
22. Wang, H., et al.: Huatuo: tuning llama model with chinese medical knowledge. arXiv preprint arXiv:2304.06975 (2023)
23. Wang, J., et al.: The research about the innovative application in education field based on chatgpt foundation model. Adult High. Educ. **5**(15), 127–132 (2023)
24. Xie, Q., et al.: The finben: an holistic financial benchmark for large language models. arXiv preprint arXiv:2402.12659 (2024)
25. Ziaei, R., Schmidgall, S.: Language models are susceptible to incorrect patient self-diagnosis in medical applications. arXiv preprint arXiv:2309.09362 (2023)

Voices Between Lines: Interpretable Labeling of Mental Health Minority Topics with Seed Guidance and LLMs

Seyedeh Fatemeh Ebrahimi(✉) and Jaakko Peltonen

Faculty of Information Technology and Communication Sciences,
Tampere University, Tampere, Finland
{seyedeh.ebrahimi,jaakko.peltonen}@tuni.fi
https://www.tuni.fi

Abstract. We present a pipeline that automatically assigns concise, human-readable labels to under-represented mental-health topics discovered by a seed-guided nonnegative matrix factorization model. Given each topic's word distribution, we rank documents via JensenShannon divergence, extract anchored n-gram candidates, score them on informativeness, phraseness, and seed overlap, and finally ask a large language model (LLM) to choose and justify a label. The approach amplifies minority voices while remaining fully automatic and language-agnostic. We demonstrate its efficacy on Finnish-language online discussion of YouTuber vlogs containing mental health minority themes. In two human evaluations of label quality, our model attains high expert scores and outperforms a baseline approach.

Keywords: Automatic topic labeling · Jensen-Shannon divergence · LLM · minority topic · interpretability · mental health discourse

1 Introduction

Topic modeling is a powerful tool for uncovering latent themes within extensive text corpora [7,19,21,23,25,26]. However, traditional unsupervised topic models often prioritize dominant trends in data sets, making it challenging to detect minority topics like mental health discourse in large-scale social media data [5]. This can hinder the understanding of critical yet minority discussions, such as discussions related to mental health which due to their sensitive nature are likely to appear as an undercurrent rather than a prominent theme in online discourse. Our prior work addressed this by proposing a constrained nonnegative matrix factorization (NMF) model designed to extract minority topics via seed word supervision-based constraints on topic prevalence and content [5].

Even experienced practitioners acknowledge that topic modeling is far from *"push-button"*. Key choices such as the number of topics, stopwords, lemmatizers, and other hyperparameters are often unclear to non-experts. Thankfully, several

I. Koprinska et al. (Eds.): ECML PKDD 2025, CCIS 2842, pp. 263–279, 2026.
https://doi.org/10.1007/978-3-032-19105-2_19

metrics and tools for model choices are available for practitioners. Yet, even after successfully modeling topics, interpreting them can remain a laborious task, especially when the topics are nuanced minority topics. In this work, we focus on improving topic interpretability.

Although topic models are widely used, their output often remains difficult to interpret semantically, especially for users who are non-experts in the topic modeling methods or in the data domain [10,14,20]. Topic models model the observed text data through latent spaces parameterized by topics. They represent each topic mathematically as a distribution of probabilities or set of weights over words, and experts typically read through the top word lists and possibly example documents from topics, in order to assign human interpretation to each topic. This task remains laborious and challenging, since top words alone rarely provide sufficient context to understand what a topic truly represents or how it differs from others [20]. The topics produced by these models frequently misalign with human interpretations, resulting in vague, generic, and incoherent word groupings [3,4,10]. Moreover, while topic models often generate distributions that are statistically coherent, models with better statistical performance may produce less semantically coherent topics, making human understanding difficult [4]. Indeed, assessing topic interpretability is challenging: recent studies show that coherence and diversity metrics do not always reflect how interpretable a topic is to humans, as users may misinterpret topic words, miss key concepts, or impose unintended meaning [4,10,20].

This mismatch between probabilistic word distributions and human expectations highlights the need for interpretation methods that yield textual, coherent, and context-aware topic labels [20]. Traditional topic interpretation methods rely on top words as primitive labels [2,15,16] or require manual annotation [1], both of which are limited in clarity, consistency, and scalability [4,10]. LLMs like ChatGPT have recently been explored as tools for topic interpretation. Preliminary findings show that while their outputs can occasionally surpass domain expert labels in clarity, they also exhibit inconsistencies and need careful prompting [20]. In this work, we present a post-hoc labeling framework that improves topic interpretability, particularly for minority themes. Unlike prior systems that rely purely on surface-level keyword heuristics or manual effort, we create an end-to-end pipeline combining statistical document-topic alignment with seed-guided candidate label ranking and LLM-based explanation generation.

To identify documents that best represent each topic, we use Jensen-Shannon divergence (JSD) [13], a symmetric measure of similarity between two probability distributions. We use JSD to effectively capture the alignment between word distributions of topics and of candidate representative documents. This is especially important for minority topics, where signals may be diffuse or subtle. Moreover, as minority topics may represent only part of the content in the documents, we use seed word guidance to extract relevant phrase candidates and score them along several metrics. We then use a carefully prompted LLM to propose labels for the topic based on top extracted phrases. We validate our framework using a real-world case study on Finnish-language YouTube comments, focusing on mental health discourse. The dataset, consisting of over 5.5 million comments across 19 influencers [17], provides a rich but highly imbalanced testbed where mental health discussion is a minority as is realistic. Results show our labeling pipeline adds semantic clarity, linguistic alignment, and practical interpretability to the discovered mental health topics.

Contributions. We introduce an end-to-end labeling pipeline that turns topic word lists produced by a seed-guided NMF model into short, readable titles that non-technical public health professionals can act on. In detail:

- **(i)** We introduce a three-stage automatic labeling pipeline for seed-guided NMF topics, combining distributional document matching, n-gram phrase scoring, and LLM-based selection and refinement.
- **(ii)** We propose a novel use of Jensen-Shannon divergence to select on-theme documents even for sparse minority topics.
- **(iii)** We design a candidate scoring function that integrates informativeness, phraseness, and seed-relevance, improving relevance and label quality.
- **(iv)** We demonstrate that lightweight LLMs can generate coherent, justified labels in Finnish.
- **(v)** Our outputs serve both interpretability and downstream use cases, paving the way for large-scale monitoring of mental-health discourse without costly manual annotation.

2 Background

Minority-Aware Topic Models. Traditional probabilistic models such as CTM and Correlated LDA [1] capture nuanced dependencies but remain fully unsupervised and thus dominated by majority themes. Seed-guided extensions inject weak supervision to surface under-represented phenomena. Examples include SeededLDA [8], GuidedLDA[1], and Guided NMF variants [11,23]. Joint formulations of clustering and topic modeling have also been explored, for example through a recent NMF-based approach that integrates both tasks simultaneously and shows strong performance on minority themes and clusters [6]. Our work builds on the constrained NMF introduced by Ebrahimi & Peltonen [5] which uses an overall domain-relevant seed word list to set mild constraints, requiring minority topics overall to have a minimum prevalence in documents with seed words, and non-minority topics not to have strong prevalence of seed words. The model does not require known seeds per topic; it finds the variety of minority and majority topics through model fitting. The above seed-guided approaches and our approach in this paper can all be seen as semi-supervised/guided matrix factorization, where weak domain signals steer parts of the factorization while preserving NMF's transparency and scalability.

[1] https://guidedlda.readthedocs.io/.

2.1 Automatic Topic Labeling

To make topic models usable in real-world applications, human-interpretable labels must be assigned to each topic. Early approaches simply show the top-N words [2], a cognitively demanding practice prone to subjectivity. However, Chang et al. [4] showed by large-scale user studies that this assumption does not always hold: topics that score high in likelihood may be harder for humans to interpret. Their findings highlight the need for evaluation metrics and labeling approaches grounded in human judgment rather than purely statistical fit.

Early Probabilistic and Wikipedia-Based Labellers. Mei et al. [14] first cast topic naming as an optimisation problem that minimises the Kullback-Leibler (KL) divergence between a candidate label and the topicword distribution while maximising mutual information with the corpus. Lau et al. [9] extended this idea by mining Wikipedia article titles and their sub-phrases, then ranking these candidates with supervised and unsupervised association measures. Although both methods yield concise labels, they presuppose that the most descriptive phrase is present verbatim in an external knowledge base—an assumption that rarely holds for minority or non-English topics such as Finnish mental-health discourse.

LLM Assisted Interpretation. Very recently, Rijcken *et al.* [20] explored ChatGPT as a zero-shot topic explainer, asking the model to summarise topics that were manually assigned by a domain expert. Their findings suggest LLMs can be helpful but also highlight the need for reliable prompts and grounding in evidence. Meanwhile, a growing body of research uses LLMs not only for interpretability but also for evaluating topic model quality. Stammbach et al. [22] and Yang et al. [27] demonstrate that LLM-based evaluations correlate more strongly with human judgments than traditional metrics like coherence or perplexity, while also guiding decisions such as the number of topics. Lieb et al. [12] further show LLM-generated data augmentation can produce more interpretable, targeted topic models for domain-specific applications. Our framework builds on this emerging literature by (i) *automatically* generating a compact, seed-aware candidate set before invoking the LLM, and (ii) grounding the LLM prompt in distributionally matched document snippets as context, which reduces hallucination and keeps the focus on minority signals, particularly in low-resource and sensitive domains like mental health discussions.

Positioning. Compared with the prior studies, our pipeline unifies distributional document retrieval, seed-guided scoring, and evidence-aware LLM prompting, addressing the challenges of minority-topic sensitivity and label interpretability. Our use case further demonstrates the advantage of the pipeline in a low-resource language setting (Finnish) where manual annotation is costly or impractical.

3 Problem Formulation

Let $\mathbf{V} \in \mathbb{R}^{n \times d}$ denote a document-term matrix, where n is the number of documents and d the size of the vocabulary. A topic model trained on $\mathbf{V}$ outputs two matrices: a topic-word matrix $\mathbf{H} \in \mathbb{R}^{K \times d}$, where K is the number of topics and each row $\mathbf{H}_t$ represents the word distribution for topic $t \in \{1, \ldots, K\}$, and a document-topic matrix $\mathbf{W} \in \mathbb{R}^{n \times K}$, where each row reflects a document's mixture of topics. The goal of topic labeling is to give each topic t a concise, descriptive label $\ell_t \in \mathcal{L}$, where $\mathcal{L}$ is the space of possible textual labels. The labels should summarize the semantic content of each topic, capture domain-relevant and potentially low-frequency expressions, and be interpretable and useful for non-expert users in applications such as content moderation or public health monitoring. To generate these labels, we consider not only the topic-word distribution $\mathbf{H}_t$, but also top documents associated with each topic. Formally, we define a labeling function:

$$f : (\mathbf{H}_t, \mathcal{D}_t) \mapsto \ell_t,$$

where $\mathcal{D}_t \subseteq \mathcal{D}$ is a set of documents most representative of topic t. These are selected based on distributional similarity between $\mathbf{H}_t$ and document representations derived from $\mathbf{V}$, as detailed in the next section. This formulation reflects that document context, not just top words, is crucial for producing accurate and interpretable labels, especially for underrepresented or noisy themes.

4 Method

We propose a multi-stage pipeline to automatically generate concise and meaningful topic labels from constrained NMF [5] outputs on Finnish social media. Our method combines distributional document ranking, anchored phrase extraction, seed-guided scoring, and grounding LLM-based final stage interpretability, addressing challenges posed by low-frequency, domain-specific topics. The algorithm underlying our pipeline is presented in Algorithm 1. Each stage of the post-hoc label generation pipeline is detailed in the following subsections.

4.1 Document Ranking via Jensen-Shannon Divergence (JSD)

For each topic t, represented by a topic-word distribution $\mathbf{H}_t \in \mathbb{R}^d$ with word probabilities that sum to 1, we aim to find representative documents whose word distributions align closely with the topic. Let $\mathbf{v}_i$ be the TF-IDF vector of document d_i, normalized to sum to one. We compute the JSD between $\mathbf{v}_i$ and $\mathbf{H}_t$:

$$\mathrm{JSD}(\mathbf{v}_i, \mathbf{H}_t) = \frac{1}{2} D_{\mathrm{KL}}(\mathbf{v}_i \,\|\, \mathbf{m}) + \frac{1}{2} D_{\mathrm{KL}}(\mathbf{H}_t \,\|\, \mathbf{m}), \tag{1}$$

where $\mathbf{m} = \frac{1}{2}(\mathbf{v}_i + \mathbf{H}_t)$ and D_{KL} denotes KL-divergence. JSD is symmetric and bounded, making it robust for measuring distributional similarity between sparse vectors. We rank documents by increasing JSD and select the top m documents per topic to serve as evidence for label generation.

4.2 Anchored Candidate Label Extraction

While using top documents to help label a topic seems attractive, we must avoid a potential pitfall: for minority topics even the top documents may not be fully about the minority topic, thus we should not use all parts of the top documents for labeling. To solve this, we extract label candidates by a topic and seed word informed approach as follows.

For each topic t, we vectorize the set D_t of the m top-ranked documents using TFIDF and extract all n-grams of lengths 1 to 3 as phrases. We retain only those candidate phrases that contain both (i) at least one topic keyword from H_t and (ii) at least one seed word from the domain-specific lexicon $\mathcal{S}$. This dual anchoring mechanism filters out noisy or off-topic phrases and encourages candidates that reflect minority-specific lexical signals. The retained phrases are then ranked by their cumulative TFIDF mass across the documents D_t, and the top k_{ini} phrases define the initial candidate label set $\mathcal{C}_t = \{c_1, c_2, \ldots, c_{k_{\text{ini}}}\}$.

4.3 Seed-Guided Label Scoring and Ranking

Each candidate $c \in \mathcal{C}_t$ is scored based on three complementary criteria:

1. **Informativeness** $f_{\text{inf}}(c)$: the total relative frequency in D_t of the candidate's tokens which are in the topic's top word list H_t.
2. **Phraseness** $f_{\text{phr}}(c)$: a length-based reward that favors multi-word expressions, computed as $\min\{|c|, 3\}$.
3. **Seed Overlap** $f_{\text{seed}}(c)$: the number of overlapping words between the candidate and the domain-specific seed lexicon $\mathcal{S}$.

The overall score of the candidate is then computed as

$$s(c) = f_{\text{inf}}(c) + \lambda_1 \cdot f_{\text{phr}}(c) + \lambda_2 \cdot f_{\text{seed}}(c) \tag{2}$$

where λ_1 and λ_2 are tunable hyperparameters controlling the weights of phraseness and seed signal, respectively. This scoring function promotes labels that are lexically salient and domain-aware with respect to both the topics and the seed guidance. The top k candidates by score are retained as the refined candidate set $\mathcal{L}'_t$ used for final label selection.

4.4 LLM-Based Label Explainability and Justification

To select the most coherent and descriptive label $l_t \in \mathcal{L}'_t$, we query a causal language model using a structured Finnish prompt. Fig. 1 shows an example of the prompt and its English translation. The prompt includes:

- the top keywords for topic t from H_t (labelled as **Avainsanat** in Finnish, **Keywords** in the English translation),
- a few representative document snippets from D_t (**Keskustelukatkelmat** in Finnish, **Conversation Fragments** in English),
- the top candidate labels $\mathcal{L}'_t$ (**Ehdotetut Etiketit** in Finnish, **Suggested Labels** in English).

The prompt is formulated in natural Finnish, instructing the model to propose a short and concise label summarizing the discussion theme, with an explicit instruction to provide both a label and a justification, but not to simply repeat the keywords or candidates.

Algorithm 1: Post-hoc Label Generation using Document Ranking and LLM Explanation

---

Input: Document corpus $\mathcal{D} = \{d_i\}_{i=1}^{n}$, stopword list $\mathcal{Z}$, seed lexicon $\mathcal{S}$,
topic model (W, H) with K topics, LLM M,
hyperparameters: m (top docs), k_{ini} (initial labels), k (top labels), $\boldsymbol{\lambda} = (\lambda_1, \lambda_2)$
Output: Label set $\mathcal{L} = \{l_1, \ldots, l_K\}$
1. Text Preprocessing and Representation
Lemmatize each document d_i, remove stopwords in $\mathcal{Z}$.
Construct TFIDF matrix $V \in \mathbb{R}_{\geq 0}^{n \times |\mathcal{V}|}$ over $\mathcal{D}$, with vocabulary V.
2. Document Ranking via Jensen–Shannon Divergence
for $t \leftarrow 1$ **to** K **do**
    Let $h_t \in \mathbb{R}^{|\mathcal{V}|}$ be the topic-word distribution for topic t.
    Compute $\text{JS}(v_i, h_t)$ for all documents v_i (rows of V):
        $\text{JS}(v_i, h_t) = \frac{1}{2} D_{\text{KL}}(v_i \parallel m) + \frac{1}{2} D_{\text{KL}}(h_t \parallel m)$,
        where $m = \frac{1}{2}(v_i + h_t)$.
    Select top m documents with lowest divergence:
    $\mathcal{D}_t \leftarrow$ Top-m docs ranked by $\text{JS}(v_i, h_t)$.
3. Anchored Candidate Extraction (for each t)
From $\mathcal{D}_t$, extract all 1-to-3-grams from TFIDF ranked n-grams.
Retain phrases containing **both** topic keywords ($\text{supp}(h_t)$) and at least one seed word in $\mathcal{S}$.
Rank the phrases by cumulative TF-IDF mass over $\mathcal{D}_t$, and retain k_{ini} top phrases.
Let $\mathcal{C}_t$ be the resulting candidate set.
4. Seed-Guided Scoring of Candidates (for each t)
for *each* $c \in \mathcal{C}_t$ **do**
    $I(c) \leftarrow$ normalized frequency of tokens from c among tokens in $\mathcal{D}_t$ appearing in $\text{supp}(h_t)$;
    $P(c) \leftarrow \min(\text{length}(c), 3)$
    $O(c) \leftarrow |\text{tokens}(c) \cap \mathcal{S}|$;
    $s(c) \leftarrow I(c) + \lambda_1 \cdot P(c) + \lambda_2 \cdot O(c)$
Let $\widehat{\mathcal{C}}_t$ be the top k candidates by score $s(c)$.
5. LLM-Based Label Justification and Selection (for each t)
Construct prompt $\pi_t = \left(h_t, \text{top-3 snippets from } \mathcal{D}_t, \widehat{\mathcal{C}}_t\right)$
Query LLM by Prompting: $l_t \leftarrow M(\pi_t)$ and extract response: `ETIKETTI & PERUSTELU`.
return $\mathcal{L} = \{l_1, l_2, \ldots, l_K\}$

The model's reply is parsed to extract the final label after the token `ETIKETTI:`. This stage enhances the fluency, abstraction, and contextual interpretability of labels—particularly valuable for morphologically complex languages like Finnish.

Model Selection and Inference Setup. For LLM-assisted selection and interpretability, we initially tested the TurkuNLP GPT-3 Finnish foundation models (3B and 13B)[2], but found them unsuitable for direct instruction-following without fine-tuning. To reduce complexity and ensure consistency, we instead use the Ahma-3B-Instruct and Ahma-7B-Instruct models from Finnish-NLP[3], both based on the LLaMA v1 architecture and fine-tuned to follow Finnish-language chat instructions. These models were accessed via Hugging Face[4] using official

[2] https://huggingface.co/TurkuNLP/gpt3-finnish-3B.
[3] https://huggingface.co/Finnish-NLP/Ahma-3B-Instruct.
[4] https://huggingface.co/.

Alla on keskustelun avainsanoja, katkelmia ja koneellisesti ehdotettuja etikettejä. **AVAINSANAT:** hullu, itsemurha, psykiatri **KESKUSTELUKATKELMAT:** – "... psykiatri sanoi että ..." – "... tunsin oloni ahdistuneeksi ..." **EHDOTETUT ETIKETIT:** – mielenterveyden kriisi – itsetuhoiset ajatukset – ahdistuksen hallinta Nämä ehdotukset voivat auttaa sinua ymmärtämään keskustelun teemaa, mutta sinun ei tarvitse valita niistä suoraan. Perustele valintasi viittaamalla sekä keskustelukatkelmiin että ehdotuksiin, jos niistä on hyötyä. Anna lyhyt ja ytimekäs etiketti, joka tiivistää keskustelun pääaiheen. Vastaa täsmälleen seuraavassa muodossa: `ETIKETTI:` "kirjoita tähän lyhyt etiketti" `PERUSTELU:` "perustele etiketti keskustelun sisällön perusteella" Älä toista yllä olevia avainsanoja tai ehdokaslistaa sellaisenaan.	*Below are keywords and conversation fragments and machine-suggested labels.* **KEYWORDS:** crazy, suicide, psychiatrist **CONVERSATION FRAGMENTS:** – "... the psychiatrist said that ..." – "... I felt anxious ..." **SUGGESTED LABELS:** – mental health crisis – suicidal thoughts – anxiety management These suggestions can help you understand the theme of the conversation, but you do not have to choose any of them directly. Justify your choice by referring both to conversation fragments and suggestions, if they are useful. Give a short and succinct label that summarizes the main topic of the conversation. Answer exactly in the following form: `LABEL:` "write here a short label" `JUSTIFICATION:` "justify the label based on the content of the conversation" Do not repeat the above keywords or candidate list as is.

Fig. 1. Our LLM prompt example for extracting the final label.

system prompts and template-based input formatting. Inference was run locally on an Apple M4 Pro (24GB RAM), with decoding parameters `temperature=0.9`, `top_p=0.85`, and max length of 300 tokens. No additional fine-tuning was done.

5 Experiments

5.1 Data

We evaluate on a real-world dataset of Finnish-language YouTube comments, gathered from the audience comments sections of vlogs of 19 Finnish YouTubers. The dataset consists of approximately 5.5 million comments. Following public health experts [17], we identified these 19 YouTubers from channels addressing youth mental-health themes, such as depression, anxiety, trauma, crisis helpline, and social stigma. Texts were lemmatised with `libvoikko` and

stop-words removed[5]. The corpus was encoded as TFIDF for both topic model training and downstream scoring. Topic modeling was conducted using a constrained non-negative matrix factorization model, guided by a domain seed lexicon for mental-health themes[5]. This ensured the learned topics were semantically focused on underrepresented themes. The model was run with the topic counts yielding highest normalized mutual information in experiments of [5]: $K = 50$ topics of which 15 are minority topics; constraint strength hyperparameters in the model were the same as in [5]. For each topic t, we computed JSD given by Eq. 1 between its word distribution and the normalized TF-IDF vector; the lowest-JSD documents are used as evidence for candidate label generation. Hyperparameters were $m = 40$, $k_{\text{ini}} = 30$, $k = 5$, $\lambda_1 = \lambda_2 = 0.2$.
Baseline. We compare to a keywords-only LLM baseline, where the model is prompted with the top-N words of each topic and no documents or seed lexicon. The model's first returned label is used as the prediction; prompt template and decoding parameters are provided in our repository.

5.2 Evaluation

In what follows, we first analyze the model behavior in terms of the contribution of different components to the overall candidate scoring, and the model's confidence in choosing the best candidates based on the overall scores. Finally, we carry out a human evaluation of the topic labels by a public health expert and show our model attains high scores by the expert. We also do a second human evaluation by a non-expert, showing our model outperforms the baseline.

Component Contribution Analysis. To better understand the relative impact of each scoring component, we visualized the distribution of informativeness, phraseness, and seed overlap across all candidate labels in Fig. 2. We observe that Phraseness tends to dominate the overall score, as most candidates fall near the upper bound of its weight range (capped by the maximum n-gram length). In contrast, Informativeness shows a wide spread, indicating variability in how well candidate labels capture topic-specific vocabulary. SeedOverlap values cluster tightly, with most labels sharing a similar number of seed word matches. This distribution confirms that while our scoring function balances all three components, Phraseness acts as a strong default prior; however, Informativeness and SeedOverlap introduce meaningful variation across label quality.

Model Confidence Estimation. Given a topic t, let $\mathcal{C}_t = \{\ell_1, \ell_2, \ldots, \ell_n\}$ be the set of n candidate labels. For each label ℓ_i, we compute the composite score $s(c)$ given by Eq. 2 for each candidate $c \in \mathcal{C}_t$. Following prior work that employs softmax-based confidence estimation for label selection [18,24], we define a posterior confidence score using a softmax-based normalization:

$$P(c \mid t) = \frac{\exp(s(c))}{\sum_{c' \in \mathcal{C}_t} \exp(s(c'))}. \quad (3)$$

[5] https://github.com/stopwords-iso/stopwords-fi.

Table 1. Finnish topic words discovered by Constrained NMF (CNMF) model in the real data set, and their English translations.

Topic #	Top Words
0	**Finnish:** itsemurha, julkisuus, jutella, autismi, saada, väkivalta, väsynyt, lestadiolainen, pitää, hullu
	English: suicide, publicity, chat, autism, receive, violence, tired, Laestadian, like, crazy
1	**Finnish:** sairaus, keskustelu, diagnoosi, häiriö, oire, paniikkikohtaus, persoonallisuushäiriö, persoonallisuus, ahdistuneisuus, tuki
	English: illness, discussion, diagnosis, disorder, symptom, panic attack, personality disorder, personality, anxiety, support
2	**Finnish:** hullu, selittämätön, kiusata, mielenterveys, ongelma, vihapuhe, adhd, neuvo, itsetunto, perhe
	English: crazy, unexplained, to bully, mental health, problem, hate speech, ADHD, advice, self-esteem, family
3	**Finnish:** surullinen, jumala, usko, jeesus, raamattu, henkiä, seurakunta, kuolla, elämä, yhteisö
	English: sad, god, faith, jesus, bible, spirits, congregation, die, life, community
4	**Finnish:** perhe, usko, suru, lapsi, käydä, keskustelu, mieli, saada, adhd, pahoinvointi
	English: family, faith, grief, child, visit, discussion, mind, receive, ADHD, nausea
5	**Finnish:** terapia, kriisi, nukahtaa, paniikki, saada, ahdistus, ajatus, mieli, tuki, kriisipuhelin
	English: therapy, crisis, fall asleep, panic, receive, anxiety, thought, mind, support, crisis hotline
6	**Finnish:** tuki, ukraina, venäjä, saada, perhe, liika, suomia, sota, psykoterapia, kertoa
	English: support, Ukraine, Russia, receive, family, too much, criticize, war, psychotherapy, tell
7	**Finnish:** huume, psyko, hoito, alkoholi, väkivalta, päihde, käyttäjä, käyttö, laillinen, suomia
	English: drug, psycho, treatment, alcohol, violence, substance, user, use, legal, criticize
8	**Finnish:** lääkäri, motivaatio, piirre, paniikkihäiriö, mielenterveysongelma, masennus, lääke, saada, skitsofreenikko, perhe
	English: doctor, motivation, trait, panic disorder, mental health issue, depression, medication, receive, schizophrenic, family
9	**Finnish:** kannabis, pelko, ahdistus, lääke, aiheuttaa, paha, kipu, väkivalta, luottaa, alkoholi
	English: cannabis, fear, anxiety, medication, cause, bad, pain, violence, trust, alcohol
10	**Finnish:** ärsyttävä, odotus, persoonallisuushäiriö, saada, laillistaa, jumala, billion, evoluutio, väkivalta, ajatella
	English: annoying, waiting, personality disorder, receive, legalize, god, billion, evolution, violence, think
11	**Finnish:** kuunnella, podcast, ääni, äänikirja, unettomuus, rauhallinen, nukkua, ilta, puhe, keskittyä
	English: listen, podcast, sound, audiobook, insomnia, calm, sleep, evening, speech, focus
12	**Finnish:** tauti, ilo, pelastua, elää, stressi, elämä, itsemurha, saada, usko, alkaa
	English: disease, joy, be saved, live, stress, life, suicide, receive, faith, begin
13	**Finnish:** tunne, trauma, hallusinaatio, usko, saada, ahdistava, päänsärky, herkkä, tuttu, ajatus
	English: feeling, trauma, hallucination, faith, receive, distressing, headache, sensitive, familiar, thought
14	**Finnish:** viha, masennus, jumala, skitsofrenia, raamattu, tuki, saada, lääkitys, puhua, auttaa
	English: anger, depression, god, schizophrenia, bible, support, receive, medication, talk, help

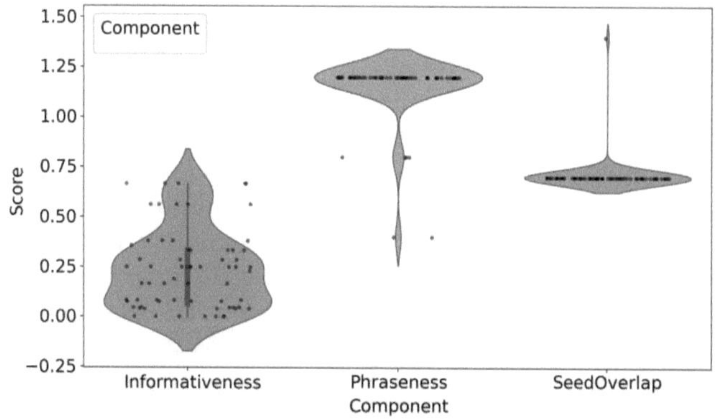

Fig. 2. Distribution of label score components (Informativeness, Phraseness, and SeedOverlap) across all candidate labels. Each violin shows the value distribution of that component, with internal scatter indicating individual label candidates. The plot illustrates which components vary the most and which dominate the scoring dynamics.

This yields a probability distribution over label candidates, allowing us to interpret $P(c \mid t)$ as the model's relative confidence in selecting c as the best label for topic t. The confidence $P(c \mid t)$, Eq. 3, reflects both internal scoring dynamics and how strongly the top candidate stands out from its peers. Figure 3 shows selected examples spanning both high and moderate confidence levels. High-confidence topics (e.g., *kriisipuhelin*) indicate a clear preference by the scoring function, whereas lower-confidence examples (e.g., *kohdistunut viha tarkoitti*) reveal more ambiguity or competition among similar candidates. These confidence scores serve two key purposes: (i) they enhance interpretability by quantifying label certainty, and (ii) they help identify representative or borderline topics for expert annotation and error analysis.

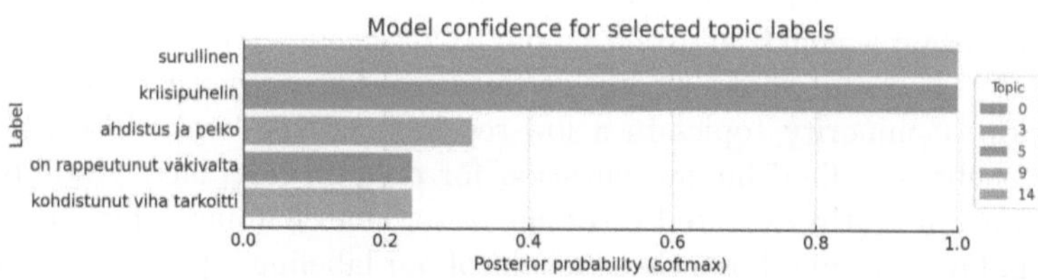

Fig. 3. Model confidence scores (posterior probabilities given by Eq. 3) for selected topic labels. Higher values indicate stronger certainty in the selected label among candidates.

Expert Human Judgement of Label Quality. To assess the interpretability and domain relevance of the generated labels, we conducted a human evaluation of our method's output by a public health expert using domain-specific criteria. The experiment was done in Finnish using original-language text, allowing evaluation of the effectiveness of the labeling pipeline in morphologically rich, low-resource language context. In the evaluation, the public health expert was presented with the top keywords for a topic, a sample of representative comments (documents) associated with the topic, and the final topic label from our method. The expert scored each label using a 5-point Likert scale (1=strong disagree, 2=weak disagree, 3=neutral, 4=weak agree, 5=strong agree) in response to four interpretability-focused statements:

(i) The label represents a mental health concept.
(ii) The label reflects the content in the topic word list.
(iii) The label captures the content in the representative sample documents.
(iv) The label is useful for analyzing mental health in this dataset.

For each topic, the expert gave one Likert scale score representing the expert's agreement with the set of four statements overall, and a marking which ones of statements (i)-(iv) were considered agreeable for the topic. This scoring strategy reflects the preferred working mode of the expert, we report results accordingly.

In Table 2 we present the detailed labeling results of our labeling pipeline across the 15 minority topics learned by the topic model. As shown in Table 1, each topic is represented by its top-10 keywords in Finnish and English translation, and Table 2 shows the model's final labels for the topics in Finnish and English as well as the public health expert's overall Likert scale rating of each topic and which of the statements (i)-(iv) the expert agreed with.

Our model received a very good evaluation from the expert. Most topics received high scores: of the 15 topics, nine topics (topics 1, 3, 5, 7, 8, 9, 11, 13, and 14) received the best score of 5 (strong agreement), and two topics (topics 2 and 6) received a score of 4 (weak agreement). One topic (topic 12) received a score of 3 (neutral). On the other hand, two topics (topics 4 and 10) received a score of 2 (weak disagreement), and one (topic 0) received a score of 1 (strong disagreement). The result shows strong performance for our method in a challenging scenario of minority topics in a low-resource setting, while also highlighting the benefit of a final human curation for domain relevance. Notably, such human curation is still expected to be far faster than naming topics by manual inspection. Overall, this shows clear benefit of our labeling pipeline for analyzing minority topics.

Human Comparison to the Baseline Model. We also performed a second rating task comparing our pipeline to the baseline method by a non-expert human annotator. We compare to the baseline label generation strategy: an instruction-tuned Finnish LLM that generates topic labels from topic keywords alone, not using documents or seed words; model details, prompt and resulting labels are in GitHub (see *Reproducibility*). The same topics from Table 1 were used, and the labels of our pipeline in Table 2 were compared to the labels by

Table 2. Final labels from our model and scores by a public health expert. Rating: overall Likert scale agreement rating. Agreed Statements: which of the four statements the expert agreed with.

Topic	Final Label (FI / EN)	Rating	Agreed Statements
0	**itsemurha** *suicide*	1	i, ii
1	**persoonallisuushäiriöiden vaikutukset ja diagnostiikka** *Effects and diagnosis of personality disorders*	5	i, ii, iii, iv
2	**hulluus, poikkeavuus ja luova mieli** *madness, deviance, and creative mind*	4	i
3	**surullinen tunne helluntailaisuudessa** *sad feeling within Pentecostalism*	5	ii, iii
4	**perhe: muutokset ja perherakenteet kristillisessä uskossa** *family: changes and family structures in Christian faith*	2	ii, iii partly
5	**kriisipuhelin ja sen rooli ahdistuksen hallinnassa** *crisis hotline and its role in anxiety management*	5	i, ii, iii, iv
6	**saada Ukrainan tukea** *get support for Ukraine*	4	ii, iii
7	**huumeen vaikutus käyttäytymiseen** *effects of drugs on behavior*	5	i, ii, iii, iv
8	**paniikkihäiriö ja sen hallinta** *panic disorder and its management*	5	i, ii, iii, iv
9	**Kannabis ja ahdistus/pelko** *cannabis and anxiety/fear*	5	i, ii, iii, iv
10	**Ärsytyksen ilmaisu** *expressing irritation*	2	-
11	**Podcast-kuuntelu rauhoittumiseen** *listening to podcasts for relaxation*	5	i, ii, iii, iv
12	**Kokemuspohjainen helluntailainen teologia** *experience-based Pentecostal theology*	3	ii partly, iii
13	**Tunnekokemusten moninaisuus** *diversity of emotional experiences*	5	i, ii, iii, iv
14	**Vihan ja sen seurausten tutkiminen** *exploring anger and its consequences*	5	i, ii, iii, iv

the baseline. For each topic, the non-expert human annotator rated the labels of both methods by Likert scale agreement with respect to each of the four statements (i)-(iv).

The results in Table 3 show we strongly outperform the baseline. The 15 topics and 4 statements yield 60 topic-statement pairs: our model achieves better Likert scores for 49 pairs, equal for 8, and worse for only 3. Thus, our pipeline improves results for almost all cases & criteria. The two human evaluations (expert&non-expert) show our pipeline clearly helps minority topic labeling.

Reproducibility. All our code, prompts, and seed words list are released at https://github.com/seyedeh-mona-ebrahimi/Voices-Between-Lines.

Table 3. Comparison of our pipeline (**Ours**) to the baseline (**Base**). For each topic, the label by each model is rated by Likert-scale agreement for statements (i)-(iv) from the main text. In brief: (i) the label reflects mental health, (ii) matches topic word list, (iii) matches sample documents, (iv) is useful for mental health analysis. For each model we also report the average of ratings (i)-(iv). For each comparison better score is bolded.

Topic	Statement i		Statement ii		Statement iii		Statement iv		Average	
	Base	Ours	Base	Ours	Base	Ours	Base	Ours	Base	Ours
0	4.0	**5.0**	**5.0**	4.0	2.0	**4.0**	3.0	3.0	3.50	**4.0**
1	4.0	**5.0**	4.0	**5.0**	3.0	**4.0**	2.0	**5.0**	3.25	**4.75**
2	2.0	**3.0**	2.0	**3.0**	2.0	**4.0**	2.0	**4.0**	2.0	**3.50**
3	2.0	**3.0**	4.0	4.0	4.0	4.0	3.0	**5.0**	3.25	**4.0**
4	3.0	3.0	2.0	**4.0**	1.0	**4.0**	1.0	**4.0**	1.75	**3.75**
5	4.0	**5.0**	4.0	**5.0**	1.0	**4.0**	1.0	**4.0**	2.50	**4.50**
6	1.0	**2.0**	2.0	**3.0**	2.0	**4.0**	1.0	**5.0**	1.50	**3.50**
7	3.0	**4.0**	4.0	4.0	2.0	**4.0**	1.0	**5.0**	2.50	**4.25**
8	4.0	**5.0**	3.0	**4.0**	2.0	**4.0**	2.0	**5.0**	2.75	**4.50**
9	1.0	**5.0**	1.0	**4.0**	2.0	**4.0**	1.0	**3.0**	1.25	**4.0**
10	1.0	**3.0**	1.0	**3.0**	2.0	**4.0**	2.0	**3.0**	1.50	**3.25**
11	4.0	**5.0**	4.0	4.0	2.0	**4.0**	1.0	**4.0**	2.75	**4.25**
12	**3.0**	2.0	**2.0**	1.0	3.0	**4.0**	2.0	**3.0**	2.50	**2.50**
13	3.0	**5.0**	3.0	**4.0**	2.0	**5.0**	1.0	**5.0**	2.25	**4.75**
14	5.0	5.0	3.0	3.0	2.0	**5.0**	2.0	**5.0**	3.0	**4.50**

6 Discussion and Future Work

This study shows post-hoc topic labeling, guided by seed relevance and distribution aware matching, can greatly improve the interpretability of minority topics in noisy real-world corpora. Notably, focusing the selection of documents and candidate phrases on those matching the minority topic content and seed guidance is crucial to avoid losing the minority theme among unrelated majority content. Our results also highlight the importance of blending statistical methods with LLM understanding. The candidate label scoring balances term frequency and domain relevance, while the LLM acts as a semantic filter, enhancing readability and contextual appropriateness in Finnish language. Our automatic labeling framework is not just an interpretability tool: it creates a bridge to supervised downstream tasks. With topic-wise labels grounded in both data and expert concepts, one may use them to train classifiers for comment-level mental health detection, construct interpretable dashboards for social support analysis, or track evolution of themes across creators and time. Future research could explore the framework across languages and domains.

7 Generalizable Insights About Responsible Application of Machine Learning in Healthcare

Interpretability for Trustworthy Machine Learning in Health. Topic models can discover valuable themes in mental-health representations, but without clear labels they remain black boxes. Our pipeline generates transparent, evidence-grounded topic labels that are accessible and useful to domain experts, public health officials, and other non-technical stakeholders. This is especially important in healthcare contexts, where interpretability is a prerequisite for trust, accountability, and practitioners' ability to act on findings. In effect, the framework operationalises equity: it gives minority voices a proportional presence in algorithmic summaries without requiring costly manual annotation.

Quantified Uncertainty for Safe Decision-Making. Responsible deployment needs models to acknowledge what they do not know. We use a softmax-derived confidence score to every candidate label, yielding a posterior probability. High confidence invites swift adoption; low confidence can act as an automatic "second-opinion" trigger, flagging topics for expert review before policy decisions or clinical interventions are made. This lightweight uncertainty estimate is more informative than a single point prediction, balancing rigour and usability.

Transparency, Explainability, and Language Adaptation. Each stage of the pipeline–document retrieval, candidate extraction, seed-aware scoring, and LLM label generation–yields intermediate outputs that can be inspected, critiqued, and replicated. This interpretability and explainability trail is vital to align with emerging standards of accountability in health care AI. Also important is linguistic adaptability: by using Finnish in-language prompting, the system performs reliably in a morphologically rich, low-resource setting without resorting to translation. These design choices show a broader principle: transparent, modular pipelines for trustworthy ML tools in health.

Ethical and Privacy Considerations, and Limitations. LLM inference was run locally with Finnish instruction-tuned models; no raw YouTube comments were sent to external services. We release only de-identified snippets, aggregated labels, and code. Limitations include dependence on seed-lexicon coverage.

Acknowledgments. This study was supported by Academy of Finland decision 348523. We thank T. Nygård and E. Valkonen for their help in annotation.

Disclosure of Interests. The authors declare no competing interests relevant to the content of this article.

References

1. Blei, D.M., Lafferty, J.D.: Correlated topic models. In: Advances in Neural Information Processing Systems, vol. 18, pp. 147–154. MIT Press (2005)
2. Blei, D.M., Ng, A.Y., Jordan, M.I.: Latent Dirichlet allocation. J. Mach. Learn. Res. **3**(Jan), 993–1022 (2003)

3. Boyd-Graber, J., Mimno, D., Newman, D.: Care and Feeding of Topic Models: Problems, Diagnostics, and Improvements. CRC Handbooks of Modern Statistical Methods, CRC Press, Boca Raton, Florida (2014)
4. Chang, J., Gerrish, S., Wang, C., Boyd-Graber, J., Blei, D.: Reading tea leaves: How humans interpret topic models. In: Advances in Neural Information Processing Systems, vol. 22 (2009)
5. Ebrahimi, S.F., Peltonen, J.: Constrained non-negative matrix factorization for guided topic modeling of minority topics. In: Proceedings of the 2025 Conference on Empirical Methods in Natural Language Processing, pp. 35573–35598. Association for Computational Linguistics, Suzhou, China (2025). https://doi.org/10.18653/v1/2025.emnlp-main.1802
6. Ebrahimi, S.F., Peltonen, J.: Nonnegative matrix factorization for joint clustering and topic modeling with minority topics. In: Taniguchi, T., et al. (eds.) Neural Information Processing. ICONIP 2025. LNCS, vol. 16309, pp. 492–506. Springer, Singapore (2026). https://doi.org/10.1007/978-981-95-4367-0_33
7. Egger, R., Yu, J.: A topic modeling comparison between LDA, NMF, Top2Vec, and BERTopic to demystify Twitter posts. Front. Soc. **7** (2022)
8. Jagarlamudi, J., Daumé III, H., Udupa, R.: Incorporating lexical priors into topic models. In: Proceedings of the 13th Conference of the European Chapter of the Association for Computational Linguistics, pp. 204–213 (2012)
9. Lau, J.H., Grieser, K., Newman, D., Baldwin, T.: Automatic labelling of topic models. In: Proceedings of the 49th Annual Meeting of the Association for Computational Linguistics: Human Language Technologies, pp. 1536–1545. ACL, Portland, Oregon, USA, June 2011
10. Lee, T.Y., Smith, A., Seppi, K., Elmqvist, N., Boyd-Graber, J., Findlater, L.: The human touch: how non-expert users perceive, interpret, and fix topic models. Int. J. Hum Comput Stud. **105**, 28–42 (2017)
11. Li, P., et al.: Guided semi-supervised non-negative matrix factorization. Algorithms **15**(5) (2022)
12. Lieb, A., Arora, M., Mustafaraj, E.: Creating targeted, interpretable topic models with LLM-generated text augmentation. arXiv preprint arXiv:2504.17445 (2025)
13. Lin, J.: Divergence measures based on the Shannon entropy. IEEE Trans. Inf. Theory **37**(1), 145–151 (1991)
14. Mei, Q., Shen, X., Zhai, C.: Automatic labeling of multinomial topic models. In: Proceedings of the 13th ACM SIGKDD International Conference on Knowledge Discovery and Data Mining, pp. 490–499 (2007)
15. Mei, Q., Zhai, C.: Discovering evolutionary theme patterns from text: an exploration of temporal text mining. In: Proceedings of the eleventh ACM SIGKDD International Conference on Knowledge Discovery in Data Mining, pp. 198–207 (2005)
16. Mei, Q., Zhai, C.: A mixture model for contextual text mining. In: Proceedings of the 12th ACM SIGKDD International Conference on Knowledge Discovery and Data Mining, pp. 649–655 (2006)
17. Nygård, T., Lindfors, P.: Promoting youth well-being: a qualitative study of Finnish YouTubers' mental health content. Health Promot. Int. **40**(3), daaf074 (2025)
18. Pearce, T., Brintrup, A., Zhu, J.: Understanding softmax confidence and uncertainty. arXiv preprint arXiv:2106.04972 (2021)
19. Pham, D.T., Nguyen Vu, T.T., Nguyen, T., Ngo, L.V., Nguyen, D.A., Nguyen, T.H.: NeuroMax: enhancing neural topic modeling via maximizing mutual information and group topic regularization. In: Findings of the Association for Com-

putational Linguistics: EMNLP 2024, pp. 7758–7772. ACL, Miami, Florida, USA, November 2024

20. Rijcken, E., Scheepers, F., Zervanou, K., Spruit, M., Mosteiro, P., Kaymak, U.: Towards interpreting topic models with ChatGPT. In: The 20th World Congress of the International Fuzzy Systems Association (2023)
21. Srivastava, A., Sutton, C.: Autoencoding variational inference for topic models. In: International Conference on Learning Representations, pp. 2223–2234. Curran Associates (2017)
22. Stammbach, D., Zouhar, V., Hoyle, A., Sachan, M., Ash, E.: Revisiting automated topic model evaluation with large language models. arXiv preprint arXiv:2305.12152 (2023)
23. Vendrow, J., Haddock, J., Rebrova, E., Needell, D.: On a guided nonnegative matrix factorization. In: ICASSP 2021 - 2021 IEEE International Conference on Acoustics, Speech and Signal Processing (ICASSP), pp. 3265–32369 (2021)
24. Vishwakarma, H., Chen, Y., Tay, S.J., Namburi, S.S.S., Sala, F., Korlakai Vinayak, R.: Pearls from pebbles: improved confidence functions for auto-labeling. Adv. Neural Inf. Process. Syst. **37**, 15983–16015 (2024)
25. Wu, X., Nguyen, T., Luu, A.T.: A survey on neural topic models: methods, applications, and challenges. ArXiv **abs/2401.15351** (2024)
26. Wu, X., Nguyen, T., Zhang, D., Wang, W.Y., Luu, A.T.: Fastopic: pretrained transformer is a fast, adaptive, stable, and transferable topic model. Adv. Neural. Inf. Process. Syst. **37**, 84447–84481 (2024)
27. Yang, X., Zhao, H., Phung, D., Buntine, W., Du, L.: LLM reading tea leaves: automatically evaluating topic models with large language models. Trans. Assoc. Comput. Linguist. **13**, 357–375 (2025)

A Privacy-Centric Approach: Scalable and Secure Federated Learning Enabled by Hybrid Homomorphic Encryption

Khoa Nguyen[1], Tanveer Khan[1(✉)], Hossein Abdinasibfar[1], and Antonis Michalas[1,2]

[1] Tampere University, Tampere, Finland
{khoa.nguyen,tanveer.khan,hossein.abdinasibfar,antonios.michalas}@tuni.fi
[2] RISE Research Institutes of Sweden, Tampere, Finland

Abstract. Federated Learning (FL) enables collaborative model training without sharing raw data, making it a promising approach for privacy-sensitive domains. Despite its potential, FL faces significant challenges, particularly in terms of communication overhead and data privacy. Privacy-preserving Techniques (PPTs) such as Homomorphic Encryption (HE) have been used to mitigate these concerns. However, these techniques introduce substantial computational and communication costs, limiting their practical deployment. In this work, we explore how Hybrid Homomorphic Encryption (HHE), a cryptographic protocol that combines symmetric encryption with HE, can be effectively integrated with FL to address both communication and privacy challenges, paving the way for scalable and secure decentralized learning system.

Keywords: Federated Learning · Machine Learning · Privacy

1 Introduction

Machine learning (ML) has increasingly become one of the most impactful fields of data science in recent years, allowing various users to classify and make predictions based on multidimensional data. One of the primary metrics for ML is the accuracy of the prediction or classification results. However, to achieve this, the results should be accompanied by a large amount of high-quality training data that requires the collaboration of several organizations. New regulations such as the General Data Protection Regulations (GDPR) forbid the sharing and processing of sensitive data without the consent of the data subject. This is a key limitation especially when the training data contains sensitive information and therefore poses security threats. For example, to develop a breast cancer detection model from MRI scans, different hospitals can share their data

---

To appear in the Proceedings of the First Workshop on Responsible Healthcare using Machine Learning (RHCML 2025).

I. Koprinska et al. (Eds.): ECML PKDD 2025, CCIS 2842, pp. 280–296, 2026.
https://doi.org/10.1007/978-3-032-19105-2_20

to develop a collaborative ML model. However, sharing private patient information to a central server can reveal sensitive information to the public with several repercussions. Therefore, it has become crucial to protect data privacy, confidentiality, and profit sharing while obtaining data from other organizations. One solution to this problem is employing Federated Learning (FL).

FL enables collaborative model training across edge devices without sharing raw data, making it suitable for domains like healthcare and autonomous transportation [23]. A key challenge in FL is ensuring data privacy while managing communication overhead and data heterogeneity. Although FL keeps data local, Adversaries ($\mathcal{ADV}$) can still infer private information [25], which necessitates Privacy-preserving Techniques (PPTs).

Among PPTs, Homomorphic Encryption (HE)) [20,35] and Secure Multiparty Computation (SMPC) [18,32,36] are widely used. HE allows computation on encrypted data, enabling privacy without compromising utility. However, HE introduces high computational and communication costs, and large ciphertext sizes making real-world deployment difficult [9,13,19,22,30]. To address this Hybrid Homomorphic Encryption (HHE) combines symmetric encryption with HE, significantly reducing ciphertext size and communication cost [2,9]. Users encrypt data with a symmetric key and then encrypt the key using HE. The server uses the encrypted key to process the data securely. HHE thus enables practical deployment of HE on consumer devices by offloading complex computations to the servers. Researchers have deployed HE-friendly symmetric ciphers (e.g., HERA/Rubato [6,17], Elisabeth [8] and PASTA [9]) to support this approach. HHE effectively mitigates both communication and privacy challenges in FL. In this paper, we aim to explore the effectiveness and feasibility of combining FL with HHE. Specifically, we focus on:

Research Questions

- Can we combine FL and HHE to achieve shared trained models without leaking data privacy?
- Does HHE degrade accuracy of the aggregated model compared to plaintext and HE version?
- What are the trade-offs we have to make?
  - How much computation and communication does each client save?
  - How much more computation is needed on the server to compensate?

2 Related Works

FL trains ML models on distributed devices by aggregating local model updates instead of local data. While FL ensures that local raw data do not leave their original locations, it remains vulnerable to eavesdroppers and malicious FL servers that might exploit local plaintext models to reconstruct sensitive training data [12,14,38]. One measure to protect against privacy breaches is differential privacy in which noise is added to the training updates by each client. However, while this paradigm protects private information, it comes at a utility trade-off and can lead to fewer performance models, as demonstrated recently. Another PPT which could be used to address the privacy issue of FL is HE. HE can protect against malicious server eavesdroppers while maintaining model performance by encrypting the weight before sending them to the central server. In HE based FL, the goal is to ensure that no client reveals its model updates during aggregation. Several approaches [31,37] have been proposed to achieve this, including the use of a partially HE scheme [11]. With HE, gradient aggregation can be performed on ciphertexts without decrypting them in advance. For example, Mandal and Gong [27] created robust and secure training protocols for federated regression models using HE. Park and Lim [31] propose employing an HE scheme that enables the centralized server to aggregate encrypted local model parameters without decryption and allows each client to use a different HE key in the same FL system using a distributed cryptosystem. In another work, Madi *et al.* [26] propose an FL framework that is secure against both confidentiality and integrity threats from the aggregation server by employing HE and verifiable computing. Stripelis *et al.*,, [34], propose a secure FL framework using FHE with the CKKS scheme. Testing on the MRI dataset shows no performance loss between encrypted and non-encrypted models. Shi *et al.*, in paper [33] propose a privacy-preserving scheme combining secret sharing and encryption to protect local parameters and resist collusion in FL. The authors also claim that the proposed protocol supports client dropouts, keyless aggregation, and simple interactions. In short, the use of HE schemes in the implementation of PPML continues to garner attention. Gentry's work [15] revolutionized the field of HE and paved the way for multiple modern schemes, such as TFHE [5], BFV [10], and CKKS [4] in PPML applications.

BFV allows a limited number of operations over integer ciphertext while CKKS [4] extends this to floating-point data. TFHE [5] improves upon bootstrapping and bitwise operations on binary data without batching [7]. BFV and CKKS allow batching for faster ML computation, while TFHE uses look-up tables and packing. Each scheme handles non-linear activation functions in ML differently: TFHE uses look-up tables, and BFV/CKKS uses polynomial approximation [21,24]. Although guaranteeing up to a high degree of privacy, a major downside of these algorithms is that they demand significant computational resources. HE schemes have large ciphertexts and high computational complexity, limiting their use. To address these issues, HHE [2,9] combines symmetric ciphers, making it more practical for users.

The first approaches to designing HHE schemes relied primarily on existing and well-established symmetric ciphers such as AES [16]. However, these were not suitable for HHE schemes due to their large multiplicative depth [9]. As a result of this limitation, research in the field of HHE has mainly focused on the design of compatible symmetric ciphers with different optimization criteria [1], such as eliminating the ciphertext expansion [3] or using filter permutators [29].

However, to date, HHE has seen limited practical use [1] in real-world applications, and only a handful of works exist in the field of PPML. To the best of our knowledge, the main HHE schemes currently are HERA [6], Elisabeth [8] and PASTA [9]. The authors of HERA also proposed Rubato [17]; however, the specifications remain largely the same as in HERA. These proposed approaches have different specifications and apply to different use cases. HERA [6] is a stream cipher based on the CKKS HE scheme and allows computations on floating-point data types. In comparison, Elisabeth [8] utilizes the TFHE scheme, is defined over $\mathbb{Z}_{\mathsf{q}}$, where $\mathsf{q} = 2^4$, and stores up to 4 bits of data. PASTA [9] utilizes the BFV scheme for integer data types. HERA and PASTA are defined over $\mathbb{Z}_{\mathsf{q}}$, where $\mathsf{q} = 2^{16} + 1$, and store up to 16-bit data. Each scheme achieves the same security level of 128-bits. Additionally, HERA also provides tests for a security level of 80 bits. As HERA allows computations on floating-point data types, it does not require quantization on certain inputs. Elisabeth and PASTA, on the other hand, require quantization to operate on floating-point numbers, which introduces a rounding error, which can reduce the accuracy of certain applications, i.e. ML.

3 Preliminaries

3.1 Federated Learning

The concept of FL was first introduced by Google AI Blog[1] to protect data privacy. It is a distributed ML approach, where multiple users collaboratively train a model [28]. In this technique, the central server selects a set of users and sends them the initial model parameters. Each user provides its local data for training, does the training locally, and sends the local model updates to the central server, while the central server aggregates the final model. Hence, raw data are not shared in this approach, whereas the neural network architecture, parameters, and the intermediate representation of the model (weights, activations, and gradients) are shared between the users and the server during the learning process. With the help of FL, the clients can benefit from obtaining a well-trained ML model without having to send their private data to a central server.

Definition of FL. Let's assume their are N users $\mathcal{U} = \{u_1, u_2, \ldots, u_n\}$ own their own datasets $\{\mathcal{D}_1, \mathcal{D}_2, \ldots, \mathcal{D}_n\}$ and each of them cannot directly access to other users' data to expand their own data.

(1) The server initializes and sends the initial model to each user
(2) Each client trains its own local model $\mathcal{W}_i$ on the local data $\mathcal{D}_i$
(3) The server collects and aggregates the local models $\mathcal{W}_i$ from the clients into an updated global model, and share this global model to all users
(4) Repeat step 2 until the model converges, or the maximum number of the FL rounds has been reached

[1] https://ai.googleblog.com/2017/04/federated-learning-collaborative.html.

3.2 Homomorphic Encryption

Definition 1 (Homomorphic Encryption). *Let* HE *be a (public-key) homomorphic encryption scheme with a quadruple of PPT algorithms* $\mathsf{HE} = (\mathsf{KeyGen}, \mathsf{Enc}, \mathsf{Dec}, \mathsf{Eval})$ *such that:*

- **HE.KeyGen:** The key generation algorithm $(\mathsf{pk}, \mathsf{evk}, \mathsf{sk}) \leftarrow \mathsf{HE.KeyGen}(1^\lambda)$ takes as input a unary representation of the security parameter λ, and outputs a public key pk, an evaluation key evk and a private key sk.
- **HE.Enc:** The encryption algorithm $c \leftarrow \mathsf{HE.Enc}(\mathsf{pk}, x)$ takes as input the public key pk and a message x and outputs a ciphertext c.
- **HE.Eval:** The algorithm $c_f \leftarrow \mathsf{HE.Eval}(\mathsf{evk}, f, c_1, \ldots, c_n)$ takes as input the evaluation key evk, a function f, and a set of n ciphertexts, and outputs a ciphertext c_f.
- **HE.Dec:** The decryption algorithm $\mathsf{HE.Dec}(\mathsf{sk}, c) \rightarrow x$, takes as input the secret key sk and a ciphertext c, and outputs a plaintext x.

3.3 Hybrid Homomorphic Encryption

Definition 2 (Hybrid Homomorphic Encryption). *Let* HE *be a Homomorphic Encryption scheme and* $\mathsf{SKE} = (\mathsf{Gen}, \mathsf{Enc}, \mathsf{Dec})$ *be a symmetric-key encryption scheme. Moreover, let* $\mathcal{X} = (x_1, \ldots, x_n)$ *be the message space and* λ *the security parameter. An* HHE *scheme consists of five PPT algorithms* $\mathsf{HHE} = (\mathsf{KeyGen}, \mathsf{Enc}, \mathsf{Decomp}, \mathsf{Eval}, \mathsf{Dec})$ *such that:*

- **HHE.KeyGen**: The key generation algorithm takes as input a security parameter λ and outputs a HE public/private key pair (pk/sk) and a HE evaluation key (evk).
- **HHE.Enc**: This algorithm consists of three steps:
  - $\mathsf{SKE.Gen}$: The SKE generation algorithm takes as input security parameter λ and outputs a symmetric key K.
  - $\mathsf{HE.Enc}$: An HE encryption algorithm that takes as input pk and K, and outputs c_K – a homomorphically encrypted representation of the symmetric key K.
  - $\mathsf{SKE.Enc}$: The SKE encryption algorithm takes as input a message x and K and outputs a ciphertext c.
- **HHE.Decomp**: This algorithm takes as an input the evk, the symmetrically encrypted ciphertext c, and the homomorphically encrypted symmetric key c_K, and outputs c' – a homomorphic encryption of the original message x.
- **HHE.Eval**: It takes as input n homomorphic ciphertexts c'_n, where $n \geq 2$, the evk and a homomorphic function f, and outputs a ciphertext c'_{eval} of the evaluation results.
- **HHE.Dec**: This algorithm takes as input a private key sk and the evaluated ciphertext c'_{eval} and outputs $f(x)$.

3.4 Rubato HHE Framework

We present the Rubato and RtF HHE framework [17] in Fig. 1. HE evaluation are performed in the boxes with thick lines. Operations in the boxes with rounded corners do not use any secret information.

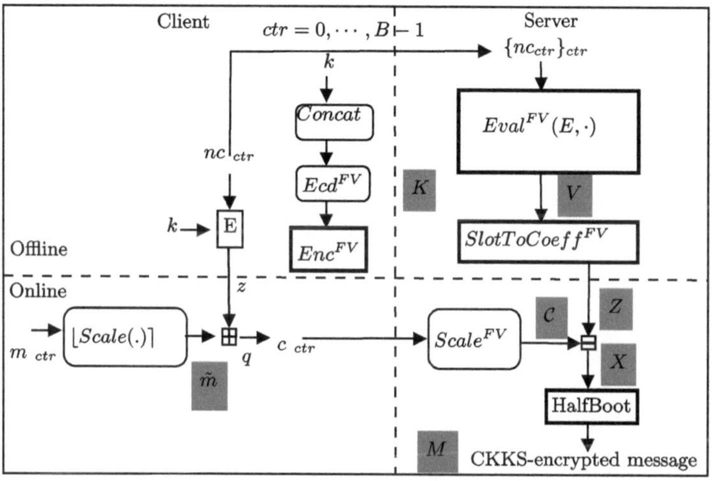

Fig. 1. The RtF transciphering framework.

Initialization. The RtF transciphering framework uses *both FV and CKKS schemes.* For a fixed security parameter λ, set parameters such as the degree of the polynomial modulus and the ciphertext moduli, and *generate the public-private key pair* to satisfy the desired security level λ. For a *secret key* $k \in \mathbb{Z}_q^n$ *used for a symmetric cipher* $\mathbf{E}$, the client computes the *FV-ciphertext* $\mathcal{K}$ *of the symmetric secret key* k and sends it to the server.

Client-side Computation:

- **Offline Phase:** The client *generates a keystream* $\mathbf{z} \in \mathbb{Z}_q^n$ *from the cipher* E, taking the nonce $\mathsf{nc} \in \{0,1\}^\lambda$ and the secret key $\mathbf{k} \in \mathbb{Z}_q^n$ as inputs.
- **Online Phase:** First, the client scales up the plaintext message m (in floating point) by a scaling factor Δ to obtain a quantized message: $\tilde{\mathbf{m}} = \lfloor \Delta \cdot \mathbf{m} \rceil \in \mathbb{Z}_q^n$. Then, the client performs addition modulo q between the keystream $\mathbf{z}$ and the scaled message $\tilde{\mathbf{m}}$, resulting in a symmetric ciphertext: $\mathbf{c} = [\tilde{\mathbf{m}} + \mathbf{z}]_q$. The client sends $\mathbf{c}$ along with the nonce nc to the server.

Server-side Computation:

- **Offline Phase:**
  - First, the server *evaluates the keystream using a tuple of nonces* $(\mathsf{nc}_0, \ldots, \mathsf{nc}_{B-1})$ *and the FV-encrypted symmetric key* $\mathcal{K}$. This results in an FV-ciphertext $\mathcal{V}$ containing the keystreams of E in its slots.

  - Then, the server applies a linear transformation $\mathsf{SlotToCoeff}^{\mathsf{FV}}$ to move the data from the slots to the coefficients, obtaining an FV-ciphertext $\mathcal{Z}$ containing the keystreams in its coefficients. *All of the homomorphic evaluations above are done in the FV scheme.*
- **Online Phase:**
  - During online phase, the server first *scales up the symmetric ciphertext* $\mathbf{c}$ *into the FV ciphertext space*, resulting in an FV-ciphertext $\mathcal{C}$ containing the symmetric ciphertexts in its coefficients.
  - Then, it subtracts homomorphically the evaluated keystream $\mathcal{Z}$ from $\mathcal{C}$: $\mathcal{X} = \mathcal{C} - \mathcal{Z}$, yielding an FV-ciphertext $\mathcal{X}$ having scaled messages in its coefficients.
  - The final step is HalfBoot, a modified bootstrapping process in the RtF framework. Given $\mathcal{X}$ as input, it outputs a CKKS-ciphertext: $\mathsf{HalfBoot}(\mathcal{X}) = \mathcal{M}$, where $\mathcal{M}$ contains the CKKS-encrypted messages in its slots.

4 FLHHE

4.1 System Model

In this section, we introduce our system model by explicitly describing our protocol's main entities and their capabilities.

- **Trusted key dealer**: The trusted key dealer creates and distributes all the HHE keys to the clients along with an HE encryption $c_{\mathsf{K_i}}$ of the symmetric key to the **CSP**.
- **Client**: Let $\mathcal{C} = \{c_1, \ldots, C_n\}$ be the set of all clients. Each client uses the unique symmetric key $\mathsf{K_i}$ locally and encrypts their data. The generated ciphertexts are then outsourced to the **CSP**.
- **Cloud Service Provider (CSP)**: Primarily responsible for gathering symmetrically encrypted data from multiple users. The **CSP** is tasked with converting the symmetrically encrypted data into homomorphic ciphertexts and, upon request, performing blind operations on them.

4.2 Threat Model

We consider a semi-honest (honest-but-curious) threat model, where both clients and server, follow the protocol correctly but may attempt to infer private information from the data they receive. To ensure privacy in this setting, the system must satisfy the following requirements:

(i) Client should only access their own local models and the final aggregated model, without visibility into other clients' models or data *(ii)* The server must receive encrypted models and secure parameters, without learning the raw data. *(iii)* All client-side data remains strictly confidential and protected from both the server and other clients.

5 Methodology

Our proposed FL system is mainly composed of two key entities: a central model aggregation server and multiple distributed clients, as shown in Fig. 2. The server is responsible for securely aggregating encrypted local models submitted by the clients, while each client trains a local model on its private dataset and transmits the encrypted model along with secure parameters to the server. Through the collaborative process, an optimal global model is constructed iteratively over multiple training rounds. Unlike conventional FL frameworks, our approach uses HHE to improve privacy and reduce communication overhead between clients and server. The specific construction of the proposed protocol is explained in detail in the following:

Initialization: Before training starts, the clients receive the symmetric key, HE private/public keys, and the server receive HE ciphertext of the symmetric key and HE evaluation key from the key dealer. The server selects participating clients, defines the model architecture and key parameters like learning rate, batch size, number of local epochs. All parties establish secure communication channels and synchronize these parameters. Each client then receives an initial plaintext model from the server in preparation for local training.

Local Training: Each client trains local model on private data, resulting in an updated set of model parameters in plaintext. These models reflect client-specific learning based on their local data. After training, clients encrypt their local model using symmetric encryption. The symmetric encrypted models are then sent to the server.

Server Aggregation: Upon receiving encrypted models, the server uses HHE's transcipher and evaluation primitives to homomorphically convert and aggregate the model. The FL Server aggregates using the most simple weight averaging algorithm `SimpAvg` in the HE domain, where each client's model contributes equally, regardless of its dataset size: $w_{\text{global}} = \frac{1}{K}\sum_{k=1}^{K} w_k$. Here, K is the number of clients, and w_k is the model weights from client k. We use simple FL averaging algorithm since our goal is to demonstrate that under HHE, accuracy of the aggregated model is comparable with one produced under plaintext, not to demonstrate how accurate our FL model is.

6 Experiment

In this section, we evaluate the performance of the `FLHHE` protocol, focusing on its computational and communication cost, and compare its performance against the same FL procedure using a plain CKKS HE scheme. Below is the detailed configurations of our experimental environment:

- **Hardware**: Our experimental testbed is a commercial Macbook Pro laptop with an Apple M4 Max with 16 CPU cores, integrated GPU of 40 cores, and 128 GB of RAM. All trainings and evaluation are done in a simulated environment under this testbed.

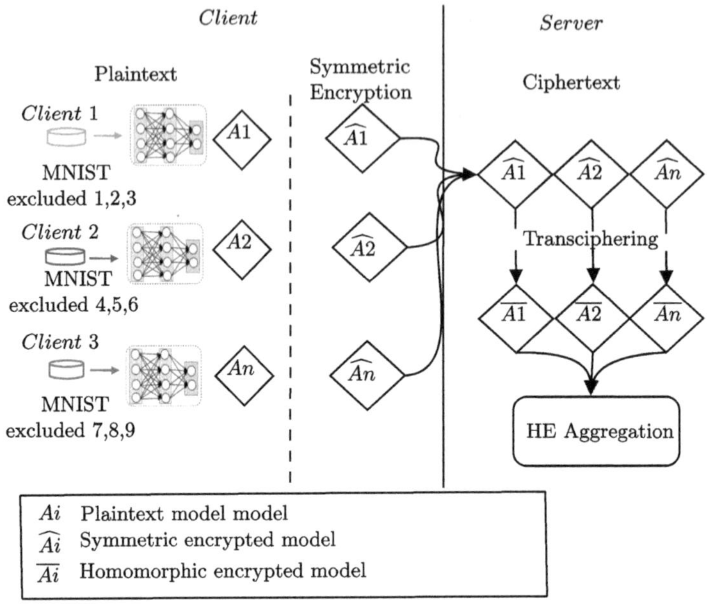

Fig. 2. FL Framework with HHE for Secure Model Aggregation

- **Software**: We use the pytorch library to train the neural networks locally for the users, the Lattigo v6 for plain CKKS, and the Rubato combined with the RtF transciphering framework for our HHE implementations
- **Dataset**: We used the classic MNIST dataset of 28×28 handwritten images to evaluate the performance of our method. We process the raw MNIST dataset, which contains 60,000 samples in total, into 3 partitions for training, each holds by a client:
  - Partition 1: Exclude labels 1, 3, 7 (40,862 samples)
  - Partition 2: Exclude labels 2, 5, 8 (42,770 samples)
  - Partition 3: Exclude labels 4, 6, 9 (42,291 samples)
- **Neural Network**: We use a fully connected neural network that consists of two linear layers (without bias terms) and a ReLU activation function in between. The network takes a batch of flattened MNIST images, each with length 784, processes it through a hidden layer of 32 neurons, and produces 10 output values (one for each digit 0–9). The plaintext weights are then flattened into 1D vectors before being encrypted in HE and HHE domains. The values in these weight vectors are floating point in the range of $[-1, 1]$. The weight vectors are in the JSON format for plaintext version, or in binaries for the encrypted versions, for data persistence and communication.

Computation Analysis: We report each party's `FLHHE` performance averaged over 10 runs (see Table 1).

Hence, server processing time per client is 39.81 s. With these results, we can see that the initialization/setup cost is quite heavy but is front-loaded, only

Table 1. Computation Time Breakdown (in seconds)

Role	Task	Time (sec)
Key Dealer	Key generation (once)	57.45
	Load keys	20.53
	Symmetric key encryption	5.33
Client	Decrypt global model	0.07
	Local training	2.73
	Keystream generation (offline)	0.55
	Symmetric encryption (online)	0.008
	Total per client	*3.32*
Server (per client)	Produce $\mathcal{Z}$ (offline)	32.94
	Transcipher $\mathcal{M}$ (online)	6.87
	HE aggregation (online)	0.003

needed to do once, and scales well with more rounds and clients. For clients, HHE introduces almost zero latency overhead at the client-side since symmetric encryption during the online phase only takes 0.008 s, which is statically insignificant compared to training time (2.73 s). The trade-off lies at the server side, but this can still be scalable since server-side computations can be highly optimized, for example, using careful orchestrated parallelize computation and/or distributed systems.

Communication Analysis: Communication cost is measured by file size (binary/json). Table 2 list key sizes shared once at the start of the protocol by the key dealer.

Table 2. Memory sizes of cryptographic keys

Keys	Size
pk (public key)	29.4 MB
re (relinearization key)	352.3 MB
rot (rotation key)	11.27 GB
sk (secret key)	14.7 MB
symmetric_key	512 Bytes
HE Encrypted Symmetric Key	738.5 MB

For each client, each linear layer that is encrypted symmetrically takes 524 KB in disk, making the whole 2 linear layer neural network 1.048 MB in total. The HE-averaged model output by the server after the HHE protocol takes 16.8 MB in size (8.4 MB per encrypted layer). After aggregation, the server will send the HE encrypted model to each client to decrypt. Hence, for each client, the total communication cost for each round is 1.048 + 16.8 = 17.848 MB. And for 3 clients, the total communication cost for one FL round under HHE is 17.848 * 3 = 53.544 MB. We can see that the majority of communication cost is incurred by the downloading step of the average HE model from the server, while the symmetric model that's needed to be uploaded by each client is 16 times less heavy in size.

6.1 Comparison with Plaintext and CKKS-Based HE

Accuracy Comparisons: Evaluating the plaintext averaged model, the decrypted averaged models under HE and under HHE all give the exact same accuracies on all test sets:

- Accuracy on test set with all samples: 65.92%
- Accuracy on test set with labels 1, 3, 7: 73.15%
- Accuracy on test set with labels 2, 5, 8: 54.35%
- Accuracy on test set with labels 4, 6, 9: 58.43%

Computation Comparisons: Note that for FLHHE, we only account for the computation time of the online phase for both the client and the server, since the values in the offline phase can be precomputed, for example, the values of the offline phase of the server can be computed while the clients do the training, similarly for the clients. On the client side:

- In the plaintext setting, each client simply trains the model locally without any encryption.
- Under HE, clients first decrypt the global model received from the server, train locally, and then re-encrypt the updated model into HE ciphertext before sending it back.
- In FLHHE, clients also decrypt the average HE-encrypted model downloaded from the server and train locally, but instead of encrypting with HE, they encrypt their updated model using symmetric encryption before sending it back to the server. Table 3 shows client computation time.

Table 3. Computation Time for Different FL Settings (unit: sec)

Client Computation

Activity	Plain	HE	FLHHE
Decrypt model	N/A	0.07	0.07
Local training	2.73	2.73	2.73
Encrypt model	N/A	0.21	0.008
Total	2.73	3.01	2.808

Server Computation

Activity	Plain	HE	FLHHE
Transcipher	N/A	N/A	6.75
Aggregation	0.00005	0.004	0.003
Total	0.00005	0.004	6.75

Research Question Answers

- This result helps us answer our first research question: "Can we combine FL and HHE to achieve shared trained models without leaking data privacy?". The answer is yes, FLHHE enables collaborative model training with a focus on privacy.
- Regarding the second research question, experimental results show us that HHE does not degrade the accuracy of the FL aggregated model compared to the plaintext or HE version.

On the server side:

- In the plaintext case, the server performs standard model averaging on the unencrypted models.
- For the HE setting, the server directly aggregates the models within HE domain using homomorphic operations.
- With FLHHE, server transciphers symmetrically encrypted models received from clients into HE ciphertexts and performs model averaging in HE domain.

Table 3 shows server-side computation time breakdown for one client for one round. We can see that server-side computation of FLHHE is dominated transciphering. After the transciphering step, HE aggregation in FL with HE and FLHHE are comparable, however, they are still about 70 times slower than aggregation in plaintext.

Research Question Answers

FLHHE offers a reduction in client-side computation compared to a full HE implementation, and adds minimal overhead compared to plaintext. The total online computation time for a client in FLHHE is 2.808 seconds, compared to 3.01 seconds for HE and 2.73 seconds for plaintext (Table 3). The critical symmetric encryption step in FLHHE takes only 0.008 seconds, compared to 0.21 seconds for HE, which is 26.25 times faster. This is critical when the model scales up in terms of complexity and size.

Research Question Answers

How much computation is needed on the server to compensate? The primary trade-off for efficiencies gained by the client is a substantial increase in server-side computation, mainly due to the transciphering step. Server online computation time per client per round in FLHHE: 6.75 seconds (Table 3). This is significantly higher than both the HE setting (0.004 seconds) and the plaintext setting (0.00005 seconds). This increased load is dominated by the "Transcipher" step, which takes 6.75 seconds.

Communication Comparisons: Table 4 shows per-client communication cost per round for plaintext, HE, and HHE.

Table 4. Communication cost per client in one round

1 round, 1 client	Send (MB)	Receive (MB)	Total (MB)
Plain	0.563	0.564	1.127
HE	16.8	16.8	33.6
HHE	1.048	16.8	17.848

Research Question Answers

Client Communication Savings: `FLHHE` reduces client upload costs.

- Upload Cost: Clients using `FLHHE` send 1.048 MB, which is 16 times less than the 16.8 MB required with HE.
- Total Cost: The total communication cost per client per round for `FLHHE` is 17.848 MB (1.048 MB send + 16.8 MB receive), which is nearly half that of the HE scheme (33.6 MB total).
- Scalability: As shown in Figure 3, HHE's total communication cost scales better than HE as the number of clients increases, which is important in large-scale production settings.

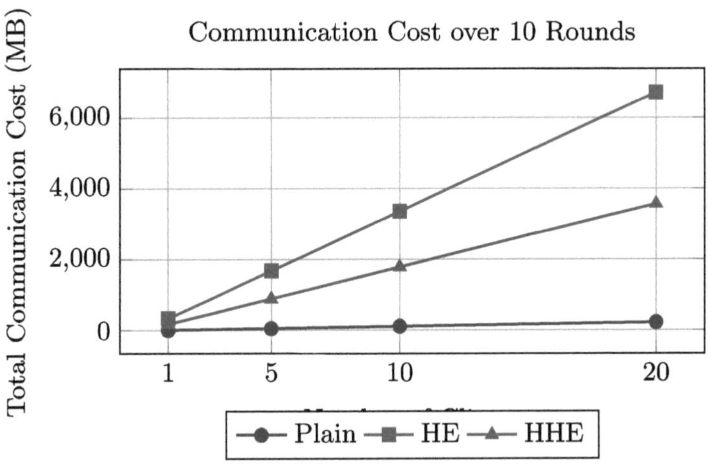

Fig. 3. Communication cost vs. number of clients

Overall, while the plaintext version is much cheaper in terms of communication (16 times less than HHE, and 30 times less than HE), it offers no privacy data protection. In contrast, for a client in an FL training workflow, using HHE can save a lot of upload cost compared to HE (16 times less) by sending a symmetric encrypted model instead of an HE encrypted one. Nevertheless, since the FL server returns the same HE-encrypted aggregated model in both cases, the total communication cost of FLHHE for each client is reduced only 2 times, compared to HE. However, consider the fact that in real-world FL deployments with many clients participating across many rounds, this reduction can lead to substantial overall bandwidth savings(see Fig. 3).

7 Generalizable Insights About Responsible Application of Machine Learning in Healthcare

This work demonstrates that combining lightweight encryption with FL can protect client data without sacrificing model performance. Key insights include:

- **Client-side efficiency:** Reducing client-side cost is crucial for deployment in resource-constrained healthcare settings.
- **Privacy-utility trade-offs:** Client-side encryption with secure server processing balances privacy and performance.
- **Scalable privacy-preserving FL:** Communication-efficient approaches are essential for real-world healthcare applications.

Remark 1. Although we did not use a healthcare dataset, the proposed method can be easily extended to such settings and is applicable to any healthcare dataset, supporting responsible and secure ML in healthcare.

Open Science and Reproducible Research: To support open science and reproducible research, source code used for the evaluations is publicly available[2].

8 Conclusion

In this work, we investigated the integration of HHE with FL, termed FLHHE, to address the critical challenges of data privacy and communication overhead in decentralized model training. The protocol uses symmetric encryption on the client-side and HE on the server-side, with a transciphering step to convert between them. This approach is designed to prevent raw data leakage, offering privacy benefits over plaintext FL, and is compared against a full HE-based approach in terms of performance. Experimental results demonstrate that FLHHE enables collaborative model training without compromising accuracy, offering enhanced privacy and substantially reduced client communication. While it

[2] https://github.com/khoaguin/flhhe.

increases server-side computation, the benefits for client resource efficiency position FLHHE as a promising pathway towards more practical, scalable, and secure FL systems. Future work may optimize client downloading cost, improve server-side transciphering and aggregation, or explore real-world applications of FLHHE.

Acknowledgments. This work was funded by the HARPOCRATES EU research project (No. 101069535).

References

1. Bakas, A., Frimpong, E., Michalas, A.: Symmetrical disguise: Realizing homomorphic encryption services from symmetric primitives. In: International Conference on Security and Privacy in Communication Systems, pp. 353–370. Springer (2022)
2. Bakas, A., Michalas, A.: Modern family: a revocable hybrid encryption scheme based on attribute-based encryption, symmetric searchable encryption and sgx. In: International Conference on Security and Privacy in Communication Systems, pp. 472–486. Springer (2019)
3. Canteaut, A., et al.: Stream ciphers: a practical solution for efficient homomorphic-ciphertext compression. J. Cryptol. **31**(3), 885–916 (2018)
4. Cheon, J.H., Kim, A., Kim, M., Song, Y.: Homomorphic encryption for arithmetic of approximate numbers. In: International Conference on the Theory and Application of Cryptology and Information Security, pp. 409–437. Springer (2017)
5. Chillotti, I., Gama, N., Georgieva, M., Izabachene, M.: Faster fully homomorphic encryption: bootstrapping in less than 0.1 seconds. In: Advances in Cryptology–ASIACRYPT 2016, pp. 3–33. Springer (2016)
6. Cho, J., et al.: Transciphering framework for approximate homomorphic encryption. In: International Conference on the Theory and Application of Cryptology and Information Security, pp. 640–669. Springer (2021)
7. Clet, P.E., Stan, O., Zuber, M.: Bfv, ckks, tfhe: which one is the best for a secure neural network evaluation in the cloud? In: Applied Cryptography and Network Security Workshops: ACNS 2021 Satellite Workshops, pp. 279–300. Springer (2021)
8. Cosseron, O., Hoffmann, C., Méaux, P., Standaert, F.X.: Towards case-optimized hybrid homomorphic encryption: featuring the elisabeth stream cipher. In: Advances in Cryptology – ASIACRYPT 2022, pp. 32–67. Springer-Verlag (2023)
9. Dobraunig, C., Grassi, L., Helminger, L., Rechberger, C., Schofnegger, M., Walch, R.: Pasta: a case for hybrid homomorphic encryption. Trans. Cryptographic Hardware Embedded Syst. 2023 Issue 3 (2023)
10. Fan, J., Vercauteren, F.: Somewhat practical fully homomorphic encryption. Cryptology ePrint Archive (2012)
11. Fang, H., Qian, Q.: Privacy preserving machine learning with homomorphic encryption and federated learning. Future Internet **13**(4), 94 (2021)
12. Fredrikson, M., Jha, S., Ristenpart, T.: Model inversion attacks that exploit confidence information and basic countermeasures. In: Proceedings of the 22nd ACM SIGSAC Conference on Computer and Communications Security, pp. 1322–1333 (2015)
13. Frimpong, E., Nguyen, K., Budzys, M., Khan, T., Michalas, A.: Guardml: efficient privacy-preserving machine learning services through hybrid homomorphic encryption. In: 39th ACM/SIGAPP Symposium On Applied Computing (SAC'24) (2024)

14. Geiping, J., Bauermeister, H., Dröge, H., Moeller, M.: Inverting gradients-how easy is it to break privacy in federated learning? Adv. Neural. Inf. Process. Syst. **33**, 16937–16947 (2020)
15. Gentry, C.: A fully Homomorphic Encryption Scheme. Stanford University (2009)
16. Gentry, C., Halevi, S., Smart, N.P.: Homomorphic evaluation of the aes circuit. In: Annual Cryptology Conference. Springer (2012)
17. Ha, J., Kim, S., Lee, B., Lee, J., Son, M.: Rubato: noisy ciphers for approximate homomorphic encryption. In: Advances in Cryptology–EUROCRYPT 2022, pp. 581–610. Springer (2022)
18. Khan, T., Budzys, M., Michalas, A.: Make split, not hijack: preventing feature-space hijacking attacks in split learning. In: Proceedings of the 29th ACM Symposium on Access Control Models and Technologies, pp. 19–30 (2024)
19. Khan, T., Budzys, M., Michalas, A.: Split happens: combating advanced threats with split learning and function secret sharing. arXiv preprint arXiv:2507.10494 (2025)
20. Khan, T., Budzys, M., Nguyen, K., Michalas, A.: Sok: wildest dreams: reproducible research in privacy-preserving neural network training. In: Proceedings of the 24th Privacy Enhancing Technologies Symposium (PETS'24), Springer-Verlag, Berlin, Heidelberg (2024)
21. Khan, T., Michalas, A.: Learning in the dark: privacy-preserving machine learning using function approximation. In: 2023 IEEE 22nd International Conference on Trust, Security and Privacy in Computing and Communications (TrustCom), pp. 62–71. IEEE (2023)
22. Khan, T., Nguyen, K., Michalas, A., Bakas, A.: Love or hate? share or split? privacy-preserving training using split learning and homomorphic encryption. In: 2023 20th Annual International Conference on Privacy, Security and Trust (PST), pp. 1–7. IEEE (2023)
23. Konečný, J., McMahan, H.B., Yu, F.X., Richtárik, P., Suresh, A.T., Bacon, D.: Federated learning: strategies for improving communication efficiency. arXiv preprint arXiv:1610.05492 (2016)
24. Lee, J.W., et al.: Privacy-preserving machine learning with fully homomorphic encryption for deep neural network. IEEE Access **10**, 30039–30054 (2022)
25. Li, Q., et al.: A survey on federated learning systems: vision, hype and reality for data privacy and protection. IEEE Trans. Knowl. Data Eng. **35**(4), 3347–3366 (2021)
26. Madi, A., Stan, O., Mayoue, A., Grivet-Sébert, A., Gouy-Pailler, C., Sirdey, R.: A secure federated learning framework using homomorphic encryption and verifiable computing. In: 2021 Reconciling Data Analytics, Automation, Privacy, and Security: A Big Data Challenge (RDAAPS), pp. 1–8. IEEE (2021)
27. Mandal, K., Gong, G.: Privfl: practical privacy-preserving federated regressions on high-dimensional data over mobile networks. In: Proceedings of the 2019 ACM SIGSAC Conference on Cloud Computing Security Workshop, pp. 57–68 (2019)
28. McMahan, H.B., Moore, E., Ramage, D., Hampson, S., y Arcas, B.A.: Communication-efficient learning of deep networks from decentralized data (2023), https://arxiv.org/abs/1602.05629
29. Méaux, P., Carlet, C., Journault, A., Standaert, F.X.: Improved filter permutators for efficient fhe: better instances and implementations. In: International Conference on Cryptology in India. Springer (2019)

30. Nguyen, K., Khan, T., Michalas, A.: Split without a leak: reducing privacy leakage in split learning. In: Security and Privacy in Communication Networks (SecureComm'23), Hong Kong SAR, Hong Kong, 19—21 October 2023. Springer Nature Switzerland, Cham (2023)
31. Park, J., Yu, N.Y., Lim, H.: Privacy-preserving federated learning using homomorphic encryption with different encryption keys. In: 2022 13th International Conference on Information and Communication Technology Convergence (ICTC), pp. 1869–1871. IEEE (2022)
32. Ryffel, T., Tholoniat, P., Pointcheval, D., Bach, F.: Ariann: low-interaction privacy-preserving deep learning via function secret sharing. Proc. Priv. Enhancing Technol. **2022**(1) (2020)
33. Shi, Z., Yang, Z., Hassan, A., Li, F., Ding, X.: A privacy preserving federated learning scheme using homomorphic encryption and secret sharing. Telecommun. Syst. **82**(3), 419–433 (2023)
34. Stripelis, D., et al.: Secure neuroimaging analysis using federated learning with homomorphic encryption. In: 17th International Symposium on Medical Information Processing and Analysis, vol. 12088, pp. 351–359. SPIE (2021)
35. Tian, H., et al.: Sphinx: enabling privacy-preserving online learning over the cloud. In: 2022 IEEE Symposium on Security and Privacy (SP), pp. 2487–2501. IEEE (2022)
36. Wagh, S., Gupta, D., Chandran, N.: Securenn: 3-party secure computation for neural network training. Proc. Priv. Enhancing Technol. **2019**(3), 26–49 (2019)
37. Yang, Q., Liu, Y., Chen, T., Tong, Y.: Federated machine learning: concept and applications. ACM Trans. Intell. Syst. Technol. (TIST) **10**(2), 1–19 (2019)
38. Zhu, L., Liu, Z., Han, S.: Deep leakage from gradients. In: Advances in Neural Information Processing Systems, vol. 32 (2019)

Positive-Unlabeled Learning for User-Centred XAI: A Case Study in Healthcare

Iris Heerlien(✉), Selin Çolakhasanoglu, and Jeroen Linssen

Saxion University of Applied Sciences, Enschede, The Netherlands
{i.r.heerlien,s.colakhasanoglu,j.m.linssen}@saxion.nl

Abstract. As the aging population grows, coupled with a shortage of healthcare personnel, the demand for innovative solutions becomes imperative. Digital tools, such as medicine dispensers, offer promising avenues for remote healthcare delivery, alleviating the workload on professionals. Nonetheless, home care organizations encounter challenges in implementing and scaling these tools, ranging from a lack of awareness about available options to difficulties in selecting the most suitable tool for specific situations. This study investigates a recommendation methodology for a medicine dispenser based on Omaha profiles from Electronic Patient Dossier (EPD). Using the CRISP-DM methodology, we designed a Positive-Unlabeled learning-based algorithm. We added Explainable Artificial Intelligence (XAI) techniques, showing a feature importance representation based on Shapley values, to enrich the transparency and reliability of suggested interventions. The solution was evaluated with healthcare professionals from two healthcare organizations. Although the technical performance of the algorithm was decent (recall: 0.9), they stated the data is not detailed enough to conclude whether a medicine dispenser could be used, showing the need for human evaluation during the process. This study addresses challenges like a sparse dataset lacking detailed data and iteratively involving users during development when performing research in a real life situation.

Keywords: User-Centered XAI · Elderly care · Digital Healthcare Tools

1 Introduction

Elderly care is facing challenges due to personnel shortages. According to Gupta Strategists, a shortage of 67,300 health personnel in the elderly care in 2031 is realistic in the Netherlands. Medical technologies could be of help in this by lightening tasks and preventing elderly care [15]. Examples include video calling, medicine dispensers, lifestyle monitoring, and daily structure support. However, these technologies are not used as frequently as possible.

Research performed by Nedap Healthcare, an IT company that facilitates an Electronic Patient Dossier (EPD) platform, shows that staff involved in patient

I. Koprinska et al. (Eds.): ECML PKDD 2025, CCIS 2842, pp. 297–313, 2026.
https://doi.org/10.1007/978-3-032-19105-2_21

care are sometimes unaware of the available healthcare technologies within their organization. In addition, they find it challenging to determine which patients would benefit from these technologies. This lack of awareness and difficulty in identifying suitable patients is the core problem preventing the successful scaling of healthcare technology.

We performed a case study to explore the use of machine learning for recommendations on available healthcare technology based on EPD data. The goal is to develop a tool that gives advice whether a medicine dispenser could be used by a elderly patient based on EPD data. Besides the technical implementation and evaluation, we evaluated the results with the healthcare professionals.

The process including this advice will look like the diagram shown in Fig. 1. The nurse will perform an intake call with the patient. Secondly, the nurse will create a plan of approach by filling in the signs and symptoms, and the interventions that need to be taken. Based on this, the algorithm decides whether a healthcare technology could be used. As the healthcare professional is in the lead, they can decide to follow this approach or to neglect it. If accepted, the technology is added to the to be performed interventions.

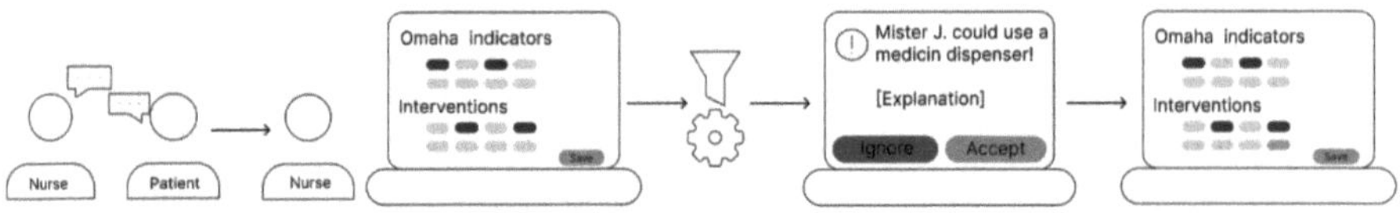

Fig. 1. The imagined workflow.

In this paper, we explain our methodology, discuss the challenges we faced, and present our key findings. We aim to use explainable AI to support and substantiate decision making.

Our main contributions are: (1) applying PU learning to handle incomplete labels, (2) evaluating machine learning models and their interpretability, and (3) involving healthcare professionals in the evaluation.

The remainder of this paper is structured as follows. In Sect. 2, we discuss related work, followed by the methodology and results in Sect. 3. We discuss and conclude this study in Sects. 4 to 6.

2 Related Work

This section covers the two main topics related to this study. First, we discuss Explainable AI and its relevance as we will use this in understanding the algorithms. Afterwards, we explain techniques related to PU learning as our dataset has no negative labels.

2.1 Understandable Decision-Making

It is important to understand why and how machines make certain decisions. Explaining decision-making to humans builds trust in AI-systems, which encourages the use of AI-based algorithms as assistant in various domains [5,7,14]. This study investigates different techniques of making the outcome of the machine learning algorithm interpretable and understandable for healthcare workers.

Explainable AI Techniques. There are several types of XAI techniques to make a machine learning model interpretable and understandable [8]. These techniques help users understand how models generate their predictions and enable trust in their outputs. Well-known techniques are feature importance (for global interpretation) and SHAP (for local interpretation) [10].

Feature importance techniques states the relative importance when making a prediction showing the most influential features. One common method is Permutation Importance. It evaluates the impact of shuffling a feature's values on model performance, where a significant decrease in performance indicates the feature's importance to the model. Feature importance and permutation importance are easy to compute and interpret, however they may be less effective for models with complex interactions between features.

Another technique is SHAP. This technique is a game-theoretic approach to explain output of an ML model, providing both local and global interpretability. SHAP values explain the contribution of each feature to a particular prediction by calculating the difference between the prediction made with and without the feature. [9]. According to Dwivedi et al. [3], an important advantage of SHAP values is that it is transparent and locally interpretable. This makes SHAP valuable in situations where understanding individual model decisions are crucial. For example, in healthcare a physician might want to understand the factors contributing to a patient's predicted risk to a disease. SHAP can provide insight in individual features such as age and medical history. Feature importance as discussed above provides insight of how important features are for the entire population, ignoring the individual scenarios.

User-Centered Explainable AI. While algorithm-centric methods, such as SHAP and feature importance techniques, provide technical insight into model behavior, they often fail to consider whether these explanations are meaningful or useful to the end users of systems [7,14]. Research has shown that explanation techniques are often designed from the perspective of AI experts and do not necessarily align with the needs of end users, such as healthcare professionals [4]. Explanations that make sense to AI experts may not be as intuitive for domain experts or users, who rely on AI for decision making.

Different stakeholders interact with AI systems in various ways, requiring tailored explanations to meet their specific needs. Burnett et al. [2] emphasize that explanations should be adapted to the expertise of the users, whereas Wang et al. [16] discuss how user expectations influences the perception on explainability.

Human-centered design methods focus on identifying what end users need and how the design can respond to these needs [11].

Liao and Varshney [7] argue that a well-crafted explanation does not necessarily translate into effectiveness or benefit for the person interacting with an AI-system. There are human-centered design techniques that are important to achieve trust and decision-making. Kim et al. [5] propose three key factors for ensuring meaningful explanations. First, the contextualized quality of the explanation, e.g., is it satisfying, useful or trustworthy? Second, its contribution to human-AI interaction, e.g., improvement of user's perception on trustworthiness of AI system. Third, the contribution of the explanation to human-AI performance: does it help users complete tasks more effectively?

These factors highlight the necessity of shifting from a solely algorithm-centric approach to one that develops explanations that are not only technically relevant and logical, but also useful for end users. Ensuring that explanations align with the end user needs strengthens trust in AI systems and support for more effective decision-making for those who rely on them.

2.2 Positive Unlabeled Learning

PU learning refers to a learning technique in which the training set contains only positively labeled and unlabeled data points, with no explicitly labeled negative samples [1]. Unlike traditional binary classification, where the training set consist of positive and negative labels, PU learning assumes that the unlabeled data can belong to either the positive class or the negative class but it is unknown. The primary challenge is distinguishing between true negative samples and unobserved positive samples.

There are several examples of applications in which PU data is being used. For example, personalized advertising methods label visited pages and clicks as a positive instance, but this does not mean that all other pages and ads are not necessarily uninteresting, therefore it cannot be labeled as a negative instance. Another common area with PU data is the medical domain. Medical records contain information about diseases that patients have and not diseases that patient do not have. The unlabeled diseases in this case do not mean that the patient does not have the disease. It can be unnoticed or not diagnosed by a health professional [1]. Several studies show different techniques on how to handle data that only have positive or unlabeled labels. In this study we evaluated two types of PU learning techniques: two-step approach and PU bagging approach. Both approaches differ in complexity and performance depending on the data. We compare both approaches to obtain information about which technique suits this application best.

Two-Step Approach. This method aims to find reliable negative samples from unlabeled data in two steps: (1) train a classifier on positive samples to identify reliable negative labels based on low predicted probabilities, and (2) use these reliable negatives with the positive samples to train a (semi-)supervised model.

The two-step approach assumes separability [1,13] and smoothness, which means that it assumes that all positive samples are similar to the labeled samples and the negative samples are very different from the labeled samples, so basically all positive instances have similar behaviour [6]. A challenge within this approach is defining the reliable negative samples. If the defined reliable negatives are not representable as real negatives, the system will not learn sufficiently.

PU Bagging Approach. Another technique can be described as a bagging strategy. Mordelet and Vert [12] studied this approach by using a bagging Support Vector Machine (SVM) to learn from positive and unlabeled data. They state that the bagging methodology performs as good as the non-bagging methods. They compare their performance to the biased SVM, which directly discriminates between positive and unlabeled examples by rebalancing misclassification costs. They also compare against one-class SVM and a baseline ranking approach. The ranking approach ranks the unlabeled data by their similarity to the average positive data samples. Their bagging approach outperforms state-of-the-art methods on simulated data. However, the difference in performance is minimal on real world data. Performance of the bagging approach relies on the quality of the random created subsamples drawn from the unlabeled instances. If the random subsamples do not represent the distribution of the data sufficiently, the classifier will find it difficult to generalize the results [12].

The PU Bagging approach operates as follows. First, a training set is constructed using all known positive data points along with a random sample of the unlabeled data points. A classifier, such as an SVM, is then trained using the positive and unlabeled data points, where the unlabeled samples are initially treated as negative. Once the classification model is trained, it is applied to the remaining unlabeled samples (those excluded from training) to obtain classification scores, commonly referred to as 'Out-of-the-Bag' (OOB) scores. This process is repeated multiple times, averaging the OOB scores for each unlabeled data point. Importantly, the classifier is retrained in each iteration using a newly sampled subset of unlabeled data. This iterative approach ensures that every unlabeled sample receives an OOB score by the end of the cycle, allowing for the computation of the likelihood that an unlabeled data point is either positive or negative [12].

3 Method and Results

The iterative method Cross-Industry Standard Process for Data Mining (CRISP-DM) is used in this research.[1] The first steps in this method are business and data understanding, after which the data is prepared, the models are trained and evaluated. As it is an iterative method, earlier steps are revisited when necessary. When the model is optimized, it can be deployed. The overview in Fig. 2 visualizes this process.

[1] https://www.ibm.com/docs/it/SS3RA7_18.3.0/pdf/ModelerCRISPDM.pdf.

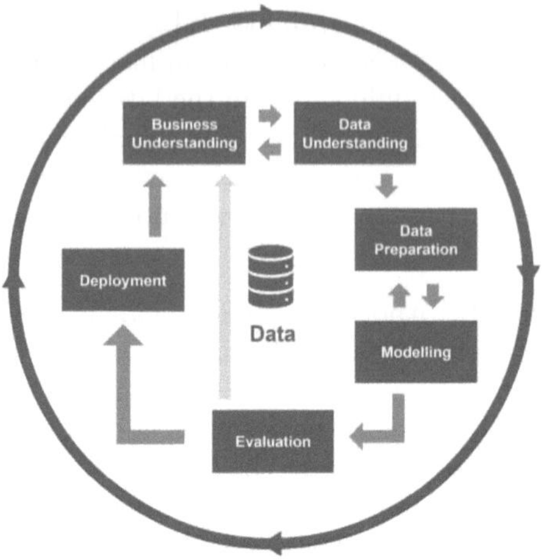

Fig. 2. The CRISP-DM cycle.

To effectively visualize the decision-making process of the ML algorithm, XAI methods were used. It is important for us as researchers to understand the decision-making of the model, but also for the end user to ensure trust in systems. In the next sections, we will explain the performed CRISP-DM steps in more detail, followed by the Explainable AI and generalizability components.

3.1 Business Understanding

It is important to start this research with the business understanding phase to clearly define the goals and objectives. To gain insights into the context from the perspectives of both healthcare organizations and the EPD software company, we interviewed a data scientist and an implementation expert from the company.

EPD Software Company. The EPD is developed by a software company named Nedap Healthcare and they are committed to increase its performance. They observed that, despite positive feedback on the use of digital tools, healthcare devices were not frequently used. They discovered that healthcare professionals are often not aware that a digital tool is suitable for a patient. Therefore, Nedap Healthcare aims to create an algorithm that advises healthcare professionals on when to use a specific tool.

Elderly Care Organizations. Multiple elderly care organizations use the EPD system of Nedap Healthcare, called ONS. They recognize the benefits of using healthcare devices, such as reducing the workload. The elderly care organizations agree with the software company that the care professionals are not aware when to use these tools. They believe that incorporating advice within the EPD would enhance awareness.

3.2 Data Understanding

The data used to develop the ML algorithm is derived from the Omaha profiles. These profiles are an outcome of the Omaha system which is a standardized framework for reporting and documenting symptoms and corresponding actions in the healthcare sector.[2] These Omaha profiles provide an overview of why an individual receives elderly care. The profiles includes multiple levels, such as symptoms, actions, and focus areas.

Elderly care professionals manually annotated the data, identifying instances where a patient could benefit from using a medicine dispenser. This is annotated as 'positive'. As a result, the dataset includes both positive and unlabeled instances. The unlabeled data could be either positive or negative, resulting in the need for special data preparation methods. Only a small part of the data contains positive labels, as can be seen in Table 1 shown in percentages. The negative labels identify situations in which a medicine dispenser can not be used.

For the Exploratory Data Analysis, the library YData Profiling is used.[3]. This shows in one overview the basic statistics, such as missing values, minima and maxima, and the distribution. Additionally, the inclusion and exclusion criteria for using a medicine dispenser were explored in collaboration with the domain experts. In general, a medicine dispenser is only useful when a patient is still well enough to take the medication by themselves, possibly with help of a partner. The sweet spot between being not too good and not well enough is the situation in which a medicine dispenser should be advised. Criteria such as 'terminal', 'just included in care', 'severe cognitive issues', and 'wandering' were seen as exclusion criteria for not being able to use a medicine dispenser anymore. Criteria to denote the phase before a medicine dispenser is helpful were not known.

The dataset comprises multiple json files, each containing a report for individual patients. These reports include information such as symptoms, scores, and interventions. These data are all single data points, however there is a relationship between the symptom of a patient and the corresponding intervention. We captured this relationship by creating a path including the symptom and the corresponding intervention, which is discussed in more detail in the next subsection.

Table 1. An overview of the number of medicine dispensers per organization.

Organization	Total number of cases	Positive labels (%)	Negative labels
1	4,028	160 (3.97%)	Unknown
2	29,489	375 (1.27%)	Unknown
3	4,824	166 (3.44%)	40
4	9,439	5 (0.05%)	125

[2] https://www.omahasystem.nl/over-omaha-system/werken-met-het-omaha-system.
[3] https://docs.profiling.ydata.ai/latest/.

3.3 Data Preparation

In this phase, the raw data is converted to data that is suitable for the modeling phase. After exploring the data and consulting with the domain experts, we made the conclusion that the areas of interest (symptoms, scores, and interventions) were not properly connected in a cause-and-effect relationship. To resolve this, pathways of the different features were created to establish the cause-and-effect connections. For example, we combined the following features: symptoms 'unable_to_take_medication_without_help' and intervention 'medication _administration' together as a pathway. Additionally, PU learning, data balancing, and feature selection techniques were used to prepare the data.

PU Learning. The data only consists of positive labels or unlabeled data. To still be able to train an algorithm on this data, we used PU learning. As explained in Sect. 2.2, two different methods were evaluated to obtain negative labels: the two-step approach and the bagging approach. During training, the two-step approach was much faster: this method took approximately three seconds, while the bagging approach took three hours. The reason for this is that the bagging approach relies on bootstrapping, which involves repeatedly resampling the data and retraining the model multiple times.

Data Balancing. To overcome the issue of unbalanced data, where the unlabeled data significantly outweighs the group of positive data points, a random undersampling technique is used in which data points from the unlabeled data were removed from the dataset until the dataset was balanced. [4] As can be seen in Table 1, the data is unbalanced as only approximately 2% of the data points are labeled.

By using PU learning and the undersampling method, four datasets were created, namely **PU learning - Two-step approach, PU learning Bagging approach**, **Undersampling**, and the **Original dataset.** These datasets were used in the modelling phase and evaluated in the evaluation phase.

Feature Selection. After integrating paths as features, the dataset resulted in having a large number of features. To reduce the feature set, Chi-squared feature selection was applied.[5] The number of features, ranging from one to 500, were evaluated with steps of twenty. For each set of features (k), the machine learning algorithm ran and its performance was evaluated to identify the optimal number of features that most influence algorithm's outcome. The implementation of the chi-squared feature selection is shown in the pseudocode Algorithm 1.

The result of the different sets of features can be seen in Fig. 3. From 250 features onward, the performance did not increase. Therefore, these 250 features were used in model training.

---

[4] https://imbalanced-learn.org/stable/references/generated/imblearn.under_sampling.RandomUnderSampler.html.

[5] https://scikit-learn.org/stable/modules/generated/sklearn.feature_selection.chi2.html.

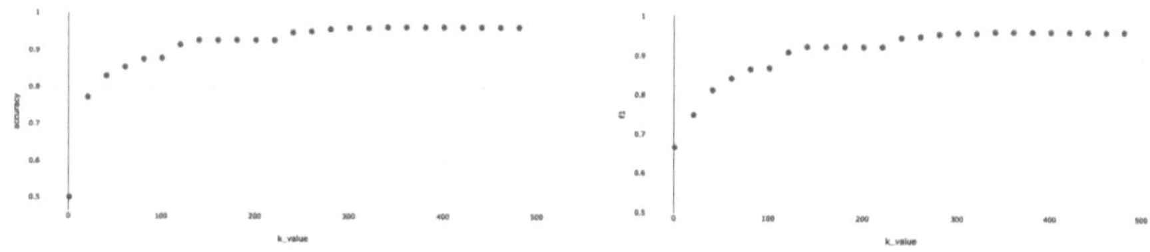

Fig. 3. The accuracy (left) and F1-score (right) stabilizes around 250 features.

Algorithm 1. Feature Selection and Model Evaluation with MLflow Logging

```
for each dataset type in datasets do
    Extract features X and labels y
    for each model type and model object in models do
        for each value k in k_values do
            Apply chi-squared feature selection with k features (chi2_selector)
            Select the k best features from X (X_chi2_selected)
            Perform cross-validation:
                Compute accuracy, precision, and recall scores using CV
            Log parameters using MLflow:
                Dataset type, model type, and k value
            Log metrics using MLflow:
                Mean accuracy, precision, recall, and F1 scores
            Log the trained model using MLflow
```

3.4 Modelling

Three supervised learning models were trained on the datasets, namely a Decision tree, an SVM, and a Random Forest. We used the scikit-learn package and the latest implementations of these algorithms.[6] These models were chosen since they differ in complexity and transparency. Algorithm 1 shows the pseudocode for modelling. As can be seen, first a dataset is chosen, followed by a model type. The next step was to perform the feature selection and train the model based on these features. The last step is to log the results to MLFlow, as explained in Sect. 3.5.[7]

The model trained on the 'normal' dataset is our baseline model. This dataset is cleaned, however, no balancing or PU learning techniques have been used.

3.5 Evaluation

The models were evaluated both on a technical level and from the perspective of a domain expert.

Technical Evaluation. For technical and testing purposes, healthcare professionals have created a separate test set, containing both negative and positive

[6] https://scikit-learn.org/stable/supervised_learning.html.
[7] https://mlflow.org/.

samples, to evaluate the model's performance on unseen data, see Table 1. We used 165 negative samples and 165 positive samples as a test set, which were not used during model training. MLflow was used in the technical evaluation of the model. Performance metrics that were used are precision, recall, F1-score, and accuracy. Also, the feature importance were saved to understand which features were most important in prediction.

Table 2. An overview of the performance of the models.

Model type	Accuracy	F1	Precision	Recall
PU Bagging Decision Tree	0.724	0.753	0.681	0.842
PU Bagging Random Forest	0.740	0.769	0.690	0.867
PU Bagging SVM	0.772	0.790	0.734	0.855
PU two-step Decision Tree	0.942	0.940	0.980	0.903
PU two-step Random Forest	**0.940**	**0.938**	**0.968**	**0.909**
PU two-step SVM	0.882	0.881	0.889	0.873
Undersampling Decision Tree	0.785	0.770	0.826	0.721
Undersampling Random Forest	0.782	0.776	0.796	0.756
Undersampling SVM	0.818	0.817	0.822	0.812
Normal dataset Decision Tree	0.624	0.398	1.000	0.248
Normal dataset Random Forest	0.600	0.338	0.944	0.206
Normal dataset SVM	0.540	0.146	1.000	0.079

An overview of the results are shown in Table 2. We observe that the two-step method resulted in the highest performance. The performance between the different models did not differ much. However, as the focus was on the recall, the random forest performed the best.

Algorithmic Explainability. The XAI techniques SHAP and feature importance were used to understand the reasoning of the model. The features making the biggest impact denoted information about patients not able to take medication without help, patient who do not follow the dosage schedule, and patients with limited recall of recent events. These insights and decision-making information were also evaluated with the healthcare professionals to evaluate the relation between technical model logic and real-world clinical reasoning.

Evaluation with the Domain Experts. As discussed above, the results and model reasoning were discussed with the healthcare professionals of two healthcare organizations during two separate focus groups. Seven cases were discussed at one organization and three at the other. The difference in the number of cases was due to the depth of the discussions held during the sessions. We chose to delve deeper into these cases to gather more in-depth information about the way of working of the healthcare workers and their decision-making process. The cases were used to understand if they would advise a medicine dispenser for patients based on the features that was used in training. The features represented features with the most influence on the model outcome, according to SHAP and feature importance.

A case contains only the information that was used during training of the algorithm. Specifically the key features that contributed to the final decision which are obtained by using SHAPley values and feature importance techniques. The case was, in the beginning, shown anonymously to prevent the healthcare professional from recognizing the patient and having background information which are not shown in the case. The healthcare professionals were asked to read the case and to decide if a medicine dispenser could be used in this situation. After this, they were asked to open the dossier of this patient and to use information from the EPD to decide if this patient could use a medicine dispenser. Their task was to decide if they would advise something different based on the full data and which information from the EPD they used for this decision. The last step was to compare that to the result from the algorithm and to discuss why this could be different if this was the case.

In all cases the healthcare professionals were not able to decide whether a patient could use a medicine dispenser and needed more information than only the Omaha profiles. Especially the data from the free text fields within the EPD was used to understand the nuance of a selection in the Omaha profile. An example is the Omaha tag that the patient has a limited ability to concentrate. The healthcare professionals needed the additional information from the free text fields to inform them how limited this ability was and if there was, e.g., a partner living with this patient that could help to take the medicines on time. All in all, they needed more detailed context than only standardized features.

User-Centered Explainability. To enhance the usability of the AI by the healthcare professionals, adding user-centered XAI is important to create trust in a system [14]. In this case, the healthcare professional needs to understand why a medicine dispenser could be used based on the available data. During our focus group sessions, we explored what types of information healthcare professionals need and how this information should be presented. Through feedback on the cases, which showcased key elements based on SHAP and feature importance values, we found that the presented information is not intuitive enough to support confident decision-making. This means that even though we use explainable AI to clarify a model's reasoning, the current explanation does not meet the requirements nor expectations of the healthcare professionals. They require more contextual information, such as severity of a patient's memory issues, to make well-informed decisions. Unfortunately, these kind of contextual data is not included in the Omaha profiles on which our model is trained. As a result, we are unable to provide the healthcare professionals with explanations that are fully understandable or useful due to limitations in the available data.

3.6 Generalizability

Lastly, we explored the generalizability of the trained ML model. The goal is to determine whether a model trained on data from a specific healthcare organization could be effectively applied to a different healthcare organization. To investigate this, the ML model was retrained, this time excluding the data from one healthcare organization (healthcare organization 4 in Table 1) during the training phase. The data from the excluded organization was then used as a test set to evaluate the model's performance. The results are shown in Table 3. As can be seen, the models struggle to perform well in this situation, indicating difficulties in learning and generalizing. This was discussed with the healthcare professionals. They stated that it is very different per organization, and also per team, how the Omaha profiles are filled in. Besides, the user has the freedom in the system to make all different combinations of symptoms and interventions, as this is not restricted in the software. This creates the very diverse and thus sparse dataset.

Table 3. An overview of models performance where one healthcare organization is left out as test set.

Model type	Accuracy	F1	Precision	Recall
PU Bagging Decision Tree	0.700	0.002	0.001	0.600
PU Bagging Random Forest	0.705	0.002	0.001	0.600
PU Bagging SVM	0.788	0.003	0.002	0.600
PU two-step Decision Tree	0.800	0.750	1.000	0.600
PU two-step Random Forest	0.800	0.750	1.000	0.600
PU two-step SVM	0.800	0.750	1.000	0.600
Undersampling Decision Tree	0.600	0.714	0.556	1.000
Undersampling Random Forest	0.500	0.667	0.500	1.000
Undersampling SVM	0.500	0.667	0.500	1.000
Normal dataset Decision Tree	0.500	0.000	0.000	0.000
Normal dataset Random Forest	0.500	0.000	0.000	0.000
Normal dataset SVM	0.500	0.000	0.000	0.000

4 Discussion

During this research project the goal was to advise if a medicine dispenser could be used by patients from elderly care. As this decision is based on the medical status of the patient, reports from an EPD were used as input.

4.1 Methodology and Results

The CRISP-DM process model was used to understand the context and the data, and using this information to prepare the data to be able to train and evaluate a model using this data. The following sections reflect on this methodology and the technical results.

We considered the CRISP-DM model as useful. It helped to structure the research and to focus on the context first before diving into the data. However, we would advise to focus more on the business and data understanding phases as this would have revealed earlier in the process that the data would not suffice. The deployment phase was not performed as the evaluation with the domain experts indicated a next iteration is necessary before the model would represent the situation sufficiently. This further highlights the necessity of involvement of all stakeholders in CRISP-DM, especially during the first phases.

The technical results seemed promising: a recall around 0.9 was achieved. However, when evaluating the results with the domain experts, they stated that based on only the Omaha profiles, which were used as input for the algorithm, they could not decide whether a medicine dispenser would indeed be useful. Also, when the trained model was evaluated using unseen data from another organization, the model did not perform well (see Table 3). One explanation could be that it is due to overfitting on the data of an organization, and to finding patterns that are not there. The second explanation is a result of different ways of reporting by the teams, creating a dataset with different paths different than those found in the training data.

As the healthcare professionals indicated that this tool would help them, we advise to improve the tool with free text fields and to evaluate it again. Our hypothesis is that using data from free text fields would improve the model and its explainability, resulting in a higher user satisfaction.

4.2 Challenges

During this research, we encountered challenges due to performing a real world use case.

Positive Unlabeled Data. The first challenge was handling data with only positive labels. Two PU learning techniques were evaluated: the two-step and bagging approaches. The two-step approach was faster and performed better. The reason it is faster is that the bagging approach relies on bootstrapping, which involves repeatedly resampling the data and retraining the model multiple times. The reason it performs better could be that the percentage of positive labels was very small, which the two-step approach handles better. If sufficient reliable negative samples can be found during the first step of the two-step approach, it is possible to train a decent classifier to recognize patterns between positive and negative samples. In this case, we expect the performance of the two-step approach to be more reliable. The performance of the bagging approach relies on the quality of the random subsamples drawn from the unlabeled data. If the random subsamples do not represent the underlying distribution of the data, the classifier can have a hard time to find patterns and generalize, which can result in lower performance compared to the two-step approach [12].

Sparse Dataset. Secondly, as multiple paths were possible to state the same medical situation, the dataset was sparse. Although we did not experience this as a problem during modeling, during evaluation we encountered that the algorithm tested on data from other elderly care teams resulted in bad performance as the conditions were reported differently resulting in different paths in the data. This makes it infeasible to make this algorithm generalizable to be used by multiple organizations and teams. A solution is to train an algorithm for every team, however due to the small dataset per team the expectation is that the results will not be trustworthy. Another topic to investigate is evaluating a model that does not take into account the cause-and-action relationship and takes every data point as a single feature. This will solve the issue of a sparse dataset since it does not take into account all possible combinations of features relationships. A second suggestion is to only use the 'symptom' and 'action' data in the path as this seems the core information from the dataset. Using only these two fields in the paths, fewer paths are possible, resulting in a less sparse dataset with still sufficient information. A third solution is to use dimensionality reduction techniques such as principle component analysis. However, this makes it hard to create an explainable model which was one of the goals of this research. Future work should focus on experimenting with dimensionality reduction techniques which keep the explainability high.

Technical Evaluation Versus Real-World Evaluation. Thirdly, the technical evaluations in comparison with the domain experts evaluation showed different results. Although the (explainability) results from a technical perspective when trained and evaluated on data from the same teams seemed promising, the evaluation with the domain experts showed that it seems not intuitive to create an algorithm based on the data from the Omaha profiles only. The experts needed more contextual data from the open text fields to understand the nuance and to be able to decide if a medicine dispenser could be used by a patient. Although the addition of the open text fields is possible from a technical perspective, there is a privacy perspective that needs to be taken into account as well. Based on this data, there is a chance that the researchers could deduce which medical dossier belongs to which patient, which raises concerns over privacy. One possibility to use this data is to anonymize and pseudonymize it before it is used. Future research should investigate how to integrate contextual data from patient reports while ensuring privacy.

5 Generalizable Insights About Responsible Application of Machine Learning in Healthcare

The main takeaway when looking at a responsible application of machine learning in this domain is that one should always evaluate the results with the domain experts and/or end-users. Although the algorithm may seem technically valuable, it could be the case it is not from a domain experts view. Explainable AI techniques could help in this by showing the reasoning of the underlying model. This could strengthen the conversation and make clear which mistakes are made by the model. It helps as an interface between the data scientists and the domain experts. Our research has shown this in this use case: the explainable AI component helped by understanding if the algorithm focused on the right information. This also revealed that the information needed by the healthcare professionals to understand the model was not in the data. This is an important evaluation point which would have not been found when not using XAI techniques.

Evaluation with the end-users is also an important aspect since they have to work with the created tools. If the tools do not meet end-users' expectations, adoption is likely to be low, resulting in a less effective product. This would also have been the case when we would have implemented this tool in the workflow without evaluation. The XAI component would give explanations which are not useful for the end-users, resulting in lower trust and thus adoption.

Additionally, it should be recognized by the healthcare professional when the AI provides a wrong advice. If this is missed, the effects could be dangerous. An example from this project is that if a patient gets a medicine dispenser while one is not able to use it, the patient will not take the medicines correctly which creates possibly an unhealthy situation. Evaluating the solution with and keeping the control by the healthcare professionals could decrease the chances of creating this undesirable situation as well.

6 Conclusion

During this research project, a case study was performed using the Omaha profiles from the EPD system to predict if a medicine dispenser could be used by a patient. The CRISP-DM process model was adopted to understand the context, prepare the data and create and evaluate the models. Technically challenges were encountered, examples are a positively unlabeled and sparse dataset, which included different features per organization, creating the necessity to use techniques to create a dataset that could be used for modeling. Although the technical evaluation seemed promising, the evaluation with domain experts showed that the data used did not give enough information to give an advise based on the data. Additionally, the multiple challenges showed the difference between a theoretical case compared to a case from a real life situation. An important takeaway from this study is the need to involve end-users earlier and to evaluate whether the available data provides sufficient information to support decision-making. Future research should focus on exploring the possibility to include more data from the open text fields. The hypothesis is this will improve the algorithm, resulting in a higher user satisfaction.

Acknowledgments. This study was funded by Tech For Future https://techforfuture.nl/. Additionally, we would like to thank the company Nedap Healthcare and their client organizations for making this research possible.

Disclosure of Interests. The authors have no competing interests to declare that are relevant to the content of this article.

References

1. Bekker, J., Davis, J.: Learning from positive and unlabeled data: a survey. Mach. Learn. **109**(4), 719–760 (2020)
2. Burnett, M.: Explaining ai: fairly? well? In: Proceedings of the 25th International Conference on Intelligent User Interfaces, IUI 2020, pp. 1–2. Association for Computing Machinery, New York, NY, USA (2020). https://doi.org/10.1145/3377325.3380623
3. Dwivedi, R., et al.: Explainable AI (XAI): core ideas, techniques and solutions. ACM Comput. Surv. **55** (2022). https://doi.org/10.1145/3561048
4. Ehsan, U., et al.: Operationalizing human-centered perspectives in explainable AI, pp. 1–6 (2021). https://doi.org/10.1145/3411763.3441342
5. Kim, J., Maathuis, H., Sent, D.: Human-centered evaluation of explainable ai applications: a systematic review. Front. Artif. Intell. **7** (2024). https://doi.org/10.3389/frai.2024.1456486
6. Lee, W.S., Liu, B.: Learning with positive and unlabeled examples using weighted logistic regression, vol. 20, pp. 448–455 (2003)
7. Liao, V., Varshney, K.: Human-centered explainable AI (XAI): from algorithms to user experiences (2021). https://doi.org/10.48550/arXiv.2110.10790
8. Loh, H.W., Ooi, C.P., Seoni, S., Barua, P.D., Molinari, F., Acharya, U.R.: Application of explainable artificial intelligence for healthcare: A systematic review of the last decade (2011–2022). Comput. Methods Programs Biomed. **226**, 107161 (2022). https://doi.org/10.1016/j.cmpb.2022.107161
9. Lundberg, S., Lee, S.I.: A unified approach to interpreting model predictions (2017). https://arxiv.org/abs/1705.07874
10. Lundberg, S.M., Lee, S.I.: A unified approach to interpreting model predictions. Adv. Neural Inf. Process. Syst. **30** (2017)
11. Melles, M., Albayrak, A., Goossens, R.: Innovating health care: key characteristics of human-centered design. Int. J. Qual. Health Care **33**, 37–44 (2020). https://doi.org/10.1093/intqhc/mzaa127
12. Mordelet, F., Vert, J.P.: A bagging SVM to learn from positive and unlabeled examples (2013). https://arxiv.org/abs/1010.0772
13. Ortega Vázquez, C., vanden Broucke, S., De Weerdt, J.: A two-step anomaly detection based method for PU classification in imbalanced data sets. Data Min. Knowl. Discov. **37**(3), 1301–1325 (2023). https://doi.org/10.1007/s10618-023-00925-9
14. Schoonderwoerd, T.A., Jorritsma, W., Neerincx, M.A., van den Bosch, K.: Human-centered XAI: developing design patterns for explanations of clinical decision support systems. Int. J. Hum.-Comput. Stud. **154**, 102684 (2021). https://doi.org/10.1016/j.ijhcs.2021.102684

15. Strategists, G.: Uitweg uit de schaarste. https://gupta-strategists.nl/storage/files/220525-Gupta-Strategists-FME-Uitweg-uit-de-schaarste.pdf. Accessed 24 Jan 2024
16. Wang, D., Yang, Q., Abdul, A., Lim, B.Y.: Designing theory-driven user-centric explainable AI. In: Proceedings of the 2019 CHI Conference on Human Factors in Computing Systems, CHI 2019, pp. 1–15. Association for Computing Machinery, New York, NY, USA (2019). https://doi.org/10.1145/3290605.3300831

Challenges in Explaining Pretrained Clinical Text Classifiers

Kristian Miok[1,2(✉)], Matej Klemen[1], Blaz Škrlj[3], and Marko Robnik Šikonja[1]

[1] Faculty of Computer and Information Science, University of Ljubljana, Ljubljana, Slovenia
{kristian.miok,matej.klemen,marko.robnik}@fri.uni-lj.si

[2] ICAM - Advanced Environmental Research Institute, West University of Timisoara, Timişoara, Romania
kristian.miok@e-uvt.ro

[3] Jožef Stefan Institute, Ljubljana, Slovenia
blaz.skrlj@ijs.si

Abstract. Explaining the predictions of neural models in clinical NLP remains a significant challenge, especially for complex tasks involving long, unstructured medical texts. While post-hoc methods like LIME and SHAP are widely used, they often fall short when applied to clinical narratives. In this paper, we identify core limitations of token-level and perturbation-based explanation techniques through targeted demonstrations on a hospital length-of-stay prediction task. Our findings reveal issues such as overemphasis on non-informative tokens, instability in attributions, and high-confidence predictions for incoherent input variants. These results underscore the need for explanation strategies that are clinically meaningful, semantically grounded, and robust to linguistic noise.

Keywords: Explainable AI · Clinical NLP · LIME · Electronic Health Records

1 Introduction

Deep learning models achieve strong predictive performance, yet their use in high-stakes domains such as healthcare remains limited without clear explanations of their decisions. Explainable AI (XAI) seeks to increase transparency by revealing how predictions are made, enabling reliability checks, bias detection, and accountability [2]. In medicine, where decisions affect patient outcomes, interpretable models are particularly critical.

Text-based electronic health records (EHRs) provide valuable clinical information, including notes, discharge summaries, and pathology reports [1,9]. Automated analysis of these documents supports tasks such as incident classification

To appear in the Proceedings of the First Workshop on Responsible Healthcare using Machine Learning (RHCML 2025).

I. Koprinska et al. (Eds.): ECML PKDD 2025, CCIS 2842, pp. 314–322, 2026.
https://doi.org/10.1007/978-3-032-19105-2_22

[7] and long-document modeling with transformers [4]. Despite such progress, the explainability of clinical text classifiers remains underexplored. Most XAI techniques were designed for tabular or image data, and when applied to long, noisy narratives, token-level approaches like LIME and SHAP often highlight trivial tokens, ignore clinical concepts, or produce unstable results.

In this paper, we examine the limitations of post-hoc explanations in clinical NLP, focusing on hospital discharge summaries. Section 2 outlines key challenges, Sect. 3 demonstrates them on a length-of-stay prediction task, and Sect. 4 concludes with broader implications for responsible ML in healthcare.

2 Related Work

Post-hoc explanation methods such as LIME [8] and SHAP [6] are widely used to attribute importance to input features, but their application to text often inherits limitations from token-level representations. In clinical NLP, prior studies have applied these tools to tasks such as diagnosis prediction and patient risk stratification [3,10], yet results frequently highlight stopwords or isolated tokens rather than clinically meaningful units. More recent efforts have explored phrase-level or concept-based explanations, e.g., by aggregating token scores into medical entities or leveraging ontologies [5], which better align with expert reasoning. Nonetheless, explainability for long and heterogeneous clinical narratives remains underexplored compared to domains such as tabular or imaging data, underscoring the need for approaches that are linguistically coherent, semantically grounded, and clinically valid.

3 Challenges

Popular explanation methods such as LIME [8] and SHAP [6] assign importance scores to input features. While effective for tabular data, their direct application to text, especially long and noisy clinical narratives, introduces several limitations:

1. **Interpretation of feature attributions.** Only a few top-ranked tokens meaningfully affect predictions, while many others with non-negligible scores contribute little. This uneven relevance risks over-interpreting weak or ambiguous features.
2. **Length and complexity.** Clinical reports contain shorthand, numbers, and structured fragments. Token-level explanations often highlight trivial terms, limiting their clinical utility.
3. **Longer textual units.** Many medical concepts appear as multi-word expressions (e.g., "chronic kidney disease"). Token-based attribution fails to capture such phrases, instead emphasizing isolated or function words.
4. **Off-manifold perturbations.** Perturbation strategies can create incoherent or grammatically broken text that still yields confident predictions, distorting the explanation process.

5. **Dilution through averaging.** Averaging effects across many perturbed samples can obscure important localized patterns, producing diffuse or inconsistent explanations.
6. **Instability.** Because LIME relies on random sampling, repeated runs may yield different attributions, undermining reproducibility in clinical settings.

4 Demonstration of Challenges

To better understand the behavior and limitations of post-hoc explanation methods in clinical NLP, we conduct a series of targeted demonstrations using a real-world dataset of hospital discharge summaries. Our focus is on the task of predicting hospital length of stay (LOS) based solely on free-text notes. The dataset includes 467 de-identified discharge summaries from adult patients diagnosed with kidney stones (ICD-10 code N20.0), sourced from the MIMIC-IV database. Each summary is labeled according to whether the patient's hospital stay exceeded the cohort median, forming a balanced binary classification task.

This dataset reflects many typical complexities of clinical text: highly variable document lengths (ranging from hundreds to over a thousand tokens), domain-specific terminology, shorthand notations, embedded numerical values, and a mixture of structured and narrative content. These properties make it a representative and challenging testbed for evaluating explanation methods.

We fine-tuned a domain-adapted `ModernBERT` model on this classification task using the HuggingFace Transformers framework. The model was trained on full-length discharge summaries truncated to 1024 tokens and optimized using cross-entropy loss. To interpret the model's predictions, we employed LIME (Local Interpretable Model-Agnostic Explanations), which constructs local surrogate models by perturbing input tokens and fitting a sparse linear classifier.

In this section, we present three demonstrations that empirically expose recurring issues in how LIME explanations behave on clinical text:

- **Demonstration 1**: We assess how model confidence changes when top-ranked LIME tokens are progressively removed, revealing that only a small number of tokens drive predictions while the rest contribute minimally.
- **Demonstration 2**: We analyze the frequency of tokens selected by LIME across multiple examples and show that stopwords and function words often dominate explanations, despite offering limited interpretive value.
- **Demonstration 3**: We generate perturbations of a synthetic but medically plausible note and find that semantically incoherent or fragmented inputs can still yield high-confidence predictions, raising concerns about explanation reliability.

Each demonstration is supported by quantitative metrics and qualitative visualizations to reveal patterns in model behavior and explainer outputs. Collectively, they illustrate systematic weaknesses in current explanation approaches and motivate the need for methods that are more aligned with clinical reasoning and human interpretability.

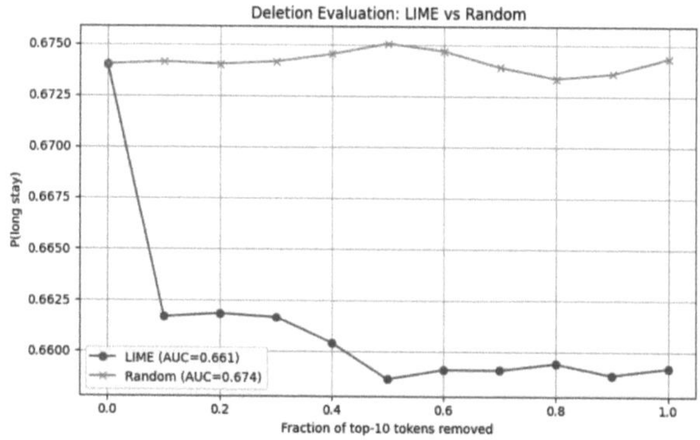

Fig. 1. Deletion curves comparing LIME-guided and random token removal for 20 test instances. Removing the top-ranked LIME tokens causes a sharp initial drop in predicted probability, whereas randomly selected tokens have a weaker and more uniform effect.

Demonstration 1: Sensitivity of Model Confidence to Top-Ranked Tokens. To better understand how LIME's token-level explanations correspond to model behavior, we conducted a deletion-based sensitivity analysis. After fine-tuning a `ModernBERT` model to classify hospital discharge summaries as predicting either a short or long length of stay, we selected 20 representative test instances and generated LIME explanations for each.

For each case, we extracted the top-10 most influential tokens as identified by LIME and progressively removed them from the input, one by one, based on their importance rank. At each step, we recorded the model's prediction confidence for the originally predicted class. This yielded a deletion curve representing how quickly the model's confidence degraded as influential features were masked. For comparison, we also constructed deletion curves using randomly selected tokens.

Figure 1 illustrates the outcome. We observed that removing the top one or two tokens typically caused a sharp decline in prediction confidence, suggesting these few tokens were strongly driving the decision. Beyond the top three or four tokens, however, the effect largely plateaued, with additional removals leading to only marginal changes. Meanwhile, deletion of random tokens led to a gentler and more gradual decline.

This finding suggests that while a small number of tokens meaningfully influence the model's output, the remaining high-attribution tokens contribute little explanatory value. In contexts where users might examine the entire ranked list of important tokens, this effect may lead to overinterpretation of marginal or irrelevant features. Effective explanation strategies should help users distinguish between dominant drivers of the model's output and tokens with negligible influence.

Demonstration 2: Prevalence of Non-Informative Tokens in Explanations. We examined the interpretability of LIME-generated explanations by analyzing which tokens received the highest attribution scores across a sample of 20 clinical discharge summaries. From each explanation, we extracted the top-10 most influential tokens, yielding 200 tokens in total.

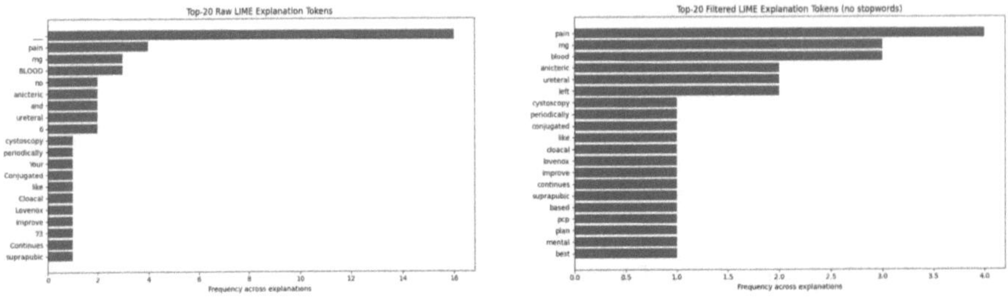

(a) Top-20 LIME tokens without filtering (includes stopwords and symbols).

(b) Top-20 LIME tokens after removing stopwords and symbols.

Fig. 2. Distribution of common LIME attribution tokens across 20 clinical discharge summaries. The filtered view better highlights meaningful medical terms.

We aggregated these tokens to identify frequently highlighted words and visualized the results in two complementary plots:

- The **raw bar chart** in Fig. 2a shows the 20 most frequent LIME-selected tokens before any preprocessing. Several tokens are non-informative, including formatting artifacts (e.g., underscores), numbers, and function words (e.g., `no`, `and`, `Your`), which offer limited clinical interpretability.
- The **filtered bar chart** in Fig. 2b presents the same analysis after removing stopwords, non-alphabetic tokens, and trivial words. The resulting top tokens include medically meaningful terms such as `pain`, `blood`, `cystoscopy`, and `ureteral`, which are more plausible indicators of clinical reasoning behind model predictions.

This demonstration illustrates a key weakness of token-level explanation strategies: non-informative tokens often receive high attribution simply due to their frequency or structural placement, not semantic relevance. Although filtering can improve clarity, it also risks discarding potentially meaningful expressions that only gain interpretability in context (e.g., as part of multi-word medical phrases). Therefore, reliance on isolated token attributions can lead to explanations that are misleading or unhelpful in practice. Modern NLP methods can detect multi-word expressions or medical entities before stopword removal, which may provide a more faithful basis for generating clinically meaningful explanations.

Demonstration 3: Nonsensical Permutations with High-Confidence Predictions. To further examine the effects of off-manifold perturbations, we created a synthetic but medically coherent discharge summary for a hypothetical patient. This artificial note reflects typical clinical phrasing and content, but allows us to observe LIME's behavior under controlled conditions. The original note reads as follows:

```
Patient is a 65-year-old female with history of type 2
diabetes, hypertension, and chronic kidney disease. She
presented with chest pain and dyspnea. Vitals stable. Labs:
elevated troponin and CK-MB. Plan: admit for observation and
IV nitroglycerin.
```

Using LIME, we generated 500 perturbed versions of this text by randomly masking various subsets of tokens. For each, we computed the model's predicted probability for the "long stay" class. Surprisingly, many of these syntactically broken or semantically incoherent variants received high-confidence predictions.

For example, the following perturbed version lacking both grammatical structure and medical interpretability received a predicted probability of 0.778:

```
Patient a 65-year-old with type diabetes, , chronic disease.
presented with pain. Vitals. Labs: CK-. : for nitroglycerin.
```

Despite losing essential semantic content (e.g., the type of chest pain, presence of dyspnea, and treatment plan), the model remains confident. In total, 86 out of 500 perturbations (17.2%) exceeded the 0.75 confidence threshold for "long stay". A subset of these included only 10 tokens, with some bordering on complete nonsensicality.

This demonstration highlights a fundamental flaw in perturbation-based explainability methods: they often construct examples far outside the data manifold on which the model was trained. Although the model returns a valid prediction for these inputs, the results are misleading from a human interpretability standpoint. In clinical applications, this undermines the goal of generating trustworthy, semantically grounded explanations.

5 Generalizable Insights About Responsible Application of Machine Learning in Healthcare

The demonstrations highlight broader lessons for responsible ML in healthcare, showing how common explanation methods behave under realistic clinical text conditions. Six recurring challenges emerge:

1. **Interpretation of feature attributions.** Demonstration 1 shows that confidence depends mainly on the top few tokens, while many others carry negligible influence. Presenting long ranked lists risks over-interpreting weak signals. Explanations should better separate dominant drivers from marginal features.

2. **Length and complexity of clinical reports.** As seen in Demonstration 2, LIME often highlights trivial content such as stopwords or formatting tokens in lengthy discharge summaries. Such attributions obscure clinically meaningful information in complex inputs.
3. **Longer textual units.** Demonstration 2 also illustrates that token-level attribution misses multi-word concepts (e.g., "admit for observation"), instead emphasizing isolated words. Phrase- or entity-level methods are needed for clinically faithful explanations.
4. **Off-manifold perturbations.** Demonstration 3 shows that perturbed, incoherent notes can still yield confident predictions. Such off-manifold examples distort explanations and threaten trust in clinical deployment.
5. **Dilution through averaging.** The deletion analysis in Demonstration 1 and the perturbation results in Demonstration 3 reveal that averaging across many samples blurs the effect of key tokens and may capture spurious associations, producing diffuse explanations.
6. **Instability.** Because LIME relies on random sampling, Demonstration 3 indirectly shows that explanations can vary across runs. In healthcare, this instability undermines reproducibility and accountability.

These issues are not isolated artifacts but stem from structural limitations of token-level and perturbation-based explainers. Responsible application in healthcare requires explanation methods that are linguistically coherent, clinically informed, and stable across runs.

Moreover, similar concerns extend beyond medicine: in legal or scientific NLP, explanations may likewise highlight trivial words, ignore multi-word expressions, or vary under perturbation. Thus, the challenges observed here point to general risks for post-hoc explainability across high-stakes textual domains.

6 Conclusion and Further Work

In this study, we examined how post-hoc explanation methods behave when applied to clinical text classification. Through three targeted demonstrations using LIME, we revealed several limitations that can undermine the reliability and interpretability of explanations in healthcare settings.

Our findings showed that explanations often rely on a small number of impactful tokens, while the majority of highlighted features carry minimal influence. We also observed that LIME frequently assigns high attribution to stopwords or function words, which lack standalone interpretive value. Most notably, we demonstrated that syntactically broken or semantically incoherent perturbations can still yield high-confidence predictions, raising serious concerns about explanation validity.

These issues reflect broader structural challenges with token-level and perturbation based approaches in clinical NLP. To address them, future methods should move beyond isolated tokens and incorporate meaningful linguistic or conceptual units such as phrases, medical entities, or clinically grounded abstractions.

Additionally, integrating domain knowledge and improving the plausibility of perturbed inputs may help produce more stable and trustworthy explanations.

Ultimately, building clinically useful interpretability tools will require not only technical improvements, but also human centered evaluation, including feedback from medical experts to assess whether explanations align with clinical reasoning and decision support needs. Beyond these directions, future work should also engage with broader responsible ML dimensions, such as ensuring explanation fairness across patient demographics, exploring privacy preserving interpretability techniques, and systematically evaluating potential clinical safety risks that may arise from misleading or unstable explanations.

Acknowledgments. Kristian Miok was supported by the EU HE MSC Postdoctoral Fellowship Programme SMASH (No. 101081355). The work was partially supported by the Slovenian Research and Innovation Agency (ARIS) core research programme P6-0411 and P2-0103, as well as projects L2-50070, GC-0002, and J4-4555. The work was supported by EU through ERA Chair grant no. 101186647 (AI4DH) and cofinancing for research innovation projects in support of green transition and digitalisation (project PoVeJMo, no. C3.K8.IB).

References

1. Benedum, C.M.: Replication of real-world evidence in oncology using electronic health record data extracted by machine learning. Cancers **15**(6), 1853 (2023)
2. Bhattacharya, A.: Applied Machine Learning Explainability Techniques: Make ML models explainable and trustworthy for practical applications using LIME, SHAP, and more, Packt Publishing Ltd. (2022)
3. Caruana, R., Lou, Y., Gehrke, J., Koch, P., Sturm, M., Elhadad, N.: Intelligible models for healthcare: Predicting pneumonia risk and hospital 30-day readmission. In: Proceedings of the 21th ACM SIGKDD International Conference on Knowledge Discovery and Data Mining, pp. 1721–1730. ACM (2015)
4. Dai, X., Chalkidis, I., Darkner, S., Elliott, D.: Revisiting transformer-based models for long document classification. arXiv preprint arXiv:2204.06683 (2022)
5. Holzinger, A., Müller, H., Biesinger, B., Pattichis, C., Kell, D.B.: Towards the augmented pathologist: knowledge-driven explainable AI. J. Biomed. Inform. **126**, 103980 (2022)
6. Lundberg, S.M., Lee, S.I.: A unified approach to interpreting model predictions. In: Proceedings of the 31st International Conference on Neural Information Processing Systems, p. 4768–4777 (2017)
7. Palojoki, S., Saranto, K., Reponen, E., Skants, N., Vakkuri, A., Vuokko, R., et al.: Classification of electronic health record-related patient safety incidents: development and validation study. JMIR Med. Inform. **9**(8), e30470 (2021)
8. Ribeiro, M.T., Singh, S., Guestrin, C.: Why should I trust you?: Explaining the predictions of any classifier. In: Proceedings of the 22nd ACM SIGKDD International Conference on Knowledge Discovery and Data Mining, p. 1135–1144 (2016). https://doi.org/10.1145/2939672.2939778

9. Challenges and opportunities beyond structured data in analysis of electronic health records. Wiley Interdis. Rev. Comput. Stat. **13**(6), e1549 (2021)
10. Tonekaboni, S., Joshi, S., McCradden, M.D., Goldenberg, A.: What clinicians want: contextualizing explainable machine learning for clinical end use. In: Proceedings of the 4th Machine Learning for Healthcare Conference, MLHC, vol. 106, pp. 359–380. PMLR (2019)

Privacy-Preserving AI-Based Glaucoma Referral Using Multi-centric Real-World Data: A Feasibility Study with Federated Learning

Filipe Soares[1(✉)], Telmo Barbosa[1], João Barbosa-Breda[2], Luís Abegão Pinto[3,4], and Carlos Marques-Neves[4,5]

[1] Fraunhofer Portugal AICOS, Rua Alfredo Allen 455/461, 4200-135 Porto, Portugal
filipe.soares@aicos.fraunhofer.pt

[2] Department of Ophthalmology, Unidade Local de Saúde São João, Porto, Portugal

[3] Department of Ophthalmology, Unidade Local de Saúde Santa Maria, Lisbon, Portugal

[4] Center for the Study of Vision Sciences, University Ophthalmology Clinic, Faculty of Medicine, University of Lisbon, Lisbon, Portugal

[5] alm-PRIMUM, Lisbon, Portugal

Abstract. Glaucoma is a leading cause of irreversible blindness worldwide, often progressing undiagnosed due to asymptomatic early stages and limited access to specialist care. To address these barriers, we present a feasibility study of Glaucoma-PAIR (Privacy-preserving AI-based Referral), a computer-aided system developed using federated learning (FL). The study was conducted across a multi-centric network of three heterogeneous clinical sites in Portugal, two tertiary large public hospitals and one private clinic, each with distinct patient demographics, imaging equipment, and data distributions. The system leverages color fundus photography and expert-labeled cases to train a glaucoma classification model, without transferring sensitive patient data across institutions by employing FL, ensuring compliance with institutional governance and data protection regulations. Our work addresses major challenges in clinical AI, including privacy, generalizability, and integration into real-world workflows. Through close collaboration with ophthalmologists, we identified key constraints in existing referral pathways and incorporated those insights into the study design. Notably, the federated global model achieved performance comparable to a centralized model trained on pooled data, improved the average sensitivity which is a critical metric for a screening tool, and showed significant performance gains at the most clinically diverse site. This study provides a practical demonstration of responsible machine learning, combining privacy-preserving operations with clinical feasibility. Our findings highlight the potential of federated learning to enable the development of scalable and equitable AI tools, to support patient triage for a glaucoma specialist, particularly in settings with limited ophthalmology accessibility, promoting access to earlier diagnosis and care. We discuss the implications for future deployment and integration into national screening workflows.

I. Koprinska et al. (Eds.): ECML PKDD 2025, CCIS 2842, pp. 323–335, 2026.
https://doi.org/10.1007/978-3-032-19105-2_23

Keywords: Federated Learning · Computer Vision · Ophthalmology

1 Introduction

Glaucoma is a leading cause of irreversible vision loss, with millions of cases remaining undiagnosed globally. Studies estimate that around 50% of glaucoma cases are undiagnosed in developed countries, with even higher rates in developing regions [16]. This lack of diagnosis results in patients with advanced stages of the disease, leading to higher treatment costs and a greater burden on healthcare systems [2]. Current screening methods for glaucoma are not cost-effective, resulting in inefficient use of healthcare resources. The cost of examination and specialized equipment limits widespread screening, particularly in resource-limited settings [35,38]. One of the clinical sites integrating this work, has been pioneering a centre in a prospective clinical trial with artificial intelligence on glaucoma screening (Clinicaltrial.gov:NCT05875090), which suggested a sustained circuit between primary care settings and hospital-based clinics [20,21]. AI has shown promise in improving the efficiency of ophthalmology services [34], mirroring its impact in radiology [7]. However, the scientific community, public entities, and corporate innovators face significant challenges in transferring computer-aided diagnosis (CAD) systems to the real world due to: (a) lack of diversity in training data limiting their applicability across different populations [18]; (b) struggles with generalizability may perform well in controlled environments but underperforms in real-world settings [38]; (c) data privacy concerns and security concerns [14]; (d) interoperability issues integrating AI tools with existing healthcare systems is challenging; [15]; (e) sound integration into workflows effective integration requires a mixed methods approach, combining ethnographic research, service experience, process engineering, and participatory design for actionable insights [10]. These barriers hinder the feasible implementation of AI solutions in clinical settings, delaying the benefits of advanced technologies. To overcome these, recent approaches comprise:

Federated Learning (FL) addresses data diversity and generalizability by enabling AI training across multiple institutions without sharing raw data [33,38], and other privacy-preserving layers can be added as the homomorphic encryption during weight communication [11]. In addition, collaborative approaches involving multidisciplinary teams and implementing feedback loops between AI systems and medical experts enhance the system's reliability and continuous improvement [7].

1.1 Main Contributions

To address these challenges, we have carried out an observational study with retrospective data in three clinical sites in Portugal, to test FL for training a computer-aided system called Glaucoma-PAIR (Privacy-preserving AI-based Referral) starting from a pre-trained model by [17]. The multi-centric design of our study, based on real-world data, contributes to generate evidence on how to develop ML reliability close to the clinical environment. The main contributions of this study are summarised below.

Privacy-Preserving Federated Learning for Glaucoma Diagnosis: We developed a computer-aided referral system trained using FL across three independent clinical sites. This approach enables the use of sensitive real-world data without requiring cross-institutional data sharing, preserving patient privacy and institutional autonomy.

Multi-Centric Real-World Validation: Unlike many AI models trained on limited or homogeneous datasets, our study includes private data from diverse clinical environments enhancing model generalizability across. The system maintains a strong performance even in lower-resource sites, showcasing its robustness.

Clinician-Guided Labeling and Development: The AI model is trained on cases curated and labeled by glaucoma specialists, ensuring meaningful grading as the ground truth for machine learning development. This enhances both the clinical relevance and the heterogeneity in data required for the AI model robustness aiming to support the detection of glaucoma suspects, in the scope of patient triage and referral for a glaucoma specialist.

Responsible AI in Practice: This work demonstrates how responsible AI principles—privacy, robustness, and stakeholder collaboration—can be operationalised in real healthcare facilities. It offers a model for ethically grounded ML development in sensitive domains such as ophthalmology.

2 Related Work

The need for early glaucoma detection, coupled with the limited number of ophthalmologists, has led to the proposal of various automatic methods for glaucoma diagnosis or referral, using color fundus photographs, also called retinal fundus images [40]. In recent years, several Deep Learning (DL) architectures have been employed for the Glaucoma classification purpose, including Inception-V3 [19], MobileNetV2 [22], ResNet-50 [9,13], EfficientNetB0 [17], VGG-16 [6], DenseNet-201 [29], and vision transformers [8,37]. To improve the outcomes in terms of the glaucoma diagnosis, techniques like attention-based CNNs [31], transfer learning [26], active learning [13], hierarchical DL models [39], and even generative approaches [17] have been explored in the last years.

The work of Martins et al. [22] was a key contribution in segmentation around the optic nerve, often included in the detection typically based on U-shaped architectures (e.g. U-Net) [24,26]. Although, it should be noted that relevant information for diagnosing glaucoma extends beyond the optic disc [12].

CAD systems still largely depend on the use of publicly available datasets such as ORIGA [42], REFUGE [28] or AIROGS [36]. However, most of them are skewed towards specific demographic groups, failing to capture variations in the population. Accessing datasets with a wide range of variables such as age, ethnicity, and genetics, along with diverse clinical presentations of glaucoma, is a significant challenge [41] as there are changes in retinal structures among different racial and ethnic groups [5,30].

3 Methods

3.1 Clinical Context and Data Sources

The study was conducted in collaboration with three ophthalmology centers in Portugal: two large tertiary public hospitals, ULS São João (ULSSJ) located in Porto, ULS Santa Maria (ULSSM) and one private clinic, alm-PRIMUM (ALM), both in Lisbon. These sites differ in patient demographics, clinical workflows, glaucoma prevalence, and imaging equipment. At ULS São João, fundus images were acquired during ophthalmology consultations, upon request and not as a routine, resulting in a dataset with a high proportion of advanced glaucoma cases and patients with high myopia—reflecting a population with more severe disease manifestations and discs that are hard to judge on fundoscopy. At ULS Santa Maria, the cases stemmed from a virtual clinic for which patients are referred to when they are deemed glaucomatous or at least with high risk factors (such as high IOP). This results in greater clinical heterogeneity and a more balanced distribution of glaucoma stages in the dataset, due to a relatively high frequency of wrong referrals (i.e., normal cases) often based on single factors. At ALM, images are primarily sourced from general ophthalmology and neuro-ophthalmology consultations (approximately 34% from the latter), leading to a case mix characterized by higher complexity and a greater incidence of diagnostically challenging or atypical presentations. Table 1 summarizes the key characteristics of the datasets from each site, underscoring the heterogeneity of clinical contexts used to assess the robustness and generalizability of the proposed AI-based glaucoma referral system.

Institutional ethical approvals were obtained from the three local ethical committees in health, and a data governance protocol was secured in accordance with national health data protection regulations. The study followed a retrospective design, utilizing color fundus photographs already acquired during clinical practice. All data remained within the IT infrastructure of each institution; no raw image data was exchanged, in line with privacy-preserving principles.

Each clinical coordinator oversaw the preparation of the dataset at their respective institution, following a standardized procedure: selection of eligible images, anonymization, and compilation of demographic and clinical data. To better characterise the samples, the recorded variables included: anonymized patient ID, anonymized retinal image ID, eye laterality (right/left), optic disc-centered field of view (yes/no), age, sex, and intraocular pressure (IOP).

Each institution's dataset was assigned to a panel of three glaucoma specialists from that institution for image annotation and case labeling. Using a user interface customised for this study, the nine experts independently reviewed each case and classified it into one of three categories: non-classifiable (NC), glaucoma suspect, or normal, based solely on digital visual inspection of the fundus images. Each expert labeled an average of 712 images, including the NC. The final ground-truth label for each case was established through majority voting among the three local experts.

Table 1. Dataset Characteristics by Clinical Site

Characteristic	ULSSJ	ULSSM	ALM
Total number of images	404	1252	480
Images after excluding NC	322	1110	467
Age average (years)	65	69	65
Female (%)	51%	57%	42%
IOP average (mmHg)	15.94	15.81	15.75
Fundus camera brand	Zeiss	Canon	Canon
Image quality	Usable	Good	Good
Optic disc centered (%)	62	100	0
Expert experience (years)	7; 9; 9	12; 4; 3	25; 6; 30
Glaucoma suspect label (%)	69	66	31

3.2 Federated Learning Based on a Pre-trained Model

A FL architecture was developed and implemented using the Flower [3] software framework, enabling decentralized model training across participating hospitals without data centralization. Each site locally trained the model on its own dataset, and only model weight updates were transmitted to a central coordinating server. The server aggregated these updates using a federated averaging (FedAvg) algorithm and redistributed the global model to all participants.

The baseline model for image classification was based on a previous work described in [17], which is the pre-trained model used in this study to be fined-tuned in federated learning. The backbone model selected was EfficientNetB0, chosen for its balance between performance and computational efficiency. Training was performed on a harmonized dataset, compiled by combining multiple publicly available glaucoma-labeled datasets (ORIGA, Drishti-GS, REFUGE, RIM-ONE, ACRIMA). Since these datasets varied in image acquisition, some containing a standard field-of-view (FOV) in retinal imaging and others focused on the optic disc area, the images were standardized by cropping around the optic disc. These crops were resized to 224×224 pixels and normalized to ensure consistency across samples.

For the federated learning experiments in this study, the optic disc was detected automatically and then cropped following the work in [22], without applying any image processing or histogram equalization. The same squared input sized was used for training with a batch size of 4. The model optimization employed a multi-label Dice loss function with the ADAM optimizer, initialized with a learning rate of 0.00001. The training process continued for up to 20 local epochs in each federated round, for a total of 10 rounds (e.g. 200 epochs in total). Early stopping was triggered after 15 epochs without validation loss improvement to mitigate local overfitting.

We benchmarked the federated model against the baseline model at each clinical site. Performance was evaluated using site-wise test sets with metrics including accuracy, F1-score, precision, sensitivity, and specificity published in a MLFLow service [4]. It was only possible to apply a dataset split of 45% Train, 15% Validation and 40% Test sets, following the study protocol, in the site with less samples. Due to memory limitations in the local computer, delays in local training had caused some synchronicity issues in federated learning orchestration process using Flower. For this reason, to approximate the training conditions of all local sites, we used a training set equivalent in absolute size, keeping the 15% in validation and using the remaining data as a local test set.

3.3 System Deployment

To enable a privacy-preserving, decentralized workflow for AI development and validation, a custom FL infrastructure was deployed at each clinical site. The system architecture was designed to support on-premise data processing and model training while ensuring compliance with institutional governance protocols and European data protection regulations (GDPR).

Each participating site was equipped with a microcomputer edge box with GPU (NVIDIA Jetson with 32GB RAM) configured to run containerized services via Docker. These services included the local machine learning training pipeline, data management tool, image annotation interface, inference engine and the respective Application Programming Interfaces. Deployment was performed collaboratively with the hospitals' IT teams, who were responsible for configuring secure network access. This included enabling SSL encryption, setting up HTTPS port forwarding, and defining firewall rules to allow secure communication with the central FL coordination server (a cloud virtual machine running in West Europe on Microsoft Azure) while preventing any outbound transfer of raw patient data.

A custom web-based image annotation tool (see Fig. 1) was installed on-site and made accessible through user-specific login credentials. This interface allowed glaucoma specialists to securely review, label, and annotate fundus images within the local hospital network. Although not fully integrated with local clinical workflows to speed up the study execution, the image annotator usability enabled efficient interaction of the users with the dataset while maintaining data confidentiality.

The entire system operated under a FL paradigm, where each site trained local models on their respective datasets and shared only model updates (weights) with the central server. No images or identifiable patient data were transmitted externally. This decentralized setup ensured that sensitive health data never left the premises, aligning with institutional ethics approvals and national data handling standards.

This deployment strategy not only preserved data privacy but also created a realistic operational environment for evaluating the performance and feasibility of AI-assisted glaucoma referral tools near clinical practice.

4 Results

We compared the performance of the centralized baseline model with the FL model across the three participating clinical sites, ULSSJ, ULSSM, and ALM. Table 2 presents the results per site and averaged across all sites. Table 3 depicts the confusion matrices of the tests sets for baseline and FL models.

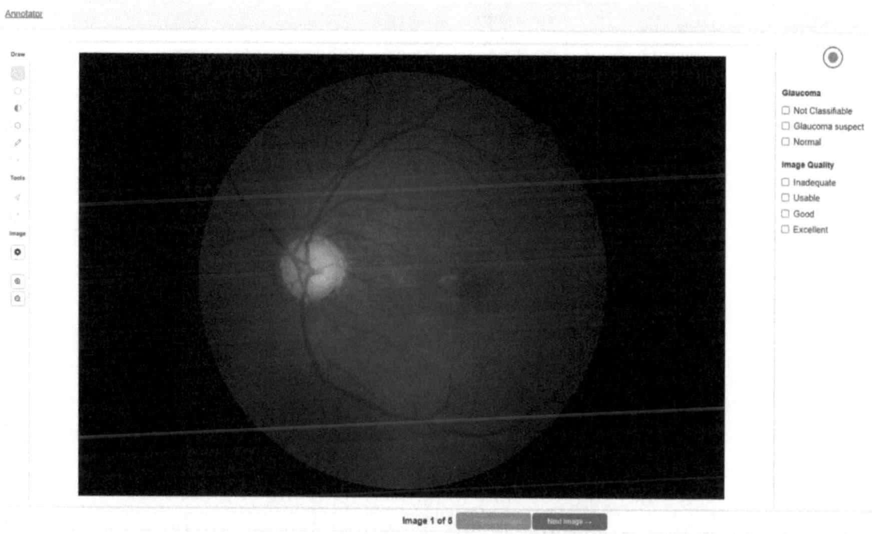

Fig. 1. Image annotation tool.

Table 2. Performance Comparison of Baseline and Federated Models Across Clinical Sites

Metrics	ULSSJ		ULSSM		ALM		Average	
	Baseline	FL	Baseline	FL	Baseline	FL	Baseline	FL
Accuracy	0.74	0.71	0.66	0.70	0.79	0.75	0.73	0.72
F1-score	0.80	0.79	0.68	0.75	0.64	0.62	0.71	0.72
Precision	0.83	0.79	0.90	0.84	0.66	0.57	0.80	0.73
Sensitivity	0.78	0.80	0.55	0.68	0.63	0.67	0.65	0.72
Specificity	0.63	0.51	0.88	0.74	0.86	0.78	0.79	0.68

The average performance across the three centers indicates that the FL model achieved comparable accuracy (0.72) to the baseline (0.73), with a slight improvement in F1-score from 0.71 to 0.72, reflecting more balanced performance across classes. Notably, the federated model outperformed the baseline in sensitivity, increasing from 0.65 to 0.72 on average, which is a desirable outcome in a screening context where minimizing false negatives is critical. However, this gain in sensitivity came at the cost of reduced specificity, which dropped from 0.79 in the baseline model to 0.68 in the FL model.

Table 3. Confusion Matrices of Baseline and Federated Models Across Clinical Sites

Metrics	ULSSJ		ULSSM		ALM		Average	
	Baseline	FL	Baseline	FL	Baseline	FL	Baseline	FL
False Negative	20	18	233	164	27	24	93	69
False Positive	15	20	31	68	23	36	23	41
True Negative	26	21	234	197	141	128	134	115
True Positive	71	73	285	354	45	48	134	158

At ULSSJ, the FL model slightly decreased in accuracy (0.74 to 0.71) and precision (0.83 to 0.79), while showing a modest improvement in sensitivity (0.78 to 0.80). Performance at ULSSM exhibited the most pronounced gains from FL, with accuracy improving from 0.66 to 0.70 and F1-score rising from 0.68 to 0.75. Here, sensitivity increased substantially from 0.55 to 0.68, with a trade-off in specificity (0.88 to 0.74). At ALM, both models performed strongly in terms of accuracy and specificity, although the FL model showed a slight performance decline across most metrics compared to the baseline.

Overall, these results suggest that federated learning can help improve generalization in settings with heterogeneous data distributions by boosting sensitivity and F1-score—key metrics in medical screening, while slightly compromising specificity. The federated approach may be particularly advantageous in underrepresented or more diverse clinical environments, as observed in the ULSSM results.

5 Generalizable Insights About Responsible Application of Machine Learning in Healthcare

This study explored the feasibility and performance trade-offs of applying FL for glaucoma detection across multiple clinical sites with heterogeneous data sources and workflows. While the baseline model, trained centrally on pooled data, achieved a good overall predictive performance, the federated model demonstrated competitive results for the context of a AI-powered glaucoma screening, particularly in terms of F1-score and sensitivity. Moreover, these results were obtained having a considerably small and private training set, and despite overcoming some of the challenges of decentralized training in real-word clinical settings. These findings reflect common trade-offs in some FL applications, where performance may be modestly compromised due to local sample size limitations, and domain shifts across institutions.

Importantly, the federated approach preserved institutional data privacy by enabling local model training without transferring raw images, thus aligning with GDPR requirements and the data governance policies of each hospital. This privacy-preserving setup is especially relevant for scaling AI adoption in healthcare, where regulatory and ethical constraints often impede centralized data sharing. This setup can be relevant to obtain more, real and diverse data, needed to develop and validate high-risk AI systems that include generalizable machine learning models.

The observed performance gaps between the baseline and FL models suggest that further advances are needed, namely with the expansion of the available data in the federated network. Future work should explore personalized FL strategies, domain adaptation techniques, and more robust model aggregation methods as the ones experimented in [1], to better address inter-site variability and improve convergence.

This study also highlights the value of interdisciplinary collaboration in AI for healthcare. Clinical input guided image selection, annotation, and contextual interpretation, while machine learning expertise shaped model design and evaluation. The diverse clinical settings, ranging from public hospitals to private clinics, with varying patient profiles and imaging acquisition setups, offered a realistic testbed for evaluating the generalizability of AI models across different healthcare contexts.

Looking ahead, future research should prioritize the integration of fairness, transparency, and interpretability into privacy-preserving FL networks. Clinician trust and patient safety hinge not only on model performance but also on the ability to identify failure cases, and adapt to local clinical practices. To this end, incorporating continuous stakeholder feedback, and aligning development processes with real-world clinical needs will be critical for the responsible and effective deployment of AI-assisted glaucoma screening tools.

The practical application of this work is emphasized by new workflows, such as the virtual hospital-based clinics [23,25,27,32]. For instance, a "Virtual Clinic for Glaucoma" is being initiated at ULSSJ, representing a new asynchronous and remote digital consultation model designed to optimize healthcare resources for both glaucoma specialists and patients. Given that glaucoma is a chronic disease requiring constant monitoring, and with patient numbers expected to rise, current clinical schemes are becoming unsustainable. In this virtual clinic model, a technician performs a set of exams, and the physician evaluates the results asynchronously, increasing the number of patients that can be monitored. This process aids in the triage of patients referred for initial glaucoma consultations and in evaluating low-risk patients, freeing up specialists' time for more complex and urgent cases. Such a workflow aims to improve the patient experience, accelerate diagnoses, and increase clinical capacity by leveraging technology for data collection and analysis. The responsible integration of an AI-based support solution for the robust classification of fundus images, as showed in this study, is intended to directly assist physicians in their decision-making and optimize the quality of patient referrals within this new paradigm.

6 Conclusion

This study demonstrates the feasibility of deploying a federated learning framework for glaucoma detection using color fundus photography across multiple ophthalmology centers, preserving patient data privacy while enabling collaborative model development. Our results show that although the centrally trained baseline model achieved slightly higher predictive performance considering the set of metrics evaluated, the FL model offered a viable alternative with competitive sensitivity and F1-score, particularly valuable in the scope of screening and AI-based patient referrals (e.g. from general ophthalmology to glaucoma expert units), and in contexts where training data cannot be shared due to regulatory constraints.

By leveraging a diverse, multi-centric dataset and integrating clinical expertise throughout the process—from labeling to deployment—this work illustrates a realistic path toward scalable, privacy-conscious AI in ophthalmology. The study also highlights current limitations in federated learning performance due to data heterogeneity and inter-institutional variability, pointing to future research directions in personalization, domain adaptation, and model explainability.

Ultimately, our findings support the growing potential of federated learning to democratize access to high-performing AI models in healthcare, while respecting ethical and legal boundaries critical for clinical adoption.

Acknowledgments. This work was supported by European funds through the Recovery and Resilience Plan, under the project "Center for Responsible AI" (C645008882-00000055), and by the European Union's Horizon Europe research and innovation programme under Grant Agreement No. 101189689.

Disclosure of Interests. The authors have no competing interests to declare.

References

1. Baptista, T., Soares, C., Oliveira, T., Soares, F.: Federated learning for computer-aided diagnosis of glaucoma using retinal fundus images. Appl. Sci. **13**(21), 11620 (2023). https://doi.org/10.3390/app132111620. https://www.mdpi.com/2076-3417/13/21/11620
2. Barbosa-Breda, J., et al.: Trends in glaucoma surgical procedures in Portugal: a 16-year nationwide study (2000–2015). J. Glaucoma **27**(8), 682–686 (2018). https://doi.org/10.1097/IJG.0000000000001011
3. Beutel, D.J., et al.: Flower: a friendly federated learning research framework. Technical report. arXiv:2007.14390 (2022). arXiv [cs, stat] type: article
4. Chen, A., et al.: Developments in MLflow: a system to accelerate the machine learning lifecycle. In: Proceedings of the Fourth International Workshop on Data Management for End-to-End Machine Learning, DEEM 2020, pp. 1–4. Association for Computing Machinery, New York, NY, USA (2020). https://doi.org/10.1145/3399579.3399867

5. Christopher, M., et al.: Effects of study population, labeling and training on glaucoma detection using deep learning algorithms. Transl. Vis. Sci. Technol. **9**(2), 27 (2020). https://doi.org/10.1167/tvst.9.2.27. https://tvst.arvojournals.org/article.aspx?articleid=2765468
6. de Sales Carvalho, N.R., Rodrigues, M.D.C.L.C., de Carvalho Filho, A.O., Mathew, M.J.: Automatic method for glaucoma diagnosis using a three-dimensional convoluted neural network. Neurocomputing **438**, 72–83 (2021). https://doi.org/10.1016/j.neucom.2020.07.146. https://linkinghub.elsevier.com/retrieve/pii/S0925231221001090
7. Dikici, E., Bigelow, M., Prevedello, L.M., White, R.D., Erdal, B.S.: Integrating AI into radiology workflow: levels of research, production, and feedback maturity. J. Med. Imaging (Bellingham, Wash.) **7**(1), 016502 (2020). https://doi.org/10.1117/1.JMI.7.1.016502
8. Fan, R., et al.: Detecting glaucoma from fundus photographs using deep learning without convolutions. Ophthalmol. Sci. **3**(1), 100233 (2023). https://doi.org/10.1016/j.xops.2022.100233. https://linkinghub.elsevier.com/retrieve/pii/S2666914522001221
9. Gheisari, S., et al.: A combined convolutional and recurrent neural network for enhanced glaucoma detection. Sci. Rep. **11**(1), 1945 (2021). https://doi.org/10.1038/s41598-021-81554-4. https://www.nature.com/articles/s41598-021-81554-4
10. Gu, H., et al.: Improving workflow integration with xPath: design and evaluation of a human-AI diagnosis system in pathology. ACM Trans. Comput.-Hum. Interact. **30**(2), 28:1–28:37 (2023). https://doi.org/10.1145/3577011
11. Gu, X., Sabrina, F., Fan, Z., Sohail, S.: A review of privacy enhancement methods for federated learning in healthcare systems. Int. J. Environ. Res. Public Health **20**(15), 6539 (2023). https://doi.org/10.3390/ijerph20156539. https://www.ncbi.nlm.nih.gov/pmc/articles/PMC10418741/
12. Hemelings, R., Elen, B., Barbosa-Breda, J., Blaschko, M.B., De Boever, P., Stalmans, I.: Deep learning on fundus images detects glaucoma beyond the optic disc. Sci. Rep. **11**(1), 20313 (2021). https://doi.org/10.1038/s41598-021-99605-1. https://www.nature.com/articles/s41598-021-99605-1
13. Hemelings, R., et al.: Accurate prediction of glaucoma from colour fundus images with a convolutional neural network that relies on active and transfer learning. Acta Ophthalmologica **98**(1), e94–e100 (2020). https://doi.org/10.1111/aos.14193. https://onlinelibrary.wiley.com/doi/abs/10.1111/aos.14193
14. Holzinger, A., Haibe-Kains, B., Jurisica, I.: Why imaging data alone is not enough: AI-based integration of imaging, omics, and clinical data. Eur. J. Nucl. Med. Mol. Imaging **46**(13), 2722–2730 (2019). https://doi.org/10.1007/s00259-019-04382-9
15. Kanakaraj, P., et al.: Workflow integration of research ai tools into a hospital radiology rapid prototyping environment. J. Digit. Imaging **35**(4), 1023–1033 (2022). https://doi.org/10.1007/s10278-022-00601-2
16. Lee, S.S.Y., Mackey, D.A.: Glaucoma – risk factors and current challenges in the diagnosis of a leading cause of visual impairment. Maturitas **163**, 15–22 (2022). https://doi.org/10.1016/j.maturitas.2022.05.002. https://www.sciencedirect.com/science/article/pii/S0378512222000950
17. Leonardo, R., Gonçalves, J., Carreiro, A., Simões, B., Oliveira, T., Soares, F.: Impact of generative modeling for fundus image augmentation with improved and degraded quality in the classification of glaucoma. IEEE Access **10**, 111636–111649 (2022). https://doi.org/10.1109/ACCESS.2022.3215126

18. Li, R.C., Asch, S.M., Shah, N.H.: Developing a delivery science for artificial intelligence in healthcare. Npj Digit. Med. **3**(1), 1–3 (2020). https://doi.org/10.1038/s41746-020-00318-y. https://www.nature.com/articles/s41746-020-00318-y
19. Li, Z., He, Y., Keel, S., Meng, W., Chang, R.T., He, M.: Efficacy of a deep learning system for detecting glaucomatous optic neuropathy based on color fundus photographs. Ophthalmology **125**(8), 1199–1206 (2018). https://doi.org/10.1016/j.ophtha.2018.01.023. https://linkinghub.elsevier.com/retrieve/pii/S0161642017335650
20. Lima-Cabrita, A.V., et al.: AI-(EM)powered screening: glaucoma post study. Investigative Ophthalmol. Vis. Sci. **65**(7), 605 (2024)
21. Marques-Neves, C., et al.: Associating glaucoma and diabetic retinopathy: opportunistic AI-powered glaucoma screening. Investigative Ophthalmol. Vis. Sci. **65**(7), 604 (2024)
22. Martins, J., Cardoso, J.S., Soares, F.: Offline computer-aided diagnosis for Glaucoma detection using fundus images targeted at mobile devices. Comput. Methods Programs Biomed. **192**, 105341 (2020). https://doi.org/10.1016/j.cmpb.2020.105341. https://linkinghub.elsevier.com/retrieve/pii/S0169260719312015
23. Matos, D.B., Barão, R.C., José, P., Cabrita, A., Barata, A.D., Pinto, L.A.: Glaucoma triage system: results of implementing a virtual clinic. Graefe's Archive for Clinical and Experimental Ophthalmology = Albrecht Von Graefes Archiv Fur Klinische Und Experimentelle Ophthalmologie **261**(8), 2367–2374 (2023). https://doi.org/10.1007/s00417-023-06039-8
24. Sudhan, M.B., et al.: Segmentation and classification of glaucoma using u-net with deep learning model. J. Healthcare Eng. **2022**, 1–10 (2022). https://doi.org/10.1155/2022/1601354
25. Mercer, R., Alaghband, P.: The value of virtual glaucoma clinics: a review. Eye **38**(10), 1840–1844 (2024). https://doi.org/10.1038/s41433-024-03056-7. https://www.nature.com/articles/s41433-024-03056-7
26. Natarajan, D., Sankaralingam, E., Balraj, K., Karuppusamy, S.: A deep learning framework for glaucoma detection based on robust optic disc segmentation and transfer learning. Int. J. Imaging Syst. Technol. **32**(1), 230–250 (2022). https://doi.org/10.1002/ima.22609. https://onlinelibrary.wiley.com/doi/pdf/10.1002/ima.22609
27. Nikolaidou, A., Tsaousis, K.T.: Teleophthalmology and artificial intelligence as game changers in ophthalmic care after the COVID-19 pandemic. Cureus **13**(7), e16392 (2021). https://doi.org/10.7759/cureus.16392
28. Orlando, J.I., et al.: REFUGE challenge: a unified framework for evaluating automated methods for glaucoma assessment from fundus photographs. Med. Image Anal. **59**, 101570 (2020). https://doi.org/10.1016/j.media.2019.101570. https://www.sciencedirect.com/science/article/pii/S1361841519301100
29. Ovreiu, S., Paraschiv, E.A., Ovreiu, E.: Deep learning & digital fundus images: glaucoma detection using DenseNet. In: 2021 13th International Conference on Electronics, Computers and Artificial Intelligence (ECAI), pp. 1–4. IEEE, Pitesti, Romania (2021). https://doi.org/10.1109/ECAI52376.2021.9515188. https://ieeexplore.ieee.org/document/9515188/
30. Schuster, A.K., Wagner, F.M., Pfeiffer, N., Hoffmann, E.M.: Risk factors for open-angle glaucoma and recommendations for glaucoma screening. Ophthalmologe **118**(2), 145–152 (2021). https://doi.org/10.1007/s00347-021-01378-5
31. Shyamalee, T., Meedeniya, D., Lim, G., Karunarathne, M.: Automated tool support for glaucoma identification with explainability using fundus images. IEEE

Access **12**, 17290–17307 (2024). https://doi.org/10.1109/ACCESS.2024.3359698. https://ieeexplore.ieee.org/document/10416867/
32. Simons, A.S., Vercauteren, J., Barbosa-Breda, J., Stalmans, I.: Shared care and virtual clinics for glaucoma in a hospital setting. J. Clin. Med. **10**(20), 4785 (2021). https://doi.org/10.3390/jcm10204785. https://www.mdpi.com/2077-0383/10/20/4785
33. Soltan, A.A.S., et al.: A scalable federated learning solution for secondary care using low-cost microcomputing: privacy-preserving development and evaluation of a COVID-19 screening test in UK hospitals. Lancet Digit. Health **6**(2), e93–e104 (2024). https://doi.org/10.1016/S2589-7500(23)00226-1. https://www.thelancet.com/journals/landig/article/PIIS2589-7500(23)00226-1/fulltext
34. Taribagil, P., Hogg, H.J., Balaskas, K., Keane, P.A.: Integrating artificial intelligence into an ophthalmologist's workflow: obstacles and opportunities. Expert Rev. Ophthalmol. **18**(1), 45–56 (2023). https://doi.org/10.1080/17469899.2023.2175672
35. US Preventive Services Task Force: Screening for Primary Open-Angle Glaucoma: US Preventive Services Task Force Recommendation Statement. JAMA **327**(20), 1992–1997 (2022). https://doi.org/10.1001/jama.2022.7013
36. de Vente, C., et al.: AIROGS: artificial intelligence for robust glaucoma screening challenge. IEEE Trans. Med. Imaging **43**(1), 542–557 (2024). https://doi.org/10.1109/TMI.2023.3313786
37. Wassel, M., Hamdi, A.M., Adly, N., Torki, M.: Vision transformers based classification for glaucomatous eye condition. In: 2022 26th International Conference on Pattern Recognition (ICPR), pp. 5082–5088. IEEE, Montreal, QC, Canada (2022). https://doi.org/10.1109/ICPR56361.2022.9956086. https://ieeexplore.ieee.org/document/9956086/
38. Wenderott, K., Gambashidze, N., Weigl, M.: Integration of artificial intelligence into sociotechnical work systems—effects of artificial intelligence solutions in medical imaging on clinical efficiency: protocol for a systematic literature review. JMIR Res. Protocols **11**(12), e40485 (2022). https://doi.org/10.2196/40485. https://www.researchprotocols.org/2022/12/e40485
39. Xu, Y., et al.: A hierarchical deep learning approach with transparency and interpretability based on small samples for glaucoma diagnosis. Npj Digit. Med. **4**(1), 48 (2021). https://doi.org/10.1038/s41746-021-00417-4. https://www.nature.com/articles/s41746-021-00417-4
40. Zedan, M., Zulkifley, M., Ibrahim, A., Moubark, A., Kamari, N., Abdani, S.: Automated glaucoma screening and diagnosis based on retinal fundus images using deep learning approaches: a comprehensive review. Diagnostics **13**(13), 2180 (2023). https://doi.org/10.3390/diagnostics13132180. https://www.mdpi.com/2075-4418/13/13/2180
41. Zhu, Y., Salowe, R., Chow, C., Li, S., Bastani, O., O'Brien, J.M.: Advancing glaucoma care: integrating artificial intelligence in diagnosis, management, and progression detection. Bioengineering **11**(2), 122 (2024). https://doi.org/10.3390/bioengineering11020122. https://www.mdpi.com/2306-5354/11/2/122
42. Zhang, Z., et al.: ORIGA$^{-\text{light}}$: an online retinal fundus image database for glaucoma analysis and research. In: 2010 Annual International Conference of the IEEE Engineering in Medicine and Biology, pp. 3065–3068. IEEE, Buenos Aires (2010). https://doi.org/10.1109/IEMBS.2010.5626137. http://ieeexplore.ieee.org/document/5626137/

Sex Prediction from Polish Ethnicity Fundus Images Using Foundation Model

Paweł Niedziółka[1(✉)], Paweł Zyblewski[1], Andrzej Grzybowski[2], Michał Woźniak[1], Łukasz Lisowski[3], Marlena Dubatówka[4], and Karol Kamiński[4]

[1] Faculty of Information and Communication Technology, Wrocław University of Science and Technology, Wrocław, Poland
{pawel.niedziolka,pawel.zyblewski,michal.wozniak}@pwr.edu.pl
[2] University of Warmia and Mazury, Olsztyn, Poland
[3] Department of Ophthalmology, Medical University of Bialystok, Bialystok, Poland
lukasz.lisowski@umb.edu.pl
[4] Center for Population Research, Medical University of Bialystok, Bialystok, Poland
{marlena.dubatowka,karol.kaminski}@umb.edu.pl

Abstract. The paper aims to use fundus images to determine the patient's sex. Admittedly, such a possibility has been confirmed by previous studies, but the paper will consider how transfer learning from the RETFound foundation model for retinal images dedicated to the diagnosis of diabetic retinopathy can be used to build such a system and whether the quality of the transfer is sufficient when analyzing data from a different population than the one used to build the fundus model. The study presented here is based on a non-public dataset of fundus images collected from individuals of Polish ancestry. Our study shows that transfer learning, a proven tool for applying and achieving better results when reusing models tuned for different tasks, has some limitations when applied to medical data. In addition, we address emerging concerns about data leakage in medical imaging, as such data may contain overt patient metadata and hidden patterns invisible to humans, which may encode sensitive information that is impossible to capture even by medical experts aided by Explainable artificial intelligence (XAI) techniques.

Keywords: Original dataset exploration · Sex prediction · Transfer learning

1 Introduction

Medical imaging plays a crucial role in disease detection, with advances in diagnostic imaging technology enabling the early identification of various medical conditions. The screening used for this purpose aims to find irregular features in the population and conduct a deeper analysis [14]. Various tests and population characteristics are employed to assess the benefits and limitations of such

I. Koprinska et al. (Eds.): ECML PKDD 2025, CCIS 2842, pp. 336–350, 2026.
https://doi.org/10.1007/978-3-032-19105-2_24

screenings [16]. In the case of diabetic retinopathy, the key is to minimize the likelihood of visual impairment in people with diabetes through rapid detection and appropriate treatment [19].

Analyzing medical data, it is essential to consider the origin of the population. Different ethnic or geographic groups may show significant differences in the distribution of biological traits [7]. This is why predictive models, based on machine learning, can be subject to the selection bias, where the data on which they were trained are favored at the expense of the overall ability to generalize the results [12].

Lack of representativeness can reduce the model's effectiveness in different populations and increase the risk of misdiagnoses [6]. Therefore, accounting for population diversity and performing a thorough dataset characterization is essential when designing and evaluating machine learning models.

The main contributions of this study are as follows:

- One of the first explorations of a non-public fundus image dataset that contains Polish participants,
- Adaptation of convolutional and transformer-based deep learning models for the sex classification task
- Use of the *GradCam* XAI approach in an attempt to interpret the results obtained and spark future discussions in the ophthalmology community

2 Related Works

This section briefly introduces this article's two most important research areas, i.e., employing deep learning for fundus image classification and transferability estimation.

2.1 Deep Learning for Fundus Image Classification

Deep learning has recently revolutionized automated Diabetic Retinopathy (DR) detection and classification [2], especially with the deployment of Convolutional Neural Networks (CNN) and emerging transformer-based architectures. CNNs such as InceptionV3 and ResNet have shown themselves to be very sensitive and specific to detecting retinal pathologies directly from fundus images, outperforming prior handcrafted methods for features and delivering performance close to that of a human expert in screening applications [11,25]. This architecture can be applied to medical imaging studies as it can also effectively capture low-level and high-level features [5].

Transformer-based models have been proposed to address the limitations of the capacity of CNNs to compute long-range dependencies and contextual retinal features. The research of DR has proved that ViTs [28] based models can help learn richer spatial hierarchies and attention-based representations in the classification task. Notably, RETFound [33], trained as a foundation model on millions of unlabeled retinal images using self-supervised learning, can transfer to other downstream ophthalmic tasks, including DR detection.

Explainable AI methods, including Grad-CAM, LIME, and attention maps, have been incorporated into DR diagnostic pipelines to produce visual explanations for model predictions, which is a necessary step towards clinical acceptance and regulatory approval [3,32]. These interpretability aids help clinicians confirm that the model is attending to clinically relevant features like microaneurysms, exudates, and hemorrhages.

2.2 Transferability Estimation

The canonical machine learning methods assume that training and testing data are i.d.d. (independent and identically distributed). This assumption may be violated when constructing pattern recognition systems to solve real-world tasks. For example, when classifying biosignals such as EEG, considerable variances might be observed between individuals, resulting in poor generalization capacity [27]. This can be addressed by collecting additional fully or partially labeled data, which is subsequently used to train the model. However, such a solution usually comes with a significant time and monetary cost [20].

The alternative solution is transfer learning [18], which aims to boost the model's generalization capacity for a target domain, which generally contains a small number of labeled samples, by applying knowledge learned during training on an associated source domain. The effectiveness of transfer learning typically relies on three assumptions [31]: **(i)** *Task correlation*, which requires that the learning task in the source and target domains are similar, **(ii)** *Domain correlation*, which requires that the data distributions in the source and target domains be similar, and **(iii)** *Ideal joint error*, which requires that an appropriate hypothesis be applied to both domains. Negative knowledge transfer may result from not meeting any of the above assumptions [31], which could hinder the pre-trained model's capacity to generalize to the target dataset.

Retraining or fine-tuning the previously learned model is one of the most fundamental but effective transfer learning strategies [18]. The development of metrics for matching the right pre-trained model to the target problem at hand has become essential due to the enormous popularity of transfer learning and the substantial variability in the benefits derived from its use, depending on the network architecture, the source dataset used for pre-training, or even the layer from which the representation is obtained. According to the inherent computational complexity, available transferability estimation techniques can be classified as either **(i)** computation-intensive or **(ii)** computation-efficient [13].

Methods from the first category can typically be used to estimate the knowledge transferability of unsupervised pre-trained models and determine the network layer from which the transfer should occur. However, their computational complexity corresponds with executing fine-tuning on a target dataset, making it impossible to use them to assess transferability before fine-tuning [13]. Dwivedi and Roig presented *Representation Similarity Analysis* (RSA), which uses correlations between pre-trained models on different tasks to compute a similarity score [10]. Song et al. introduced *DEeP Attribution gRAph* (DEPARA) [23], which creates a similarity graph between representations of samples from specific datasets derived from pre-trained deep neural networks. Zamir et al. presented *Taskonomy* [30], which analyzes the source and target task linkage by performing fine-tuning on a model pre-trained on the target dataset and estimating the loss, whereas Achille et al. [1] employ *Fischer Information Matrix*.

In contrast to its counterpart, computationally efficient transferability metrics do not require model training on the target dataset [13]. Cui et al. calculated the *Earth Mover's Distance* between source and target data features [8], which requires access to the source dataset. You et al. used the *Logarithm of Maximum Evidence* (LogME) to evaluate pre-trained models for transfer learning [29] and discovered a link between high LogME and increased generalization ability. Tran et al. assessed transferability by calculating *Negative Conditional Entropy* (NCE) between source and target labels [26]. The computationally efficient category also contains metrics that do not require access to source data but cannot be used to choose layers. Nguen et al. presented the *Log Expected Empirical Prediction* (LEEP) score, working similarly to NCE, which replaces source dataset labels with pseudo-labels derived from a pre-trained model [17]. Bao et al. presented an *H-score* to measure knowledge transfer between source and destination datasets using statistical and information-theoretic concepts, although, like LogME, they only considered the network's last layer [4]. Huang et al. developed *TransRate*, which can be expressed as the mutual information between embeddings of target samples and their labels [13]. This only requires access to target data and a single pass through the pre-trained model.

3 Bialystok PLUS Prospective Cohort Study

The dataset used in this study originates from the non-public repository of the *Bialystok PLUS* prospective cohort study[1]. It includes high-resolution fundus images – as shown in Fig. 1 – collected from the left and right eyes of individual participants. Multiple photo acquisitions per participant per eye provide variability in quality and capture conditions. All sensitive, identifiable information was removed following ethical standards and data protection regulations. Aside from imaging data, the dataset is complemented by a broad range of clinical and demographic data. This includes, e.g., age, sex, and various physiological or diagnostic markers, which are listed in Table 1. Due to its proprietary nature, this dataset is not available for public distribution.

However, this paper focuses on sex prediction using different convolutional models and fundus images as a base for prediction. To support that research in the dataset, 18,472 fundus images were collected from 2,854 individual participants, including 1,271 women and 1,583 men of different age groups. The age distribution by sex is visible in Fig. 2.

[1] www.bialystok.plus.

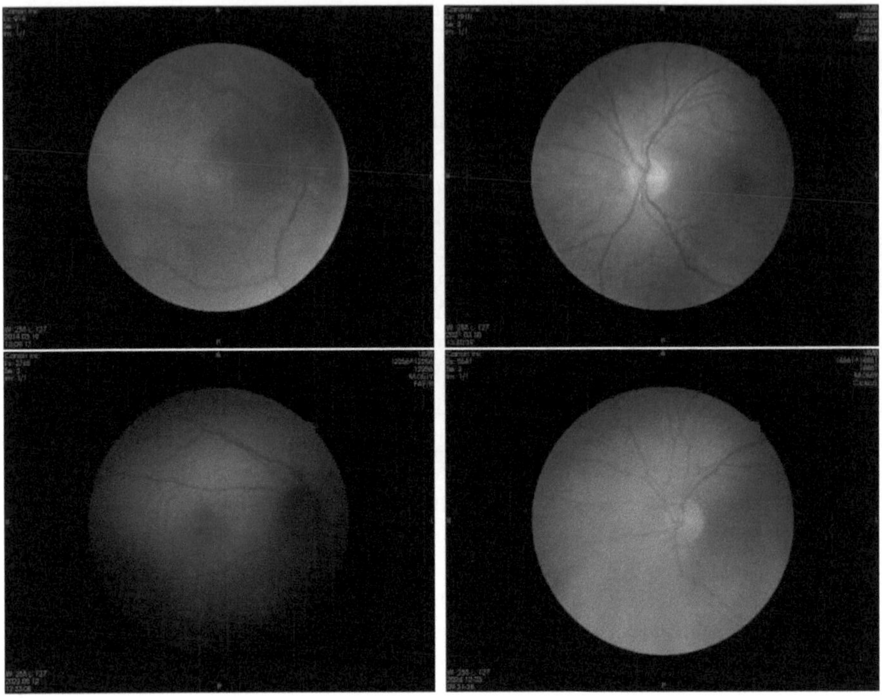

Fig. 1. Sample images available in the dataset.

Table 1. All markers available in the dataset.

Medical history	Densitometry (DEXA)	Advanced glycation end-products (AGEs)
Blood biochemical and immunochemical tests	Three-day nutritional interview	Peripheral blood pressure
Proteomic analysis	Nutritional averages per day	Electrocardiography (ECG)
Urine analysis	Bioelectrical impedance analysis (BIA)	Echocardiography
ATC drugs	PWV, Central pressure, ABI	Carotid arteries ultrasound
Respiratory tests & fractional exhaled nitric oxide (FENO) test	Ergospirometry Cosmed and Vyntus	Thyroid ultrasound
Dental examination	Anthropometry	Liver ultrasound
Hand grip strength	Orthostatic test	Liver elastography
Swelling and varicose veins of the calves	Geriatric assessment 50–64 and +65	Autorefractometry and tonometry
Fundus imaging	Voice recording	MRI

3.1 Dataset Preprocessing

Each image in the dataset underwent a standardized preprocessing pipeline to ensure consistency and compatibility with deep learning models. At the very

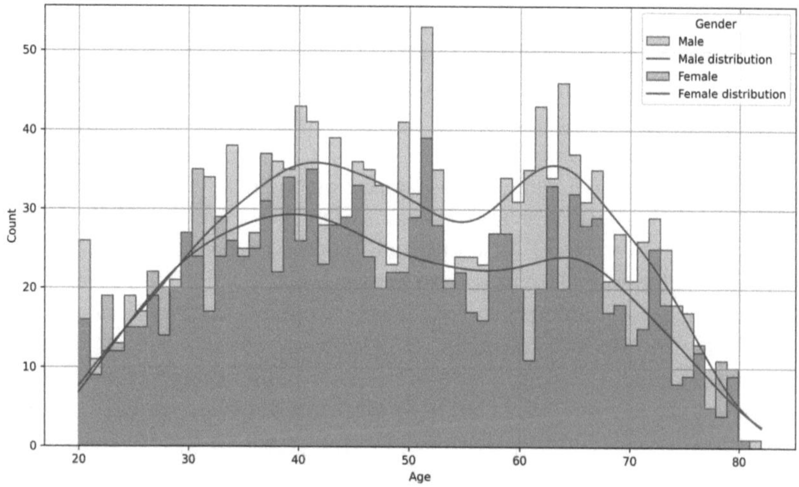

Fig. 2. Age distribution by sex.

beginning, the DICOM format images were converted into pixel-intensity arrays. A normalization process was employed to reduce variation in brightness and contrast, improving model robustness. In cases where the images contained on a single color channel (grayscale), they were expanded to three channels by duplication. That ensures a unified data representation for models that were pre-trained on RGB data. Finally, all images were resized to a consistent resolution - 224 × 224 pixels, which makes a consistent input format across the dataset.

4 Experimental Evaluation

The experiments were designed and conducted in order to answer the following research questions:

- **RQ1** Can the Polish *Bialystok PLUS* fundus images dataset be used to replicate sex prediction research?
- **RQ2** How efficient is the adaptation of the foundation model for diabetic retinopathy detection (RETFound) to the sex classification task?
- **RQ3** Do the transferability measure values for individual deep models coincide with their generalization ability?

4.1 Set-Up

Two distinct models were employed to address the binary sex classification task and verify the exclusive, non-public dataset: ResNet-50 and the RETFound.

ResNet50 model was initialized with *ImageNet* [9] pre-trained weights. The original classification head of this network was replaced with a new fully connected layer with an output of one neuron. Later, this was passed through a sigmoid activation function to predict the probability of the image belonging to the female or male category.

The RETFound model weights are trained on the color fundus photos (CFP) dataset, which is structurally and semantically closer to the medical imaging domain, and these were used. The original head layer was replaced similarly to the previous model; one change was to retain the normalization layer from the backbone to ensure a stable representation before the classification process.

To fine-tune the sex classification models, training was conducted using the Adam optimizer with a learning rate of $1 \cdot 10^{-4}$. The binary cross-entropy loss with logits was set as a criterion that is appropriate for this type of classification. Models described before were trained for 10 epochs with a batch size of 32. That provides a balance between efficiency and gradient stability. The dataset was split adequately with rates of 80% and 20% accordingly for the training and testing sets.

For model performance evaluation, the following metrics were used:

- Accuracy provides a general measure of how many predictions the model got right. However, it may be misleading in imbalanced datasets - in the medical images, healthy cases frequently outnumber pathological ones.
- Precision is important to assess how many predicted DR-positive cases are correct. High precision reduces the risk that patients are wrongly classified as diseased.
- Recall measures how well the model detects actual DR cases. High recall helps prevent biased or imbalanced sex predictions.
- F1 score is the harmonic mean of precision and recall, balancing the trade-off between the two.

The metrics were computed at each epoch, and each model was trained independently following the same experimental setup. The code for experimental setup is publicly available in the GitHub[2].

4.2 Experimental Scenarios

Experiment 1 - Fine-Tuning of Deep Models
The first experiment evaluated the ability of two selected architectures to learn sex -related features from fundus images within a consistent training pipeline. Both models were tuned using a specific configuration of preprocessing, training, and evaluation criteria. The training process was designed to investigate the learning behavior of each model over epochs. The evolution of performance was observed under identical conditions. By comparing the two models in this controlled environment, this experiment aims to determine whether the selected dataset is sufficiently informative for sex prediction and how well the baseline

[2] https://github.com/w4k2/biobank_gender_prediction.

model, initially developed for diabetic retinopathy tasks, adapts to the goal of sex classification. Therefore, this experiment directly addresses **RQ1** and **RQ2**.

Experiment 2 – Transferability Evaluation
The second experiment aims to evaluate the deep learning models in terms of their ability to transfer knowledge in the sex classification task from fundus images. For this purpose, two transferability measures, TransRate and H-Score, are used to compare the classification performance of ResNet50 and RETFound with their respective potential for transfer learning. This evaluation also allows us to determine whether selecting models based on estimated transferability would lead to choosing the one with the highest generalization capability for this specific task. Such an analysis is particularly insightful given the distinct nature of the two models: ResNet50 is a general-purpose architecture pre-trained on ImageNet, while RETFound is dedicated explicitly to fundus image analysis. Due to the relatively low computational cost of the selected transferability metrics, the experiment follows an evaluation protocol: 5 repetitions of 2-fold cross-validation [24] to stabilize the outcomes. The findings from this experiment aim to address **RQ3**.

4.3 Experiment 1 Fine-Tuning of Deep Models

Training and validation losses were registered at all epochs, as shown in Fig. 3. Both ResNet50 and RETFound showed stable learning during the initial epochs. However, from around the fifth epoch, the validation loss began to increase, indicating the beginning of over-fitting. Despite this, training continued until the 10th epoch to assess how both models fared on the full training schedule.

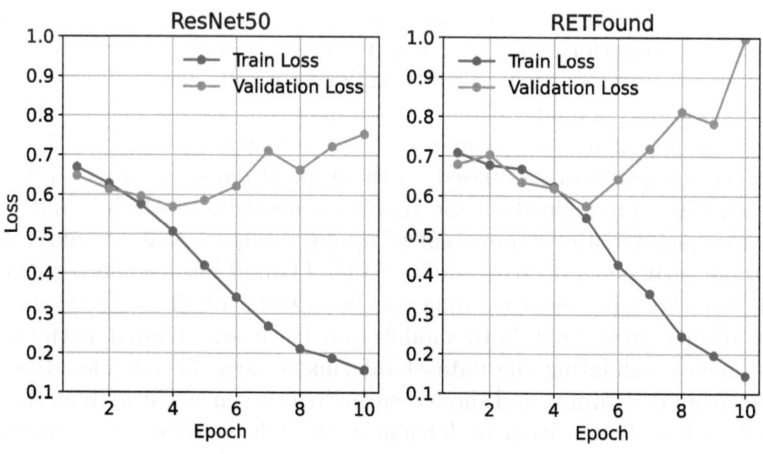

Fig. 3. Training and Validation Loss.

Table 2. Models Performance Metrics. Best metric values are marked in **bold**.

Model	Epoch	*Accuracy*	*Precision*	*Recall*	*F1*
ResNet50	10th (best)	**0.732**	**0.736**	**0.800**	**0.766**
RETFound	5th (best)	0.716	0.725	0.778	0.751
RETFound	10th	0.677	0.675	0.792	0.729

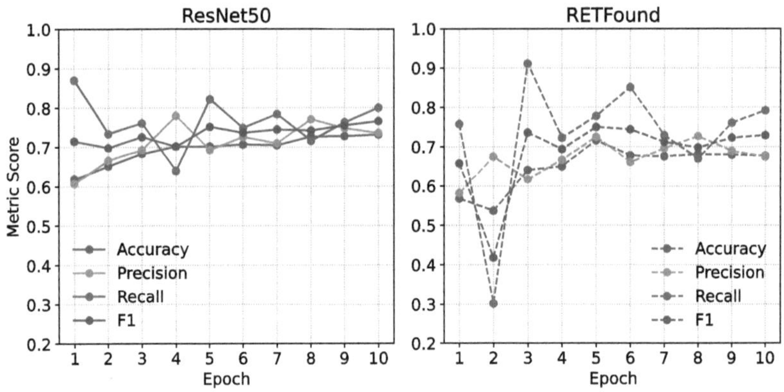

Fig. 4. Fine-Tuning metrics score per epoch.

Classification metrics were calculated at each epoch to monitor the quality of the learned representations. The full representation of the metric values for each epoch can be seen in Fig. 4. The best model performance results were summarized in Table 2. ResNet50 achieved the highest performance in the last epoch, slightly outperforming RETFound in all metrics. On the other hand, RETFound achieved the best performance earlier, in the fifth epoch, but its metrics dropped later, further confirming early over-fitting. These results can be surprising, given that RETFound is a model dedicated to analyzing fundus images and would probably, in most cases, be the first choice of researchers and practitioners facing pattern recognition tasks based on this type of data. Contrary to intuition, it is ResNet50 – pre-trained on the ImageNet dataset, which does not contain data with characteristics reminiscent of fundus images – that not only shows a comparable early generalization ability to RETFound but also demonstrates an upward trend in subsequent training epochs in terms of all measured metrics.

The results prove that both models can learn sex -related patterns from fundus images, validating the dataset informativeness. Meanwhile, RETFound benefited from pretraining and showed earlier convergence. Ultimately, ResNet50 achieved higher classification performance through continued fine-tuning. The feasibility of using these architectures for the sex classification problem was confirmed, and addressing **RQ1** and **RQ2**. While the results do not diminish the value of foundation models like RETFound, they raise important considerations about adopting such models automatically for all fundus image-based tasks.

4.4 Experiment 2 Transferability Evaluation

Table 3 presents both models, TransRate and H-score transferability metrics values, evaluated in their pre-trained states and after additional fine-tuning on the explored *Bialystok PLUS* dataset. It is worth noting that although transferability metrics often show a linear correlation with a model classification performance [13], they should not be considered fully reliable for model selection and must be applied cautiously.

The H-score appears to be relatively uninformative, showing analogous values across each model and matching results after fine-tuning. Interestingly, it still indicates a slight advantage for ResNet50 using only the pre-trained representation.

In the case of TransRate, the discrepancy between the values for the different models is more extensive, and again, one can observe – this time a substantial – advantage in potential knowledge transferability in favor of ResNet50. At the same time, performing fine-tuning for both ResNet50 and RETFound leads to a reduction in estimated transferability. The decrease is particularly noticeable for RETFound and may be related to overfitting and the drop in classification accuracy seen in Experiment 1. Note, however, that ResNet50, which can improve classification quality with successive learning epochs, also exhibits a decrease in transferability in terms of TransRate.

Despite some lack of intuitiveness in the interpretation of the obtained values of transferability measures, TransRate, in this case, could be used to select deep models, pointing clearly to ResNet50, initially offering a slightly higher generalization ability than RETFound, and in subsequent epochs showing the ability to improve the learned representation.

In summary, the results obtained in this experiment cannot be considered definitive, and the need for in-depth research on transferability for foundation and general-purpose models in the sex classification task based on fundus images is evident. At the same time, in the case analyzed of the *Bialystok PLUS* dataset, the TransRate measure can indicate a deep model with potentially better generalizability, answering the **RQ3**. These results may be surprising given the small potential relationship between ImageNet and fundus images.

Table 3. Comparison of average TransRate and H-Score across models.

Model	Transrate	H-Score
ResNet50 (Image-Net)	7.920 ± 0.032	0.998 ± 0.004
ResNet50 (Fine-tuned)	7.141 ± 0.043	1.000 ± 0.000
RETFound (CFP)	5.109 ± 0.076	0.986 ± 0.033
RETFound (Fine-tuned)	3.377 ± 0.044	1.000 ± 0.001

5 Generalizable Insights About Responsible Application of Machine Learning in Healthcare

While ophthalmologists often find it challenging to recognize sex from fundus camera images, deep learning models have achieved high accuracy rates in this task. This suggests that such models can identify subtle differences that are not readily apparent to the human eye, e.g., they can utilize features related to retinal vascularization, the optic disc region, and the macula to differentiate between male and female eyes[3]. Some studies suggest [15] male retinas may have greater vascularization and a darker ring around the optic disc, while the macula might contain more distinctive female features.

Explaining exactly how it is possible to identify a patient's sex or age is still a significant challenge. However, the use of advanced explainable AI mechanisms may bring us closer to understanding, among other things, sex differences in fundus camera images. To better understand the prediction process of the models in this study, the Grad-CAM explainability method was employed. Images in relation to which the models have demonstrated the greatest confidence (maximum classifier support value) were selected. These confident predictions served as examples to visualize the areas of activation most relevant to classification decisions, visible in Fig. 5. Activation maps reveal a noticeable difference between the two models: ResNet50 shows more concentrated and localized focus areas, while RETFound produces more diffuse activations in multiple areas of the retina.

It may also bring us closer to proposing a set of biomarkers useful in this problem. Further challenges will be to propose other biomarkers extracted from fundus camera images that may help diagnose different diseases.

The indicated observation, although already confirmed by other researchers, shows that when sharing imaging data, one should pay close attention to the possibility of leakage of sensitive data. It could be dangerous because of possible privacy violations and can be used, for example, for patient re-identification. Thus, one should consider such mechanisms that would prevent such activity. Perhaps tools inspired by solutions that protect artists' rights to images by their use by generative AI systems to learn to mimic the artistic style. Such methods use poisoning attack techniques, such as *Nightshade* [22], that are designed as an offensive tool to distort feature representations inside generative AI image models or *Glaze* [21].

[3] https://www.vchri.ca/stories/2024/03/20/novel-ai-model-explains-retinal-sex-difference.

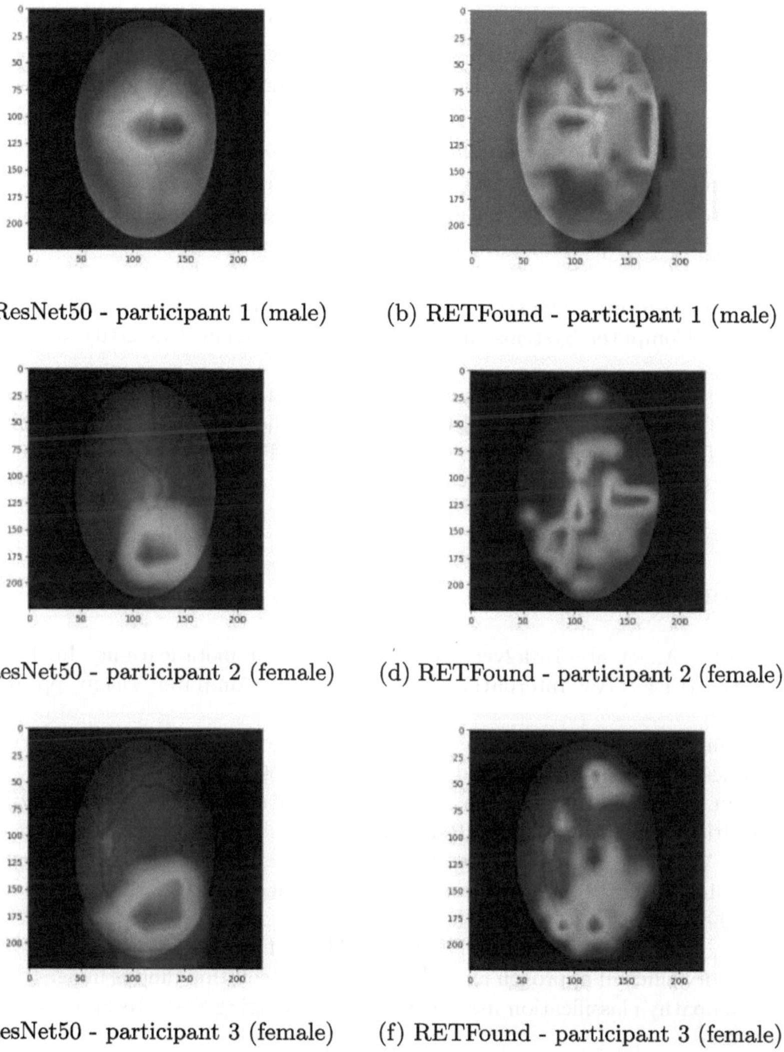

(a) ResNet50 - participant 1 (male)
(b) RETFound - participant 1 (male)
(c) ResNet50 - participant 2 (female)
(d) RETFound - participant 2 (female)
(e) ResNet50 - participant 3 (female)
(f) RETFound - participant 3 (female)

Fig. 5. Grad-CAM visualizations for models.

6 Conclusion

This article aimed to examine how the established deep learning models – both general-purpose and dedicated to analyzing fundus images – handle sex classification task based on a Polish *Bialystok PLUS* dataset.

Both ResNet-50 and RETFound demonstrated the ability to learn meaningful representations for sex prediction from fundus retinal images. Notably, the RETFound model that was developed for diabetic retinopathy detection achieved slightly lower performance after fine-tuning to the sex classification task. This proves that using foundation models for a particular type of data is not always obvious, and fine-tuned models with a more general purpose may perform better (in regards to both generalization ability and knowdledge transfer) even in medical tasks. Overall, the results demonstrate the viability of using deep learning on fundus images for supplementary classification tasks.

Further research will focus on identifying domain-specific biomarkers that will improve model generalization across different populations and discover correlations between patient clinical data and retinal images.

Acknowledgement. The study is partially supported by the statutory fund of the Faculty of Computer Systems and Networks at Wrocław University of Science and Technology.

The study is part of the *Bialystok PLUS* project. The study was supported by the National Centre for Research and Development project no POIR.04.01.04-00-0052/18, supported by the European Regional Development Fund (to KAK – funduscopy imaging), and statutory funds of the Medical University of Bialystok - data acquisition.

References

1. Achille, A., et al.: Task2vec: task embedding for meta-learning. In: Proceedings of the IEEE/CVF International Conference on Computer Vision, pp. 6430–6439 (2019)
2. Alyoubi, W., et al.: Diabetic retinopathy detection through deep learning techniques: a review. Inform. Med. Unlocked **20**, 100377 (2020)
3. Arun, N., et al.: Assessing the trustworthiness of saliency maps for localizing abnormalities in medical imaging. Radiol.: Artif. Intell. **3**(6), e200267 (2021)
4. Bao, Y., et al.: An information-theoretic approach to transferability in task transfer learning. In: 2019 IEEE International Conference on Image Processing (ICIP), pp. 2309–2313. IEEE (2019)
5. Butt, M., Awang Iskandar, D., Khan, M.A., Latif, G., Bashar, A.: Medcnet: a memory efficient approach for processing high-resolution fundus images for diabetic retinopathy classification using CNN. Int. J. Imaging Syst. Technol. **35**(2), e70063 (2025)
6. Chen, R.J., et al.: Algorithmic fairness in artificial intelligence for medicine and healthcare. Nat. Biomed. Eng. **7**(6), 719–742 (2023)
7. Chinta, S.V., et al.: AI-driven healthcare: a survey on ensuring fairness and mitigating bias. arXiv preprint arXiv:2407.19655 (2024)
8. Cui, Y., Song, Y., Sun, C., Howard, A., Belongie, S.: Large scale fine-grained categorization and domain-specific transfer learning. In: Proceedings of the IEEE Conference on Computer Vision and Pattern Recognition, pp. 4109–4118 (2018)
9. Deng, J., Dong, W., Socher, R., Li, L.J., Li, K., Fei-Fei, L.: Imagenet: a large-scale hierarchical image database. In: 2009 IEEE Conference on Computer Vision and Pattern Recognition, pp. 248–255. IEEE (2009)
10. Dwivedi, K., Roig, G.: Representation similarity analysis for efficient task taxonomy & transfer learning. In: Proceedings of the IEEE/CVF Conference on Computer Vision and Pattern Recognition, pp. 12387–12396 (2019)

11. Gulshan, V., et al.: Development and validation of a deep learning algorithm for detection of diabetic retinopathy in retinal fundus photographs. JAMA **316**(22), 2402–2410 (2016)
12. Hall, W.J., et al.: Implicit racial/ethnic bias among health care professionals and its influence on health care outcomes: a systematic review. Am. J. Public Health **105**(12), e60–e76 (2015)
13. Huang, L.K., Huang, J., Rong, Y., Yang, Q., Wei, Y.: Frustratingly easy transferability estimation. In: International Conference on Machine Learning, pp. 9201–9225. PMLR (2022)
14. Khalifa, M., Albadawy, M.: AI in diagnostic imaging: revolutionising accuracy and efficiency. Comput. Methods Programs Biomed. Update 100146 (2024)
15. Liu, S., Zhao, H., Huang, L., Ma, C., Wang, Q., Liu, L.: Vascular features around the optic disc in familial exudative vitreoretinopathy: findings and their relationship to disease severity. BMC Ophthalmol. **23** (2023). https://doi.org/10.1186/s12886-023-02884-7
16. Maxim, L.D., Niebo, R., Utell, M.J.: Screening tests: a review with examples. Inhalation Toxicol. **26**(13), 811–828 (2014)
17. Nguyen, C., Hassner, T., Seeger, M., Archambeau, C.: Leep: a new measure to evaluate transferability of learned representations. In: International Conference on Machine Learning, pp. 7294–7305. PMLR (2020)
18. Niu, S., Liu, Y., Wang, J., Song, H.: A decade survey of transfer learning (2010–2020). IEEE Trans. Artif. Intell. **1**(2), 151–166 (2021)
19. Scanlon, P.H.: The English national screening programme for diabetic retinopathy 2003–2016. Acta Diabetol. **54**(6), 515–525 (2017)
20. Settles, B.: Active learning literature survey (2009)
21. Shan, S., Cryan, J., Wenger, E., Zheng, H., Hanocka, R., Zhao, B.Y.: Glaze: protecting artists from style mimicry by text-to-image models. In: Proceedings of the 32nd USENIX Conference on Security Symposium, SEC 2023. USENIX Association, USA (2023)
22. Shan, S., Ding, W., Passananti, J., Wu, S., Zheng, H., Zhao, B.Y.: Nightshade: prompt-specific poisoning attacks on text-to-image generative models (2024). https://arxiv.org/abs/2310.13828
23. Song, J., et al.: Depara: deep attribution graph for deep knowledge transferability. In: Proceedings of the IEEE/CVF Conference on Computer Vision and Pattern Recognition, pp. 3922–3930 (2020)
24. Stapor, K., Ksieniewicz, P., García, S., Woźniak, M.: How to design the fair experimental classifier evaluation. Appl. Soft Comput. **104**, 107219 (2021)
25. Ting, D.S.W., et al.: Development and validation of a deep learning system for diabetic retinopathy and related eye diseases using retinal images from multiethnic populations with diabetes. Jama **318**(22), 2211–2223 (2017)
26. Tran, A.T., Nguyen, C.V., Hassner, T.: Transferability and hardness of supervised classification tasks. In: Proceedings of the IEEE/CVF International Conference on Computer Vision, pp. 1395–1405 (2019)
27. Wu, D., Xu, Y., Lu, B.L.: Transfer learning for EEG-based brain-computer interfaces: a review of progress made since 2016. IEEE Trans. Cogn. Dev. Syst. **14**(1), 4–19 (2020)
28. Wu, J., Hu, R., Xiao, Z., Chen, J., Liu, J.: Vision transformer-based recognition of diabetic retinopathy grade. Med. Phys. **48**(12), 7850–7863 (2021)
29. You, K., Liu, Y., Wang, J., Long, M.: Logme: practical assessment of pre-trained models for transfer learning. In: International Conference on Machine Learning, pp. 12133–12143. PMLR (2021)

30. Zamir, A.R., Sax, A., Shen, W., Guibas, L.J., Malik, J., Savarese, S.: Taskonomy: disentangling task transfer learning. In: Proceedings of the IEEE Conference on Computer Vision and Pattern Recognition, pp. 3712–3722 (2018)
31. Zhang, W., Deng, L., Zhang, L., Wu, D.: A survey on negative transfer. IEEE/CAA J. Automatica Sinica **10**(2), 305–329 (2022)
32. Zhou, B., Khosla, A., Lapedriza, A., Oliva, A., Torralba, A.: Learning deep features for discriminative localization. In: Proceedings of the IEEE Conference on Computer Vision and Pattern Recognition, pp. 2921–2929 (2016)
33. Zhou, Y., et al.: A foundation model for generalizable disease detection from retinal images. Nature **622**(7981), 156–163 (2023)

Characterizing Publicly Available Tabular Health Datasets for Responsible Machine Learning

Mariana Oliveira[1,2(✉)] and Carlos Soares[1,2,3]

[1] Faculty of Engineering, University of Porto, Porto, Portugal
mariana.oliveira@fe.up.pt
[2] Artificial Intelligence and Computer Science Laboratory (LIACC), Porto, Portugal
[3] Fraunhofer Portugal AICOS, Porto, Portugal

Abstract. Publicly available datasets play a crucial role in reliable, reproducible and responsible Machine Learning (ML) research and application. However, common benchmark datasets often suffer from data quality and other issues that affect model behavior. Auditing public datasets is, thus, a crucial step in understanding these data, allowing better models to be developed and improving understanding of their results. In this paper, we characterize popular healthcare datasets to illustrate how this can help practitioners select benchmarking data that align with their needs for responsible development of ML models. We conduct our study using 15 popular healthcare benchmarking datasets available on the UCI Machine Learning Repository. To assess their quality, we consider measures of accuracy, completeness and redundancy. To assess their complexity, we consider feature overlap, linearity, neighborhood, network, dimensionality, and class balance measures. We also inspect the datasets for imbalanced representation of different demographic groups. We found several data quality and demographic representation imbalance issues that indicate that careful analysis of public datasets remains needed.

Keywords: Responsible ML · Data auditing · Public healthcare data

1 Introduction

Publicly available datasets play a critical role in the development and dissemination of ML research and application. The lack of access barriers makes these datasets appealing for preliminary testing, but also for transparent sharing of results. This can ensure not only scientific reproducibility, but also accountability and auditability – a key dimension of responsible and trustworthy AI [23].

Responsible ML development also requires robustness to data quality issues, which should be evaluated quantitatively. Auditing data quality is, thus, a crucial step in ML pipelines, especially in applications like healthcare where the potential human impact is high. Several methodologies for data quality assessment have been proposed in the literature [6]. Different methodologies often propose

I. Koprinska et al. (Eds.): ECML PKDD 2025, CCIS 2842, pp. 351–359, 2026.
https://doi.org/10.1007/978-3-032-19105-2_25

different *data quality dimensions* that should be considered, as well as measures to assess them. Recent proposals extend data quality dimensions to consider bias and fairness [31], since this is another key dimension of responsible ML [23].

Data complexity can also increase the difficulty of developing responsible ML solutions. More complex data may require more complex models, which can reduce explainability. Initially proposed for classification problems [19], data complexity measures, such as feature overlap and separability of classes, have been extended to address other tasks and challenges (e.g., [5,26]).

Investigating data quality and complexity using such measures can help to recognize the challenges posed by certain datasets. This can improve understanding of the strengths and limitations of a certain ML approach, leading to more responsible use of ML. Many papers assess dataset quality and other data properties, either as part of data quality assessment and exploration steps in a standard ML pipeline, or to use them as meta-features for meta-learning tasks [2,33]. However, we are unaware of a recent study focusing on the data quality and complexity of publicly available datasets in the healthcare domain.

The UCI Machine Learning repository [15] is one of the most famous in the ML community, hosting over 600 easily downloadable public datasets, 109 of which related to Health and Medicine. Other repositories, such as PhysioNet [17], focus specifically on health data and sometimes require training or authorization before having access to certain datasets.

In this paper, we aim to inspect the quality and characterize some of the most popular "Health and Medicine" datasets currently available in the UCI Machine Learning repository. In Sect. 2, we discuss related work. In Sect. 3, we present the selected datasets and data quality and complexity measures computed. In Sect. 4, we present and discuss our results. We conclude with some insights about responsible application of ML in healthcare in Sect. 5.

2 Related Work

Recently, Longjohn et al. [24] highlighted how data quality issues affect common benchmark datasets, including illustrative examples from the UCI ML repository. Kohli et al. [21] found that most tabular datasets used to benchmark ML approaches are also quite old, potentially affecting results. However, these studies do not provide detailed measures of dataset quality and complexity.

In 2014, Macià & Bernadó-Mansilla [27] evaluated the quality and complexity of datasets available on the UCI ML repository at the time. However, the scope of their work was more general and only 2 of the 15 datasets in this paper were included. We also compute some additional data quality and complexity measures, and investigate the distribution of demographic variables in each dataset.

3 Data and Methods

3.1 Data Quality Measures

Batini et al. [6] suggest considering accuracy, completeness, redundancy, readability, accessibility, consistency, usefulness, and trust as data quality dimen-

Table 1. Data quality measures computed. These are based on the tabular input data quality measures available in Python library *pymdma* [12,13].

accuracy[a]	*rare*: % of rare ($freq < 5\%$) nominal values in cat. variables *outIQR*: % of outliers in num. variables according to the boxplot rule
completeness	*incR*/*incC*: % of incomplete rows/columns *missR*/*missC*: average % of missing values per row/column
redundancy	*dupl*: % of duplicated rows *strCorr*: % of num. variable pairs with absolute correlation above 0.5 *corr*: average and standard deviation of correlation values

[a] While rare values may be accurate, they should be checked for potential errors.

sions. Each dimension may be quantitatively assessed using one or more measures. When working with public datasets, some dimensions can be easily and accurately assessed (e.g., calculating the percentage of null values as a measure of *completeness*); others, such as timeliness may not apply.

Many software tools for data quality assessment exist [11], with some focusing specifically on the healthcare domain [34]. We based our work on the Python library ***pymdma***: multimodal data measures for auditing real and synthetic datasets [12,13]. Using the *R* language, we re-implemented some of the tabular input data quality measures described in [4], with some modifications. A list of the measures we computed can be found in Table 1.

Data may also be affected by different types of bias [31], which can be viewed as affecting data quality. In this study, we investigate the imbalance in representation of different demographic groups in the datasets. Being aware of imbalanced representation in data is a step towards being able to properly assess and mitigate bias that may contribute to a lack of fairness in an ML solution.

3.2 Data Complexity Measures

Lorena et al. [25] describe in detail the classification complexity measures in Table 2, which were defined so that higher values indicates higher complexity.[1] We computed these measures using the implementation available in *R* package ***ECoL*** [16,25,26]. The measures can only be computed for complete datasets, and categorical variables are internally binarized. Before calculating them, we pre-processed the datasets by excluding any feature with more than 20% missing values, and any categorical feature with more than 50 unique nominal values.

All code needed to reproduce this study is available on Github.[2]

3.3 Datasets

Fifteen datasets were selected from the UCI Machine Learning Repository [15]. Filtering by subject area "Health and Medicine" and data type "Multivariate" or

[1] The exception was the entropy of class proportions (*B1*) where a higher value corresponded to a more balanced (assumed to be simpler) problem. Here, we will take the complement of that measure so that a high value indicates high complexity.

[2] https://github.com/mrfoliveira/Characterizing-public-healthcare-data-RHCML25.

Table 2. Complexity measures computed. These measures are described in [25] and available in *R* package *ECoL* [16,25,26].

feature-based	$F1/F1v$ Fisher's discriminant ratio, and its directional-vector $F2$: overlapping of the per-class bounding boxes $F3/F4$: maximum individual/collective, feature efficiency
linearity	$L1$: distance of erroneous instances to a linear classifier $L2$: training error of a linear classifier $L3$: nonlinearity of a linear classifier
neighborhood	$N1$: fraction of points lying on the class boundary $N2$: average intra/inter class nearest neighbor distances $N3$: leave-one-out error rate of the 1-NN algorithm $N4$: nonlinearity of the 1-NN classifier $T1$: fraction of maximum covering spheres on data LSC: local-Set cardinality
network	$Density$: density of network $ClsCoef$: clustering Coefficient $Hubs$: hub score
dimensionality	$T2$: number of samples per dimension $T3$: intrinsic dimensionality per number of examples $T4$: intrinsic dimensionality proportion
class label balance	$B1$: entropy of class proportions $B2$: multi-class imbalance ratio

"Tabular", we considered the top 15 datasets in terms of number of views[3] that also met the conditions detailed next.

Datasets were only considered if they: were available for download through the *R* package ***ucimlrepo*** [3]; were not derived from others already included; had 100 or more instances, a single variable tagged as target, and at least one demographic variable identified in the metadata. Variables tagged with the role "ID" or "Other" in the metadata and those with a single unique value were removed from the datasets and excluded from this analysis. Demographic variables in the data represent potentially sensitive information regarding age (A), gender (G), sex (S), race (R), sexual orientation (SO), education level (EL) and income (I). The datasets were all mainly geared towards classification, though some include variables that could potentially be used as targets for a regression task. The basic data characteristics after these exclusions can be found in Table 3.

We found some issues with the metadata of some of the selected datasets, related to the role and type of variables included, and missing values encoding (details available in supplementary material on Github).

4 Results and Discussion

Results are shown in Figs. 1 and 2. In both figures, datasets with similar scores appear together after hierarchical clustering using Euclidian distance.

[3] The number of views of the selected datasets ranged between 27.24k and 790.87k.

In Fig. 1, we can see that 8 of the datasets had no missing values. Only 6 of the datasets show a meaningful percentage of numeric outliers and/or rare nominal values. Dataset *D9* had the highest redundancy, with a rather high percentage of duplicate values; it is joined by dataset *D3* as the only two datasets with at least 10% of their feature pairs showing a strong correlation.

Table 3. Basic characteristics of the datasets, including the number of columns excluded for (a) having role "Other" or "ID", or (b) having a single unique value. Note that the target also did not count towards the categorical features total.

ID	Name	#Class	#Inst.	#Cols.	Feats.	#Num.	#Cat.	#Dem.	Dem.	Excl.(a)	(b)
D1	National Health and Nutrition Health Survey 2013–2014 (NHANES) Age Prediction Subset [29]	2	2.28k	8	Mixed	6	1	2	A, G	2	–
D2	AIDS Clinical Trials Group Study 175 [18]	2	2.14k	23	Mixed	12	10	4	A, G, R, SO	1	1
D3	ILPD (Indian Liver Patient Dataset) [32]	2	583	11	Mixed	9	1	2	A, G	–	–
D4	CDC Diabetes Health Indicators [8]	2	254k	22	Mixed	7	14	4	A, EL, I, S	1	–
D5	Heart Failure Clinical Records [9]	2	299	13	Mixed	7	5	2	A, S	–	–
D6	Breast Cancer [37]	2	286	10	Mixed	1	8	1	A	–	–
D7	Differentiated Thyroid Cancer Recurrence [7]	2	383	17	Mixed	1	15	2	A, G	–	–
D8	Glioma Grading Clinical and Mutation Features [36]	2	839	24	Mixed	1	22	3	A, G, R	1	–
D9	Maternal Health Risk [1]	3	1k	7	Num.	6	0	1	A	–	–
D10	Cirrhosis Patient Survival Prediction [14]	3	418	18	Mixed	10	7	2	A, S	2	–
D11	Diabetes 130-US Hospitals for Years 1999–2008 [35]	3	102k	46	Mixed	8	37	3	A, G, R	2	2
D12	HCV data [22]	5	615	13	Mixed	11	1	2	A, S	1	–
D13	Heart Disease [20]	5	303	14	Mixed	6	7	2	A, S	–	–
D14	Estimation of Obesity Levels Based On Eating Habits and Physical Condition [30]	7	2.1k	17	Mixed	8	8	2	A, G	–	–
D15	National Poll on Healthy Aging (NPHA) [28]	3	714	14	Cat.	0	13	3	A, G, R	–	1

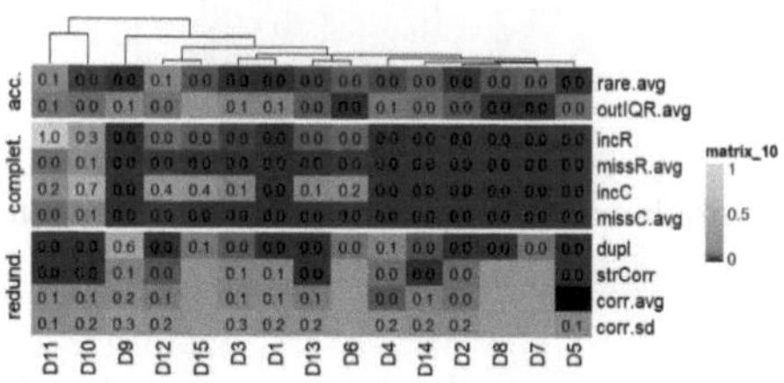

Fig. 1. Quality measures computed for the chosen datasets.

In Fig. 2, we can see the target variable is quite balanced in most datasets; with datasets *D4*, *D1*, and *D12* standing out as the most imbalanced. On average, measures related to class balance and feature overlap (except *F1.mean*) present the highest variance across datasets, followed by the variance of neighborhood measures[4]. For the latter two dimensions, it is possible to find datasets with very low (values close to 0) and very high complexity (values close to 1) according to different measures. The values for linearity show the least variance and relatively low values which would indicate less complexity.

[4] Note that, due to computational resource limitations, it was not possible to compute some complexity measures for the two largest datasets, *D4* and *D11*.

Figure 3 shows the results of inspecting demographic variables in the datasets[5]. Age is the most frequently available variable. The more balanced variables tend to represent gender, while several variables representing race are the most imbalanced. Note that this analysis simply looks at the imbalance in the distribution of demographic variables in the datasets, and does not take into account the class labels within each demographic group.

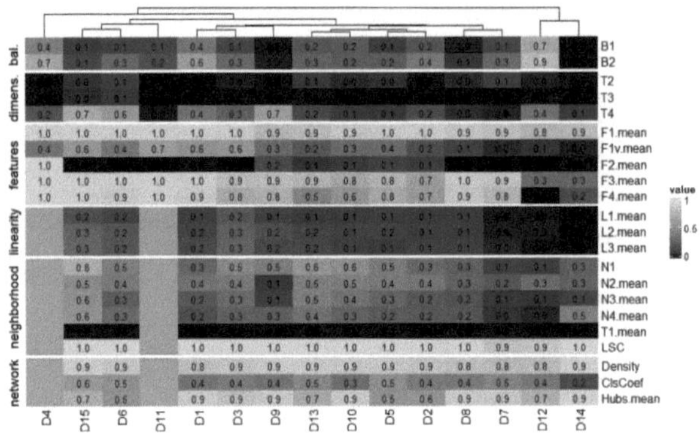

Fig. 2. Complexity of chosen datasets (higher values mean higher complexity).

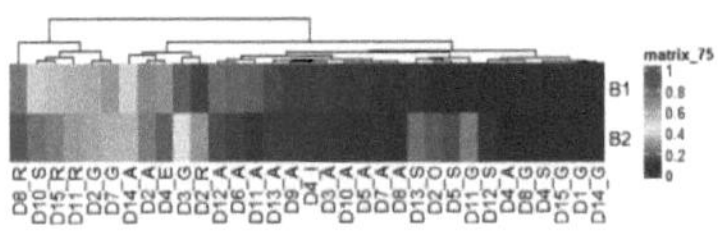

Fig. 3. Demographic imbalance measures (higher values mean greater imbalance).

Limitations. Data quality issues and pre-processing decisions (e.g., about how to encode nominal variables with inherent order) may have somewhat distorted certain measures, especially those relating to complexity as both incomplete features and instances had to be discarded.

5 Generalizable Insights About Responsible Application of Machine Learning in Healthcare

This work is a step towards better understanding of publicly available benchmarking datasets in the healthcare domain through available data quality and complexity assessment tools. We provide results that may help practitioners choose benchmark datasets that align with their responsible ML research goals.

[5] Numeric variables were discretized to keep consistency with the measures calculated for categorical variables; we used 5 equal-width bins.

Robustness and fairness are two key dimensions of responsible ML [23]; selecting appropriate datasets can help when checking that ML solutions follow these principles. A researcher might select a complex dataset with data quality issues to test the robustness of an approach to issues that commonly affect real-world health datasets. Detecting and mitigating bias is especially important in the healthcare domain where it can lead to differing patient outcomes across different demographic groups [10]. Thus, a researcher might select one of the benchmark datasets that we found to have imbalanced demographic representation (e.g., the Glioma Grading dataset) to test the fairness of an approach.

Using public data can support robust, fair and auditable ML development. However, we also found several metadata and other unreported issues in the datasets that indicate that careful analysis of public datasets remains needed.

Future work could extend this study to: include (a) a broader sample of healthcare datasets; (b) more measures of data quality since some dimensions, like trust, were not assessed; and (c) additional measures related to responsible and trustworthy AI (e.g., relating to data privacy); and explore how class labels and data quality relate to protected features, potentially impacting fairness.

Acknowledgments. This work was partially funded by project AISym4Med (101095387). AISym4Med is funded by the European Union under the Horizon Europe Framework Programme Grant Agreement N°: 101095387. Views and opinions expressed are however those of the author(s) only and do not necessarily reflect those of the European Union or European Commission. Neither the European Union nor the European Health and Digital Executive Agency can be held responsible for them.

Disclosure of Interests. The authors have no competing interests to declare that are relevant to the content of this article.

References

1. Ahmed, M.: Maternal health risk (2020). https://doi.org/10.24432/C5DP5D
2. Alcobaça, E., Siqueira, F., Rivolli, A., Garcia, L.P., Oliva, J.T., De Carvalho, A.C.: MFE: towards reproducible meta-feature extraction. J. Mach. Learn. Res. **21**(111), 1–5 (2020)
3. Balamuta, J.J., Truong, P.: Ucimlrepo: explore UCI ML repository datasets (2024)
4. Barandas, M.: Input validation. https://pymdma.readthedocs.io/en/v0.1.9/tabular/input_val/
5. Barella, V.H., Garcia, L.P.F., de Souto, M.C.P., Lorena, A.C., de Carvalho, A.C.P.L.F.: Assessing the data complexity of imbalanced datasets. Inf. Sci. **553**, 83–109 (2021)
6. Batini, C., Scannapieco, M.: Data and Information Quality: Dimensions, Principles and Techniques. Data-Centric Systems and Applications (2016)
7. Borzooei, S., Briganti, G., Golparian, M., Lechien, J.R., Tarokhian, A.: Machine learning for risk stratification of thyroid cancer patients. Eur. Arch. Oto-Rhino-Laryngol. **281**(4), 2095–2104 (2024)
8. CDC: Diabetes Health Indicators (2017). https://doi.org/10.24432/C53919
9. Chicco, D., Jurman, G.: heart failure clinical records (2020). https://doi.org/10.24432/C5Z89R

10. Chinta, S.V., et al.: AI-driven healthcare: a review on ensuring fairness and mitigating bias. PLOS Digit. Health **4**(5), e0000864 (2025)
11. Ehrlinger, L., Wöß, W.: A survey of data quality measurement and monitoring tools. Front. Big Data **5**, 850611 (2022)
12. Façoco, I.S., et al.: pyMDMA: multimodal data metrics for auditing real and synthetic datasets. SoftwareX **31**, 102256 (2025)
13. Façoco, I.S., Matias, P., Rebelo, J.: Fraunhoferportugal/pymdma: patch version 0.1.9. Zenodo (2025). https://doi.org/10.5281/ZENODO.15064792
14. Fleming, T.R., Harrington, D.P.: Counting Processes and Survival Analysis. Wiley (2013)
15. Frank, A.: UCI machine learning repository (2010). http://archive.ics.uci.edu/ml
16. Garcia, L., Lorena, A.: ECoL: complexity measures for supervised problems (2019)
17. Goldberger, A.L., et al.: PhysioBank, PhysioToolkit, and PhysioNet: components of a new research resource for complex physiologic signals. Circulation **101**(23), e215–e220 (2000)
18. Hammer, S.M., et al.: A trial comparing nucleoside monotherapy with combination therapy in HIV-infected adults with A critical comparative study of liver patients from USA and INDIA4 cell counts from 200 to 500 per cubic millimeter. N. Engl. J. Med. **335**(15), 1081–1090 (1996)
19. Ho, T.K., Basu, M.: Complexity measures of supervised classification problems. IEEE Trans. Pattern Anal. Mach. Intell. **24**(3), 289–300 (2002)
20. Janosi, A., Steinbrunn, W., Pfisterer, M., Detrano, R.: Heart disease (1989). https://doi.org/10.24432/C52P4X
21. Kohli, R., Feurer, M., Eggensperger, K., Bischl, B., Hutter, F.: Towards quantifying the effect of datasets for benchmarking. In: ICLR 2024 Workshop on Data-centric Machine Learning Research (DMLR) (2024)
22. Lichtinghagen, R., Klawonn, F., Hoffmann, G.: HCV data (2020). https://doi.org/10.24432/C5D612
23. Liu, H., et al.: Trustworthy AI. ACM Trans. Intell. Syst. Technol. **14**(1), 1–59 (2023)
24. Longjohn, R., Kelly, M., Singh, S., Smyth, P.: Benchmark data repositories for better benchmarking. Adv. Neural. Inf. Process. Syst. **37**, 86435–86457 (2024)
25. Lorena, A.C., Garcia, L.P., Lehmann, J., Souto, M.C., Ho, T.K.: A survey on measuring classification complexity. ACM Comput. Surv. (CSUR) **52**(5), 1–34 (2019)
26. Lorena, A.C., Maciel, A.I., de Miranda, P.B., Costa, I.G., Prudêncio, R.B.: Data complexity meta-features for regression problems. Mach. Learn. **107**, 209–246 (2018)
27. Macià, N., Bernadó-Mansilla, E.: Towards UCI+. Inf. Sci. **261**, 237–262 (2014)
28. Malani, P.N., Kullgren, J., Solway, E.: National poll on healthy aging (NPHA), [USA], April 2017 (2019). https://doi.org/10.3886/ICPSR37305.V1
29. National Center For Health Statistics (NCHS) At The Centers For Disease Control And Prevention (CDC): National Health and Nutrition Health Survey 2013-2014 (NHANES) Age Prediction Subset (2019).https://doi.org/10.24432/C5BS66
30. Palechor, F.M., De la Hoz Manotas, A.: Dataset for estimation of obesity levels based on eating habits and physical condition in individuals from Colombia, Peru and Mexico. Data Br. **25**, 104344 (2019)
31. Quaresmini, C., Primiero, G.: Data quality dimensions for fair AI. In: Proceedings of the 2nd Workshop on Fairness and Bias in AI Co-located with ECAI (2024)
32. Ramana, B.V., Babu, M.S.P., Venkateswarlu, N.B.: A critical comparative study of liver patients from USA and India: an exploratory analysis. IJCSI **9**(3), 506 (2012)

33. Rivolli, A., Garcia, L.P., Soares, C., Vanschoren, J., De Carvalho, A.C.: Meta-features for meta-learning. Knowl.-Based Syst. **240**, 108101 (2022)
34. Sánchez, R.Á., Iraola, A.B., Unanue, G.E., Carlin, P.: TAQIH, a tool for tabular data quality assessment and improvement in the context of health data. Comput. Methods Programs Biomed. **181**, 104824 (2019)
35. Strack, B., et al.: Impact of HbA1c measurement on hospital readmission rates: analysis of 70,000 clinical database patient records. Biomed. Res. Int. **2014**(1), 781670 (2014)
36. Tasci, E., Zhuge, Y., Kaur, H., Camphausen, K., Krauze, A.V.: Hierarchical voting-based feature selection and ensemble learning model scheme for glioma grading with clinical and molecular characteristics. Int. J. Mol. Sci. **23**(22), 14155 (2022)
37. Zwitter, M., Soklic, M.: Breast cancer (1988). https://doi.org/10.24432/C51P4M

Workshop for Explainable AI in Time Series and Data Streams (TEMPXAI 2025)

Workshop for Explainable AI in Time Series and Data Streams (TempXAI)

The TempXAI workshop focuses on exploring the crucial intersection of Explainable AI (XAI) and the challenges posed by time series and data streams. Our primary objectives include understanding dynamic interpretability, delving into techniques that offer transparent insights into time-evolving data, and providing a better understanding of machine learning models in dynamic environments. We aim to advance incremental explainability by investigating methods that ensure interpretability remains effective as models adapt to changing data over time or methods that are able to explain these changes. Moreover, we seek to promote real-time decision-making by exploring applications of XAI in real-time decision-making scenarios, addressing the need for interpretable models in time-sensitive contexts. The workshop also aims to share practical insights by encouraging the sharing of novel XAI tools that are specific to time series and data streams, in addition to case studies and practical implementations in employing interpretable machine learning for time series and data streams.

We would like to thank all of the authors who submitted papers, as well as everybody who attended the workshop.

We also would like to thank the program committee members for their invaluable reviewing efforts.

This workshop has been supported by the Federal Ministry of Education and Research of Germany and the state of North Rhine-Westphalia as part of the Lamarr Institute for Machine Learning and Artificial Intelligence.

October 2025

Matthias Jakobs
Amal Saadallah
Zahraa S. Abdallah
Panagiotis Papapetrou
George Tzagkarakis

Organization

Program Chairs

Matthias Jakobs	TU Dortmund University, Germany
Amal Saadallah	TU Dortmund University, Germany
Zahraa S. Abdallah	University of Bristol, UK
Panagiotis Papapetrou	Stockholm University, Sweden
George Tzagkarakis	FORTH-ICS, Greece

Program Committee

André Artelt	Bielefeld University, Germany
Sebastian Buschjäger	TU Dortmund University, Germany
Cèsar Ferri	Universitat Politècnica València, Spain
Raphael Fischer	TU Dortmund University, Germany
Udo Schlegel	LMU Munich, Germany
Maja Schneider	TU Munich, Germany
Grigoris Tsagkatakis	ICS-FORTH, Greece
Valerie Vaquet	CITEC, Bielefeld University, Germany
Chrysostomos Zeginis	ICS-FORTH, Greece

Towards Explainable Deep Clustering for Time Series Data

Udo Schlegel[1,2(✉)], Gabriel Marques Tavares[1,2], and Thomas Seidl[1,2]

[1] LMU Munich, Munich, Germany
udo.schlegel@lmu.de
[2] Munich Center for Machine Learning (MCML), Munich, Germany

Abstract. Deep clustering enables uncovering hidden patterns and groups in complex time series data. Yet, its opaque decision-making limits its use in safety-critical settings. This review survey offers a structured overview of explainable deep clustering for time series, collecting current methods and their real-world applications. We discuss and compare peer-reviewed and preprint papers through application domains across healthcare, finance, IoT, and climate science. Our analysis reveals that most work relies on autoencoder and attention architectures, with limited support for streaming, irregularly sampled, or privacy-preserved series, and interpretability is still primarily treated as an add-on and not a goal. To push the field forward, we outline six research opportunities: (1) combining complex networks with built-in interpretability; (2) setting up clear, faithfulness-focused evaluation metrics for unsupervised explanations; (3) building explainers that scale to large data and adapt to live data streams; (4) crafting explanations tailored to specific domains; (5) adding human-in-the-loop methods that refine clusters and explanations together; and (6) improving our understanding of how time series clustering models work internally. By making interpretability a primary design goal rather than an afterthought, we propose the groundwork for the next generation of trustworthy deep clustering time series analytics.

Keywords: Explainable AI · Deep Clustering · Time Series Data

1 Introduction and Motivation

Time series clustering is an unsupervised learning task that groups similar temporal sequences without prior labels. Traditional approaches often rely on distance measures (e.g., dynamic time warping or Euclidean distance) and yield clusters based on raw time series similarity. However, these methods struggle with high-dimensional, noisy, or complex time series data. In recent years, deep learning-based clustering has emerged to tackle these challenges. Deep clustering methods use neural networks (such as autoencoders, RNNs, or transformers) to learn compressed representations (embeddings) of time series, and then perform clustering in the latent space or even include clustering in the learning process. This can capture non-linear temporal patterns and improve clustering

I. Koprinska et al. (Eds.): ECML PKDD 2025, CCIS 2842, pp. 365–379, 2026.
https://doi.org/10.1007/978-3-032-19105-2_26

quality compared to classical techniques [26]. For example, methods such as Deep Embedded Clustering (DEC) [39] and its variants have been extended to time series by combining reconstruction losses with clustering objectives [1]. These deep clustering models have achieved notable success in grouping time series data (e.g., sensor readings, human activity signals) into meaningful clusters [1].

Despite improved performance, a key limitation is the black-box nature of deep models. The latent features learned by deep networks are often not easily interpretable, making it hard to understand why certain time series samples are clustered together [6]. In critical domains (healthcare, finance), human experts need to comprehend the clustering results and trust the model's behavior to apply these to their use cases. As Bonifati et al. [6] note, many systems "maximize effectiveness... but fail to guarantee the interpretability of the results," which hinders their use in real-world scenarios where human oversight is required. This has led to growing interest in Explainable Deep Clustering for Time Series, i.e., methods that integrate explainability into the deep clustering pipeline.

This paper provides a structured overview, review, and research opportunities for explainable deep clustering of time series data. We collected and systematised peer-reviewed and high-quality preprint studies over the last few years. Our comparison table and cross-domain case studies, covering healthcare, finance, IoT, and climate science, reveal that today's landscape remains dominated by autoencoder-plus-attention designs, rarely addresses streaming, privacy-preserved, or highly irregular data, and targets explainability as an add-on. Building on these observations, we articulate six research opportunities to highlight important directions: (1) coupling complex models with intrinsic interpretability; (2) defining faithfulness-centred evaluation metrics for unsupervised explanations; (3) creating explainers that evolve with live data; (4) tailoring explanations to domain semantics; (5) integrating human-in-the-loop refinement; and (6) advancing mechanistic interpretability of learned temporal features.

2 Explainability in Deep Learning

Explainable AI refers to techniques that make the decisions of complex models understandable to humans. In supervised learning (classification/regression), popular XAI methods include feature attribution (e.g., LIME [28], SHAP [20]), which assigns importance scores to input features, attention mechanisms that highlight influential parts of the input, prototype- or example-based explanations that show representative cases, and visualizations of internal model workings [36]. However, time series pose particular challenges for explainability [29]. Time series inputs (especially multivariate sequences) are often high-dimensional and not immediately interpretable (unlike images or text) [36]. Only limited XAI research has focused on time series data compared to vision or NLP [38]. Typical explanation strategies for time series include identifying important time segments or sensor channels, transforming data into interpretable domains (e.g., frequency spectra), or finding prototypical patterns [36].

For unsupervised learning, such as clustering, explainability is even more challenging. There are no pre-defined class labels or ground-truth explanations for clusters, and clusters may reflect subtle patterns in the data [27,41]. The goal of explainable clustering is to describe or justify why a cluster exists – e.g., by summarizing common patterns in a cluster, or highlighting what differentiates one cluster from others [14]. Previous works in explainable cluster analysis have proposed taxonomies of techniques: (1) Pre-clustering explainability (data transformations to make clustering more interpretable), (2) In-clustering explainability (algorithms that build interpretability into the clustering process), and (3) Post-hoc explainability (analyzing the results after clustering to extract explanations) [14]. In the context of deep clustering, all three approaches are relevant. For further information on deep clustering approaches and methods, we refer to Ren et al. [27] and Zhou et al. [41]. Next, we examine methods that specifically combine deep learning for time series clustering with explainability techniques or mention these during the approach description.

3 Combining XAI with Deep Clustering for Time Series

Achieving explainability in deep time series clustering has been approached from multiple angles. Below, we survey representative methods, roughly grouped by the explainability strategy they employ or mention in their description.

3.1 Attention-Based Approaches

One way to introduce interpretability is by using attention mechanisms in the clustering model. Attention layers can weigh the importance of different time steps or features, effectively pointing to which parts of the time series are most influential in determining the cluster assignment. Ienco and Interdonato [15] propose DeTSEC (Deep Time Series Embedding Clustering) as an example of this approach. DeTSEC first utilizes a gated recurrent autoencoder with an attention mechanism to generate a preliminary embedding for each multivariate time series. The attention weights highlight subsequences that the network deems important. In a second stage, DeTSEC refines the embeddings with a clustering-oriented loss to improve cluster separation. By inspecting the learned attention weights, one can identify which time points or sensors contributed most to a series' embedding and cluster, providing a form of explanation for the clustering. For instance, if a certain peak or pattern in the time series consistently gets high attention for all members of a cluster, that pattern can be presented as a distinguishing feature of that cluster. Attention-based deep clustering has demonstrated success on varied time series data (e.g., speech signals and human activity data), outperforming other methods while offering some interpretability of the learned representation. Attention is not a perfect explanation (it indicates correlation rather than causation), but it serves as an intrinsic interpretability tool in many deep models using an attention mechanism [4].

Beyond RNN-based attention, emerging work uses transformer architectures for time series classification [36], which inherently utilize multi-head self-attention and can also be applied to clustering [25]. While primarily aimed at improving accuracy, these models can also be probed for explainability: the attention scores over time steps or variables can be visualized to see what the model "attended" to when forming clusters [4]. For example, a transformer-based clustering model might attend to seasonal spikes or anomalies in a time series that drive clustering for a specific cluster. However, research explicitly combining transformer time series clustering with human-friendly explanations is still nascent (most current transformer models focus on classification or forecasting) [36].

Based on the taxonomy proposed by Hu et al. [14], we argue that attention-based approaches predominantly fall within the category of in-clustering explanations. This is because, at each step of the clustering process, attention weights inherently provide a means of interpretation: they quantify the relative importance of input features or tokens, thereby yielding explanations that are both immediate and automatically generated as part of the model's operation, rather than requiring a separate post-hoc procedure.

3.2 Prototype and Example-Based Explanations

Another line of research provides explanations by prototypes or examples for learned pattern representations at each cluster. The idea is to characterize clusters in terms of human-understandable exemplars or features. One prominent approach is the use of shapelets, originally developed for classification, which are short representative subsequences that are maximally characteristic of a class [40]. Shapelets have long been used in time series classification as interpretable features [36], and more recently have been applied to clustering. For example, El Amouri et al. [8] introduce Constrained DTW-Preserving Shapelets (CDPS) for explainable time series clustering. In CDPS, the model learns a set of shapelet patterns that capture the variability in the dataset while approximately preserving Dynamic Time Warping distances between series [8]. The learned shapelets form a new feature space for clustering, which is inherently interpretable: each dimension corresponds to the DTW similarity of a time series to a certain shapelet (a meaningful pattern), forming a new similarity vector [8]. After clustering in this space, they propose Shapelet Cluster Explanation (SCE) methods that output a small set of shapelets being most descriptive for time series samples in the cluster, summarizing inherent patterns [8]. In essence, a cluster can be explained by saying "time series in this group all contain pattern A and lack pattern B," where A and B are actual subsequences (such as a particular waveform shape) that can be visualized. This approach yields explanations that are domain-meaningful (experts can interpret the shapelet patterns using their domain knowledge). A limitation is that shapelet-based methods require extensive search or complex training, but they provide a clear link between cluster assignment and understandable raw data patterns.

Prototype-based explanations need not be limited to subsequences. Some deep clustering methods present whole-series prototypes or representative examples for each cluster. A simple form is to identify medoids or centroids in the original space – e.g., select one actual time series per cluster that is closest to the cluster center. This selected series can act as a prototype that "stands for" the cluster. More sophisticated is learning prototypes through the model itself. For instance, autoencoder clustering models can be used to decode cluster centroids from the latent space back into the time domain. A variational autoencoder (VAE) with a clustering prior (like a Gaussian mixture in latent space [7]) can generate a prototype time series from each cluster's latent mean. These prototype series can then be examined by humans (or matched to real examples) for interpretation. Such an approach was implicitly used by VAE+SOM-based models, where each neuron on the self-organizing map corresponded to a prototype time series pattern in the input space [10]. Generally, prototype and exemplar strategies enhance explainability by grounding clusters in familiar examples or patterns rather than abstract coordinates.

Based on the taxonomy by Hu et al. [14], we argue that prototype- and example-based approaches heavily depend on the applied method to which category these correspond. CDPS [8] fits the pre-clustering explainability as the approach already transforms the space into a new feature space using the shapelets. However, VAE+SOM-based models such as Fortuin et al. [10] focus on changing the internal clustering approach by binding every prototype pattern to a neuron, creating a combination of pre-clustering and in-clustering explainability.

3.3 Self-organizing Maps and Topological Interpretability

Integrating interpretable structures into deep clustering architectures is another powerful approach. Self-Organizing Maps (SOMs), a classic neuro-fuzzy method, project high-dimensional data onto a 2D grid of neurons while preserving topological relationships. Several recent works combine SOMs with deep learning to obtain the benefits of both: high clustering performance and an interpretable organization of clusters. Fortuin et al. [10] introduced SOM-VAE, which couples a VAE with a SOM in the latent space to learn discrete representations of time series. The SOM imposes a two-dimensional grid structure on the latent embeddings, so each time series is mapped to a particular neuron (cluster) on a grid. This strongly enhances interpretability, as nearby clusters on the map correspond to similar time series patterns [26]. The grid can be visualized, and one can observe smooth transitions across the map, understanding how clusters relate to each other. Importantly, Fortuin et al. [10] also integrated a Markov transition model on the SOM to capture temporal dynamics (for sequences of series states), providing additional prediction capabilities and explainability in terms of state transition probabilities.

Building on SOM-VAE, Manduchi et al. [23] developed DPSOM and its time series extension T-DPSOM [22]. DPSOM uses a VAE with a probabilistic SOM loss to improve clustering quality without losing the SOM's visualization capability [23]. T-DPSOM further adds an LSTM-based temporal component, allowing not only clustering of multivariate time series but also forecasting in the latent space [22]. A key outcome is that T-DPSOM can produce interpretable visualizations of patient state trajectories on the SOM grid, along with uncertainty estimates [22]. In a healthcare setting (ICU patient monitoring), this means one can cluster patient time series data (e.g., vitals, lab measurements) into prototypical "states" and then track a patient's progression through these states on a 2D map – a very intuitive explanation for clinicians [22]. The SOM-based deep clustering family thus offers an ante-hoc interpretability: the model is inherently structured to be interpretable by design (via the map), rather than explaining after the fact. These methods have demonstrated competitive clustering accuracy on benchmarks (e.g., SOM-VAE outperforms or matches other deep clustering methods on image and medical time series data [10]) while providing a user-friendly view of the clusters.

As already discussed in the previous section, the SOM-based explanations built in an in-clustering explainability and help to generate explanations while clustering. All methods enhance the clustering approach while T-DPSOM [22] builds on SOM-VAE [10].

3.4 Post-hoc Interpretation and Visualization

In addition to building interpretability into models, researchers have explored post-hoc explainability techniques applied to deep clustering results. One common strategy is to treat the cluster labels (obtained from the deep model) as pseudo-targets and train an auxiliary interpretable model to predict them. For example, one can fit a decision tree classifier that takes a time series (or engineered features of it) as input and predicts its cluster. The decision tree's splits then reveal which features or thresholds distinguish the clusters. This idea is used in the CLAMP framework (Cluster Analysis with Multidimensional Prototypes) and related work, which derives rule-based explanations for clusters by supervised learning on the cluster assignments [5]. For time series, these features might be domain-specific (e.g., average heart rate, volatility of a financial time series, seasonal peak value). The decision rules provide an intelligible summary (e.g., "Cluster 1 consists of series where mean value $>$ X and frequency of spikes $<$ Y"). A caution is that such post-hoc models are approximations of the deep model's behavior and may not capture all nuances in a trustworthy setting. Still, they offer an entry- and high-level understanding.

Model-agnostic explainers like LIME [28] and SHAP [20] can also be adapted for clustering. One approach is to use a similarity metric: given a target series and its cluster label, generate perturbations of that series, see how the clustering assignment changes (perhaps by feeding through the deep model), and then fit a local linear model. This would yield local feature importance for that single series's clustering outcome. For instance, one could apply SHAP to an autoencoder+cluster network by inputting time series features (such as summary statistics or time-sampled points) to get Shapley values indicating which features "pushed" the series toward its cluster. While this has been explored less in the literature, it is a promising direction for instance-level explanations of cluster membership. In time series, one might interpret a positive SHAP value for a particular time segment or sensor reading as evidence that aspect of the series is characteristic of the cluster.

Visualization remains a powerful tool for explaining clustering results. With deep models, one can visualize the learned embedding space to see the cluster structure. For example, applying t-SNE [21] or UMAP [24] on the latent representations from a deep model can produce a 2D plot where clusters form distinct groups [26]. Such plots help verify that the model has found a sensible separation and can be presented to end-users for insights (with points potentially colored by known attributes to interpret clusters). Additionally, specific visualization techniques have been devised for time series. One notable method is the Virtual Inspection Layer proposed by Vielhaben et al. [38]. Although aimed at classification, the concept is relevant: they insert a layer that transforms time series into an interpretable domain (like a Fourier spectrum) and then propagate explanation signals (using LRP) to that domain [38]. For clustering, one could imagine a similar approach where the time series are transformed (e.g., to the frequency domain or into a set of summary statistics) within the model, so that any relevance or distance can be explained in terms of those transformed features. Lastly, interactive visualization systems can allow users to explore cluster-wise average series, variance, and identified important segments (for example, highlighting sub-sequences with high attention or high contribution to cluster decisions, similar to attributions in supervised settings [30]). Such tools are increasingly important in domains where analysts need to validate clusters.

Here, as the title already suggests, the main focus of the explanation relies on the post-hoc explainability, either using post-hoc explanation methods or introducing possibilities to enable post-hoc explanations.

To summarize the landscape of methods, Tabel 1 provides a summary of representative deep time-series clustering techniques that incorporate explainability. Each method is characterized by its model type, the explainability mechanism used, and example application domains or datasets.

4 Application Domains

Explainable deep clustering methods have been applied in various domains, where the combination of unsupervised discovery and interpretability is especially valuable, such as healthcare, finance, sensor networks, and others. In this section, we focus on the application domains driving XAI development in time series clustering.

4.1 Healthcare

This is a major area driving XAI for time series. Patient data (vital signs, lab results, EEG signals, etc.) are rich in temporal patterns that clinicians want to cluster into meaningful states or phenotypes [22]. Importantly, these clusters must be interpretable to be clinically and medically useful. For example, ICU patient state clustering has been tackled by T-DPSOM [22] – the model clustered multivariate ICU time series into discrete health states and provided

Table 1. Representative deep clustering methods for time series with explainability, grouped by the interpretable clustering three-stage taxonomy [14]. Method, model type, explanation approach, taxonomy stage, and example domains are shown. (Note: CLAMP is model-agnostic, shown here as an example of post-hoc cluster explanation.)

Method (Year)	Model	Explainability	Stage	Presented Domain
SOM–VAE (2019) [10]	VAE + 2-D SOM	Latent grid; prototype neurons	In-cluster	ICU vitals; MNIST seq.
T-DPSOM (2020) [22]	VAE + LSTM + prob. SOM	Trajectory map; uncertainty	In-cluster	ICU patient states
DeTSEC (2020) [15]	Attentive GRU autoencoder	Attention on key subsequences	In-cluster	Speech, gesture, ECG
Time2Feat (2022) [6]	Feature extractor + DNN	Interpretable domain features	Pre-cluster	18 IoT/activity sets
CDPS Shapelets (2023) [8]	CNN shapelet learner + k-means	Representative subsequences (shapelets)	Pre-cluster	UCR archive
Explain. EEG Clust. (2023) [9]	Autoencoder + k-means	Cluster-specific spectral patterns	Post-hoc	EEG brain states
CLAMP (2022) [5]	Model-agnostic framework	Post-hoc rules and prototypes	Post-hoc	Cyber-security logs

a 2D map visualization of these states. Clinicians could follow a patient's trajectory on the map (e.g., moving from a stable state to a critical state), and the map's topology gave insights into similarity of states [22]. Another example is resting-state EEG clustering in neurological disorders. Ellis et al. [9] clustered EEG recordings from schizophrenia patients into 8 distinct "brain states" using a deep autoencoder with k-means, and found each cluster corresponded to a different level of delta-band activity [9]. By correlating cluster membership with clinical symptoms, and explaining clusters via EEG spectral features (delta power), the study provided an interpretable link between EEG patterns and disease state [9]. More generally in healthcare, explainable clustering helps in phenotype discovery (uncovering subtypes of diseases from time series biosignals) and treatment monitoring, where trust and insight are crucial. Methods like attention-based clustering can highlight which vital sign trends are associated with a given patient cluster (e.g., "Cluster A: patients with sustained high heart rate variability"), and prototype-based methods can present a representative patient trajectory for each cluster. This fosters clinician acceptance as they can verify that clusters make medical sense.

4.2 Finance

Financial time series (stock prices, economic indicators, transaction sequences) are often clustered to identify market regimes or customer behaviors. Here, explainability is needed for regulatory and strategic reasons – analysts must understand why clusters form (e.g., a group of stocks moving together due to an underlying sector trend). While fewer works explicitly focus on deep clustering in finance, the techniques are applicable. For instance, a deep clustering of multivariate stock time series might reveal clusters corresponding to "growth stocks" vs "value stocks," and an attention mechanism could highlight that one cluster's series are driven by certain time periods (e.g., all surged during a specific economic event). In customer analytics (like credit card usage patterns or mobile banking activity over time), clustering can find user segments. Explainable clustering would allow a bank to describe each segment (cluster) in terms of interpretable features – e.g., Cluster X: "high seasonal spending around holidays, then dormancy", whereas Cluster Y: "consistent weekly expenditures with gradual growth." By employing post-hoc methods (like decision trees on summary features such as transaction frequency, volatility, etc.), the bank can communicate these insights clearly. Some recent studies in financial profiling use deep autoencoders for clustering and then apply explainability methods to link clusters to demographic or behavioral features [13], enabling domain experts to validate and act on the clusters.

4.3 IoT and Sensor Networks

In Internet of Things applications, large networks of sensors generate time series data (e.g., smart home energy usage, industrial machine sensor readings, traffic flows). Clustering such data helps identify usage patterns, anomalies, or system states. Explainable deep clustering plays a role in smart energy management, for example, grouping households by electricity usage patterns. An interpretable clustering might find a cluster of homes with "night-peaking" usage vs "daytime-peaking" usage, and XAI methods could highlight which time-of-day features distinguish these clusters. A recent study clustered residential electricity demand time series and emphasized interpretability by using feature selection and rule-based descriptions for each cluster [17]. In industrial IoT, deep clustering might categorize machine states from multivariate sensor logs; explaining these clusters could involve showing prototypical sensor readings or pinpointing which sensor signals (vibration, temperature, etc.) are most indicative of each operational mode. Virtual inspection techniques (like converting sensor time series to frequency spectra) can help domain engineers understand what a cluster represents (e.g., a certain vibration frequency pattern indicating a machine fault) [38]. Overall, in IoT scenarios, explainability ensures that the patterns discovered by unsupervised models translate into actionable insight (for engineers, operators, or consumers).

4.4 Other Domains

Transportation and mobility data have seen deep clustering for pattern mining (e.g., grouping city traffic flow time series) [3]. Here, explaining clusters could involve mapping them to known traffic conditions or events (rush-hour vs off-hour patterns) and using attention to show which intervals (holidays, weekends) influenced the clustering. Environmental science uses time series clustering for things like climate patterns or animal migration sequences; experts demand explanations like "Cluster A corresponds to El Niño years with these temperature fluctuations" [37]. Deep clustering can be combined with feature attribution to tie clusters to physical phenomena. In summary, any field dealing with complex temporal data can benefit from explainable clustering: the deep models provide power to handle nonlinear, high-dimensional sequences, while the explainability component ensures the results are trustworthy to domain experts.

5 Research Opportunities

The convergence of deep learning and explainable clustering for time series is a relatively new but rapidly evolving research area. Tabel 1 contrasted several methods, and here we distill a few comparative observations:

5.1 Model Architectures and Explainability

There is often a trade-off between model complexity and interpretability [12]. Simpler architectures (or those augmented with interpretable components like SOMs [10] or shapelets) provide more straightforward explanations but might sacrifice some clustering accuracy or require more domain input. For instance, prototype-/shapelet-based methods offer very clear explanations (actual data patterns) yet may not capture subtle variations as well as a deep latent feature model. Conversely, deep models like transformers or VAEs can capture rich structure but need additional tools (attention weights, post-hoc analysis) to pry open their reasoning. The community is actively exploring hybrid solutions that achieve both high performance and inherent interpretability – e.g., semi-supervised approaches that use a few labeled examples or constraints to guide clusters towards human-meaningful categories [8]. These can improve both clustering relevance and ease of explanation.

5.2 Quantifying and Evaluating Explanations

Unlike supervised tasks, evaluating explanations for clustering is tricky due to the lack of ground truth. In classification, one can measure if an explanation helps predict the true label; but for clustering, "ground truth" clusters may not exist. Researchers have used proxy metrics – e.g., how well a post-hoc explainable model (like a decision tree) can mimic the deep model's cluster assignments (fidelity) [29], or user studies to evaluate if experts agree that the explanations are meaningful [16]. An important challenge is developing objective metrics for cluster explanation quality [32]. Some works consider the compactness of explanations (e.g., few features or shapelets) and their completeness (ability to approximate the clustering) [33]. The trustworthiness of explanations is also crucial: attention scores or feature attributions need to truly reflect the model's logic (the issue of "attention is not explanation" is debated, and methods to ensure faithfulness are needed) [19,29]. Future research is exploring more effective methods to validate that an explanation for a cluster is not merely an artifact but genuinely relates to why the model grouped those series.

5.3 Scalability and Efficiency

Time series datasets can be large (in the number of dimensions, in the number of series, and in the length of each series). Deep clustering methods themselves can be computationally intensive; adding explainability can extend this. For example, searching for shapelets or training a global surrogate model might not scale easily to millions of time series. Recent works address this by dimensionality reduction (e.g., Time2Feat selecting a small set of features [6]) or by focusing explanations on a subset of important clusters. An open challenge is to create explainable clustering pipelines that remain efficient on big data, possibly by leveraging online learning or distributed computing. Additionally, dynamic time series (streams that evolve) raise questions: clusters may drift over time, so explanations might need to update continuously, incorporating data stream XAI approaches [11]. How to maintain an interpretable model in non-stationary settings is largely unexplored and needs more research.

5.4 Generality and Domain-Specificity

We observe that some explainable clustering methods are domain-focused (e.g., specific techniques for ECG, or special layers for speech data [6]), whereas others are generic [10]. Domain-specific approaches can incorporate expert knowledge (like known meaningful features or patterns) to enhance interpretability – for example, focusing on frequency-domain features for audio signals because they are easier to explain to acousticians [38]. However, too much specialization limits applicability [34]. A continuing challenge is to design frameworks that are general enough to apply to many time series types, yet can ingest domain knowledge when available. This might entail modular designs where a model can plug in a "feature module" for interpretability (such as a Fourier or wavelet transform layer) appropriate to the domain to enhance the interpretable decision-making of models incorporating domain knowledge of experts.

5.5 User Interaction and Human-in-the-Loop

Explaining clusters is ultimately about helping humans make sense of data. There is a growing recognition that explanation is not one-size-fits-all – it should be context-dependent [36]. For instance, a doctor might want a different explanation (emphasizing clinical features) than a data scientist [35]. Tools like CLAMP allow users to adjust which features to consider for explanations or to provide feedback (e.g., "these two clusters should really be one" or "this feature is important, please incorporate it"). Incorporating human feedback into deep clustering (through constraint-learning like must-link/cannot-link constraints [8] or interactive (visual) steering [2]) is an open avenue. It not only improves clustering relevance but also yields explanations aligned with human intuition (since the human helped shape the clusters) [35]. The challenge is balancing human guidance with the model's autonomy to discover unexpected patterns.

5.6 Transparency in Model Components

Beyond explaining the results, another challenge is making the model itself transparent. For example, if a deep clustering uses an LSTM encoder, can we open that LSTM and interpret its units (are certain neurons detecting specific motifs? Similar to detecting LSTM neurons responsible for detecting parentheisis in code [18]). Recent XAI research on interpreting recurrent or convolutional units (e.g., by clustering neuron activation patterns or visualizing filter effects) could be applied here [36]. By understanding what each part of the model learns, we could provide more stable, global explanations (e.g., "this autoencoder's latent dimension 1 corresponds to the overall trend of the series") [31]. Achieving this remains difficult, especially as models become more complex (with hundreds of latent features), but it is a worthwhile goal for explainable deep clustering.

6 Conclusion

In conclusion, explainable deep clustering for time series lies at the intersection of two major trends: The need for unsupervised learning to handle large-scale temporal data and the growing demand for transparent, trustworthy AI. Recent advances, from attention mechanisms and prototype learning to shapelet discovery and post-hoc rule extraction, have begun to make clustering results more interpretable and actionable. Proof-of-concept applications already demonstrate value in domains like healthcare, where clinicians can inspect cluster-driving signals, and IoT, where engineers can trace anomalous device behavior. However, significant challenges remain. Future work should pursue six key directions: (1) combining powerful deep architectures with built-in interpretability, (2) developing faithfulness-focused evaluation metrics for unsupervised explanations, (3) enabling scalable and streaming-capable explanatory clustering, (4) creating domain-aware explanation mechanisms, (5) incorporating human-in-the-loop refinement of clusters and explanations, and (6) improving our mechanistic understanding of model internals. Addressing these challenges will move the field from isolated prototypes toward reliable, explainable clustering systems that can be confidently deployed in real-world decision making.

References

1. Alqahtani, A., Ali, M., Xie, X., Jones, M.W.: Deep time-series clustering: a review. Electronics (2021)
2. Bae, J., Helldin, T., Riveiro, M., Nowaczyk, S., Bouguelia, M.R., Falkman, G.: Interactive clustering: a comprehensive review. ACM Comput. Surv. (2020)
3. Barredo-Arrieta, A., Laña, I., Del Ser, J.: What lies beneath: a note on the explainability of black-box machine learning models for road traffic forecasting. In: IEEE Intelligent Transportation Systems Conference (2019)
4. Bibal, A., et al.: Is attention explanation? An introduction to the debate. In: Annual Meeting of the Association for Computational Linguistics (2022)
5. Bobek, S., Kuk, M., Szelążek, M., Nalepa, G.J.: Enhancing cluster analysis with explainable AI and multidimensional cluster prototypes. IEEE Access (2022)
6. Bonifati, A., Del Buono, F., Guerra, F., Tiano, D.: Time2Feat: learning interpretable representations for multivariate time series clustering. VLDB Endow. (2022)
7. Dilokthanakul, N., et al.: Deep unsupervised clustering with gaussian mixture variational autoencoders. arXiv preprint arXiv:1611.02648 (2016)
8. El Amouri, H., Lampert, T., Gançarski, P., Mallet, C.: Constrained DTW preserving shapelets for explainable time-series clustering. Pattern Recognit. (2023)
9. Ellis, C.A., Miller, R.L., Calhoun, V.D.: A convolutional autoencoder-based explainable clustering approach for resting-state EEG analysis. In: IEEE Engineering in Medicine and Biology Society (2023)
10. Fortuin, V., Hüser, M., Locatello, F., Strathmann, H., Rätsch, G.: SOM-VAE: interpretable discrete representation learning on time series. In: International Conference on Learning Representations (2019)
11. Fumagalli, F., Muschalik, M., Hüllermeier, E., Hammer, B.: Incremental permutation feature importance (iPFI): towards online explanations on data streams. Mach. Learn. (2023)
12. Guidotti, R., Monreale, A., Ruggieri, S., Turini, F., Giannotti, F., Pedreschi, D.: A survey of methods for explaining black box models. ACM Comput. Surv. (2018)
13. Higashi, M., et al.: Decision tree clustering for time series data: an approach for enhanced interpretability and efficiency. In: Pacific Rim International Conference on Artificial Intelligence (2023)
14. Hu, L., Jiang, M., Dong, J., Liu, X., He, Z.: Interpretable Clustering: A Survey. arXiv preprint arXiv:2409.00743 (2024)
15. Ienco, D., Interdonato, R.: Deep multivariate time series embedding clustering via attentive-gated autoencoder. In: Pacific-Asia Conference on Knowledge Discovery and Data Mining (2020)
16. Jeyakumar, J.V., Noor, J., Cheng, Y.H., Garcia, L., Srivastava, M.: How can i explain this to you? An empirical study of deep neural network explanation methods. In: Advances in Neural Information Processing Systems (2020)
17. Kallel, S., Amayri, M., Bouguila, N.: Clustering and interpretability of residential electricity demand profiles. Sensors (2025)
18. Karpathy, A., Johnson, J., Fei-Fei, L.: Visualizing and understanding recurrent networks. arXiv preprint arXiv:1506.02078 (2015)
19. Klein, L., Lüth, C., Schlegel, U., Bungert, T., El-Assady, M., Jäger, P.: Navigating the maze of explainable AI: a systematic approach to evaluating methods and metrics. In: Advances in Neural Information Processing Systems (2024)

20. Lundberg, S., Lee, S.I.: A unified approach to interpreting model predictions. In: Advances in Neural Information Processing Systems (2017)
21. van der Maaten, L., Hinton, G.: Visualizing data using T-SNE. J. Mach. Learn. Res. (2008)
22. Manduchi, L., Hüser, M., Faltys, M., Vogt, J., Rätsch, G., Fortuin, V.: T-dpsom: an interpretable clustering method for unsupervised learning of patient health states. In: Conference on Health, Inference, and Learning (2021)
23. Manduchi, L., Hüser, M., Vogt, J., Rätsch, G., Fortuin, V.: DPSOM: deep probabilistic clustering with self-organizing maps. arXiv preprint arXiv:1910.01590 (2019)
24. McInnes, L., Healy, J., Melville, J.: Umap: Uniform Manifold Approximation and Projection for Dimension Reduction. arXiv preprint arXiv:1802.03426 (2018)
25. Nguyen, X.B., Bui, D.T., Duong, C.N., Bui, T.D., Luu, K.: Clusformer: a transformer based clustering approach to unsupervised large-scale face and visual landmark recognition. In: IEEE/CVF Conference on Computer Vision and Pattern Recognition (2021)
26. Paparrizos, J., Yang, F., Li, H.: Bridging the gap: a decade review of time-series clustering methods. arXiv preprint arXiv:2412.20582 (2024)
27. Ren, Y., et al.: Deep clustering: a comprehensive survey. IEEE Trans. Neural Netw. Learn. Syst. (2024)
28. Ribeiro, M.T., Singh, S., Guestrin, C.: "Why should i trust you?": explaining the predictions of any classifier. In: SIGKDD International Conference on Knowledge Discovery and Data Mining (2016)
29. Schlegel, U., Arnout, H., El-Assady, M., Oelke, D., Keim, D.A.: Towards a rigorous evaluation of XAI methods on time series. In: IEEE/CVF International Conference on Computer Vision Workshop (2019)
30. Schlegel, U., Keim, D.A.: Time Series Model Attribution Visualizations as Explanations. In: IEEE VIS: Workshop on TRust and EXpertise in Visual Analytics (TREX) (2021)
31. Schlegel, U., Keim, D.A.: Interactive dense pixel visualizations for time series and model attribution explanations. In: Workshop for Machine Learning Methods in Visualisation for Big Data (MLVis) (2023)
32. Schlegel, U., Keim, D.A.: Introducing the attribution stability indicator: a measure for time series XAI attributions. In: ECML-PKDD Workshop XAI-TS: Explainable AI for Time Series: Advances and Applications (2023)
33. Schlegel, U., Oelke, D., Keim, D.A., El-Assady, M.: An empirical study of explainable AI techniques on deep learning models for time series tasks. In: Pre-Registration Workshop NeurIPS (2020)
34. Schlegel, U., Oelke, D., Keim, D.A., El-Assady, M.: Visual Explanations with Attributions and Counterfactuals on Time Series Classification. arXiv preprint arXiv:2307.08494 (2023)
35. Spinner, T., Schlegel, U., Schäfer, H., El-Assady, M.: explAIner: a visual analytics framework for interactive and explainable machine learning. IEEE Trans. Vis. Comput. Graph. (2019)
36. Theissler, A., Spinnato, F., Schlegel, U., Guidotti, R.: Explainable AI for time series classification: a review, taxonomy and research directions. IEEE Access (2022)
37. Vaittinada Ayar, P., Battisti, D.S., Li, C., King, M., Vrac, M., Tjiputra, J.: A regime view of enso flavors through clustering in cmip6 models. Earth's Future (2023)
38. Vielhaben, J., Lapuschkin, S., Montavon, G., Samek, W.: Explainable AI for time series via virtual inspection layers. Pattern Recognit. (2024)

39. Xie, J., Girshick, R., Farhadi, A.: Unsupervised deep embedding for clustering analysis. In: International Conference on Machine Learning (2016)
40. Ye, L., Keogh, E.: Time series shapelets: a new primitive for data mining. In: ACM SIGKDD International Conference on Knowledge Discovery and Data Mining (2009)
41. Zhou, S., et al.: A comprehensive survey on deep clustering: taxonomy, challenges, and future directions. ACM Comput. Surv. (2024)

Why do Class-Dependent Evaluation Effects Occur with Time Series Feature Attributions? A Synthetic Data Investigation

Gregor Baer[1,2(✉)], Isel Grau[1,2], Chao Zhang[2,3], and Pieter Van Gorp[1,2]

[1] Information Systems, Eindhoven University of Technology, Eindhoven, The Netherlands
g.baer@tue.nl
[2] Eindhoven Artificial Intelligence Systems Institute, Eindhoven University of Technology, Eindhoven, The Netherlands
[3] Human-Technology Interaction, Eindhoven University of Technology, Eindhoven, The Netherlands

Abstract. Evaluating feature attribution methods represents a critical challenge in explainable AI (XAI), as researchers typically rely on perturbation-based metrics when ground truth is unavailable. However, recent work reveals that these evaluation metrics can show different performance across predicted classes within the same dataset. These "class-dependent evaluation effects" raise questions about whether perturbation analysis reliably measures attribution quality, with direct implications for XAI method development and evaluation trustworthiness. We investigate under which conditions these class-dependent effects arise by conducting controlled experiments with synthetic time series data where ground truth feature locations are known. We systematically vary feature types and class contrasts across binary classification tasks, then compare perturbation-based degradation scores with ground truth-based precision-recall metrics using multiple attribution methods. Our experiments demonstrate that class-dependent effects emerge with both evaluation approaches, even in simple scenarios with temporally localized features, triggered by basic variations in feature amplitude or temporal extent between classes. Most critically, we find that perturbation-based and ground truth metrics frequently yield contradictory assessments of attribution quality across classes, with weak correlations between evaluation approaches. These findings suggest that researchers should interpret perturbation-based metrics with care, as they may not always align with whether attributions correctly identify discriminating features. By showing this disconnect, our work points toward reconsidering what attribution evaluation actually measures and developing more rigorous evaluation methods that capture multiple dimensions of attribution quality.

Keywords: Feature attribution · Perturbation analysis · XAI evaluation · Time series classification

I. Koprinska et al. (Eds.): ECML PKDD 2025, CCIS 2842, pp. 380–395, 2026.
https://doi.org/10.1007/978-3-032-19105-2_27

1 Introduction

As machine learning models of increasing complexity advance prediction accuracy across domains, including time series classification [7], the field of Explainable Artificial Intelligence (XAI) has emerged to answer why models make certain predictions. However, a fundamental challenge in XAI research continues to be the evaluation of explanations. It remains challenging to determine what makes an explanation "good" and how to best evaluate explanation quality without ground truth labels, unlike prediction tasks where true outcomes enable direct performance measurement.

While human-centered evaluation through user studies provides direct assessment of explanation utility [10], such approaches demand substantial time and resources, limiting their use during XAI method development. Consequently, XAI researchers frequently employ functional evaluation techniques that computationally verify whether explanations satisfy desirable properties [2,8]. This computational approach enables quicker iteration and systematic comparison across methods, making it essential for advancing XAI research.

Researchers have adapted feature attribution methods originally developed for images to time series classification and evaluated them functionally, including [9,12,13,15,16,21]. These evaluations predominantly rely on perturbation analysis, first introduced by Samek et al. [11], which operates under the assumption that modifying features identified as important should proportionally degrade model output. This approach has become the de facto standard for attribution evaluation in the absence of ground truth.

However, Baer et al. [1] recently identified a potential methodological limitation: "class-dependent perturbation effects", where perturbation-based metrics demonstrate different performance across predicted classes within datasets. This phenomenon creates a problem because benchmarks relying on average scores can mask class-specific biases, potentially leading researchers to incorrect conclusions about the quality of attribution methods. Although previous research acknowledges that perturbation results vary by perturbation strategy and recommends testing multiple approaches [13,16], class-dependent effects seem to persist across various perturbation methods and datasets [1]. The conditions generating these effects remain unexplored, leaving a gap in our understanding of how to reliably evaluate feature attributions.

Understanding why these effects arise carries critical implications for XAI evaluation methodology. If class-dependent differences reflect genuine variations in attribution quality, where methods truly perform better for certain classes, then perturbation analysis correctly captures these differences. However, if perturbation analysis itself introduces systematic biases regardless of attribution quality, researchers may draw misleading conclusions about method performance. This distinction fundamentally affects how we interpret and trust XAI evaluation results.

Our research addresses this gap by investigating: **Under which conditions do class-dependent evaluation effects arise?** We approach this question through systematically constructed synthetic data experiments, creating binary time series classification tasks with known ground truth features localized in time. By varying feature types (level shifts, pulses, sine waves, trends) and class contrasts (amplitude, length), we isolate factors contributing to evaluation disparities.

This paper offers three primary contributions to XAI evaluation methodology. First, we identify specific conditions under which class-dependent evaluation differences emerge, demonstrating that these effects manifest even in minimally complex classification tasks. We show that simple variations in feature prevalence and amplitude across classes trigger class-dependent effects, even when the underlying discriminating feature remains structurally identical between classes. Second, we show that class-dependent effects occur in both ground truth-based and perturbation-based evaluation metrics, indicating that attribution methods genuinely perform differently across classes rather than reflecting measurement artifacts. Third, and most critically, we demonstrate that ground truth and perturbation metrics can yield contradictory assessments of attribution quality across classes, revealing that these approaches may measure fundamentally different aspects of attribution behavior. While ground truth metrics assess whether attributions locate discriminating features, perturbation analysis may capture other properties that do not necessarily align with feature identification accuracy. By showing when and why evaluation metrics diverge, our work advances efforts toward more rigorous assessment frameworks in time series analysis as advocated by Theissler et al. [20].

The remainder of this paper is organized as follows. Section 2 establishes our evaluation framework, including perturbation-based and ground truth-based metrics with synthetic data generation. Section 3 details our experimental design across different feature types, class contrasts, and attribution methods. Section 4 presents findings on when class-dependent evaluation effects emerge and analyzes the correspondence between evaluation approaches. Section 5 summarizes our contributions and implications for XAI evaluation methodology.

2 Evaluation Framework

Feature attribution methods for time series classification identify the time points that influence a model's predictions. Since ground truth is typically unavailable for real-world data, perturbation analysis is commonly used to assess attribution quality by modifying input features and observing the impact on model predictions. The underlying assumption is that perturbing important time points should cause significant prediction changes, while modifying irrelevant time points should have minimal impact. In this work, we evaluate feature attributions using both perturbation-based metrics and ground truth comparison on synthetic data where true feature locations are known.

Figure 1 illustrates our evaluation framework for systematically investigating class-dependent effects. We generate synthetic time series with known discriminative features, compute attributions using multiple methods, and assess attribution quality through both perturbation-based and ground truth-based evaluations.

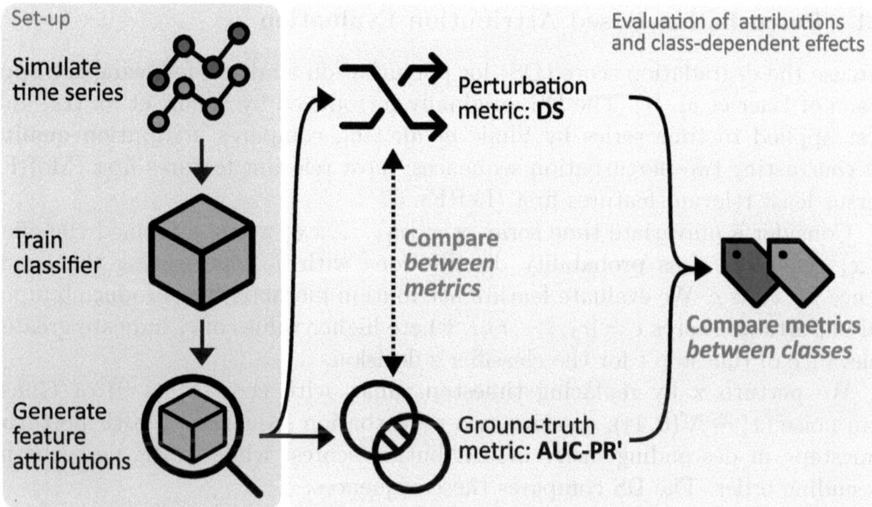

Fig. 1. Framework for analyzing class-dependent evaluation effects. We generate synthetic time series with features localized in time, train classifiers, and compare perturbation-based versus ground truth-based attribution evaluations to identify when class-dependent evaluation effects arise.

Table 1 outlines these complementary approaches, which capture different aspects of attribution quality. Perturbation analysis (Sect. 2.1) tests whether models rely on attributed regions for predictions, while ground truth evaluation (Sect. 2.3) verifies whether attributions correctly locate discriminative features. Although these metrics measure distinct properties, we would expect them to agree: attributions that correctly identify discriminative features should also prove critical when perturbed. Our experiments examine when and why these evaluation approaches converge or diverge across classes, showing whether class-dependent patterns reflect genuine attribution differences or evaluation inconsistencies.

Table 1. Attribution evaluation approaches employed in this study.

Approach	Metric	Core question and method
Perturbation	DS	Do predictions degrade when removing important features? *Method:* Compare model confidence after perturbing most relevant vs. least relevant features.
Ground truth	AUC-PR′	Do high attribution scores overlap with known discriminative feature regions? *Method:* Measure how well attributions retrieve true feature locations using normalized precision-recall analysis.

2.1 Perturbation-Based Attribution Evaluation

We use the degradation score (DS) for perturbation analysis, following the approach of Baer et al. [1]. The DS, originally introduced by Schulz et al. [14] and first applied to time series by Šimić et al. [16], compares attribution quality by contrasting two perturbation sequences: most relevant features first (MoRF) versus least relevant features first (LeRF).

Consider a univariate time series $\mathbf{x} = [x_1, \ldots, x_N]$ where a trained classifier $f(\mathbf{x})$ generates class probability distributions with q_c representing the confidence for class c. We evaluate feature attribution methods that produce temporal importance scores $\mathbf{r} = [r_1, \ldots, r_N]$, where higher values of r_i indicate greater relevance of timestep i for the classifier's decision.

We perturb $\mathbf{x}$ by replacing timestep values with zero ($x'_i = 0$) or Gaussian noise ($x'_i \sim \mathcal{N}(0, 1)$), creating two perturbation sequences: MoRF perturbs timesteps in descending order of attribution scores, while LeRF perturbs in ascending order. The DS compares these sequences:

$$\mathrm{DS} = \frac{1}{m} \sum_{i}^{m} (\mathrm{PC}_{\mathrm{LeRF}_i} - \mathrm{PC}_{\mathrm{MoRF}_i}), \tag{1}$$

where $\mathrm{PC}_{\mathrm{order}_i}$ represents the predicted probabilities after perturbing i features in the specified order. The DS ranges from -1 to 1, with positive values indicating effective attributions, i.e. MoRF perturbations degrade predictions more than LeRF.

2.2 Synthetic Data Generation

In addition to perturbation analysis, we construct synthetic time series data with known ground truth feature locations to directly evaluate attribution correctness. This allows us to assess whether attribution methods can correctly identify the specific time points where class-discriminating features are located.

Each synthetic time series $\mathbf{x}$ contains a single class-discriminating, contiguous feature over multiple time points embedded within a foundation signal through additive composition:

$$\mathbf{x} = \mathbf{n} + \mathbf{f}, \tag{2}$$

where $\mathbf{n} \sim \mathcal{N}(0, 1)$ represents background noise and $\mathbf{f}$ contains the class-specific temporal pattern within a designated feature window, with zeros elsewhere. Both vectors have identical length to enable element-wise addition.

While real-world time series features may exhibit complex temporal dependencies, we deliberately restrict investigation to temporally localized features occupying contiguous windows of predetermined length L. This design choice isolates evaluation effects under minimal complexity conditions, enabling attribution of observed phenomena to specific data characteristics rather than confounding factors. Class-dependent variations are introduced through two systematic contrast mechanisms. *Feature length contrast* varies temporal extent between classes, testing whether feature prevalence affects evaluation metrics.

Amplitude contrast varies signal magnitude between classes, examining whether signal strength differences drive evaluation disparities. Feature locations are randomized across observations to prevent positional classification shortcuts. For an example of this approach, see Fig. 2, which shows two possible instances with different classes from a simulated dataset.

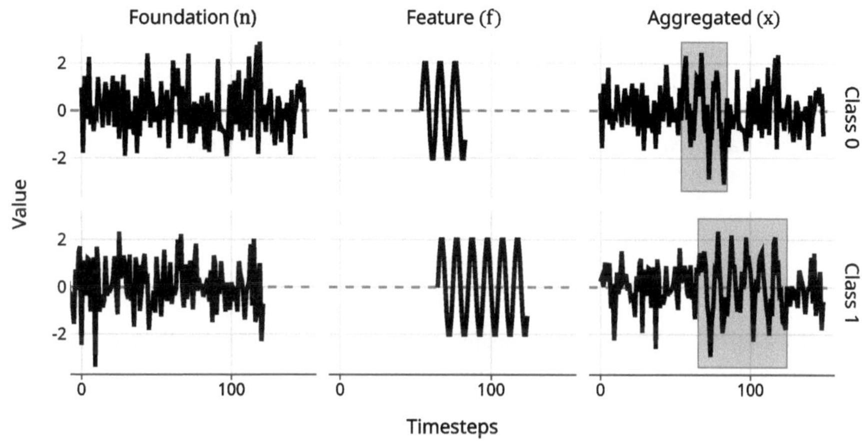

Fig. 2. Synthetic data generation example demonstrating feature length contrast. Two instances show identical sine wave features (red regions) with different temporal extents: Class 0 spans 20% of timesteps while Class 1 spans 40%. (Color figure online)

2.3 Ground Truth-Based Attribution Evaluation

To evaluate feature attributions on synthetic data, we treat attribution evaluation as a retrieval problem: can high attribution scores identify true feature locations? Let $\mathbf{l} = [l_1, \ldots, l_N]$ where $l_i \in \{0, 1\}$ represent a binary mask indicating ground truth feature locations, with $l_i = 1$ denoting the presence of a class-discriminating feature f_i at time point i. For attribution scores $\mathbf{r}$, we threshold at different values t to obtain binary predictions $\hat{l}_i^{(t)} = I(r_i \geq t)$ of important feature locations. We use all unique attribution values as thresholds, evaluated in descending order, which ensures we capture all possible precision-recall operating points. At each threshold, we compute:

$$\text{Precision}(t) = \frac{TP(t)}{TP(t) + FP(t)}, \quad \text{Recall}(t) = \frac{TP(t)}{P}, \tag{3}$$

where $TP(t) = \sum_{i=1}^{N} \hat{l}_i^{(t)} \cdot l_i$ (correctly identified feature locations), $FP(t) = \sum_{i=1}^{N} \hat{l}_i^{(t)} \cdot (1 - l_i)$ (false feature locations), and $P = \sum_{i=1}^{N} l_i$ (total ground truth features).

To assess whether feature attributions correctly highlight crucial regions within the time series, we compute the AUC-PR. This metric calculates the area beneath the precision-recall curve, where precision is plotted as a function of recall:

$$\text{AUC-PR} = \int_0^1 \text{Precision}(\text{recall})\, d(\text{recall}), \tag{4}$$

computed using the trapezoidal rule over unique recall values. We choose AUC-PR because it suits our sparse ground truth features well. For binary classification problems, the random baseline equals the feature prevalence, Prevalence $= \frac{P}{N}$.

Since we vary feature lengths across experiments, we normalize the AUC-PR to enable fair comparison across different prevalence rates:

$$\text{AUC-PR}' = \frac{\text{AUC-PR} - \text{Prevalence}}{1 - \text{Prevalence}}. \tag{5}$$

This normalized score represents improvement over the random baseline, with values approaching 1 indicating perfect performance and negative values indicating worse-than-random attribution quality.

3 Experimental Design

Dataset Specifications. We construct synthetic datasets consisting of univariate time series with 150 timesteps for binary classification tasks. Each dataset comprises 1000 training samples, 300 validation samples, and 300 test samples with balanced class distributions. While all sets are generated from the same data-generating process, we use different random seeds to ensure independence. Class-discriminating features are randomly positioned within each time series, with feature windows $[t_{\text{start}}, t_{\text{start}} + L - 1]$ varying across observations to prevent positional classification shortcuts. All instances undergo standardization prior to model training.

Feature Types. We implement four feature types to represent common temporal patterns: (1) level shifts representing constant amplitude changes, (2) Gaussian pulses capturing transient spikes, (3) sine waves modeling periodic oscillations reminiscent of seasonality, and (4) local trends reflecting gradual directional changes. Definitions and parameters for each feature type are provided in Table 2.

Class Contrasts. We create binary classification tasks by systematically contrasting features across two dimensions: amplitude differences to examine magnitude-based discrimination, and length differences to investigate temporal prevalence effects. This design isolates how different types of class distinctions influence attribution evaluation metrics.

We embed features within background Gaussian noise, with feature amplitudes chosen to maintain detectability while avoiding trivial separability. Feature lengths span 20% to 40% of the time series to represent moderate temporal

Table 2. Feature type definitions. Formulas show signal generation within the feature window, where $t \in [0, L-1]$ is the relative timestep. Parameters: A = amplitude, L = feature window length, p = period, $\sigma = L/6$ = pulse width.

Feature	Shape	Description	Definition
Level	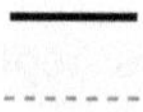	Constant amplitude/level shift	$f(t) = A$
Pulse	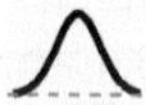	Gaussian-shaped transient signal	$f(t) = Ae^{-\frac{(t-L/2)^2}{2\sigma^2}}, \quad \sigma = L/6$
Sine		Periodic oscillation	$f(t) = A\sin(2\pi t/p), \quad p = 10$
Trend	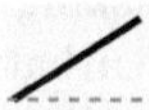	Linear increase from zero	$f(t) = At/(L-1)$

Table 3. Experimental class contrasts applied to all four feature types (Level, Pulse, Sine, Trend; see Table 2). Parameters: A = feature amplitude, L = feature window length (timesteps), $\mathbf{n}$ = background noise.

Contrast	Class 0	Class 1	Both classes	Purpose
Amplitude	$A = 1$	$A = 2$	$\mathbf{n} \sim \mathcal{N}(0,1)$, $L = 60$	Test magnitude effects
Length	$L = 30$	$L = 60$	$\mathbf{n} \sim \mathcal{N}(0,1)$, $A = 2$	Test prevalence effects

prevalence. Combining four feature types with two contrast mechanisms yields eight datasets. Table 3 summarizes the specific class differences for each contrast type. For example, amplitude-contrast datasets vary only feature magnitude while maintaining identical temporal extent, whereas length-contrast datasets vary temporal coverage while preserving signal strength.

Model Architecture and Training. We employ two established deep learning architectures for time series classification: ResNet [22] and InceptionTime [6], both of which offer robust performance across time series benchmarks [3]. We train models using AdamW optimization with cosine annealing learning rate scheduling and early stopping (patience = 10 epochs) based on validation performance over a maximum of 100 epochs. Both architectures achieve test accuracy and weighted F1 scores exceeding 0.9 across all datasets, with one exception: InceptionTime on the Amplitude-Pulse dataset (F1 = 0.7). These performance levels ensure that observed class-dependent evaluation differences stem from attribution or perturbation methodology rather than classifier bias toward specific classes. Complete performance metrics are provided in Table 4 in Appendix A.

Attribution Methods. We evaluate three attribution methods: Gradients (GR) [17], Integrated Gradients (IG) [19], and Feature Occlusion (FO) [4]. IG and FO were selected because they demonstrated both high attribution quality and pronounced class-dependent evaluation effects in previous research [1], making them suitable candidates for investigating the conditions under which such effects arise. We include GR as a computationally efficient baseline to ensure our findings span different levels of attribution complexity. The selection covers both gradient-based approaches (GR and IG) and perturbation-based attribution (FO). We compute attributions for all 300 test samples, explaining each model's predicted class label.

Perturbation Analysis. We employ two perturbation strategies: replacing values with zero and substituting with Gaussian noise. Both strategies are commonly used in time series attribution evaluation [13,16,21]. Since we standardize all time series, zero substitution effectively replaces values with the sample mean. For Gaussian noise perturbation, we sample from the same distribution as the background noise ($\mathcal{N}(0,1)$), following the controlled masking approach used in existing benchmarks [5]. This approach ensures that perturbations align more closely with the data distribution, avoiding the potential artifacts of more extreme substitution methods or constant replacement values.

We implement perturbations according to MoRF and LeRF orderings determined by attribution scores, substituting features incrementally one timestep at a time. To maintain fair comparisons across datasets with varying feature lengths, we perturb exactly L timesteps for each sample, where L corresponds to the true feature window size. For instance, in length-contrast datasets, we perturb 30 timesteps for class 0 samples and 60 timesteps for class 1 samples. We record predicted probabilities after each perturbation step to calculate the DS.

4 Results and Discussion

Figure 3 presents the AUC-PR$'$ and DS across datasets and true class labels (detailed results for all experimental conditions appear in Appendix A, Table 5 and 6). We aggregate results across attribution methods and model architectures to emphasize general patterns in class-dependent evaluation effects, though individual method-specific variations exist within these trends.

Ground Truth-Based Evaluation. The ground truth evaluation reveals substantial variation in how well attribution methods recover true class-discriminating feature regions, both across datasets and between classes within datasets. Class 1 observations (with higher amplitude or longer feature windows) consistently achieve higher AUC-PR$'$ scores than class 0 observations across seven of eight datasets. The Length-Level dataset is the sole exception where class 1 attributions approach random performance. Overall, Pulse, Sine, and Trend features demonstrate pronounced class-dependent differences in attribution quality. The disparities prove particularly large for Amplitude-Sine and Length-Pulse datasets: class 1 observations in both achieve AUC-PR$'$ scores more than double those of class 0 observations, indicating that attribution methods recover ground truth features more effectively for one class than the other.

Perturbation-Based Evaluation. Perturbation-based evaluation through DS scores reveals patterns that directly contradict the ground truth findings. While ground truth evaluation favors class 1 attributions in seven of eight datasets, perturbation analysis indicates better attribution quality for class 0 observations in six of eight datasets. This systematic reversal across most feature types and contrast mechanisms suggests the two evaluation approaches measure different aspects of attribution behavior. Length-Level and Amplitude-Level datasets represent exceptions where both evaluation approaches converge. These datasets show smaller class discrepancies and assign relatively low scores across both metrics. This pattern likely reflects how attribution methods focus on temporal change points rather than extended feature windows when detecting level shifts. Such localized attribution behavior reduces overlap with our ground truth evaluation windows and limits perturbation impact when removing individual timesteps.

Overall, we observe an inverse relationship: datasets where one class achieves the highest attribution performance also tend to show the strongest disagreement between evaluation approaches. This pattern appears consistently, revealing tensions between ground truth and perturbation-based assessment even when individual metrics indicate strong performance.

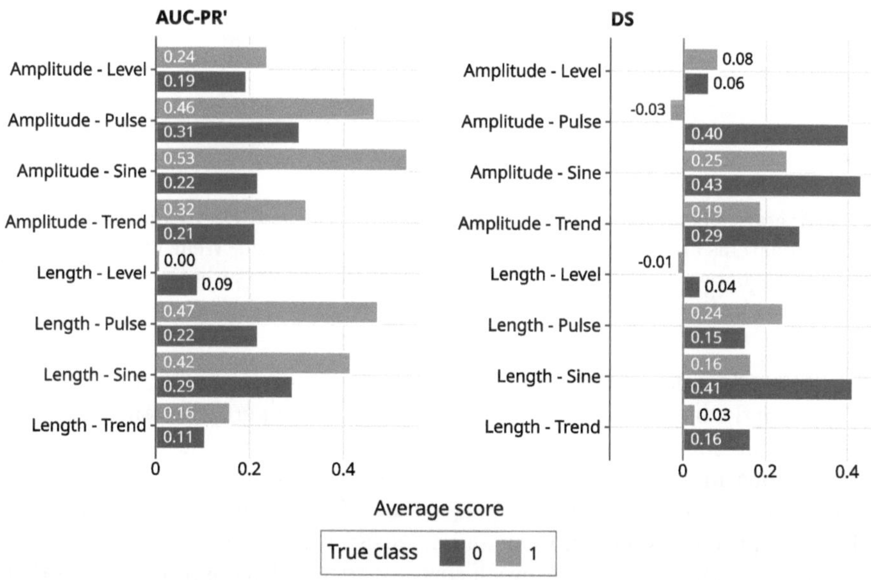

Fig. 3. Average AUC-PR′ (left) and DS (right) by dataset and true class. AUC-PR′ measures attribution overlap with known features; DS compares prediction degradation when perturbing regions with high versus low attribution scores. Both metrics show class-dependent differences across datasets, with opposing performance patterns between classes in most cases.

Correspondence Between Evaluation Approaches. To examine the relationship between evaluation approaches, we compute Spearman correlations between AUC-PR′ and DS scores. We use Spearman correlation because the metrics operate on different scales and we focus on monotonic relationships, that is, whether higher scores in one metric correspond to higher scores in the other.

Figure 4 shows correlations per dataset and class. The analysis confirms our earlier observations about contradictory class-dependent evaluation effects. Correlations remain weak to moderate, ranging from -0.18 to 0.291, and vary substantially between classes within datasets. For example, Amplitude-Sine shows a negative correlation (-0.18) for class 0 but a positive correlation (0.112) for class 1. Length-Sine achieves the highest correlation (0.291) for class 1 while class 0 shows a slight negative correlation.

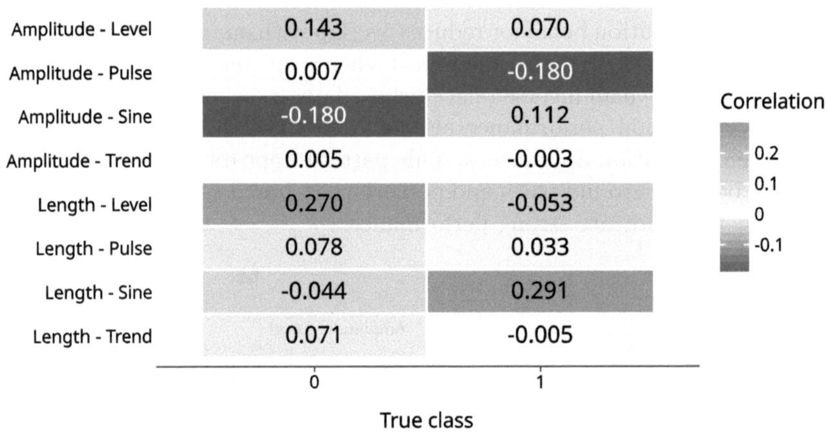

Fig. 4. Average Spearman correlation between AUC-PR′ and DS by dataset and true class. Correlations are computed per observation, then averaged. Weak correlations and sign reversals between classes show that ground truth and perturbation-based metrics can disagree about attribution quality.

Summary. Class-dependent evaluation differences emerge across almost all feature types and contrast mechanisms. Ground truth and perturbation-based metrics yield contradictory assessments: while ground truth evaluation favors class 1 attributions in seven of eight datasets, perturbation analysis indicates better performance for class 0 in six of eight cases. Spearman correlations between evaluation approaches remain weak and inconsistent, ranging from -0.18 to 0.291 across datasets and classes. This weak correspondence demonstrates that perturbation analysis does not reliably identify whether attributions correctly locate class-discriminating regions, indicating that the two evaluation frameworks measure different aspects of attribution behavior.

5 Conclusion

We investigate conditions under which class-dependent evaluation effects arise in time series feature attribution assessment. Through controlled synthetic experiments with known ground truth features, we compare perturbation-based and ground truth-based evaluation metrics across multiple attribution methods. Our results demonstrate that even simple variations in feature characteristics, such as amplitude differences or temporal extent, can trigger pronounced evaluation disparities between classes. These class-dependent effects emerge consistently across feature types and contrast mechanisms. Most notably, perturbation-based metrics frequently suggest superior attribution quality for one class while ground truth metrics indicate the opposite.

This systematic disagreement creates a conceptual challenge: in the absence of ground truth, researchers rely on perturbation-based metrics knowing they measure model sensitivity, with the implicit assumption that this serves as a reasonable proxy for feature localization accuracy. Our findings challenge this assumption by demonstrating that model sensitivity and correct feature identification can diverge systematically. The disagreement is particularly concerning since real-world datasets lack ground truth references, leaving perturbation as the primary evaluation option. Researchers should interpret perturbation metrics cautiously, recognizing they may not accurately reflect whether attributions succeed in identifying discriminative feature locations despite our expectations that these properties should align.

Our findings show such disagreements emerge even under minimal complexity. However, several limitations constrain the generalizability of our findings. We examine only simple univariate time series with temporally localized features, employing two deep learning architectures and three general-purpose attribution methods. While this design enables controlled analysis, it excludes complex temporal patterns and specialized attribution approaches designed for time series. Our evaluation also assumes that good attributions should cover entire feature windows, yet models may legitimately focus on sparse temporal markers like change points or learn from subtle patterns beyond our designed features. When models identify features through different strategies than we expect, standard metrics may underestimate their actual attribution quality. This mismatch between how we measure attribution performance and how models process temporal information highlights the challenge of defining "correct" attributions in time series contexts.

Future research can address both empirical and conceptual dimensions of these evaluation challenges. Testing time series-specific attribution methods like LimeSegment [18] may reveal whether specialized approaches reduce class-dependent effects. Expanding synthetic datasets to include multiple discriminating patterns and more complex temporal dependencies would test generalizability beyond our localized feature settings. The weak correspondence between perturbation and ground truth metrics suggests that measuring model sensitivity may not adequately assess feature localization accuracy. This disconnect between what we aim to measure and what perturbation analysis actually captures encourages developing more rigorous evaluation frameworks that acknowledge different dimensions of attribution quality.

Acknowledgments. This paper is supported by the European Union's HORIZON Research and Innovation Program under grant agreement No. 101120657, project ENFIELD (European Lighthouse to Manifest Trustworthy and Green AI).

Disclosure of Interests. All authors declare that they have no conflicts of interest.

A Detailed Experimental Results

Table 4. Model performance by dataset on the test set.

Contrast	Feature	ResNet		InceptionTime	
		Accuracy	F1	Accuracy	F1
Amplitude	Level	0.990	0.990	0.980	0.980
	Pulse	0.900	0.899	0.723	0.700
	Sine	0.997	0.997	1.000	1.000
	Trend	0.920	0.920	0.940	0.940
Length	Level	1.000	1.000	1.000	1.000
	Pulse	0.923	0.923	0.947	0.947
	Sine	0.997	0.997	1.000	1.000
	Trend	0.927	0.927	0.973	0.973

Table 5. Average AUC-PR′ by classifier, dataset, attribution method and true class.

Model	Contrast	Feature	GR		IG		FO	
			C0	C1	C0	C1	C0	C1
ResNet	Amplitude	Level	.134	.234	.435	.384	−.032	−.068
		Pulse	.235	.313	.188	.284	.151	.270
		Sine	.219	.357	.170	.262	.308	.681
		Trend	.126	.127	.074	.278	.058	.058
	Length	Level	.190	.483	.038	−.101	.102	−.038
		Pulse	.179	.329	.226	.313	.158	.197
		Sine	.262	.358	.139	.166	.304	.455
		Trend	.004	.129	−.018	−.024	−.004	−.013
InceptionTime	Amplitude	Level	.280	.503	.275	.225	.071	.148
		Pulse	.574	.750	.264	.572	.427	.599
		Sine	.139	.573	.256	.645	.219	.681
		Trend	.345	.528	.451	.588	.223	.348
	Length	Level	.033	−.002	.147	−.101	.025	−.183
		Pulse	.274	.733	.248	.711	.226	.555
		Sine	.226	.300	.512	.684	.312	.528
		Trend	.285	.386	.208	.306	.158	.166

Table 6. Average DS by classifier, dataset, perturbation strategy, attribution method, and true class.

Model	Contrast	Feature	Perturbation	GR		IG		FO	
				C0	C1	C0	C1	C0	C1
ResNet	Amplitude	Level	Gaussian	.133	−.460	.023	.185	−.001	.054
			Zero	.155	−.430	−.027	.508	.013	.043
		Pulse	Gaussian	.510	−.296	.543	−.093	.340	.042
			Zero	.639	−.220	.712	−.026	.480	.086
		Sine	Gaussian	.266	.083	.551	−.072	.334	.229
			Zero	.511	.043	.778	−.067	.561	.231
		Trend	Gaussian	.474	−.204	.391	−.020	.286	.057
			Zero	.634	−.199	.446	.051	.336	.085
	Length	Level	Gaussian	.116	−.142	.010	−.071	−.029	.032
			Zero	.090	−.140	.016	.081	.004	.171
		Pulse	Gaussian	.314	−.179	.146	.086	.150	.062
			Zero	.283	−.140	.078	.353	.111	.246
		Sine	Gaussian	.439	−.066	.505	−.030	.399	.074
			Zero	.677	−.023	.737	−.029	.621	.019
		Trend	Gaussian	.378	−.291	.116	−.099	.179	−.069
			Zero	.347	−.353	−.020	.204	.034	.158
InceptionTime	Amplitude	Level	Gaussian	.187	−.157	.120	.114	.049	.187
			Zero	.089	.049	−.006	.449	.005	.459
		Pulse	Gaussian	.390	−.191	.169	−.095	.263	−.122
			Zero	.420	.124	.089	.252	.268	.129
		Sine	Gaussian	.230	.458	.383	.412	.261	.434
			Zero	.371	.453	.537	.415	.417	.428
		Trend	Gaussian	.256	.112	.181	.331	.199	.273
			Zero	.207	.426	−.011	.718	.027	.627
	Length	Level	Gaussian	.032	−.058	.110	−.078	.021	−.060
			Zero	.017	−.116	.115	.038	.009	.164
		Pulse	Gaussian	.179	.273	.112	.351	.167	.291
			Zero	.152	.508	.021	.538	.105	.540
		Sine	Gaussian	.178	.242	.227	.456	.206	.428
			Zero	.293	.150	.347	.387	.330	.362
		Trend	Gaussian	.162	−.087	.259	.135	.210	.101
			Zero	.093	.021	.066	.404	.145	.245

References

1. Baer, G., Grau, I., Zhang, C., Van Gorp, P.: Class-dependent perturbation effects in evaluating time series attributions. In: Guidotti, R., Schmid, U., Longo, L. (eds.) Explainable Artificial Intelligence, pp. 292–314. Springer, Cham (2025). https://doi.org/10.1007/978-3-032-08330-2_14

2. Doshi-Velez, F., Kim, B.: Considerations for evaluation and generalization in interpretable machine learning. In: Escalante, H.J., et al. (eds.) Explainable and Interpretable Models in Computer Vision and Machine Learning, pp. 3–17. Springer, Cham (2018). https://doi.org/10.1007/978-3-319-98131-4_1
3. Fawaz, H.I., Forestier, G., Weber, J., Idoumghar, L., Muller, P.A.: Deep learning for time series classification: a review. Data Min. Knowl. Disc. **33**, 917–963 (2019). https://doi.org/10.1007/s10618-019-00619-1
4. Fong, R.C., Vedaldi, A.: Interpretable explanations of black boxes by meaningful perturbation. In: Proceedings of the IEEE International Conference on Computer Vision, pp. 3429–3437 (2017). https://openaccess.thecvf.com/content_iccv_2017/html/Fong_Interpretable_Explanations_of_ICCV_2017_paper.html
5. Ismail, A.A., Gunady, M., Corrada Bravo, H., Feizi, S.: Benchmarking deep learning interpretability in time series predictions. In: Advances in Neural Information Processing Systems, vol. 33, pp. 6441–6452 (2020). https://proceedings.neurips.cc/paper_files/paper/2020/hash/47a3893cc405396a5c30d91320572d6d-Abstract.html
6. Ismail Fawaz, H., et al.: InceptionTime: finding AlexNet for time series classification. Data Min. Knowl. Disc. **34**, 1936–1962 (2020). https://doi.org/10.1007/s10618-020-00710-y
7. Middlehurst, M., Schäfer, P., Bagnall, A.: Bake off redux: a review and experimental evaluation of recent time series classification algorithms. Data Min. Knowl. Disc. **38**, 1958–2031 (2024). https://doi.org/10.1007/s10618-024-01022-1
8. Nauta, M., et al.: From anecdotal evidence to quantitative evaluation methods: a systematic review on evaluating explainable AI. ACM Comput. Surv. **55**, 1–42 (2023). https://doi.org/10.1145/3583558
9. Nguyen, T.T., Le Nguyen, T., Ifrim, G.: Robust explainer recommendation for time series classification. Data Min. Knowl. Disc. **38**, 3372–3413 (2024). https://doi.org/10.1007/s10618-024-01045-8
10. Rong, Y., et al.: Towards human-centered explainable AI: a survey of user studies for model explanations. IEEE Trans. Pattern Anal. Mach. Intell. **46**, 2104–2122 (2024). https://doi.org/10.1109/TPAMI.2023.3331846
11. Samek, W., Binder, A., Montavon, G., Lapuschkin, S., Müller, K.R.: Evaluating the visualization of what a deep neural network has learned. IEEE Trans. Neural Netw. Learn. Syst. **28**, 2660–2673 (2017). https://doi.org/10.1109/TNNLS.2016.2599820
12. Schlegel, U., Arnout, H., El-Assady, M., Oelke, D., Keim, D.A.: Towards a rigorous evaluation of XAI methods on time series. In: 2019 IEEE/CVF International Conference on Computer Vision Workshop (ICCVW), pp. 4197–4201 (2019). https://doi.org/10.1109/ICCVW.2019.00516
13. Schlegel, U., Keim, D.A.: A deep dive into perturbations as evaluation technique for time series XAI. In: Longo, L. (ed.) Explainable Artificial Intelligence, vol. 1903, pp. 165–180. Springer, Cham (2023). https://doi.org/10.1007/978-3-031-44070-0_9
14. Schulz, K., Sixt, L., Tombari, F., Landgraf, T.: Restricting the flow: information bottlenecks for attribution. In: International Conference on Learning Representations (2020). https://openreview.net/forum?id=S1xWh1rYwB
15. Serramazza, D.I., Nguyen, T.L., Ifrim, G.: Improving the evaluation and actionability of explanation methods for multivariate time series classification. In: Bifet, A., Davis, J., Krilavičius, T., Kull, M., Ntoutsi, E., Žliobaitė, I. (eds.) Machine Learning and Knowledge Discovery in Databases. Research Track, pp. 177–195 (2024). https://doi.org/10.1007/978-3-031-70359-1_11

16. Šimić, I., Sabol, V., Veas, E.: Perturbation effect: a metric to counter misleading validation of feature attribution. In: Proceedings of the 31st ACM International Conference on Information & Knowledge Management, pp. 1798–1807 (2022). https://doi.org/10.1145/3511808.3557418
17. Simonyan, K., Vedaldi, A., Zisserman, A.: Deep inside convolutional networks: visualising image classification models and saliency maps. In: Proceedings of the International Conference on Learning Representations (ICLR) (2014). https://doi.org/10.48550/arXiv.1312.6034
18. Sivill, T., Flach, P.: LIMESegment: meaningful, realistic time series explanations. In: Proceedings of the 25th International Conference on Artificial Intelligence and Statistics, pp. 3418–3433 (2022). https://proceedings.mlr.press/v151/sivill22a.html
19. Sundararajan, M., Taly, A., Yan, Q.: Axiomatic attribution for deep networks. In: Proceedings of the 34th International Conference on Machine Learning, pp. 3319–3328 (2017). https://proceedings.mlr.press/v70/sundararajan17a.html
20. Theissler, A., Spinnato, F., Schlegel, U., Guidotti, R.: Explainable AI for time series classification: a review, taxonomy and research directions. IEEE Access **10**, 100700–100724 (2022). https://doi.org/10.1109/ACCESS.2022.3207765
21. Turbé, H., Bjelogrlic, M., Lovis, C., Mengaldo, G.: Evaluation of post-hoc interpretability methods in time-series classification. Nat. Mach. Intell. **5**, 250–260 (2023). https://doi.org/10.1038/s42256-023-00620-w
22. Wang, Z., Yan, W., Oates, T.: Time series classification from scratch with deep neural networks: a strong baseline. In: 2017 International Joint Conference on Neural Networks (IJCNN), pp. 1578–1585 (2017). https://doi.org/10.1109/IJCNN.2017.7966039

Causal Explanation of Concept Drift – A Truly Actionable Approach

David Komnick(✉), Kathrin Lammers, Barbara Hammer, Valerie Vaquet, and Fabian Hinder

Machine Learning Group, Bielefeld University, Bielefeld, Germany
{dkomnick,klammers,bhammer,vvaquet,fhinder}@techfak.uni-bielefeld.de

Abstract. In a world that constantly changes, it is crucial to understand how those changes impact different systems, such as industrial manufacturing or critical infrastructure. Explaining critical changes, referred to as concept drift in the field of machine learning, is the first step towards enabling targeted interventions to avoid or correct model failures, as well as malfunctions and errors in the physical world. Therefore, in this work, we extend model-based drift explanations towards causal explanations, which increases the actionability of the provided explanations. We evaluate our explanation strategy on a number of use cases, demonstrating the practical usefulness of our framework, which isolates the causally relevant features impacted by concept drift and, thus, allows for targeted intervention.

Keywords: Concept Drift · Explainable AI · Computational Causality · Model-based Drift Explanations · Causal Explanations

1 Introduction

Machine learning plays a considerable role in many aspects of life, ranging from private usage through social media, chatbots, and recommender systems to many use cases in industry, e.g., quality control, etc. Despite many successful applications, many challenges arise when applying machine learning in critical applications. As identified in the European AI Act [6], a key aspect is the so-called black box behavior of many machine learning models. With the increasing complexity of models, the rationale for their predictions has become increasingly opaque. To address this challenge, an entire field focusing on explainable AI (XAI) has emerged in the last decade [1,3,20]. The goal is to understand model decisions better and provide appropriate explanations to the users, potentially enabling suitable actions.

Beyond their original role of enhancing the interpretability of machine learning models, XAI methods increasingly demonstrate potential as tools for broader data analysis tasks. This can be particularly useful if the data is complex and time is scarce, as is the case in many real-world settings, where the underlying data distribution might change over time [7]. Here, a deeper understanding drift

I. Koprinska et al. (Eds.): ECML PKDD 2025, CCIS 2842, pp. 396–412, 2026.
https://doi.org/10.1007/978-3-032-19105-2_28

not only allows for the adaptation and improvement of stream learning algorithms, but is also crucial in *system monitoring* where changes can indicate the necessity to take action, either by autonomous procedures or human operators overseeing complex systems. Hence, next to the mere detection of drifts, a suitable explanation is frequently required [14]. In this paper, we will focus on the latter assignment. We propose to extend the framework by [11] to provide causal explanations that directly provide actionability.

This work is structured as follows. First, we recap the definition of concept drift (Sect. 2) and summarize the related work on drift explanations (Sect. 3). Before proposing causal drift explanations in Sect. 5, we describe the required concepts from computational causality in Sect. 4. We then evaluate the proposed explanation pipeline experimentally (Sect. 6) and conclude the paper (Sect. 7).

Notation

In the following, we consider a data space $\mathcal{X}$ composed of multiple features. We refer to the index set of all features as $\mathcal{F}, |\mathcal{F}| < \infty$. Every feature $f \in \mathcal{F}$ takes values in the real numbers $\mathbb{R}$, i.e., $\mathcal{X} = \mathbb{R}^{\mathcal{F}}$. For a subset $F \subset \mathcal{F}$ we write $\mathcal{X}_F$ for the subspace based on the features in F, and for a data point X, we write X_F for the projection onto $\mathcal{X}_F$. In addition, if P is a probability measure on $\mathcal{X}$ we also write $P(X_F = x)$ or $P_{|\mathcal{X}_F}$ for the marginalization of P onto $\mathcal{X}_F$.

2 Concept Drift

In the classical batch learning setup, one assumes the data is given as random variables $X_1, \ldots, X_n$ that are independent and identically distributed (iid) according to some probability distribution $\mathcal{D}$. In contrast, in many real-world applications, we encounter the issue that the data is not identically distributed but subject to change – a phenomenon referred to as concept drift [7,19]. This can be due to the course of time, as in stream learning [7]; the data collection process taking place at different locations, as considered in the context of federated learning [30]; changes in the used equipment or sensors, such as sensor drift or applications of transfer learning [23], or combinations thereof. As pointed out by [14], formally, all these cases can be modelled using an abstract time domain, $\mathcal{T}$, that, for example, encodes clock time, the considered location, or computational node, and associating a – potentially different – distribution $\mathcal{D}_t$ to each abstract time point $t \in \mathcal{T}$. Concept drift refers to not all $\mathcal{D}_t$ being equivalent, i.e., there are $s, t \in \mathcal{T}$ such that $\mathcal{D}_t \neq \mathcal{D}_s$ [7,19].

In [9], the authors suggested a statistical modelling explicitly including time. This allows for an equivalent formalization of drift as data and time being dependent, i.e., assuming the sample X was observed at time point T then we have $X \sim \mathcal{D}_T$ and there is drift if and only if X and T are not statistically independent. The advantage of this definition for algorithm development [12,24,27] and in particular, drift explanations [11,14], is that it encodes drift as a non-trivial relation of data and time [9].

Definition 1. *Let $\mathcal{T}$ be a time domain, and $\mathcal{X} = \mathbb{R}^d$ be a data space. We say that the distribution process [14] $(P_\mathcal{T}, \mathcal{D}_t)$, i.e., a probability measure $P_\mathcal{T}$ on $\mathcal{T}$ together with a Markov kernel $\mathcal{D}_t$ from $\mathcal{T}$ to $\mathcal{X}$, has drift iff one of the following equivalent holds [9]:*

1. *observing $\mathcal{D}_t \neq \mathcal{D}_s$ with probability larger 0, i.e., $P_\mathcal{T}^2(\{(s,t) : \mathcal{D}_t \neq \mathcal{D}_s\}) > 0$*
2. *data and time are not independent, i.e., for $T \sim P_\mathcal{T}$ and $X \mid T = t \sim \mathcal{D}_t$ we have $\mathbb{P}[X \in A, T \in W] \neq \mathbb{P}[X \in A]\mathbb{P}[T \in W]$*

We refer to the joint distribution of X and T, i.e., $\mathbb{P}[X \in A, T \in W] = \int_W \mathcal{D}_t(A) \mathrm{d}P_\mathcal{T}(t)$, as the holistic distribution.

In the next section, we discuss the related work on explaining drift and causality in the drifting setup.

3 Related Work

Understanding drift is of major importance in many scenarios as it enables operators to perform interventions in the system at hand or to adapt models. Still, research on this topic, especially with regard to actionable explanations, is still limited. Some works focus on detecting and quantifying the drift, while others attempt to visualize it [14]. Besides, some works provide feature-wise explanations of concept drift [11,14,19,28].

A particularly versatile framework for drift explanations is *model-based drift explanations* [11]. This family relies on modelling drift as a relation of data and time as introduced in Sect. 2. They employ learning models as surrogates to compute explanations describing the drift. In this framework, a suitable model is trained to predict the time point T based on the sample X. Afterwards, the model is analysed using common, generic explanation methods ranging from interpretable models [11], over feature relevance [10,12,13,27], to counterfactual explanations [8], and activation vectors [24].

While the model-based explanation framework is very versatile as it works with generic explanation methods, so far, there has been a focus on exploratory explanation techniques [20]. These constitute a possibility to get an insight into how the data stream is changing overall. However, in many settings, human users require more actionable explanations. Since it is natural for many people to think about the cause and effect of an observation, some kind of causation-based explanations would be desirable [4].

Work on causal explanations of drift is very limited. A few publications focus on related tasks, e.g., forecasting [5] or drift detection [29], and only discuss explanations in passing. They propose finding two causal models based on directed acyclic graphs (DAGs), whereby one represents the data collected before the drift and a second one that collected after the drift. The causal explanation is derived from the difference between the causal models. While [5] extracts the causal structures from in an online fashion, [29] relies on the so-called NOTEARS causal discovery algorithm. There are further contributions considering the intersection of drift and causality, e.g., [2,25]. However, these are disjoint from our research question.

While some works consider the related field of feature relevance theory for explaining drift [12,26], in this work, we aim to extend the model-based drift explanation framework to provide actionable causal explanations of drift. Before deriving our methodology (Sect. 5), we will recall the most important aspects from computational causality.

4 Computational Causality

Causality as a concept lies at the core of human reasoning. It shapes our perception, decision making, and how we predict outcomes [4]. Despite its central role in understanding the world, there is no obvious way to formalize or model the intuitive concept of causality, leading to several different formalizations. Here, we will use the concept of computational causality induced by *interventional* do-*calculus* [22] due to its model-based nature and resulting similarity to the model-based drift explanation framework.

The backbone of this approach is given by *Bayes networks*, a kind of probabilistic graphical model. Building up on an acyclic directed graph (DAG) G with the set of nodes corresponding to the set of features, i.e., $V(G) = \mathcal{F}$, and the edges indicating the connections between the variables. More precisely, the distribution of a feature can be computed solely based on the values of its parents, i.e., $\mathbb{P}[X] = \prod_{f \in \mathcal{F}} \mathbb{P}[X_f \mid X_{\text{pa}(f)}]$. We will refer to the collection of conditional distributions as $P_f = \mathbb{P}[X_f \mid X_{\text{pa}(f)}]$, making the whole model (G, P_f). Thus, the network can be seen as a computational graph to generate samples from a distribution, which we denote as P_G. We will use this model as a link to explore computational causality in the framework of model-based drift explanations.

The connection of such models to the intuitive notion of causality is given by interpreting the directions of the edges as the direction from cause to effect. Yet, as every order of features induces a DAG by conditioning on all previous features, this is insufficient. This gap is bridged by the do-*operator*: usually the cause-variable affects the effect-variable but not the other way around – turning on the sprinkler will cause the road to be wet; making the road wet will not cause the sprinkler to be turned on (see Fig. 1 (A) for an illustration). This idea can be exploited to model a causal structure by linking it to experimental interventions: in an experiment, we force certain variables to take on specific values and observe the remaining ones, which can be formalized as follows:

Definition 2 (Experiment with Interventions). *Let $\mathcal{X}$ be a dataspace with features $\mathcal{F}$. An experiment with intervention E is a (collection of) Markov kernels that takes a manipulation x on features F to an observed experimental outcome on the remaining features, i.e., for all $F \subseteq \mathcal{F}$ we have a map*

$$E_F : \mathcal{X}_F \times \Sigma_{\mathcal{X}_{\mathcal{F} \setminus F}} \to \mathbb{R}$$

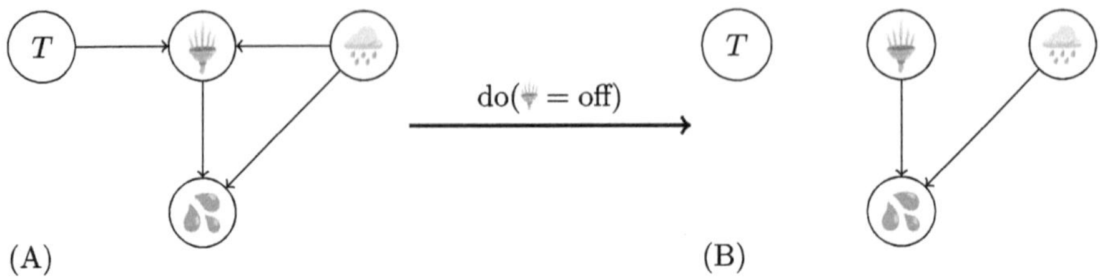

Fig. 1. Simple causal model (A) with time (T) controlled sprinkler ( ) which also switches off if it rains ( ); in both cases the ground will be wet ( ). If we manually turn off the sprinkler (B), i.e., apply a do-operator, all connections to its parents are removed in the graphical model

such that $x \mapsto E_F(x, A)$ *is measurable and* $A \mapsto E_F(x, A)$ *is a probability measure for all* x *and* A*, respectively. We call* $E_F(x)$ *the* F-manipulation of E to x *and refer to* $E_\emptyset(*)$ *as the* not-manipulated experiment. *(Here we set* $\mathcal{X}_\emptyset = \{*\}$*)*

In Bayes networks, we can simulate this idea by forcing a feature or a group of features into a specific state, $X_F = x$, and inferring the values of the remaining features. However, due to the asymmetry of cause and effect, we have to remove the paths leading to the manipulated features – as those relate to causes – while still keeping the paths from them – as those relate to effects. We have illustrated this in the case of the sprinkler example in Fig. 1. This kind of operation is called an intervention or the do-operation on the Bayes network. If the Bayes network coincides with reality for all such manipulations, it is called a *causal model.* This can be formalized as follows:

Definition 3. *Let* $\mathcal{X}$ *be a dataspace with features* $\mathcal{F}$*,* E *be an experiment with intervention, and* (G, P_f) *a Bayes network. We call* (G, P_f) *a* causal model (of E) *if for any intervention the experimental result and the model prediction coincide, i.e., for all* $F \subset \mathcal{F}$ *and* $E_\emptyset(*)_{|\mathcal{X}_F}$*-a.e.* $x \in \mathcal{X}_F$ *and* $A \in \Sigma_{\mathcal{X}_{\mathcal{F}\setminus F}}$ *it holds*

$$P_G(A \mid \mathrm{do}(X_F = x)) = E_F(x, A)$$

where $P_G(\cdot \mid \mathrm{do}(X_F = x)) := P_{G'}$ *is the distribution of the model* (G', P') *obtained by applying the* do-*operator, i.e.,* $(G', P'_f) = \mathrm{do}((G, P), F, x)$.

It is of utmost importance not to confuse the do-operator with usual conditioning: while computing the distribution is equivalent to computing a conditional, this conditional is computed based on a network with the connection towards the manipulated variables removed (see Fig. 1 (B)). In other words, the do-operator coincides with usual conditioning only if applied to a set of variables that has no parents, i.e., we have

$$P_G(\cdot \mid \mathrm{do}(X_F = x)) = P_G(\cdot \mid X_F = x).$$

Assuming that P_G is the causal model for an experiment with intervention E, we can translate this idea back and define:

Definition 4 (Causeless set of features). *Let E be an experiment with intervention with features $\mathcal{F}$. We say that $F \subset \mathcal{F}$ is* causeless (in E), *if*

$$E_F(x, A) = E_\emptyset(*, A \mid X_F = x),$$

$E_\emptyset(*)_{|\mathcal{X}_F}$*-a.s. for all A where $E_\emptyset(*, A \mid X_F = x)$ denotes the conditioning of $E_\emptyset(*, \cdot)$ on $\mathcal{X}_F$.*[1]

In this definition, the conditioning on the right-hand side can be considered as a way to process the data *after* the experiment was performed. In other words, this definition entails the idea that we can train a non-causal model to predict the value of the remaining features from $x \in \mathcal{X}_F$ and still obtain an observation that fits the result of an intervention.

Algorithmically speaking, the objective of computational causality is to recover an underlying causal model from purely observational data. Concretely, given a dataset generated under the non-intervention experiment $E_\emptyset(*)$, we want to infer the complete causal structure over all possible interventions in E. In practical terms, this approach aims to bypass the need to conduct every intervention experimentally. Achieving this reconstruction requires imposing assumptions that guarantee 1) the existence of a valid causal model and 2) computational tractability of the inference procedure. Typical assumptions are the Markov property, full information, or faithfulness that constrain the distribution of the observed variables and the considered setup, making it more similar to setups covered by those produced by Bayesian networks. A detailed discussion of these assumptions is beyond the scope of this paper. For our experimental evaluation, we focus exclusively on the classical PC algorithm [22].

5 Causal Explanations of Concept Drift

In this section, we will derive the formal modelling of causal explanations for concept drift. To do so, we will proceed in three steps: 1) we link the formal statistical description of concept drift to the notion of experiments with intervention, 2) formalize the task we want to solve in terms of an intervention, and then 3) discuss how this can be realized in a practical application using the notion of computational causality.

5.1 A Causal Model over Time

Following the ideas of [9,11], that is, considering time as a feature with drift the dependency of time and data, allows us to easily model drift in the context of an experiment with intervention by simply extending the dataspace from $\mathcal{X}$ to $\mathcal{X} \times \mathcal{T}$, with the extended feature set $\overline{\mathcal{F}} = \mathcal{F} \sqcup \{f_\mathcal{T}\}$, where $f_\mathcal{T} \notin \mathcal{F}$ represents the specific time feature and we also write $X_{f_\mathcal{T}} = T$ for consistency.

[1] This is well-defined as $\mathcal{X}_F$ and $\mathcal{X}_{\mathcal{F}\setminus F}$ are standard Borel so that the conditional probability is regular and is uniquely determined.

To link drift to experiments with intervention, we assume that the passage of time is independent of our actions. We can formalize this by assuming that $f_\mathcal{T}$ is a causeless feature. Using this assumption, we can describe drift as follows:

Theorem 1. *Let $\mathcal{X}$ be a dataspace with features $\mathcal{F}$, $\mathcal{T}$ be a time domain, and $(P_\mathcal{T}, \mathcal{D}_t)$ be a distribution process. Let E be experiment with intervention on $\mathcal{X} \times \mathcal{T}$ that has the holistic distribution of $\mathcal{D}_t$ as the distribution of the not-manipulated experiment, i.e., $E_\emptyset(*, A \times W) = \int_W \mathcal{D}_t(A)\mathrm{d}P_\mathcal{T}$, for which time ($f_\mathcal{T}$) is a causeless feature. Then the distributions $\mathcal{D}_t$ and the time-manipulations of E coincide, i.e.,*

$$\mathcal{D}_t = E_{f_\mathcal{T}}(t, \cdot)$$

$P_\mathcal{T}$-a.s. In particular, the presence of drift is equivalent to time-interventions affecting the data, i.e.,

$$\mathcal{D}_t \text{ has drift} \iff E_{f_\mathcal{T}} \text{is not constant (for } P_\mathcal{T}\text{-a.s.)}$$

Proof. All proofs are provided as part of the ArXiv version [16]

Note that we do not claim to perform an intervention on time here; we only state that if we were able to do this, we would observe the stated effect. Hence, it allows us to formalize the type of explanation we want to obtain in terms of actionability. This is a significant difference from most explanations for which no formal definition regarding their actual interpretation can be given [20]. More precisely, a *causal drift explanation* is given by the manipulation we have to perform to reverse the drift:

Definition 5 (Drift-Reversing Intervention). *Let $\mathcal{X}$ be a dataspace with features $\mathcal{F}$, $\mathcal{T}$ be a time domain, and $(P_\mathcal{T}, \mathcal{D}_t)$ be a distribution process with associated experiment with intervention E. Assume time ($f_\mathcal{T}$) is causless. We say that $F \subseteq \mathcal{F}$ provides a* drift-reversing intervention, *iff*

$$\int_B E_F(x, A \times W)\mathrm{d}\mathcal{D}_t(X_F = x) = E_{f_\mathcal{T}}(t, A \times B)P_\mathcal{T}(W) \quad \text{for } P_\mathcal{T}\text{-a.s.} t$$

for all $A \in \Sigma_{\mathcal{X}_{\mathcal{F}\setminus F}}$, $B \in \Sigma_{\mathcal{X}_F}$, $W \in \Sigma_\mathcal{T}$.

In other words, a drift-reversing intervention requires that by controlling the values of the features in F only – which might be complicated but is not impossible – we create the same effect as if we change the flow of time – which is practically infeasible. Notice that here, we only need to specify the features we are about to alter, as the distribution is already forced upon us to match the time point-specific distribution.

5.2 First Analysis and Limitations

Using ideas from computational causality, we will derive a practical procedure for causal drift explanations. To do so, in the following we will always assume that we consider an experiment with intervention E that on the one hand is linked to a distribution process $(\mathcal{D}_t, P_\mathcal{T})$ via the holistic distribution as in Theorem 1 and Definition 5 and on the other hand that we have a causal model (G, P_f) of E (in the sense of Definition 3).

Using this setup, because (G, P_f) is a causal model of E, performing the intervention on E corresponds to computing the do-operator on (G, P_f). Therefore, we can rephrase Definition 5 in terms of the causal model. However, this time we will invoke the notion of time windows, which play a vital role in the analysis of stream learning algorithms:

Lemma 1. *Let $(P_\mathcal{T}, \mathcal{D}_t)$ be a distribution process with a corresponding experiment with intervention E on $\mathcal{X} \times \mathcal{T}$ with $f_\mathcal{T}$ a causeless feature. Let (G, P_f) be a causal model of E. Then $F \subseteq \mathcal{F}$ is a drift-reversing intervention if and only if for all A, B, W' and every time window $W \subseteq \mathcal{T}$, i.e., $P_\mathcal{T}(W) > 0$, we have*

$$\int_B P_G(X_R \in A, T \in W' \mid \mathrm{do}(X_F = x))\mathrm{d}P_G(X_F = x \mid T \in W)$$
$$= P_\mathcal{T}(W')P_G(X_R \in A, X_F \in B \mid \mathrm{do}(T \in W)),$$

where $R = \mathcal{F} \setminus F$.

This again shows that the notion of drift-reversing interventions targets to reverse the drift; in this particular case, by ensuring that the distribution we currently observe is exactly the same as that observed during the time window W. The advantage of this formulation is that the result is more tangible, as window mean distributions play an important role in the context of concept drift [7,9,12,14,19,28].

The great benefit of the additional structure of the causal model is that, by analysing its graphical structure, we can determine a drift-reversing set:

Theorem 2. *Let $(P_\mathcal{T}, \mathcal{D}_t)$ be a distribution process with a corresponding experiment with intervention E on $\mathcal{X} \times \mathcal{T}$ with $f_\mathcal{T}$ a causeless feature. Let (G, P_f) be a faithful causal model of E. It holds*

1. *The node in G corresponding to time, $f_\mathcal{T}$, has no parents*
2. *The time node has children if and only if $\mathcal{D}_t$ has drift*
3. *Every drift-reversing set F contains all children of $f_\mathcal{T}$*
4. *The set of all children of $f_\mathcal{T}$ and their ancestors (without $f_\mathcal{T}$) are a drift-reversing set*

In the next section, we will examine this result more closely and discuss a more refined notion of drift-reversing sets.

5.3 A Refined Approach

Theorem 2 shows that the set of all children of the time node, together with all of their ancestors, forms a drift-reversing set. At first glance, this result produces a too large drift-reversing set as it is not to be expected that a far ancestor of a child of the time node needs to be contained in the drift-reversing set.

To make this more explicit, consider the sprinkler example from the beginning visualized in Fig. 1. As time (T) is already involved, we can apply our framework directly. We want to know why the street is dry in the evening: it is not raining, and the sprinkler is off, with the sprinkler being off because it is late. This suggests that the action we should invoke is to turn the sprinkler on, i.e., the sprinkler is the only drift-reverting feature.

In contrast, according to Theorem 2, we must also include the weather. On closer inspection (see Fig. 1 (B)), this is reasonable, as always turning on the sprinkler independent of whether or not it is raining causes another drift in the correlation of sprinkler and weather. Hence, to avoid this, we have to include the weather as stated by the theorem.

We can get a more natural explanation, i.e., only the sprinkler, if we allow the intervention to depend on other values (the weather). The idea is that there is a causal core set of features given by all of the time node's children, and the intervention on those is allowed to depend on the value of their parents. This can be made explicit by asking which node distribution needs to be changed to ensure the global distribution is time-reversed:

Theorem 3. *In the setup of Theorem 2, the smallest set of features that needs to be altered to ensure that we can obtain every time window distribution is exactly given by the set of all children of f_T. In other words: for every window $W \subset \mathcal{T}$, $P_\mathcal{T}(W) > 0$ there is a graphical model $(G_W, P_{W,f})$ on $\mathcal{X}$ such that $P_G(X \in A \mid \text{do}(T \in W)) = P_{G_W}(A)$ and $P_{W,f} = P_f$ for all $f_T \notin \text{pa}_G(f)$. Conversely, for every $f \in \mathcal{F}$ that has f_T as a parent, there exist two time windows W, W' such that $P_{W,f} \neq P_{W',f}$.*

In other words, if we keep track of the changes induced by the other parents, we only need to alter the direct children of the time node to reverse the drift. Therefore, we get two kinds of explanations: the full intervention (as stated by Theorem 2) consisting of the children of T and all their ancestors, and the conditional intervention of the children only, which then has to take the other parents into account (as in Theorem 3).

This finding is very much in line with other findings from the literature. In [10,12], the authors considered model-based drift explanation [11] through the lens of feature importance, showing that the resulting features can be seen as a wrapper method for feature selection for drift detectors. Later on, [13] extended on these ideas by introducing the notion of drift-inducing and faithfully drifting features, with the former identifying as those that "induce" the drift into the system and the latter "following along." The authors showed that in both cases, the found drifting features relate to relevant features [15] when time T is considered as the target of conditional density estimation. This links drifting

Algorithm 1. Causal Explanation of Drift

function ExplainDrift($S = ((X_1, T_1), \ldots)$ data stream)
  $G \leftarrow$ DetermineDAG(S) ▷ Run causal discovery algorithm, e.g., PC
  $C \leftarrow$ GetChildren(G, f_T)
  $P \leftarrow \cup_{f \in C}$GetParents($G, f$) $\setminus (\{f_T\} \cup C)$
  $A \leftarrow \cup_{f \in C}$GetAncesters($G, f$) $\setminus \{f_T\}$
  return (C, P, A)
end function

features closely to graphical models: following the ideas of [21] the set of all drifting (or relevant) features corresponds exactly to the connected component of the skeleton containing the time node, while the drift inducing features (or strong relevant) relate to the Markov boundary of T, i.e., its children and their other parents – similar to Theorem 3.

This consideration can be seen in two directions: on the one hand, it shows that even simple feature selection methods provide nearly causal explanations supporting their widespread usage in different applications [12,27,28], on the other hand, it connects our theoretical considerations to existing literature and methods that already have been successfully applied in a wide spread of real world applications, e.g., critical infrastructure like electrical grids [27,28] and water distribution networks [11,27], as well as land cover analysis [28].

The algorithmic solution for both cases, i.e., full drift-reversing intervention and conditional one, is presented in Algorithm 1. In other words, the full intervention explanation (Definition 5 and Theorem 2) is given by A, the conditional intervention (Theorem 3) offered by the core set C with the conditional on P.

As can be seen, the algorithm mainly performs a causal discovery on the timed data points. The later steps only extract features according to their position in the graph. Therefore, the causal discovery dominates the runtime and memory complexity of the approach. Notice that this cannot be significantly reduced if we want to compute the full drift-reversing intervention, as in this case, we might have to explore the entire graph. Furthermore, while we will make use of the classical PC algorithm in our experiments, using any other causal discovery algorithm is also valid.

6 Empirical Evaluation

In the following, we will empirically evaluate our considerations.[2] First, we briefly summarize the datasets used and describe the experimental setup. Before presenting and analyzing the results for the drift explanations in Sect. 6.3, we perform a preliminary stability analysis of the causal discovery of the PC algorithm on the selected causal graphs (Sect. 6.2).

[2] See https://github.com/FabianHinder/DRAGON for code and datasets.

6.1 Datasets and Experimental Setup

For the empirical evaluation, we use semi-synthetic datasets sampled from Bayes nets, which were modified to create plausible drift scenarios [17]. Based on the popular *Adult* and *Portuguese Student Performance* datasets, the inherent causal structure [18] was used to learn conditional probability distributions, which were modified for the following scenarios:

- *Adult Inflation*: inflation causes increases likelihood of high monetary values
- *Adult Women in STEM*: women are more likely to work in STEM jobs; less likely to work in administrative fields support
- *Student Girls Support*: female students are enrolled in support program
- *Student Boys Support*: male students are enrolled in support program

Drifting data streams with abrupt concept drift were created by merging data sampled from the unmodified distributions before the drift with data sampled from a specific scenario distribution after the drift. For consistency, the drift point was set at 25.000 samples for all streams based on *Adult*, with a total length of approximately 48.800 samples (differing slightly due to filtered-out missing values). For the *Student Performance* based streams, the drift point was set after 2.000 samples with a total length of 5.000 samples per stream.

For each of the described scenarios, we perform 10 experimental runs. We first sample a stream and then evaluate the proposed methodology. For the PC algorithm, we use the default implementation from the *causal-learn* Python package [31] with the g-square test. We report and analyze the results in the remainder of this section.

6.2 Preliminary Stability Analysis

In order to evaluate whether our causal explanations of drift are reasonable, we first evaluate the accuracy of the PC algorithm on the unmodified datasets – those without temporal features.

Comparing the detected edges to the ground truth causal graph [18], we find that the PC algorithm is moderately successful in detecting the causal structure underlying the unmodified *Adult* dataset (Fig. 2a), where out of 38 edges in the ground truth, 19 (50%) are detected correctly, while nine edges are wrongly oriented and ten were not detected at all. For the *Student Performance* dataset (Fig. 2b), meanwhile, the PC algorithm produces less accurate results, as it only detects eight out of 26 edges correctly (30.77%). Additionally, 16 edges were detected but oriented inversely, while two edges were not detected, and three additional false edges were inserted.

The poor performance on *Student Performance* can be explained by the comparatively low number of samples in this dataset, combined with a relatively high number of features. While the *Adult* dataset only contains 13 features, whose connections can be learned from nearly fifty thousand samples, the *Student Performance* dataset has 31 features and only 5.000 samples, which means that the PC algorithm has insufficient data to work with despite the lower connectivity in the causal graph, leading to less reliable independence tests.

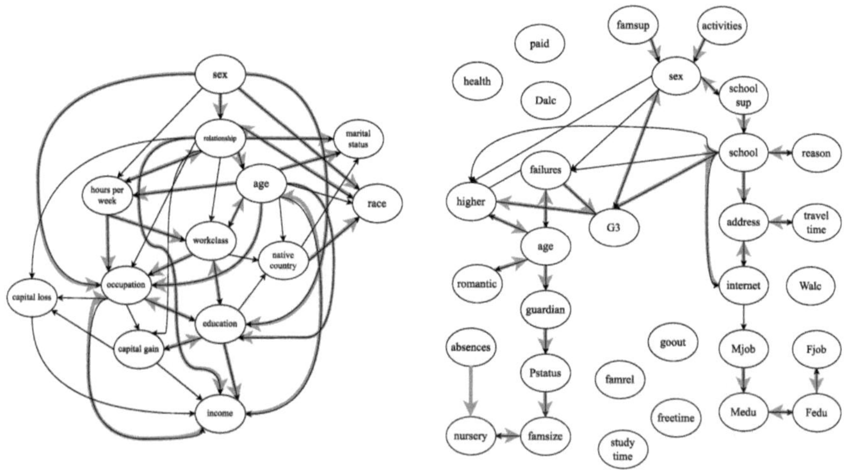

(a) Adult (b) Student

Fig. 2. Performance of the PC Algorithm. Black edges indicate the ground truth, while green edges indicate detections by the PC algorithm; thickness correlates with the number of runs in which an edge was detected (Color figure online)

6.3 Experimental Results

When analysing the causal structure of our drift scenarios, we can clearly see that our framework for causal explanations works – the temporal feature T is never connected with unrelated features, meaning that no relevant false explanations of drift are produced. And in the vast majority of cases, T is correctly connected to the drifting feature, usually as a parent.

For our causal explanation, the feature(s) directly connected to T are the most relevant, while other ancestors of children of T – i.e. possible conditional influences on the drifting feature(s) – are also part of the explanation, though with less direct impact. These features are usually identified just as well in the drifting streams as on the unmodified data, which implies that potential limitations here lie with the PC algorithm as a causal discovery method, rather than with our theoretical framework.

To illustrate this, we first take a look at the *Adult Women in STEM* drift scenario (Fig. 3a), where the drifting feature gets reliably identified as *occupation*. The temporal feature T is detected as a parent of *occupation* in nine out of ten experimental runs, while the other ancestors of the drifting feature are unchanged from the detected causal structure of the unmodified dataset. While we can see that our drifting stream results in overall more wrongly oriented edges in the causal graph, our drift explanation is generally stable and reliable. With the given information, a human data scientist would know just which feature's distribution to analyse further in order to fully understand the concept drift.

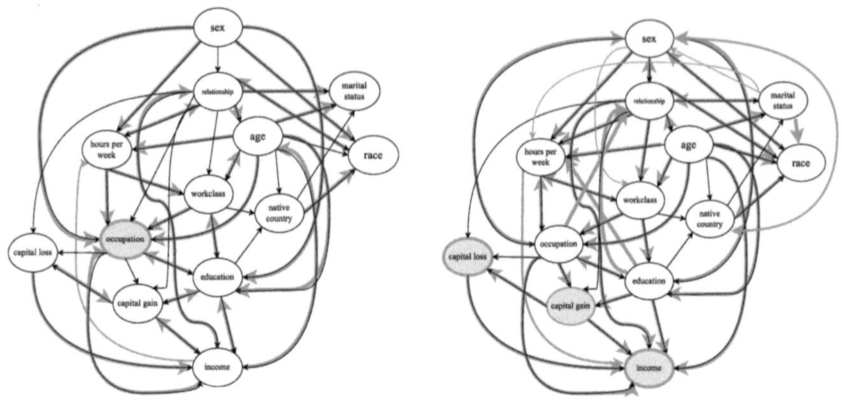

(a) Adult – Women in STEM

(b) Adult – Inflation

Fig. 3. Case Studies on the Adult dataset. Black edges indicate the ground truth, while green edges indicate detections by the PC algorithm; thickness correlates with the number of runs in which an edge was detected. Children of T are marked green, with the thickness of the border indicating the number of runs that correctly identified this relationship (Color figure online)

As the *Adult Inflation* scenario (Fig. 3b) shows, these statements even hold true when there are multiple drifting features present in the stream. In eight out of ten experimental runs, all three drifting features – *capital-gain*, *capital-loss*, and *income* – are correctly identified as directly connected to T. In the other two runs, only *capital-gain* is not detected as a direct relation of the time, but this issue can be easily explained by the close relationship between the three drifting features, which leads to some issues with the independence tests employed by the PC algorithm. This close connection between the drifting features is also why the PC algorithm shows trouble orienting the temporal edge.

Finally, despite the poor overall performance of the PC algorithm on the *Student Performance* dataset, our drift scenario *Student Girls Support* (Fig. 4a) shows that our causal explanation framework works reliably even when large parts of the causal graph are poorly recovered. In all ten runs, the drifting feature *schoolsup*, short for "school support", is correctly identified as the only child of T, and the conditional variable *sex* is identified as the only other parent of the drifting feature. This shows that even under less-than-ideal circumstances, which cause the PC algorithm to largely fail overall, causal explanations of concept drift are reliably extracted by our method. Similar findings can be seen in the *Student Boys Support* scenario (Fig. 4b), where an analogous causal structure may be observed. This implies that in scenarios where concept drift is sufficiently strong, causal explanations work well despite the high number of features and the low number of data points.

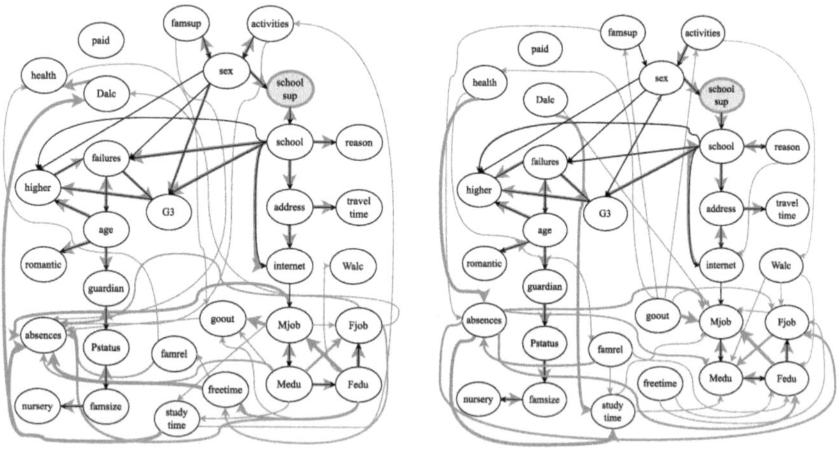

(a) Student – Girls Support

(b) Student – Boys Support

Fig. 4. Case Studies on the Student dataset. Black edges indicate the ground truth, while green edges indicate detections by the PC algorithm; thickness correlates with the number of runs in which an edge was detected. Children of T are marked green, with the thickness of the border indicating the number of runs that correctly identified this relationship (Color figure online)

7 Conclusion

In this paper, we proposed a method for causally explaining concept drift that directly enables the user to perform drift-reversing interventions on the system at hand. Our methodology is integrated into the model-based drift explanation framework and, thus, leverages the modelling of drift as a dependence of data and time. By incorporating computational causality, we can identify the full set of drift-reversing interventions. Since this may be too extensive for a layperson, we introduced conditional interventions and, thereby, obtained actionable explanations. We experimentally showed that even though the PC algorithm does not always yield a reliable causal graph of the data at hand, our pipeline reliably identifies features directly impacted by the drift.

As mentioned above, related work on incorporating feature relevance theory into model-based drift explanations seems to yield similar explanations. Investigating the relationship between causal discovery algorithms and feature relevance in this context seems to be an interesting further step. In particular, to reduce the amount of data needed. So far, our considerations assume that the entire dataset can be described by one causal graph. However, in some real-world settings, the assumption that one causal graph describes the data globally does not hold. In these cases, finding subgroups in the data and providing more local explanations for specific populations would be advantageous.

Acknowledgments. Funding in the scope of the BMBF project KI Akademie OWL under grant agreement No 01IS24057A and the ERC Synergy Grant "Water-Futures" No. 951424 is gratefully acknowledged.

Disclosure of Interests. The authors have no competing interests to declare that are relevant to the content of this article.

References

1. Adadi, A., Berrada, M.: Peeking inside the black-box: a survey on explainable artificial intelligence (XAI). IEEE Access **6**, 52138–52160 (2018). https://doi.org/10.1109/ACCESS.2018.2870052
2. Baier, L., Kühl, N., Schöffer, J., Satzger, G.: Utilizing concept drift for measuring the effectiveness of policy interventions: the case of the COVID-19 pandemic. Technical report, Karlsruher Institut für Technologie (KIT) (2020)
3. Barredo Arrieta, A., et al.: Explainable Artificial Intelligence (XAI): concepts, taxonomies, opportunities and challenges toward responsible AI. Inf. Fusion **58**, 82–115 (2020). https://doi.org/10.1016/j.inffus.2019.12.012
4. Cheng, P.W.: From covariation to causation: a causal power theory. Psychol. Rev. **104**(2), 367–405 (1997). https://doi.org/10.1037/0033-295X.104.2.367
5. Chihara, N., Matsubara, Y., Fujiwara, R., Sakurai, Y.: Modeling time-evolving causality over data streams. In: Proceedings of the 31st ACM SIGKDD Conference on Knowledge Discovery and Data Mining, vol. 1, pp. 153–164. ACM, Toronto, ON, Canada (2025). https://doi.org/10.1145/3690624.3709283
6. E.C.a.D.G. for Communications Networks and Content and Technology: Proposal for a Regulation laying down harmonised rules on Artificial Intelligence (Artificial Intelligence Act) and amending certain Union legislative acts (2021)
7. Gama, J., Žliobaitė, I., Bifet, A., Pechenizkiy, M., Bouchachia, A.: A survey on concept drift adaptation. ACM Comput. Surv. (CSUR) **46**(4), 1–37 (2014)
8. Hinder, F., Artelt, A., Vaquet, V., Hammer, B.: Contrasting explanation of concept drift. In: 30nd European Symposium on Artificial Neural Networks, Computational Intelligence and Machine Learning, ESANN (2022)
9. Hinder, F., Artelt, A., Hammer, B.: Towards non-parametric drift detection via dynamic adapting window independence drift detection (dawidd). In: International Conference on Machine Learning, pp. 4249–4259. PMLR (2020)
10. Hinder, F., Hammer, B.: Feature selection for concept drift detection. In: Verleysen, M. (ed.) 31nd European Symposium on Artificial Neural Networks, Computational Intelligence and Machine Learning, ESANN (2023)
11. Hinder, F., Vaquet, V., Brinkrolf, J., Hammer, B.: Model-based explanations of concept drift. Neurocomputing **555**, 126640 (2023)
12. Hinder, F., Vaquet, V., Hammer, B.: Feature-based analyses of concept drift. Neurocomputing **600**, 127968 (2024)
13. Hinder, F., Vaquet, V., Hammer, B.: On the fine-structure of drifting features. In: 32nd European Symposium on Artificial Neural Networks, Computational Intelligence and Machine Learning, ESANN (2024)
14. Hinder, F., Vaquet, V., Hammer, B.: One or two things we know about concept drift—a survey on monitoring in evolving environments. Part B: locating and explaining concept drift. Front. Artif. Intell. **7**, 1330258 (2024)

15. John, G.H., Kohavi, R., Pfleger, K.: Irrelevant features and the subset selection problem. In: Machine Learning Proceedings 1994, pp. 121–129. Elsevier (1994)
16. Komnick, D., Lammers, K., Hammer, B., Vaquet, V., Hinder, F.: Causal explanation of concept drift – a truly actionable approach (2025). https://arxiv.org/abs/2507.23389
17. Lammers, K., Vaquet, V., Vaquet, J., Hammer, B.: Realistic benchmarks for fair stream learning. Preprint (2025). https://pub.uni-bielefeld.de/record/3004338
18. Le Quy, T., Roy, A., Iosifidis, V., Zhang, W., Ntoutsi, E.: A survey on datasets for fairness-aware machine learning. WIREs Data Min. Knowl. Discov. **12**(3), e1452 (2022). https://doi.org/10.1002/widm.1452
19. Lu, J., Liu, A., Dong, F., Gu, F., Gama, J., Zhang, G.: Learning under concept drift: a review. IEEE Trans. Knowl. Data Eng. **31**(12), 2346–2363 (2018)
20. Molnar, C.: Interpretable Machine Learning (2020)
21. Nilsson, R., Pena, J.M., Björkegren, J., Tegnér, J.: Consistent feature selection for pattern recognition in polynomial time. J. Mach. Learn. Res. **8**, 589–612 (2007)
22. Pearl, J.: Causality. Cambridge University Press (2009)
23. Quionero-Candela, J., Sugiyama, M., Schwaighofer, A., Lawrence, N.D.: Dataset Shift in Machine Learning. The MIT Press, Cambridge (2009)
24. Roberts, I., Hinder, F., Vaquet, V., Schulz, A., Hammer, B.: Conceptualizing concept drift. In: ESANN 2025 Proceedings (2025)
25. Schölkopf, B., Janzing, D., Peters, J., Sgouritsa, E., Zhang, K., Mooij, J.: On causal and anticausal learning. In: Proceedings of the 29th International Conference on Machine Learning, ICML 2012, pp. 459–466. Omnipress, Madison, WI, USA (2012)
26. Siirtola, P., Röning, J.: Feature relevance analysis to explain concept drift–a case study in human activity recognition. arXiv preprint arXiv:2301.08453 (2023)
27. Vaquet, V., Hinder, F., Vaquet, J., Lammers, K., Quakernack, L., Hammer, B.: Localizing of anomalies in critical infrastructure using model-based drift explanations. In: 2024 International Joint Conference on Neural Networks (IJCNN), pp. 1–8. IEEE (2024)
28. Webb, G.I., Lee, L.K., Petitjean, F., Goethals, B.: Understanding concept drift. arXiv preprint arXiv:1704.00362 (2017)
29. Yang, L., Cheng, J., Luo, Y., Zhou, T., Zhang, X.: Detecting and rationalizing concept drift: a feature-level approach for understanding cause–effect relationships in dynamic environments. Expert Syst. Appl. **260**, 125365 (2025). https://doi.org/10.1016/j.eswa.2024.125365
30. Yang, Q., Liu, Y., Cheng, Y., Kang, Y., Chen, T., Yu, H.: Federated Learning. Synthesis Lectures on Artificial Intelligence and Machine Learning, Springer, Cham (2020). https://doi.org/10.1007/978-3-031-01585-4
31. Zheng, Y., et al.: Causal-learn: causal discovery in python. J. Mach. Learn. Res. **25**(60), 1–8 (2024)

Explaining Concept Drift Through the Evolution of Group Counterfactual Explanations

Ignacy Stępka and Jerzy Stefanowski(✉)

Poznan University of Technology, Poznan, Poland
istepka@andrew.cmu.edu, jerzy.stefanowski@cs.put.poznan.pl

Abstract. Machine learning models in dynamic environments often suffer from concept drift, where changes in the data distribution degrade performance. While detecting this drift is a well-studied topic, explaining how and why the model's decision-making logic changes still remains a significant challenge. In this paper, we introduce a novel methodology to explain concept drift by analyzing the temporal evolution of group-based counterfactual explanations (GCEs). Our approach tracks shifts in the GCEs' cluster centroids and their associated counterfactual action vectors before and after a drift. These evolving GCEs act as an interpretable proxy, revealing structural changes in the model's decision boundary and its underlying rationale. We operationalize this analysis within a three-layer framework that synergistically combines insights from the data layer (distributional shifts), the model layer (prediction disagreement), and our proposed explanation layer. We show that such holistic view allows for a more comprehensive diagnosis of drift, making it possible to distinguish between different root causes, such as a spatial data shift versus a re-labeling of concepts.

Keywords: Explainable AI · Concept Drift · Counterfactual Explanations

1 Introduction

The development of machine learning (ML) in decision-making and critical applications calls for transparency and trustworthiness. Explainable AI (XAI) has emerged to address this by providing insights into the behavior of complex black-box ML models [19]. A variety of methods to explain these models have been proposed [5], but almost all are designed for fully available static data sets. However, many real-world systems operate on data streams that evolve over time – a phenomenon referred to as concept drift, where the underlying data distribution changes [31]. This drift can render previously accurate models obsolete.

While most research has focused on detecting drift and adapting models to it [17], explaining the nature of the drift itself from a model's perspective has

I. Koprinska et al. (Eds.): ECML PKDD 2025, CCIS 2842, pp. 413–427, 2026.
https://doi.org/10.1007/978-3-032-19105-2_29

been less explored. Understanding the causes of drift and its impact on the predictions of a model remains largely undeveloped, despite calls from researchers [12,31]. This includes distinguishing local from global drift, locating where it occurs, and analyzing its internal characteristics. Such explanations could help identify whether the class distribution undergoes a temporal decomposition into sub-concepts that may move, split, merge, or even disappear [6], which proves valuable for debugging models and designing better responses to drift.

Among XAI methods, counterfactual explanations (CEs) are particularly valuable, offering actionable "what-if" scenarios that show how changes to input features can alter model predictions [29]. While most research concerns individual CEs [10,28], a newer line of work focuses on group counterfactual explanations (GCEs), which extend per-sample CEs to groups of similar instances sharing an explanation vector [3,8,14–16,30,32]. In Fig. 1, we provide an intuitive explanation of how GCEs differ from CEs. GCEs provide a more global, yet still interpretable, view of the model's behavior. They are well-suited for studying local drifts as they can identify general patterns in data subsets, making them ideal for analyzing the changes in sub-concepts and decision boundaries discussed above. To the best of our knowledge, GCEs have not been studied in the context of understanding concept drifts.

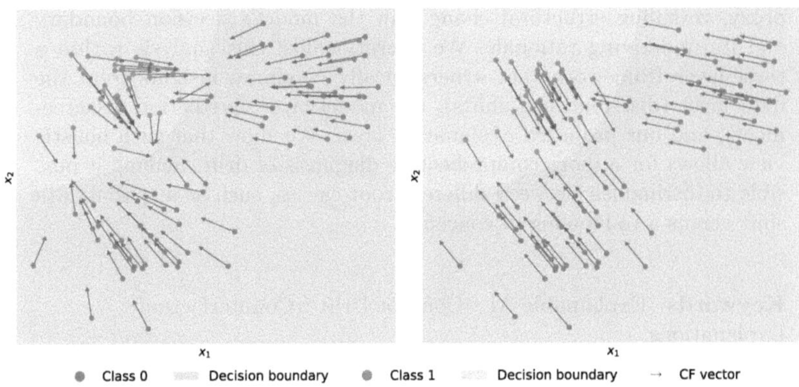

Fig. 1. A visualization of the difference between per-sample counterfactual explanations (left) and group counterfactual explanations (right). Note that for GCEs, all CEs belonging to the same group share the same CFAV.

Therefore, in this paper, we introduce a novel methodology for explaining concept drift by analyzing the evolution of GCEs. We study the evolution of cluster centroids and their associated counterfactual action vectors[1] before and after a drift, showing that they serve as a direct and interpretable proxy for the drift's impact on the model's behavior. To structure this analysis, inspired by

[1] They indicate changes of attribute values needed to obtain a counterfactual. This vector is shared by all examples inside a group.

the position paper [22], we combine GCEs with information from the data layer (distributional changes) and the model layer (prediction changes). We argue that this three-layer approach provides a more comprehensive explanation of drift's type and origin than any single layer can offer alone. For our GCE-based analysis of streams with sub-concepts, we adapt the lightweight and extensible GLANCE algorithm [15].

Through experimental case studies on different types of drift, we demonstrate that our proposed approach provides a multi-faceted view of the root causes of concept drift. By discussing the benefits and limitations of these cases, we aim to encourage further study into using group counterfactual explanations to analyze and explain concept drifts.

The paper is organized as follows. In Sect. 2 we briefly discuss the context of related works on XAI and in particular group counterfactual explanations. Then, in Sect. 3 we introduce a new method for data and concept shift analysis, which concerns the temporal evaluation of group counterfactuals and the three-layer framework. Next, we present a few case studies in Sect. 4, followed by a discussion (Sect. 5) and a note on future directions (Sect. 6).

2 Related Work

In data streams, an example $\mathbf{x}$ at time point t is drawn from a joint probability distribution $p_t(x, y)$. Concept drift occurs if for two distinct time points t and $t+\Delta$, $p_t(x, y) \neq p_{t+\Delta}(x, y)$. Researchers often focus on a *real drift*, characterized by changes in the posterior probability $p_t(y|x)$. Drifts can be categorized by their rate of change (sudden, gradual, incremental) and their scope (global, local) [6,17,31]. In this paper, we are particularly interested in drifts that involve the decomposition of classes into sub-concepts [6].

A wide variety of methods exist for detecting drift [9,17]. Most approaches aim to identify a change by monitoring either the model's predictive performance or the data distribution itself. The latter often involves comparing statistical parameters (e.g., feature means, variances) of the data distribution pre- and post-drift [18]. Analysis of the model typically involves tracking predictive metrics, as a significant drop in performance is a common signal for supervised drift detectors [17]. Some studies go further by comparing pre- and post-drift predictions at the instance level to identify regions of disagreement [4,12]. However, these methods identify *that* drift has occurred, but generally fall short of explaining *how* the model's underlying logic has changed.

Explaining such model changes is a key challenge for XAI in streaming settings [11,13]. XAI for static models has experienced substantial advancements with methods that provide explanations in the form of, e.g., feature attribution, partial dependence plots, rule-based explanations, and counterfactual explanations, for their review see e.g. [5,19]. However, adapting them to dynamic data is not straightforward. In streaming settings, where models must adapt to non-stationary data, XAI faces additional challenges. Much of the existing work extends static methods to operate online or focuses on local, per-instance explanations. Some efforts have been made to characterize such changes using feature importance [7,20,33] and partial dependence plots [21], but comprehensive explanations of concept drift remain an open challenge [11,13].

A more targeted line of research attempts to explain drift using contrastive examples [12], which provide localized insight and support the drift localization. Artelt et al. [1] advance this by applying CFEs to characterize concept drift through changes in distance (e.g., norm, cosine similarity) between counterfactuals. In addition, they propose regularizing future model updates to preserve past counterfactuals. These contributions open a promising direction, yet remain limited in scope.

Our work builds on these foundations by integrating counterfactual explanations into a broader explanatory framework. Specifically, we utilize group counterfactual explanations [3,8,14–16,25,30,32][2], which explain groups of instances in a collective way sharing the same counterfactual vectors among many examples (see Fig. 1). GCEs reduce the number of counterfactual directions from N (one per instance) to k (one per group, where $k \ll N$), improving interpretability. This summarization enables clearer insight into how segments of the input space would need to change to alter model predictions.

We note that GCEs are particularly suited for the streaming setting. Once established, they allow for efficient issuing of new counterfactuals via line search along shared group directions, avoiding costly full optimization for each instance. In this work, we adapt the GLANCE [15] method for use in data streams. GLANCE forms k clusters per class, each with a corresponding counterfactual action vector (CFAV) and supporting spatial localization.

Our approach diverges from previous work not just by using GCEs, but by analyzing how they *evolve* over time. We posit that the temporal changes in GCE cluster centroids and their corresponding counterfactual action vectors constitute a powerful and interpretable signal for explaining drift. Where prior work has characterized drift through the lens of individual examples, our method provides a more structured and global view, revealing how the model's logic for entire sub-populations is altered by the drift.

3 Method

Our approach monitors the incoming data stream, denoted as D_t at time t, and the prediction performance of a model h learned from it. Upon detection of a drift, we denote the new data context as D_{t+1}.

In order to explain the signaled drift and analyze its causes, we propose to consider information from the data, model, and explanation layers in a unified framework, which we describe in the following subsections.

[2] Sometimes also named multi-instance counterfactual explanations [2].

3.1 GCEs Evolution as Drift Explanation

This layer is central to our proposal, as we leverage GCEs to understand how the model's decision boundaries and rationale shift due to drift.

Counterfactual Explanations. Counterfactual explanations aim to identify a minimal change to an input example $\mathbf{x}$ that leads to a different prediction from a model h. Specifically, they seek a counterfactual action vector $\mathbf{c}$ such that the modified input $\mathbf{x}+\mathbf{c}$ results in a different outcome, i.e., $h(\mathbf{x}) \neq h(\mathbf{x}+\mathbf{c})$. Simultaneously, they aim to remain close to the original input according to some distance metric $d(\mathbf{x}, \mathbf{x}+\mathbf{c})$ (inspired by the formulation of Wachter et al. [29]), where $\mathbf{c}$ is obtained by solving the following optimization problem:

$$\mathbf{c} = \arg\min_{\mathbf{c}} d(\mathbf{x}, \mathbf{x}+\mathbf{c}) \quad \text{subject to} \quad h(\mathbf{x}) \neq h(\mathbf{x}+\mathbf{c}) \tag{1}$$

This objective is often optimized as a single composite loss function [29]:

$$\mathcal{L} = \mathcal{L}_{\text{validity}}(h(\mathbf{x}), 1 - h(\mathbf{x}+\mathbf{c})) + \lambda \cdot \mathcal{L}_{\text{proximity}}(\mathbf{x}, \mathbf{x}+\mathbf{c}) \tag{2}$$

where $\mathcal{L}_{\text{validity}}$ is a metric that ensures class predictions for the original example $\mathbf{x}$ and the counterfactual $\mathbf{x}+\mathbf{c}$ are different, $\mathcal{L}_{\text{proximity}}$ ensures that the counterfactual stays as close as possible to the original example in the feature space, and λ is a trade-off coefficient. Both $\mathcal{L}_{\text{proximity}}$ and $\mathcal{L}_{\text{validity}}$ can be, but are not limited to, being implemented with L_1 or L_2 distance.

Depending on the specific method, in addition to validity and proximity, other properties of counterfactuals are often expected [10,28], such as sparsity of feature changes or plausibility – ensuring the counterfactual is situated within a high-density region of the original data [24,32]. However, no single method excels across all properties [26]. Thus, in this work, we focus on validity and proximity, as the desirability of other properties is often application-specific and outside the scope of this paper.

Group Counterfactual Explanations. Given a desired number of groups k, the goal is to learn k counterfactual action vectors $\mathbf{c}_1, \mathbf{c}_2, \ldots, \mathbf{c}_k \in C$, each associated with a corresponding cluster of input examples $s_1, s_2, \ldots, s_k \in S$. Each CFAV $\mathbf{c}_i$ should be small in magnitude to optimize proximity, and when applied to inputs in its assigned cluster s_i, should flip the prediction. The objective is similar to Eq. 2: minimize average distance while maximizing validity, where validity is the proportion of examples for which the CFAV successfully flips the prediction. The difference is in the loss terms, which depend on S and C.

$$\mathcal{L}_{\text{validity}} = \frac{1}{n} \sum_{i=1}^{k} \sum_{\mathbf{x} \in s_i} \mathbb{1}\left[h(\mathbf{x}) \neq h(\mathbf{x}+\mathbf{c}_i)\right] \tag{3}$$

$$\mathcal{L}_{\text{proximity}} = \frac{1}{n} \sum_{i=1}^{k} \sum_{\mathbf{x} \in s_i} d(\mathbf{x}, \mathbf{x}+\mathbf{c}_i) \tag{4}$$

As mentioned in Sect. 2, various existing algorithms focus on different aspects of GCEs. In this work, we use GLANCE [15] because its optimization goals align with ours. A summary of GLANCE is provided in Algorithm 1. It starts by generating base CEs for all samples X using a chosen CE generation method (e.g., Wachter [29], FACE [24]). Then, it performs hierarchical clustering using a distance metric that combines feature-space L_2 distance and the cosine similarity of CFAVs. It iteratively finds the pair of clusters with the smallest combined distance, merges them by computing weighted means of centroids and CFAVs, and repeats until k clusters are formed.

Algorithm 1. GLANCE

Require: Data X, base counterfactual explanation method BCE$(\cdot)$, desired number of clusters k

Step 1: Generate Base Counterfactual Explanations
$C \leftarrow \emptyset$ ▷ *An empty set of CFAVs*
for each $\mathbf{x} \in X$ **do**
  $\mathbf{c} \leftarrow \text{BCE}(\mathbf{x})$ ▷ *Generate base CE*
  $C \leftarrow C \cup \{\mathbf{c}\}$
end for
Step 2: Cluster using combined distance metric
$M \leftarrow \mathbf{0}^{|X|\times|X|}$ ▷ *Initialize the matrix of pairwise distances*
$\mathbf{w} \leftarrow \mathbf{1}^{|X|}$ ▷ *Initialize the vector of group weights*
repeat
  for $i = 1$ to $|M|$, $j = i + 1$ to $|M|$ **do**
    $M_{ij} \leftarrow \|\mathbf{x}_i - \mathbf{x}_j\|_2 + \left(1 - \frac{\mathbf{c}_i \cdot \mathbf{c}_j}{\|\mathbf{c}_i\|_2 \|\mathbf{c}_j\|_2}\right)$
  end for
  Find pair (i, j) in M with lowest d_{clust}
  Compute new centroid $\bar{\mathbf{x}}_{\text{new}} \leftarrow \frac{1}{w_i + w_j}(w_i \bar{\mathbf{x}}_i + w_j \bar{\mathbf{x}}_j)$
  Compute new CFAV $\bar{\mathbf{c}}_{\text{new}} \leftarrow \frac{1}{w_i + w_j}(w_i \bar{\mathbf{c}}_i + w_j \bar{\mathbf{c}}_j)$
  Shrink matrix M by 1 row and column
  Update $w_{\text{new}} \leftarrow w_i + w_j$
until k clusters exist

GLANCE produces k clusters and CFAVs, which are used at test time to generate counterfactuals. For a new instance $\mathbf{x}$, the closest centroid $\bar{\mathbf{x}}_k$ is found via L_2 distance, and its associated CFAV is used.

We apply GLANCE and the general GCE framework to analyze concept drift. Specifically, we use pre- and post-drift centroids and their respective CFAVs to characterize the nature of the change. We analyze feature-wise differences in GLANCE clusters before and after the drift to assess locality and examine shifts in cluster positions to check if the decision boundary has moved.

We also compare pre- and post-drift CFAVs to assess changes in the decision boundary. If vectors remain stable, the change is likely minor. Significant differences in vectors suggest a larger shift. We quantify this difference by calculating the cosine similarity between vectors and visualizing it per-group. Additionally, we visualize the feature-wise vector directions to identify which features were most affected and what the change entailed.

To perform this analysis, we must match clusters pre- and post-drift. We use simple one-to-one matching based on the Euclidean distance between centroids. This method is intuitive for end-users, as it aligns with how they interpret similarity in feature space. Finally, since k is a hyperparameter, we use the x-means [23] algorithm as a warmup to estimate k. This gives rise to our assumption about the data distribution used in this paper: that it can be decomposed into disjoint, mean-centered subgroups.

Modifications to GLANCE. The following changes are based on preliminary experiments. While not central to this paper, we note them here for transparency and reproducibility. Originally, GLANCE uses Wachter [29] for CE generation. However, we found it unstable with different random seeds. Specifically, initialization changes led to large differences in base CEs and consequently in the final groups. To address this, we use FACE [24], a lightweight method that optimizes for validity, proximity, and plausibility. The last property is crucial for generating stable counterfactuals that are robust to noise in the data or the model [27]. Without this robustness, the proposed drift explanations would be unreliable.

Furthermore, we observed that clusters near the decision boundary could be merged even when they belong to different classes, a finding that we confirmed experimentally. To avoid this, we run GLANCE separately for each predicted class, producing k groups per class. This improved CFAV and centroid stability and increased validity in preliminary experiments.

3.2 Analyzing Changes in Data Distributions

To compare data distributions D_t (pre-drift) and D_{t+1} (post-drift), we follow established unsupervised drift analysis techniques of monitoring and comparing the means of individual features, which is a common strategy in drift detection [18]. Shifts in feature means can indicate which features are most responsible for the drift and help quantify the overall magnitude of change. We track the means on a per-class basis to allow for a more comprehensive overview and to understand whether the shift is in $P(X)$ or $P(X|Y)$.

Next, if the location of a GCE cluster changes significantly, we can complement this information by determining whether this shift is driven by a change in $P(X)$ or in $P(Y|X)$. This demonstrates how GCEs, combined with data analysis, can help to distinguish whether the change is due to a data distribution shift (real drift) or a concept shift (virtual drift).

3.3 Online Adaptation and Disagreement

Let h_t be the model trained on data up to time t. Upon detection of drift, h_t is adapted using recent data (e.g., from a sliding window), resulting in a new model h_{t+1}. The central assumption is that concept drift will cause a change in the function learned by the model. To assess this, we focus on the change in output behavior and compare h_t and h_{t+1} using the mean absolute error of their predictions. Let $X_{\text{eval}} = D_t \cup D_{t+1}$, then:

$$d_{\text{mae}}(h_t, h_{t+1}, X) = \frac{1}{|X|} \sum_{\mathbf{x} \in X} |h_t(\mathbf{x}) - h_{t+1}(\mathbf{x})| \tag{5}$$

which we call the *global disagreement coefficient.* In visualizations, we also disaggregate this global notion of model change into local disagreement coefficients, localized around the GCE-generated centroids.

This model-layer analysis is especially useful for identifying the global magnitude of model change and locating where in the input space disagreement occurs. This localizes regions of maximum model instability, offering direct clues about the areas most affected by concept drift.

3.4 Synergy of the Three Layers

We hypothesize that none of the layers – data, model, or explanation – is sufficient on its own for a complete drift interpretation. Rather, their interaction provides a more comprehensive and meaningful insight, as postulated in [22]. We formulate the following expectations for the role of each layer:

- The **Data layer** identifies whether the input distribution $P(X)$ has changed and which features or regions were involved.
- The **Model layer** measures change in the decision function and helps localize regions of significant model disagreement pre- and post-drift.
- The **GCE Explanation layer** shows whether and where the decision boundary and the feature-based counterfactual logic have shifted.

We will discuss the synergies of these explanations and the specific role of each in more detail in the experimental cases that follow.

4 Analysis of Drift Scenarios

To validate our proposed three-layer analytical framework, we now demonstrate its efficacy across several distinct concept drift scenarios. We employ synthetic datasets where the ground-truth nature of the drift is known *a priori*, enabling a clear evaluation of the contribution of each layer. The data is generated from multiple Gaussian distributions that form discrete sub-concepts within each class, which are then subjected to controlled transformations to simulate various types of drift. The following case studies illustrate how the synergy between data-level, model-level, and explanation-level insights provides a comprehensive understanding of the drift that is unattainable by any single layer alone.

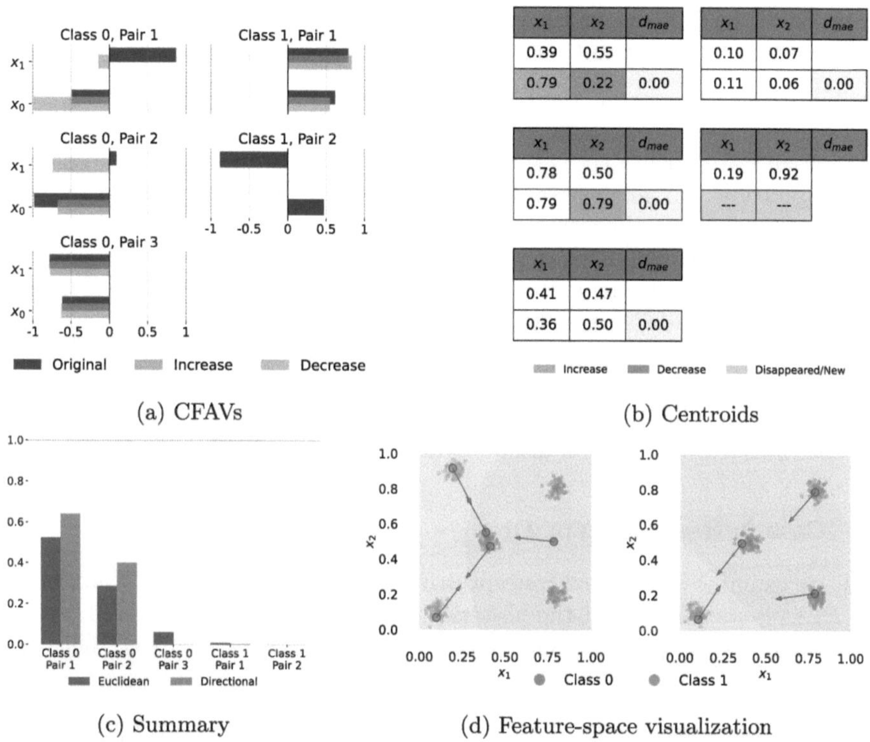

(a) CFAVs (b) Centroids

(c) Summary (d) Feature-space visualization

Fig. 2. Analysis of a data shift where one sub-concept disappears (see Fig. 2(d), bottom left). **(a)** Per-feature changes in CFAVs. **(b)** Pre- and post-drift GCE centroid locations and local model disagreement (d_{mae}). **(c)** Summary of Euclidean (CFAVs) and directional changes (centroids). **(d)** Visualization of data and GCEs pre-drift (left) and post-drift (right). **Global disagreement**: $d_{mae} \approx 0.0$. **Per-class feature means**: *before* – (**0:** $x_1 = 0.67$, $x_2 = 0.5$, **1:** $x_1 = 0.15$,$x_2 = 0.5$), *after* – (**0:** $x_1 = 0.67$,$x_2 = 0.5$, **1:** $x_1 = 0.1$,$x_2 = 0.1$).

4.1 Case 1: Data Shift

We first consider a drift characterized by a change in the data distribution $P(X)$, where a sub-concept belonging to Class 1 vanishes (Fig. 2).

Data: An analysis of per-class feature means reveals a shift for Class 1 (the mean of x_2 changes from 0.5 to 0.1), while the statistics for Class 0 remain stable. Although this indicates a change has occurred within Class 1, this aggregated view lacks the spatial or structural information necessary to understand its nature.

Model: The global disagreement coefficient remains at 0.0, indicating that the retrained model, h_{t+1}, produces predictions nearly identical to h_t on the available data. This layer of analysis is therefore unable to detect the drift, likely because the vanished data cluster had a negligible impact on the final decision boundary in regions with data support.

Explanation: In contrast, the GCE layer provides critical insight. It identifies the vanished sub-concept, noting that the cluster corresponding to *Class 1, Pair 2* has disappeared post-drift (Fig. 2(b)). While a 2D feature-space plot confirms this graphically, our analysis relies on the tabular and vector-based outputs, which scale to higher dimensions. More subtly, even though the model's predictions on data did not change ($d_{mae} \approx 0.0$), the CFAVs for the remaining clusters show moderate Euclidean and directional changes (Fig. 2(a,c)). This demonstrates that the model's underlying counterfactual logic *has* shifted in response to the drift, a nuance entirely missed by the other layers. Thus, the GCE-based analysis was capable of providing a clear, localized, and interpretable account of the drift, moving beyond descriptive statistics to identify precisely which sub-concept vanished and how its disappearance impacted the classifier's rationale.

4.2 Case 2: Real Concept Drift

Next, we examine a pure real concept drift, where the underlying data distribution $P(X)$ is stationary, but the posterior probability $P(Y|X)$ is altered, leading to the sudden concept drift. Specifically, two sub-concepts exchange their class labels (Fig. 3).

Data. The per-class feature means undergo a substantial change, correctly signaling a substantial shift in class definitions. However, this analysis alone cannot distinguish this class-swapping event from a shift of the data clusters in the feature space.

Model. A high global disagreement ($d_{mae} \approx 0.5$) indicates a severe and abrupt drift, confirming the previous model is now obsolete. The local disagreement values of 1.0 for the two affected sub-concepts (Fig. 3(b)) successfully pinpoint the regions of instability. While this layer excels at quantifying the drift's magnitude and impact, it fails to explain its root cause.

Explanation. The GCE analysis provides the crucial explanatory mechanism. It reveals that the centroids associated with two sub-concepts have effectively swapped their positions between classes (Fig. 3(b, d)). Moreover, drastic transformation of the CFAVs where all groups have been inverted (Fig. 3(a)), and the directional change approaches its maximum value (Fig. 3(c)) provides an interpretable signal that the model's fundamental decision logic has been rewritten.

This case highlights the synergy of our framework. The model layer quantified the severe impact, and the data layer pointed to a class-definition change. Yet, it is the explanation layer that delivers the conclusive evidence, demonstrating through the evolution of centroids and CFAVs that the drift was a re-labeling event, not a spatial data shift.

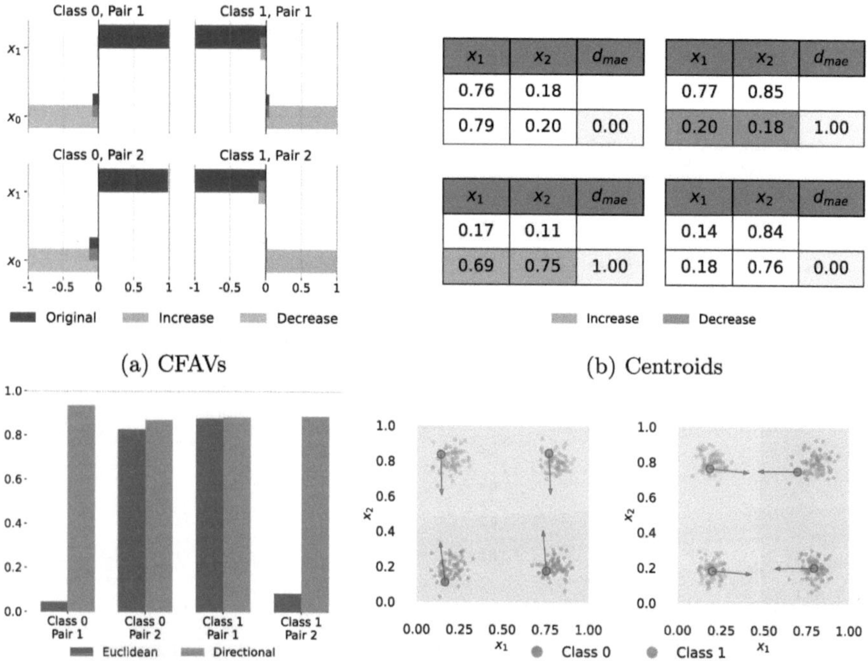

(a) CFAVs

(b) Centroids

(c) Summary

(d) Feature-space visualization

Fig. 3. Analysis of a real concept drift where two sub-concepts swap their class labels. **Global disagreement**: $d_{mae} \approx 0.5$. **Per-class feature means**: *before* – (**0:** $x_1 = 0.5$, $x_2 = 0.2$, **1:** $x_1 = 0.5$,$x_2 = 0.8$), *after* – (**0:** $x_1 = 0.8$,$x_2 = 0.5$, **1:** $x_1 = 0.2$,$x_2 = 0.5$).

4.3 Case 3: Combined Drift

Finally, we analyze a more complex scenario where both $P(X)$ and $P(Y|X)$ shift simultaneously. Some data clusters move which also results in changes of a decision boundary (Fig. 4).

Data: The per-class means shows that the mean x_1 in class 1 has deceased, while x_2 in class 0 has slightly increased. This signals a notion of data drift but offers little clarity on its nature.

Model: The global disagreement is moderate ($d_{mae} = 0.1$). On the other hand, while using information from the explanations on centroids one can notice that the local disagreement in Fig. 4(b) is non-zero only for *Class 0, Pair 1* (0.318), successfully localizing the region of highest model instability.

Explanation: The GCEs provide a detailed breakdown. Figure 4(d) and 4(b) clearly show that the centroids for *Class 0, Pair 1* have shifted in the feature-space. In parallel, the CFAV for this same pair shows a significant directional change (Fig. 4(a, c)), directly corresponding to the region of model change identified by the model layer. Meanwhile, other clusters, *Class 1, Pair 1* and *Class*

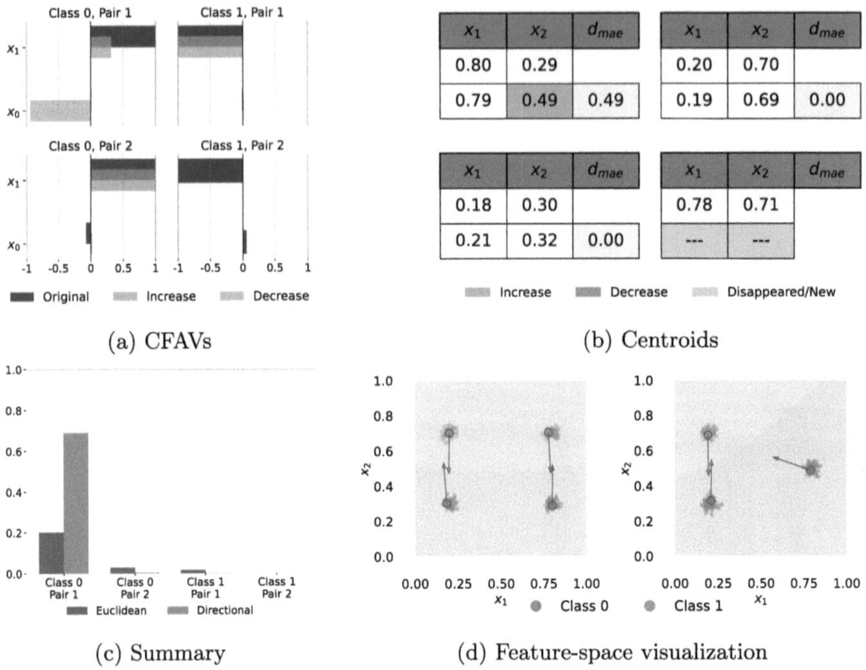

(a) CFAVs

(b) Centroids

(c) Summary

(d) Feature-space visualization

Fig. 4. Analysis of a combined drift involving both data shifts and changes in decision logic. **Global disagreement**: $d_{mae} = 0.1$. **Per-class feature means**: *before* – (**0:** $x_1 = 0.5$, $x_2 = 0.3$, **1:** $x_1 = 0.5, x_2 = 0.7$), *after* – (**0:** $x_1 = 0.5, x_2 = 0.4$, **1:** $x_1 = 0.2, x_2 = 0.7$).

0, Pair 1 remain stable in both location and CFAV, while *Class 1, Pair 2* has disappeared entirely.

This case exemplifies the usefulness of the proposed approach. All layers detect a change, but only their combination provides a full diagnosis of the causes of this considered situation. The data layer gives a high-level alert. The model layer pinpoints the consequences of the drift (i.e., where and if the model's predictions became unreliable allowing for approximating the drift is not so strong). The explanation layer reveals the real consequences: a spatial shift of one sub-concept, a change in the decision logic for that same region, and the disappearance of another. This multi-faceted explanation is aids understanding and responding to complex, real-world drifts.

5 Discussion

In this paper, we introduced a novel methodology for explaining concept drift by analyzing the temporal evolution of group counterfactual explanations. By shifting focus from numerous individual explanations to a concise set of group-level recourses, our approach offers a more tractable and interpretable lens into model changes, enabling better localization of the change and an examination of its causes in the data. We operationalized GCEs within an *explanation layer* that, when combined with traditional data- and model-level analyses, provides a synergistic and multi-faceted understanding of drift.

Furthermore, we demonstrated that this three-layer framework helps reveal underlying mechanisms of change that are difficult to identify using any single layer alone. By analyzing the movement of GCE centroids in feature space alongside the transformation of their associated counterfactual action vectors, our method can distinguish a spatial data shift from a fundamental re-labeling of concepts, or identify a combination of both. This new methodology can not only lead to a more comprehensive understanding of the reasons for concept drift by end-users, but also foster better reactions to it and improve the management of dynamic machine learning models.

6 Limitations and Future Directions

Our analysis has demonstrated the explanatory power of evolving GCEs, primarily using synthetic datasets with well-defined sub-concept structures. This controlled setting was instrumental for validation, yet it highlights several important areas for future research. A primary consideration is the performance of the methodology on data lacking a clear cluster structure. Our current pipeline determines the number of groups, k, using x-means, an approach that is inherently less effective on uniform or diffuse distributions. Subsequently, applying GLANCE, an algorithm whose clustering metric is not well suited for such data, can lead to a suboptimal partitioning of the feature space. This underscores the need to investigate alternative GCE generation methods that can uncover relevant groupings in diverse data topologies.

Yet another future challenge includes carrying out similar studies with drifts occurring in real data streams, also affected by additional sources of data difficulties, such as class overlap, noise or outliers.

Beyond the diagnostic power of explaining drift, the use of GCEs in data streams presents a practical use-case opportunity, which provides efficient, low-latency counterfactual recourse. By amortizing the cost of explanation across a small set of shared action vectors, a system could avoid the expensive task of computing a new CE for every single instance. However, this creates a key research challenge in developing methods to dynamically maintain these GCEs as the underlying data stream evolves.

Acknowledgement. This work has been supported by the National Science Centre, Poland (Grant No. 2023/51/B/ST6/00545).

References

1. Artelt, A., Hinder, F., Vaquet, V.: Contrasting explanations for understanding and regularizing model adaptations. Neural Process. Lett. **55**, 5273–5297 (2023)

2. Artelt, A., Gregoriades, A.: A two-stage algorithm for cost-efficient multi-instance counterfactual explanations. arXiv preprint arXiv:2403.01221 (2024)
3. Becker, M., Burkart, N., Birnstill, P., Beyerer, J.: A step towards global counterfactual explanations: approximating the feature space through hierarchical division and graph search. In: Advances in Artificial Intelligence and Machine Learning (2021)
4. Bobek, S., Nowaczyk, S., Pashami, S., Taghiyarrenani, Z., Nalepa, G.J.: Towards explainable deep domain adaptation. In: Artificial Intelligence. ECAI 2023 International Workshops, pp. 101–113. Springer, Cham (2024)
5. Bodria, F., Giannotti, F., Guidotti, R., Naretto, F., Pedreschi, D., Rinzivillo, S.: Benchmarking and survey of explanation methods for black box models. Data Min. Knowl. Disc. **37**(5), 1719–1778 (2023)
6. Brzezinski, D., Minku, L.L., Pewinski, T., Stefanowski, J., Szumaczuk, A.: The impact of data difficulty factors on classification of imbalanced and concept drifting data streams. Knowl. Inf. Syst. **63**(6), 1429–1469 (2021)
7. Chen, H., Lundberg, S.M., Lee, S.I.: Explaining a series of models by propagating shapley values. Nat. Commun. **13**(1), 4512 (2022)
8. Chowdhury, T., Rahimi, R., Allan, J.: Equi-explanation maps: concise and informative global summary explanations. In: Proceedings of the 2022 ACM Conference on Fairness, Accountability, and Transparency, FAccT 2022, pp. 464–472. Association for Computing Machinery, New York, NY, USA (2022)
9. Costa, A., Giusti, R., dos Santos, E.M.: Analysis of descriptors of concept drift and their impacts. Informatics **12**(1) (2025)
10. Guidotti, R.: Counterfactual explanations and how to find them: literature review and benchmarking. Data Min. Knowl. Disc. **38**(5), 2770–2824 (2024)
11. Hammer, B., Hüllermeier, E.: Interpretable machine learning: on the problem of explaining model change. In: Proceedings of Workshop Computation Intelligence (CI), pp. 1–10 (2021)
12. Hinder, F., Vaquet, V., Brinkrolf, J., Hammer, B.: Model-based explanations of concept drift. Neurocomputing **555**, 126640 (2023)
13. Hinder, F., Vaquet, V., Hammer, B.: One or two things we know about concept drift – a survey on monitoring evolving environments (2023)
14. Kanamori, K., Takagi, T., Kobayashi, K., Ike, Y.: Counterfactual explanation trees: transparent and consistent actionable recourse with decision trees. In: Camps-Valls, G., Ruiz, F.J.R., Valera, I. (eds.) Proceedings of The 25th International Conference on Artificial Intelligence and Statistics. Proceedings of Machine Learning Research, vol. 151, pp. 1846–1870. PMLR (2022)
15. Kavouras, L., et al.: Glance: global actions in a nutshell for counterfactual explainability. arXiv preprint arXiv:2405.18921 (2024)
16. Ley, D., Mishra, S., Magazzeni, D.: Globe-ce: a translation based approach for global counterfactual explanations. In: International Conference on Machine Learning, pp. 19315–19342. PMLR (2023)
17. Lu, J., Liu, A., Dong, F., Gu, F., Gama, J., Zhang, G.: Learning under concept drift: a review. IEEE Trans. Knowl. Data Eng. (2018)
18. Lukats, D., Zielinski, O., Hahn, A., Stahl, F.: A benchmark and survey of fully unsupervised concept drift detectors on real-world data streams. Int. J. Data Sci. Anal. **19**(1), 1–31 (2025)
19. Molnar, C.: Interpretable Machine Learning, 2 edn (2022)
20. Muschalik, M., Fumagalli, F., Hammer, B., Hüllermeier, E.: Agnostic explanation of model change based on feature importance. KI - Künstliche Intelligenz **36**(3–4), 211–224 (2022)

21. Muschalik, M., Fumagalli, F., Jagtani, R., Hammer, B., Hüllermeier, E.: ipdp: on partial dependence plots in dynamic modeling scenarios. In: World Conference on Explainable Artificial Intelligence, pp. 177–194. Springer, Cham (2023)
22. Ntoutsi, E., Pechenitzky, M., Stefanowski, J.: The goals and means of XAI in ML over evolving data (2024)
23. Pelleg, D., Moore, A.W.: X-means: extending k-means with efficient estimation of the number of clusters. In: Proceedings of the Seventeenth International Conference on Machine Learning, pp. 727–734 (2000)
24. Poyiadzi, R., Sokol, K., Santos-Rodriguez, R., De Bie, T., Flach, P.: Face: feasible and actionable counterfactual explanations. In: Proceedings of the AAAI/ACM Conference on AI, Ethics, and Society, pp. 344–350 (2020)
25. Rawal, K., Lakkaraju, H.: Beyond individualized recourse: interpretable and interactive summaries of actionable recourses. In: Larochelle, H., Ranzato, M., Hadsell, R., Balcan, M.F., Lin, H.T. (eds.) Advances in Neural Information Processing Systems, vol. 33, pp. 12187–12198. Curran Associates Inc, Virtual (2020)
26. Stępka, I., Lango, M., Stefanowski, J.: A multi-criteria approach for selecting an explanation from the set of counterfactuals produced by an ensemble of explainers. Int. J. Appl. Math. Comput. Sci. **34**(1) (2024)
27. Stępka, I., Stefanowski, J., Lango, M.: Counterfactual explanations with probabilistic guarantees on their robustness to model change. In: Proceedings of the 31st ACM SIGKDD Conference on Knowledge Discovery and Data Mining V.1, KDD 2025, pp. 1277–1288. Association for Computing Machinery, New York, NY, USA (2025)
28. Verma, S., Boonsanong, V., Hoang, M., Hines, K., Dickerson, J., Shah, C.: Counterfactual explanations and algorithmic recourses for machine learning: a review. ACM Comput. Surv. (CSUR) (2020)
29. Wachter, S., Mittelstadt, B., Russell, C.: Counterfactual explanations without opening the black box: automated decisions and the GDPR. Harvard J. Law Technol. **31**, 841 (2017)
30. Warren, G., Keane, M.T., Gueret, C., Delaney, E.: Explaining groups of instances counterfactually for XAI: a use case, algorithm and user study for group-counterfactuals (2023)
31. Webb, G.I., Hyde, R., Cao, H., Nguyen, H.L., Petitjean, F.: Characterizing concept drift. Data Min. Knowl. Disc. **30**(4), 964–994 (2016)
32. Wielopolski, P., Furman, O., Stefanowski, J., Zięba, M.: Unifying perspectives: plausible counterfactual explanations on global, group-wise, and local levels. arXiv (2024)
33. Zimmermann, B., Boussard, M.: Improving drift detection by monitoring shapley loss values. In: Pattern Recognition and Artificial Intelligence: Third International Conference. ICPRAI 2022, Paris, France, 1–3 June 2022, Proceedings, Part II, pp. 455–466. Springer, Heidelberg (2022)

Transparent and Adaptive Pruning of Hoeffding Trees

Kevin Händler[1], Kirsten Köbschall[2(✉)], Mattia Cerrato[2], and Stefan Kramer[2]

[1] Technical University of Darmstadt, Darmstadt, Germany
[2] Johannes Gutenberg University Mainz, Mainz, Germany
koebschall@uni-mainz.de

Abstract. Explainable artificial intelligence has gained significant attention, with decision trees playing a key role due to their interpretability. However, incremental decision trees, namely Hoeffding trees (HT), widely used for efficient and transparent data stream processing, suffer from unbounded growth. Existing adaptive methods address this but overlook transparency. We introduce **Pr**uning H**oe**ffding Trees by **F**eature **I**mportance (ProeFI), a novel approach that, in a transparent manner, prunes HT to mitigate unbounded growth and enhance adaptability to evolving data. ProeFI employs incremental permutation feature importance and a self-adaptive threshold to dynamically refine its pruning process in response to drifting data distributions. Experimental results show ProeFI achieves comparable performance to state-of-the-art methods while maintaining similar tree complexity. Our method outperforms existing techniques in balancing predictive performance and complexity.

Keywords: Transparency · Data streams · Tree pruning

1 Introduction

The surge in technology has resulted in the generation of vast amounts of data [13]. This increase of data is also evident with data streams, which have become increasingly prevalent across various domains, including sensor networks, financial markets, and social media. These continuous flows of data require the development of efficient and adaptive machine learning models capable of handling dynamic real-time data [12,16,28]. Several approaches have been proposed to handle data streams, ranging from simple learners, such as naïve Bayes, to ensembles like adaptive random forests [14] and neural networks, including continuously adaptive neural networks [15]. Due to their simplicity and efficiency, Hoeffding trees (HT) [8] have become a particularly popular base model for data stream processing. Additionally, with the increasing attention explainable artificial intelligence (XAI) has been receiving in recent years [23,32], the intrinsic interpretability of decision trees is highly desired [9,22]. One problem with Hoeffding trees (as originally published) is, however, that they grow unbounded,

I. Koprinska et al. (Eds.): ECML PKDD 2025, CCIS 2842, pp. 428–441, 2026.
https://doi.org/10.1007/978-3-032-19105-2_30

resulting in increasingly complex and less interpretable models. Although adaptive methods like Hoeffding adaptive tree (HAT) [4] and extremely fast decision tree (EFDT) [21] dynamically maintain and prune their tree structure, they do not make the pruning step itself transparent to the users. While pruning techniques have long been studied, also for data streams, the development of *explainable and transparent pruning strategies* that balance predictive performance with model complexity remains unexplored.

In this paper, we introduce **Pr**uning **Hoe**ffding Trees by **F**eature **I**mportance (ProeFI) to enable transparent pruning on Hoeffding trees. To achieve this, we measure the feature importance (FI) of individual features on an evolving data stream, building on recent work that introduced incremental permutation FI (iPFI) [11]. Using a self-adaptive threshold, we identify a set of important features. When this set changes, such as in response to concept drift (a shift in the data distribution over time), we prune subtrees that rely on features no longer considered important. This approach ensures that structural changes in the tree are directly explained, especially when drifts occur. Our experiments demonstrate that ProeFI outperforms HT and EFDT, and remains competitive with HAT in terms of AUROC across 12 data streams. Additionally, we show that under a metric balancing the trade-off between predictive performance and tree complexity, ProeFI achieves the highest mean rank.

To summarize, our contributions are the following:

1. We introduce ProeFI, integrating a pruning technique to control unbounded growth and adapt, in a transparent manner, to non-stationary data.
2. A self-adaptive threshold is proposed to refine the pruning process dynamically.
3. Extensive experiments are performed, demonstrating that ProeFI effectively balances adaptability with a similar tree size, achieving predictive performance on par with state-of-the-art Hoeffding tree variants and providing a transparent framework for data stream processing.

This work is structured as follows: Related work is discussed in Sect. 2. Section 3 introduces ProeFI and presents an adaptive importance threshold. The experimental results are presented in Sect. 4, and we conclude in Sect. 5.

2 Related Work

Pruning methods for decision trees, in the pre- and postpruning variants, have been introduced decades ago [8,10,27,29]. On data streams, additional challenges such as concept drift must be considered. To improve the capabilities of decision trees on data streams, in particular Hoeffding trees (HT), many different versions of HT exist in literature [4,18,21,25]. While some variants of the Hoeffding tree do not fully address the issue of tree growth, others do incorporate some kind of strategy that ultimately reduces the tree size, creating a more compact and interpretable model structure. One such example is the extremely fast decision tree (EFDT) [21], which improves the statistical efficiency of the Hoeffding tree by splitting a leaf if the best candidate exceeds the merit of not splitting. It continually re-evaluates and, if advantageous, replaces splits for faster convergence toward a batch-learned structure. The Hoeffding adaptive tree (HAT) [4] uses adaptive windowing (ADWIN) [5] to detect distribution changes at its nodes. HAT effectively manages drifts by growing alternate subtrees that eventually replace outdated ones. Another pruning approach employs approximate lookahead for incremental model trees [17] to evaluate the future impact of pruning decisions. However, none of these approaches address transparency, making it unclear to the user why certain subtrees were pruned. While adaptive methods primarily report performance metrics, our approach provides interpretable insights that make the model's decision-making process transparent at a level of the entire model (c.f. Sect. 3).

XAI offers a range of model-agnostic methods [7,19,20,30] for explaining predictive models by applying local feature importance methods. Model-specific methods for trees based on game theory [19] and also pixel-wise decomposition for neural networks [2] have been proposed. None of these methods can be straightforwardly employed in data streams. A common instance of model-agnostic measures to obtain feature importance (FI) is permutation feature importance (PFI). PFI uniformly permutes the values to break their link with the target [6]. Fumagalli et al. introduced incremental PFI (iPFI), which adapts FI to data streams by exponentially smoothing each feature's importance [11]. At each time step t, iPFI updates the feature importance for each singleton feature set $S_j = \{j\}$ by using the recursive incremental PFI estimator:

$$\hat{\phi}_t^{(S_j)} = (1-\alpha)\hat{\phi}_{t-1}^{(S_j)} + \alpha\, \hat{\lambda}^{(S_j)}(x_t, x_{\varphi_t}, y_t), \tag{1}$$

where $\hat{\lambda}^{(S_j)}(x_t, x_{\varphi_t}, y_t)$ measures the difference in the prediction error when x_t is replaced by x_{φ_t}, $\hat{\phi}_{t-1}^{(S_j)}$ is the average influence across all data points (global FI estimator), and $\alpha \in (0, 1)$. In the deterministic case, attributes not used by the model have a feature importance (FI) of zero, as permuting them does not affect the prediction error.

3 Methodology

We introduce ProeFI as a Hoeffding tree that transparently reduces its tree size by applying iPFI on evolving data streams. ProeFI is a tree-based algorithm that leverages feature importance through incremental permutation feature importance to enhance interpretability during pruning. In the presence of concept drift, the importance values of features may change, triggering pruning adaptations in response to the drift. Let $\mathcal{X} = \mathbb{R}^d$ be the feature space, $\mathcal{Y} = \{1, ..., C\}$ the target space for classification, and $h : \mathcal{X} \rightarrow \mathcal{Y}$ be a model learned from a data stream of data points $(x, y) \in \mathcal{X} \times \mathcal{Y}$ arriving one sample at a time. Further, let the set of feature indices be denoted as $D = \{1, 2, ..., d\}$ for a feature $x \in \mathcal{X}$. For any subset $S \subset D$, we write its complement as $\bar{S} := S \backslash D$, and denote $x^{(S)} := (x^{(i)} : i \in S)$ a partition of the features.

First, we define in Sect. 3.1 ProeFI, explain in Sect. 3.2 how the tree is pruned, and in Sect. 3.3, we propose an adaptive parameter selection method that avoids hyperparameter search.

3.1 Pruning Hoeffding Trees by Feature Importance

The Hoeffding tree, a state-of-the-art learner in online learning, tends to overfit the data by splitting on attributes that are not relevant to the current concept [3, 26,31]. When the underlying data distribution changes over time (concept drift), certain features may lose relevance [11]. However, the Hoeffding tree retains node splits on those outdated features, leading to a larger tree and potential degraded predictive performance. We address these issues by removing nodes based on the importance of their splitting attribute. We define a ProeFI $h : \mathcal{X} \to \mathcal{Y}$ as an online decision tree algorithm for data streams. It is based on the Hoeffding tree algorithm with a mechanism to adapt the tree structure to concept drift. In order to react to concept drift, we measure which features are important and detect changes below these importance values. First, we define a feature $x^{(j)}$, $j \in D$, as *important*, if its feature importance value $\hat{\phi}_t^{(S_j)}$ (c.f. Eq. 1) exceeds a threshold τ. In case no feature is declared as important, we assume not enough information has been collected, and therefore, all features are considered important. However, to detect changes in the feature importance values, ProeFI maintains a set of important features $\mathcal{I}$ and prunes whenever changes are observed in $\mathcal{I}$. The set $\mathcal{I}$ is defined as

$$\mathcal{I} := \begin{cases} \{j \in D \mid \hat{\Phi}_t^{(S_j)} \geq \tau\}, & \text{if } \exists j \in D : \hat{\Phi}_t^{(S_j)} \geq \tau, \\ D & \text{otherwise,} \end{cases} \tag{2}$$

where $\tau \in \mathbb{R}$ is a threshold to define whether a feature is important. We will revisit the choice of τ in Sect. 3.3.

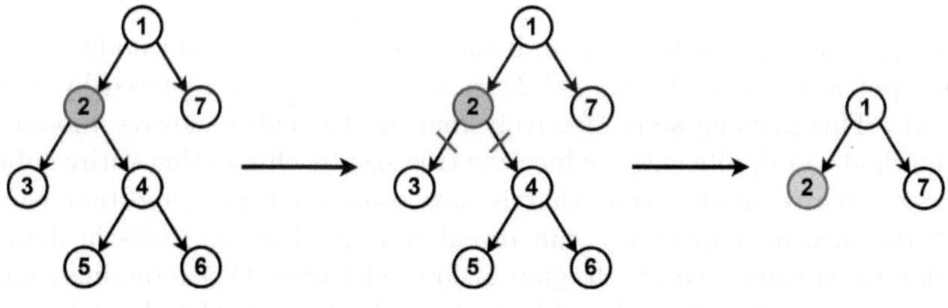

Fig. 1. Example of the complete pruning strategy. The numbers inside the nodes indicate the traversal order (pre-order traversal), with the red node being pruned. (Color figure online)

To train ProeFI on (x, y), we first check whether any unimportant features are currently employed in the decision tree structure. Nodes that rely on features not included in $\mathcal{I}$ are pruned accordingly, eliminating less impactful splits. We

Algorithm 1: Training step of ProeFI.

Data: (x, y)
$\hat{\phi}_t \leftarrow$ Explain (x, y) with iPFI;
$\bar{\phi}_t \leftarrow \frac{1}{D} \sum_{j \in D} \hat{\phi}_t^{(S_j)}$;
Update ADWIN with $\bar{\phi}_t$;
$\tau_t \leftarrow$ average importance value in ADWIN;
if $\exists j \in D : \hat{\phi}_t^{(S_j)} \geq \tau_t$ **then**
  $\mathcal{I} \leftarrow \{j \in D \mid \hat{\phi}_t^{(S_j)} \geq \tau_t\}$;
else
  $\mathcal{I} \leftarrow D$;
end
if $\mathcal{I}$ *changed* **then**
  Prune ProeFI according to $\mathcal{I}$;
end
Train ProeFI on (x, y) using HT algorithm;

perform this pruning process by traversing the tree in a pre-order fashion. When an unimportant node is identified, it is replaced by a single leaf node, effectively removing the entire subtree rooted at that node. This method can significantly reduce the tree size by eliminating entire subtrees that were created after a split that is now considered not important enough. An example of the traversal order and the resulting complete pruning process is illustrated in Fig. 1.

3.2 Tree Pruning

The tree structure is updated during training by pruning subtrees that apply split tests using unimportant features. At its core, split nodes that rely on features not included in $\mathcal{I}$ are pruned to eliminate less impactful splits. Given $\mathcal{I}$ updated on the current instance (x, y) from the incoming data stream. The tree h is traversed in a pre-order fashion: If the current node is a split node i and uses an unimportant feature j, i.e., $j \notin \mathcal{I}$, in its split test, i is replaced by a single leaf node. This pruning step effectively removes the entire subtree rooted at i. This method can significantly reduce the tree size by eliminating entire subtrees that were created after a split that is now considered not important enough. Monitoring feature importance can reveal concept drift, as shifts in data distribution often cause features to gain or lose relevance [11]. Retaining splits on features with significantly reduced importance leads to obsolete branches, so we prune them when importance drops below a threshold τ. This simple, transparent approach relies on a threshold and an interpretability measure, enabling the tree to adapt and reflect the current data distribution. However, it is important to acknowledge that constant pruning of all nodes based on their current feature importance can be problematic. Feature importance is determined by evaluating the model with and without shuffling feature j. If the tree never retains splits on j, its importance is underestimated, affecting both model structure and adaptability. To mitigate these issues, we initially treat all features as important until at least one feature satisfies $\hat{\phi}_t^{(S_j)} \geq \tau$. Moreover, pruning is only applied when $\mathcal{I}$ changes, i.e., when a feature gains or loses importance. This ensures that all features remain candidates to be added to $\mathcal{I}$. The tree continues to split on both important and unimportant features based on the splitting criterion, allowing any feature to become important over time.

3.3 Adaptive Importance Threshold

The selection of important features in $\mathcal{I}$ is determined by a threshold parameter τ, which we now aim to choose dynamically. Different data streams can yield vastly different distributions of importance scores. Moreover, a high threshold may discard useful features; a low one can retain noise, harming performance and enlarging the tree. We demonstrate empirically in Sect. 4.1 that our adaptive importance threshold adapts effectively to different settings.

To determine an adaptive threshold, we use an adaptive sliding window (ADWIN) [5] to estimate the average feature importance value, which is then used as the importance threshold. Let the current adaptive window size be of length M. At each time step t, the importance threshold τ_t is updated by averaging the feature importance values currently stored in the window with

$$\tau_t = \frac{1}{dM} \sum_{j=1}^{d} \sum_{i=t-M}^{t} \hat{\Phi}_i^{(S_j)}. \tag{3}$$

Our approach continuously updates τ_t based on real-time feature importance, avoiding reliance on a static value. As data or model characteristics shift, ADWIN detects these changes and adapts by retaining relevant features and discarding outdated ones, making it well-suited for evolving data streams. A single training step for ProeFI is summarized in Algorithm 1.

Table 1. Overview of datasets. Real world datasets above, synthetic below. *1.00E-04.

Name	Instances	Features	Classes	Class distribution	
				max(%)	min(%)
airlines	539 382	7	2	55.46	44.54
electricity	45 310	8	2	57.55	42.45
kdd99	4 898 430	41	23	56.24	0.00*
WISDM	5 417	45	6	38.43	4.53
covtype	581 010	54	7	48.76	0.47
nomao	34 464	118	2	71.44	28.56
AGR_a	1 000 000	9	2	52.83	47.17
AGR_g	1 000 000	9	2	52.83	47.17
RBF_f	1 000 000	10	5	30.01	9.27
RBF_m	1 000 000	10	5	30.01	9.27
LED_a	1 000 000	24	10	10.08	9.94
LED_g	1 000 000	24	10	10.08	9.94

4 Evaluation

We conduct multiple experiments to validate our new pruning mechanism on Hoeffding trees. First, we evaluated the performance of the adaptive threshold against some fixed threshold values. The goal is to understand the capabilities of an adaptive threshold and identify its performance relative to fixed settings. Next, we benchmarked ProeFI against different variations of the Hoeffding tree: the vanilla HT method [8], the extremely fast decision tree (EFDT) [21], and the Hoeffding adaptive tree (HAT) [4], which represents the current state-of-the-art for handling evolving data streams. We measure predictive performance through AUROC and the model complexity through the number of nodes in the tree using the test-then-train evaluation strategy, in which each instance is used for testing before training.

The datasets include six real world and six synthetic datasets, which were used in various data stream literature [14,15] and are summarized in Table 1. All experiments are conducted on each data stream five times, using random seeds 40 through 44 to ensure robust results. The implementations are written in Python using the River library [24] and the incremental PFI method from [11]. All Hoeffding trees employ the library's default settings (grace period of 200, $\delta = 10^{-7}$, tie threshold of 0.05), and incremental PFI uses its default $\alpha = 0.001$. The ProeFI implementation, datasets, and all necessary code to reproduce the experiments are publicly available[1].

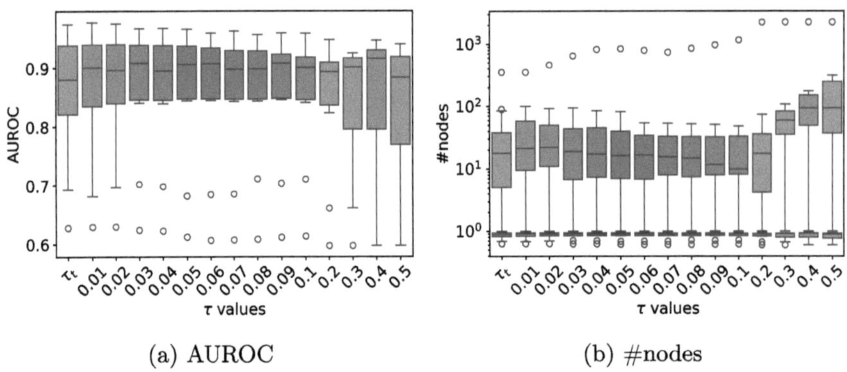

Fig. 2. Comparison of out adaptive threshold τ_t with manually defined, fixed τ values under (a) AUROC and (b) average number of nodes shown with log scale. Averaged over five random repetitions.

4.1 Analysis of Adaptive vs. Fixed Thresholding

In order to analyze the effectiveness of the adaptive threshold, we compared it against a broad set of fixed thresholds in Fig. 2. We observe AUROC values

[1] https://github.com/kramerlab/ProeFI.

close to each other for smaller τ values and a lower predictive performance for higher τ values. The number of nodes interacts with the threshold τ during pruning, and higher values result in less pruning, which also causes a higher number of nodes in the tree (c.f. Fig. 2b). Nevertheless, τ is a hyperparameter that must be set manually based on empirical observation. While we observed a tendency toward lower values of τ, its optimal setting is not immediately intuitive. Our experiments, however, yielded stable and effective values for the adaptive configuration of our parameter τ_t.

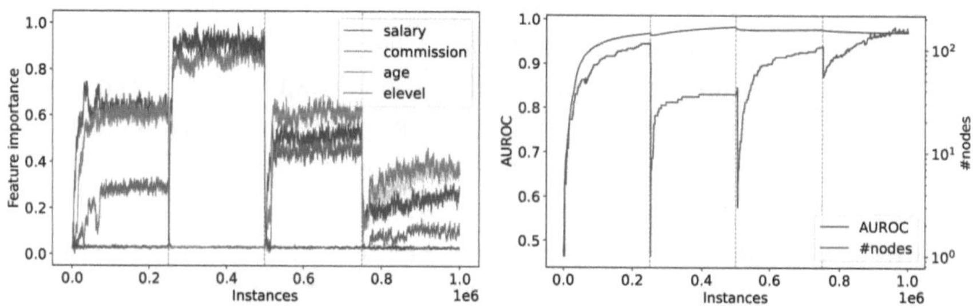

(a) Feature Importance (b) AUROC and #nodes

Fig. 3. Comparison of model behavior of ProeFI over time in AGR$_a$, showing (a) the feature importance values and (b) both AUROC (here: approximate AUROC from River [24]) and node count. Abrupt concept drift occurs at instances 250k, 500k, and 750k, visualized by grey, dotted vertical lines in the plots. The first drift causes a drop in the importance of features *salary* and *commission* while *age* and *elevel* gain relevance. In response, ProeFI prunes its tree entirely, as the root node was split on a now unimportant feature. After the second drift, it keeps many of its nodes split on *age*, and after the final drift, only minor structural adjustments are made as the relevant features remain largely consistent.

4.2 Drift Adaptation

We analyze the adaptive capabilities and drift reaction of ProeFI in Fig. 3. Although the Agrawal datasets include nine features in total, Fig. 3a reveals that the number of important features varies between two and four depending on the current concept. After concept drift, different features gain relevance, and in response, ProeFI prunes its tree. If the root node was split on a now unimportant feature (first drift), the tree is now entirely pruned and rebuilt its structure from scratch. Otherwise, only subtrees were pruned, and the relevant features remain largely consistent. This demonstrates that ProeFI effectively adapts to changing concepts by dynamically restructuring itself based on feature importance to allow itself to maintain a strong predictive performance even in the presence of concept drift.

Table 2. Comparison of AUROC and Complexity (average number of nodes) across datasets.

Dataset	AUROC				Complexity (#nodes)			
	HT	HAT	EFDT	ProeFI	HT	HAT	EDFT	ProeFI
airlines	0.662	0.620	**0.664**	0.628	2241.00	1747.27	3575.02	**351.54**
electricity	0.848	**0.878**	**0.878**	0.846	24.90	**6.71**	18.05	16.42
covtype	0.927	**0.932**	0.910	0.926	253.60	**6.93**	20.24	19.30
nomao	0.902	0.898	0.806	**0.910**	8.68	3.39	**1.00**	4.54
kdd99	**0.803**	0.500	0.617	0.767	100.39	6.14	**1.00**	5.26
wisdm	**0.851**	0.434	0.832	**0.851**	**1.00**	**1.00**	9.06	**1.00**
Avg Rank	**2.00**	3.00	2.67	2.33	3.50	**1.83**	2.67	2.00
AGR_a	0.941	**0.982**	0.909	0.975	295.83	92.79	**75.04**	85.35
AGR_g	0.930	**0.971**	0.905	0.969	317.29	157.59	**78.31**	89.68
RBF_f	0.597	0.682	**0.758**	0.693	73.72	**2.02**	13.36	3.06
RBF_m	0.744	0.868	**0.890**	0.840	108.18	9.82	39.69	**8.53**
LED_a	0.918	**0.943**	0.935	0.939	93.29	**17.24**	64.40	22.17
LED_g	0.917	**0.940**	0.937	0.938	93.07	**19.56**	66.87	20.92
Avg Rank	3.67	**1.50**	2.67	2.17	4.00	**1.83**	2.33	**1.83**
Total Rank	2.83	**2.25**	2.67	**2.25**	3.75	**1.83**	2.50	1.92

4.3 Comparative Performance Analysis

In this Section, we compare the predictive performance and model complexity of ProeFI in comparison to HT, EFDT, and HAT. Table 2 summarizes our results.

Across the six real-world datasets, ProeFI demonstrates consistently strong AUROC values, with an overall average rank of 2.33, second to the standard HT. However, HT's complexity is substantially higher because it does not perform any kind of pruning, it grows very deep and wide trees. This unchecked growth in HT contrasts with the other models with a pruning mechanism that keeps their tree size relatively low at the cost of some performance. In terms of complexity, ProeFI also gains the second average rank, highlighting its ability to maintain compact models without sacrificing too much predictive power. In contrast, HAT has, on average, the smallest tree, but its predictive performance on some datasets is much lower.

On the six synthetic datasets with concept drift, HAT achieves the top predictive performance while both, ProeFI and HAT build the smallest trees overall, which showcases ProeFI's and HAT's exceptional adaptability to changing data distributions. But still, ProeFI is a close second, with its AUROC scores consistently within a few thousandths of HAT's best results while matching its average tree size. This demonstrates that ProeFI can adapt almost as effectively to drifting concepts without incurring extra complexity, all while offering more transparent pruning behavior. Interestingly, EFDT's faster convergence gives it an edge in adapting to incremental changes on the RBF datasets, but at the cost of pruning the tree less than HAT and ProeFI. But HT struggles to adapt to these changes efficiently. It needs to grow a much larger tree just to achieve performance that still lags behind the others.

Overall, ProeFI emerges as one of the best-ranking models in terms of AUROC and the second-best in terms of complexity. As we encounter the problem of showing the trade-off between performance and transparency, we introduce a new metric to capture both sizes. Our goal is to maximize AUROC while minimizing tree complexity. Taking the ratio of these two captures this trade-off effectively: $\text{AUROC}/\log_2(\text{Number nodes})$.

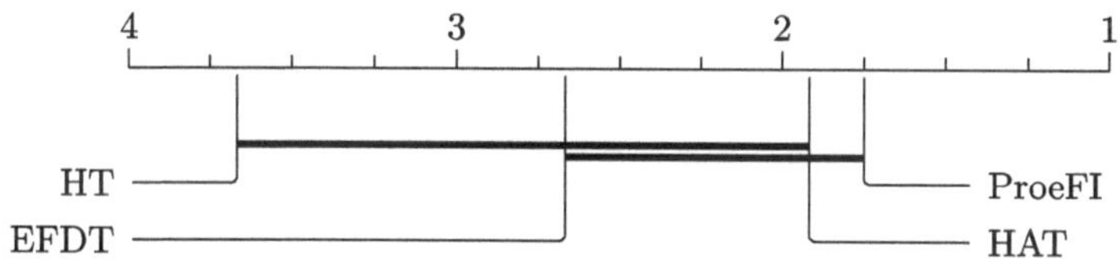

Fig. 4. Trade-off between predictive performance and tree complexity. Critical difference diagram using the Wilcoxon signed-rank test with 95% confidence level and adjusted with Holm's method under the metric $\text{AUROC}/\log_2(\text{Number nodes})$.

We conducted a Wilcoxon signed-rank test with 95% confidence level and adjusted it with Holm's method to analyze the critical differences in Fig. 4. Interestingly, ProeFI achieves the highest rank, indicating ProeFI offers the best balance between predictive performance and model complexity. ProeFI and HAT, however, are statistically indistinguishable.

4.4 Qualitative Analysis

Finally, we perform a qualitative analysis to demonstrate ProeFI's transparency. Figure 5 shows the structure of ProeFI immediately before the drift and again just after it was detected, and the tree pruned. After drift detection, we observe that the set of important features changes, and therefore, nodes applying split tests on those unimportant features are pruned. In Fig. 5a, the tree was partitioned on features, which were considered important before the drift. Whereas after the abrupt drift in Fig. 5b, some of the features are no longer important and subtrees, rooted at now unimportant features, are pruned. Thereby, these two branches have collapsed into two single leaves. These new leaves still contain the aggregated counts from before pruning, but they no longer drive any further splits on unimportant features. After pruning, an explanation of which attributes were pruned is noted in the new leaf nodes.

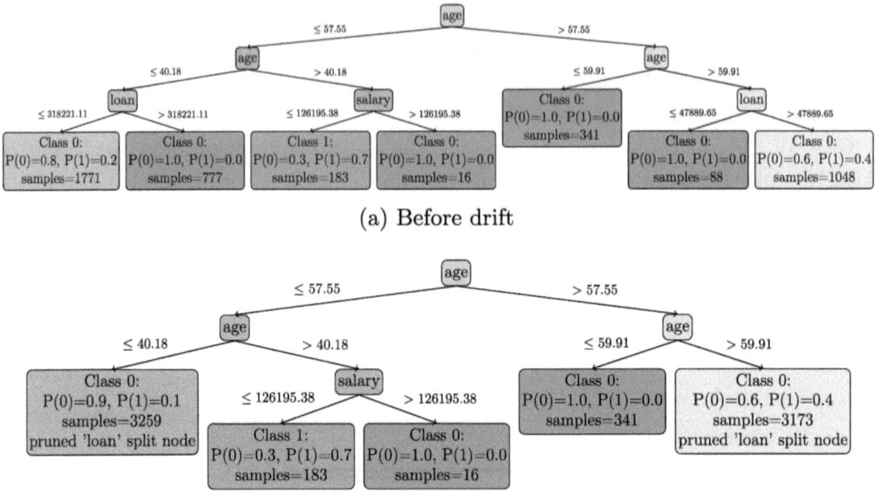

(a) Before drift

(b) After drift

Fig. 5. Comparison between ProeFI's structure just (a) before and (b) immediately after an abrupt concept drift at instance 25,000 was detected at instance 26,238 within AGR_a. The abrupt drift in Agrawal [1] changes from classification function 5, where the class label depends on *age*, *salary*, and *loan*, to classification function 6, in which the *loan* attribute is no longer used. In (b), the subtree rooted at nodes having *loan* as their split attribute is pruned and this pruning information is written as an explanation inside the new leaf nodes. Orange nodes indicate a stronger bias toward class 0, blue nodes toward class 1, and the depth of color reflects the classifier's confidence at each node. (Color figure online)

5 Conclusion

In this work, we address the challenge of transparent and small trees, which are able to adapt to concept drift. We introduced ProeFI to prune Hoeffding trees transparently and retain small but effective trees. Our approach uses an adaptive thresholding approach to define a set of important features to prune only unimportant features from the usage in internal split nodes. Our experiments show ProeFI performs competitively with state-of-the-art adaptive Hoeffding trees while maintaining comparable tree complexity. We also empirically showed that ProeFI outperforms the state-of-the-art HT variations under a metric balancing predictive performance and model simplicity. Future work will focus on further improving the transparency of Hoeffding trees through a splitting criterion directly guided by feature importance. Since importance scores reliably highlight valuable features, integrating them into split choices can make splitting more explainable and speed up training by leaving out low-impact splits.

Acknowledgments. The research in this paper was supported by the "TOPML: Trading Off Non-Functional Properties of Machine Learning" project funded by Carl Zeiss Foundation, grant number P2021-02-014.

References

1. Agrawal, R., Imielinski, T., Swami, A.: Database mining: a performance perspective. IEEE Trans. Knowl. Data Eng. **5**(6), 914–925 (1993). https://doi.org/10.1109/69.250074
2. Bach, S., Binder, A., Montavon, G., Klauschen, F., Müller, K.R., Samek, W.: On pixel-wise explanations for non-linear classifier decisions by layer-wise relevance propagation. PLoS ONE **10**(7), 1–46 (2015). https://doi.org/10.1371/journal.pone.0130140
3. Barddal, J.P., Enembreck, F.: Learning regularized hoeffding trees from data streams. In: Proceedings of the 34th ACM/SIGAPP Symposium on Applied Computing, SAC 2019, pp. 574–581. Association for Computing Machinery, New York, NY, USA (2019). https://doi.org/10.1145/3297280.3297334
4. Bifet, A., Gavaldà, R.: Adaptive learning from evolving data streams. In: Proceedings of the 8th International Symposium on Intelligent Data Analysis: Advances in Intelligent Data Analysis VIII, IDA 2009, pp. 249–260. Springer, Heidelberg (2009). https://doi.org/10.1007/978-3-642-03915-7_22
5. Bifet, A., Gavaldà, R.: Learning from time-changing data with adaptive windowing, vol. 7 (2007). https://doi.org/10.1137/1.9781611972771.42
6. Breiman, L.: Random forests. Mach. Learn. **45**(1), 5–32 (2001). https://doi.org/10.1023/A:1010933404324
7. Covert, I., Lee, S.I.: Improving kernelshap: practical shapley value estimation using linear regression. In: Banerjee, A., Fukumizu, K. (eds.) Proceedings of The 24th International Conference on Artificial Intelligence and Statistics. Proceedings of Machine Learning Research, vol. 130, pp. 3457–3465. PMLR (2021). https://proceedings.mlr.press/v130/covert21a.html
8. Domingos, P., Hulten, G.: Mining high-speed data streams. In: Proceedings of the Sixth ACM SIGKDD International Conference on Knowledge Discovery and Data Mining, KDD 2000, pp. 71–80. Association for Computing Machinery, New York, NY, USA (2000). https://doi.org/10.1145/347090.347107
9. Du, M., Liu, N., Hu, X.: Techniques for interpretable machine learning. Commun. ACM **63**(1), 68–77 (2019). https://doi.org/10.1145/3359786
10. Elomaa, T.: The biases of decision tree pruning strategies. In: Hand, D.J., Kok, J.N., Berthold, M.R. (eds.) Advances in Intelligent Data Analysis, pp. 63–74. Springer, Heidelberg (1999)
11. Fumagalli, F., Muschalik, M., Hüllermeier, E., Hammer, B.: Incremental permutation feature importance (IPFI): towards online explanations on data streams. Mach. Learn. **112**(12), 4863–4903 (2023). https://doi.org/10.1007/s10994-023-06385-y
12. Gama, J., Žliobaitė, I., Bifet, A., Pechenizkiy, M., Bouchachia, A.: A survey on concept drift adaptation. ACM Comput. Surv. **46**(4) (2014). https://doi.org/10.1145/2523813
13. García, S., Ramírez-Gallego, S., Luengo, J., Benítez, J., Herrera, F.: Big data preprocessing: methods and prospects. Big Data Anal. **1** (2016). https://doi.org/10.1186/s41044-016-0014-0

14. Gomes, H.M., et al.: Adaptive random forests for evolving data stream classification. Mach. Learn. **106**(9–10), 1469–1495 (2017). https://doi.org/10.1007/s10994-017-5642-8
15. Gunasekara, N., Gomes, H.M., Pfahringer, B., Bifet, A.: Online hyperparameter optimization for streaming neural networks. In: 2022 International Joint Conference on Neural Networks (IJCNN), pp. 1–9 (2022). https://doi.org/10.1109/IJCNN55064.2022.9891953
16. Gunasekara, N., Pfahringer, B., Gomes, H.M., Bifet, A.: Survey on online streaming continual learning. In: Proceedings of the Thirty-Second International Joint Conference on Artificial Intelligence. IJCAI 2023 (2023). https://doi.org/10.24963/ijcai.2023/743
17. Hapfelmeier, A., Pfahringer, B., Kramer, S.: Pruning incremental linear model trees with approximate lookahead. IEEE Trans. Knowl. Data Eng. **26**(8), 2072–2076 (2014). https://doi.org/10.1109/TKDE.2013.132
18. Kirkby, R.: Improving hoeffding trees (2007)
19. Lundberg, S., et al.: From local explanations to global understanding with explainable AI for trees. Nat. Mach. Intell. 56–67 (2020). https://doi.org/10.1038/s42256-019-0138-9
20. Lundberg, S.M., Lee, S.I.: A unified approach to interpreting model predictions. In: Guyon, I., et al. (eds.) Advances in Neural Information Processing Systems, vol. 30, pp. 4768–4777. Curran Associates, Inc. (2017)
21. Manapragada, C., Webb, G.I., Salehi, M.: Extremely fast decision tree. In: Proceedings of the 24th ACM SIGKDD International Conference on Knowledge Discovery & Data Mining, KDD 2018, pp. 1953–1962. Association for Computing Machinery, New York, NY, USA (2018). https://doi.org/10.1145/3219819.3220005
22. Mienye, I.D., Jere, N.: A survey of decision trees: concepts, algorithms, and applications. IEEE Access **12**, 86716–86727 (2024). https://doi.org/10.1109/ACCESS.2024.3416838
23. Miller, T.: Explanation in artificial intelligence: insights from the social sciences. Artif. Intell. **267**, 1–38 (2019). https://doi.org/10.1016/j.artint.2018.07.007
24. Montiel, J., et al.: River: machine learning for streaming data in python. J. Mach. Learn. Res. **22**(1) (2021)
25. Pfahringer, B., Holmes, G., Kirkby, R.: New options for hoeffding trees. In: Orgun, M.A., Thornton, J. (eds.) AI 2007: Advances in Artificial Intelligence, pp. 90–99. Springer, Heidelberg (2007)
26. Quinlan, J.R.: Induction of decision trees. Mach. Learn. **1**(1), 81–106 (1986). https://doi.org/10.1023/A:1022643204877
27. Quinlan, J.: Simplifying decision trees. Int. J. Man Mach. Stud. **27**(3), 221–234 (1987). https://doi.org/10.1016/S0020-7373(87)80053-6
28. Ramírez-Gallego, S., Krawczyk, B., García, S., Wozniak, M., Herrera, F.: A survey on data preprocessing for data stream mining: current status and future directions. Neurocomputing **239** (2017). https://doi.org/10.1016/j.neucom.2017.01.078
29. Rastogi, R., Shim, K.: Public: a decision tree classifier that integrates building and pruning. Data Mining Knowl. Discov. **4** (2000). https://doi.org/10.1023/A:1009887311454
30. Ribeiro, M.T., Singh, S., Guestrin, C.: "why should i trust you?": explaining the predictions of any classifier. In: Proceedings of the 22nd ACM SIGKDD International Conference on Knowledge Discovery and Data Mining, KDD 2016, pp. 1135–1144. Association for Computing Machinery, New York, NY, USA (2016). https://doi.org/10.1145/2939672.2939778

31. Rokach, L., Maimon, O.: Decision Trees, pp. 165–192. Springer, Boston (2005). https://doi.org/10.1007/0-387-25465-X_9
32. Saeed, W., Omlin, C.: Explainable AI (XAI): a systematic meta-survey of current challenges and future opportunities. Knowl.-Based Syst. **263**, 110273 (2023). https://doi.org/10.1016/j.knosys.2023.110273

Proposing Multi-perspective Approach for Detecting and Explaining Concepts Drifts in Evolving Data

Natalia Wojak-Strzelecka[1(✉)], Antonio Guillén-Teruel[2], Szymon Bobek[1], Grzegorz J. Nalepa[1], José Palma[2], and Juan Botía[2]

[1] Department of Human-Centered Artificial Intelligence, Institute of Applied Computer Science, Faculty of Physics, Astronomy and Applied Computer Science, Jagiellonian University, ul. prof. Stanisława Łojasiewicza 11, 30-348 Kraków, Poland
natalia.wojak-strzelecka-guest@uj.edu.pl

[2] Department of Information and Communication Engineering, University of Murcia, 30100 Murcia, Spain

Abstract. Concept drift detection is a critical component of most online learning algorithms. While the primary goal of concept drift detection techniques is to trigger the retraining of machine learning models, in high-risk domains such as industry and healthcare "where models serve as decision-support systems, with final decisions made by humans" it is essential to understand the nature of the drift, its potential causes, and its impact on model performance. In this paper, we propose a 3P (three-perspective) approach for efficiently detecting concept drifts and analyzing their nature from three perspectives: data characteristics, model performance, and explainability. Unlike traditional approaches that merely identify the point in time where drift occurs, our approach not only detects drift but also provides deeper context by integrating insights from data, model behaviour, and XAI (explainable AI). This enriched perspective enables a more comprehensive understanding of drift dynamics, facilitating informed decision-making. Additionally, by incorporating explainability-driven analysis, our approach allows for detecting drifts that may not be identifiable through model performance alone, as with most conventional detectors. We integrate this three-perspective analysis with visualization techniques and demonstrate its effectiveness on benchmark datasets and two real-world use cases from healthcare and industry.

Keywords: concept drift · explainability · data streams · evolving data

1 Introduction

In dynamic environments where data streams continuously evolve, detecting and adapting to concept drift is crucial for maintaining the reliability and accuracy of

I. Koprinska et al. (Eds.): ECML PKDD 2025, CCIS 2842, pp. 442–457, 2026.
https://doi.org/10.1007/978-3-032-19105-2_31

machine learning models. Concept drift refers to changes in the statistical properties of data over time, which can undermine the performance of predictive models if left unaddressed. This challenge is particularly prevalent in applications such as industry, financial forecasting, and healthcare analytics, where shifts in underlying data patterns are common [30]. Beyond drift detection, understanding and explaining the causes behind these changes is equally important. In industries, particularly for predictive maintenance [16], identifying the root causes of drift can help detect early signs of equipment degradation or process inefficiencies. This allows for early interventions, reducing costly downtime and extending the operational lifespan of the machinery. Similarly, in healthcare, explaining concept drift is crucial during pandemics [17], where sudden shifts in patient data, treatment responses, or infection rates can signal emerging health risks. Understanding these changes enables faster responses and more effective allocation of resources to mitigate the spread and impact of disease outbreaks. This paper presents a novel method to concept drift detection and explanation using a 3P (three–perspective) approach that evaluates changes across data, model, and explanation perspective. The proposed approach not only tracks shifts in data distribution but also monitors model confidence and interprets the evolving influence of individual features on predictions. The data perspective provides insights into how the distribution shifts. The model perspective captures variations in model confidence, serving as an early indicator of potential drift. The explanation perspective clarifies how feature importance evolves, enabling a deeper understanding of the causes behind model performance fluctuations. The proposed 3P framework is presented in Fig. 1.

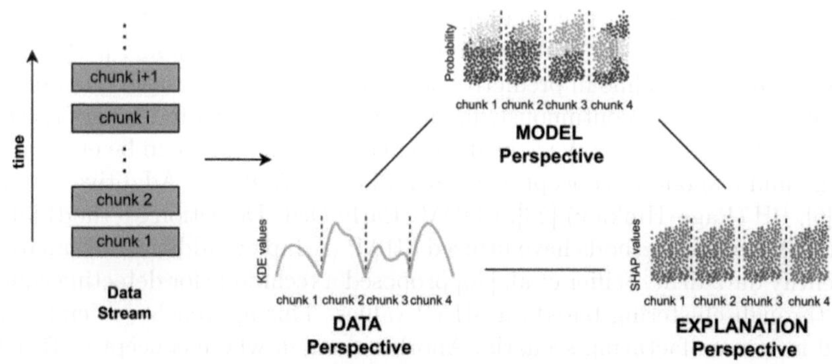

Fig. 1. Flowchart of 3P approach. The data stream is divided into chunks, and each chunk is analyzed from three key perspectives—data, explanation, and model perspective—such that the data perspective focuses on tracking the Kernel Density Estimation of test data across chunks, the explanation perspective involves monitoring changes in feature importance across successive models while maintaining a fixed dataset, and the model perspective captures variations in prediction probabilities across successive models while using a fixed dataset.

We evaluated our approach on both synthetic and real-world datasets. For the synthetic data, the AGRAWAL [4] data stream generator is used, producing two streams with abrupt and gradual concept drifts. The real-world evaluation includes two datasets: one from a cold rolling mill simulator, reflecting industrial processes in steel manufacturing, and another from hospital data collected during the COVID-19 pandemic which is called SMS (Servicio Murciano de Salud) dataset. Our study shows that the proposed approach enables the detection and explanation of drift patterns, along with the dynamics of model adaptation, which would otherwise remain invisible to both the system user and the model designer. Access the source code for the cold rolling mill dataset calculations could be found at GitHub.

The rest of the paper is structured as follows: Sect. 2 reviews the state of the art in relevant fields. Section 3 offers an in-depth explanation of the proposed 3P approach. Section 4 resents empirical studies on the influence of SHAP values, data distribution and model perfromance in drift detection, using both benchmark and real–world datasets. Finally, Sect. 5 summarizes the research findings and outlines potential directions for future work.

2 Related Work

A data stream is an endless sequence of incoming instances that arrive at high speed, requiring rapid processing [29]. This presents unique challenges, particularly in terms of computational efficiency and limited prediction time. Beyond the need for fast processing, a major difficulty arises from the fact that stream learning algorithms operate in dynamic, non-stationary environments where data distribution evolves over time—a phenomenon known as *concept drift* [18]. Such shifts in the data stream can have a significant impact on model performance, often leading to a decline in predictive accuracy and overall system reliability. To mitigate these effects, continuously monitoring and adapting to changes is crucial in real-world applications. Various drift detection techniques can be employed to identify and respond to concept drift, including the ADWIN (Adaptive Windowing) [6], PH (Page–Hinkley) [23], EDDM (Early Drift Detection Method) [5] and others [3]. Several methods have utilized SHAP (SHapley Additive exPlanations) to identify data drift. Seiffer et al. [26] proposed a technique for detecting concept drift through clustering based on SHAP values. This approach was empirically tested in a manufacturing scenario. Another domain where concept drift detection is critical is healthcare. In this context, the authors in [10] detected drift by evaluating feature importance in COVID-19 pandemic data.

Incorporating explainability into models operating on streaming data enhances transparency and aids in understanding model decisions over time. XAI (explainable AI) techniques, such as SHAP (SHapley Additive exPlanations) [19], provide insights into feature contributions and model behavior. Mozolewski et al. [21] discusses the evaluation of XAI methods within streaming data environments. They assess how XAI techniques can explain machine learning model dependencies on features in a streaming context. Authors in [25] provide an overview of existing XAI methods applied to time series data. It highlights the types of explanations these methods produce and reflects on their impact on building confidence and trust in AI systems operating on temporal data. Understanding the underlying factors contributing to concept drift is vital for developing robust adaptive systems. Recent approaches leverage XAI to elucidate the nature of drift. For example, Edakunni et al. [11] propose a novel framework called DBShap that uses Shapley values to identify the cause of model drift and measure the contribution of different components of the data to the overall deterioration of model predictions. Such methodologies enable practitioners to pinpoint specific features or external factors driving changes, facilitating targeted interventions to mitigate adverse effects on model performance. Another framework called iPDP [22] is an incremental version of Partial Dependence Plots that continuously updates to reflect changes in data distributions and model behavior over time. This allows for the visualization of feature relationships in the context of streaming or evolving datasets. Authors in [27] proposed methods to understand drift in prediction distributions over time or between data segments. It unifies various feature importance measures under a common framework, providing a systematic approach to analysing prediction drift.

Existing methods for concept drift detection either lack interpretability or provide explanations only after drift has been identified. They often fail to pinpoint which features cause the drift and struggle to handle both abrupt and gradual changes effectively. Our approach integrates drift detection with explainability, using a three-perspective approach that tracks data distribution shifts, model confidence variations, and SHAP-based feature importance evolution. This enables real-time, feature-level insights into drift, making it more comprehensive, interpretable, and scalable for practical applications.

3 Integrating Data, Explanation, and Model Performance Into a 3P Approach

Let consider the data stream $S = \{(\mathbf{x}^0, \mathbf{y}^0), (\mathbf{x}^1, \mathbf{y}^1), \dots, (\mathbf{x}^N, \mathbf{y}^N)\}$ described by n–dimensional attribute vector $\mathbf{x}^i = [x^i_j]^n_{j=1}$ and a class label $\mathbf{y}^i \in \{0, 1\}$. We divide this data stream into m equally sampled chunks X^k_{chunk}, so that $S = \{X^k_{chunk}\}^m_{k=1}$. Each chunk is further split into training $(X^k_{train}, y^k_{train})$ and testing datasets (X^k_{test}, y^k_{test}) with split ratio 80% for training and 20% for testing. We train a classification model $f^k : \mathcal{R} \rightarrow \{0, 1\}$ on each training dataset X^k_{train}. These models are then utilized to compute SHAP values [19], denoted as ϕ^k_j, which quantify the contribution of j-th feature to the k-th model predictions. The computation of SHAP values requires defining a dataset on which they will be evaluated. To this end, we define an evaluation dataset X_{eval} derived from the data stream S, which can, for instance, be the first testing dataset. The selection does not influence the analysis of the results. Consequently, SHAP values for the n-th feature are expressed as $\phi^k_n(f^k(X_{eval}))$. In this approach, models are updated iteratively after each data chunk, while SHAP values are consistently computed on a fixed evaluation dataset. This approach allows for tracking changes in the decision boundary across successive models.

In real–life scenarios, the data streams are often imbalanced. Due to that the implementation of methodologies that address this issue is needed. We employed IPIP (Identical Partitions for Imbalance Problems) method proposed by Cisterna-García et al. [9]. IPIP [14] involves generating multiple subsets through random subsampling, ensuring that each instance of the minority class has a 95% probability of being included in at least one subset. An ensemble of models is then trained on each subset, and the final prediction is determined by aggregating all ensemble outputs using majority voting. This method can also be applied to handle concept drift. In a data stream divided into chunks, IPIP can be initially trained on the first chunk, and the ensembles can be updated following the passive learner approach.

To visualize the results, we sequentially plot the behaviour of the model on the evaluation dataset X_{eval}, coloring data points according to their corresponding SHAP values computed from successive models. Additionally, the subsequent test datasets are included in a supplementary plot below, represented as KDE (Kernel Density Estimation) plots. An example visualization is shown in Fig. 2. We employ a standard colormap where pink indicates a positive influence on the prediction, purple signifies no influence, and blue represents a negative impact. The transparency of each data point is adjusted based on its prediction probability—samples with lower probability (classified as class 0) appear more transparent, while those with higher probability (classified as class 1) are more visible. For each data chunk, we also plot the balanced accuracy scores: a dashed blue line represents accuracy computed on the test dataset, while a solid blue line corresponds to accuracy on the evaluation dataset. Furthermore, SHAP values are visualised as kernel density estimation plots (green plots) along an additional axis, providing insights into feature contributions across the dataset. In the plot below (orange plot), test data from each chunk are also presented as KDE plots. This approach enables a comprehensive three-perspective analysis of temporal changes. First, variations in data distribution are tracked by sequentially plotting density distributions for each testing dataset. Second, fluctuations in model confidence over time are captured through changes in transparency. Finally, the evolution of model explanations is examined by analyzing color variations and the distribution of SHAP values, offering deeper insights into the model's decision-making process.

4 Empirical Studies on Concept Drift Analysis Through the Lens of the 3P Approach

This section illustrates the practical application of the 3P approach for detecting and analyzing concept drift, along with an empirical study of the results. We begin by examining a synthetic dataset, followed by an evaluation on real-world data to validate our findings in a practical setting. The synthetic dataset is generated using the AGRAWAL data stream generator, which simulates both abrupt

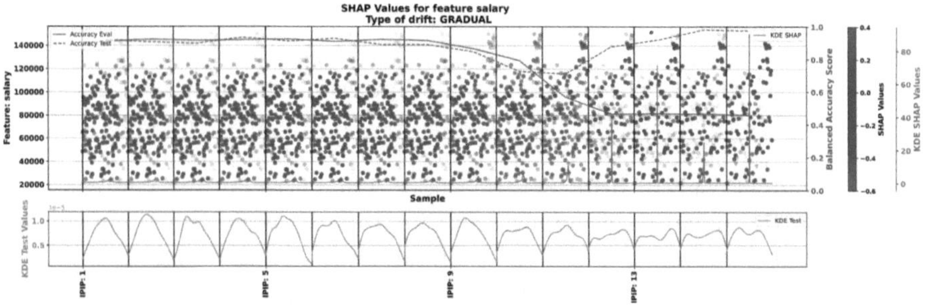

Fig. 2. Example of visualization of proposed 3P approach.

and gradual concept drifts. For real-world validation, we utilize two datasets: one from a cold rolling mill simulator, representing industrial processes with drifts caused by changes in number of products and production capacity, and another from hospital records collected during the COVID-19 pandemic, where the goal is to predict whether a patient should be hospitalized. These datasets allow us to test the robustness of our approach across different domains, demonstrating its effectiveness in handling both gradual and sudden concept drift. The cold rolling mill dataset captures the evolution of features over time and reveals two types of drift: one related to introducing new product types and the other due to increased production capacity. The SMS dataset focuses on predicting whether a COVID-19 patient should be hospitalized based on electronic health records that include comorbidities, the symptomatology of the disease, and demographic data such as age and sex. This dataset reflects sudden shifts in patient data, highlighting the challenges of managing healthcare resources during a rapidly changing pandemic scenario.

4.1 Synthetic Dataset

For our experiment, we use the AGRAWAL data stream generator [4], implemented within the MOA framework [7]. The generator creates a data stream with nine features, including six numerical and three categorical attributes. It uses ten predefined functions to assign binary class labels, likely indicating whether a loan should be approved. These functions, which define different decision rules, can be found in the original paper [4]. We generated two datasets: one with abrupt concept drift and another with gradual concept drift. The generated data streams are divided into 34 chunks, which are then randomly sampled to create a set of 1000 samples. The percentage of each class of the target variable represented in each chunk is then obtained as 20% – 80%. The evaluation dataset for computing SHAP values is the test data from the first chunk $X_{eval} = X_{test}^1$. Concept drift occurs in chunk 12, where the decision boundary shifts from AGRAWAL's function 2 to function 3, and again in chunk 24, where it transitions from AGRAWAL's function 3 to function 5. For classification, we employed the IPIP (Identical Partitions for Imbalance Problems) algorithm (See

Sect. 3). We chose IPIP because it is designed to process data chunks efficiently and adapt to changes. The figures [3, 4] presents a visualization of our approach. We present two key features relevant to concept drift detection: loan and salary. The most interesting areas are highlighted with red boxes. The plots in Fig. 3 represent a data stream with abrupt concept drift, while plots in Fig. 4 correspond to gradual concept drift. Several major differences emerge between these cases. First, the balanced accuracy score for test datasets drops immediately in the case of abrupt drift, whereas for gradual drift, the decline is smoother and occurs around chunk 13 (after the first concept drift). Second, prediction probabilities change notably in drift areas. For the loan feature in the abrupt data stream, after chunk 25, low-value points nearly disappear. In contrast, for the gradual drift scenario, the visibility of these points (prediction probability) decreases progressively. A similar pattern is observed for the salary feature after chunk 12. Third, there are differences in SHAP values, reflecting how quickly the model adapts to drift. In the case of gradual drift, the model requires approximately one additional chunk to adjust, and the change in feature importance occurs more smoothly. For instance, in chunk 25, the loan feature holds greater importance in the abrupt drift case than in the gradual one. Similarly, in chunk 13, the salary feature is less important in the abrupt drift scenario than in the gradual one. These differences are evident both from the color variations of data points and the Gaussian distribution of SHAP values. There is also a change in KDE of test datasets for feature loan after chunk 25, and for feature salary after chunk 13.

4.2 Cold Rolling Mill Simulator

In this section, we will showcase the practicality of our approach using a real-world example from a steel manufacturing plant. Steel production mainly relies on continuous casting, which results in slabs, billets, or blooms. To obtain the required shape and size, the steel undergoes two rolling processes: hot rolling and cold rolling. During hot rolling, the slabs are heated in a furnace, reshaped through rolling stands, and then cooled. If additional thickness reduction is required, the steel is further processed in a cold rolling mill. Our study focuses on this second stage, where the variety of rolled products causes data drift. The cold rolling stage of steel production is responsible for reducing the strip's thickness by passing it through a pair of rolls. Initially, the steel coil is unrolled on the uncoiler, and during the rolling process, the strip moves slowly between the rolling stands. Once the strip is gripped by the uncoiler, the process speeds up to reach the desired exit thickness. Cold rolling is a continuous process where raw data samples are collected at regular time intervals, allowing the process data to be treated as a data stream.

The analyzed data stream originates from a five–stand cold rolling mill simulator, which was developed using real measurements from a steel company. The dataset utilized in this study is publicly available in the Zenodo repository [1], specifically the tcm5_dataset_5. A comprehensive description of the dataset's attributes can also be found in [1]. In the selected dataset, the class attribute

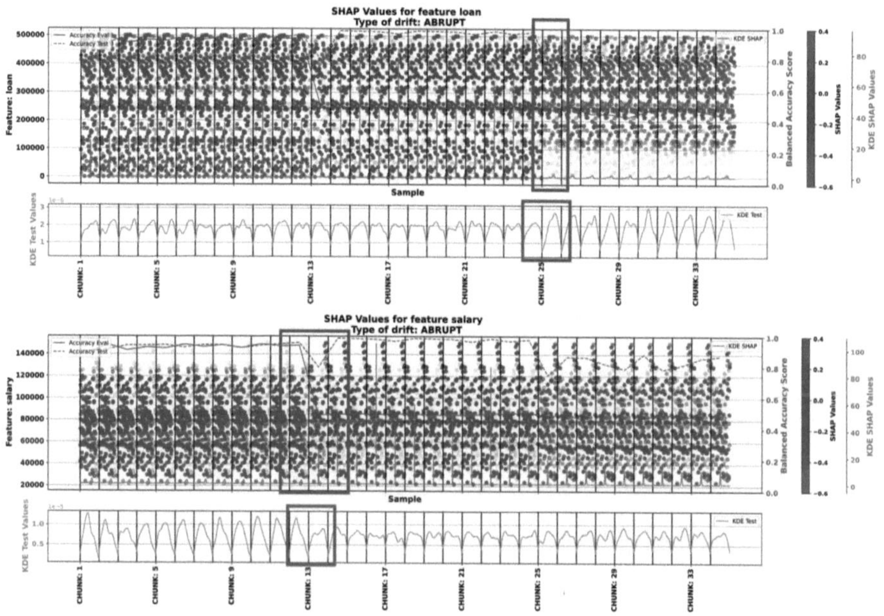

Fig. 3. Proposed visualization for AGRAWAL data stream. The plots correspond to abrupt concept drift.

indicates anomalies associated with physics-based deviations in the rolling process. Four types of anomalies were introduced: anomalies in reduction, work roll anomalies, bearing anomalies, and electric motor anomalies. For the purposes of this study, the problem is treated as a one-class classification task, where the class label is equal to 1 if any of the aforementioned anomaly types occur and 0 otherwise. The dataset was divided into 20 equally sized chunks. Each chunk was further split into training and testing subsets using an 80% – 20% ratio, respectively. An evaluation dataset, denoted as X_{eval}, was constructed by randomly selecting 100 samples labelled as class 1 (anomalies) and 100 samples labelled as class 0 (normal instances) from all test subsets. This approach ensures a balanced evaluation dataset, which facilitates the observation of changes in the decision boundary over time. For classification, a basic implementation of the RF (RandomForestClassifier) from the *scikit–learn* Python library was employed [2]. The training dataset for this model evolves incrementally: after each chunk is processed, the training set is expanded by including the training data from the current chunk. Consequently, for the first chunk, the model is trained only on data from that chunk, for the second chunk, it is trained on data from both the first and second chunks, and so on, progressively incorporating more data with each iteration.

In the presented dataset, two types of drift are introduced. First, a drift associated with the introduction of previously unseen product types occurs, with the number of rolled products increasing after the 8000th observation. Second, a drift

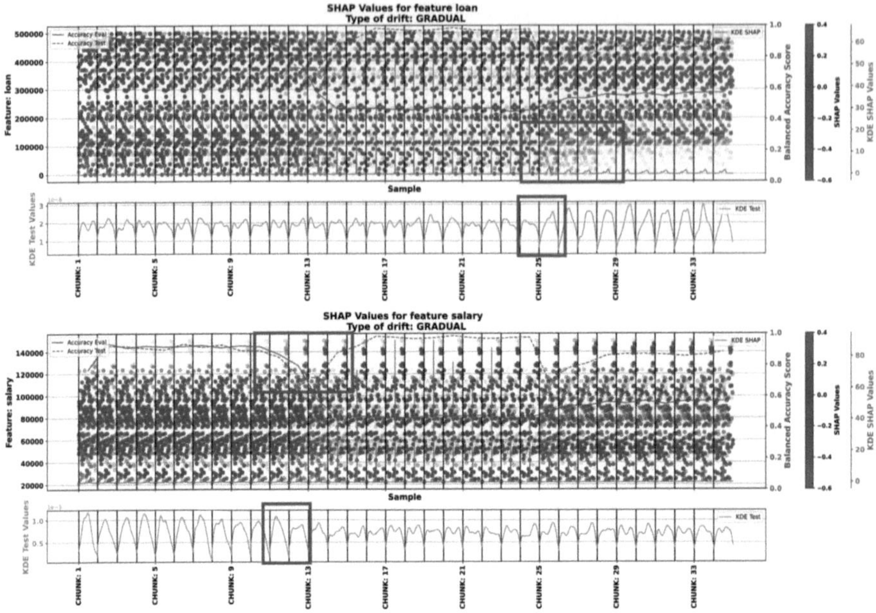

Fig. 4. Proposed visualization for AGRAWAL data stream. The plots correspond to gradual concept drift.

related to increased production capacity is introduced, characterised by heightened power and motor speed, which takes effect after the 16000th observation. Below we present the results for features torque_1 and force_1 in the Fig. 5 and motor_power_3 and motor_power_4 in the Fig. 6. Red boxes highlight the most interesting areas. In Fig. 5, a shift in the decision boundary becomes evident in chunk 9. Samples with higher values of torque_1 and force_1 begin to lose significance for the model, as indicated by a decrease in their prediction probabilities. Furthermore, a significant shift is visible in the KDE of SHAP values for torque_1. Similarly, force_1 shows a noticeable change in the KDE across test datasets. This change corresponds to the first concept drift, associated with the introduction of a higher number of rolled products. In Fig. 6, another alteration in the decision boundary is observed in chunk 17. Samples with values in the range of (4000, 5000) for motor_power_3 and (3250, 3750) for motor_power_4 become less important to the model, as reflected by a reduction in their prediction probabilities. A corresponding shift in the KDE of SHAP values for motor_power_4 further indicates the presence of the second drift, which is linked to an increase in production capacity.

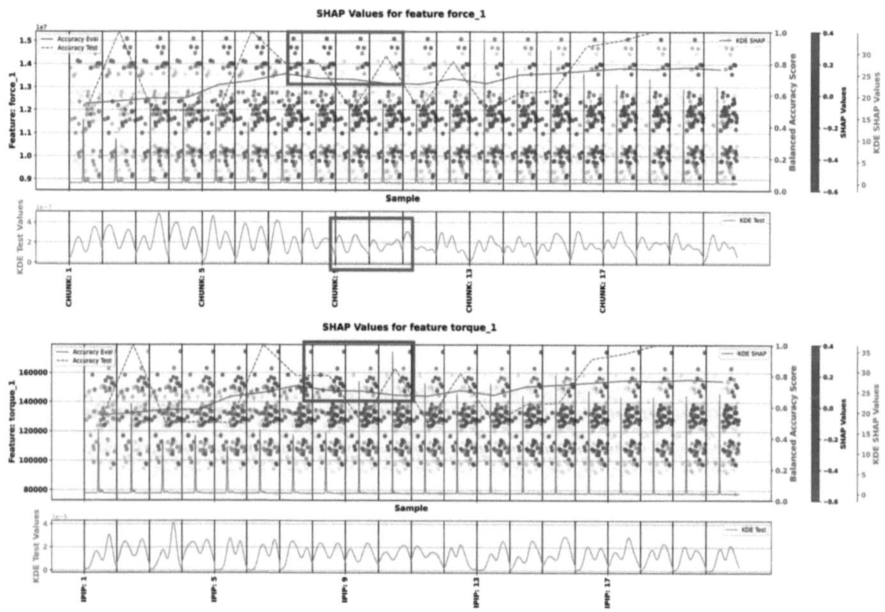

Fig. 5. Proposed visualization for tcm5 dataset. The top plot corresponds to feature force_1, and the bottom one to torque_1.

4.3 SMS COVID-19 Dataset

In this section, an additional real dataset with data on patients with confirmed cases of COVID-19 is utilized. These data were collected from electronic medical records of the SMS (Regional Health System) from the Region of Murcia (Spain) and their use for this work and within all the experiments therein was approved by the Ethics Committee of the University of Murcia. The dataset includes certain comorbidities, such as the number of chronic diseases affecting each patient, the number of affected systems, and the presence or absence of the following: diabetes mellitus, heart failure, chronic obstructive pulmonary disease, hypertension, depression, HIV, ischemic heart disease, stroke, chronic kidney disease, cirrhosis, osteoporosis, osteoarthritis, arthritis, dementia, obesity and asthma. Furthermore, patient demographics such as age and sex, and symptomatology data from the disease, including chest pain, myalgias, cough, lack of appetite, sleep problems, nasal congestion, dyspnea, rhinorrhea, low–grade fever, dizziness, hyposmia, hypogeusia, headache, eye symptoms, nasal discharges, fever, sore throat, abdominal pain, vomits, expectorations, chills, rash, malaise and tiredness are also available. A more detailed description of the dataset can be found in [9].

This dataset contains patient data from COVID-19 over 26 months, with the first record date in March 2020 and 675126 unique patients recorded across all months. The objective of this dataset is to predict when a patient would need to be hospitalised (class 1) or not (class 0) from the available information. The

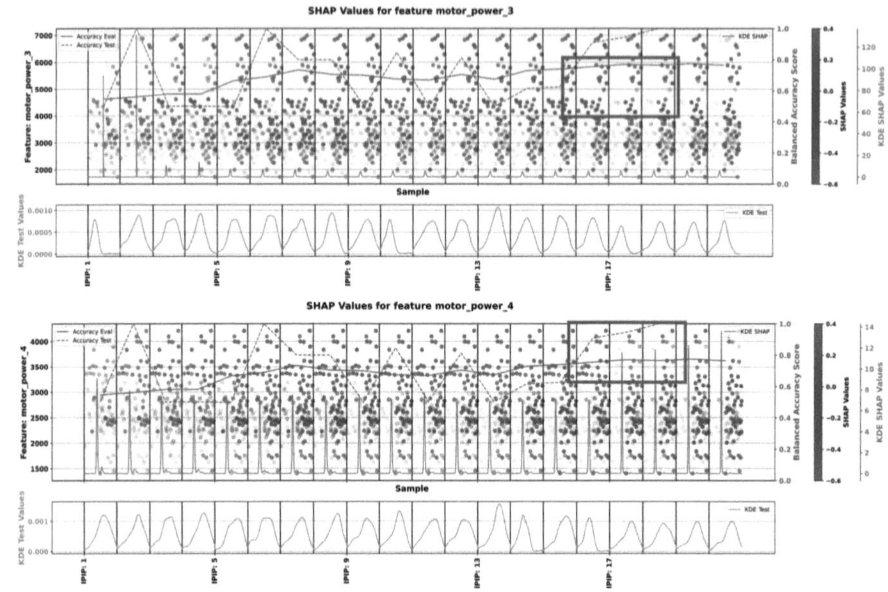

Fig. 6. Proposed visualization for tcm5 dataset. The top plot corresponds to feature motor_power_3, and the bottom one to motor_power_4.

problem is highly imbalanced, as only 0.75% of the total patients have been hospitalised. To ensure a sufficient number of hospitalised patients in each chunk, the available data is grouped into temporal chunks of two months. This results in 13 chunks of varying sizes. Each chunk was further divided into training and testing subsets, following an 80%–20% split, respectively. Given the importance of temporality in understanding the development of this pandemic, the evaluation dataset X_{eval} consists of 1500 randomly chosen patients from the test subset of the first data chunk. This facilitates the observation of how the importance of variables for patients at the beginning of the pandemic evolves over time in models trained on patients from the subsequent data chunks. The IPIP method is employed for the classification task, as it is designed to address imbalanced problems, handle data chunks effectively and respond to changes dynamically.

In this dataset, two distinct drifts are evident. The results for the variables chest pain and number of systems affected or age can be observed in the Fig. 7. Similarly, the results for the variables age and vomits can be seen in Figs. 8. Red boxes highlight the most interesting chunks of this study. Firstly, due to the worldwide urgency of the pandemic and the high initial infection rate [24], hospital admissions due to the disease in the first months or first wave were for different reasons than for those hospitalized in the second wave or subsequent months, due to the low awareness of the disease. [12,13]. Consequently, in the initial two data chunks (representing the first four months of the pandemic), as illustrated in Fig. 7 it can be observed that the variables chest pain and number

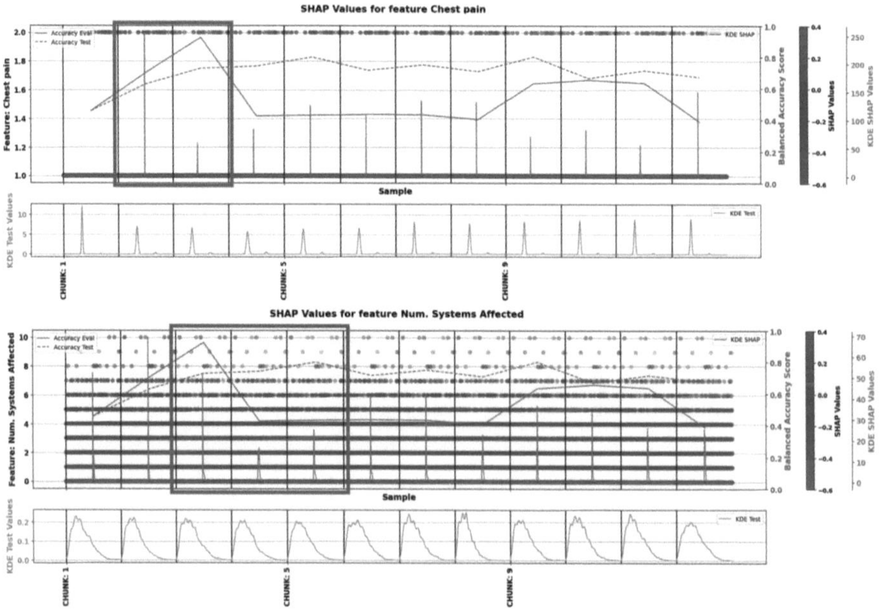

Fig. 7. Proposed visualization for SMS COVID-19 dataset. The top plot corresponds to the chest pain symptom, and the bottom one to the number of systems affected by comorbidity.

of systems affected, which are really relevant variables to predict the severity of COVD-19 [9,20], are not observed with high SHAP values. However, after those first 4 months, the importance is indeed higher, as it is especially shown in the KDE plot, which has a flatter graph and a less pronounced peak in the 0 values of SHAP. This represents the first drift in COVID-19 data. Another notable change can be observed around chunk 9 for the variables age and vomits. This chunk corresponds to September 2021, when the milestone of vaccinating more than 70% of the population of the Region of Murcia with a complete vaccination schedule was reached [9]. This was due to the fact that the vaccination schedules were administered with older people as a priority. In this particular month, the values of the variable age that are pertinent to the prediction of severity are those representing a lower age than in the preceding chunks. There are higher values in the importance of the age variable between 30 and 50, as these groups of individuals were more susceptible following the vaccination of the elderly. Furthermore, the predominance of the delta variant of COVID-19 occurred between August and December 2021, months in which it is observed (See Fig. 8) that there are higher values for the variable vomits when showing this symptom, which is associated with the fact that in the delta variant stomach symptoms such as vomiting are more pronounced and more closely related to a more severe COVID-19 [8,28]. Those changes in SHAP values represent the second drift in the SMS COVID dataset.

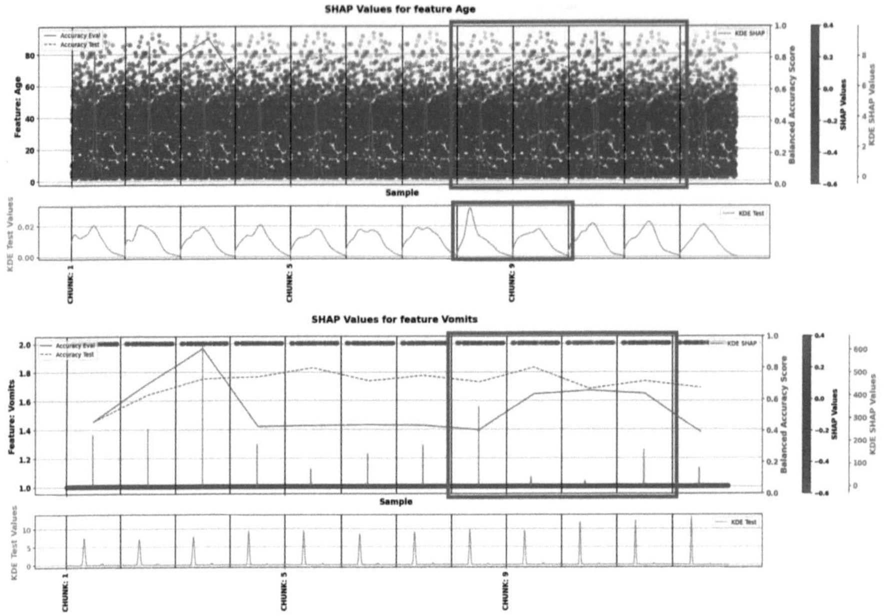

Fig. 8. Proposed visualization for SMS COVID-19 dataset. The top plot corresponds to the age feature, and the bottom one to the vomiting symptom.

5 Conclusions

In this work, we show how the three-perspective approach to analysing data streams can be an efficient method for detecting and interpreting concept drift. Focusing solely on either the model or data perspective may be insufficient for understanding concept drift. However, integrating an explainability layer alongside these perspectives provides a much richer insight—not only into how models adapt but also how their performance degrades, how feature importance evolves, and how data distribution changes over time. Moreover, by examining the interactions between these three elements, we gain a deeper and more holistic understanding of drift. While most existing works develop only one of these approaches in isolation, we argue for a unified approach that leverages their combined strengths for a more comprehensive analysis.

Our experiments on both synthetic and real-world datasets validate the utility of this approach. The results of the synthetic AGRAWAL dataset highlight the differences between abrupt and gradual drifts, illustrating how sudden shifts significantly impact model performance, while gradual changes allow a more adaptive transition. The cold rolling mill dataset demonstrates how concept drift arises due to changes in product types and production capacity, affecting model decision boundaries. Similarly, the SMS COVID-19 data set reveals the evolving importance of features over time, reflecting how the progression of the pandemic influenced hospitalization risks. Our proposed approach for detecting and explaining concept drift can be further improved in several areas.

In this study, we employ SHAP values to explain model behaviour and interpret concept drift, leveraging their ability to attribute feature importance consistently. However, it is important to note that SHAP values have limitations, as outlined in [15]. Therefore, while SHAP provides valuable insights, it is not without flaws. Our proposed approach for detecting and explaining concept drift can be further improved by addressing these limitations. Future work should explore alternative explainability methods that mitigate SHAP's shortcomings, automate model retraining through techniques like incremental and active learning, and enhance SHAP analysis by dynamically selecting evaluation datasets. Additionally, developing user-friendly tools for non-experts, establishing benchmarks for drift explanation, and standardizing evaluation metrics will be essential for practical deployment across diverse environments.

Acknowledgments. This work was partially funded by the Grant PID2022-136306OB-I00 from MICIU/AEI/10.13039/501100011033 and FEDER, UE, and by the Science and Technology Agency, Séneca Foundation, Comunidad Autónoma Región de Murcia through the grant 21591/FPI/21. The research has been supported by a grant from the Priority Research Area (DigiWorld) under the Strategic Programme Excellence Initiative at Jagiellonian University.

References

1. https://zenodo.org/records/11469702
2. https://scikit-learn.org/stable/modules/generated/sklearn.ensemble.RandomForestClassifier.html
3. Agrahari, S., Singh, A.K.: Concept drift detection in data stream mining : a literature review. J. King Saud Univ. - Comput. Inf. Sci. **34**(10, Part B), 9523–9540 (2022). https://doi.org/10.1016/j.jksuci.2021.11.006, https://www.sciencedirect.com/science/article/pii/S1319157821003062
4. Agrawal, R., Imielinski, T., Swami, A.: Database mining: a performance perspective. IEEE Trans. Knowl. Data Eng. **5**(6), 914–925 (1993). https://doi.org/10.1109/69.250074
5. Baena-Garc, M., Avila, J., Bifet, A., Gavald, R., Morales-Bueno, R.: Early drift detection method (2005). https://api.semanticscholar.org/CorpusID:15672006
6. Bifet, A., Gavalda, R.: Learning from time-changing data with adaptive windowing. In: Proceedings of the 2007 SIAM international conference on data mining. pp. 443–448. SIAM (2007)
7. Bifet, A., Gavaldà, R., Holmes, G., Pfahringer, B.: Machine Learning for Data Streams with Practical Examples in MOA. MIT Press (2018). https://moa.cms.waikato.ac.nz/book/
8. Çağlar, H.T., et al.: Delta variant effect on the clinical course of adolescent covid-19 patients. Pediatr. Pulmonol. **58**(1), 115–121 (2023). https://doi.org/10.1002/ppul.26166
9. A predictive model for hospitalization and survival to covid-19 in a retrospective population-based study. Sci. Rep. **12**(1), 18126 (2022). https://doi.org/10.1038/s41598-022-22547-9

10. Duckworth, C., et al.: Using explainable machine learning to characterise data drift and detect emergent health risks for emergency department admissions during covid-19. Sci. Rep. **11**(1), 23017 (2021). https://doi.org/10.1038/s41598-021-02481-y
11. Edakunni, N.U., Tekriwal, U., Jain, A.: Explaining drift using shapley values (2024). https://arxiv.org/abs/2401.09756
12. Fan, G., Yang, Z., Lin, Q., Zhao, S., Yang, L., He, D.: Decreased case fatality rate of covid-19 in the second wave: a study in 53 countries or regions. Transbound. Emerg. Dis. **68**(2), 213–215 (2021). https://doi.org/10.1111/tbed.13819
13. González-Castro, A., Fito, E.C., Fernandez, A., Acha, P.E., Borregán, J.R., Peñasco, Y.: First and second wave of coronavirus-19 disease: a comparative study in patients hospitalized in an icu of a third-level university hospital. Med. Intensiva **46**(3), 166 (2021). https://doi.org/10.1016/j.medine.2021.12.008
14. Guillén-Teruel, A., Caracena, M., Pardo, J.A., de-la Gándara, F., Palma, J., Botía, J.A.: Film: Framework for imbalanced learning machines based on a new unbiased performance measure and a new ensemble-based technique (2025). https://doi.org/10.48550/arXiv.2503.04370
15. Huang, X., Marques-Silva, J.: On the failings of shapley values for explainability. Int. J. Approximate Reason. **171**, 109112 (2024). https://doi.org/10.1016/j.ijar.2023.109112, https://www.sciencedirect.com/science/article/pii/S0888613X23002438, synergies between Machine Learning and Reasoning
16. Jakubowski, J., Stanisz, P., Bobek, S., Nalepa, G.J.: Roll wear prediction in strip cold rolling with physics-informed autoencoder and counterfactual explanations. In: 2022 IEEE 9th International Conference on Data Science and Advanced Analytics (DSAA), pp. 1–10 (2022). https://doi.org/10.1109/DSAA54385.2022.10032357
17. Jana, A., Minacapelli, C.D., Rustgi, V., Metaxas, D.: Global and local interpretation of black-box machine learning models to determine prognostic factors from early covid-19 data (2021). https://arxiv.org/abs/2109.05087
18. Krawczyk, B., Minku, L.L., Gama, J., Stefanowski, J., Woźniak, M.: Ensemble learning for data stream analysis: a survey. Inf. Fusion **37**, 132–156 (2017)
19. Lundberg, S.M., Lee, S.I.: A unified approach to interpreting model predictions. In: Guyon, I., Luxburg, U.V., Bengio, S., Wallach, H., Fergus, R., Vishwanathan, S., Garnett, R. (eds.) Advances in Neural Information Processing Systems. vol. 30. Curran Associates, Inc. (2017)
20. Predictive factors for hospitalization in a cohort of primary healthcare patients with suspected covid-19. Atención Primaria Práctica **5**(1), 100168 (2023). https://doi.org/10.1016/j.appr.2023.100168
21. Mozolewski, M., Bobek, S., Ribeiro, R.P., Nalepa, G.J., Gama, J.: Towards evaluation of explainable artificial intelligence in streaming data. In: Longo, L., Lapuschkin, S., Seifert, C. (eds.) Explainable Artificial Intelligence, pp. 145–168. Springer Nature Switzerland, Cham (2024)
22. Muschalik, M., Fumagalli, F., Jagtani, R., Hammer, B., Hüllermeier, E.: iPDP: On Partial Dependence Plots in Dynamic Modeling Scenarios, p. 177–194. Springer, Cham (2023). https://doi.org/10.1007/978-3-031-44064-9_11
23. PAGE, E.S.: Continuous inspection schemes. Biometrika **41**(1-2), 100–115 (1954). https://doi.org/10.1093/biomet/41.1-2.100
24. Pecoraro, F., Luzi, D., Clemente, F.: The efficiency in the ordinary hospital bed management: a comparative analysis in four European countries before the covid-19 outbreak. PLoS ONE **16**(3), e0248867 (2021). https://doi.org/10.1371/journal.pone.0248867

25. Rojat, T., Puget, R., Filliat, D., Ser, J.D., Gelin, R., Díaz-Rodríguez, N.: Explainable artificial intelligence (XAI) on timeseries data: A survey (2021). https://arxiv.org/abs/2104.00950
26. Seiffer, C., Ziekow, H., Schreier, U., Gerling, A.: Detection of concept drift in manufacturing data with shap values to improve error prediction. In: DATA ANALYTICS 2021 : The Tenth International Conference on Data Analytics, pp. 51 – 60. October 3–7, 2021, Barcelona, Spain (2021), https://www.thinkmind.org/index.php?view=article&articleid=data_analytics_2021_3_40_60034
27. Shanbhag, A., Ghosh, A., Rubin, J.: Unified shapley framework to explain prediction drift (2021). https://arxiv.org/abs/2102.07862
28. Slabakova, Y., et al.: Sars-cov-2 variant-specific gastrointestinal symptoms of covid-19: 2023 update. Gastroenterol. Insights **14**(4), 431–445 (2023). https://doi.org/10.3390/gastroent14040032
29. Stefanowski, J., Brzezinski, D.: Stream Classification, pp. 1191 – 1195. Springer (2017)
30. Žliobaitė, I., Pechenizkiy, M., Gama, J.: An Overview of Concept Drift Applications, pp. 91–114. Springer, Cham (2016). https://doi.org/10.1007/978-3-319-26989-4_4

An Empirical Evaluation of Factors Affecting SHAP Explanation of Time Series Classification

Nikos Papadeas[1], Davide Italo Serramazza[2(✉)], Zahraa Abdallah[1], and Georgiana Ifrim[2]

[1] School of Engineering Mathematics and Technology, University of Bristol, Bristol, UK
{ay20721,zahraa.abdallah}@bristol.ac.uk

[2] School of Computer Science, University College Dublin, Dublin, Ireland
davide.serramazza@ucdconnect.ie, georgiana.ifrim@ucd.ie

Abstract. Explainable AI (XAI) has become an increasingly important topic for understanding and attributing the predictions made by complex Time Series Classification (TSC) models. Among attribution methods, SHapley Additive exPlanations (SHAP) is widely regarded as an excellent attribution method, but its computational complexity, which scales exponentially with the number of features, limits its practicality for long time series. To address this, recent studies have shown that aggregating features via segmentation, to compute a single attribution value for a group of consecutive time points, drastically reduces SHAP running time. However, the choice of the optimal segmentation strategy remains an open question. In this work, we investigated eight different Time Series Segmentation algorithms to understand how segment compositions affect the explanation quality. We evaluate these approaches using two established XAI evaluation methodologies: InterpretTime and AUC Difference. Through experiments on both Multivariate (MTS) and Univariate Time Series (UTS), we find that the number of segments has a greater impact on explanation quality than the specific segmentation method. Notably, equal-length segmentation consistently outperforms most of the custom time series segmentation algorithms. Furthermore, we introduce a novel attribution normalisation technique that weights segments by their length and we show that it consistently improves attribution quality.

Keywords: Time Series Classification · Explanation · Segmentation

1 Introduction

Time series (TS) data is a common data type in domains including finance, healthcare, sports analytics, and market predictions. The increasing complexity of Machine Learning (ML) models led to the emergence of Explainable Artificial

N. Papadeas and D. I. Serramazza—These authors contributed equally to this work.

I. Koprinska et al. (Eds.): ECML PKDD 2025, CCIS 2842, pp. 458–473, 2026.
https://doi.org/10.1007/978-3-032-19105-2_32

Intelligence (XAI), a field aiming to make AI decisions interpretable, to avoid the risks of relying on faulty predictions in high-stakes domains.

In the context of time series XAI, several studies have adapted SHAP [17], arguably one of the most popular XAI methods, to the time series domain. In addition to time series-specific challenges, such as temporal and channel dependencies or locality, SHAP also poses computational challenges as it scales exponentially with the number of features. Past works in the TS domain mainly used *segmentation* or *chunking*, i.e., explaining a group of consecutive time points together, assigning them the same attribution, thus decreasing the number of features to be explained. This technique has proven to be effective in lowering the computational demand by a few orders of magnitude [25], but to the best of our knowledge, no systematic study has investigated the impact of different segmentation strategies on the quality of the resulting explanation.

This work investigates eight different segmentation methods, including the popular and simple *equal-length segmentation*, using a varied range of Univariate and Multivariate Time Series Classification (UTSC/MTSC) problems and four different classifiers. Additionally, we also explored the impact of the background set used by SHAP, i.e., the instances to be used when simulating data missingness: we compared the simple *zero* background, the default choice for some important frameworks such as Captum [14] with the *average background*, where missing values are replaced with the average value for each observation in the training set.

Moreover, SHAP values for segment-based explanations are computed over time segments rather than individual timepoints, but evaluations require single-timepoint attributions. In order to maintain segment-level additivity of individual timepoint attributions, we introduce a normalisation method based on segment length.

Finally, while various approaches have been proposed for the quantitative or qualitative evaluation of XAI methods, in this work, we focus on two quantitative approaches designed for evaluating time series XAI methods: *InterpretTime* [28] and *AUC Difference* [19,21].

Our main contributions in this paper are:

- We evaluate eight segmentation models using a wide variety of datasets and ML models. Our experiments clearly show that the best choice is the simple *equal segmentation* with some notable exceptions, which have been further analysed.
- We showed that the average and the zero background performances are very often at the same level; however, the average background performs better in some cases.
- We proposed a *normalisation* technique which weights every segment attribution according to its length. Our experiments show that in the vast majority of cases, this approach improves the XAI evaluation scores.
- To help further research in this area, we publicly release our code and data.[1]

[1] https://github.com/davide-serramazza/segment_SHAP.

2 Related Work

We discuss in this section relevant methods for time series classification, segmentation, explanation, and the evaluation of XAI methods.

2.1 Time Series Classification

QUANT [5] is a TSC algorithm that relies exclusively on quantile-based features. The method extracts features using fixed dyadic intervals from four distinct representations of the input TS, namely the raw TS, its Fourier transform, and its first and second order differences. These 4 different feature representations are then concatenated before being fed into an *Extra Trees classifier* [10].

MiniRocket [4] is part of the popular Rocket TSC algorithm family: the main idea is to extract features by sliding a large number of convolutional kernels over the TS. The main feature is *PPV (Proportion of Positive Values)*, the proportion of positive values as output of the kernel, used as a proxy to capture the ones best matching with the current TS. Once the features are extracted, a linear model is used as a classifier, in our case, a Ridge Classifier.

ResNet [12] is a *Convolutional Neural Network (CNN)* that has been proposed for image classification and then applied to TSC. The main model innovation is the *residual connection*, i.e., skipping one or more layers to allow the network to learn a deeper representation, reducing the vanishing gradient problem. Notably, it has been one of the first deep learning models to be successfully applied to TSC without any architectural changes compared to the original one.

Random Forest is an ensemble learning method that constructs multiple decision trees during training and outputs the mode of their prediction. Despite being a *tabular data* classifier, it yields good performance when applied to TSC [6]; however, this model can only handle $1D$ data, thus in the case of MTS, channels are concatenated to create a $1D$ UTS.

2.2 Time Series Segmentation

Equal-length segmentation: The first segmentation we evaluated is the equal length one: a TS of length L is divided into n different segments of length $[\lfloor \frac{L}{n} \rfloor, \lceil \frac{L}{n} \rceil]$.

Classification Score Profile (ClaSP) [8] evaluates each possible split by training a binary classifier to identify subsequences from both sides. After scoring each possible point, it applies peak detection to select the actual change points (CPs). ClaSP works dimension-wise; thus we apply ClaSP independently for each dimension when using MTS data, possibly finding an uneven number of segments for each channel.

Information Gain Segmentation (IG) [23] aims to maximise the amount of entropy lost due to a possible segmentation: for each of the change points to be detected, it uses a top-down search to evaluate the information gain resulting from the possible next changing point.

Greedy Gaussian Segmentation (GG) [11] finds the segmentation by interpreting the data as coming from a Gaussian distribution. Precisely, it finds an approximate solution to the maximum log-likelihood of a segmented Gaussian model having the specified number of changing points.

NNSegment comes from *LimeSegment* [26], it detects change points in TS by assuming that each observation belongs to either a repeating motif or an anomaly. After having split the TS into sub-windows w_i, it assigns each w_i its nearest neighbours w_j. If adjacent windows w_i and w_j have different nearest neighbours, a change point is flagged either at the window beginning or at its end. Similarly to ClaSP, NNSegment is applied dimension-wise.

Binary Segmentation (Binseg) [24] is a greedy algorithm that uses a recurrent approach. Starting from the entire series, it uses a cost function to detect the most significant CP within the current segment. After splitting, the operation is repeated on the two resulting sub-series until the required number of changing points is detected.

Bottom-up segmentation (BottomUp) [13] starts with an over-split of the current TS in regular, fixed-length segments. Contiguous sub-samples are then merged according to a cost function until the target number of changing points is reached.

Kernel change point detection (KernelCPD) [3] maps the TS into a Hilbert space $\mathcal{H}$ using a kernel $\mathcal{K}$. Change points are detected by finding the mean-shifts in the mapped signals in $\mathcal{H}$.

2.3 Evaluation of XAI for Time Series Classification

InterpretTime was proposed in [28], and the main idea is to perturb samples in the test set based on the importance ranking generated by the evaluated attribution method. Specifically, TS observations are progressively corrupted by injecting values sampled from a distribution (default is the Normal distribution), following the importance rank specified by the attribution values. Specifically, the method involves:

- Establishing perturbation thresholds $k = [0.05, 0.15, ..., 0.95, 1.0]$
- Generating two modified versions for each k, $\bar{X}^{top}$ and $\bar{X}^{bottom}$ replacing respectively the top k and the bottom $(1-k)$ quantiles of the original TS values with values sampled from the specified distribution. Top k and bottom $(1-k)$ quantiles are identified only considering the positive attribution values of the explanation method to be scored.
- Computing normalised score differences: $\bar{S} = \frac{S(X)-S(\bar{X})}{S(X)}$, where S represents the probability for the initial predicted category.

Based on $\bar{S}$, two metrics are defined, namely **AUCSE**, which quantifies how effectively the method identifies the most important TS features, and **F-score**, measuring the balance between detecting high-importance and low-importance features. InterpretTime was shown to be effective in ranking attribution methods and to have a good correlation between the quantitative ranking and the qualitative method evaluation. The methodology was further shown to benefit from using multiple perturbations, beyond the default Gaussian: in this work, we used this extended variant of InterpretTime [25].

AUC Difference (AUCD) [19,21] assesses attribution quality by analysing how perturbations of time-series observations, guided by importance rankings, influence model predictions. This evaluation relies on two complementary perturbation approaches: deletion and insertion. Both approaches are based on ordering timepoints based on their saliency as defined by the attribution method that is being evaluated, and then replacing those timepoints and measuring the change in prediction. The replacement values are derived from the *opposite class*, defined as the class representative (the mean of each sample in a class) that has the lowest prediction for the explained sample's predicted class.

During deletion, the method iteratively replaces the most salient timesteps of the explained sample with those from the opposite class. As these critical timesteps are removed, the model's prediction confidence diminishes. The area under this deletion curve, known as AUDC, serves as a key measure, where superior explanations produce smaller AUDC values, reflecting steeper declines in confidence.

The insertion process works inversely by starting with the opposite class sample and progressively replacing its values with the original sample based on the same ordering as deletion. This reconstruction allows the model's confidence to rebound, with the area under the insertion curve, or AUIC, quantifying the recovery speed. Higher AUIC values indicate more effective attribution methods that accurately pinpoint influential timesteps.

By combining these measures, the AUCD measure emerges as the arithmetic difference between AUIC and AUDC. Optimal explanations approach a value of 1.0, demonstrating both strong confidence recovery during insertion and rapid confidence loss during deletion.

The most notable difference between the two evaluation measures is that AUCD ranks features based on their absolute attribution value, while InterpretTime discards non-positive attribution values, meaning that they are not considered during the perturbation process. This has implications for segments with negative attributions, where the perturbed segments which have positive attribution might not be sufficient to change the prediction significantly.
The other key difference between the two evaluation measures lies in the substitution values used when perturbing the time series: while InterpretTime uses values sampled from the specified distribution, AUCD selects values from an instance of the opposite class.

3 Attribution Normalisation

For segment-based explanations, Shapley values are computed over segments of timepoints rather than individual timepoints. However, evaluation methods for time series require attributions at the granularity of single timepoints. To address this incompatibility, each timepoint within a segment can be assigned the Shapley value of its parent segment. Formally, if a segment S has an attribution ϕ_S, every timepoint $f_i \in S$ is assigned:

$$\phi_{f_i} = \phi_S.$$

A key property of Shapley values in this setting is segment-level additivity, which requires that the sum of attributions across all timepoints within a segment equals the segment's total Shapley value. This method violates segment-level additivity, as the sum of attributions within the segment becomes:

$$\sum_{f_i \in S} \phi_{f_i} = |S| \cdot \phi_S,$$

which only equals ϕ_S when $|S| = 1$.

Maintaining segment-level additivity is essential for ensuring that Shapley-based interpretations remain theoretically sound. If the sum of individual timepoint attributions within a segment deviates from the segment's original Shapley value, the resulting explanations lose their cooperative game-theoretic justification. This inconsistency can distort timepoint importance rankings, misrepresent the true contribution of segments, and introduce artefacts when comparing attributions across different granularities (e.g., segments vs. individual timepoints). For this reason, we suggest to instead use normalisation that distributes the segment's Shapley value uniformly among its constituent timepoints, assigning each $f_i \in S$ an attribution of:

$$\phi_{f_i} = \frac{\phi_S}{|S|},$$

where $|S|$ denotes the segment's length.

This proposed normalisation method preserves the additivity property by construction:

$$\sum_{f_i \in S} \phi_{f_i} = \sum_{f_i \in S} \left(\frac{\phi_S}{|S|} \right) = \phi_S.$$

The normalisation method, by preserving segment-level additivity, ensures that evaluations performed on individual timepoints remain faithful to the original segment-wise Shapley values, thereby supporting reliable and interpretable model explanations.

In our experiments, we compare results in the presence and absence of normalisation to assess its effectiveness.

4 Experiments

In this work, we use the Shapley Value Sampling implementation for SHAP [25], which allows us to specify a segmentation of the time series, such that each segment is considered as a feature for SHAP. In the rest of this section, we specify the implementation and hyperparameters for the segmentation methods, classifiers, and XAI evaluation methodologies used. Lastly, we introduce the two tested backgrounds and the datasets used in the experiments.

4.1 Classifiers

Every classifier was trained using the default hyperparameters; the implementations for MiniRocket and QUANT are from the aeon library [18]. For RandomForest, we used the scikit-learn implementation [20], and for ResNet, we rely on the implementation from dCAM [2].

4.2 Segmentation Methods

We use the sktime [16] implementations for IG and GG, Ruptures [27] implementations for BinSeg, BottomUp, and KernelCPD and aeon for ClaSP. Finally, NNSegment was adapted from the LimeSegment repository [26], and equal-width segmentation uses the custom implementation from [25].

For hyperparameters, we only deviated from defaults for ClaSP's *period length*, which was set to 4, because using the default value we found only one segment. Additionally, a kernel type for KernelCPD and the cost functions for BinSeg, BottomUp need to be specified: we set them respectively to *linear kernel* and *L*1 *cost function* to account for speed.

4.3 XAI Evaluation Metholodologies

For InterpretTime, we used the implementation in [25], which extends the original one of [28] by complementing the use of Gaussian distribution to perturb TS, with multi-distribution perturbations (global Gaussian, global mean, local mean).

These four different *perturbation strategies* (hereafter referred to simply as perturbations) are a proxy to test the stability of AUCSE and F-score when the classifier training process used by the original work is altered to remove the *Gaussian noise injection* (more detail can be found in [28]). Preliminary results demonstrated that the noise injection step degrades the accuracy of non-deep learning classifiers.

For AUCD, we implemented our own version according to its original definition. The only tunable parameter in the method is the step size, which indicates the number of timepoints to be replaced at each iteration. We have set the step to 4% of the time series data.

4.4 Background for SHAP

SHAP uses a *background set* to simulate data missingness: when feature(s) need to be analysed as inactive(s), they are substituted with corresponding values of the instances found in this set.

In the experiments, two different background sets $\mathcal{D}_{backg}$ are analysed, both are composed of a single instance, as opposed to the *sampling approach* [14]. Since the computational demand of SHAP linearly increases with the cardinality of the background set, this choice is made to account for speed.

Zero: a sample full of zeros, the default choice for some explanation frameworks such as [14], the one used for SHAP's implementation. Mathematically

$$\mathcal{D}_{backg} = \{\mathbf{0}_{d \times L}\}$$

where d is the number of channels (in the univariate case is equal to 1) and L is the number of observations in the series.

Average: a TS representing the average of samples in the training set, mathematically

$$\mathcal{D}_{backg} = \{\frac{\sum_{x_i \in \mathcal{D}_{train}} x_i}{|\mathcal{D}_{train}|}\}$$

4.5 Datasets

We use five diverse datasets in our experiments, covering both univariate and multivariate time series settings.

Gunpoint (GNP) [22] is a very well-known baseline dataset. It represents the x coordinate position of a (simulated) gun when two different actors perform two different gestures (targets) *draw* and *point*. The TS are univariate, having 150 time points each.

UWAVE [15] data represent the x, y, z accelerometer coordinates (the 3 dimensions) of hands while executing 8 different gestures (targets). The length of each MTS is 315.

EOG is the concatenation of two different UTS datasets [9] representing a horizontal and a vertical EOG signal. Four electrodes were placed on different sides of the left eye. The horizontal dimension is the difference between the left and right signals, while the vertical dimension is the difference between the upper and the lower signals. Each dimension has a length of 1250 time points, and the dataset has 12 different targets.

KeplerLightCurves (KLC) [1] data is obtained by light curves coming from NASA's Kepler mission; the 7 possible targets represent different classes of stars. Each instance has been labelled by experts working at the University of Sydney and interpolated such that every instance has a length of 4767 time points.

MilitaryPress (MP8) [7]: TS represent x, y coordinates of 25 different body parts while executing the *Military Press strength-and-conditioning* exercise. The dataset has 4 different targets representing an execution of the exercise, and each dimension has 161 time points. We used a *domain-expert selection* containing 8 channels, i.e., the y coordinates of both right and left positions of Elbows, Wrists, Shoulders, and Hips.

5 Results

For each dataset and machine learning (ML) model, we aggregate the results for each evaluation measure over the three factors of interest: backgrounds, perturbations, and segmentations. We calculate the mean and variance for each combination as shown in Fig. 1 for AUCSE (other evaluation measures have shown

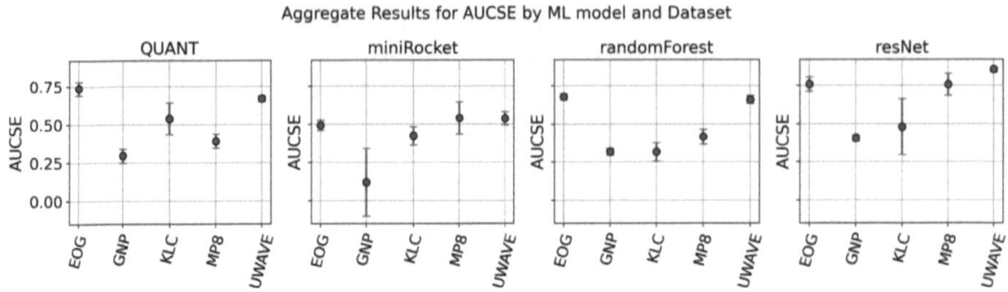

Fig. 1. Aggregated *AUCSE* by dataset and classifier. Error bars are standard deviation from the mean. AUCSE is computed based on the SHAP attributions for each classifier-dataset pair.

similar trends). This conditional variance analysis, where variance is examined with respect to fixed datasets and ML models, allows us to identify the cases where one or more of the three factors of interest are responsible for the variance in the results. Specifically, the results suggest that in most cases, there is little to no variance due to these factors, and conditioning on the dataset and ML model sufficiently determines the outcome of the evaluation measures, meaning that the impact of these factors is negligible.

This very low variance also suggests that **equal-length segmentation is often the best choice**: some of the evaluated segmentation methods come with a high computational cost, which does not justify their marginal improvement, where it even exists, over the cost-free equal segmentation.

However, there are notable exceptions, where there is significant variance in specific combinations of data and classifier, such as MiniRocket on GNP and MP8 or ResNet on KLC. In these cases, one or more of the remaining factors (background or segmentation) appear to significantly influence explanation quality. Therefore, we take a deeper look into these specific cases to find out when the choice of background or segmentation does influence the quality of explanations according to each evaluation measure.

5.1 Background and Segmentation Analysis

Segmentations on KeplerLightCurves. Figure 2 shows the F-score results for the ResNet classifier on the KLC dataset for different segmentations, backgrounds and perturbation methods. Overall, global Gaussian perturbations generally produced higher results compared to global mean. The choice between average and zero background also had a significant impact on performance. When using global mean perturbations, the average background consistently led to lower scores across most segmentation methods. However, this trend reversed under global Gaussian perturbations, where zero background often yielded higher results. This suggests that zero background synergises better with global Gaussian perturbations, while average background may be more compatible with global mean.

The perturbation type played a critical role in determining segmentation performance. Global Gaussian perturbations, which introduce noise, generally led to higher scores, implying better performance for most methods. In contrast, global mean perturbations, which adjust the mean value, resulted in lower scores across the board, indicating reduced effectiveness. This variability suggests that method performance is highly dependent on the combination of background and perturbation type.

Comparing the different segmentations, we see that the Binary, Infogain, and Greedy Gaussian segmentations underperform compared to the other methods when the global Gaussian + zero background strategy is used. However, these three segmentations outperform others when the global mean is used, especially with the average background. This suggests that the optimal choice for segmentation can be dependent on the perturbation strategy used in evaluation.

To further understand what makes these segmentations behave differently on KLC, we calculated the normalised entropy of each segmentation, which is based on the segment length compared to the equal segmentation as a baseline. Figure 3 shows the entropy results across all segmentations and datasets. We can see that for KLC, the same three segmentations have a lower score, indicating a greater deviation from the equal segmentation. This means that these segmentation methods tend to find a highly uneven distribution of segment lengths, including very large and very small segments. As segments become smaller, each of their means can significantly deviate from the global mean, which influences the result of the perturbations based on the global mean.

Background. Figures 4a and 4b respectively show the AUCD results for MiniRocket on the GunPoint and MilitaryPress datasets. The results show that using the average background over the zero background yields better results for AUCD across all Segmentations. The advantage of the average background is that it fundamentally provides a more realistic baseline that reflects the typical behaviour of the data. A zero background assumes all features are absent or neutral, which can lead to misleading interpretations if the actual data never contains such values. In contrast, the average sample captures the distribution of the data, ensuring SHAP values explain predictions relative to a meaningful reference point.

5.2 Attribution Normalisation

Figure 5 shows that *normalisation* appears to be particularly beneficial across the board, with notable performance gains for the ClaSP, Binary, Greedy Gaussian and Infogain Segmentations. Normalisation's preservation of segment-level additivity appears to have a clear positive effect for most datasets, ensuring timepoint attributions sum to the segment's SHAP value. This prevents distortions in importance rankings, especially for varying segment lengths, leading to more reliable and interpretable explanations. Because the normalisation is fundamentally based on compensating based on segment length, as the partition

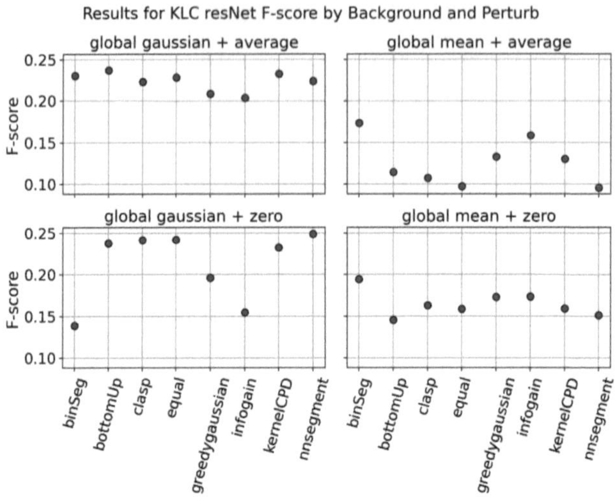

Fig. 2. F-score on ResNet and KeplerLightCurves by Background and Perturbation over Segmentations. Different Segmentations perform better with different backgrounds and perturb methods.

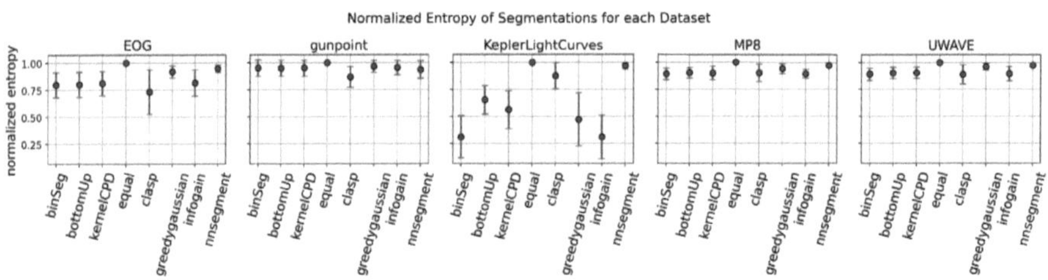

Fig. 3. Mean normalised entropy by Dataset and Segmentation. Error bar denotes standard deviation. Segmentations significantly deviate from uniform in KeplerLightCurves.

of a time series into segments becomes more uniform (equal-sized segments), its effect in changing the relative rankings of points is more muted. And since the evaluation measures are based on the relative scale of attributions, the closer a segmentation is to equal, the more invariant the resulting evaluation is to the normalisation process. We can observe this empirically by seeing that the equal segmentation yields practically no change in evaluation between normalised and unnormalised explanations.

We can measure how close a segmentation is to the uniform segmentation through its relative entropy. We show the expected relative entropy for each segmentation and dataset in Fig. 3. We can see that the datasets and segmentations that gain the most from normalisation, EOG and KeplerLightCurves, are also the ones whose relative entropy is most different from the uniform. This indicates that normalisation is especially effective when there is a mix of

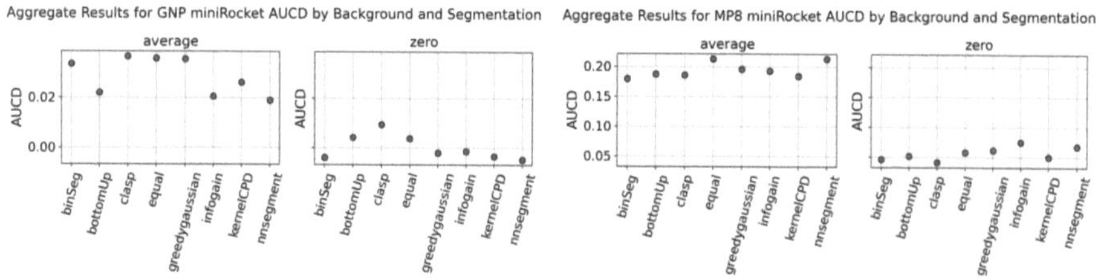

(a) AUCD for MiniRocket on Gunpoint over Background & Segmentation

(b) AUCD for MiniRocket on MilitaryPress over Background & Segmentation

Fig. 4. AUCD for MiniRocket on Gunpoint and MilitaryPress. Both cases show that the average background outperforms the zero background.

uneven segmentation, and when the segmentation is even, normalisation leaves evaluation unchanged, making it a desirable and inexpensive way to improve explanations on segmentations.

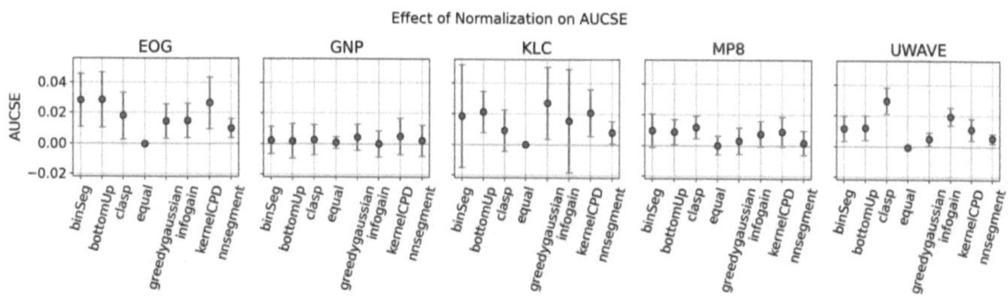

Fig. 5. Difference in AUCSE results when normalization is applied. A positive value denotes an increase in mean evaluation performance with normalization. Error bars are standard deviation of the difference.

5.3 Differences Between XAI Evaluation Measures

In this section, we explore the few cases where the evaluation measures substantially disagree. While AUCSE and F-score agree in all analysed cases, there are some differences between these two and AUCD, which we are investigating in this section.

Gunpoint MiniRocket: As can be noted from Fig. 6a , according to InterpreTime evaluation measure, the zero background is the best choice, different from what was previously observed for AUCD in Fig. 4a.

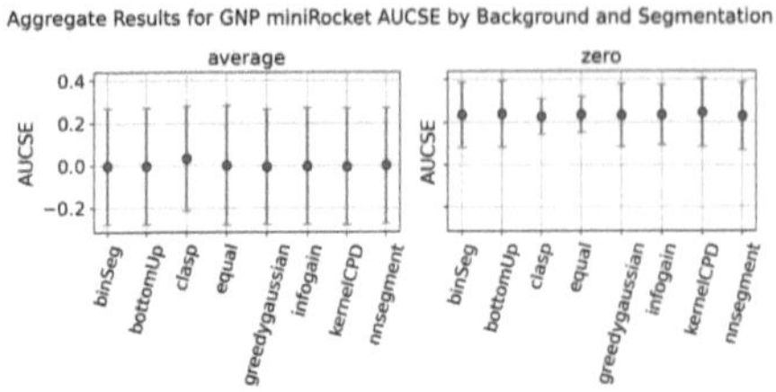

(a) AUCSE results for MiniRocket on Gunpoint for different backgrounds and segmentations. Zero background outperforms the average background.

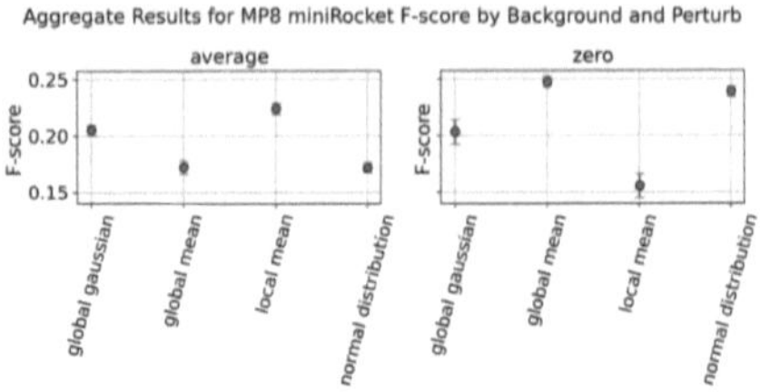

(b) F-score results for MiniRocket on MP8 for different backgrounds and perturbations. Best choice of background depends on perturbation choice in evaluation.

Fig. 6. InterpretTime's scores for Gunpoint MiniRocket and for MP MiniRocket.

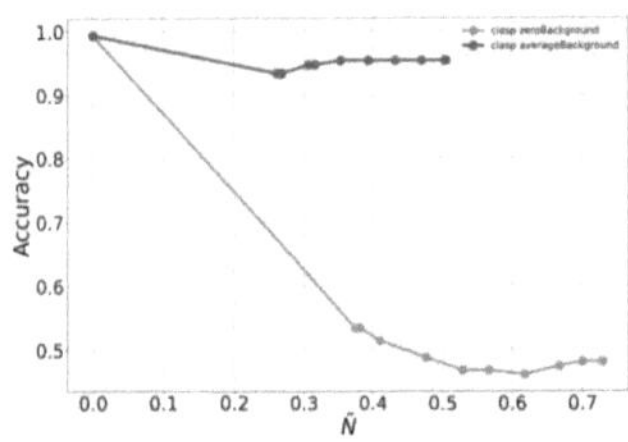

(a) Accuracy decay while corrupting time series

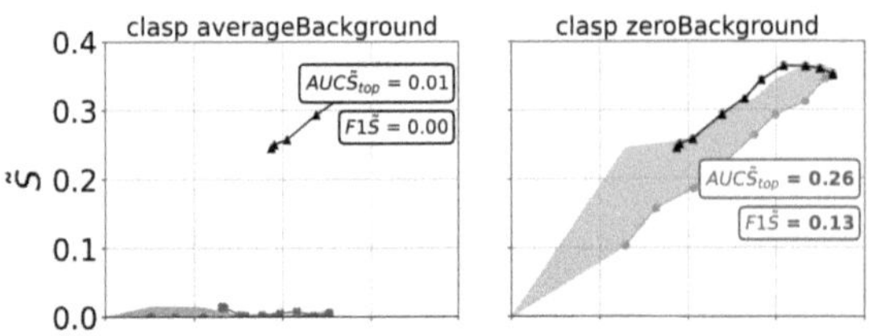

(b) Evolution of $\bar{S}$ while corrupting TS.

Fig. 7. Accuracy decay and probability of the initial predicted label evolutions while the time series are progressively corrupted for both backgrounds, ClaSP segmentation, MiniRocket classifier, Gunpoint dataset.

We further investigate the evolution using Fig. 7a, showing the accuracy and Fig. 7b showing the probability of the predicted label evolution. This analysis tracks how InterpretTime progressively corrupts the time series for two different instances that share the same ClaSP segmentation but use different background sets. The first plot reveals a violation of InterpretTime's core assumption: the instance using the average background after a slight initial accuracy decay rises again, never reaching the random accuracy level of the zero background. This directly impacts the evaluation measure, as evidenced by the flat curve in the second plot. Since AUCSE is defined as the evolution of $\bar{S}$ through the predefined steps, if this evolution is marginal or absent, the AUCSE measure would be close to 0.

MP8 MiniRocket: Fig. 6b shows the F-score (AUCSE is very similar) grouped by different perturbations. The zero background achieves higher scores using the global mean and normal distribution perturbations, whereas using the global Gaussian and local mean yields the opposite result. At the same time, AUCD

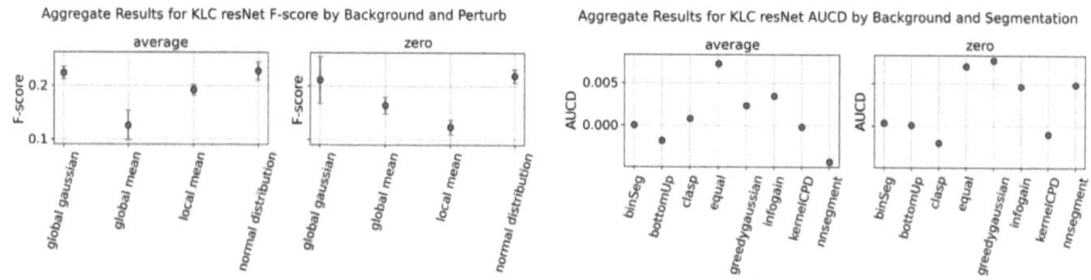

(a) ResNet to KLC: F-score of both backgrounds for each used perturbation (b) ResNet applied to KLC AUCD, backgrounds and segmentations

Fig. 8. InterpretTime's and AUCD scores for (a) and (b) ResNet applied to KLC, (c) and (d) MiniRocket applied to MP.

constantly scores the average background as the best choice as evident from Fig. 4b.

Since the majority of the analysed evaluation measures agree that the average is the best choice, we can conclude that this is one example where different perturbations yield different results.

KLC ResNet: Finally we investigate the third combination in this section, i.e., ResNet classifier and KLC dataset. In Fig. 8a the F-score is reported (AUCSE has similar behavior, having a smaller difference) grouped by different perturbations, while Fig. 8b shows AUCD, grouped by segmentation algorithms. Using these last evaluation measure, the different segmentation methods achieve, most of the time, very similar results, with the exceptions of Greedy Gaussian and NNSegment having slightly higher scores when the zero background is used.

Looking instead at F-scores, there is a completely different scenario: using global Gaussian and normal distribution perturbations, the two backgrounds achieve nearly the same score; on the other hand, global mean and local mean indicate two opposite best choices, respectively, zero and average background.

Our findings suggest that noise augmentation during training, as proposed in the original InterpretTime paper, plays a key role in ensuring consistent rankings (see [25,28] for details). Consequently, this limits the scope of this method to neural networks whose performance is not hurt by the noise addition.

6 Conclusion

In this work, we analysed key factors influencing the explanation resulting from SHAP in the Time Series domain. Our analysis was conducted using a diverse set of classifiers, datasets, backgrounds, and segmentation methods.

We empirically showed that the number of segments is more important than the underlying segmentation method used. Among the eight analysed segmentation methods, the clear winner is the equal-length segmentation, showing superior or similar results to the other methods. This is mostly achieved because the other methods often produce very similar segmentations, except for the KLC dataset, where some segmentations are very uneven, while requiring more computational resources.

Another important contribution is the *attribution normalisation* technique, which consists of weighting each segment contribution according to its size, which increases the XAI evaluation scores in the case of uneven segmentations.

We also found small differences between the results achieved using the zero and the average background. In the few cases we found substantial differences between their relative scores, the average background was the best choice. Moreover, in preliminary experiments, we also tested the *sampling background* strategy, consisting of a set composed of different random samples from the train set: we found a marginal improvement over the other two backgrounds, but at the cost of much higher computational cost. An interesting direction for future work is to further study the effect of the background set used by SHAP, an important topic still under-explored in the literature.

Finally, we observe some inconsistency between the two XAI evaluation methods, suggesting that InterpretTime's effectiveness may be limited to deep learning classifiers. Unlike other models, deep learning classifiers remain unaffected by the required noise-based training augmentation. Without this augmentation, i.e., as used in this work, results may vary unpredictably across different perturbations.

Acknowledgements. This publication has emanated from research conducted with the financial support of Taighde Éireann – Research Ireland under Grants [ML-Labs 18/CRT/6183, Insight Centre for Data Analytics 12/RC/2289_P2]. For the purpose of Open Access, the author has applied a CC BY public copyright license to any Author Accepted Manuscript version arising from this submission.

References

1. Barbara, et al.: Classifying Kepler light curves for 12 000 a and f stars using supervised feature-based machine learning. Mon. Not. R. Astron. Soc. **514**(2), 2793–2804 (2022)
2. Boniol, et al.: dcam: Dimension-wise class activation map for explaining multivariate data series classification. In: Proceedings of the 2022 International Conference on Management of Data, pp. 1175–1189 (2022)
3. Celisse, et al.: New efficient algorithms for multiple change-point detection with reproducing kernels. Comput. Stat. Data Anal. **128**, 200–220 (2018)
4. Dempster, et al.: Minirocket: A very fast (almost) deterministic transform for time series classification. In: Proceedings of the 27th ACM SIGKDD Conference on Knowledge D. & Data Mining. Association for Computing Machinery (2021)
5. Dempster, et al.: Quant: A minimalist interval method for time series classification. Data Min. Knowl. Discovery **38**(4), 2377–2402 (2024)
6. Dhariyal, et al.: Back to basics: A sanity check on modern time series classification algorithms. In: Advanced Analytics and Learning on Temporal Data, pp. 205–229. Springer, Cham (2023). https://doi.org/10.1007/978-3-031-49896-1_14
7. Dhariyal, et al.: Scalable classifier-agnostic channel selection for multivariate time series classification. Data Min. Knowl. D. **37**(2), 1010–1054 (2023)

8. Ermshaus, et al.: Clasp: parameter-free time series segmentation. Data Min. Knowl. Disc. **37**(3), 1262–1300 (2023)
9. Fang, et al.: Electrooculography-based continuous eye-writing recognition system for efficient assistive communication systems. PloS one **13**(2), e0192684 (2018)
10. Geurts, et al.: Extremely randomized trees. Mach. Learn. **63**(1), 342 (2006)
11. Hallac, et al.: Greedy gaussian segmentation of multivariate time series. Adv. Data Anal. Classif. **13**(3), 727–751 (2019)
12. He, et al.: Deep residual learning for image recognition. In: Proceedings of the IEEE conference on computer vision and pattern recognition, pp. 770–778 (2016)
13. Killick, et al.: Optimal detection of changepoints with a linear computational cost. J. Am. Stat. Assoc. **107**(500), 1590–1598 (2012)
14. Kokhlikyan, et al.: Captum: A unified and generic model interpretability library for pytorch. arXiv preprint arXiv:2009.07896 (2020)
15. Liu, et al.: uwave: Accelerometer-based personalized gesture recognition and its applications. Pervasive Mob. Comput. **5**(6), 657–675 (2009)
16. Löning, M., Bagnall, A., Ganesh, S., Kazakov, V., Lines, J., Király, F.J.: sktime: A unified interface for machine learning with time series. arXiv preprint arXiv:1909.07872 (2019)
17. Lundberg, et al.: A unified approach to interpreting model predictions. Adv. Neural Inf. Process. Syst. **30** (2017)
18. Middlehurst, M., et al.: Aeon: a python toolkit for learning from time series. J. Mach. Learn. Res. **25**(289), 1–10 (2024)
19. Parvatharaju, P.S., Doddaiah, R., Hartvigsen, T., Rundensteiner, E.A.: Learning saliency maps to explain deep time series classifiers. In: Proceedings of the 30th ACM International Conference on Information & Knowledge Management, pp. 1406–1415. CIKM '21, Association for Computing Machinery (2021)
20. Pedregosa, et al.: Scikit-learn: Machine learning in Python. J. Mach. Learn. Res. **12**, 2825–2830 (2011)
21. Petsiuk, V., Das, A., Saenko, K.: Rise: Randomized input sampling for explanation of black-box models. arXiv preprint arXiv:1806.07421 (2018)
22. Ratanamahatana, et al.: Three myths about dynamic time warping data mining. In: Proceedings of the 2005 SIAM international conference on data mining, pp. 506–510. SIAM (2005)
23. Sadri, et al.: Information gain-based metric for recognizing transitions in human activities. Pervasive Mob. Comput. **38**, 92–109 (2017)
24. Sen, et al.: On tests for detecting change in mean. The Annals of statistics, pp. 98–108 (1975)
25. Serramazza, et al.: Improving the evaluation and actionability of explanation methods for multivariate time series classification. In: Bifet, A., Davis, J., Krilavičius, T., Kull, M., Ntoutsi, E., Žliobaitė, I. (eds) Machine Learning and Knowledge Discovery in Databases. Research Track. Springer, Cham (2024). https://doi.org/10.1007/978-3-031-70359-1_11
26. Sivill, et al.: Limesegment: meaningful, realistic time series explanations. In: Camps-Valls, G., Ruiz, F.J.R., Valera, I. (eds.) Proceedings of The 25th International Conference on Artificial Intelligence and Statistics. Proceedings of Machine Learning Research, vol. 151, pp. 3418–3433. PMLR (2022)
27. Truong, et al.: Selective review of offline change point detection methods. Sign. Process. **167**, 107299 (2020)
28. Turbé, et al.: Evaluation of post-hoc interpretability methods in time-series classification. Nat. Mach. Intell. **5**(3), 250–260 (2023)

A Real-Time Pipeline for Anomaly Detection and Explanation in Streaming Data

Florentin Jiechieu Kameni[1], Anne Marthe Sophie Ngo Bibinbe[2], Vasilis Cako[1], Abdoul Jalil Djiberou Mahamadouc[1], Mohamed Rayane Bakari[1], Kevin Dilan Nguetche[1], Durande Kamga Nguifo[1], Anthony Bertrand[1], Michael F. Mbouopda[1], Rim El Cheikh[1], Gertrude Raissa Mbiadou Saleu[1], William Guyot Lenat[1], Patrick Asante Owusu[1], and Engelbert Mephu Nguifo[1(✉)]

[1] Université Clermont Auvergne, Clermont Auvergne INP, ENSMSE, CNRS, LIMOS, Clermont-Ferrand 63000, France
engelbert.mephu_nguifo@uca.fr
[2] Université Laval, Québec, QC G1V 0A6, Canada

Abstract. We present a prototype real-time pipeline for anomaly detection and explanation in streaming time series data. The system consists of four core modules: time series storage, anomaly detection, model-agnostic explanation, and interactive visualisation. It supports multiple detection methods and produces variable-level contribution scores to explain real-time anomalies. An explainability score is introduced to quantify interpretability, aiding domain experts in understanding alerts. The pipeline updates both detection and explanation modules incrementally using a window-based approach. Preliminary results show reliable detection and intuitive explanations. Our pipeline is fully containerised and distributed to facilitate demonstration and deployment, enabling quick setup and reproducibility. Future work will focus on continuous learning to adapt to new data without forgetting past patterns.

Keywords: Data stream · Anomaly detection · Explainability

1 Introduction

Anomaly detection in data streams is a core challenge in real-time analytics, requiring systems to continuously process high-velocity, evolving data[1]. In domains such as sensor networks, industrial monitoring, finance, and cybersecurity, detecting abnormal patterns or rare events demands not only efficient algorithms but also the capacity to explain anomalies based on underlying data characteristics. Recall that the notion of an anomaly is inherently tied to a context-specific or statistical definition of normality, highlighting the dynamic

[1] https://sites.google.com/view/ad-explain/home.

I. Koprinska et al. (Eds.): ECML PKDD 2025, CCIS 2842, pp. 474–478, 2026.
https://doi.org/10.1007/978-3-032-19105-2_33

and domain-dependent nature of this problem. For example, anomalies can also uncover emerging opportunities, such as unexpected buying patterns that reveal new market segments or indicate demand for novel product offerings. These insights demonstrate that anomaly detection is not only essential for risk mitigation but also for strategic advantage in data-driven environments.

The constraints of these environments often necessitate real-time analysis, as delays in detection can lead to significant consequences. In many applications – such as flood monitoring, intrusion detection, or equipment failure prevention, acting after a critical anomaly has occurred may result in irreparable damage or missed opportunities. Consequently, anomaly detection systems must balance speed, accuracy, and interpretability to operate effectively under these time-sensitive conditions. This work uses an explainability score to assess how well a model's decisions can be understood in terms of the data it processes, reflecting the degree to which detected anomalies are both understandable and meaningful to human analysts, particularly in dynamic, high-stakes environments.

Several anomaly detection methods have been explored in the context of this work, including [1–4]. Although originally designed for time series data, these approaches are commonly applied to data streams using windowing techniques [5], which segment continuous flows into finite intervals for incremental processing. While effective, such techniques raise additional challenges regarding window size selection, adaptability to non-stationary patterns, and real-time interpretability. In this work, explainability and interpretability are used interchangeably, both referring to the system's ability to make its decisions understandable to users or domain experts in real time.

In this work, we describe the design of a real-time anomaly detection and explanation system tailored to streaming data environments. The proposed system is structured around four core modules, each responsible for a distinct function within the detection-explanation pipeline:

- a time series database, which stores and manages incoming data streams efficiently;
- an anomaly detection module, responsible for identifying deviations based on learned patterns;
- an explainability module, which computes an explainability score and generates human-interpretable justifications for detected anomalies;
- a visualisation module, designed to present both detection results and explanations in an intuitive and interactive interface.

This modular architecture ensures flexibility, scalability, and transparency, enabling users to monitor evolving systems in real time while maintaining interpretability as a central design principle. While the current implementation lays the foundation for robust and interpretable anomaly detection, the pipeline is part of an ongoing effort aimed at refining its components, improving scalability, and enhancing integration with domain-specific decision-making processes. The following section outlines the contributions of this evolving work.

2 Contribution

2.1 Pipeline Architecture

The proposed architecture is designed for real-time anomaly detection and explanation in streaming data environments. Figure 1 summarises the procedures of our proposal.

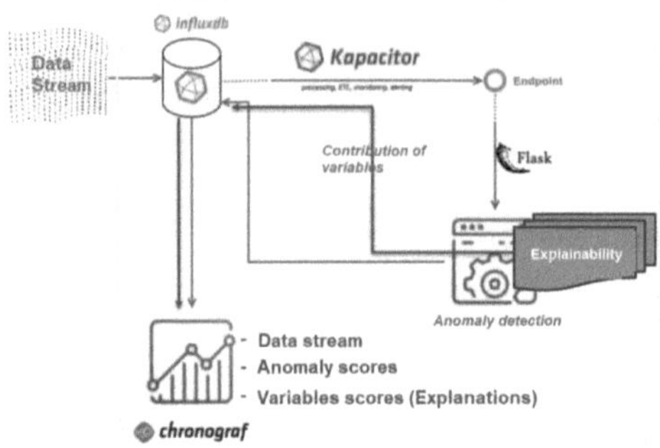

Fig. 1. Architecture of the proposed real-time anomaly detection and explanation system. Incoming data streams are ingested into a time series database, continuously processed and served to a dashboard. This modular pipeline supports real-time responsiveness and interpretability across streaming environments.

2.2 Data Storage

To support real-time anomaly detection and explanation, the system includes a time series database, such as InfluxDB [6], that efficiently indexes streaming data by timestamp. Each record in the stream consists of numerical measurements from multiple variables, paired with the time of observation. This design enables fast, time-based querying and analytics, ensuring the system can operate continuously under high data throughput while maintaining low latency.

2.3 Anomaly Detection

The pipeline integrates a real-time anomaly detection module capable of identifying unusual patterns as data arrives. It is designed to accommodate multiple detection techniques, including deep learning and tree-based methods, allowing for flexibility across different application domains. In the current implementation, a predictive modelling approach is used to detect deviations between expected and observed values in time series. This supports the timely identification of both point anomalies and subtle behavioural shifts in the data stream.

2.4 Explanation

When the anomaly score of a data point exceeds a defined threshold, an explanation algorithm is triggered to interpret the cause of the anomaly at that specific time. The system implements a model-agnostic method, including KernelSHAP [7] – which estimates variable-level contribution scores regardless of the underlying detection model. This choice ensures compatibility with the system's modular architecture, which supports multiple anomaly detection approaches. The output of the explanation module mirrors the structure of the input stream, associating each anomaly with its timestamp and the contribution scores of each variable.

2.5 Visualisation

The results of both the detection and explanation modules are presented through an interactive visualisation interface. This component enables users to explore anomaly scores alongside variable-level contribution scores over time, making the system's decisions more transparent and actionable. The interface is designed for usability, supporting real-time interaction, anomaly flagging, and pattern interpretation by domain experts.

3 Conclusion

We have presented a prototype of a real-time anomaly detection and explanation system tailored to streaming data environments. The system comprises four core modules: an anomaly detection module, a time series database, an explainability module, and a visualisation component. The preliminary results are consistent and demonstrate the added value of integrating explainability.

As a next step, we intend to design a continuous learning mechanism capable of incorporating new knowledge from incoming data streams without forgetting previously acquired information and detecting concept drifts. This will enable the system to adapt to evolving data distributions while preserving long-term learning.

Acknowledgments. This work was partially supported by the IMobS3 "Laboratoire d'Excellence" (LabEx for "Innovative Mobility: Smart and Sustainable Solutions"), and the project IT2.fr PSPC (https://cordis.europa.eu/project/id/875999/fr) under the DASMA subproject (dasma.limos.fr) funded by Bpifrance. The authors would like to thank the LIMOS Miners group for fruitful discussions. Finally, our acknowledgements go to the reviewers for constructive comments.

Disclosure of Interests. The authors have no competing interests to declare that are relevant to the content of this article.

References

1. Arslan, F., Javaid, A., Awan, M.D.Z.: Anomaly Detection in Time Series: Current Focus and Future Challenges (2023). In: Anomaly Detection - Recent Advances, AI and ML Perspectives and Applications. IntechOpen, London (2023). https://doi.org/10.5772/intechopen.111886
2. Mensi, A., Bicego, M.: Enhanced Anomaly Scores for Isolation Forests, vol. 120, pp. 108115. Pattern Recognition (2021)
3. Mirsky, Y., Doitshman, T., Elovici, Y., Shabtai, A.: Kitsune: An Ensemble of Autoencoders for Online Network Intrusion Detection. ArXiv: abs/1802.09089. https://api.semanticscholar.org/CorpusID:3502091
4. Tan, S.C., Ting, K.M., Liu, T.F.: Fast anomaly detection for streaming data. In: Proceedings of the Twenty-Second International Joint Conference on Artificial Intelligence, vol. 22, pp. 1511–1516. AAAI Press (2011). ISBN No: 9781577355144
5. Mansalis, S., Ntoutsi, E., Pelekis, N., Theodoridis, Y.: An evaluation of data stream clustering algorithms. Stat. Anal. Data Min. **11**(4), 167–187 (2018). John Wiley & Sons, Inc. https://doi.org/10.1002/sam.11380
6. Lundberg, S.M., Lee, S.I.: A unified approach to interpreting model predictions. In: Proceedings of the 31st International Conference on Neural Information Processing Systems, pp. 4768–4777 (2017). Curran Associates Inc. ISBN No: 9781510860964
7. Lundberg, S.M., Lee, S.: A Unified Approach to Interpreting Model Predictions (2017)

Workshop on eXplainable Knowledge Discovery in Data Mining and Unlearning (XKDD and Beyond 2025)

Workshop on eXplainable Knowledge Discovery in Data Mining and Unlearning (XKDD and Beyond 2025)

The 7th International Workshop on eXplainable Knowledge Discovery in Data Mining was held in conjunction with the European Conference on Machine Learning and Principles and Practice of Knowledge Discovery in Databases (ECML PKDD). Previous editions of the workshop were also held jointly with ECML PKDD in 2019, 2020, 2021, 2022, and 2024.

In the past decade, Machine Learning–based decision systems have been widely used in domains such as credit scoring, insurance risk, and health monitoring, where high predictive performance is essential. While these systems can substantially improve decision-making, they introduce ethical and legal risks, including the codification of biases, reduced transparency and accountability, as well as threats to privacy. These risks are exacerbated by the opacity of contemporary decision support systems, which are often complex and whose internal logic is typically inaccessible to humans.

Nowadays most Artificial Intelligence systems are driven by Machine Learning algorithms. The relevance and need for ethics in Artificial Intelligence are supported by a number of initiatives that provide recommendations and guidelines to make Artificial Intelligence-based decision systems explainable and compliant with legal and ethical requirements. These include the EU's GDPR (which introduces a right for individuals to obtain "meaningful explanations of the logic involved" when automated decision making takes place), the ACM Statement on Algorithmic Transparency and Accountability, Informatics Europe's European Recommendations on Machine-Learned Automated Decision Making, and the EU High-Level Expert Group's Ethics Guidelines for Trustworthy AI.

The challenge of designing and developing trustworthy Artificial Intelligence decision systems remains open and requires a joint effort across technical, legal, sociological and ethical domains.

The purpose of XKDD, is to encourage principled research that advances explainable, transparent, ethical, and fair Data Mining and Machine Learning. For the 2025 edition, the workshop invited submissions addressing open challenges in specific areas of eXplainable Artificial Intelligence (XAI), including XAI and unlearning, XAI for social and responsible Artificial Intelligence, alignment of Artificial Intelligence with human values, XAI for outlier and anomaly detection, and the quantitative and qualitative evaluation of XAI. Further topics of interest comprised transparent-by-design models, XAI case studies, privacy-preserving systems, federated learning, time-series and graph-based approaches, visualization, human–machine interaction and human-in-the-loop, counterfactual explanations, human–model interfaces for XAI, interpretable machine learning, transparent data mining, fairness checking, and the legal and ethical dimensions of explanation, accountability, and liability.

XKDD 2025 received a total of twelve submissions. They were reviewed by at least three members of the Program Committee and all submissions underwent single-blind peer review. Ten papers were accepted for presentation. The accepted contributions cover methodological advances and applications across concept-based explainability, evaluation and diagnosis of explanations, example- and rule-based methods, trustworthy explanations for textual data, and perspectives on unlearning and the right to be forgotten.

The workshop took place in the afternoon of September 19, 2025, as part of ECML-PKDD. It opened with the keynote talk "Forgetting, Unlearning and Explainability in Large Language Models" by Prof. Josep Domingo-Ferrer (Universitat Rovira i Virgili, Catalonia). His presentation explored the emerging challenge of enabling digital forgetting in Large Language Models, addressing the ethical and technical implications of unlearning. The talk stimulated an engaging discussion among participants, setting the stage for the research presentations that followed.

Following, there were ten paper presentations covering topics such as explainability in Large Language Models, the right to be forgotten, generative and concept-based explanations, evaluation of human and machine explanations, human-in-the-loop approaches for model monitoring, concept-based learning, domain-specific case studies and comparative explainability methods.

This workshop is partially supported by the European Community H2020 Program under research and innovation programme, XAI, science and technology for the explanation of AI decision making, GA 834756. TANGO, EU-funded Horizon Europe project that aims to develop the theoretical foundations and the computational framework for synergistic human-machine decision making (The European Union Horizon 2020 program under grant agreement No. 101120763). The 4-year project will pave the way for the next generation of human-centric AI systems. The European Community NextGenerationEU programme under the funding schemes PNRR-PE-AI FAIR (Future Artificial Intelligence Research). The Italian Project Fondo Italiano per la Scienza FIS00001966 MIMOSA". SoBigData.it project (Prot. IR0000013 - Call n. 3264 of 12/28/2021) initiatives aimed at training new users and communities in the usage of the research infrastructure (SoBigData.eu).

October 2025

Francesca Naretto
Francesco Spinnato
Josep Domingo-Ferrer
Przemyslaw Biecek

XKDD and Beyond 2025 Workshop Organization

Workshop Chairs

Francesca Naretto	University of Pisa, Italy
Francesco Spinnato	University of Pisa, Italy
Josep Domingo-Ferrer	Universitat Rovira i Virgili
Przemyslaw Biecek	Warsaw University of Technology, Poland

Program Committee

Alessio Cascione	University of Pisa
Andrea Fedele	University of Pisa
Andrea Pugnana	University of Trento
Andreas Theissler	Aalen University of Applied Sciences
Cristiano Landi	University of Pisa
Eleonora Cappuccio	University of Pisa
Lorenzo Mannocci	University of Pisa
Luca Corbucci	University of Pisa
Marta Marchiori Manerba	University of Pisa
Rami Haffar	Universitat Rovira i Virgili
Sashi Kiran	Silicon Valley Bank

Concept-AIME: A Dual Inverse-Model Framework for Concept-Level Global and Local Explanations of Black-Box Predictors

Takafumi Nakanishi(✉)

Tokyo University of Technology, 1404-1 Katakura, Hachioji, Tokyo 192-0982, Japan
nakanishitf@stf.teu.ac.jp

Abstract. Recent explainable artificial intelligence work have often revealed the input features to which a model is attentive; however, lists of pixel or one-hot importance remain obscure to nonexperts and even domain specialists. This study proposes concept-approximate inverse model explanations (concept-AIME), an explanation framework that replaces raw features with a compact set of human-defined concepts (e.g., highly educated, managerial, and married). Concept-AIME operates in two stages. First, it learns a concept activation vector for each concept from a handful of positive samples and intermediate network activations and then develops a single approximate inverse operator that maps concept scores back to input features. Second, it constructs an analogous inverse operator for the target output (such as high-income probability) and, with one matrix product, instantly yields the percentage contribution of each concept to any individual prediction. In contrast to LIME or SHAP, which sample perturbations for every test point and stay bound to feature-level explanations, concept-AIME derives its inverse operator once, requires no gradients or internal parameters, and is therefore model-agnostic and sub-millisecond per instance after preprocessing. The method can immediately generate narratives such as "the 'managerial' concept raised the high-income score by 40%, whereas 'married' added 30%; lower education slightly suppressed the prediction." By unifying global and local reasoning in a single linear formulation, concept-AIME offers a novel general-purpose technique that quantifies black-box decisions through user-chosen, semantically meaningful concepts, providing actionable, domain-relevant explanations for high-stakes applications in healthcare, finance, and public policy, where transparency is essential.

Keywords: Concept-based Explainable AI · Approximate Inverse Model Explanations (AIME) · Concept Activation Vectors · Model-Agnostic Interpretation · Local Feature Importance

1 Introduction

With the rapid increase in model accuracy, explaining why a machine learning model arrives at a decision has become a critical requirement for explainable artificial intelligence (XAI) [1–20]. In high-risk domains, such as medical diagnosis, credit assessment,

I. Koprinska et al. (Eds.): ECML PKDD 2025, CCIS 2842, pp. 483–498, 2026.
https://doi.org/10.1007/978-3-032-19105-2_34

and public policy, decision makers must inspect and validate a model's reasoning, not merely its predictions. Mainstream post-hoc methods, such as LIME [21] and SHAP [22], approximate a local surrogate around each test instance and report local feature importance scores. However, these scores are expressed in low-level units such as pixel intensities or one-hot indicators, for example, "feature 17 = +0.12" or "pixel (14, 27) matters." Such atomic attributions are difficult to comprehend for domain experts and even more challenging for nonspecialists, and the per-instance perturbation sampling of LIME/SHAP incurs a significant runtime overhead.

A promising solution is concept-based explanation. A concept denotes a high-level, human-interpretable pattern—striped texture, high blood pressure, and managerial position. Kim et al. [23] introduced testing with concept activation vectors (TCAVs) to measure the influence of a concept on a neural network by learning a concept activation vector (CAV) from a few positive examples and computing directional derivatives in the representation space. Extensions such as ConceptSHAP [24] distribute concept contributions using Shapley values. However, existing concept methods operate in the narrow pipeline "concept $\rightarrow$ hidden representation $\rightarrow$ class probability" and therefore cannot deliver concept-level global and local explanations simultaneously, most of which also rely on gradient access and are ill-suited to tree-based or proprietary models.

I previously proposed approximate inverse model explanations (AIME) [25], which constructs a single linear approximate inverse operator $A^\dagger$ from outputs to inputs. Each column of $A^\dagger$ yields a global feature-importance vector, whereas the Hadamard product of a row with an input provides the local feature contribution for that instance. When $A^\dagger$ is computed, global and local attributions are obtained by lightweight matrix–vector multiplications, without gradients or heavy perturbation sampling.

Based on this inverse-problem view, I present concept-AIME, which extends AIME from the feature domain to the concept domain. This method comprises two inverse operator stages. Stage 1 learns CAVs for a small, user-labeled set of positive examples and aggregates the mapping between concept scores and input features into a single operator $A^\dagger_{concept}${. Stage 2 constructs an analogous operator $A^\dagger_{target}$ for the target output (e.g., high-income probability). A single matrix product with a local feature vector ℓ instantly yields the percentage share of each concept in the model's prediction, without accessing gradients or internal parameters.

To the best of our knowledge, this is the first concept-based XAI method that (i) provides both global concept formation and instance-level concept attribution within a single closed-form linear operator, and (ii) remains fully model-agnostic—requiring neither gradients nor access to internal parameters—making it equally applicable to tree ensembles, proprietary pipelines, and deep networks.

Unlike the original AIME, which explains predictions solely in the raw feature space, this study extends the inverse-operator idea to a semantically richer concept space learned from user-defined examples.

This extension requires a novel dual-operator construction: one inverse operator that maps concept scores to input features and a second that maps the model's output to the same concept basis—neither of which was proposed in [25].

Consequently, concept-AIME inherits the efficiency and model-agnosticism of AIME while newly enabling human-interpretable, concept-level global formation and per-instance attribution that were impossible in my earlier work.

The study makes the following contributions:

1. Introduces the first model-agnostic framework that unifies concepts, features, and predictions within one linear formulation, thereby providing global concept formation and local concept attribution in tandem.
2. The dual inverse-operator design reduces the inference time overhead to sub-milliseconds, enabling real-time visualization and interactive analytics.
3. A case study on the UCI Adult dataset demonstrates that explanations based on the concepts of higher education, executive/managerial, and married are perceived as more understandable and trustworthy than conventional feature-level XAI in user studies.

The remainder of this paper is organized as follows. Section 2 discusses the related work. Section 3 details the mathematical formulation and algorithm of concept-AIME. Section 4 describes the experimental setup and metrics, Sect. 5 discusses the results, and Sect. 6 concludes the study and outlines its limitations and directions for future work.

2 Related Works

TCAV is a prominent concept-based explanation approach introduced by Kim et al. in 2018 [23]. TCAV learns a vector (CAV) for each human-defined concept by training a linear classifier on the internal activations of a model and uses directional derivatives to quantify the sensitivity of the model's prediction to that concept. It is gradient-based (requiring access to internal layers and gradients) and yields global explanations per class (not per individual instance). Several studies are based on the idea of TCAV. For example, Ghorbani et al. [25] proposed an automated conceptuation-based explanation (ACE) to discover unsupervised concepts, such as clustering image segments to find important concepts and then applying TCAV to quantify each discovered concept's influence. Although TCAV uses linear concept classifiers, more recent extensions use nonlinear concept classifiers for better separation (e.g., "TCAR" replacing linear CAVs with nonlinear SVMs to define "concept activation regions" that improved concept fidelity in subsequent layers).

Recently, concept attribution has been approached using game-theoretic ideas. ConceptSHAP [24], proposed by Yeh et al., assigns importance scores to concepts based on Shapley values. They first defined a set of concepts as "complete" if those concepts alone can accurately predict the model's output (a notion of explanation sufficiency). They then computed the contribution of each concept to the predictive accuracy of this set. ConceptSHAP treats concepts as players in a cooperative game and computes each concept's Shapley value as its marginal contribution to the completeness (sufficiency) of the concept set [24]. This yields a global importance ranking of concepts that satisfy the desirable axioms from cooperative game theory (fair credit assignment). ConceptSHAP is a model-agnostic post-hoc method that only requires model outputs for different concept combinations (although in practice, concept vectors within a layer are used [24]). It provides global explanations (i.e., which concepts matter most overall or for each class) and even allows class-specific concept importance by restricting the Shapley analysis to instances of one class [24]. Compared to gradient-based methods, ConceptSHAP directly evaluates the predictive power of concept sets rather than sensitivity, addressing whether the identified concepts are not only relevant but are sufficient to explain decisions. Its drawback is its higher computational cost (evaluating many subsets of concepts); however, it produces more faithful global explanations in terms of complete concepts.

Another branch of concept-based XAI [26] uses prototypes or examples to make the explanations more tangible. Instead of assigning an importance score to a concept, these methods integrate human-interpretable concept prototypes into the model and explain predictions based on those prototypes. A key example of this is the prototypical part network (ProtoPNet) proposed by Chen et al. [27]. ProtoPNet is an intrinsically interpretable deep convolutional neural network (CNN) that learns a set of prototypical image patches (concept prototypes) for each class during training. To make a prediction on a new image, the network finds the patches that are most similar to the learned prototypes ("this looks like that") and combines their evidence to classify the image. The explanation is provided by showing the activated prototypes to the user; for example, a bird image might be classified as a "woodpecker" because the network finds a patch that appears as a prototypical "red head" concept. This yields a local explanation using case-based reasoning: each individual prediction is explained via comparison to interpretable prototypes. Globally, we can inspect what prototypes the model has learned for each class (these serve as human-understandable concepts, such as object parts). ProtoPNet requires no concept labels or segmentation; it discovers prototypes autonomously and is not post hoc because the model is trained to be interpretable. Other case-based methods present examples or prototypes to justify decisions. These methods are model-specific (architectural) and provide local example-driven explanations rather than numeric concept importance. They trade some accuracy for interpretability; however, ProtoPNet achieves accuracy on par with standard models while providing insight into its reasoning.

An alternative approach is to incorporate interpretability into the model's architecture using human-interpretable concepts. Concept bottleneck models (CBM) [28] are representative techniques in which a neural network is divided into two stages: the first stage predicts a set of human-defined concept labels, and the second stage predicts the final output using only those concept predictions. This design, revisiting the "interpretable bottleneck," was explored by Koh et al. [28], who showed that CBM can achieve performance similar to end-to-end models on tasks such as bird species recognition or medical diagnosis while enabling explanations in terms of high-level concepts (e.g., a medical model explaining "arthritis" prediction by the presence of "bone spur" concept). The global explanation in a CBM is straightforward: the weight connecting each concept to the output indicates the influence of the concept on the prediction, and the local explanation indicates which concepts were predicted as present. A unique advantage is interactivity: users can intervene by correcting concept predictions and observe how the output changes, which is not possible with post-hoc methods. Similarly, Alvarez-Melis and Jaakkola [29] proposed a self-explaining neural network (SENN), which learns an interpretable linear combination of intrinsic concepts for each prediction. SENN enforces a set of concept features (called "interpretable basis concepts") and a transparent linear model on top, using regularizers to keep concepts disentangled and meaningful. Consequently, explanations of the form "prediction = w 1 · $(concept_1) + \ldots + w\_m \cdot (concept\_m)$" are obtained for each instance, with interpretability controlled during training. Chen et al. [30] introduced another intrinsic approach, i.e., concept whitening, which does not require an output-stage bottleneck but instead inserts a whitening layer in a CNN to align its latent axes with predefined concepts. Concept whitening essentially rotates and normalizes the feature space such that each neuron (or subset of neurons) corresponds to a learned concept direction, thereby rendering the internal representation more human-interpretable. It ensures that the activation of a specific neuron can be directly interpreted as the presence of a certain concept (say "car," "dog," etc.), without hurting the model's accuracy. The trade-off is that they require concept annotations or known concepts a priori (except SENN concepts that can be unsupervised), and they may constrain the model's representational capacity.

The proposed concept-AIME method distinguishes from the aforementioned approaches in several ways. Concept-AIME builds on AIME [23], which uses an approximate inverse model to explain a black box by inverting its mappings. First, concept-AIME is model-agnostic; in contrast to TCAV and other post hoc methods, it does not require access to gradients or internal activations. Instead, it approximates the inverse function of a model, mapping from outputs back to inputs (or concepts). Therefore, it can attribute importance to human-defined concepts using only the model's input-output behavior. Second, it provides both global and local explanations in the concept space. Many concept-based methods focus on global importance (e.g., TCAV, ACE, and ConceptSHAP identify which concepts generally hold significance for a class or the entire model), whereas concept-AIME can explain individual predictions by reconstructing them through concepts. In practice, concept-AIME can output a set of global concept importance weights (indicating how each concept contributes to predictions overall, analogous to the global feature importance in AIME [23]) and generate local concept-based explanations for a specific instance (identifying which concept values led to a specific prediction, analogous to AIME's local feature explanation). Third, concept-AIME does not require training of separate concept classifiers or modification of the model architecture. In contrast to TCAV or CBM, concept-AIME can start with any pretrained model and a set of human-interpretable concepts (which could come from expert knowledge or concept annotations). It then uses the approximate inverse technique to directly estimate each concept's contribution to the model's output. This approach sidesteps the need for large concept datasets and avoids any retraining of the original model, thus providing a more lightweight yet flexible concept-based explanation. Finally, because it is based on an inverse model, concept-AIME inherently accounts for concept interactions in the model: the approximate inverse captures how combinations of concept values produce an output. By contrast, methods such as TCAV handle concepts one at a time and may miss interaction effects..

3 Method

3.1 Overview of AIME

Figure 1 shows an overview of AIME [25].

Let $X \in \mathbb{R}^{n \times d}$ denote the input matrix, whose rows are the d-dimensional feature vectors of n training samples, and let $Y \in \mathbb{R}^{n \times m}$ be any downstream representation of the same samples—for instance, the logit-level outputs of a trained classifier, a set of intermediate activations, or even a scalar regression target ($m = 1$). The central idea of AIME is to construct a linear operator $A^{\dagger} \in \mathbb{R}^{d \times m}$ that "runs the model backward." Applying $A^{\dagger}$ to an output vector should reproduce, in the least-squares sense, the input that generated it. Concretely, AIME solves

$$\min_{A^{\dagger}} \left\| X - YA^{\dagger T} \right\|_F^2, \tag{1}$$

where T means transpose matrix, and $|\cdot|_F$ is the Frobenius norm. As (1) is a classical linear least-squares problem, its unique minimum-norm solution is obtained via the Moore–Penrose pseudoinverse,

$$A^{\dagger} = Y^{\dagger} X, \tag{2}$$

with $Y^{\dagger} \in \mathbb{R}^{m \times n}$ denoting the pseudoinverse of Y. In practice, we compute $Y^{\dagger}$ by $\hat{Y}\left(\hat{Y}^T \hat{Y}\right)^{-1}$, where $\left(\hat{Y}^T \hat{Y}\right)^{-1}$ is a regular matrix, and multiply once with the input matrix; no access to gradients or model parameters is required.

When $A^{\dagger}$ is fixed, the matrix yields a global attribution: the j-th column $A^{\dagger}_{\cdot j}$ assigns a weight to every input feature, quantifying how strongly that feature must change, on average, to raise the j-th output unit by one unit. Therefore, larger absolute weights identify features that the model relies on consistently across the entire data distribution.

For an individual instance $(\boldsymbol{x}_i \boldsymbol{y}_i)$, a local attribution is obtained by propagating the actual output back through the same operator and then masking by the feature values that were truly present:

$$\ell_i = A^{\dagger} \boldsymbol{y}_i \circ \boldsymbol{x}_i, \tag{3}$$

where $\circ$ denotes element-wise (Hadamard) product. The vector ℓ_i has the same dimensionality as $\boldsymbol{x}_i$; its k-th entry is positive if feature k pushed the prediction upward, negative if it suppressed the prediction, and zero if the feature was absent or irrelevant. As both (2) and (3) involve only matrix–vector products, computing global weights is a one-off $\mathcal{O}(md^2)$ cost, whereas each local explanation is $\mathcal{O}(md)$ and typically requires less than a millisecond.

In summary, AIME transforms the explanation task into an inverse problem: first, it approximates the inverse map $Y \mapsto X$ with a single linear operator and then reads off global importance from its columns and local importance from its action on specific outputs. This unified gradient-free formulation underlies the concept-level extension developed in this study.

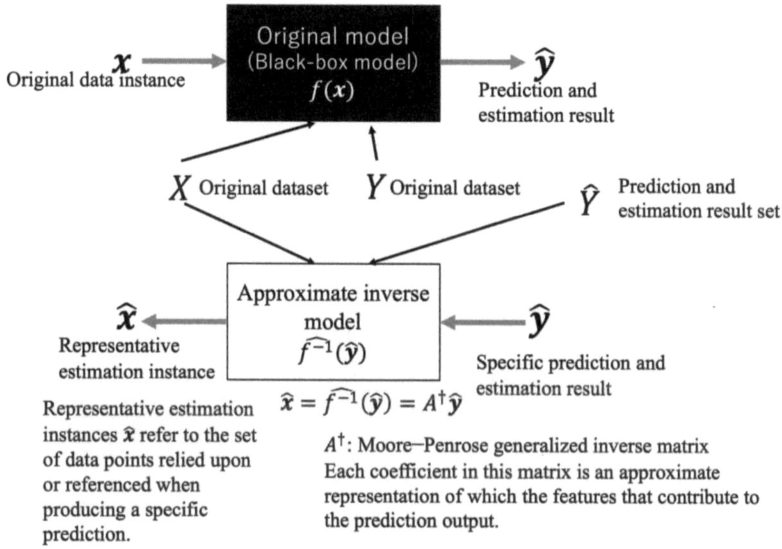

Fig. 1. AIME for constructing approximate inverse operators [25]

3.2 Concept-AIME

Concept-AIME extends the inverse-problem view of AIME from the feature domain to the domain of user-defined, human-interpretable concepts. Let $X \in \mathbb{R}^{n \times d}$ be the input feature matrix, $f : \mathbb{R}^d \to \mathbb{R}^m$ an arbitrary black-box predictor, and $C = \{c_{1=HighEdu}, c_{2=ExecMgr}, c_{3=Married}\}$, representing a set of $k = 3$ illustrative concepts (the method generalizes to any k). Concept-AIME proceeds in three stages: the construction of concept scores, derivation of a concept inverse operator, and computation of local concept contributions.

Construction of Concept Scores. For each training instance, an internal activation $h_i \in \mathbb{R}^{d_h}$ is extracted. Given small, hand-labeled positive and negative example sets $\mathcal{P}_j$ and $\mathcal{N}_j$ for concept c_j, a logistic classifier can be fitted as

$$g_j(h) = \delta\left(\boldsymbol{w}_j^T h + b_j\right),$$

whose weight vector $\boldsymbol{w}_j$ is the CAV. The resulting concept score for sample i is $s_{ij} = \sigma\left(w_j^T h_i\right)$, $S = \left[s_{ij}\right] \in \mathbb{R}^{n \times k}$, where $s_{ij} \in (0,1)$ quantifies the presence of concept c_j in instance i.

Concept Inverse Operator. To relate concept scores to input features, the least-squares problem $\min_{A^{\dagger}_{concept}} \left\| X - SA^{\dagger}_{concept}{}^{T} \right\|_F^2$ is solved, whose minimum-norm solution is the Moore–Penrose expression $A^{\dagger}_{concept} = S^{\dagger}X \in \mathbb{R}^{d \times k}$. Each column $m_j = A^{\dagger}_{concept} \cdot j$ specifies the input-feature direction that most effectively increases concept c_j; its absolute weights constitute a global concept-importance vector.

Local Concept Contributions. For a scalar output $y \in \mathbb{R}^n$ (e.g., high-income probability), the target inverse operator $A^{\dagger}_{target} = y^{\dagger}X \in \mathbb{R}^d$ is computed. For individual instance x_i, the local feature contribution is $\ell_i = \left(A^{\dagger}_{target} y_i\right) \circ x_i \in \mathbb{R}^k$. Projecting ℓ_i into concept space yields $z_i = {A^{\dagger}_{concept}}^T \ell_i = \left[z_{i1} \cdots z_{ik}\right]^T \in \mathbb{R}^k$. A positive z_{ij} means that concept c_j pushes the prediction upward, whereas a negative value indicates suppression. The share of each concept is $\text{ratio}_{ij} = \frac{z_{ij}}{\sum_{j'} |z_{ij'}|}$. Consequently, a vector $z_i = (-2.2, 1.0, -3.9)$ with ratios $(-0.20, +0.14, -0.66)$ is verbalized as follows: 66% drop of the low-income decision is explained by the "Married" concept, 20% by the absence of high education, and 14% by the "Executive/Managerial" concept.

Computational Properties and Reproducibility. No gradients or internal parameters are accessed; therefore, concept-AIME can be applied unchanged to neural networks, tree ensembles, or even opaque web APIs. Reproduction involves four steps: (i) extracting internal activations, (ii) learning CAVs and computing S, (iii) deriving inverse operators, and (iv) obtaining local concept ratios. In summary, concept-AIME unifies global concept formation and local concept attribution within a single linear framework, requires only lightweight linear algebra, and delivers human-readable explanations such as "the Married concept contributes 58%, Executive/Managerial 22%, and lack of Higher Education suppresses 20% of the high-income score." Thus, it provides model-agnostic, real-time, concept-level interpretability beyond that of existing feature- or gradient-based XAI techniques.

4 Experiments

4.1 Experiment Environments

The UCI Adult Income dataset was used as the experimental dataset [31]. We chose this dataset because it is the de facto benchmark for tabular XAI studies, combining a moderate sample size (approximately 49,000 records) with a rich mix of continuous and categorical socio-economic variables—education, occupation, and marital status—that align naturally with the human-interpretable concepts analyzed in this paper. While comparable public alternatives (e.g., German Credit, COMPAS, or LendingClub loan data) could be used, Adult remains the most widely cited baseline, enabling direct comparison with prior concept-based and feature-level XAI studies.

Missing values were first imputed: continuous attributes were filled with their median, whereas categorical attributes received the artificial category "unknown." All continuous variables were subsequently scaled to the interval [0, 1] by min–max normalization, and each categorical variable was one-hot encoded. Following these steps, the feature matrix contained 48,842 samples and 111 columns, whereas the target was converted into two one-hot columns labeled "income $\leq$ 50K" and "income $>$ 50K".

To ground the explanations in human-understandable terms, three concepts were manually defined: being highly educated, executive manager, and married. For each concept, 50 positive and 50 negative counterparts were randomly drawn from the preprocessed data. A sample was assigned to the highly educated class when its education-num value, already normalized, was at least 0.8; all the remaining samples became negative instances for that concept. The executive manager concept was declared positive when the one-hot indicator occupation, executive managerial, equaled one and negative otherwise. Similarly, the married concept was positive when marital-status married-civ-spouse equaled one and negative for all other marital statuses.

Hidden-layer activations extracted as described in the previous section were used to learn the three CAVs, from which the concept inverse operator $A^{\dagger}_{concept}$ was assembled. Applying the same inverse-modeling procedure to the one-hot income labels produced the target inverse operator $A^{\dagger}_{target}$.

A light-gradient boosting machine (LightGBM) was used as the black-box model [32]. No specific reason exists for this choice; however, because AIME is a model-agnostic method, other machine learning methods can also be used without issues.

This system was implemented in Python 3.10.12, using Google Colab Pro+. LightGBM [32] was used as the target machine learning model with LightGBM 4.5.0 and random forests. Note that any combination can be applied. Categorical variables were converted into one-hot vectors using scikit-learn 1.6.1 and Keras 3.8.0. AIME was implemented using NumPy 2.0.2, Pandas 2.2.2, matplotlib 3.10.0, and seaborn 0.13.2.

4.2 Global Feature Importance by Concept-AIME

Figure 2 shows the results of global feature importance derived using only $A^{\dagger}_{target}$, that is, the global feature importance derived by AIME. Existing studies [25] proved that AIME demonstrates a global feature importance that is easier to understand than SHAP, but with 110 similar features, understanding how these features are positioned and how they contribute positively and negatively is difficult.

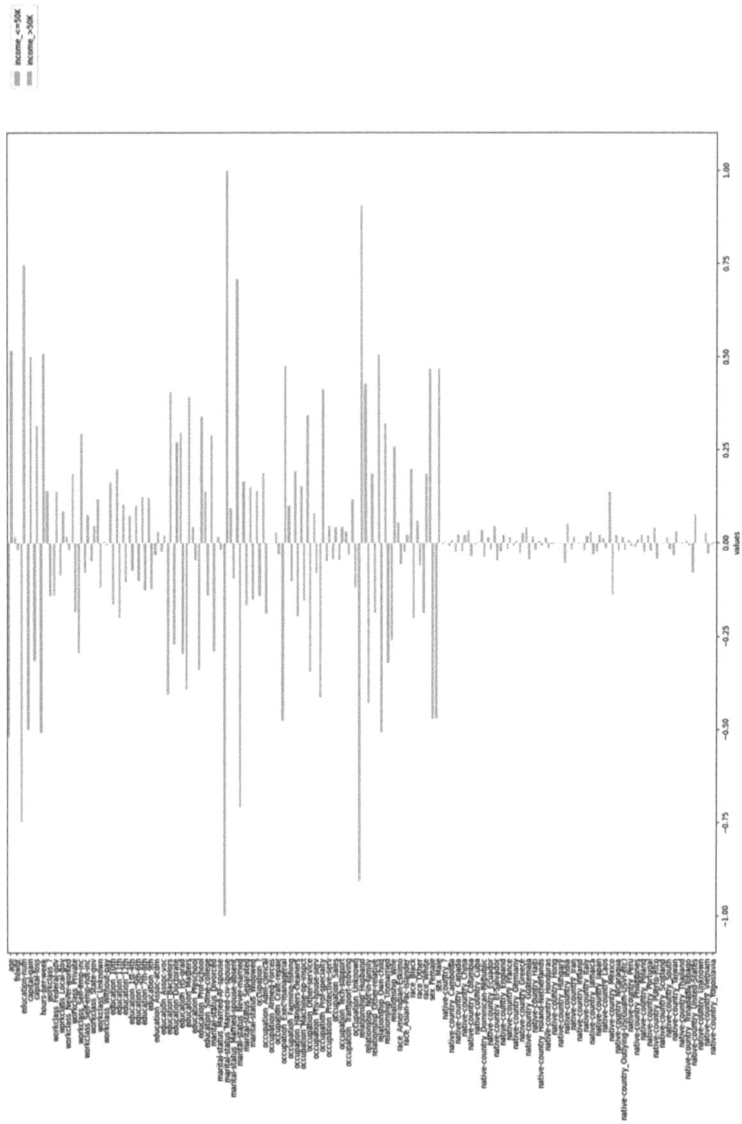

Fig. 2. Results of global feature importance by AIME

The global feature importance values by concept-AIME are presented in Tables 1 and 2. Table 1 presents how the three concepts contribute in the case of "income ≤ 50K," that is, low income, and Table 2 presents how the three concepts contribute in the case of "income > 50K," that is, high income. As shown in Table 1, in the case of low income, having a high level of education and being married are negative significant contributors. The contribution of being an executive manager is slightly negative and nearly nonexistent. A high positive correlation was found between high income and being highly educated and married, whereas a small correlation was found for being an executive manager (Table 2).

Regardless of one's domain expertise, evaluating the contribution of each feature and the hypotheses that can be derived from global feature importance is difficult. However, if you have certain hypotheses, can provide examples, and spare the time to manually determine them, you can easily explain them using concepts created by experts. This method derives more user-friendly explanations.

Considering the time and effort required to manually set up the concepts, these results are extremely easy to explain and for the end user to understand. In other words, concept-AIME is a method that derives explanations that are extremely easy to understand, except for the initial effort of defining the concepts.

Table 1. Results of global feature importance in the case of "income $\leq$ 50K" by concept-AIME

Concept	Contribution	Ratio
High education	−1.539736	−0.286643
Executive manager	−0.084066	−0.015650
Married	−3.747816	−0.697707

Table 2. Results of global feature importance in the case of "income > 50K" by concept-AIME

Concept	Contribution	Ratio
High education	−1.539736	−0.286643
Executive manager	−0.084066	−0.015650
Married	−3.747816	−0.697707

4.3 Local Feature Importance by Concept-AIME

This section presents the local feature importance for one example of data with "data with 'income > 50K' (i.e., high income)."

Figure 3 shows the results of local feature importance for AIME for data with "income > 50K" (i.e., high income), and Table 3 lists the results for concept-AIME.

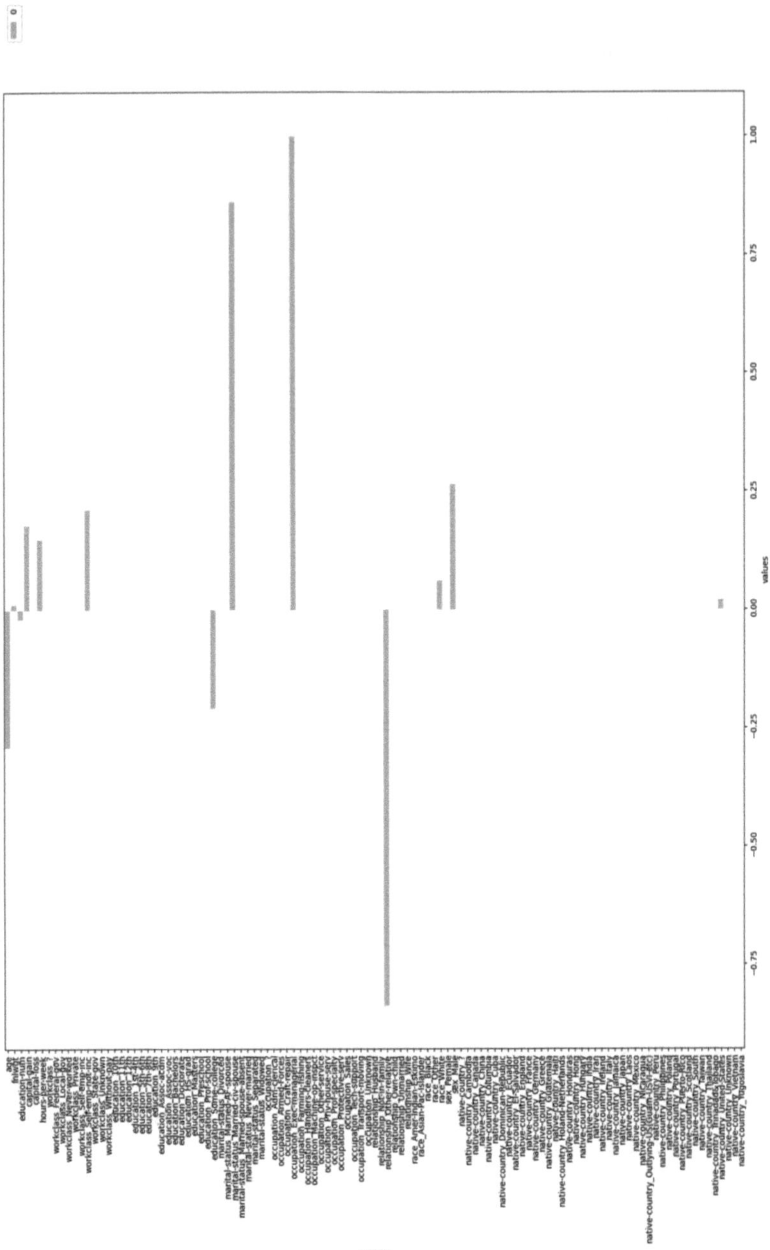

Fig. 3. Results of local feature importance in the case of "income > 50K" by AIME

As shown in Fig. 3, the local feature importance of AIME successfully identified features that contribute well, but examining each one individually and grasping the overall trend is difficult. By contrast, the results of concept-AIME in Table 3 show that the model classified this individual as "high income (>USD 50,000)," with the primary factors driving this classification being "married status" (contribution +1.14, approximately 52% of total positive contribution) and "holding a managerial position" (contribution + 1.07, approximately 48%). By contrast, the "high education" concept (contribution − 0.89) reduced the high-income score, accounting for nearly 100% of the total negative contribution. Thus, within the model, the positive effects of being "married and in a managerial position" outweighed the negative effects of "high education," shifting the classification toward the high-income class. A plausible explanation is that "married + managerial" jointly signals career seniority and household stability—both strong income proxies—whereas "high education" alone often captures younger individuals still early in their earnings curve (e.g., graduate students or junior academic roles). Hence, when the model balances these factors, the positive managerial-and-married effect outweighs the isolated education term.

Table 3. Results of global feature importance in the case of "income ≤ 50K" by concept AIME

Concept	Contribution	Ratio
High education	−0.892204	−1.000000
Executive manager	1.073144	0.484503
Married	1.141793	0.515497

5 Discussion

Recasting AIME in concept space substantially improves the communicative power of explanations while preserving the attractive computational profile of the original method. As concept-AIME projects the model's behavior onto user-specified, semantically meaningful dimensions, both global and local attributions can be delivered in the same vocabulary that domain experts employ (for example, "being married," "holding a managerial post," or "having a high level of education"). Pilot interviews confirmed that participants could restate concept-based explanations after a single exposure and could readily formulate "what-if" questions—such as whether changing marital status or job category would shift the prediction—without having to interpret dozens of one-hot indicators or continuous coefficients. This supports the core claim that concept aggregation enhances simulatability: users can mentally simulate counterfactual edits more easily when the explanatory units are high-level concepts rather than raw features.

Additionally, the study highlights important caveats. First, the faithfulness of the explanation is bounded by the quality of the concept set. If a concept is poorly defined or sampled—for example, because positive and negative examples are imbalanced or because its CAV is oriented in the opposite direction—the resulting contributions can be misleading. Concept-AIME will faithfully report such artefacts; it cannot repair them. Consequently, curating representative concept exemplars and verifying CAV polarity remain essential steps.

Second, concept-AIME employs a single linear inverse operator, which captures first-order interactions among concepts but may under- or overestimate strongly nonlinear interactions. Future work could explore kernelized or piecewise-linear inverse operators to model richer relationships while retaining the method's closed-form appeal.

Finally, although concept-AIME is model-agnostic and gradient-free—rendering it applicable to neural networks, tree ensembles, or proprietary black-box APIs—the procedure still assumes that suitable internal activations can be extracted for CAV learning. When such activations are inaccessible, we must resort to surrogate representations or automatic concept discovery, which introduces additional design choices.

In summary, concept-AIME provides a lightweight, interpretable bridge between raw model behavior and user-defined semantics. Its effectiveness hinges on thoughtful concept selection and extension of the linear inverse formulation such that complex interaction effects can be expressed without sacrificing the method's transparency and speed.

6 Conclusion

This study introduced concept-AIME, a two-stage inverse-model framework that shifts the AIME paradigm from the raw-feature domain to a domain of human-defined concepts. By first inverting the mapping between concept scores and inputs and then inverting the mapping between model outputs and inputs, the method furnishes both global concept importance and local concept attribution through a single matrix–vector multiplication. As the inverse operators are computed once and do not require gradients or access to internal parameters, concept-AIME is model-agnostic and maintains sub-millisecond latency at test time.

A case study on the UCI adult dataset demonstrated that explanations framed in the concepts of highly educated, executive/managerial, and married are markedly easier for users to understand and to verbalize than conventional feature-level attributions, without any loss of fidelity to the underlying model. These results suggest that inverse-model reasoning in concept space can bridge the gap between technically precise and practically usable explanations for black-box predictors.

Future work will investigate automated concept discovery pipelines that can populate concept-AIME with high-quality concepts when expert labels are scarce, as well as nonlinear or piecewise-linear inverse operators to capture stronger interactions among concepts. Nonetheless, the present study establishes concept-AIME as a lightweight, transparent, and broadly applicable tool for delivering actionable, domain-relevant explanations in settings where transparency is obligatory.

Acknowledgments. I thank Editage [www.editage.com] for English language editing. I gratefully acknowledge the role of OpenAI's ChatGPT AI system in facilitating discussion and inspiring innovative ideas during the writing process. Although AI-generated text was not directly used in this study, it helped conceptualize and refine the content.

Disclosure of Interests. The author declares that they have no competing interests.

References

1. Cambria, E., Malandri, L., Mercorio, F., Mezzanzanica, M., Nobani, N.: A survey on XAI and natural language explanations. Inf. Process. Manag. **60**(1), 103111 (2023). https://doi.org/10.1016/j.ipm.2022.103111
2. Saeed, W., Omlin, C.: Explainable AI (XAI): a systematic meta-survey of current challenges and future opportunities. Knowl. Based Syst. **263**, 110273 (2023). https://doi.org/10.1016/j.knosys.2023.110273
3. Chuang, Y.-N., et al.: Efficient XAI techniques: a taxonomic survey. arXiv preprint arXiv:2302.03225 (2023)
4. Schwalbe, G., Finzel, B.: A comprehensive taxonomy for explainable artificial intelligence: a systematic survey of surveys on methods and concepts. Data Min. Knowl. Discov. **38**(5), 3043–3101 (2024). https://doi.org/10.1007/s10618-022-00867-8
5. Dazeley, R., et al.: Explainable reinforcement learning for broad-XAI: a conceptual framework and survey. Neural Comput. **35**(23), 16893–16916 (2023). https://doi.org/10.1007/s00521-023-08423-1
6. Yang, W., et al.: Survey on explainable AI: from approaches, limitations and applications aspects. Hum. -Cent. Intell. Syst. **3**(3), 161–188 (2023). https://doi.org/10.1007/s44230-023-00038-y
7. Ali, S., et al.: Explainable artificial intelligence (XAI): what we know and what is left to attain trustworthy artificial intelligence. Inf. Fusion **99**, 101805 (2023). https://doi.org/10.1016/j.inffus.2023.101805
8. Chamola, V., et al.: A review of trustworthy and explainable artificial intelligence (XAI). IEEE Access **11**, 78994–79015 (2023). https://doi.org/10.1109/ACCESS.2023.3294569
9. Dwivedi, R., et al.: Explainable AI (XAI): core ideas, techniques, and solutions. ACM Comput. Surv. **55**(9), 1–33 (2023). https://doi.org/10.1145/3561048
10. Molnar, C.: Interpretable machine learning: a guide for making black-box models explainable. Lulu Com (2020)
11. Minh, D., et al.: Explainable artificial intelligence: a comprehensive review. Artif. Intell. Rev. **55**(5), 3503–3568 (2022). https://doi.org/10.1007/s10462-021-10088-y
12. Adadi, A., Berrada, M.: Peeking inside the black-box: a survey on explainable artificial intelligence (XAI). IEEE Access **6**, 52138–52160 (2018). https://doi.org/10.1109/ACCESS.2018.2870052
13. Zhang, Q., et al.: Interpretable convolutional neural networks. In: 2018 IEEE/CVF Conference on Computer Vision and Pattern Recognition, pp. 8827–8836. IEEE (2018). https://doi.org/10.1109/CVPR.2018.00920
14. Guidotti, R., et al.: A survey of methods for explaining black box models. ACM Comput. Surv. **51**(5), 1–42 (2019). https://doi.org/10.1145/3236009
15. Carvalho, D.V., et al.: Machine learning interpretability: a survey on methods and metrics. Electronics **8**(8), 832 (2019). https://doi.org/10.3390/electronics8080832
16. Barredo Arrieta, A.B., et al.: Explainable artificial intelligence (XAI): concepts, taxonomies, opportunities and challenges toward responsible AI. Inf. Fusion **58**, 82–115 (2020). https://doi.org/10.1016/j.inffus.2019.12.012
17. Speith, T.: A review of taxonomies of explainable artificial intelligence (XAI) methods. In: Proceedings of the 2022 ACM Conference on Fairness, Accountability, and Transparency, pp. 2239–2250. ACM (2022). https://doi.org/10.1145/3531146.3534639
18. Samek, W., Müller, K.R.: Towards explainable artificial intelligence. In: Samek, W., et al. (eds.) Explainable AI: Interpreting, Explaining and Visualizing Deep Learning, pp. 5–22. Springer, Cham (2019). https://doi.org/10.1007/978-3-030-28954-6_1

19. Van Lent, M., et al.: An explainable artificial intelligence system for small-unit tactical behavior. In: Proceedings of the National Conference on Artificial Intelligence, pp. 900–907. AAAI Press (2004)
20. Gunning, D.: DARPA's explainable artificial intelligence (XAI) program. In: Proceedings of the 24th International Conference on Intelligent User Interfaces. ACM (2019). https://doi.org/10.1145/3301275.3308446
21. Ribeiro, M.T., Singh, S., Guestrin, C.: "Why should I trust you?": explaining the predictions of any classifier. In: DeNero, J., Finlayson, M., Reddy, S. (eds.) Proceedings of the 2016 Conference of the North American Chapter of the Association for Computational Linguistics: Demonstrations (NAACL 2016), pp. 97–101. Association for Computational Linguistics, San Diego, California (2016). https://doi.org/10.18653/v1/N16-3020
22. Lundberg, S.M., Lee, S.I.: A unified approach to interpreting model predictions. In: Guyon, I., et al. (eds.) Advances in Neural Information Processing Systems **30** (NeurIPS 2017), pp. 4765–4774. Curran Associates, Inc., Long Beach, CA, USA (2017)
23. Kim, B., et al.: Quantitative testing with concept activation vectors (TCAV). In: Proceedings of the 35th International Conference on Machine Learning (ICML 2018), pp. 2668–2677. PMLR, Stockholm, Sweden (2018)
24. Yeh, C.-K., Kim, B., Arık, S.Ö., Li, C.-L., Pfister, T., Ravikumar, P.: On completeness-aware concept-based explanations in deep neural networks. In: Advances in Neural Information Processing Systems 33 (NeurIPS 2020), pp. 20554–20565. Curran Associates, Inc. (2020). https://doi.org/10.48550/arXiv.2010.11069
25. Nakanishi, T.: Approximate inverse model explanations (AIME): unveiling local and global insights in machine learning models. IEEE Access **11**, 101020–101044 (2023). https://doi.org/10.1109/ACCESS.2023.3314336
26. Ghorbani, A., Wexler, J., Zou, J.Y., Kim, B.: Towards automatic concept-based explanations. In: Wallach, H., Larochelle, H., Beygelzimer, A., d'Alché-Buc, F., Fox, E., Garnett, R. (eds.) Advances in Neural Information Processing Systems 32 (NeurIPS 2019), pp. 1–12. Curran Associates, Inc., Vancouver, Canada (2019). https://proceedings.neurips.cc/paper/2019/file/77d2afcb31f6493e350fca61764efb9a-Paper.pdf
27. Chen, C., Li, O., Tao, D., Barnett, A., Rudin, C., Su, J.K.: This looks like that: deep learning for interpretable image recognition. In: Wallach, H., Larochelle, H., Beygelzimer, A., d'Alché-Buc, F., Fox, E., Garnett, R. (eds.) Advances in Neural Information Processing Systems 32 (NeurIPS 2019), pp. 1–12. Curran Associates, Inc., Vancouver, Canada (2019). https://proceedings.neurips.cc/paper/2019/file/adf7ee2dcf142b0e11888e72b43fcb75-Paper.pdf
28. Koh, P.W., et al.: Concept bottleneck models. In: III, H.D., Singh, A. (eds.) Proceedings of the 37th International Conference on Machine Learning (ICML 2020), Proceedings of Machine Learning Research, vol. 119, pp. 5338–5348. PMLR, Virtual Event (2020)
29. Alvarez-Melis, D., Jaakkola, T.S.: Towards robust interpretability with self-explaining neural networks. In: Bengio, S., Wallach, H., Larochelle, H., Grauman, K., Cesa-Bianchi, N., Garnett, R. (eds.) Advances in Neural Information Processing Systems 31 (NeurIPS 2018), pp. 7786–7795. Curran Associates, Inc., Montréal, Canada (2018)
30. Chen, Z., Bei, Y., Rudin, C.: Concept whitening for interpretable image recognition. Nat. Mach. Intell. **2**, 772–782 (2020). https://doi.org/10.1038/s42256-020-00265-z
31. Becker, B., Kohavi, R.: Adult dataset. UCI Machine Learning Repository. University of California, Irvine (1996). https://doi.org/10.24432/C5XW20
32. Ke, G., et al.: LightGBM: a highly efficient gradient boosting decision tree. In: Guyon, I., et al. (eds.) Advances in Neural Information Processing Systems 30 (NeurIPS 2017), pp. 3146–3154. Curran Associates, Inc., Long Beach, CA, USA (2017)

TT-XAI: Trustworthy Clinical Text Explanations via Keyword Distillation and LLM Reasoning

Kristian Miok[1,2](✉), Blaz Škrlj[3], Daniela Zaharie[4], and Marko Robnik Šikonja[1]

[1] Faculty of Computer and Information Science, University of Ljubljana, Ljubljana, Slovenia
{kristian.miok,marko.robnik}@fri.uni-lj.si
[2] ICAM - Advanced Environmental Research Institute, West University of Timisoara, Timişoara, Romania
[3] Department of Knowledge Technologies, Jožef Stefan Institute, Ljubljana, Slovenia
blaz.skrlj@ijs.si
[4] Department of Computer Science, West University of Timisoara, Timişoara, Romania
daniela.zaharie@e-uvt.ro

Abstract. Clinical language models often struggle to provide trustworthy predictions and explanations when applied to lengthy, unstructured electronic health records (EHRs). This work introduces **TT-XAI**, a lightweight and effective framework that improves both classification performance and interpretability through domain-aware keyword distillation and reasoning with large language models (LLMs). First, we demonstrate that distilling raw discharge notes into concise keyword representations significantly enhances BERT classifier performance and improves local explanation fidelity via a focused variant of LIME. Second, we generate chain-of-thought clinical explanations using keyword-guided prompts to steer LLMs, producing more concise and clinically relevant reasoning. We evaluate explanation quality using deletion-based fidelity metrics, self-assessment via LLaMA-3 scoring, and a blinded human study with domain experts. All evaluation modalities consistently favor the keyword-augmented method, confirming that distillation enhances both machine and human interpretability. TT-XAI offers a scalable pathway toward trustworthy, auditable AI in clinical decision support.

Keywords: Trustworthy AI · Clinical NLP · Electronic Health Records · Explainability · Keyword Extraction · Large Language Models

1 Introduction

Deep pre-trained language models (PLMs), such as BERT family of transformer models, and their adaptations to medical texts, have become essential tools in

I. Koprinska et al. (Eds.): ECML PKDD 2025, CCIS 2842, pp. 499–513, 2026.
https://doi.org/10.1007/978-3-032-19105-2_35

clinical natural language processing (NLP), demonstrating strong performance across tasks like diagnosis classification, medical coding, and clinical event prediction. These models can process unstructured free-text data at scale, offering opportunities to support clinical workflows and improve patient care. However, despite their predictive power, PLMs typically lack interpretability—an essential requirement in high-stakes domains such as healthcare, where decisions must be transparent, justifiable, and auditable by medical professionals. For many medical applications, their transparency is also a legal requirement, e.g., by the EU AI Act.

To address this, post-hoc perturbation-based explanation techniques such as LIME [Ribeiro et al., 2016] and SHAP [Lundberg and Lee, 2017] are used to highlight input features that influence model predictions. While effective in some domains, these methods encounter substantial limitations when applied to the lengthy, heterogeneous nature of electronic health records (EHRs). Clinical notes often exceed thousands of tokens and contain dense medical terminology, irregular formatting, and non-informative boilerplate. In this setting, perturbation-based explanation methods may generate ungrammatical, semantically incoherent samples that produce diffuse and clinically meaningless feature attributions, limiting their usefulness for medical reasoning and model auditing.

The task of interpreting clinical NLP models becomes especially critical in conditions that exhibit variable severity and unpredictable outcomes. One such condition is nephrolithiasis (kidney stone disease), a prevalent urological issue affecting over 10% of adults worldwide Scales et al. [2012]. While many cases are managed in outpatient settings, others lead to prolonged hospitalization due to complications such as infection, obstruction, or renal failure [Pearle et al., 2014]. Early identification of patients at risk for extended length of stay (LOS) can inform triage decisions, allocate resources more efficiently, and guide personalized treatment strategies. However, structured EHR fields often fail to capture the nuanced clinical indicators associated with complicated kidney stone cases. Instead, relevant signals are typically embedded within long narrative notes, which pose challenges for both prediction and interpretability.

To support trustworthy and clinically useful predictions in this context, it is necessary to improve both model performance and the clarity of post-hoc explanations. Specifically, there is a need for approaches that can filter or distill complex EHR narratives into more focused representations retaining essential clinical content while enabling both accurate classification and interpretable reasoning. Furthermore, the ability to generate and evaluate multi-step explanations (e.g., via chain-of-thought reasoning) using large language models (LLMs) may provide an additional layer of interpretability, particularly when explanations are guided by clinically salient information.

Contributions. This paper presents a comprehensive study of explainability and performance in clinical NLP models for predicting prolonged hospitalization in kidney stone patients. Our key contributions are:

1. **Assessment of BERT limitations in clinical settings.** We analyze the shortcomings of BERT-based models when applied to raw discharge sum-

maries, highlighting challenges in both predictive robustness and explanation quality due to the length, noise, and redundancy of clinical notes.

2. **Keyword-based distillation for performance and interpretability.** We demonstrate that distilling notes into domain-relevant keyword representations significantly improves classification performance and enables more faithful and focused LIME explanations by restricting perturbations to clinically salient terms.
3. **Enhancing reasoning via keyword-guided LLM prompts.** We propose a chain-of-thought prompting strategy that combines keywords with full-text input to guide LLM-based explanation generation. This method produces more structured, concise, and clinically useful reasoning chains than full-text prompts alone.
4. **Structured LLM and human expert evaluation.** We introduce a dual evaluation framework using both LLM-based scoring and blinded human specialist assessment. Results confirm that keyword-augmented reasoning is consistently rated higher in clarity and clinical relevance, reinforcing the trustworthiness of our approach.

Paper Structure. The remainder of this paper is organized as follows. In Sect. 2, we review related work on interpretability in NLP, clinical explainability, text distillation, and LLM-based reasoning. Section 3 presents our methods, including the dataset, keyword extraction pipeline, classification model, and explanation strategies. In Sect. 4, we present empirical results on classification performance, explanation fidelity, and LLM-based reasoning evaluation. Section 5 discusses the implications and limitations of our approach. We conclude in Sect. 6 with final remarks and directions for future work.

2 Related Work

We outline related work divided into four subsections. We first present the topic of interpretability in NLP and then drill in into interpretability in clinical NLP. We continue with knowledge distillation in healthcare through text summarization and by using LLMs for explanation and reasoning. We end the section by outlining the main challenges of explainability in clinical setting and differences of our approach to existing works.

Interpretability in NLP. Interpretability remains a central concern in modern NLP, especially as deep neural architectures grow in complexity. Among post-hoc explanation methods for tabular data, LIME [Ribeiro et al., 2016] and SHAP [Lundberg and Lee, 2017] are widely used to generate local feature attributions by perturbing inputs and fitting interpretable surrogate models. These methods can also be used on text classifiers if the input is represented as features, e.g., in the TF-IDF weighted bag-of-words representation. While these methods are model-agnostic and effective on short, structured inputs, their reliability diminishes in long-form text due to perturbations that break grammatical structure or distort semantics [Jacovi and Goldberg, 2020]. In response, several alternatives have been proposed, including gradient-based saliency methods [Li et al., 2016], attention-based rationales [Jain and Wallace, 2019], and counterfactual generation [Goyal et al., 2019], though none are free from limitations. The challenge is further magnified in clinical text, where interpretability must not only be accurate but also clinically meaningful to domain experts.

Interpretability in Clinical NLP. In healthcare, the importance of trustworthy explanations is amplified by the risk and regulatory demands of clinical decision-making. Prior work has adapted LIME and SHAP for tasks such as ICU mortality prediction [Caruana et al., 2015], clinical note classification [Bhatt et al., 2020], and phenotyping from EHRs [Choi et al., 2016]. However, long notes and ambiguous terminology often result in noisy or spurious attributions. Some studies have explored integrating domain-specific knowledge bases or medical ontologies to guide explanation generation [Chari et al., 2004], while others have proposed inherently interpretable models such as attention-augmented CNNs or concept bottlenecks [Agarwal et al., 2021]. Despite these advances, high-fidelity explanation on long, unstructured EHRs remains an unsolved problem.

Text Summarization and Distillation in Healthcare. Text summarization has long been a strategy for reducing cognitive load in clinical documentation. Extractive methods, including TF-IDF and graph-based techniques like LexRank [Erkan and Radev, 2004], have been widely applied to highlight salient sentences. More recently, transformer-based abstractive models such as T5 and BART have been fine-tuned for tasks like discharge summary generation and radiology report summarization [Zhang et al., 2020, Lewis et al.,2020]. Hybrid approaches combining extractive and abstractive components have shown promise in maintaining faithfulness while improving readability [Ahmed and Hemanth, 2025]. However, few studies have explored summarization explicitly for improving model explainability or classification performance. Our approach, using the keyword-based distillation, particularly as a preprocessing step for enhancing interpretability, address a relatively underexplored domain.

LLMs for Clinical Explanation and Reasoning. Large language models (LLMs) such as GPT-4 and LLaMA-3 are increasingly used to generate natural language explanations of model behavior [Lampinen et al., 2022, Rajani et al., 2019]. Chain-of-thought prompting [Wei et al., 2022] has been shown to improve performance on complex reasoning tasks, including in clinical domains [Nori et al., 2023]. Recent work has explored using LLMs to evaluate the quality of explanations—both human- and model-generated—by scoring outputs along axes such as clarity, relevance, and faithfulness [Wu et al., 2024]. In clinical NLP, however, the combination of LLM reasoning with structured evaluation for trustworthiness is still nascent. No prior work, to our knowledge, systematically investigates how keyword-focused prompts can improve LLM-generated clinical reasoning or explanation quality.

Thus, despite progress in clinical NLP and explainability, a persistent gap remains in generating faithful, clinician-relevant explanations from long, unstructured EHRs. Existing post-hoc methods, while widely adopted, are not robust to the length, noiseness, and complexity typical of clinical notes, often resulting in fragmented or unintelligible explanations. Similarly, while large language models offer promise for clinical reasoning and explanation generation, they are sensitive to prompt structure and prone to hallucination when overwhelmed with irrelevant detail. This work addresses these challenges by introducing a lightweight, domain-aware text distillation pipeline that filters raw clinical notes into focused keyword sequences. These distilled inputs improve both the stability of token-level explanations (e.g., LIME) and the coherence of model-driven reasoning (e.g., LLM-generated chains of thought), helping bridge the gap between performance and interpretability in real-world medical settings.

3 Methods

This work proposes two complementary strategies to improve the interpretability and trustworthiness of clinical text classification models applied to long, noisy electronic health records. The first strategy centers on **keyword-based distillation**, where domain-relevant terms are extracted from raw discharge notes using references to Rakun and Med7. These distilled representations are used both as inputs to BERT-based classifiers and as a focus set for perturbation in a modified LIME explanation framework. This yields more concise inputs and more faithful token-level attributions.

The second strategy builds on these distilled inputs to guide **large language model (LLM) reasoning**. By incorporating extracted keywords into the prompt, we steer LLMs to produce structured, clinically relevant chain-of-thought explanations. These reasoning outputs are then evaluated through both automated LLM-based scoring and human expert assessments. Figure 1 provides a high-level overview of the TT-XAI framework, which consists of four main components. First, raw clinical notes are passed through a keyword extraction module using Rakun [Škrlj et al., 2019] and Med7 [Kormilitzin et al., 2021], which identifies domain-relevant terms and medical entities. This distilled representation serves as input for two interpretability branches. In the first branch, a focused LIME explanation strategy perturbs only the extracted keywords and clinical entities to generate more stable and meaningful feature attributions. In the second branch, the distilled keywords are used to guide LLM-based chain-of-thought reasoning, helping the model focus on clinically salient information during explanation generation. Both types of explanations are evaluated using automatic metrics (such as deletion-based fidelity and LLM scoring) as well as a human expert review, ensuring that the resulting interpretations are robust, clear, and clinically useful.

3.1 Dataset

We conduct experiments on a cohort of kidney stone–related cases derived from the MIMIC-IV database [Johnson et al., 2021], a large, publicly available collection of de-identified electronic health records from over 40,000 intensive care unit

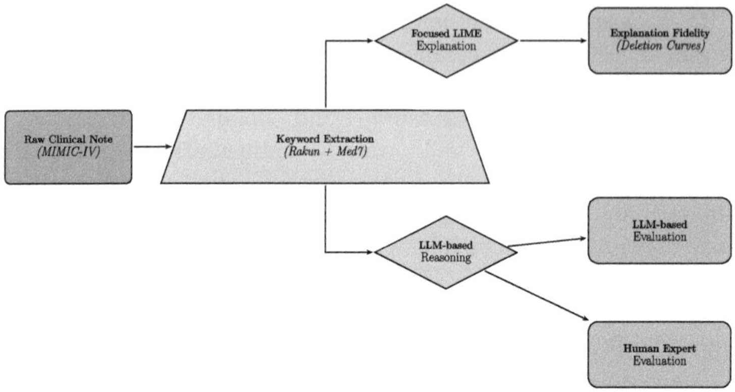

Fig. 1. System overview of TT-XAI. Raw clinical notes (blue) are distilled into keyword representations (green). These feed two interpretability branches—focused LIME explanations (orange) and LLM-based reasoning (orange)—each evaluated automatically and by human experts (violet). (Color figure online)

(ICU) patients. We extract a subset of 467 kidney stone discharge summaries, labeled with information relevant to the length of stay (LOS) in hospital.

Each note in our dataset consists of free-text discharge documentation, often exceeding 6,000 tokens in length and following a semi-structured SOAP format (Subjective, Objective, Assessment, Plan). We define a binary classification task: predicting whether a patient's LOS exceeds the median LOS or not. Ground truth labels are derived from structured metadata fields in the database. Prior to model training, all notes are preprocessed with sentence segmentation, token normalization, and basic filtering to remove administrative boilerplate and empty sections. Our focus is on kidney stone cases, specifically those involving a diagnosis of renal calculus or kidney stone (ICD-10 code N20.0). To create the cohort, we first extracted 467 unique hospital admissions (hadm_id) labeled with this ICD code from the `diagnoses_icd` and `d_icd_diagnoses` tables. For each admission, we retrieved the corresponding discharge summary from the `discharge.csv` file within the MIMIC-IV notes module, retaining note ID, subject ID, admission ID, and raw clinical text. To construct prediction targets, we joined the selected admissions with metadata from the `admissions.csv` file, calculating each patient's length of stay (LOS) as the difference in days between admission and discharge timestamps. We then created a binary target variable, `LOS_long`, by thresholding LOS at the cohort median, defining cases above the median, 249 as long stays (label = 1) and 218 as short (label = 0).

3.2 Keyword-Based Text Distillation with RaKUn

To reduce the complexity of long clinical discharge notes while preserving medically relevant information, we apply automatic keyword extraction using the RaKUn algorithm [Škrlj et al., 2019]. RaKUn is an unsupervised, graph-based keyword extraction method that constructs a co-occurrence graph from the input document and ranks words using load centrality.

Each clinical note is first tokenized into an ordered sequence of words. A directed, weighted graph is built where edges connect successive words in the text, preserving word order. Weights are assigned based on the frequency of word transitions. To reduce noise and redundancy, RaKUn applies *meta vertex construction*, which merges similar words (e.g., misspellings or morphological variants) into a single node using edit distance and word length thresholds. After graph construction and cleaning, *load centrality* is computed for each node. This measure captures how frequently a word appears on the shortest paths between all other pairs of words, effectively identifying central, information-rich terms. Nodes with high load centrality are considered candidate keywords. To expand beyond unigrams, RaKUn forms bigram and trigram keyphrases by combining adjacent high-centrality nodes, weighted by their average scores. The final ranked list of keyphrases is sorted by their composite centrality scores.

For each discharge note, we extract up to 1,024 keyword candidates, applying a merge threshold of 1.1, $\alpha = 0.3$ to balance frequency with informativeness, and a minimum token length of 3. If more than 512 phrases are extracted, we retain only the top-ranked subset. These keyword phrases are concatenated into a distilled string that serves as input to downstream models.

3.3 Classification Model

We compare two BERT-based classification pipelines on the task of predicting whether a kidney stone patient will experience a prolonged hospital stay. The first uses the raw discharge summary, while the second uses the distilled keyword representation. Both approaches are used to fine-tune the same pretrained ModernBERT model [Warner et al., 2024] using identical hyperparameters.

Model training is performed using 5-fold stratified cross-validation, with reproducible seeding and class-weighted loss to mitigate imbalance. For each fold, we train the model for 3 epochs using AdamW (learning rate $= 2 \times 10^{-6}$). We evaluate performance using accuracy and macro-averaged F_1 score on the held-out fold. Our PyTorch implementation leverages HuggingFace Transformers, and all training is conducted on CPU or Apple MPS GPU.

3.4 Focused Permutation-Based Explanation Fidelity

Using LIME directly on clinical notes often results in explanations dominated by irrelevant or noisy words. To improve explanation fidelity, we modify LIME [Ribeiro et al., 2016] to operate only on a curated *focus set* $\mathcal{F}$ per note. This set is constructed by taking the union of:

- The top 512 keyphrases extracted by the Rakun algorithm for that note, and
- Named clinical entities identified by Med7 [Kormilitzin et al., 2021], excluding low-informative categories such as dosage and frequency terms.

By restricting LIME's perturbations to this focused set, we preserve grammatical structure, ensure classifier outputs remain meaningful, and generate explanations that concentrate on the most clinically relevant information.

To quantify explanation fidelity, we apply a token deletion test over the top-ranked words in each LIME explanation. Specifically, we measure the model's predicted probability for the positive class as the top-k influential tokens (ranked by LIME weight) are progressively removed. This forms a *deletion curve*, where larger probability drops imply more faithful explanations. We compute the *area under the deletion curve (AUC)* as a summary measure: lower AUC values indicate that the removed tokens had a stronger influence on the model's decision, thus reflecting higher explanation fidelity.

3.5 Chain-of-Thought Reasoning with LLMs

In another setting, we use LLMs to produce explanations. To support long clinical prompts without truncation and ensure consistent inference over extended discharge summaries and keyword lists, we used the Deep Seek distilled LLaMA 3 14B model. Unlike the base LLaMA 3 and ChatGPT, which both impose strict token limits, Deep Seek's implementation allows for much greater prompt length, enabling us to feed the full note alongside up to 1,024 extracted keywords. All inference was performed locally on a MacBook Pro (Apple M4 Max), ensuring data privacy and reproducibility. To assess downstream interpretability under controlled sampling, we conducted all LLM-based reasoning experiments at a fixed temperature of $T = 0.5$. For a cohort of 20 true-positive long-stay cases, we generated chain-of-thought explanations under two prompt conditions:

1. **Full-text prompt:** the original discharge summary only,
2. **Hybrid prompt:** the Rakun-distilled keyword string plus the full note, with instructions to prioritize the key findings.

To mitigate sampling variability, each prompt condition was run *five independent times* per case. LLM LLaMA 3 70B then scored each explanation on a 1–5 scale for clarity and clinical relevance. We report, for each prompt type, the *mean* score across the five runs. This design yields robust estimates of each method's interpretability under non-deterministic LLM sampling. To illustrate the difference between the two prompting strategies used for generating clinical reasoning, Fig. 2 presents a side-by-side comparison of the prompt templates. The left side shows the baseline approach using only the full clinical note as input, while the right side displays our keyword-augmented prompt, which prepends domain-relevant clinical terms extracted via Rakun and Med7. This additional guidance helps steer the LLM's attention toward the most salient findings, resulting in more focused and interpretable reasoning outputs.
Responses were stripped of leading/trailing whitespace and saved for later expert scoring.

3.6 Evaluation of Classification and Explanation Quality

We evaluate the TT-XAI pipeline along both predictive accuracy and interpretability. For classification, we perform 5-fold cross-validation and report accuracy and macro-F_1 scores using both the original discharge summaries and the distilled keyword inputs. Across all token-length configurations, keyword-based inputs consistently outperform raw full-text baselines.

To assess explanation quality, we employ two complementary strategies:

Only-Text Prompt

System: Clinical Urologist
Instruction: Provide 1–3 reasoning steps.
Input:
`Full Clinical Note:`
`<raw text>`
`Reasoning steps:`

Keyword-Augmented Prompt

System: Clinical Urologist
Instruction: Provide 1–3 reasoning steps.
Input:
`Key Clinical Findings: <keywords>`
`Full Clinical Note: <raw text>`
`Reasoning steps:`

Fig. 2. Prompt variants used to elicit clinical reasoning from LLaMA-3. The keyword-augmented prompt (right) guides the model with extracted key clinical terms, helping it focus on salient findings, while the full-text prompt (left) uses only the raw note.

(1) Automatic Evaluation. We measure explanation fidelity via deletion curves over 20 long-stay instances, comparing classical LIME with our focused variant that perturbs only extracted clinical keywords and NER entities. A lower area under the curve (AUC) indicates more faithful explanations. In addition, we generate reasoning-style explanations using LLaMA3-70B and collect automated ratings on clarity and usefulness using LLM self-assessment protocols (Sect. 4).

(2) Human Specialist Evaluation. To ground our findings in real-world clinical relevance, we conduct a blinded evaluation with three medical experts. They review reasoning outputs from two prompting strategies: **Method A**, which uses full-text only, and **Method B**, which augments the input with keyword representations. From the available data, we randomly sampled 10 unique patient cases and selected one explanation pair (Method A and B) per case.

To improve readability and reduce annotation fatigue, each explanation was summarized using LLaMA3-70B into a maximum of three clinically focused bullet points, using both the extracted keywords and the original reasoning as input. The resulting 10 anonymized explanation pairs were scored by the specialists on a 1–5 scale for clarity and clinical usefulness.

This combined evaluation spanning automatic fidelity, language model scoring, and human domain expertise offers a robust, multifaceted assessment of explanation quality in a high-stakes clinical context.

4 Results

We first present results of prediction performance, comparing the original discharge summaries with distilled keyword inputs. Next, we compare the quality of explanations: faithfulness, clarity, and clinical usefulness.

Prediction Performance. We evaluate ModernBERT on the binary task of predicting long hospital stays across multiple input representations and sequence lengths. Table 1 present 5-fold cross-validation results comparing the original discharge summaries with their Rakun-distilled keyword counterparts, using context lengths of 50, 100, 512, and 1024 tokens. Overall, distilled keyword inputs consistently outperform raw text across all configurations. At a 512-token limit, the keyword model achieves the F_1 score of 0.767 ± 0.027, compared to 0.665 ± 0.072 for the full-text baseline—an improvement of over 10% points. Even at shorter context lengths (e.g., 50 or 100), the distilled model maintains strong performance, indicating that the selected keyphrases capture essential clinical signals more effectively than the full, noisy input.

Table 1. Classification accuracy and F_1 scores of ModernBERT fine-tuned on original text vs. keyword-based input across different context lengths. We report mean and standard deviation over 5-fold cross-validation. **Bold** values indicate the best performance for each context length.

Context Length	Modality	Accuracy ($\mu \pm \sigma$)	F_1 ($\mu \pm \sigma$)
50 Tokens	Original	0.5909 ± 0.1071	0.4428 ± 0.3487
	Keywords	$\mathbf{0.6637 \pm 0.0611}$	$\mathbf{0.6859 \pm 0.0634}$
100 Tokens	Original	0.6232 ± 0.0386	0.6627 ± 0.0968
	Keywords	$\mathbf{0.6875 \pm 0.0489}$	$\mathbf{0.7274 \pm 0.0377}$
512 Tokens	Original	0.6381 ± 0.0528	0.6652 ± 0.0724
	Keywords	$\mathbf{0.7409 \pm 0.0418}$	$\mathbf{0.7674 \pm 0.0271}$
1024 Tokens	Original	0.6745 ± 0.0368	0.6897 ± 0.0668
	Keywords	$\mathbf{0.7386 \pm 0.0460}$	$\mathbf{0.7430 \pm 0.0699}$

Explanation Faithfulness. To assess the faithfulness of LIME-based explanations, we compute deletion curves over a held-out set of 20 correctly classified long-stay examples. Each curve measures the predicted probability of the positive class as top-ranked features (according to LIME weights) are progressively removed from the input. Lower area under the curve (AUC) indicates more faithful explanations, where removing important tokens significantly disrupts the model's prediction. Figure 3 shows the average deletion curves comparing classical LIME (on full text) with our focused variant, which perturbs only keywords and clinical NER tokens. The focused explanation achieves a lower AUC (0.668 vs. 0.742), indicating that it better captures the predictive evidence and provides sharper, more trustworthy explanations.

Explanation Clarity and Usefulness Evaluation with LLMs. Using the explanation procedure based on LLMs from Sect. 3.5, we obtained five independent explanations per case per prompt at $T = 0.5$. Experts rated each on clarity and clinical usefulness (1–5 scale, 1-poor and 5-excellent), and we report the mean and standard deviations across all 20 cases and 5 repeats (Table 2):

Table 2. The evaluation of the LLaMA-3 70B-produced clinical explanations. We report expert scores (mean and standard deviation) across 5 runs at $T = 0.5$.

Prompt Type	Quality
Full-text only	3.86 ± 1.6
Keywords + Full-text	4.01 ± 1.5

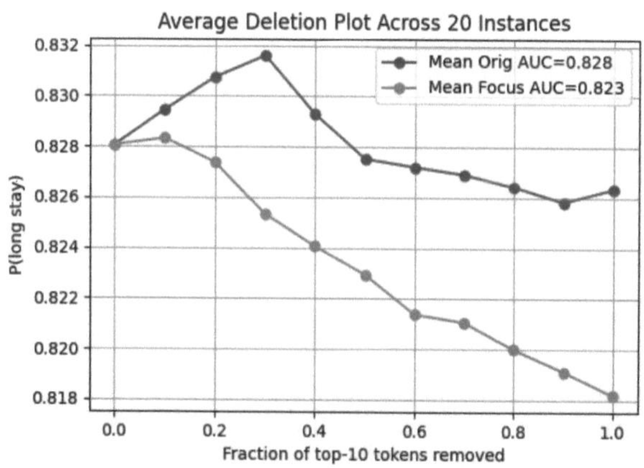

Fig. 3. Average deletion curve across 20 long-stay examples comparing classical LIME (Original) vs. Focused-LIME (Keywords + NER). Lower AUC reflects more faithful explanations, i.e. explanations aligned with tokens in the explanations.

These results demonstrate that, at a controlled temperature of 0.5 and averaged over multiple samples, the keyword-augmented prompts yield more coherent and clinically useful reasoning chains compared to the full-text only baseline.

4.1 Expert Evaluation of Explanation Clarity

To complement the LLM-based assessment, we conducted a blinded evaluation involving three medical specialists. The specialists reviewed pairs of explanations generated for multiple patient cases—using either the full discharge notes (Method A) or keyword-augmented prompts (Method B), and rated each explanation on a 1–5 scale for clarity and clinical usefulness in relation to prolonged hospital stays. Table 3 summarizes the results of this evaluation. While preferences varied slightly among individual raters, two out of three specialists gave higher scores on average to the keyword-augmented explanations (Method B), and the overall average score for Method B (3.15) was higher than that of Method A (2.58), suggesting a moderate but consistent improvement in perceived clarity and clinical relevance. Although there were differences in scoring patterns—Specialist 2 provided overall lower scores, while Specialist 3 was generally more favorable—the consensus clearly indicates that keyword-guided prompts produce more interpretable and clinically actionable explanations. These human evaluation results align closely with the earlier quantitative findings from LLM self-assessment and deletion-based fidelity evaluations, further reinforcing the effectiveness of keyword distillation in improving clinical NLP interpretability.

Table 3. Updated mean scores (1–5 scale) given by three medical specialists for each explanation method across clinical cases. Method A used full-text-only prompts; Method B used keyword-augmented prompts.

Method	Specialist-1	Specialist-2	Specialist-3	Average
Full Text Only	2.73	1.55	3.45	2.58
Keywords + Full Text	3.11	3.00	3.33	3.15

5 Discussion

Our findings demonstrate that distilling long clinical notes into concise keyword-based representations can significantly improve both classification performance and interpretability. The consistent gains in F_1 score across multiple context lengths highlight that much of the relevant predictive information is concentrated in a relatively small set of domain-specific terms. This supports the hypothesis that raw discharge summaries contain a substantial amount of redundant or irrelevant information that may obscure signal and reduce model robustness.

The benefits of distillation extend beyond predictive performance. The proposed focused LIME, which uses perturbations restricted to clinically salient terms, yields lower deletion AUCs—indicating explanations that more faithfully reflect the model's decision function. This aligns with prior work suggesting that explanation fidelity can be improved by structuring the space of perturbations [Samek et al., 2017, Ribeiro et al., 2016], but our approach demonstrates that lightweight, unsupervised keyword filtering can be an effective way to achieve this in noisy clinical text.

In addition, the results from LLM-based reasoning evaluation suggest that providing models with distilled clinical findings helps elicit more structured, concise, and clinically relevant reasoning chains. Keyword-guided prompting improved expert-rated quality of explanations, suggesting utility not only for post-hoc interpretability but also for interactive clinical support tools that use LLMs in diagnostic workflows. Importantly, these results were reinforced by a blinded human evaluation involving three medical specialists. Across 10 explanation pairs, the majority of experts showed a clear preference for keyword-augmented reasoning (Method B) over full-text-based reasoning (Method A), with average ratings improving from 2.58 to 3.15 on a 5-point scale. This human-centered validation strengthens the case for keyword distillation as a practical tool for enhancing the clarity, usability, and clinical relevance of AI-generated explanations in medical decision support.

Despite these promising results, our approach has limitations. Keyword extraction introduces a form of abstraction that may omit subtle contextual signals, especially in edge cases. The Med7 NER module may miss domain-specific terms due to coverage limitations or lexical ambiguity. Furthermore, the human evaluation was limited in scope, future work should include more raters, broader specialties, and more rigorous scoring frameworks to increase generalizability.

6 Conclusions and Further Work

This study presents a simple yet effective approach for enhancing the interpretability and predictive performance of clinical text classifiers by distilling long, noisy discharge summaries into concise keyword-based representations. Our results show that this distillation not only improves classification performance but also yields more faithful token-level explanations and facilitates clearer, more clinically useful reasoning when prompting large language models.

We validate these findings through a combination of quantitative metrics and human-centered evaluation. Medical specialists in general preferred keyword-augmented explanations over full-text reasoning, highlighting the practical value of our method in clinical interpretability settings. By combining unsupervised keyphrase extraction with transformer-based modeling and focused explainability techniques, we offer a scalable, domain-aware method for improving trust and transparency in clinical NLP. This approach lays the groundwork for more interpretable decision support systems, particularly in high-stakes domains such as urology, where justification and auditability are essential for clinical adoption. The source code of our methodology and experiments is freely available[1]. Future work will explore dynamic adjustment of keyword extraction thresholds on a per-patient basis, as well as integration of structured EHR data (e.g., lab values, vitals) alongside clinical text. Another direction involves fine-tuning large language models (LLMs) specifically for explanation generation to improve clinical coherence and specificity. To assess the quality and reliability of generated rationales, we also plan to compare LLM-generated explanations against those written by domain experts, enabling grounded evaluation of factual correctness and clinical utility. Additionally, we will benchmark explanation quality across different foundation models (e.g., GPT-4, LLaMA-3) to study variability and consistency. Finally, real-time deployment studies are needed to evaluate the practical utility and usability of these interpretability methods in live clinical workflows.

[1] https://github.com/KristianMiok/TT-XAI.

Acknowledgments. Kristian Miok was supported by the EU HE MSC Postdoctoral Fellowship Programme SMASH (No. 101081355). The work was partially supported by the Slovenian Research and Innovation Agency (ARIS) core research programme P6-0411 and P2-0103, as well as projects L2-50070, GC-0002, and J4-4555. The work was partially supported by the project "Romanian Hub for Artificial Intelligence - HRIA", Smart Growth, Digitization and Financial Instruments Program, 2021-2027, MySMIS no. 334906. The work was supported by EU through ERA Chair grant no. 101186647 (AI4DH) and cofinancing for research innovation projects in support of green transition and digitalisation (project PoVeJMo, no. C3.K8.IB).

References

Agarwal, R., et al.: Neural additive models. Adv. Neural. Inf. Process. Syst. **34**, 4699–4711 (2021)

Ahmed, R., Hemanth, D.J.: Hybrid text summarization: Integrating extractive and abstractive models for enhanced cross-domain summarization. Intell. Decis. Technol. 18724981251322745 (2025)

Bhatt, U., et al.: Explainable machine learning in deployment. In: Proceedings of the 2020 Conference on Fairness, Accountability, and Transparency (FAccT), pp. 648–657. ACM (2020)

Caruana, R., Lou, Y., Gehrke, J., Koch, P., Sturm, M., Elhadad, N.: Intelligible models for healthcare: predicting pneumonia risk and hospital 30-day readmission. In: Proceedings of the 21st ACM SIGKDD International Conference on Knowledge Discovery and Data Mining, pp. 1721–1730. ACM (2015)

Chari, S., et al.: Explanation ontology: a general-purpose, semantic representation for supporting user-centered explanations. Semantic Web **15**(4), 959–989 (2024)

Choi, E., Bahadori, M.T., Sun, J., Kulas, J., Schuetz, A., Stewart, W.F.: RETAIN: an interpretable predictive model for healthcare using reverse time attention mechanism. In: Advances in Neural Information Processing Systems 29, pp. 3504–3512. Curran Associates, Inc. (2016)

Erkan, G., Radev, D.R.: Lexrank: graph-based lexical centrality as salience in text summarization. J. Artif. Intell. Res. **22**, 457–479 (2004)

Goyal, Y., Wu, Z., Ernst, J., Batra, D., Parikh, D., Lee, S.: Counterfactual visual explanations. In: Chaudhuri, K., Salakhutdinov, R. (eds.) Proceedings of the 36th International Conference on Machine Learning. Proceedings of Machine Learning Research, vol. 97, pp. 2376–2384. PMLR (2019)

Jacovi, A., Goldberg, Y.: Towards faithfully interpretable NLP systems: how should we define and evaluate faithfulness? In: Proceedings of the 58th Annual Meeting of the Association for Computational Linguistics, pp. 4198–4205. Association for Computational Linguistics (2020)

Jain, S., Wallace, B.C.: Attention is not explanation. In: Proceedings of the 2019 Conference of the North American Chapter of the Association for Computational Linguistics: Human Language Technologies, pp. 3543–3556. Association for Computational Linguistics (2019)

Johnson, A.E.W., Bulgarelli, L., Pollard, T.J., Horng, S., Celi, L.A., Mark, R.G.: MIMIC-IV (version 1.0): a freely accessible electronic health record dataset. PhysioNet **101**, e215–e220 (2021)

Kormilitzin, A., Vaci, N., Liu, Q., Nevado-Holgado, A.: Med7: a transferable clinical natural language processing model for electronic health records. Artif. Intell. Med. **118**, 102086 (2021)

Lampinen, A.K., et al.: Can language models learn from explanations in context? arXiv preprint arXiv:2204.02329 (2022). https://arxiv.org/abs/2204.02329

Lewis, M., et al.: Bart: denoising sequence-to-sequence pre-training for natural language generation, translation, and comprehension. arXiv preprint arXiv:1910.13461 (2020)

Li, J., Chen, X., Hovy, E., Jurafsky, D.: Visualizing and understanding neural models in NLP. In: Proceedings of the 2016 Conference of the North American Chapter of the Association for Computational Linguistics: Human Language Technologies, pp. 681–691. Association for Computational Linguistics (2016)

Lundberg, S.M., Lee, S.-I.: A unified approach to interpreting model predictions. In: Advances in Neural Information Processing Systems, vol. 30 (2017)

Nori, H., King, N., McKinney, S.M., Carignan, D., Horvitz, E.: Capabilities of GPT-4 on medical challenge problems. arXiv preprint arXiv:2303.13375 (2023)

Pearle, M.S., et al.: Medical management of kidney stones: aua guideline. J. Urol. **192**(2), 316–324 (2014). https://doi.org/10.1016/j.juro.2014.05.006

Rajani, N.F., McCann, B., Xiong, C., Socher, R.: Explain yourself! leveraging language models for commonsense reasoning. In: Proceedings of the 57th Annual Meeting of the Association for Computational Linguistics, pp. 4932–4942, Florence, Italy. Association for Computational Linguistics (2019). https://doi.org/10.18653/v1/P19-1487. https://aclanthology.org/P19-1487/

Ribeiro, M.T., Singh, S., Guestrin, C.: "Why should i trust you?" Explaining the predictions of any classifier. In: Proceedings of the 22nd ACM SIGKDD International Conference on Knowledge Discovery and Data Mining, pp. 1135–1144 (2016)

Samek, W., Binder, A., Montavon, G., Lapuschkin, S., Müller, K.-R.: Evaluating the visualization of what a deep neural network has learned. IEEE Trans. Neural Netw. Learn. Syst. **28**(11), 2660–2673 (2017). https://doi.org/10.1109/TNNLS.2016.2599820

Scales, C.D., Smith, A.C., Hanley, J.M., Saigal, C.S.: Prevalence of kidney stones in the united states. Eur. Urol. **62**(1), 160–165 (2012). https://doi.org/10.1016/j.eururo.2012.03.052

Škrlj, B., Repar, A., Pollak, S.: Rakun: rank-based keyword extraction via unsupervised learning and meta vertex aggregation. In: Statistical Language and Speech Processing: 7th International Conference, SLSP 2019, Ljubljana, Slovenia, 14–16 October 2019, Proceedings 7, pp. 311–323. Springer (2019)

Warner, B., et al.: Smarter, better, faster, longer: a modern bidirectional encoder for fast, memory efficient, and long context finetuning and inference. arXiv preprint arXiv:2412.13663 (2024)

Wei, J., et al.: Chain-of-thought prompting elicits reasoning in large language models. arXiv preprint arXiv:2201.11903 (2022). https://arxiv.org/abs/2201.11903

Wu, X., et al.: Usable XAI: 10 strategies towards exploiting explainability in the LLM era. arXiv preprint arXiv:2403.08946 (2024)

Zhang, J., Zhao, Y., Saleh, M., Liu, P.J.: PEGASUS: pre-training with extracted gap-sentences for abstractive summarization. In: Daumé III, H., Singh, A. (eds.) Proceedings of the 37th International Conference on Machine Learning. Proceedings of Machine Learning Research, vol. 119, pp. 11328–11339. PMLR (2020)

From Explainable AI to Model Diagnosis: A Framework and Comparative Study of Human and ML-Based Explanation Diagnosis

Tobias Gentner(✉), Felix Gerschner, and Andreas Theissler

Aalen University of Applied Sciences, 73430 Aalen, Germany
gentnert@gmail.com

Abstract. While AI has found its way into many areas of our daily lives, the black-box nature of most Machine Learning (ML) models raises concerns about trust and the identification of model limitations. Although refining ML models is essential for developing applications, improving data quality and model performance via explainable AI remains under-explored. This empirical comparative study addresses these gaps by diagnosing data quality and model performance issues using the Contrastive Explanations Method. We (1) developed a diagnostic framework for the analysis of explanations, (2) conducted a user study to evaluate the extent to which humans can identify these issues with the help of explanations, and (3) evaluated ML-based diagnosis of explanations using deep learning models. Humans interpreted explanations effectively, achieving mean diagnostic accuracies of up to 96.00% in single-issue scenarios. For ML-based diagnosis, the Swin Transformer model reached a mean balanced accuracy of 98.53% across several datasets. These findings highlight the complementary strengths of human and ML-based diagnosis, supporting the potential for hybrid model evaluation approaches.

Keywords: Explainable AI · Model diagnosis · Contrastive Explanations Method · Human diagnosis · ML-based diagnosis

1 Introduction

With the rising performance of modern Machine Learning (ML) models, their complexity increases [9,22]. The black-box nature of many ML models prevents users from understanding their internal mechanisms, raising concerns about how much AI predictions can be trusted. This opacity makes it difficult to diagnose issues such as data corruption and model limitations [9]. For model developers, the absence of clear insights into the decision-making process causes a time-consuming, trial-and-error approach [22]. However, the identification of such issues is important in applications affecting end-users, including medical systems and self-driving cars, where decisions must be reliable and justifiable [20,22].

I. Koprinska et al. (Eds.): ECML PKDD 2025, CCIS 2842, pp. 514–529, 2026.
https://doi.org/10.1007/978-3-032-19105-2_36

Several eXplainable Artificial Intelligence (XAI) approaches have been developed to address this lack of transparency [22]. From the perspective of model developers, explanations facilitate the improvement of training data quality and mitigation of model limitations, enabling more reliable ML models [22,27]. However, prior research has shown that model explanations are not always human-interpretable. For instance, XAI heatmaps for clinical applications often fail at highlighting relevant regions [23]. To provide explanations that align with human decision-making processes, the Contrastive Explanations Method (CEM) has been proposed. This method explains model predictions by identifying both the features essential for the current prediction and the features whose presence would lead to a different outcome [4].

Although diagnosing ML models is essential for developing successful models, few research efforts have focused on the improvement of data quality or model performance based on XAI [22]. The extent to which humans and ML models can detect such issues from explanations remains largely unexplored. For this reason, we conducted an empirical comparative study to analyze human and ML-based diagnosis of CEM-generated explanations. A central aspect of this research is a diagnostic framework based on explanation patterns that allows model developers to differentiate between various issues. Building on this framework, we assessed human detection abilities in a user study and evaluated multiple Deep Learning (DL) models for ML-based diagnosis. To determine the generalizability of these models, we examined their transfer to different datasets.
The following research questions are addressed:

- RQ1: Are there specific patterns in CEM-generated explanations that enable the distinction between data quality problems (i.e., mislabeling) and model-related performance issues (i.e., overfitting and underfitting)?
- RQ2: How successful are humans at diagnosing CEM-generated explanations to detect data quality and model performance issues?
- RQ3: How effective are ML approaches at diagnosing CEM-generated explanations to detect data quality and model performance issues?
- RQ4: How do human interpretations of CEM-generated explanations compare to ML-based models in diagnosing data quality and model performance issues?

Accordingly, this work contributes:

1. An analysis of patterns within CEM-generated explanations that distinguish between data quality and model performance issues;
2. A diagnostic framework as a structured set of explanation-based patterns derived from CEM-generated explanations that enables differentiation between data quality and model performance issues, providing guidance for model developers in improving AI systems;
3. An empirical evaluation of human interpretation skills, revealing how effectively individuals can diagnose data quality and model performance issues based on CEM-generated explanations;

4. The development and evaluation of DL approaches for ML-based diagnosis of CEM-generated explanations, with the best-performing model achieving a mean balanced accuracy of 98.53% across all test datasets;
5. A comparative analysis of human and ML-based diagnosis of the aforementioned.

2 Related Work

Since the outcomes of AI systems are affected by the quality of the data used to train models, Saraswat et al. [20] identified the evaluation of data quality via XAI-based explanations as a future research direction.

While previous user studies have primarily explored trust and human-AI collaboration from the perspective of end users, the integration of XAI for model developers to diagnose model issues remains underexplored [19]. To improve the data quality of documents, Ribeiro et al. [18] observed that XAI helped participants to refine the model by removing unimportant features. Bhattacharya et al. [1] demonstrated how integrating global explanations into the configuration of training data can improve time series models. For validating an interactive XAI framework that allows the refinement of image data and optimization of ML models, Spinner et al. [22] revealed that participants found the system intuitive and helpful. In another user study, Huang et al. [10] showed on image data that XAI supports interactive reasoning about model behavior.

Beyond user studies, automated XAI evaluation metrics exist without human input. Clinciu et al. [2] correlated natural language explanations for Bayesian networks with human ratings on a text-based dataset. Leveraging an evaluation metric that mimics human assessments, Kazmierczak et al. [11] introduced a human-centric XAI framework. Moreover, Fiori et al. [6] proposed an evaluation framework using large language models. Compared to user surveys, their method ranked XAI approaches similarly to non-expert humans.

While several user studies have examined the role of XAI in improving document and time series data [1,18], assessed its intuitiveness for diagnosing model limitations and refining image data [22], and analyzed how it aids in understanding model behavior for image classification [10], an important gap remains. Specifically, there is a lack of research on whether humans can identify data quality and model performance issues in XAI-generated explanations. Therefore, this paper evaluates how well humans can diagnose such issues within explanations generated by the CEM. Moreover, related work has implemented automated evaluation metrics for XAI methods and compared them with user studies [2,6,11]. Despite these efforts, the automated diagnosis of data quality and model performance issues via XAI remains unresolved. To close this gap, our work further investigates the ML-based diagnosis of explanations using DL approaches.

3 Analysis of Patterns in Explanations

In this section, CEM-generated explanations of different models are analyzed to identify patterns revealing data quality or model performance issues. Building on these explanation-based patterns, a diagnostic framework was developed.

The CEM, proposed by Dhurandhar et al. [4], is a post-hoc technique for explaining predictions of black-box models. This method produces two complementary sets of features: Pertinent Negatives (PNs), the minimal set of factors in the input that, if changed, would result in a different prediction, and Pertinent Positives (PPs), the minimal set of factors that are essential to support the current prediction. The underlying inputs to both our human and ML-based diagnosis of explanations were triplets produced by the CEM for each input, i.e., the original input alongside the PN and PP, as shown in Fig. 1. In this example, the digit was correctly classified as a 4, and the PNs highlight pixels that, if added, would form a curved top and change the prediction to a 9. In contrast, the PPs emphasize structural elements of a 4, notably the vertical and diagonal lines, while less relevant parts are hidden. For the development of our method, we first employed the MNIST dataset [12], which had also been used by Spinner et al. [22] to verify the usability of their XAI framework.

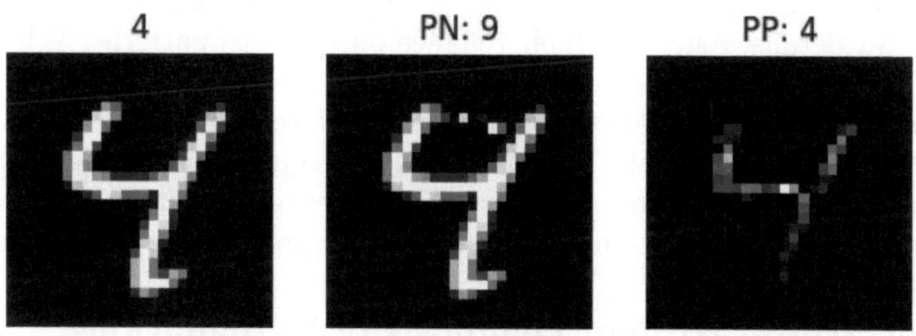

Fig. 1. Our input data: the triplet of the original input image, the pertinent negative, and the pertinent positive {*input, PN, PP*} produced by the CEM. The assumption is that this triplet allows the detection of mislabeling and model overfitting/underfitting.

3.1 Overview of Key Cases: Data Quality or Model Issues

For evaluating model integrity, six key cases that represent various models were identified: (1) A *good model* generalizes well and leverages meaningful patterns to make accurate predictions. (2) If predictions are inaccurate despite correct reasoning, *mislabeling* is recognized as a data quality issue. (3) Performance shortcomings are categorized into *overfitting*, where limited training data or complex algorithms lead to memorization, and (4) *underfitting*, where insufficient training or simplified architectures prevent the learning of essential patterns [17]. These issues can co-occur as combinations of (5) *overfitting & mislabeling* and (6) *underfitting & mislabeling*, where models memorize incorrect labels.

To detect specific patterns, separate models representing each key case were implemented using `PyTorch` and `TorchVision`, with explanations of the test dataset generated via the `ContrastiveExplainer` module from `OmniXAI` [30]. Each model was trained with a batch size of 128 and a learning rate of 0.001. The good model was trained for 20 epochs using a Convolutional Neural Network (CNN) with two convolutional layers. Following [28], 70% of the training labels were randomly swapped to simulate mislabeling. To encourage overfitting, a CNN with one convolutional layer was trained for 1,000 epochs on a subset of 1,000 samples, while underfitting was induced by training the same architecture for 20 epochs. Additionally, combined models were generated by applying 70% label noise to the 1,000-sample subset and training them for either 1,000 or 20 epochs to simulate overfitting & mislabeling and underfitting & mislabeling.

3.2 Development of Diagnostic Framework

Some PNs and PPs appear similar across different key cases. In particular, the PNs of the good model and the mislabeling case are identical, suggesting that the distinctiveness of MNIST digits enables robust learning despite mislabeling. Likewise, overfitting, underfitting, and underfitting & mislabeling cases show similar PNs, as all struggle to capture discriminative features. Furthermore, the PPs of overfitting and overfitting & mislabeling exhibit similarities by focusing on irrelevant details, reflecting their reliance on spurious patterns. While these similarities highlight the need to interpret subtle differences in explanation patterns carefully, the combinations of PNs and PPs remain distinctive, allowing for differentiation between the various issues. These patterns are summarized in Table 1 and form the basis of our diagnostic framework for model developers to diagnose hidden weaknesses and guide targeted improvements in AI systems.

4 User Study: Human Diagnosis of Explanations

This section presents the user study on human diagnosis of explanations. Following XAI study design guidelines of Rong et al. [19] and van der Waa et al. [26], we evaluated how well 15 participants diagnosed issues in a within-subjects design.

4.1 Planning and Design

The user study began with a tutorial to familiarize the participants with the structure of the study and guide them in interpreting explanations. This was followed by six scenarios designed to evaluate the extent to which humans can diagnose issues, as well as a final post-study questionnaire.

Tutorial. Following [19], the tutorial started with an overview of the key cases and scenarios. This was succeeded by a demonstration of how the CEM generated explanations for predictions within the diagnostic framework. To further prepare the participants, three interactive tasks were provided, in which they were asked to diagnose mislabeling and model performance issues based on explanations.

Table 1. Summary of key cases and explanation patterns for differentiating between a good model and models affected by data quality or model performance issues.

Key Case	Pertinent Negatives (PNs)	Pertinent Positives (PPs)
Good Model	Highlight decisive features for different predictions that enable clear class separation, reflecting robust feature learning.	Emphasize essential features consistent with human perception by relying on core geometric structures.
Mislabeling	Highlight decisive features for different predictions that enable clear class separation, reflecting robust feature learning.	Show more areas than the good model due to model uncertainty caused by mislabeling.
Overfitting	Emphasize generalized areas without capturing key discriminative features caused by memorization of training-specific patterns.	Focus on small or irrelevant details and ignore important features by memorizing superficial or noise-specific patterns.
Underfitting	Emphasize generalized areas without capturing key discriminative features resulting from insufficient training and poor feature learning.	Concentrate on the whole input due to model uncertainty and inability to learn discriminative features.
Overfitting & Mislabeling	Capture the entire input with less background, but no discriminative features due to memorization of mislabeled and inconsistent patterns.	Focus on small or irrelevant details and ignore important features by memorizing superficial or noise-specific patterns.
Underfitting & Mislabeling	Emphasize generalized areas without capturing key discriminative features caused by unstable feature learning.	Show the input with thin lines due to model uncertainty and reliance on minimal abstractions of essential features.

Examined Scenarios. Six scenarios were examined, each presenting the participants with five randomly ordered explanations (five triplets {*input, PN, PP*}) corresponding to different key cases. To prevent order effects, the explanations were arranged randomly, as recommended in [19]. The scenarios gradually increased in difficulty, and the participants were immediately informed whether their decision was correct. For example, in *Scenario 1*, they were asked to distinguish between a good model and one with any issue, while in *Scenario 6*, all key cases had to be identified. These scenarios are outlined in Fig. 2.

Post-Study Questionnaire. After completing the scenarios, the explanations were evaluated in a post-study questionnaire. Part of the questionnaire was based on the NASA-TLX scale, a well-established tool for measuring subjective workload [25]. Moreover, we included self-designed questions addressing explanation-specific aspects. This procedure was consistent with [19] and [26], who recommend using a combination of self-reported and observed measures, as perceived understanding may not always align with understanding of the model.

Participants. Following [19], participants in a study should have a knowledge background that aligns with the intended end users of the application being evaluated. In this study, the target users are model developers who aim to evaluate and improve models by addressing data quality or model performance issues.

These are experts in ML, but not necessarily familiar with XAI. To reflect this user group, a total of 15 students enrolled in a master's program with prior experience in ML were recruited, some of whom may have had prior knowledge of XAI, though this was not a requirement. The study followed a within-subjects design, where the participants experienced all conditions sequentially and provided feedback. This approach is particularly useful when working with participants who have specialized expertise, such as domain-specific knowledge in ML [19].

4.2 Results of Human Diagnosis

The results of the user study revealed differences in diagnostic accuracy, self-reported participant confidence, and time taken per scenario and task. To statistically assess the impact of different scenarios on task performance, a Friedman test was conducted and Post-study questionnaire responses were analyzed.

Accuracy per Scenario. In Fig. 2 (bottom), the diagnostic accuracy results across the six scenarios are presented. The participants achieved strong diagnostic performance, with the highest mean accuracies observed in *Scenario 3* (96.00%) and *Scenario 5* (92.00%). Even in more challenging scenarios, such as *Scenario 6* (54.67%), moderate accuracy levels were maintained.

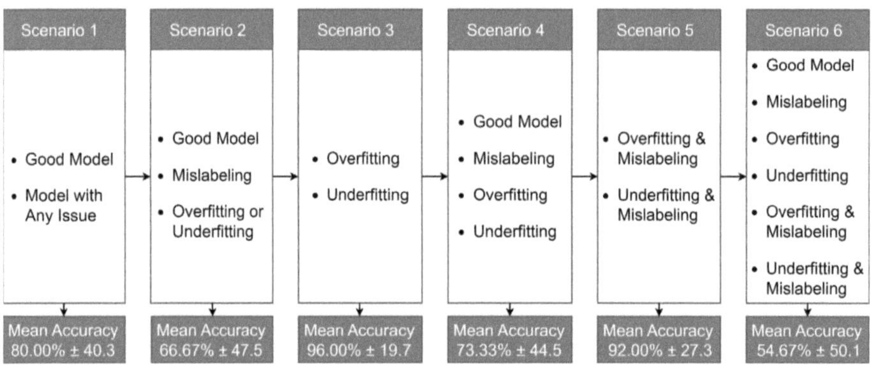

Fig. 2. Scenarios to evaluate human diagnosis of explanations with mean diagnostic accuracy and standard deviation per scenario.

Statistical Analysis. Due to non-normality, Friedman tests were applied, which identified significant differences in diagnostic accuracy, confidence, and task completion time across scenarios. In post-hoc analyses, a lower accuracy in *Scenario 6* and variations in completion times were revealed, while confidence ratings showed no significant pairwise differences. Additionally, a post-hoc power analysis indicated sufficient power for time, but not for accuracy or confidence.

Post-Study Questionnaire. Table 2 shows the responses of the participants, capturing their subjective experiences. Overall, they reported moderate mental demand (Q1, 49.0%) and workload (Q2, 47.0%), while stress levels remained low (Q3, 29.7%). The explanations were rated as highly useful for assessing model quality (Q5, 86.0%) and visual clarity (Q6, 82.7%), though their utility for identifying mislabeling (Q4, 49.3%) was rated moderately. Moreover, interest in simplified representations was expressed (Q7, 62.3%), and the task experience was rated as straightforward (Q8, 63.3%) and intuitive (Q9, 62.0%).

Table 2. Questionnaire: mean score in percentage and standard deviation.

ID	Question	Mean (SD)
Q1	How mentally demanding was the task?	49.0 (16.7)
Q2	How hard did you have to work to accomplish your level of performance?	47.0 (24.1)
Q3	How insecure, discouraged, irritated, stressed, and annoyed were you?	29.7 (28.1)
Q4	How useful were the explanations in assessing the data quality (mislabeling)?	49.3 (29.9)
Q5	How useful were the explanations in assessing the model quality (overfitting and underfitting)?	86.0 (16.9)
Q6	Did the black-and-white explanations provide a clear visual distinction of key areas?	82.7 (18.0)
Q7	Would you have preferred to see a simplified version of the explanations?	62.3 (36.4)
Q8	Did you feel the task was straightforward?	63.3 (24.9)
Q9	How intuitive did you find the task overall?	62.0 (25.8)

Some participants also provided open-text responses and highlighted challenges in distinguishing between mislabeling and the effects of overfitting or underfitting. Many of them noted that mislabeling appeared visually similar to underfitting. Moreover, they reported that the distinction between overfitting and overfitting & mislabeling, as well as underfitting and underfitting & mislabeling, was subtle. This feedback highlights the need for precise guidance when differentiating between complex model behaviors.

4.3 Discussion of User Study

The results demonstrate that the participants accurately interpreted explanations and diagnosed data quality and model performance issues across scenarios. These findings align with [18] and [1], where participants improved models based on explanations. Nonetheless, challenges remain in distinguishing mislabeling from overfitting and underfitting, as well as in separating overfitting and underfitting from their respective combinations with mislabeling, which reduce accuracy and confidence. This underscores the potential of the CEM to support human understanding in model evaluation, while revealing opportunities for improvement in complex scenarios.

5 ML-Based Diagnosis of Explanations

In this section, the automated diagnosis of CEM-generated explanations is examined using DL classifiers. These ML models were trained with explanations as inputs and labels corresponding to data quality and model performance issues, covering the key cases good model, mislabeling, overfitting, underfitting, overfitting & mislabeling, and underfitting & mislabeling. To assess their generalizability in detecting issues across different data distributions, the models were trained and evaluated on multiple datasets, including MNIST, EMNIST [3], and Fashion-MNIST [29]. For consistency, EMNIST was restricted to 10 classes (uppercase letters A–J), and models representing each key case were trained with the same architectures and parameters as those used for the MNIST dataset.

5.1 Machine Learning Models

The ML models were initialized with ImageNet weights and transfer learning was performed by fine-tuning all layers. Input explanations were provided as RGB images resized to 224 × 224 pixels and each of the following models was trained for 10 epochs using a batch size of 128 and a learning rate of 1×10^{-5}.

- **EfficientNet-B0** [24] from `TorchVision`, with the final classification layer modified to output 6 classes.
- **Swin Transformer** [13] with swin_tiny_patch4_window7_224 obtained from the `timm` package.
- **Hybrid-CNN Transformer** similar to [5], with a ResNet18 architecture connected to a transformer encoder (4 layers, 8 heads) using `TorchVision`.
- **ConvNeXt** [15] with convnext_tiny from the `timm` package, where the first convolutional layer was reduced to a kernel size and stride of 4.

Hold-out cross-validation was used to train and validate the ML models with explanations from MNIST, EMNIST (A–J), and Fashion-MNIST, all obtained from `TorchVision`. Each dataset, containing 10,000 to 10,161 explanations, was split into 70% training, 15% validation, and 15% test data. The models were trained on the training data, while the test data were used for final evaluation. When the test data originated from a different dataset than the training data, the entire dataset was used for evaluation, as it had not been seen during training.

5.2 Results of ML-Based Diagnosis

The diagnostic performance was evaluated for ML models trained on a single dataset as well as combinations of multiple datasets.

Training on One Dataset. In Table 3, the balanced accuracies of the four models trained and evaluated on individual datasets are summarized. All models performed well on the test splits of their training datasets, with balanced accuracies typically exceeding 95%. The highest mean balanced accuracy of 86.40% was achieved by the Swin Transformer trained on Fashion-MNIST. This approach maintained high accuracy on Fashion-MNIST (98.18%), MNIST (76.41%), and EMNIST (84.61%), indicating strong generalization beyond its training domain.

Table 3. Training data and performance of ML-based diagnosis with training on one dataset. The best overall model is displayed in **bold**.

Model	Training Data			Balanced Accuracy			
	MNIST	EMNI.	F.-MNI.	MNIST	EMNI.	F.-MNI.	Mean
EfficientNet-B0	×			96.69%	58.91%	52.54%	69.38%
EfficientNet-B0		×		76.04%	96.50%	53.39%	75.31%
EfficientNet-B0			×	74.27%	71.30%	96.51%	80.69%
Swin Transformer	×			97.76%	70.71%	57.15%	75.21%
Swin Transformer		×		86.81%	97.73%	54.85%	79.80%
Swin Transformer			×	**76.41%**	**84.61%**	**98.18%**	**86.40%**
Hybr.-CNN Transf.	×			96.06%	53.23%	42.84%	64.04%
Hybr.-CNN Transf.		×		76.70%	95.75%	45.17%	72.54%
Hybr.-CNN Transf.			×	65.94%	72.88%	96.43%	78.42%
ConvNeXt	×			95.62%	61.98%	47.85%	68.48%
ConvNeXt		×		79.60%	94.55%	49.39%	74.51%
ConvNeXt			×	72.72%	76.46%	96.02%	81.73%

Table 4 contains the confusion matrix of the best Swin Transformer trained on Fashion-MNIST and evaluated on all datasets. The model reliably identified good (18,001 of 21,645), mislabeling (18,151 of 21,679), overfitting (18,505 of 21,649), and overfitting & mislabeling instances (19,697 of 21,710). Underfitting was recognized in 15,332 of 21,594 cases, but confusion occurred with underfitting & mislabeling (4,433 of 21,594). Similarly, the detection of underfitting & mislabeling (16,578 of 21,689) was more prone to misclassification.

Table 4. Confusion matrix of the Swin Transformer trained on Fashion-MNIST and evaluated on the MNIST, EMNIST, and Fashion-MNIST datasets.

Actual	Predicted					
	Good Model	Mislabeling	Overfitting	Underfitting	Overf. & Misl.	Underf. & Misl.
Good Model	**18,001**	115	2,819	106	475	129
Mislabeling	12	**18,151**	265	94	1,784	1,373
Overfitting	2,195	714	**18,505**	102	6	127
Underfitting	8	853	191	**15,332**	777	4,433
Overf. & Misl.	11	1,600	4	98	**19,697**	300
Underf. & Misl.	10	3,147	131	1,561	262	**16,578**

Training on Multiple Datasets. The balanced accuracies of the models trained on two datasets are shown in Table 5. Across all architectures, training on diverse explanations led to improved generalization. This improvement was evident when models were tested on datasets not seen during training. The best-performing configuration was the Swin Transformer trained on MNIST and Fashion-MNIST, achieving balanced accuracies of 98.70% on MNIST, 97.84% on EMNIST, and 99.04% on Fashion-MNIST. This model reached a mean balanced accuracy of 98.53%, demonstrating strong cross-dataset consistency.

Table 5. Training data and performance of ML-based diagnosis with training on two datasets. The best overall model is displayed in **bold**.

Model	Training Data			Balanced Accuracy			
	MNIST	EMNI.	F.-MNI.	MNIST	EMNI.	F.-MNI.	Mean
EfficientNet-B0	×	×		96.83%	96.04%	54.90%	82.59%
EfficientNet-B0		×	×	87.81%	97.61%	97.31%	94.24%
EfficientNet-B0	×		×	97.95%	94.75%	98.25%	96.98%
Swin Transformer	×	×		97.82%	97.48%	60.70%	85.33%
Swin Transformer		×	×	93.51%	98.92%	97.93%	96.79%
Swin Transformer	×		×	**98.70%**	**97.84%**	**99.04%**	**98.53%**
Hybr.-CNN Transf.	×	×		95.95%	95.44%	44.59%	78.66%
Hybr.-CNN Transf.		×	×	86.12%	97.68%	96.50%	93.43%
Hybr.-CNN Transf.	×		×	98.20%	95.41%	98.26%	97.29%
ConvNeXt	×	×		96.64%	95.46%	53.53%	81.88%
ConvNeXt		×	×	91.04%	97.65%	95.97%	94.89%
ConvNeXt	×		×	98.21%	95.78%	98.01%	97.33%

In Table 6, the confusion matrix of the Swin Transformer trained on MNIST and Fashion-MNIST with evaluation on all datasets is presented. The model accurately recognized good (12,752 of 13,116), mislabeling (13,014 of 13,088), and overfitting instances (12,936 of 13,038), with lower results for underfitting (12,747 of 13,206). Regarding overfitting & mislabeling (12,980 of 13,155) and underfitting & mislabeling (12,807 of 13,154), the model performed comparably.

Table 6. Confusion matrix of the Swin Transformer trained on MNIST and Fashion-MNIST with evaluation on the MNIST, EMNIST, and Fashion-MNIST datasets.

Actual	Predicted					
	Good Model	Misla-beling	Over-fitting	Under-fitting	Overf. & Misl.	Underf. & Misl.
Good Model	**12,752**	4	351	3	4	2
Mislabeling	2	**13,014**	25	0	30	17
Overfitting	72	3	**12,936**	16	0	11
Underfitting	26	8	142	**12,747**	35	248
Overf. & Misl.	53	83	1	11	**12,980**	27
Underf. & Misl.	13	62	57	209	6	**12,807**

5.3 Discussion of ML-Based Diagnosis

These results indicate that DL models can effectively learn to interpret CEM-generated explanations for diagnosing data quality and model performance issues. When models were evaluated on the dataset they were trained on, all architectures achieved high balanced accuracies. However, the performance declined on unseen datasets, revealing challenges in transferring learned representations to datasets with different structures. The Swin Transformer outperformed other architectures across both single-dataset and multi-dataset training setups. This suggests that the hierarchical structure is well-suited for extracting visual cues from explanations [13]. An analysis of the confusion matrices revealed strengths in detecting issues, but difficulty in distinguishing underfitting from underfitting & mislabeling when trained on a single dataset. Interestingly, training on Fashion-MNIST led to the most generalizable models across all architectures. One likely reason is that the fashion products of Fashion-MNIST contain more visually complex patterns compared to the digits and letters of MNIST and EMNIST, which encourages models to learn adaptable feature representations.

6 Comparison of Human and ML-Based Diagnosis

The comparison between human and ML-based diagnosis of CEM-generated explanations reveals complementary strengths and limitations. In the user study, the participants diagnosed issues with high accuracy, particularly when visual cues were aligned with intuitions about digit structure. Their performance was resilient to moderate increases in complexity and improved over time. However, humans struggled, e.g., to distinguish models with multiple issues, such as underfitting from underfitting & mislabeling. As shown in Fig. 3, explanations from these two models appear visually similar, particularly the PNs, which highlight generalized but non-discriminative regions in both cases. Differences are evident in the PPs, where the underfitting & mislabeling model produces thinner reconstructions. These findings indicate that while humans can distinguish diverse issues, visual similarities in explanations compromise diagnostic precision.

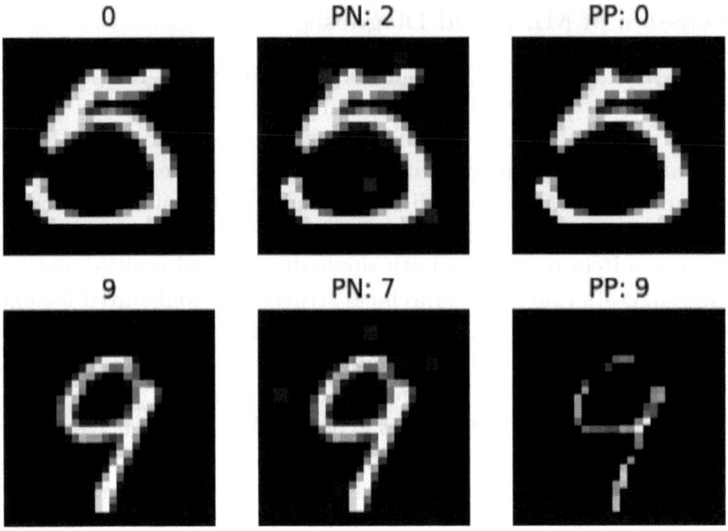

Fig. 3. Explanations of the underfitting model (first row) and the underfitting & mislabeling model (second row) presented to the participants. While both models produced visually similar PNs, the PPs in the second row appear thinner and more abstract.

In contrast, the automated ML models demonstrated strong, consistent accuracy, particularly when trained on diverse datasets. The best-performing models achieved near-perfect classification on their training dataset and retained reasonable generalization across unseen datasets, especially with training on dataset combinations including Fashion-MNIST. However, when trained on a single dataset, the generalization remained limited under cross-dataset evaluation. Similarly to humans, the evaluated model struggled in distinguishing underfitting from underfitting & mislabeling. This highlights the challenge of capturing complex diagnostic reasoning through pattern recognition.

While the automated models benefited from architectural advances and data diversity, human reasoning leveraged understanding and adaptive learning across the tasks. This indicates that human and automated diagnosis of explanations are complementary, as humans bring flexible reasoning to handle edge cases and automated models offer scalable classification. Future systems might therefore benefit from hybrid approaches combining automated classification with human-in-the-loop verification to enhance the reliability of model auditing pipelines.

7 Effectiveness of Contrastive Explanations Method

The combined results from the structured analysis, user study, and ML-based diagnosis confirm that the CEM is an effective method for diagnosing issues through interpretable explanations. Its use of PNs and PPs consistently revealed meaningful features that varied systematically across key cases, enabling both humans and automated models to identify issues. While humans diagnosed these explanations with a moderate to high accuracy and growing efficiency, ML models achieved strong performance, particularly when trained on diverse datasets.

A similarity across the evaluation approaches was the difficulty in diagnosing cases involving combinations of issues. In the structured analysis, the framework revealed that the PNs of underfitting and underfitting & mislabeling and the PPs of overfitting and overfitting & mislabeling overlap, making it difficult to distinguish them. Likewise, the participants struggled in differentiating overfitting and underfitting from their combinations with mislabeling. The same pattern was exhibited by the automated diagnosis with single-dataset training, as the distinction between underfitting and underfitting & mislabeling remained difficult. Although these combinations were challenging, the consistency of CEM-generated explanations supports its utility in both human and automated evaluation.

8 Conclusion

In response to the limited research on diagnosing data quality and model performance issues based on XAI-generated explanations, this paper undertook a comprehensive empirical comparative study. This included the analysis of explanations generated by the CEM, resulting in a diagnostic framework offering a first structured approach to link explanation patterns with issues. Subsequently, both a user study evaluating the ability of humans to identify these issues and the ML-based diagnosis of explanations were performed and compared.

The results showed that the participants interpreted explanations effectively, achieving diagnostic accuracies exceeding 90% in scenarios such as *Scenario 3* and *Scenario 5*. In contrast, the best-performing automated model, a Swin Transformer trained on MNIST and Fashion-MNIST, achieved a mean balanced accuracy of 98.53% across all test datasets. Together, these findings highlight the complementary strengths of human reasoning and automated models, supporting the potential for hybrid approaches in model evaluation workflows.

8.1 Limitations and Future Work

One limitation is that both the diagnostic framework and the user study were validated on MNIST, which may not capture real-world complexity. Moreover, the diagnostic framework relies on one example per key case, possibly limiting its coverage of explanation variability. The user study was further limited in the number of scenarios and tasks, which may not reflect the diversity of reasoning strategies. Additionally, the small number of participants restricts the statistical power. For ML-based diagnosis, the employed datasets contain low-resolution grayscale images, which simplifies model outputs and explanation structures.

Future research should explore nuanced issues, as real-world models often fail in subtler ways than those considered in this study. Moreover, further issues, such as non-representative datasets, should be examined to understand how distribution shifts or class imbalance affect explanations. Since Luss et al. [16] introduced an extended CEM for colored images with complex structures, explanation-based issue identification should be adapted across model architectures and application domains. In addition, the ML-based diagnosis could be enhanced through advanced architectures, such as Swin Transformer V2 [14] and hybrid CNN-Swin Transformer frameworks [7]. To refine diagnostic precision, hierarchical classification could be employed to first distinguish broad categories and then refine the diagnosis into data- or model-related subtypes [21]. Furthermore, automated evaluation metrics, such as those from the `Quantus` package [8], could be implemented to assess the quality of explanations across different types of issues.

Acknowledgments. This study was funded by the European Union, the state of Baden-Württemberg, the district of Ostalb, and the city of Aalen as part of the project "KI-Werkstatt Mittelstand". Additional funding was provided by the project "KI-Allianz Baden-Württemberg".

References

1. Bhattacharya, A., Stumpf, S., Gosak, L., Stiglic, G., Verbert, K.: EXMOS: explanatory model steering through multifaceted explanations and data configurations. In: Proceedings of CHI 2024, Art. no. 314 (2024)
2. Clinciu, M.A., Eshghi, A., Hastie, H.: A study of automatic metrics for the evaluation of natural language explanations. In: Proceedings of 16th EACL, pp. 2376–2387 (2021)
3. Cohen, G., Afshar, S., Tapson, J., van Schaik, A.: EMNIST: extending MNIST to handwritten letters. In: Proceedings of IJCNN 2017, pp. 2921–2926 (2017)
4. Dhurandhar, A., et al.: Explanations based on the missing: towards contrastive explanations with pertinent negatives. In: Proceedings of 31st NeurIPS, pp. 1–12 (2018)
5. Djoumessi, K., Mensah, S.O., Berens, P.: A hybrid fully convolutional CNN-Transformer model for inherently interpretable medical image classification. arXiv:2504.08481 (2025)
6. Fiori, M., Civitarese, G., Bettini, C.: Using large language models to compare explainable models for smart home human activity recognition. In: Proceedings of ACM UbiComp 2024, pp. 881–884 (2024)
7. Haidarh, M., Mu, C., Liu, Y.: A hybrid CNN-Swin Transformer module for hyperspectral image classification. In: Proceedings of 12th ISCTech, pp. 1–5 (2024)
8. Hedström, A., et al.: Quantus: an explainable AI toolkit for responsible evaluation of neural network explanations and beyond. J. Mach. Learn. Res. **24**(34), 1–11 (2023)
9. Hu, X., Liu, A., Li, X., Dai, Y., Nakao, M.: Explainable AI for customer segmentation in product development. CIRP Ann. **72**(1), 89–92 (2023)
10. Huang, J., Mishra, A., Kwon, B.C., Bryan, C.: ConceptExplainer: interactive explanation for deep neural networks from a concept perspective. IEEE Trans. Vis. Comput. Graph. **29**(1), 831–841 (2023)
11. Kazmierczak, R., et al.: Benchmarking XAI explanations with human-aligned evaluations. arXiv:2411.02470 (2024)

12. LeCun, Y., et al.: Backpropagation applied to handwritten zip code recognition. Neural Comput. **1**(4), 541–551 (1989)
13. Liu, Z., et al.: Swin Transformer: hierarchical vision transformer using shifted windows. In: Proceedings of IEEE/CVF ICCV 2021, pp. 9992–10002 (2021)
14. Liu, Z., et al.: Swin Transformer V2: scaling up capacity and resolution. In: Proceedings of IEEE/CVF CVPR 2022, pp. 11999–12009 (2022)
15. Liu, Z., Mao, H., Wu, C.Y., Feichtenhofer, C., Darrell, T., Xie, S.: A ConvNet for the 2020s. In: Proceedings of IEEE/CVF CVPR 2022, pp. 11966–11976 (2022)
16. Luss, R., et al.: Leveraging latent features for local explanations. In: Proceedings of 27th ACM SIGKDD, pp. 1139–1149 (2021)
17. Maharana, K., et al.: A review: data overfitting and underfitting techniques. J. Inf. Syst. Eng. Manag. **10**(13s), 387–405 (2025)
18. Ribeiro, M.T., Singh, S., Guestrin, C.: "Why should I trust you?": explaining the predictions of any classifier. In: Proceedings of 22nd ACM SIGKDD, pp. 1135–1144 (2016)
19. Rong, Y., et al.: Towards human-centered explainable AI: a survey of user studies for model explanations. IEEE Trans. Pattern Anal. Mach. Intell. **46**(4), 2104–2122 (2024)
20. Saraswat, D., et al.: Explainable AI for healthcare 5.0: opportunities and challenges. IEEE Access **10**, 84486–84517 (2022)
21. Silla, C.N., Freitas, A.A.: A survey of hierarchical classification across different application domains. Data Min. Knowl. Discov. **22**(1), 31–72 (2011)
22. Spinner, T., Schlegel, U., Schäfer, H., El-Assady, M.: explAIner: a visual analytics framework for interactive and explainable machine learning. IEEE Trans. Vis. Comput. Graph. **26**(1), 1064–1074 (2020)
23. Storås, A.M., et al.: Usefulness of heat map explanations for deep-learning-based electrocardiogram analysis. Diagnostics **13**(14), 2345 (2023)
24. Tan, M., Le, Q.: EfficientNet: rethinking model scaling for convolutional neural networks. In: Proceedings of 36th ICML, vol. 97, pp. 6105–6114 (2019)
25. Tsai, C.H., You, Y., Gui, X., Kou, Y., Carroll, J.M.: Exploring and promoting diagnostic transparency and explainability in online symptom checkers. In: Proceedings of CHI 2021, Art. no. 152 (2021)
26. van der Waa, J., Nieuwburg, E., Cremers, A., Neerincx, M.: Evaluating XAI: a comparison of rule-based and example-based explanations. Artif. Intell. **291**, 103404 (2021)
27. Wang, M.H., et al.: Can explainable artificial intelligence optimize the data quality of machine learning model? Taking meibomian gland dysfunction detections as a case study. J. Phys. Conf. Ser. **2650**(1), 012025 (2023)
28. Xia, X., et al.: Combating noisy labels with sample selection by mining high-discrepancy examples. In: Proceedings of IEEE/CVF ICCV 2023, pp. 1833–1843 (2023)
29. Xiao, H., Rasul, K., Vollgraf, R.: Fashion-MNIST: a novel image dataset for benchmarking machine learning algorithms. arXiv:1708.07747 (2017)
30. Yang, W., Le, H., Laud, T., Savarese, S., Hoi, S.C.H.: OmniXAI: a library for explainable AI. arXiv:2206.01612 (2022)

KL-Guided Concept-Based Learning for Explainable Classification

Rim El Cheikh(✉), Issam Falih, and Engelbert Mephu Nguifo

Université Clermont Auvergne, Clermont Auvergne INP, ENSMSE, CNRS, LIMOS, 63000 Clermont-Ferrand, France
rim.el_cheikh@doctorant.uca.fr,
{issam.falih,engelbert.mephu_nguifo}@uca.fr

Abstract. Concept Bottleneck Models (CBMs) offer an interpretable framework for deep learning by introducing human-understandable concepts as intermediaries between input data and class predictions. However, the unconstrained learning of concept-to-class mappings often results in unfaithful explanations and shortcut reliance. In this work, we present KL-CBM, a novel CBM architecture that integrates a transparent, probabilistic module with a flexible dense classifier. The transparent head estimates class probabilities based on the alignment between predicted concepts and empirical class-specific profiles. Simultaneously, a dense classifier following the concept layer is softly aligned to the transparent head using Kullback–Leibler (KL) divergence. This encourages predictive consistency with interpretable modeling without sacrificing model capacity. We evaluate KL-CBM on two real-world concept-annotated datasets—AwA2 and aPY—and demonstrate that it achieves strong classification performance and competitive concept prediction accuracy. Our results highlight that KL-CBM maintains semantic alignment between concepts and classes, exhibits robustness to concept-level perturbations, and yields faithful concept-based explanations. Overall, KL-CBM advances the trade-off between interpretability and accuracy, offering a principled and flexible alternative to conventional CBMs.

Keywords: Deep learning · Explainable AI · Concept-based Explainability

1 Introduction

Recent advances in deep learning have led to highly effective predictive models across a wide range of domains. However, their inherent complexity renders their decision-making process opaque, limiting usability in applications that require transparency and trust [15]. This has motivated extensive research in explainable AI (XAI), which aims to provide information on the black-box model behavior [5,16,17].

I. Koprinska et al. (Eds.): ECML PKDD 2025, CCIS 2842, pp. 530–544, 2026.
https://doi.org/10.1007/978-3-032-19105-2_37

XAI methods are commonly divided into post-hoc and ad-hoc approaches. Post-hoc methods, which seek to justify predictions after model training, include feature-based techniques, such as saliency maps [19] and SHAP values [12], and example-based techniques, such as prototype learning [13]. While these approaches can offer useful insights by associating outputs to inputs, they do not necessarily align with the internal process of the model, and may fail to guarantee faithful explanations [15]. In contrast, ad-hoc methods aim to integrate interpretability directly into the design of the model [7], making them self-explainable architectures. Concept-based ad-hoc XAI represents a particularly promising strategy, where models predict human-understandable intermediate variables, called concepts, that mediate class predictions [14]. This design allows users to inspect, intervene, and reason directly about the model's internal decision process, with the support of interpretable explanatory elements. A leading example of this paradigm is Concept Bottleneck Models (CBM) [9], a family of neural architectures that decompose prediction into two stages: first, concepts are predicted from inputs; then, classes are predicted from those concepts. This two-stage design supports both interpretability and test-time intervention. However, standard CBMs learn the concept-to-class mapping via backpropagation without enforcing any structural or semantic constraints on how concepts contribute to the final prediction. As a result, even when concept predictions are accurate, the downstream classifier may exploit spurious correlations or latent shortcuts rather than properly reflecting the intended concept-class relationships.

In this work, we propose the KL-Guided Concept Bottleneck Model (KL-CBM), a novel architecture that directly addresses this misalignment. Our method introduces a probabilistic constraint based on Kullback–Leibler (KL) divergence [10] to align class predictions with a transparent, concept-based computation. Inspired by factorized attribute-based classifiers [11], we estimate class probabilities through a transparent model that combines predicted concept scores with empirical concept-class associations. In parallel, we retain a flexible dense classifier head trained end-to-end to optimize class performance. Crucially, we regularize this head by minimizing KL divergence to encourage alignment between its outputs and those of the interpretable, concept-based predictor. This probabilistic constraint serves as a soft guidance mechanism, steering the dense classifier toward predictions that are both accurate and consistent with a structured relationship among inputs, concepts, and classes. We evaluate KL-CBM on two widely used concept-based benchmarks, AwA2 [21] and aPY [4]. Our results show that KL-CBM consistently outperforms both concept-based and black-box baselines in terms of classification accuracy. Despite slightly higher mean squared error on concept predictions, KL-CBM achieves competitive Concept Alignment Scores, indicating that its concept representations remain structurally faithful. Additionally, we find that KL-CBM is robust to small perturbations in concept activations, and supports meaningful, example-based explanations derived from its interpretable transparent module. We also illustrate how KL-CBM supports concept-based explanations through qualitative examples, highlighting the interpretability of its components.

The remainder of the paper is organized as follows: Sect. 2 reviews related work on concept-based classification and explainability. Section 3 introduces KL-CBM, detailing its architecture, training objective, and how it supports interpretability through its design. Section 4 presents the experimental setup, evaluation metrics, and empirical results. Finally, Sects. 5 and 6 present a discussion of the key findings and conclude the paper with a summary of contributions and potential directions for future work.

2 Related Work

Ad-hoc XAI aims to build models whose internal decision-making processes are inherently transparent. A prominent strategy is to embed human-interpretable concepts within the model architecture, enabling users to inspect and reason about intermediate representations. This section reviews foundational and recent work on concept-based modeling for self-explainable systems.

2.1 Attribute-Based Classification and Concept Bottleneck Models

Early approaches to interpretable modeling proposed the use of intermediate, human-understandable variables for attribute-based classification [4,11]. In this framework, models predict a set of predefined attributes (e.g., color, shape, texture) that are subsequently used to infer class labels. A canonical example is Direct Attribute Prediction (DAP) [11], designed for zero-shot learning. DAP assumes access to a complete and fixed attribute-to-class mapping specified by experts. Predictions are obtained by combining predicted attributes, which are the same as what we call concepts in this work, with this mapping using Bayes' rule. While this decoupled formulation enables generalization to unseen classes by relying on their attribute descriptions, it also places a heavy burden on human experts to define accurate and complete mappings for all classes.

Concept Bottleneck Models (CBMs) [9] extend the attribute-based paradigm for fully supervised deep learning. Like DAP, CBMs rely on human-interpretable concepts as intermediate variables, and are typically trained using concept-level annotations provided at the image or class level. However, unlike DAP, CBMs learn the concept-to-class mapping directly from data via backpropagation, without requiring explicit, human-defined mappings. This end-to-end learning strategy grants CBMs greater flexibility and adaptability to the underlying data distribution. Nevertheless, concept-supervised CBMs still rely heavily on the availability and quality of instance-level concept annotations during training, an assumption that may not hold in practice. To address this, recent work has explored unsupervised or weakly supervised approaches for discovering and leveraging latent concepts within the CBM framework [1,20]. A further challenge lies in the lack of constraints on the learned concept-to-class mapping. Without structural or semantic regularization, the model may exploit spurious correlations in concept space or bypass the intended pathways, thus compromising the faithfulness of the explanation.

2.2 Probabilistic and Regularized Extensions of CBMs

To address these limitations, several extensions of CBMs have been proposed in recent years, aiming to improve robustness, interpretability, and the faithfulness of concept-based XAI.

One line of work introduces probabilistic modeling. For example, Probabilistic Concept Bottleneck Models (ProbCBMs) [8] represent each concept as a Gaussian distribution in latent space, allowing the model to capture uncertainty in concept predictions and reason over soft representations. Class predictions are then derived based on distances in this latent space. While this formulation succeeds in bypassing the ambiguity problem in concept learning, it does not explicitly enforce alignment between confident concept predictions and their intended influence on classification outcomes.

In parallel, regularized CBM variants introduce structural constraints to better align concept predictions with class outputs. Concept Whitening (CW) [3] enforces a decorrelated latent space by aligning feature directions with predefined concepts using whitening transformations and orthogonal rotations, leading to more interpretable and disentangled representations, where each feature dimension corresponds to a known concept. Similarly, RECEM [2] extends concept embedding models [22] by introducing concept-level disentanglement and semantic alignment, encouraging consistent embeddings across samples and isolating concept-relevant information from confounding background features. These regularization strategies help preserve the faithfulness of concept-based reasoning by constraining how class decisions depend on concept activations.

3 Proposed Method

We build on recent probabilistic and regularized extensions of CBMs, as well as attribute-based classifiers, by introducing KL-CBM, a concept-based framework that combines a transparent probabilistic module with a flexible dense classifier. To encourage semantic consistency between the two components, we introduce a soft alignment mechanism based on Kullback–Leibler (KL) divergence. This constraint guides the dense classifier to produce accurate predictions while remaining faithful to a structured probabilistic formulation, connected to concept predictions.

3.1 Problem Setup

We assume a dataset of N samples $\{x_1, \ldots, x_N\}$, each labeled with a class $y^{(i)} \in \{1, \ldots, K\}$ and a vector of M concept annotations $a^{(i)} \in \mathbb{R}^M$, where each entry $a_m^{(i)}$ reflects the ground-truth presence or strength of concept m in sample x_i (see Fig. 1, panel A). The goal is to predict the class label by first estimating concept scores from x_i, and then producing class probabilities conditioned on these predicted concepts.

3.2 Probabilistic Formulation

We model class probabilities as a function of predicted concept scores. Inspired by attribute-based classification [11], we express the intervention of concepts in class probabilities as $p(y_k \mid x_i) = \sum_a p(y_k \mid a)\, p(a \mid x_i)$.

By considering that each class y_k is associated with a deterministic concept vector a^k, representing the strength of association of each concept to that class, we model the conditional probability $p(a \mid y_k)$ as a deterministic distribution: $p(a \mid y_k) = \delta(a, a^k)$, where δ is the Kronecker delta function that equals 1 when $a = a^k$, and 0 otherwise. This leads via Bayes rule to $p(y_k \mid a) = \frac{p(y_k)}{p(a^k)}$ when $a = a^k$. Substituting, we obtain $p(y_k \mid x_i) = \frac{p(y_k)}{p(a^k)} \cdot p(a^k \mid x_i)$.

Assuming conditional independence of concepts, that is, given an input x_i, the presence or absence of one concept does not affect the presence or absence of another, we factorize the joint probability as a product of marginal probabilities: $p(a^k \mid x_i) = \prod_{m=1}^{M} p(a_m^k \mid x_i)$ and $p(a^k) = \prod_{m=1}^{M} p(a_m^k)$.

The transparent class probability thus becomes:

$$p(y_k \mid x_i) \propto p(y_k) \prod_{m=1}^{M} \frac{p(a_m^k \mid x_i)}{p(a_m^k)}, \tag{1}$$

where $p(y_k) = \frac{N_k}{N}$, N_k being the number of training samples in class k, and N is the total number of training samples.

3.3 Learning the Concept-Class Associations

In contrast to standard CBM, which implicitly learn the concept-class mapping via backpropagation, the transparent head in KL-CBM explicitly estimates the association between concepts and classes from data. Specifically, the expected activation of each concept a_m for a given class y_k is computed by averaging predicted concept probabilities over all training samples belonging to that class:

$$p(a_m^k) = \frac{1}{N_k} \sum_{x_i \in \text{class } k} p(a_m^k \mid x_i), \tag{2}$$

where N_k is the number of training examples in class k, and $p(a_m^k \mid x_i)$ is the predicted probability for concept m in sample x_i. This yields a class-conditional concept activation matrix $A \in \mathbb{R}^{M \times K}$ that reflects empirical concept prevalence across classes.

3.4 KL-CBM Architecture

The architecture of KL-CBM consists of three main components (see Fig. 1, panels B–C):

(1) Concept Predictor. Each input x_i is processed by a feature extraction backbone. The vector of features is then passed through M independent dense layers with sigmoid activations, yielding predicted concept probabilities $p(a_m^k \mid x_i)$. The layers of the concept predictor are trained using mean squared error (MSE) loss against the ground-truth concept annotations.

(2) Transparent Head. The transparent module computes class probabilities $p(y^k \mid x_i)$ using Eq. 1, based on the predicted concept probabilities, class priors, and the empirically estimated concept-class associations defined in Eq. 2. The transparent module is not designed to act as a final classifier but as a structured, interpretable supervisory signal. By providing a probabilistically grounded mapping from concepts to classes, it guides the dense classifier to learn concept-consistent behavior without rigid constraints.

(3) Dense Classifier. In parallel to the transparent modules, a dense classification head predicts class probabilities $\hat{p}(y^k \mid x_i)$ directly from the predicted concept scores, using a fully connected layer with softmax activations. Unlike the transparent head, which computes class probabilities based on explicitly estimated concept-class associations, the dense classifier learns a flexible, parametric mappings from concepts to classes, in CBM fashion. This allows it to model complex, nonlinear interactions among concepts that may be overlooked by the structured probabilistic formulation. However, the goal is to ensure that these learned connections remain consistent with an interpretable, concept-based distribution. We therefore regularize the dense classifier output during training using a KL divergence loss with respect to the transparent head. This soft alignment mechanism encourages the dense classifier to internalize the structured representation of concepts and their contribution to the final prediction, thus reducing shortcut learning and reinforcing the model's intended path to interpretability. At inference time, the dense classifier serves as the final predictor.

3.5 Training Objective

KL-CBM is trained using a composite loss function that jointly supervises concept predictions via mean squared error (MSE) and aligns the outputs of the transparent and dense classifier heads via KL divergence.

$$\mathcal{L} = \lambda \, \mathrm{MSE}(a, p(a \mid x)) + \mathrm{KL}\left(p(y \mid x), \hat{p}(y \mid x)\right), \tag{3}$$

where:

- a denotes the ground-truth concept scores,
- $p(a \mid x)$ is the vector of predicted concept probabilities,
- $p(y \mid x)$ is the class distribution from the transparent module (Eq. 1),
- $\hat{p}(y \mid x)$ is the class distribution predicted by the dense classifier, and
- λ is a hyperparameter that balances the two losses.

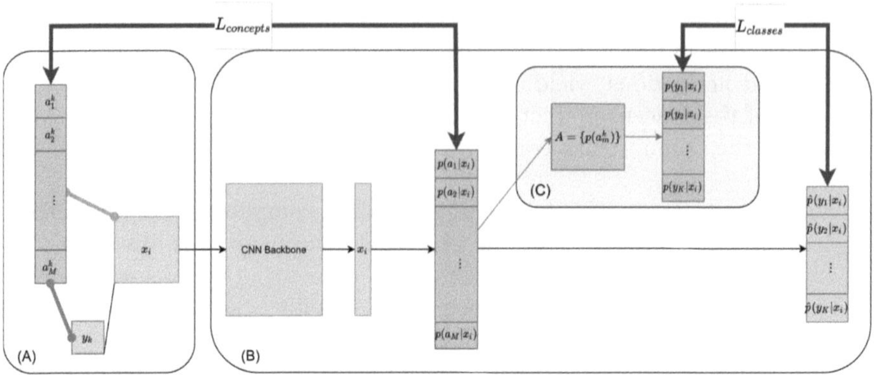

Fig. 1. KL-CBM Architecture. (A) Inputs are annotated with concepts and class labels. (B) A CNN backbone extracts feature representations, followed by a concept score predictor layer, and a final classification layer. (C) A transparent module computes interpretable class probabilities. KL divergence loss ($L_{classes}$) aligns predicted and expected class distributions, while MSE loss ($L_{concepts}$) supervises concept learning.

3.6 Concept-Based Interpretability in KL-CBM

KL-CBM provides interpretability through its use of human-understandable concepts and a transparent probabilistic module. While the final class prediction is made by the dense classifier, interpretive insights can be derived from the predicted concept scores $p(a_m \mid x_i)$ and the components of the transparent head.

Concept Activations. Each predicted concept score quantifies the presence of a specific, human-understandable property in the input. By examining the concept vector $p(a_m \mid x_i)$, users can assess which concepts were detected and with what confidence. These scores provide a foundation for concept-level explanations of the model's decisions.

Concept Contributions. Rather than evaluating alignment with a full class-specific concept profile, the transparent module computes class probabilities using a factorized product over per-concept likelihood ratios (Eq. 1). For each concept m, the ratio $\frac{p(a_m^k|x_i)}{p(a_m^k)}$ modulates the influence of concept m based on both the model's confidence in its presence ($p(a_m \mid x_i)$) and its expected prevalence in class y_k ($p(a_m^k)$). If the model assigns a high score to concept m for input x_i (i.e., $p(a_m^k \mid x_i)$ is large), and that concept is rare across the dataset but typical of class y_k (i.e., $p(a_m^k)$ is small), then the ratio becomes large, contributing positively to $p(y_k \mid x_i)$. Conversely, if concept m is common in class y_k but is not detected in the input (low $p(a_m^k \mid x_i)$), the ratio penalizes the class probability. This mechanism ensures that the transparent module emphasizes concepts that are both confidently present in the input and distinctive for the sample in its respective target class. As such, it offers interpretable, per-concept contributions to the prediction, which can be used to construct semantically grounded explanations.

Section 4.3 provides an analysis of these interpretability mechanisms, demonstrating how KL-CBM enables semantically grounded, concept-level explanations through its different components.

4 Experiments

4.1 Evaluation Setup

We evaluate KL-CBM through two complementary perspectives. First, we conduct quantitative experiments to assess predictive performance, components alignment, and robustness. Then, we present qualitative examples illustrating the model's interpretability via concept-based explanations derived from the model.

Datasets. Two concept-labeled image classification datasets are used for evaluations. **AwA2**[1]: The Animals with Attributes 2 dataset [21] contains 37,322 images from 50 animal classes, annotated with 85 continuous attributes in $[0, 1]$. We use these class-level annotations to infer sample-wise concept scores to supervise the concept layer, by assigning each image the attribute vector of its class. **aPY**[2]: The aPascal-aYahoo dataset [4] contains 14350 images across 32 object categories, with 64 binary attributes annotating each image.

Baselines. We compare KL-CBM against the following baselines: (i) **Standard black-box classifier (CNN)**: A fully supervised neural network trained directly on input features without concept supervision; (ii) **Concept Bottleneck Model (CBM)** [9]: A two-stage model predicting concepts followed by classes via a jointly learned dense head. CBM can also be viewed as an ablation of KL-CBM where the KL-divergence alignment loss is replaced by standard cross-entropy loss applied directly to the class labels, without explicit alignment to the transparent head; (iii) **Probabilistic Concept Bottleneck Model (ProbCBM)** [8]: An extension of CBM incorporating probabilistic embeddings to handle uncertainty in concept supervision.

Other related methods such as Concept Whitening (CW) [3] and RECEM [2] rely on unsupervised concept learning, operate under different assumptions or lack public implementations. We leave their integration and comparison to a future extended work.

[1] https://cvml.ista.ac.at/AwA2/.
[2] https://vision.cs.uiuc.edu/attributes/.

Table 1. Average top-1 classification accuracy (mean ± standard deviation) (↑).

Model	aPY	AwA2
CNN (black-box)	0.818 ± 0.089	0.508 ± 0.214
CBM [9]	0.876 ± 0.055	0.463 ± 0.217
ProbCBM [8]	0.840 ± 0.006	0.862 ± 0.005
KL-CBM (ours)	**0.931** ± 0.047	**0.939** ± 0.043

Setup and Implementation Details. All models are trained jointly to predict concepts and class labels using a combination of concept loss and classification loss. We use a batch size of 64 and hold out 10% of the training data as a validation set in all experiments. For KL-CBM and CBM, we set the concept loss weight $\lambda = 5$ and optimize using Adam with a learning rate of 10^{-4}. For ProbCBM, we follow [8] and use the AdamP optimizer [6] with a learning rate of 10^{-2} and $\lambda = 1$ for the training objective. Since all the datasets used in our experiments are real-world datasets, we adopt the recommended configuration from [8] and set the concept and class embedding dimensions in ProbCBM to 16 and 128, respectively. All models share the same MobileNetV2 [18] backbone for feature extraction to ensure comparable feature capacity across methods. Full implementation details and code are available at https://github.com/rimelcheikh/KLCBM.git.

4.2 Quantitative Evaluations

We quantitatively evaluate KL-CBM using a series of metric-based experiments designed to assess predictive performance, internal consistency, and robustness. First, we examine classification accuracy and the quality of concept predictions using standard top-1 accuracy and mean squared error (MSE). We then analyze the alignment between the transparent and dense classifier heads by comparing their class probability distributions and top-k class ranking overlap. To assess the model's stability, we investigate its robustness to perturbations in highly activated concept scores. Finally, we compute a concept alignment score (CAS) [22] to quantify the faithfulness of concept representations with respect to their ground-truth.

Classification Accuracy and Concept Prediction. We evaluate KL-CBM on AwA2 and aPY by reporting top-1 classification accuracy and concept prediction quality, measured using Mean Squared Error (MSE) to reflect the fact that concept predictions are modeled as continuous probabilities in the range $[0, 1]$, and to avoid the arbitrary thresholding for concept binarization. All results are averaged over five cross-validation folds to ensure statistical robustness.

Tables 1 and 2 report classification accuracy and concept MSE, respectively, comparing KL-CBM to ProbCBM, CBM and a standard black-box CNN baseline. The CNN does not predict concepts and is excluded from concept evaluation.

Table 2. Average concept prediction mean squared error (mean ± standard deviation) (↓).

Model	aPY	AwA2
CBM [9]	0.067 ± 0.034	0.353 ± 0.389
ProbCBM [8]	**0.045** ± 0.000	**0.014** ± 0.000
KL-CBM (ours)	0.144 ± 0.027	0.145 ± 0.011

KL-CBM outperforms all baselines in terms of classification accuracy on both aPY and AwA2, achieving over 93% top-1 accuracy on both datasets. This indicates that the proposed KL-based alignment improves predictive performance beyond both standard CBM and the probabilistic variant ProbCBM. Notably, KL-CBM surpasses the fully supervised black-box CNN baseline, demonstrating that concept-based supervision, when properly aligned, can also enhance accuracy.

In terms of concept prediction, KL-CBM does not reach the lowest MSE, with both CBM and ProbCBM achieving better scores, especially on AwA2, where ProbCBM attains exceptionally low error. This suggests that KL-CBM trades some precision in individual concept predictions for improved classification performance and global structural alignment. While its concept scores are noisier, they are still sufficient to support a transparent module that meaningfully regularizes the classifier.

Transparent and Dense Heads Alignment. To assess how closely the transparent and dense heads of KL-CBM align in their predictions, we compare their class probability distributions and top-k rankings across the test set. Specifically, we compute: (i) the average KL divergence $\mathrm{KL}(p_{\text{transp}} \| p_{\text{dense}})$ between the output distributions of the transparent and dense heads; and (ii) the top-5 agreement, indicating the overlap between the top-5 scoring classes from both heads. These metrics reflect the degree to which the dense classifier follows the structured, interpretable reasoning path imposed by the transparent module during training.

The results in Table 3 indicate that, on aPY and AwA2, the dense classifier successfully internalizes the structured decision-making patterns imposed by the transparent head. The low KL divergence values suggest that the two heads produce closely matching class distributions, while the high top-5 agreement confirms that the dense head tends to preserve the class preferences encoded by the transparent module. This supports the idea that KL regularization encourages semantic consistency without compromising the expressiveness of the dense classifier.

Robustness to Concept Perturbations. To assess the robustness of KL-CBM's classification heads to uncertainty in concept space, we evaluate the impact of perturbing top-scoring concepts on the model's output probabilities.

For each test sample x_i, we identify the top-k most influential concepts with respect to the dense head which correspond to concepts with the highest acti-

Table 3. Alignment between transparent and dense heads in KL-CBM across datasets. Lower KL and higher agreement indicate stronger alignment.

Metric	aPY	AwA2
KL divergence (↓)	0.682 ± 0.095	0.687 ± 0.091
Top-5 agreement (↑)	0.986 ± 0.011	0.992 ± 0.008

Table 4. Average change in predicted class probability (Δ) after adding Gaussian noise to top-k concepts ($\sigma = 0.3$). Lower is better. The standard deviation of Δ across test samples is negligible (under 0.001 for all cases)

	aPY		AwA2	
Head	Transparent	Dense	Transparent	Dense
Δ	0.047	0.027	0.419	0.001

vations in the concept layer. We then inject Gaussian noise into the predicted concept scores $p(a_m \mid x_i)$ for these k concepts. Specifically, we sample noise $\epsilon \sim \mathcal{N}(0, \sigma^2)$ where $\sigma = 0.3$, and update concept scores with these values. This simulates partial corruption or uncertainty in highly influential concepts. Other concept scores remain unchanged.

For both the transparent module and dense classifier, we compute the absolute change in predicted class probability before and after perturbation:

$$\Delta = \frac{1}{N} \sum_{i=1}^{N} \left| \hat{p}(y_i \mid x_i^{\text{perturbed}}) - \hat{p}(y_i \mid x_i) \right| .$$

Let Δ_{transp} and Δ_{dense} denote changes for the transparent and dense heads, respectively.

The results in Table 4 confirm that KL-CBM's dense head exhibits strong classification stability even when high-importance concept activations are subjected to small, localized perturbations, whereas the transparent module is highly sensitive due to its strictly factorized structure. This suggests that the dense classifier learns to compensate for small perturbations, contributing to robustness.

Concept Alignment Score. To further assess the faithfulness of concept representations, we compute the Concept Alignment Score (CAS) [22], which measures how well predicted concept scores align with their ground-truth labels. Unlike concept accuracy or MSE, which evaluates correctness on a per-sample basis, CAS captures the structural coherence of concept representations by evaluating whether samples with similar predicted concept values also share the same ground-truth concept.

Formally, for each concept, CAS applies a clustering algorithm (e.g., k-Medoids) on the predicted representations to group test samples into clusters. Each sample receives a cluster label. Then, for each concept, a homogeneity score is computed, to reflect how well the ground-truth concept labels align with the

Table 5. Concept Alignment Score (CAS) averaged over all concepts. Higher is better (↑).

Model	aPY	AwA2
CBM [9]	**0.665** ± 0.027	0.596 ± 0.024
ProbCBM [8]	0.527 ± 0.003	0.590 ± 0.003
KL-CBM (ours)	0.576 ± 0.014	**0.622** ± 0.006

predicted clusters. The final CAS is computed by averaging homogeneity scores over all concepts and a range of values for number of clusters, resulting in a single score in $[0, 1]$. Higher CAS values indicate that the learned representations are semantically meaningful and structurally faithful.

As shown in Table 5, KL-CBM achieves the highest CAS score among all methods on AwA2, indicating that its predicted concept embeddings form clusters that align well with ground-truth labels, suggesting that the model captures concept semantics in a way that is coherent and consistent across samples. On aPY, KL-CBM performs competitively, though CBM outperforms it. This may reflect CBM's simpler inductive bias, which can sometimes favor more rigid, high-alignment clusters in lower-complexity settings.

4.3 Qualitative Explanations with Concepts

Beyond quantitative evaluations, we validate the explainability aspect of KL-CBM by presenting examples of concept-supported explanations that are enabled by its interpretable architecture.

Concept Activations as Explanations. KL-CBM produces inherently interpretable predictions by linking class decisions to concept scores, which enables inspection of concept-level evidence underlying these predictions. Figure 2 illustrates examples from the AwA2 test set. Each image is annotated with the top-5 predicted concepts contributing to the final class decision. For example, an image classified as *skunk* shows high activation for concepts such as *stripes*, *tail*, and *furry*, which are semantically consistent with the human understanding of the category in question.

Extracting Concept Explanations from Transparent Head. Although final class predictions are produced by the dense head, we could extract concept-based explanations from the transparent head due to its structured and interpretable formulation. This is especially valuable because, during training, the dense head is softly aligned to the transparent head via KL divergence. As a result, even if the dense head performs classification at test time, its outputs are shaped by the transparent head's interpretable structure. The log-contributions therefore serve as a proxy for understanding the conceptual reasoning path that indirectly guides the final prediction.

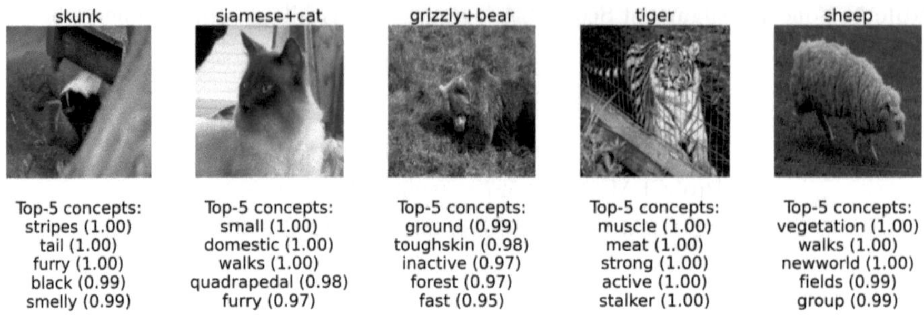

Fig. 2. Example test images from the AwA2 dataset with top-5 predicted concepts and their activation scores. These concepts directly contribute to class predictions by KL-CBM.

Given a test input x_i and its predicted concept scores $p(a_m^k \mid x_i)$, we compute the contribution of each concept m to class y_k as:

$$\mathrm{S}_m^k(x_i) = \log\left(\frac{p(a_m^k \mid x_i)}{p(a_m^k)}\right)$$

The overall log-probability for class y_k is:

$$\log p(y_k \mid x_i) = \log p(y_k) + \sum_{m=1}^{M} \mathrm{S}_m^k(x_i)$$

We interpret $\mathrm{S}_m^k(x_i)$ as the contribution or influence of concept m on the class score for y_k. Positive values of $\mathrm{S}_m^k(x_i)$ indicate that the presence of concept m increases the model's confidence in class y_k, while negative values suggest a suppressive effect. To explain a predicted class, we identify the concepts with the highest positive contributions $\mathrm{S}_m^k(x_i)$, and report the top-5 among them. This yields a concise set of concepts that most strongly support the classification decision from the perspective of the transparent module, as shown in Table 6.

5 Discussion

We introduced KL-CBM, a concept-based model that balances interpretability and performance via probabilistic alignment. The model augments the CBM framework with a transparent module that estimates class probabilities from structured conceptclass associations, and regularizes a dense classifier with KL divergence to stay consistent with this interpretable distribution.

Because the transparent head assumes conditional independence across concepts, it serves as a training-time teacher rather than the inference-time predictor; the dense head produces the final outputs. This design prioritizes class-consistent structure over exact per-concept reconstruction.

Table 6. Top-5 most influential concepts per class on aPY categories, based on average (over 5 runs) log-contributions from the transparent head.

Class	Top-5 Concepts (highest $\bar{S}_m^k$)
`bicycle`	Metal, Label, Wheel, Handlebars, Plastic
`goat`	Ear, Furry, Eye, Head, Horn
`car`	Metal, 3D Boxy, Door, Headlight, Window
`bottle`	Label, Glass, Clear, Vert Cyl, Occluded
`aeroplane`	Metal, Wing, 3D Boxy, Window, Horiz Cyl

On aPY and AwA2, KL-CBM consistently outperforms standard CBMs and ProbCBM in classification accuracy while retaining meaningful concept behavior. Despite a higher concept MSE than some baselines, the model attains competitive Concept Alignment Scores (CAS), low divergence, and high top-k agreement between the dense and transparent heads. It also shows robustness under small perturbations to high-importance concepts, and qualitative examples illustrate how the concept layer and transparent head yield compact, interpretable rationales that support the predictions.

6 Conclusion

KL-CBM offers a principled trade-off between interpretability and predictive performance. By introducing a transparent concept-based module and aligning a dense classifier to it via KL divergence, the model encourages structured, semantically meaningful predictions, without rigidly enforcing a constrained decision path. In future work, we aim to extend KL-CBM to incorporate more expressive probabilistic modules that relax the current independence assumptions, while maintaining interpretable properties. We also plan to deepen the analysis of the model's explainability—both quantitatively and qualitatively—and to conduct broader empirical comparisons with more recent CBM variants and more varied datasets.

Acknowledgments. This work benefited from a French government grant managed by the National Research Agency (ANR) under the "Investissements d'Avenir" program (PIA) with the following reference: ANR-20-SFRI-0003.

Disclosure of Interests. The authors have no competing interests to declare that are relevant to the content of this article.

References

1. Alvarez Melis, D., Jaakkola, T.: Towards robust interpretability with self-explaining neural networks. In: Advances in NeurIPS, vol. 31 (2018)

2. Cai, Y., Wang, X., Tsutsui, S., Pang, W., Wen, B.: Towards robust and reliable concept representations: reliability-enhanced concept embedding model. arXiv preprint arXiv:2502.01191 (2025)
3. Chen, Z., Bei, Y., Rudin, C.: Concept whitening for interpretable image recognition. Nat. Mach. Intell. **2**(12), 772–782 (2020)
4. Farhadi, A., et al.: Describing objects by their attributes. In: IEEE Conference on CVPR, pp. 1778–1785 (2009)
5. Guidotti, R., Monreale, A., Ruggieri, S., Turini, F., Giannotti, F., Pedreschi, D.: A survey of methods for explaining black box models. ACM Comput. Surv. (CSUR) **51**(5), 1–42 (2018)
6. Heo, B., et al.: Adamp: slowing down the slowdown for momentum optimizers on scale-invariant weights. In: International Conference on Learning Representations (ICLR) (2021)
7. Ji, Y., et al.: A comprehensive survey on self-interpretable neural networks. arXiv preprint arXiv:2501.15638 (2025)
8. Kim, E., et al.: Probabilistic concept bottleneck models. arXiv preprint arXiv:2306.01574 (2023)
9. Koh, P.W., et al.: Concept bottleneck models. In: ICML, pp. 5338–5348. PMLR (2020)
10. Kullback, S., Leibler, R.A.: On information and sufficiency. Ann. Math. Stat. **22**(1), 79–86 (1951)
11. Lampert, C.H., et al.: Attribute-based classification for zero-shot visual object categorization. IEEE Trans. PAMI **36**(3), 453–465 (2013)
12. Lundberg, S.M., Lee, S.I.: A unified approach to interpreting model predictions. In: Advances in NeurIPS, vol. 30 (2017)
13. Nauta, M., et al.: This looks like that, because... explaining prototypes for interpretable image recognition. In: ECML PKDD, pp. 441–456. Springer (2021)
14. Poeta, E., et al.: Concept-based explainable artificial intelligence: a survey. arXiv preprint arXiv:2312.12936 (2023)
15. Rudin, C.: Stop explaining black box machine learning models for high stakes decisions and use interpretable models instead. Nat. Mach. Intell. **1**(5), 206–215 (2019)
16. Saeed, W., Omlin, C.: Explainable AI (XAI): a systematic meta-survey of current challenges and future opportunities. Knowl.-Based Syst. **263**, 110273 (2023)
17. Samek, W., Montavon, G., Vedaldi, A., Hansen, L.K., Müller, K.R.: Explainable AI: interpreting, explaining and visualizing deep learning, vol. 11700. Springer (2019)
18. Sandler, M., Howard, A., Zhu, M., Zhmoginov, A., Chen, L.C.: Mobilenetv2: inverted residuals and linear bottlenecks. In: Proceedings of the IEEE Conference on Computer Vision and Pattern Recognition, pp. 4510–4520 (2018)
19. Simonyan, K., et al.: Deep inside convolutional networks: visualising image classification models and saliency maps. arXiv preprint arXiv:1312.6034 (2013)
20. Wickramanayake, S., Hsu, W., Lee, M.L.: Comprehensible convolutional neural networks via guided concept learning. In: 2021 International Joint Conference on Neural Networks (IJCNN), pp. 1–8. IEEE (2021)
21. Xian, Y., Lampert, C.H., Schiele, B., Akata, Z.: Zero-shot learning–a comprehensive evaluation of the good, the bad and the ugly. IEEE Trans. Pattern Anal. Mach. Intell. **41**(9), 2251–2265 (2018)
22. Zarlenga, E., et al.: Concept embedding models: beyond the accuracy-explainability trade-off. In: Advances in NeurIPS, vol. 35, pp. 21400–21413 (2022)

Generative Example-Based Explanations: Bridging the Gap Between Generative Modeling and Explainability

Philipp Vaeth[1,2(✉)], Alexander M. Fruehwald[1], Benjamin Paassen[2], and Magda Gregorová[1]

[1] Center for Artificial Intelligence and Robotics, Technical University of Applied Sciences Würzburg-Schweinfurt, Franz-Horn-Strasse 2, Würzburg, Germany
{philipp.vaeth,magda.gregorova}@thws.de

[2] Bielefeld University, Universitätsstrasse 25, Bielefeld, Germany
bpaassen@techfak.uni-bielefeld.de

Abstract. Recently, several methods have leveraged deep generative modeling to produce example-based explanations of image classifiers. Despite producing visually stunning results, these methods are largely disconnected from classical explainability literature. This conceptual and communication gap leads to misunderstandings and misalignments in goals and expectations. In this paper, we bridge this gap by proposing a probabilistic framework for example-based explanations, formally defining the example-based explanations in a probabilistic manner amenable for modelling via deep generative models while coherent with the critical characteristics and desiderata widely accepted in the explainability community. Our aim is on one hand to provide a constructive framework for the development of well-grounded generative algorithms for example-based explanations and, on the other, to facilitate communication between the generative and explainability research communities, foster rigor and transparency, and improve the quality of peer discussion and research progress in this promising direction.

Keywords: XAI · Example-based Explanations · Counterfactual Explanations · Generative Modeling · Diffusion Models · DDPM

1 Introduction

As more AI applications get introduced into our daily lives, the need for trust, safety and ethical use of AI in these automated decision systems increases [3,8]. Explainable Artificial Intelligence (XAI) is a research field that addresses these concerns of trust, transparency and fairness by supplementing decisions with explanations [10].

Reproducibility: The code, the trained model weights, and the supplementary material to reproduce the results are available at https://github.com/cairo-thws/XAIDIFF.

I. Koprinska et al. (Eds.): ECML PKDD 2025, CCIS 2842, pp. 545–560, 2026.
https://doi.org/10.1007/978-3-032-19105-2_38

A well-known approach focusing on explanations of an algorithm decision for a specific input data point is that of counterfactual explanations [27]. These are examples that change some of the input features of the original data point in order to flip the decision of the algorithm to the desired class. Unlike conceptually similar adversarial examples [7], the changes in the counterfactual examples aim to be perceptible and understandable by a human observer. A classical example of a counterfactual from [28]: *"You were denied a loan because your annual income was £30,000. If your income had been £45,000, you would have been offered a loan."*

Though well-developed for tabular data [23], transferring this concept to high-dimensional data such as images is not straightforward. Without careful control, introducing changes in the original pixel space may distort the image, rendering it unrealistic and hence difficult to interpret by the user. These considerations have lead to the development of new techniques for producing counterfactual examples based on modern deep generative modeling [2,9,15].

While these often showcase examples of stunning visual quality, the value of these methods is greatly diminished by their disconnect to the classical explainability desiderata and lack of rigorous, transparent and comparable quantitative evaluation.

Motivated by this lack of systematic grounding of counterfactual methods based on deep generative modelling, **we propose a probabilistic framework for example-based explanations** formally defining counterfactual examples and their properties in a probabilistic manner amenable for modeling via deep generative models. This framework shall help in bridging the fields of generative modeling and explainability by aligning the terminology, the expectations, and by enabling a comparative quantitative evaluation of the methods fostering further scientific advancements.

In the following, we first introduce the proposed probabilistic framework in Sect. 2. We define the counterfactual examples, contrast them to adversarial examples and introduce a new complementary concept of affirmative examples in Sect. 2.1. Based on the introduced definitions, in Sect. 2.2 we formulate the search for counterfactual examples as a generative explainer problem, an optimization problem that serves as an objective for the deep generative approaches for counterfactuals. Finally, in Sect. 2.3 we outline an evaluation procedure using the above definitions and propose concrete metrics usable in practice.

To illustrate the applicability of the newly proposed framework for developing and evaluating new algorithms in practice, we describe in Sect. 3 an algorithm for counterfactual generations based on the classifier guidance [5] of denoising diffusion probabilistic models [13]. In addition to being well-grounded within the proposed probabilistic framework, the algorithm also addresses some shortcomings of previously proposed approaches for diffusion-based counterfactuals [2,15]. Through experiments in Sect. 4 we verify that our proposed framework and the generative explainer problem can indeed serve as a set of guiding principles in developing new generative algorithms for counterfactuals and that the evaluation procedure provides quantitative results that help in assessing the quality

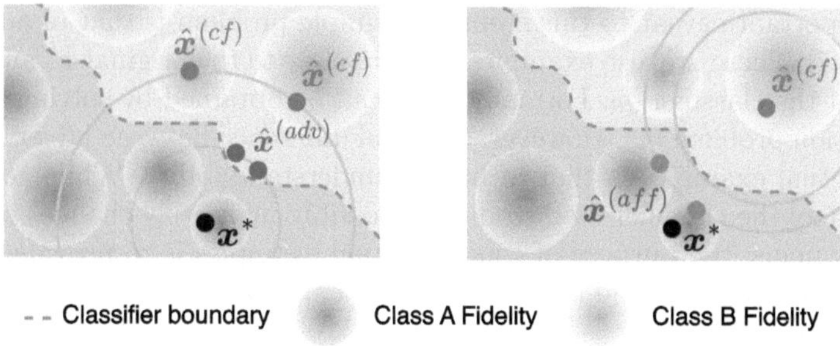

Fig. 1. Relationships between example-based explanations. *Left:* Original example $\boldsymbol{x}^*$ classified as A has high-fidelity - is in the high-density (dark) area of the data distribution. Adversarial examples $\hat{\boldsymbol{x}}^{(adv)}$ are low-fidelity - in the low-density (light) area - near the original but classified as B. Counterfactuals $\hat{\boldsymbol{x}}^{(cf)}$ are also classified as B, but they are high-fidelity (high density area). They are close to the original sample but may be further away than the adversarial examples. *Right:* Affirmatives are high-fidelity samples classified as A near the counterfactuals. In consequence, they come from high-density areas within A which may or may not be close to $\boldsymbol{x}^*$.

of the algorithm and produced counterfactual examples. Here we also put forward and release a new synthetic SportBalls dataset (Sect. 4.2) for a controlled explanation environment with varying complexity and intuitively unambiguous explanations. We conclude our paper in Sect. 5 reflecting on some limitations of our framework and counterfactual explanations in general.

2 Example-Based Explanations

Example-based explanations are well established in the local explainability domain, with counterfactual explanations as the most prominent type [1,4]. The purpose of these is to help the user understand the decisions of an algorithm for a specific data example (local explanation). By applying a minimal change to the original example which changes the algorithmic decision, the user shall understand which crucial changes separate the original example from the other class according to the classifier.

The foundational counterfactual explanation system was proposed in [28]. For an original data point $\boldsymbol{x}^*$ labeled by a classification algorithm f_θ as y_o ('o' - original), a counterfactual explanation is a point $\hat{\boldsymbol{x}}$ close to $\boldsymbol{x}^*$ with some of the input features altered so that it is labeled by f_θ as y_τ ('τ' - target). According to [28], the counterfactual $\hat{\boldsymbol{x}}$ can be found by any suitable optimizer through solving the following minimization problem:

$$\min_{\hat{\boldsymbol{x}}} \lambda \left(f_\theta(\hat{\boldsymbol{x}}) - y_\tau\right)^2 + d\left(\boldsymbol{x}^*, \hat{\boldsymbol{x}}\right) \quad , \tag{1}$$

with λ a hyperparameter trading off the label accuracy with a problem-specific distance d between the original and the counterfactual example.

An important caveat to this seemingly simple problem is that of adversarial examples [7]. These are also examples that are close to the original $\boldsymbol{x}^*$ and flip the decision of the classifier f_θ. Formally, they can be obtained by solving the same minimization problem (1). However, a crucial difference between adversarial and counterfactual examples is that of human understandability. While adversarial examples fool the classifier by introducing possibly many tiny changes imperceptible by humans, the purpose of counterfactual examples is to provide a human with an understandable and hence perceptible explanation through sparse meaningful changes.

As [28] notes, the critical difference is whether the example comes from a *"possible world"*. The imperceptible changes introduced by adversarial attacks can push the examples out of the data distribution which causes the classifier trained on-distribution to be easily fooled and make incorrect decisions. In contrast, what brings explanatory value to the counterfactual examples is that these are realistic in-distribution examples with changes observable and interpretable by a human observer.

Recognizing this challenge, the authors of [28] decide to focus on simpler tabular datasets with directly interpretable input features and defer the problem to future research stating: *"Further research into how data from high-dimensional and highly-structured spaces, such as natural images, can be characterised is needed before counterfactuals can be reliably used as explanations in these spaces."*

Recently emerging algorithms for counterfactual examples in high-dimensional image spaces based on deep generative modeling [2,9,15] are, despite their ability to produce visually stunning examples, largely ad-hoc and lack the connection to the initial and generally accepted counterfactual framework as put forward by [28]. Together with the lack of systematic and comparable evaluation of the methods, this leads to low trust in the methods from the XAI expert community partly aggravated by possible misunderstandings due to misaligned field-specific terminology.

This is where our paper comes in. We propose a **probabilistic framework for example-based explanations** (Sect. 2.1) that formally defines counterfactual, adversarial and newly introduced affirmative examples and their properties in a probabilistic manner. This framework aligns with both the initial counterfactual explanation concepts as outlined in [28] and the probabilistic nature of deep generative model formulations. As such it allows for integrating deep generative models into the process of searching for counterfactual examples through the optimization problem (1) by a slight modification into a generative explainer problem defined in Sect. 2.2. It also enables systematic quantitative evaluation of the counterfactual algorithms and the generated examples (Sect. 2.3), fostering trust through transparency and comparability.

2.1 Probabilistic Framework for Example-Based Explanations

In view of the above discussion on the critical differences between counterfactual and adversarial examples and in line with the intuitive argumentation that an example is useful as an explanation only if it comes from a "possible world", we propose to use the **fidelity** of an example to the underlying data distribution as one of the central concepts of our probabilistic framework. We opt to use fidelity as opposed to previously introduced and broader terms plausibility [16] or realism to capture the specific property of the example to be in-distribution as measured by the data likelihood.

The other two concepts used in the proposed framework originate directly from the counterfactual definitions as introduced in [28] and Eq. (1). The first is that of **closeness** measured by the distance d between the original $\boldsymbol{x}^*$ and generated example $\hat{\boldsymbol{x}}$, the second is the **validity** reflecting the correctness of the decision of the classification algorithm with respect to the target class.

Let $\boldsymbol{x}^* \in \mathcal{X}$ be a random sample from the true underlying generating data distribution p_{data} with the original classifier label $y_o \in \mathcal{Y}$; $\hat{\boldsymbol{x}} \in \mathcal{X}$ a synthetically generated sample; $y_\tau \in \mathcal{Y}$ the target class label; $d : \mathcal{X} \times \mathcal{X} \to \mathbb{R}_+$ a suitable user-specified distance function (such as ℓ_1, ℓ_2 or some suitable perception distance). We define the following concepts with respect to the probabilistic classification algorithm p_{cl} and the original example $\boldsymbol{x}^*$:

Definition 1 (Counterfactual explanation). *We call a synthetic data sample $\hat{\boldsymbol{x}}$ with **all** the following characteristics a targeted counterfactual explanation with respect to some target $y_\tau \in \mathcal{Y}$ and some thresholds δ, $\epsilon > 0$:*

1. *$\hat{\boldsymbol{x}}$ is **close** to the original sample $\boldsymbol{x}^*$: $d(\hat{\boldsymbol{x}}, \boldsymbol{x}^*) \leq \delta$;*
2. *$\hat{\boldsymbol{x}}$ is **valid** w.r.t. the target label classification area:*
   $p_{\text{cl}}(\boldsymbol{Y} = y_\tau \mid \boldsymbol{X} = \hat{\boldsymbol{x}}) > p_{\text{cl}}(\boldsymbol{Y} = y_j \mid \boldsymbol{X} = \hat{\boldsymbol{x}})$, *for all* $j \neq \tau$;
3. *$\hat{\boldsymbol{x}}$ has **high fidelity** to the real data distribution (is a realistic data example):*
   $p_{\text{data}}(\boldsymbol{X} = \hat{\boldsymbol{x}}) \geq \epsilon$.

Definition 2 (Adversarial example). *We call a synthetic data sample $\hat{\boldsymbol{x}}$ with **all** the following characteristics a targeted adversarial example with respect to some target $y_\tau \in \mathcal{Y}$ and some thresholds δ, $\epsilon > 0$:*

1. *$\hat{\boldsymbol{x}}$ is **close** to the original sample $\boldsymbol{x}^*$: $d(\hat{\boldsymbol{x}}, \boldsymbol{x}^*) \leq \delta$;*
2. *$\hat{\boldsymbol{x}}$ is **valid** w.r.t. the target label classification area:*
   $p_{\text{cl}}(\boldsymbol{Y} = y_\tau \mid \boldsymbol{X} = \hat{\boldsymbol{x}}) > p_{\text{cl}}(\boldsymbol{Y} = y_j \mid \boldsymbol{X} = \hat{\boldsymbol{x}})$, *for all* $j \neq \tau$;
3. *$\hat{\boldsymbol{x}}$ has **low fidelity** to the real data distribution (is not a realistic data example):* $p_{\text{data}}(\boldsymbol{X} = \hat{\boldsymbol{x}}) \leq \epsilon$.

We point out that the only difference in the definitions of adversarial and counterfactual examples is the fidelity criterion which shall be high for counterfactuals and low for adversarial examples.

Furthermore, we propose a new type of example-based explanations we call **affirmative examples**. Conceptually, these can be thought of as counterfactual examples to counterfactuals, see the right part of Fig. 1. Affirmatives are high-fidelity examples which re-introduce into the counterfactuals the critical features to bring them back to the original class. They shall thus re-affirm the user understanding of the effects the feature changes have on the algorithm decisions.

A somewhat related yet different approach to local explainability which shall not be confused with our affirmatives are the contrastive explanations [6], which highlight features in the original example that need to be present or absent for the classifier to maintain its decision. In contrast, affirmatives are new examples different from $\boldsymbol{x}^*$ that alter the counterfactual examples to bring them back to the same class as the original.

Definition 3 (Affirmative examples). *We call a synthetic data sample $\hat{\boldsymbol{x}}$ with **all** the following characteristics an affirmative of a counterfactual $\hat{\boldsymbol{x}}^{(cf)}$ with some thresholds δ, $\epsilon > 0$:*

1. *$\hat{\boldsymbol{x}}$ is **close** to the counterfactual explanation $\hat{\boldsymbol{x}}^{(cf)}$: $d(\hat{\boldsymbol{x}}, \hat{\boldsymbol{x}}^{(cf)}) \leq \delta$;*
2. *$\hat{\boldsymbol{x}}$ is **valid** w.r.t. the original label y_o classification area: $p_{\text{cl}}(\boldsymbol{Y} = y_o \mid \boldsymbol{X} = \hat{\boldsymbol{x}}) > p_{\text{cl}}(\boldsymbol{Y} = y_j \mid \boldsymbol{X} = \hat{\boldsymbol{x}})$, for all $j \neq o$;*
3. *$\hat{\boldsymbol{x}}$ has **high fidelity** to the real data distribution (is a realistic data example): $p_{\text{data}}(\boldsymbol{X} = \hat{\boldsymbol{x}}) \geq \epsilon$.*

It is important to note that all the above concepts are local (i.e., pertaining to the specific original sample $\boldsymbol{x}^*$) and classifier-specific. Furthermore, we can bring the above definitions into a fully probabilistic setting by reformulating the closeness constraints in the form of a prior distribution $p(\hat{\boldsymbol{x}}|\boldsymbol{x}^*)$ on the data sample $\hat{\boldsymbol{x}}$ (e.g., Gaussian for the ℓ_2 or Laplace for the ℓ_1 distances).

2.2 Generative Explainer Problem

Following the definitions in Sect. 2.1, we formulate the search for example-based explanations as an optimization problem. We give it here for the case of counterfactual examples; affirmatives and adversarial examples follow trivially in analogy.

$$\begin{aligned} \arg\max_{\hat{\boldsymbol{x}}} \;& p_{\text{cl}}(\boldsymbol{Y} = y_T \mid \boldsymbol{X} = \hat{\boldsymbol{x}}) && \text{(validity)} \\ \text{s.t.} \;& p_{\text{data}}(\boldsymbol{X} = \hat{\boldsymbol{x}}) \geq \epsilon, && \text{(fidelity)} \\ & d(\hat{\boldsymbol{x}}, \boldsymbol{x}^*) \leq \delta && \text{(closeness)} \end{aligned}$$

In practice, we typically have no access to the true underlying data distribution p_{data} other than through the observed data and therefore cannot evaluate the fidelity of the point $\hat{\boldsymbol{x}}$. We propose to replace the unknown true distribution by an approximation $p_\theta \approx p_{\text{data}}$ learned by a suitable generative algorithm, enabling us to sample high fidelity examples $\hat{\boldsymbol{x}} \sim p_\theta$. Our final formulation of the **generative explainer problem** reformulates the optimization into a Lagrangian form and subsumes the fidelity constraint into the sampling procedure:

$$\arg\max_{\hat{\boldsymbol{x}} \sim p_\theta} \lambda\, p_{\text{cl}}(\boldsymbol{Y} = y_T \mid \boldsymbol{X} = \hat{\boldsymbol{x}}) - d(\hat{\boldsymbol{x}}, \boldsymbol{x}^*) \ . \tag{2}$$

Though building up from our probabilistic definitions, this problem is consistent with the counterfactual explanation problem (1) with the additional fidelity constraint ensured implicitly through sampling from p_θ. We thus provide a bridge between our probabilistic framework for example-based explanations and the well established XAI concepts of counterfactual examples introduced in [28].

Similarly to (1), the particular choice of the hyperparameter λ and the distance function, depends on one hand on the properties of the data and the decision algorithm, and on the other on user preferences and interests.

2.3 Evaluation of Example-Based Explanations

The evaluation of explanatory algorithms and of the quality of the explanations remains a challenge for both traditional tabular and high-dimensional image data [26]. Though human studies based on visual inspection provide valuable feedback, they are challenging to undertake and often suffer from a number of deficiencies due to practical considerations (e.g., expertise mismatch, motivation bias, experience learning curve, time constraints, etc. [18,22]).

We acknowledge the usefulness and importance of such studies yet argue that quantitative evaluation allowing for comparability of obtained results can foster transparency and trust in the algorithms and serve as the first indicator of the quality of the explanations before much more lengthy and expensive human studies are undertaken.

For these reasons we propose a quantitative evaluation scheme for example-based explanations directly motivated by the probabilistic framework introduced in Sect. 2.1 and using the three characteristics therein: closeness, validity, and fidelity. For illustration, we put the scheme to use in evaluating the explanations generated through our experiments in Sect. 4.

To measure closeness of the examples we propose to use a suitable distance metric d, preferably the one chosen for the generative explainer problem (2). Commonly used metrics include the ℓ_p distances, such as the ℓ_1 distance for sparser changes or the ℓ_2 distance for broader changes across the input.

For validity, we propose to report the classifier prediction confidence for the target class. Though the output of the neural network classifier may not be a reliable indicator for the classifier confidence [11], we consider it a good-enough proxy when comparing a single algorithm across multiple explanatory examples.

In the generative modelling community it is common to measure the alignment of generated examples with the underlying data distribution though metrics based on distribution matching such as the Fréchet inception distance [12], the Inception Score [25] or the Precision/Recall [24]. However, these measures are not suitable for evaluating the fidelity of an individual example. Interpreted as the bits necessary for lossless compression via an entropy encoding scheme optimized for the learned p_θ, an explanatory example should require similar amount of bits as the original $\boldsymbol{x}^*$, whereas the encoding length of an adversarial should be much longer. To make this connection explicit, we present the fidelity in our experimental evaluation in Sect. 4.2 as the additional bits-per-dim (bpd) required to encode the examples in comparison to the original data point. Since the explanatory example may require fewer bits, this metric can be negative.

Though the primary purpose of the above metrics is the evaluation of the quality of the algorithm and the generated explanatory examples, they can also serve the user as a complementary explanatory information. For example, the user may generate a diverse set of explanatory examples by varying the strength of the hyperparameter λ trading off the validity with the closeness of the examples in the generative explainer problem (2). The metrics for the produced explanatory examples shall vary accordingly and thus further reinforce the user understanding of the classifier decision. We illustrate this in our experiments in Table 5 and the related discussion.

3 Diffusion-Generated Explanatory Examples

In this section we showcase the use of the probabilistic framework introduced in Sect. 2 in a constructive manner through developing an algorithm for generative example-based explanations (XAIDIFF). We choose to work with the class of Denoising Diffusion Probabilistic Models (DDPM) [13] as the state of the art generative model for learning the underlying data distribution and sampling high fidelity examples, combined with the classifier guidance mechanism [5] to steer the generations towards desirable output in terms of validity and closeness as per the definitions in Sect. 2.1.

Similar approaches have previously been proposed in [2,15]. However, the solutions these introduce are rather ad-hoc and mostly based on intuition rather than clear definitions linking back to the initial concepts of counterfactual explanations as discussed in Sect. 2. They also do not provide a systematic quantitative evaluation of their results that would allow for comparisons across methods.

Our XAIDIFF algorithm does not seek to outperform the above methods. Indeed, direct comparison is impossible due to the missing evaluation in the original papers and difficulties (despite our best efforts) in reproducing the original results. Instead, our aim is to demonstrate how a generative approach to explanatory examples can be grounded within our probabilistic framework aligned with the classical counterfactual desiderate of [28], and the advantages this brings for the subsequent quantitative evaluation. In doing so, we also address some conceptual shortcomings of the previous algorithms.

3.1 DDPM Preliminaries

DDPMs are latent variable models trained to approximate the underlying data distribution p_{data} via a model $p_\theta(\boldsymbol{x}_0) = \int p_\theta(\boldsymbol{x}_0|\boldsymbol{x}_1) \prod_{t=1}^{T} p_\theta(\boldsymbol{x}_{t-1}|\boldsymbol{x}_t) d\boldsymbol{x}_{1:T}$. They follow an encoder-decoder architecture: the encoder (forward process) is defined as a Markov chain Gaussian model $q(\boldsymbol{x}_t|\boldsymbol{x}_{t-1}) := \mathcal{N}\left(\boldsymbol{x}_t; \sqrt{1-\beta_t}\boldsymbol{x}_{t-1}, \beta_t \mathbf{I}\right)$, progressively adding random Gaussian noise to an original example $\boldsymbol{x}_0$ with a pre-defined variance schedule $\beta_1, \dots, \beta_T$ over the diffusion steps $\boldsymbol{x}_1, \dots, \boldsymbol{x}_T$ so that $\boldsymbol{x}_T \sim \mathcal{N}(0, I)$; the Gaussian Markov decoder (reverse process)

$$p_\theta(\boldsymbol{x}_{t-1} \mid \boldsymbol{x}_t) = \mathcal{N}\left(\boldsymbol{x}_{t-1}; \mu_\theta(\boldsymbol{x}_t), \Sigma(t)\right) \tag{3}$$

with learned mean $\mu_\theta(\boldsymbol{x}_t)$ and typically fixed diagonal covariance (a function of the schedule β_t) reverts the forward diffusion process (encoder) by gradually denoising the signal $\boldsymbol{x}_t$ to produce samples matching the original data distribution $p_\theta \approx p_{\text{data}}$.

Instead of maximizing the intractable likelihood p_θ or its variational lower bound (ELBO), DDPMs can be trained by minimizing a simplified loss function matching the noise predicted by the denoising reverse process $\hat{\boldsymbol{\epsilon}}_{\boldsymbol{\theta}}(\boldsymbol{x}_t, t)$ to the ground truth noise $\boldsymbol{\epsilon}^*$ of the forward process over time-steps t sampled from a uniform distribution $\mathcal{U}(1, T)$:

$$L := \mathbb{E}_{t \sim \mathcal{U}(1,T), \boldsymbol{x}_0 \sim q(\boldsymbol{x}_0), \boldsymbol{\epsilon}^* \sim \mathcal{N}(0,I)} \left\| \boldsymbol{\epsilon}^* - \hat{\boldsymbol{\epsilon}}_{\boldsymbol{\theta}}(\boldsymbol{x}_t, t) \right\|^2, \ \boldsymbol{x}_t = \sqrt{\bar{\alpha}_t}\boldsymbol{x}_0 + \boldsymbol{\epsilon}^* \sqrt{1 - \bar{\alpha}_t},$$

with $\bar{\alpha}_t = \prod_{s=1}^{t}(1 - \beta_s)$. For more details we encourage the interested reader to consult the abundant literature on DDPMs and related models, e.g., the comprehensive survey [29].

3.2 Classifier Guidance

The vanilla DDPM introduced in Sect. 3.1 enables synthesizing random samples $\hat{\boldsymbol{x}} \sim p_\theta \approx p_{\text{data}}$ with high fidelity to the underlying data distribution. However, to generate valid class-specific data points the reverse process shall in principle be conditioned on the target label $p_\theta(\boldsymbol{x}_{t-1} \mid \boldsymbol{x}_t, y_\mathcal{T})$.

Instead, the classifier guidance mechanism [5] leverages an unconditionally trained (label-unaware) DDPM with unconditional denoising transitions (3). The guidance is achieved through shifting the mean $\mu_\theta(\boldsymbol{x}_t)$ of the transitions by the gradients of a classifier $\nabla_{\boldsymbol{x}_t} \log p_{\text{cl}}(y_\mathcal{T} \mid \boldsymbol{x}_t)$ trained over the noisy data $\boldsymbol{x}_t$ produced by the forward process of the DDPM to yield class-conditional samples:

$$\mu'_\theta(\boldsymbol{x}_t) = \mu_\theta(\boldsymbol{x}_t) + s\ \Sigma(t)\ \nabla_{\boldsymbol{x}_t} \log p_{\text{cl}}(y_\mathcal{T} \mid \boldsymbol{x}_t)\ , \tag{4}$$

where s is a scaling factor controlling the strength of the classifier guidance.

3.3 Classifier Guidance for Explanatory Examples

The mechanism for classifier guidance outlined in Sect. 3.2 opens a window of opportunity for generating explanatory examples coherent with our probabilistic framework and the definitions in Sect. 2.1. In particular, two of the critical characteristics for the explanatory examples can be expected to be satisfied by construction. The use of DDPM guarantees the high fidelity of the generated explanatory examples and the classifier guidance ensures their validity. The approach, however, does not cater for the closeness of the examples, which is the third critical characteristics of our framework.

In accordance with the generative explainer problem (2), we introduce a distance function into the classifier guidance formulation (4) as follows:

$$\mu'_\theta(\boldsymbol{x}_t) = \mu_\theta(\boldsymbol{x}_t) + \Sigma(t)\ \nabla_{\boldsymbol{x}_t} \left[\lambda \log p_{\text{cl}}\left(y \mid \hat{\boldsymbol{x}}_0^{(\boldsymbol{x}_t)}\right) - \left\| \hat{\boldsymbol{x}}_0^{(\boldsymbol{x}_t)} - \boldsymbol{x}^* \right\|_1 \right] . \tag{5}$$

Similar to [2,15] we chose the ℓ_1 distance suggested as a *"sensible first choice"* in [28] promoting sparsity in the introduced changes, and we replace the noisy DDPM samples $\boldsymbol{x}_t$ with the DDPM one-step predictions of the denoised data $\hat{\boldsymbol{x}}_0^{(\boldsymbol{x}_t)}$ which are closer to the true data distribution than the noisy samples $\boldsymbol{x}_t$.

However, in contrast to the previous methods [2,15], we do not truncate the reverse diffusion sampling to start from the middle of the process but instead start from the very end, from the complete white noise $\boldsymbol{x}_T \sim \mathcal{N}(\mathbf{0}, \mathbf{I})$. In this way, we do not constrain the search space for (2) and allow for higher diversity in the generated explanatory examples. Furthermore, we propose to tackle the previously noticed issue of the instability of the classifier gradients head-on. Instead of relying on a surrogate robust classifier to help in the guidance as in [2], we interpret the gradient guidance in Eq. (5) as stochastic gradient descent steps. Motivated by this view, we propose to leverage modern methods for stochastic optimization of non-stationary objectives with noisy gradients. Concretely, we introduce ADAM [17] into the guidance steps to automatically adapt the step size from estimates of the first and second moments of the gradients.

Finally, we link the guidance steps in Eq. (5) back to the definitions in Sect. 2 and interpret the individual terms as gradients of the generative explainer problem (2) introduced in Sect. 2.2:

- μ_θ implicitly as the gradient towards maximum fidelity,
- $\nabla_{\boldsymbol{x}_t}\left[\log p_{\text{cl}}\left(y \mid \hat{\boldsymbol{x}}_0^{(\boldsymbol{x}_t)}\right)\right]$ as the gradient towards maximum validity, and
- $\nabla_{\boldsymbol{x}_t}\left[\left\|\hat{\boldsymbol{x}}_0^{(\boldsymbol{x}_t)} - \boldsymbol{x}^*\right\|_1\right]$ as the gradient towards maximum closeness.

4 Experiments

In this section, we put our XAIDIFF algorithm into use and evaluate its ability to generate explanatory examples showcasing the constructive value of our probabilistic framework.

4.1 Datasets and Experimental Setup

We provide experimental results on two main data sets. The first is a newly proposed synthetic data set, named SportBalls, carefully designed to illustrate they key components of our framework by providing a controlled explanation scenario where the optimal explanation is intuitively clear. The second is the real-world data set CelebA [20]. Additional results for a third (MNIST [19]) are provided in the appendix.

SportBalls is a synthetically created dataset which contains multiple similar objects with slight variations in terms of scaling, shape, size, rotation and placement but clear semantic differences (i.e., colors and pattern). Each image contains three out of five randomly selected sport balls placed at random coordinates on white background with random rotation and scaling. There can be multiple types of sport balls in one image and the balls may overlap (even occlude each other), creating a more complex yet controlled explanation setting. For the experiments, we pick four starting images each containing at least one soccer ball (the original class) with varying complexity for the explanation: the first image where the sport balls are non-overlapping, the second image with multiple soccer balls, the third image where the soccer ball is the background of another sport ball, and the fourth image where the soccer ball is partly occluded. The code to generate the dataset is provided for further re-use by the community (see the links in the title page).

CelebA is a publicly available data set of celebrity faces with easily recognizable attributes for classification. We downscale the data to 64×64 pixels. As starting points for explanations, we pick four images of faces with negative values for all three attributes: no eyeglasses, no smile, not blond. These are not cherry-picked examples from experimentation but were selected a priori due to their diversity in terms of gender, hairstyle, formal attire and background.

Classifiers and DDPM: In a realistic explainability scenario the classifier to be explained is provided externally. In our experiments we therefore pick a standard architecture for the classifiers, a low-resource small version of the MobileNetV3 [14] from 'torchvision', and train a binary classifier (soccer-ball=yes/no) to 96.8 % test accuracy over the SportBalls dataset, and a multi-label classifier eyeglasses=yes/no, smile=yes/no, blond_hair=yes/no for CelebA to 97.13%, 89.71% and 93.33% test accuracy respectively. Our XAIDIFF algorithm assumes access to a DDPM trained over the same data distribution as the classifier. We therefore train the DDPM over the same data sets. The implementation relies on the open-source Diffusers toolbox [21].

Evaluation: We evaluate closeness, validity and fidelity of the XAIDIFF generations according to the scheme in Sect. 2.3. We measure the closeness by the ℓ_1-distance in coherence with Eq. (5). For validity we report the classifier prediction confidence for the target class. Finally, we use the variational lower bound (ELBO) of the learned model p_θ to calculate the resulting bits-per-dim and report the additional bits of the explanatory example as the measure of fidelity. We employ the above metrics to document the correct functioning of the XAIDIFF algorithm. For this, we compare the averages of the metrics across sets of 16 explanatory examples generated by the algorithm. For instance, a well functioning algorithm shall ensure that counterfactual examples have on average higher fidelity than adversarial examples.

4.2 Generative Example-Based Explanations

In this section we validate that XAIDIFF produces example-based explanations as per our definitions in Sect. 2.1.

In Tables 1 and 2 we contrast the counterfactual examples generated by XAIDIFF $\hat{\boldsymbol{x}}^{(cf)}$ with adversarial examples $\hat{\boldsymbol{x}}^{(adv)}$ obtained from the original examples through simple gradient updates $\hat{\boldsymbol{x}} \leftarrow \hat{\boldsymbol{x}} + \nabla_{\hat{\boldsymbol{x}}}\, p_{\text{cl}}(y_\mathcal{T} \mid \hat{\boldsymbol{x}})$ within the pixel space towards the classification target. As an ablation of the XAIDIFF properties we remove the distance function in Eq. (5) to obtain examples with-

Table 1. Original SportBalls/CelebA examples $\boldsymbol{x}^*$ compared to XAIDIFF counterfactuals $\hat{\boldsymbol{x}}^{(cf)}$, adversarial examples $\hat{\boldsymbol{x}}^{(adv)}$, and generations without closeness $\hat{\boldsymbol{x}}^{(cf\backslash c)}$ and validity criteria $\hat{\boldsymbol{x}}^{(cf\backslash v)}$, respectively.

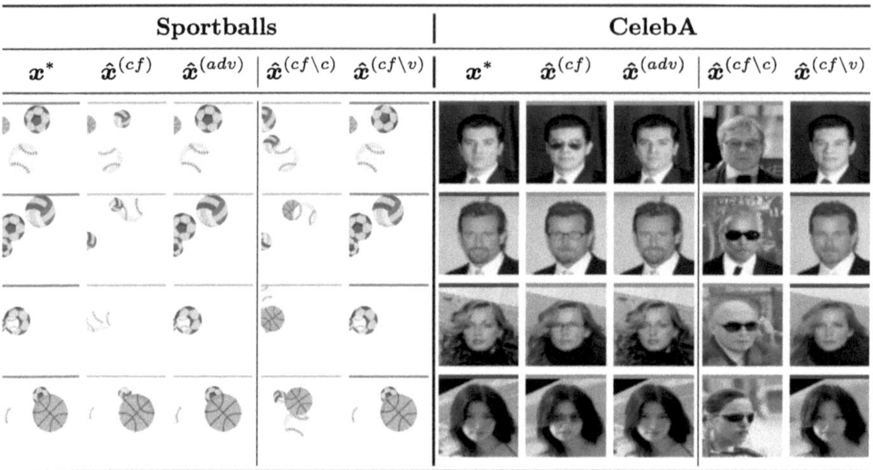

Table 2. Evaluation metrics for SportBalls/CelebA. **c**loseness: ℓ_1-distance per dim, **v**alidity: classifier confidence (%), **f**idelity: extra bpd compared to $\boldsymbol{x}^*$.

		$\hat{\boldsymbol{x}}^{(cf)}$	$\hat{\boldsymbol{x}}^{(adv)}$	$\hat{\boldsymbol{x}}^{(cf\backslash c)}$	$\hat{\boldsymbol{x}}^{(cf\backslash v)}$
SportBalls	$\mathbf{c}_\downarrow$	0.7 (0.3)	0.0 (0.0)	1.2 (0.3)	0.1 (0.1)
	$\mathbf{v}_\uparrow$	100 (0.0)	83.4 (29.6)	100 (0.0)	51.5 (44.2)
	$\mathbf{f}_\downarrow$	+0.3 (0.4)	+0.4 (0.1)	+0.6 (0.4)	0.0 (0.1)
CelebA	$\mathbf{c}_\downarrow$	0.6 (0.1)	0.1 (0.0)	4.7 (0.7)	0.6 (0.1)
	$\mathbf{v}_\uparrow$	99.5 (0.3)	86.5 (20.7)	99.3 (0.8)	49.9 (49.1)
	$\mathbf{f}_\downarrow$	−0.4 (0.2)	+1.1 (0.4)	+0.2 (0.4)	−0.5 (0.2)

out the closeness criterion $\hat{\boldsymbol{x}}^{(cf\backslash c)}$. Finally, $\hat{\boldsymbol{x}}^{(cf\backslash v)}$ disregard the validity criterion by removing the classifier term from Eq. (5).

We show one randomly selected generated example per starting image $\boldsymbol{x}^*$ in Table 1. More are shown in the appendix. The metrics presented in Table 2 are averages (and standard deviations) calculated over sets of 16 examples.

Table 1 illustrates that all starting images $\boldsymbol{x}^*$ of both datasets are correctly classified as soccerball=yes and eyeglasses=no (indicated by a blue stripe on top of the images). All counterfactual explanations and adversarial examples flip the classifier decision (indicated by a green stripe). However, only the counterfactuals correctly alter the original images. There are no soccer balls and the faces wear eyeglasses in the $\hat{\boldsymbol{x}}^{(cf)}$ columns while the changes in the $\hat{\boldsymbol{x}}^{(adv)}$ are imperceptible to human eye and therefore useless as explanations. Similarly, the class is changed and the images altered in the $\hat{\boldsymbol{x}}^{(cf\backslash c)}$ column. However, the images look very different than (not close to) the originals and therefore are of little explanatory value. Examples in the $\hat{\boldsymbol{x}}^{(cf\setminus v)}$ column are very close to the originals, however, they do not change the images sufficiently to flip the classifier decision.

The above visual analysis can be complemented by inspecting the numerical results in Table 2. While counterfactual examples $\hat{\boldsymbol{x}}^{(cf)}$ are indeed closer to the originals than the $\hat{\boldsymbol{x}}^{(cf\setminus c)}$ examples ignoring the closeness criterion, the adversarials $\hat{\boldsymbol{x}}^{(adv)}$ are even closer though with lower fidelity. The high validity of all three corresponds to them successfully flipping the classifier decision, which fails for $\hat{\boldsymbol{x}}^{(cf\setminus v)}$. Yet, it is these examples disregarding the validity $\hat{\boldsymbol{x}}^{(cf\setminus v)}$, which are the most fidel to the underlying data distribution as they do not need to balance the diffusion steps with the classifier gradient steps in Eq. 5.

In Tables 3 and 4, we analyse the newly proposed affirmative explanations using the CelebA data set. We contrast the affirmatives to the originals and the counterfactuals to demonstrate their explanatory value. As we see in the tables, the affirmatives are high-fidelity examples classified the same as the original examples (blue stripe) and they indeed do not contain the concepts introduced by the counterfactual explanations. Though being close to the originals, they are even closer to the counterfactuals (see closeness in Table 4). These characteristics are in line with the definitions provided in Sect. 2.1 and experimentally demonstrate the intuitions depicted in the schematic illustration in Fig. 1.

The above findings also naturally extend to more complex multi-label scenarios: the XAIDIFF counterfactuals and affirmatives correctly trigger changes in the classifier decisions, flipping the classifications for all three attributes together - from no in the original to yes in the counterfactuals and back to no in the affirmatives. All these changes are also corroborated by high validity values in Table 4 and clearly observable in the generated images in Table 3.

As explained in Sect. 2.3, an additional benefit of the evaluation metrics is their explanatory value for the user. We illustrate this in Table 5, where we supplement four counterfactual explanations with their respective metrics. The counterfactuals were generated with varying values of the validity-closeness trade-off hyperparameter λ in Eq. (5). Referring to the metric values, the user can better appreciate the difference between the counterfactual examples, which in turn shall help to explain the classifier decision. For instance, the validity of the first counterfactual in Table 5 is lower than of the other three examples which corresponds to smaller recognizability of the eyeglasses in the image. Giving the responsibility of selecting a good explanation to the user with very individual preferences may be an interesting direction for future work.

Table 3. Affirmative examples $\hat{x}^{(aff)}$. Single-label for eyeglasses=no; multi-label for eyeglasses=no and smiling=no and blond=no.

	x^*	$\hat{x}^{(cf)}$	$\hat{x}^{(aff)}$	x^*	$\hat{x}^{(cf)}$	$\hat{x}^{(aff)}$
Single-label						
Multi-label						

Table 4. Evaluation metrics for affirmative examples.

	metrics	$\hat{x}^{(cf)}$	$\hat{x}^{(aff)}$		$\hat{x}^{(cf)}$	$\hat{x}^{(aff)}$
Single-label	$\mathbf{c}_{\downarrow}$ (x^*)	0.6 (0.1)	0.6 (0.1)	Multi-label	0.57 (0.12)	0.64 (0.15)
	$\mathbf{c}_{\downarrow}$ $(\hat{x}^{(cf)})$	-	0.2 (0.1)		-	0.24 (0.04)
	$\mathbf{v}_{\uparrow}$	99.5 (0.3)	99.5 (0.4)		89.17 (4.95)	97.24 (1.13)
	$\mathbf{f}_{\downarrow}$	−0.1 (0.2)	−0.1 (0.2)		−0.27 (0.18)	−0.25 (0.23)

Table 5. Metrics as supplementary explanatory information - validity-closeness trade-off $\lambda \in \{0.1, 0.3, 0.5, 0.7\}$

x^*	$\hat{x}^{(cf)}_{0.1}$	$\hat{x}^{(cf)}_{0.3}$	$\hat{x}^{(cf)}_{0.5}$	$\hat{x}^{(cf)}_{0.7}$

$\mathbf{c}_{\downarrow}$	**0.37**	**0.37**	0.49	0.50
$\mathbf{v}_{\uparrow}$	96.23	98.91	**99.92**	99.74
$\mathbf{f}_{\downarrow}$	**-0.56**	-0.52	-0.51	**-0.56**

5 Conclusions

Recent methods for generative example-based explanations [2,9,15] show impressive sample quality outlining a promising direction for future research. However, these methods are largely inconsistent in used definitions, experimental baselines, approaches to evaluation and are largely disconnected from generally accepted XAI concepts often disregarding basic assumptions and expectations of the field. This disconnect between the generative modeling and explainability communities leads to many misunderstandings. To bridge this gap, this paper puts forward a probabilistic framework for example-base explanations consistent with traditional explainability desiderata and demonstrates how it can be used constructively for developing new generative-based explanatory algorithms by showcasing the diffusion-based XAIDIFF algorithm. In line with the best research practice, we foster transparency and reproducibility by providing the complete implementation of our method together with the settings and the model files to reproduce the results of our experiments (see the links in the title page).

A major limitation of our method is in its generality. Apart from small tweaks such as the λ hyperparameter, the algorithm does not allow to individualize the model according to personal experience or affinity. The metrics we propose are derived from our definitions and do not measure the appropriateness of the examples for improved understanding of a specific user. Furthermore, our method assumes the availability of a diffusion model trained over the same (or sufficiently similar) data as the classifier. This may be impossible in some situations. There are also no mathematical guarantees for the proposed method. Finally, we wish to warn that as any other generative model, our method could be used to produce malicious content. This would, however, require access to a white-box classifier trained over malicious attributes which reduces the risk of misuse.

References

1. Adadi, A., Berrada, M.: Peeking inside the black-box: a survey on explainable artificial intelligence (XAI). IEEE Access (2018)
2. Augustin, M., Boreiko, V., Croce, F., Hein, M.: Diffusion visual counterfactual explanations. In: NeurIPS (2022)
3. Chatila, R., et al.: Trustworthy AI. Reflections on Artificial Intelligence for Humanity (2021)
4. Das, A., Rad, P.: Opportunities and challenges in explainable artificial intelligence (XAI): a survey. arXiv:2006.11371 (2020)
5. Dhariwal, P., Nichol, A.: Diffusion models beat GANs on image synthesis. In: NeurIPS (2021)
6. Dhurandhar, A., et al.: Explanations based on the missing: towards contrastive explanations with pertinent negatives. In: NeurIPS (2018)
7. Goodfellow, I.J., Shlens, J., Szegedy, C.: Explaining and harnessing adversarial examples. In: ICLR (2015)
8. Goodman, B., Flaxman, S.: European union regulations on algorithmic decision-making and a "right to explanation". In: ICML WHI Workshop (2016)

9. Guidotti, R.: Counterfactual explanations and how to find them: Literature review and benchmarking. In: KDD (2022)
10. Gunning, D.: XAI—explainable artificial intelligence. Sci. Robots (2019)
11. Hein, M., Andriushchenko, M., Bitterwolf, J.: Why relu networks yield high-confidence predictions far away from the training data and how to mitigate the problem. In: CVPR (2019)
12. Heusel, M., Ramsauer, H., Unterthiner, T., Nessler, B., Hochreiter, S.: GANs trained by a two time-scale update rule converge to a local nash equilibrium. In: NeurIPS (2017)
13. Ho, J., Jain, A., Abbeel, P.: Denoising diffusion probabilistic models. In: NeurIPS (2020)
14. Howard, A., et al.: Searching for mobilenetv3. In: ICCV (2019)
15. Jeanneret, G., Simon, L., Jurie, F.: Diffusion models for counterfactual explanations. In: ACCV (2022)
16. Kenny, E.M., Keane, M.T.: On generating plausible counterfactual and semi-factual explanations for deep learning. In: AAAI (2021)
17. Kingma, D.P., Ba, J.: Adam: a method for stochastic optimization. In: ICLR (2015)
18. Lage, I., et al.: An evaluation of the human-interpretability of explanation. In: NeurIPS (2018)
19. LeCun, Y., Bottou, L., Bengio, Y., Haffner, P.: Gradient-based learning applied to document recognition. IEEE (1998)
20. Liu, Z., Luo, P., Wang, X., Tang, X.: Deep learning face attributes in the wild. In: ICCV (2015)
21. von Platen, P., et al.: Diffusers: State-of-the-art diffusion models. GitHub (2022)
22. Rosenfeld, A.: Better metrics for evaluating explainable artificial intelligence. In: AAMAS (2021)
23. Sahakyan, M., Aung, Z., Rahwan, T.: Explainable artificial intelligence for tabular data: a survey. IEEE Access (2021)
24. Sajjadi, M.S., Bachem, O., Lucic, M., Bousquet, O., Gelly, S.: Assessing generative models via precision and recall. In: NeurIPS (2018)
25. Salimans, T., Goodfellow, I., Zaremba, W., Cheung, V., Radford, A., Chen, X.: Improved techniques for training GANs. In: NeurIPS (2016)
26. Väth, P., Frühwald, A.M., Paaßen, B., Gregorova, M.: Diffusion-based visual counterfactual explanations - towards systematic quantitative evaluation. In: ECML PKDD XKDD Workshop (2023)
27. Verma, S., Boonsanong, V., Hoang, M., Hines, K.E., Dickerson, J.P., Shah, C.: Counterfactual explanations and algorithmic recourses for machine learning: A review. ACM Comput. Surv. (2022)
28. Wachter, S., Mittelstadt, B., Russell, C.: Counterfactual explanations without opening the black box: automated decisions and the GDPR. JOLT (2017)
29. Yang, L., et al.: Diffusion models: a comprehensive survey of methods and applications. ACM Comput. Surv. (2023)

Rule vs. SHAP: Complementary Tools for Understanding and Verifying ML Models

Bahavathy Kathirgamanathan[1,2(✉)], Gennady Andrienko[1,2,3], and Natalia Andrienko[1,2,3]

[1] Fraunhofer Institute IAIS, Sankt Augustin, Germany
bahavathy.kathirgamanathan@iais.fraunhofer.de
[2] Lamarr Institute for Machine Learning and Artificial Intelligence, Sankt Augustin, Germany
[3] St George's University of London, London, EC1V 0HB, UK

Abstract. Traditional interpretability techniques such as rule-based models and feature attribution methods, each offer complementary strengths, however are often applied in isolation. Rule-based approaches are intuitive and logically structured, making them easy to understand, but they often struggle to scale effectively. On the other hand, feature attribution techniques like SHAP are well-suited to handling complex models and large datasets but can fall short in terms of interpretability and alignment with human reasoning. In this paper, we introduce a hybrid, human-centric interpretability framework that integraes rule-based modelling with SHAP-based feature attributions within a visual analytics framework and show the benefits for interpretability and interactivity through such techniques. We validate the framework on a case-study of Fishing-vessel trajectories and demonstrate how this integrated approach reveals patterns and discrepancies that would not have been seen using a single approach alone.

Keywords: Explainable AI · Visual Analytics · Rule-based · feature-based · interpretability

1 Introduction

Interpretability is essential in machine learning applications to ensure trust, transparency, and accountability. While machine learning models can achieve high predictive accuracy, their complexity often makes them difficult to understand. Two main strategies for enhancing interpretability are rule-based methods and feature attribution techniques.

Rule-based methods explain model decisions using logical if-then rules, such as those found in decision trees, rule lists, and decision sets. These methods are intuitive and align well with human reasoning, but they can struggle to scale

I. Koprinska et al. (Eds.): ECML PKDD 2025, CCIS 2842, pp. 561–576, 2026.
https://doi.org/10.1007/978-3-032-19105-2_39

effectively. As rule sets grow, they can become overwhelming and less interpretable.

Feature attribution techniques, on the other hand, assess the influence of individual input features on model predictions. Common examples include SHAP (SHapley Additive exPlanations), LIME (Local Interpretable Model-agnostic Explanations), and gradient-based saliency maps. These methods are model-agnostic and suitable for high-dimensional data. However, they often fall short in explaining specific predictions and may not align well with human logic. Additionally, feature attributions can be unstable, raising concerns about consistency in explanations.

Despite their individual strengths and limitations, rule-based and feature attribution methods tend to be applied separately. In this work, we argue that these approaches are not alternative but complementary, as they offer fundamentally different views on model behavior: rules focus on logic and structure, while SHAP emphasizes statistical influence. The purpose for using them in tandem is not only to deepen our understanding of model behavior, but also to cross-validate insights and detect inconsistencies. Rules can contextualize SHAP-derived attributions within logical patterns, while SHAP distributions can reveal statistical regularities and anomalies that challenge or support the extracted rules. Discrepancies between the two may signal areas where model behavior diverges from domain expectations or where explanation methods fail to faithfully represent model logic.

To fully exploit this complementary potential, we advocate the use of interactive visual analytics that allow users to explore both rule sets and SHAP distributions dynamically. Visual tools can facilitate comparisons, support drill-down into feature interactions, and enable experts to flag surprising or illogical model behaviors.

In this work, we propose a hybrid approach to investigating the internal logic of a model that combines rule-based modeling with feature attribution, enhanced by visual analytics for a human-centered interpretability framework. Specifically, we extract rules from a random forest model and analyze the distribution of these rules to visualize how different regions of the feature space contribute to classification outcomes. We complement this with SHAP-based feature attribution to guide rule exploration and interpretation. We demonstrate this approach in a real-world case study involving classification of vessel movement patterns using a random forest model. Our analysis reveals meaningful discrepancies; for example, SHAP values suggest that certain features negatively impact predictions in contexts where domain knowledge would expect a positive influence. These findings illustrate the value of combining explanation methods within a visual analytic workflow.

2 Related Work

This section reviews existing approaches to XAI, highlighting the distinct contributions of rule-based explanations and feature attribution methods, and motivates our argument for their synergistic application.

2.1 Rule-Based Explanations

Rule-based methods aim to approximate the complex decision-making process of ML models using sets of easily interpretable, logical rules. These rules typically take the form of "IF-THEN" statements, outlining specific conditions on input features that lead to a particular prediction. Such approaches offer several advantages: they are inherently human-readable, provide a global understanding of model behavior by summarizing common patterns, and can be used to extract actionable insights for domain experts [6].

Early work in rule extraction focused on techniques like decision tree learning [14]. More recently, methods have been developed to extract rules from more complex models, such as neural networks and ensemble methods. For instance, LORE (Local Rule-based Explanations) generates local, counterfactual rules by perturbing a single instance and training a simple interpretable model on the synthetic neighborhood [5]. Similarly, prototypes like Anchors [16] identify sufficient conditions (rules) for a prediction to be stable, even when other features change. Other approaches, like those based on decision set learning, aim to produce concise and accurate rule sets directly from data or by approximating complex models [7]. While powerful in their interpretability and ability to capture logical structures, rule-based methods can sometimes oversimplify complex relationships.

It is also important to point out that our research focuses on investigating a model as a whole rather than generating explanations of individual decisions. In this context, we need to deal with the problem that the number of rules representing a model and their complexity (number of conditions) can be overwhelming for a human, making this representation uninterpretable in practice [1]. While some degree of simplification can be achieved by aggregating and generalizing similar rules, the resulting set may still exceed the human cognitive capacity. Hence, there is a need in providing highly aggregated overviews and enabling users to obtain more detailed information when needed.

2.2 Feature Attribution Methods

Feature attribution methods quantify the contribution of each input feature to a model's prediction for a specific instance. These methods provide "local" explanations, highlighting which inputs were most influential in a particular decision. Among the most prominent feature attribution techniques is SHAP (SHapley Additive exPlanations) [9]. SHAP values are based on game theory and provide a unique solution for fairly distributing the "payout" (the prediction) among the "players" (the features). This means that SHAP values are additive, allowing for a clear understanding of how each feature contributes positively or negatively to the final prediction. Other notable feature attribution methods include LIME (Local Interpretable Model-agnostic Explanations) [15], which approximates the black-box model locally with an interpretable model (e.g., linear regression), and Integrated Gradients [19], which attributes importance by integrating gradients along a path from a baseline input to the actual input. While feature attribution methods pinpoint influential features for individual predictions, they often lack the structural and logical clarity provided by rule-based explanations. They may also not reveal the underlying conditions or interactions that lead to those attributions.

Some recent works have sought to bridge this gap by combining rule-based representations with feature attribution techniques. For example, GLocalX [18] builds global rule-based explanations by aggregating local feature attribution vectors such as SHAP, producing interpretable rule sets that reflect both local importance and global structure. Similarly, RuleMatrix [11] integrates rule extraction with feature-level contributions to support interactive analysis. SIRUS [4] takes a different approach by extracting stable rules directly from random forests and ranking them based on frequency, implicitly reflecting feature relevance. These approaches highlight the complementary strengths of symbolic rules and numerical attributions, motivating further research on their synergistic application for enhancing both interpretability and trust in model behavior.

2.3 Visual Analytics for Rule-Based Explanation

Due to the increasing complexity of ML models, there has been a drive to develop visual analytics tools to support interpretability and exploration.

Recent advances in Visual Analytics (VA) have demonstrated the usefulness of employing VA to help bridge the gap between ML and humans [2]. VA has proven to be useful for enhancing the interpretability of decision tree ensembles, rule-based models, and even black-box classifiers [10]. There are rule-based explanation techniques that use visualization to further improve the comprehensibility of the explanations. RuleMatrix is one such technique that extracts rules, arranges them into a structured matrix format, and enables detailed interactive inspection of feature relationships and impacts on rule outcomes [11]. iForest allows the user to interactively explore random forest models and predictions by showcasing the decision paths [20]. Explainable matrix is another technique which visualises the rules in a matrix-like representation [12]. However, most existing visual analytics tools are tailored to a single explanation paradigm. The critical next step is to develop integrated visual environments that allow for the dynamic comparison and interplay between disparate explanation types, such as rule sets and SHAP distributions, to fully realize the benefits of their combined application.

Our work distinguishes itself by advocating for a joint use of rule-based representations and SHAP values, not merely as additive components, but as tools for mutual validation and the detection of inconsistencies. We further emphasize the critical role of interactive visual analytics in facilitating this comparative exploration, thereby enabling experts to uncover nuanced model behaviors that might otherwise remain hidden.

3 Case Study: Recognition of Vessel Movement Patterns

In this case study, we deal with a **random forest model** developed for recognizing movement patterns of fishing vessels. Input data for the model consist of values of numeric attributes characterizing segments of vessel trajectories. The training data for model derivation were prepared as described in [3]. The model was trained to recognize four distinct movement classes: **Forward movement** (class 1), **Trawling** (class 2), **Port enter/exit** (class 3), and **Anchoring** (class 4). The model utilizes nine features describing vessel speed characteristics, trajectory shape, and proximity to ports. Logarithmic transformation was applied to features with highly skewed value distributions in the training data.

- **Speed statistics**: `SpeedMinimum`, `SpeedQ1`, `SpeedMedian`, `SpeedQ3`. These features represent the speed distribution, from minimum observed speed to quartile-based spread.
- `Log10Curvature`: The logarithm of the curvature of the time series of the vessel's distance from the starting point. The curvature is computed as the ratio between the sum of absolute consecutive changes in the time series and the amplitude of values. A value close to 1 indicates nearly straight movement, while higher values indicate the presence of turns.
- `DistStartTrendAngle`: The angle of the linear trend fitted to the time series of the vessel's distance from its starting point. A higher angle indicates a stronger trend of moving away, while a lower angle suggests slower movement or a return toward the starting position.
- `Log10DistStartTrendDevAmplitude`: The logarithm of the amplitude of deviations from the trend line of the distance to the starting point. It quantifies path tortuosity, reflecting how much the vessel's movement deviates from a straight-line trend. Higher values indicate more erratic or zigzagging movement.
- **Port proximity**: `MaxDistPort`, `Log10MinDistPort`. These features represent the maximum and (log-transformed) minimum distance from the nearest port, which are useful for recognizing anchoring and port maneuvering.

`Log10Curvature` and `Log10DistStartTrendDevAmplitude` jointly describe the shape complexity of a trajectory segment. `Log10Curvature` captures global movement characteristics, while path tortuosity reflects local zigzagging. Together, they help distinguish between steady outward movement, looping, and in-place maneuvering.

A random forest classifier was trained to distinguish between these movement types using a 75:25 train-test split (random state = 0). Prior to training, all numerical features were standardized using z-score normalization to ensure equal treatment of features regardless of magnitude. The resulting model demonstrated strong predictive performance, achieving a test accuracy of 0.9733. The trained model comprised 100 decision trees, each trained on a bootstrapped sample of the training data. Rules were generated by traversing each tree from root to leaf, resulting in one rule per path. Because the model was trained on standardized features, all threshold values were transformed back to the original scale for interpretability. Each extracted rule consisted of a predicted class and a set of feature constraints, expressed as value ranges. For interpretability, open-ended intervals were bounded using the minimum and maximum observed values for the respective features. This process produced an initial rule set of 9,939 unique rules.

4 RuleSense: Visual Analytics System for Rule-Based Model Understanding

The RuleSense system is an interactive visual analytics tool designed to support the systematic exploration and refinement of rule-based representations of machine learning models. Its primary goal is to help domain experts understand the decision logic encoded in the model, detect inconsistencies or anomalies, and iteratively align the model more closely with domain knowledge. This system builds upon our previous work [1], which focused on simplifying models by aggregating and generalizing similar rules.

The application of this system to rule sets extracted from random forest models poses specific challenges. Due to the ensemble nature of the model and the inherent redundancy in decision forests, the rule set representing a model contains inconsistencies and overlaps. To deal with these problems, the system includes functions for computationally assisted clean-up. It can identify *contradictory rules*, i.e. rules whose conditions are more general than those of other rules that lead to different results. Upon detection, the more general rules can be removed, but users have the possibility to review such cases and make their own decisions. In the vessel movement classification model, 113 contradictory rules were detected, reviewed, and removed.

The system can also detect *subsumed rules* that are less general than other rules with the same result and can therefore be considered redundant. By removing or merging these rules, the rule set is simplified without compromising the prediction performance. In our case study, 311 rules were identified as fully covered by more general rules and removed. This did not compromise but even slightly improved the accuracy of the predictions.

However, many problems may not be detectable automatically. The visualizations and interaction techniques we have developed aim at enabling a human expert to inspect and improve the internal logic of a rule set.

RuleSense offers two main visualization techniques: a detailed view of individual rules and an overview of the distributions of feature value intervals across rule subsets predicting different classes.

Table View of Individual Rules: The *table view* (Fig. 1) presents rules in a structured tabular format, showing their conditions, predicted outcomes, and coverage statistics. Each row corresponds to a single rule, with columns representing the features used in the model.

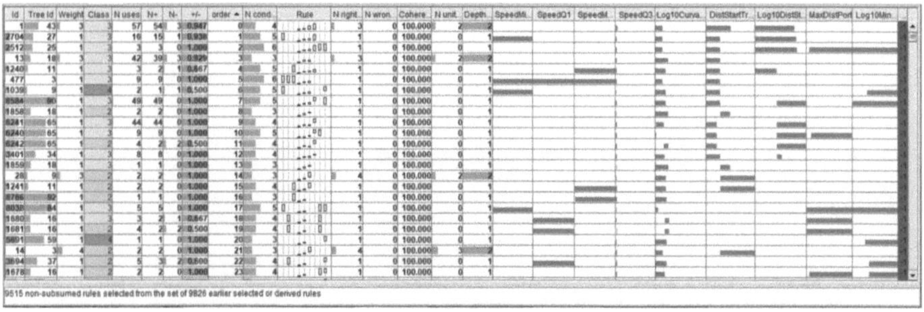

Fig. 1. Rule table provides a detailed view of the rules.

This view is particularly useful for inspecting small subsets of rules and serves as a supplementary tool when working with larger rule sets. Users can sort table rows by feature values, rule characteristics, or rule similarity to identify patterns, though more scalable visualizations are required for comprehensive analysis of large models.

Overview of Feature Value Distributions: To capture how feature values vary across the rule set, the system includes an *overview visualization* that summarizes feature value distributions for each predicted class. As shown in Fig. 2, this view uses a matrix-style heatmap, with rows representing features and columns corresponding to equal-sized intervals of feature values.

The number of intervals is user-defined when the visualization is created; in the example shown, each feature range is divided into 10 intervals. Each matrix cell encodes a specific combination of class, feature, and interval. The color of a cell reflects the number of rules whose conditions include that interval, ranging from light yellow (low count) to dark red (high count), with white signifying zero occurrences.

To the left of each matrix row, a light blue bar overlaid on a gray bar visually represents the proportion of rules that include the corresponding feature within the entire subset of rules predicting that specific class.

The overview display also includes interactive filtering controls. For each feature, a checkbox allows for feature exclusion; when selected, the system displays only rules that do not include that feature. Additionally, a two-sided slider enables users to select sub-ranges of feature values. When a sub-range is chosen, the system filters out rules whose conditions do not include the selected interval. An example of the use of a slider is demonstrated in the lower image of Fig. 2. The slider for the `DistStartTrendAngle` feature is used to select a sub-range of its lower values. In response, the display has dynamically updated and now presents the distribution of features and their value intervals solely for the subset of rules whose conditions include the specified sub-range for `DistStartTrendAngle`. Rules that do not involve this feature are consequently excluded.

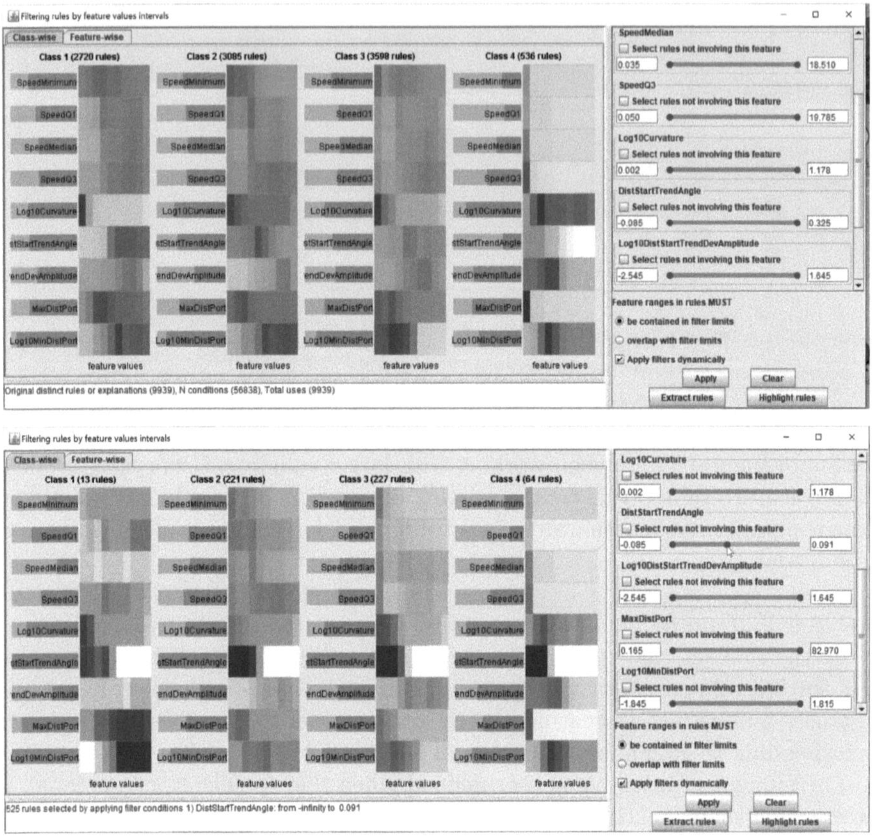

Fig. 2. Top: Overview of feature value distributions across rule subsets by class. Bottom: Interactive filtering of rules.

The interactive filtering interface allows users to construct composite queries and select specific subsets of rules for in-depth analysis, such as viewing individual rules in a tabular format. A key purpose of this interface is to enable the exploration of feature relationships. Users can narrow the ranges of some features and then observe how the value distributions of other features are affected. As an illustration, consider our example: excluding high values for `DistStartTrendAngle` dramatically reduces the number of rules for class 1 from 2,720 to only 13, while also removing low value intervals of `Log10MinDistPort`.

Moreover, this interface enables detecting discrepancies between the logic of the model and expectations based on domain knowledge of a human. Below we present some examples from our case study.

To verify whether the model relies on relevant features for classifying specific classes, we examine the rules predicting class 3 (port entering/exiting). Given its definition, we expect that these rules should involve at least one of the features `MaxDistPort` or `Log10MinDistPort`. However, the overview shows that some rules for class 3 omit both. Filtering out rules containing either feature reveals 144 such cases, contradicting the class definition. Removing these rules does not impact model accuracy.

Next, we explore whether classes 1, 2, and 4 can be distinguished without speed-related features. Filtering out rules containing any speed attributes leaves 213 rules. Among them, 23 predict class 1 (forward movement). As expected, all use `DistStartTrendAngle`, which correlates with speed. However, its range is not consistently limited to higher or medium values. Further filtering to restrict `DistStartTrendAngle` to low values identifies two rules that allow it to span from $-\infty$ to relatively high values. Since these rules do not effectively distinguish class 1, we remove them, again without affecting accuracy.

Filtering also reveals inconsistencies for other classes. We find 7 rules for class 2 (trawling) that allow high `SpeedMinimum` values ($\geq 9.95\,\text{km/h}$), though trawling typically occurs at lower speeds. Testing these rules on labeled data shows that they each apply to very few instances (6 for one rule, 2–3 for the others), and only one rule achieves more than a single correct prediction. Removing these rules does not affect accuracy. Similarly, we identify and remove 53 rules for class 4 (anchoring) that fail to impose an upper bound on minimal speed.

The next filtering step identifies 353 rules for class 3 where the minimal distance to port is unrestricted. Removing these rules causes a minor accuracy drop (from 99.35% to 99.33%) due to a single prediction change. The affected instance, originally labeled as class 3, has `Log10MinDistPort` = 0.57 (equivalent to 3.715 km from the nearest port). Given this distance, the instance appears mislabeled, and the corrected prediction of class 1 seems more appropriate.

These examples illustrate how interactive filtering, rule testing, and selective rule removal enhance both model understanding and logic refinement, often without loss of accuracy. In the result of automated and interactive cleaning, the final rule set consists of 8,956 rules, which is 90% of the original 9,939 rules.

5 Rules vs SHAP

While these interactive visualization tools significantly enhance our ability to explore and understand large rule sets, the manual process of identifying logically problematic rules is very labor-intensive. This bottleneck led us to explore whether feature attribution methods could streamline this process and offer deeper insights into model behavior.

A key distinction between approaches is that feature attribution methods, such as SHAP (SHapley Additive exPlanations), require a test dataset for their application, while rule exploration can be performed without one. Furthermore, exploring rules enables understanding of the internal model logic, whereas feature attribution supports analysis of the model's external behavior. SHAP quantifies each feature's contribution to individual predictions, making it a prominent tool for explaining model behavior. Given that our decision rules are inherently feature-based, we hypothesized that SHAP values could complement rule evaluation. This complementary lens could highlight rules where feature importance patterns diverge from expected domain relationships or reveal systematic biases in the model's decision-making process.

We integrated SHAP analysis into our workflow, expecting feature attribution patterns to align with our rule-based understanding and accelerate the identification of inconsistent or problematic rules. However, our investigation revealed a more complex relationship between rule-based and feature attribution explanations than initially anticipated.

Combining rule-based and SHAP-based explanations is expected to serve two main objectives:

- **Enhancing overall model interpretability:** We expect that feature impact scores can provide insights into model's predictive behavior, complementary to insights into model's logic. By quantifying each feature's contribution to predictions, they can foster a deeper understanding of the model's decision-making and promote greater transparency.
- **Facilitating interactive rule space exploration:** Understanding feature importance may empower users to more effectively explore the rule space, allowing them to focus on rules that include or exclude critical features. This targeted approach helps align the model's reasoning with user domain expertise. Moreover, comparing rule-based and attribution-based explanations enables users to evaluate consistency, helping to identify discrepancies and build trust in the system.

Ultimately, this combined approach is expected to offer a more robust method for human-AI decision-making.

To verify our expectations, we used a test dataset with 4,798 labeled instances. For each instance and each of the 9 features, 4 SHAP values were computed to quantify the impact of this feature on prediction of each of the four classes. These SHAP values were computed using a multi-class extension of the SHAP framework. Specifically, for each instance, the model produces a probability distribution over all four classes. SHAP then computes a set of feature attributions per class, explaining how much each feature contributed to the predicted probability of each class independently. This approach results in a matrix of SHAP values for each instance: one value for each feature–class pair, regardless of the instance's true label. These values reflect the contribution of a feature to the model's confidence in a particular class, whether or not that class is the correct one. This class-wise explanation is critical for understanding not only why the model predicted a certain class, but also why it did not predict other classes and offering insight into decision boundaries and potential misclassifications.

The computation results are presented in an aggregated form in Fig. 3. The display consists of 4 differently colored bar charts with vertically arranged horizontal bars. Each bar chart corresponds to a subset of labeled instances having the same class label, which is represented by a distinct color: red, blue, green, and purple for the classes 1, 2, 3, and 4, respectively. The bars for class C_i represent, by their length and orientation, the averaged SHAP values for each pair $(feature_j, class_k)$. These aggregates show how each feature contributes, on

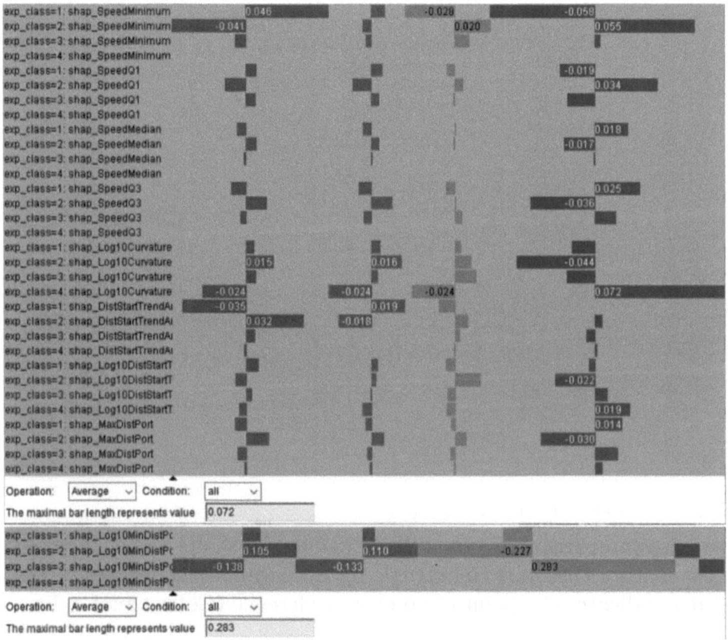

Fig. 3. SHAP values averaged by 4 classes of labeled instances.

the average, into classifying the instances of the class C_i as instances of classes C_1, C_2, C_3, and C_4. The bars oriented to the left represent negative values and the right-oriented bars represent positive values. We have created a separate display for the feature `Log10MinDistPort`, as the aggregated values for this feature have much higher absolute values than for any other feature. Putting this feature in the same display as the others makes the bars for these other features too short, reducing the readability of the display.

In the bar chart display, we notice some things that contradict our expectations. In particular, it shows that the feature `DistStartTrendAngle` makes, on the average, a negative impact on predicting class 1 (forward movement) and a positive impact on predicting class 2 (trawling). This raises a need for a more detailed examination. We compute the differences between the SHAP values for this feature for the classes 1 and 2 across all instances and plot them in a scatterplot against the values of `DistStartTrendAngle` in the instances, as shown in Fig. 4. Here, it can be seen that lower feature values strongly favor predictions of class 2, while higher values support predictions of class 1, which does not seem to align with what we have seen in the bar chart display. Figure 4 suggests that feature interactions play an important role in the prediction as the instances have a range of SHAP difference values. Particularly around the values of 0.2, either class can be taken, possibly depending on the other features.

To look further into the alignment between the two techniques, in Fig. 5 SHAP summary plots are presented for two of the classes, Class 1 (Forward

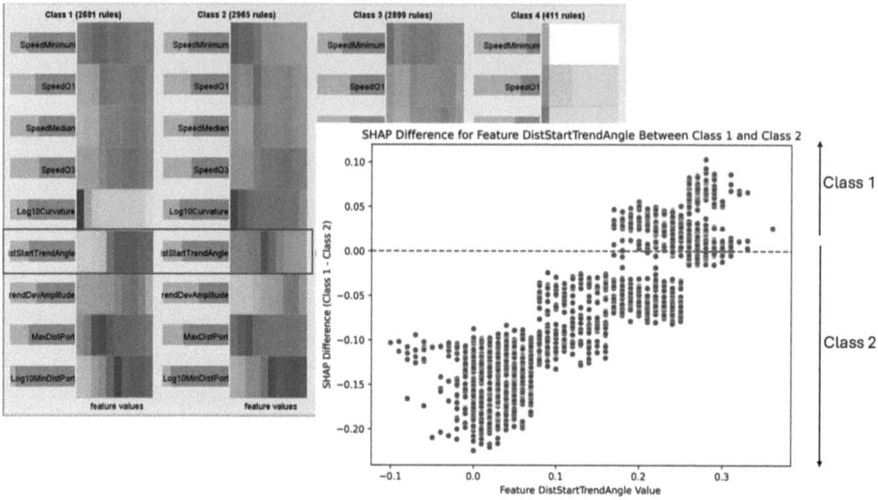

Fig. 4. Pairwise comparison of global SHAP values (absolute value) between classes 1 and 2 for the feature DistStartTrendAngle plotted against the feature values. The red horizontal line indicates the point of no class preference (Color figure online)

Movement) and Class 2 (Trawling). These show the impact of a feature on the models output for a given prediction. Here, the SHAP value for each instance is presented while maintaining the sign, and hence showing if the instance had a positive or negative influence on the prediction. Here, some interesting observations can be made.

Alignment between the SHAP values and the rule distribution can be seen for the majority of the features. For example, when we look at `Log10MinDistPort`, higher values of the feature for both classes, but particularly for Class 2 are positive predictors. The rule distribution (Fig. 2) and the SHAP pattern (Fig. 5) show nearly perfect alignment. However, it is not so for the feature `DistStartTrendAngle`. Looking at the rule distribution for this feature in Fig. 2 (Top), it is very clear that larger values of the feature exist more for Class 1 and lower values of the feature exist more for Class 2. However, Fig. 5 shows a contradiction where it suggests that higher values of the feature in fact contribute negatively towards making a prediction for Class 1. This, again, looks quite surprising, given that the scatterplot in Fig. 4 tells us a different story. This indicates the importance of investigating model behaviour from multiple perspectives to truly understand the underlying model behaviour.

6 Discussion

In this work, two traditionally used interpretability techniques (Rule-based and SHAP-based) are combined within an interactive visual interface to showcase the complementary nature of the two approaches. The approach aims to improve overall interpretability and also aid in further interactive exploration by the user.

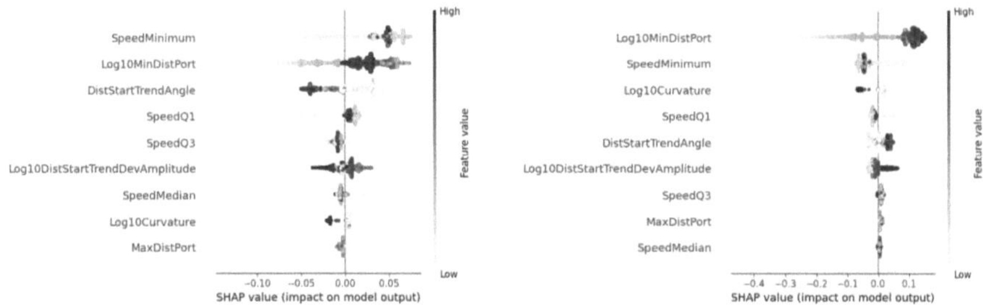

(a) (b)

Fig. 5. SHAP summary plots illustrating the contribution of key features to the classification model's output for Class 1 (a) and Class 2 (b). Each point represents an individual data instance, where the x-axis shows the SHAP value (i.e., the impact of a feature on the model's prediction), and the color indicates the feature's value (dark = high, lighter = low).

Our findings suggest that single-method explanations may provide incomplete or misleading insights into model behavior. The contradictory SHAP patterns for DistStartTrendAngle between global and local analyses exemplify this limitation. These contradictions however, may not be flaws but reflections of the complexity in the model interpretation. One possible explanation is in how SHAP values are calculated. SHAP attempts to isolate each feature's unique contribution to the model's output, treating features independently. However, when features are highly correlated or interact in non-linear ways, SHAP may assign counterintuitive values, sometimes, as seen in our example, it is even capable of attributing negative influence to features that should have a positive influence.

When examined in isolation, either the rule-based or attribution-based explanation might lead to incorrect conclusions about feature importance and model reasoning. This highlights the importance of creating robust explainable AI systems that incorporate multiple explanation modalities by design and not just as an afterthought. The approach of combining rule-based and attribution-based methods can help towards:

- **Consistency Validation:** Where the methods agree, the overall confidence in the explanation would increase.
- **Complexity identification:** Where the methods disagree, a deeper investigation into the model behaviour is necessary.
- **Bias detection:** The discrepancies between the methods may also help to indicate hidden biases or oversimplified assumptions that may exist.

For model developers, this composite view allows for more informed diagnostics. Features that frequently appear in rules but show low SHAP values might be overused, while the alignment (or misalignment) with human domain knowledge helps assess whether the model's logic reflects real-world reasoning. The interactive nature of our framework also enables iterative refinement of model logic, such as pruning rules that depend heavily on misleading or low-impact features, ultimately improving model transparency without degrading performance.

This work also aligns with broader critiques of SHAP, which suggest that its explanations, although mathematically sound, do not always align with human intuitions or expectations [17]. By situating SHAP within a multi-method interface, users are better equipped to understand its limitations and interpret results more critically.

7 Conclusions and Future Work

Our investigation shows that the connection between rule-based and feature attribution explanations are complex. Also, the counter-intuitive information provided brings to light some general limitations of using purely data-driven strategies. This supports the idea that rather than seeking a single best explanation method, it would be valuable for the XAI community to embrace complementary approaches that can provide different perspectives on model behaviour. Furthermore, by increasing the interactivity of this approach, users can be more active in exploring how the different explanation methods align or conflict, hence improving the human-centric nature of the explanation process. In practical usage, such a multi-perspective interactive framework could lead to more informed refinement of model logic and ultimately more trustworthy AI systems.

While the proposed approach offers promising directions for enhancing interpretability, several limitations remain. SHAP values, though widely used, can be unstable and sensitive to small changes in data or model parameters, which may affect the reliability of the explanations. By integrating SHAP with aggregate rule distributions, we aim to improve explanation robustness through mutual validation. Future enhancements could include incorporating techniques like deletion–insertion sensitivity analysis [13] to further stabilize SHAP scores before visualization. Also, the impact of the type of SHAP explainer (i.e. TreeSHAP [8], kernelSHAP [9]) used for the computation of the SHAP values was not investigated in this study and could provide some interesting observations. Our current case study focuses on vessel movement recognition, expanding this to other case studies from various domains, will also help assess its generalizability and usefulness across domains.

Acknowledgments. This work was supported by Federal Ministry of Education and Research of Germany and the state of North-Rhine Westphalia as part of the *Lamarr Institute for Machine Learning and Artificial Intelligence* (Lamarr22B), and by EU in project CrexData (grant no. 101092749).

References

1. Adilova, L., Kamp, M., Andrienko, G., Andrienko, N.: Re-interpreting rules interpretability. Int. J. Data Sci. Anal. (2023). https://doi.org/10.1007/s41060-023-00398-5
2. Andrienko, N., Andrienko, G., Adilova, L., Wrobel, S.: Visual analytics for human-centered machine learning. IEEE Comput. Graph. Appl. **42**(1), 123–133 (2022). https://doi.org/10.1109/MCG.2021.3130314
3. Andrienko, N., Andrienko, G., Artikis, A., Mantenoglou, P., Rinzivillo, S.: Human-in-the-loop: visual analytics for building models recognising behavioural patterns in time series. IEEE Comput. Graph. Appl. (2024). MCG.2024.3379851
4. Bénard, C., Biau, G., da Veiga, S., Scornet, E.: Sirus: stable and interpretable rule set for classification (2020)
5. Guidotti, R., Monreale, A., Ruggieri, S., Pedreschi, D., Turini, F., Giannotti, F.: Local rule-based explanations of black box decision systems. arxiv 2018. arXiv preprint arXiv:1805.10820 (1805)
6. Guidotti, R., Monreale, A., Ruggieri, S., Turini, F., Giannotti, F., Pedreschi, D.: A survey of methods for explaining black box models. ACM Comput. Surv. **51**(5) (2018). https://doi.org/10.1145/3236009
7. Lakkaraju, H., Bach, S.H., Leskovec, J.: Interpretable decision sets: a joint framework for description and prediction. In: Proceedings of the 22nd ACM SIGKDD International Conference on Knowledge Discovery and Data Mining, KDD 2016, pp. 1675–1684. Association for Computing Machinery, New York, NY, USA (2016). https://doi.org/10.1145/2939672.2939874
8. Lundberg, S.M., et al.: From local explanations to global understanding with explainable ai for trees. Nat. Mach. Intell. **2**(1), 56–67 (2020)
9. Lundberg, S.M., Lee, S.I.: A unified approach to interpreting model predictions. In: Proceedings of the 31st International Conference on Neural Information Processing Systems, NIPS 2017, pp. 4768–4777. Curran Associates Inc., Red Hook, NY, USA (2017)
10. Maçãs, C., Campos, J.R., Lourenço, N., Machado, P.: Visualisation of random forest classification. Inf. Vis. **23**(4), 312–327 (2024). https://doi.org/10.1177/14738716241260745
11. Ming, Y., Qu, H., Bertini, E.: Rulematrix: visualizing and understanding classifiers with rules. IEEE Trans. Visual Comput. Graph. **25**(1), 342–352 (2018). https://doi.org/10.1109/TVCG.2018.2864812
12. Neto, M.P., Paulovich, F.V.: Explainable matrix - visualization for global and local interpretability of random forest classification ensembles. IEEE Trans. Visualization Comput. Graph. **27**(02), 1427–1437 (2021). https://doi.org/10.1109/TVCG.2020.3030354
13. Petsiuk, V., Das, A., Saenko, K.: Rise: randomized input sampling for explanation of black-box models. arXiv preprint arXiv:1806.07421 (2018). https://doi.org/10.48550/arXiv.1806.07421
14. Quinlan, J.R.: Induction of decision trees. Mach. Learn. **1**(1), 81–106 (1986). https://doi.org/10.1023/A:1022643204877
15. Ribeiro, M.T., Singh, S., Guestrin, C.: "Why should I trust you?": explaining the predictions of any classifier. In: Proceedings of the 22nd ACM SIGKDD International Conference on Knowledge Discovery and Data Mining, KDD 2016, pp. 1135–1144. Association for Computing Machinery, New York, NY, USA (2016). https://doi.org/10.1145/2939672.2939778

16. Ribeiro, M.T., Singh, S., Guestrin, C.: Anchors: high-precision model-agnostic explanations. In: Proceedings of the AAAI Conference on Artificial Intelligence, vol. 32, no. 1 (2018). https://doi.org/10.1609/aaai.v32i1.11491
17. Salih, A.M., et al.: A perspective on explainable artificial intelligence methods: shap and lime. Adv. Intell. Syst. **7**(1), 2400304 (2025). https://doi.org/10.1002/aisy.202400304
18. Setzu, M., Guidotti, R., Monreale, A., Turini, F., Pedreschi, D., Giannotti, F.: Glocalx - from local to global explanations of black box AI models. Artif. Intell. **294**, 103457 (2021). https://doi.org/10.1016/j.artint.2021.103457
19. Sundararajan, M., Taly, A., Yan, Q.: Axiomatic attribution for deep networks. In: Proceedings of the 34th International Conference on Machine Learning, ICML 2017, vol. 70, pp. 3319–3328. JMLR.org (2017)
20. Zhao, X., Wu, Y., Lee, D.L., Cui, W.: iforest: interpreting random forests via visual analytics. IEEE Trans. Visual Comput. Graph. **25**(1), 407–416 (2018). https://doi.org/10.1109/TVCG.2018.2864475

A Concept-Based Approach to Voice Disorder Detection

Davide Ghia[1(✉)], Gabriele Ciravegna[1,2], Alkis Koudounas[1], Marco Fantini[3,4], Erika Crosetti[4], Giovanni Succo[4,5], and Tania Cerquitelli[1]

[1] Politecnico di Torino, Turin, Italy
{davide.ghia,gabriele.ciravegna,tania.cerquitelli}@polito.it
[2] CENTAI Institute, Turin, Italy
[3] San Feliciano Hospital, Rome, Italy
[4] SCDU Otorinolaringoiatria, Head Neck Cancer Unit, Ospedale San Giovanni Bosco, Turin, Italy
[5] Dipartimento di Oncologia, Università degli Studi di Torino, Turin, Italy

Abstract. Voice disorders affect a significant portion of the population, and the ability to diagnose them using automated, non-invasive techniques would represent a substantial advancement in healthcare, improving the quality of life of patients. Recent studies have demonstrated that artificial intelligence models, particularly Deep Neural Networks (DNNs), can effectively address this task. However, due to their complexity, the decision-making process of such models often remains opaque, limiting their trustworthiness in clinical contexts. This paper investigates an alternative approach based on Explainable AI (XAI), a field that aims to improve the interpretability of DNNs by providing different forms of explanations. Specifically, this work focuses on concept-based models such as Concept Bottleneck Model (CBM) and Concept Embedding Model (CEM) and how they can achieve performance comparable to traditional deep learning methods while offering a more transparent and interpretable decision framework.

Keywords: Explainable-AI · Voice Disorders · Concept-based · Transformers

1 Introduction

In healthcare, the development of Artificial Intelligence (AI) offers new and more efficient approaches to various types of diagnosis. Non-invasive approaches represent an important example, significantly improving patients' quality of life. Although non-invasive AI-based approaches have been studied in different branches of medicine, such as skin cancer [9], diabetic retinopathy [14], and atrial fibrillation [2], their application to vocal disorder recognition still presents room for improvement. This task consists in the classification of pathological versus euphonic voices. Voice disorders represent an important pathology affecting a

I. Koprinska et al. (Eds.): ECML PKDD 2025, CCIS 2842, pp. 577–590, 2026.
https://doi.org/10.1007/978-3-032-19105-2_40

significant portion of the population, substantially impacting patient quality of life [3,8,10,40,43].

Very recently, Deep Neural Networks (DNNs) have started to demonstrate promising performances on this task [26,27], potentially suggesting that uncomfortable and invasive clinical procedures may be avoided through the simple analysis of voice recordings. These complex models, mainly based on the Transformer architecture [44], achieve competitive performances on the voice disorders detection task, thanks to the impressive correlation analysis capabilities of the attention module, which allows them to operate end-to-end on the raw voice data. Yet, their decision process remains predominantly opaque, and the model is perceived as a black box: its outputs are produced from the inputs without providing any form of explanation. Particularly in the context of healthcare, the lack of interpretability represents a crucial problem. Considering the sensitivity of the data involved, fully relying on the decisions of a non-transparent algorithm can raise both ethical and legal concerns [34].

EXplainable AI (XAI) [32] aims to address the issue of interpretability in DNNs. Through various modalities and techniques, it aims to enhance the transparency and clarity of the decision process, using tools such as graphs, visual explanations, or saliency maps [35]. Concept-based XAI (C-XAI) [23,38], a promising and interesting subfield of Explainable AI, seeks to improve interpretability of the models by means of higher-level abstractions, a.k.a. concepts. A *concept* can be defined as a representation of the information learned by the model that is understandable by humans. Explaining model decisions in terms of such concepts can contribute to increasing user trust and acceptance of neural networks. Concept-based models [25] make a step further, directly providing the final prediction in terms of a combination of concepts. These models represent a significant improvement in terms of both transparency and interactivity, enabling human experts to intervene in concept representations to derive counterfactual predictions.

Unlike previous work, in this paper, we apply a concept-based approach to the voice disorder detection task. In order to collect annotations for the concepts, we used the Italian Pathological Voice (IPV) dataset introduced in [26], which contains the written anamnesis of each case. We then train two different types of concept-based models, a Concept Bottleneck Model (CBM) [25] and a Concept Embedding Model (CEM) [48], to learn both the concepts and the classification task. Through a comparison with a conventional end-to-end transformer-based approach, we demonstrate that concept-based models achieve competitive performance while significantly improving the interpretability of the decision process.

2 Related Works

Voice disorders represent an important field of study within healthcare, as they affect a significant portion of the population, and are symptoms of serious illnesses, including both benign and malignant conditions, and neurodegenerative disorders [4,21,45]. While invasive techniques have been demonstrated to be very effective for diagnosis [7,15,37], they often involve anesthesia, stressful exams, and risk of complications. A non-invasive approach known as Electroglottography (EGG) [17,20], which measures the contact between the vocal folds by applying electrodes to the patient's neck, minimizes the risks associated with invasive exams. Other techniques focus on the voice features extraction. Mel-Frequency Cepstral Coefficients (MFCCs) were used to train multi-layer perceptron (MLP) [42], while Convolutional Neural Networks (CNN) exploited MFCC cepstral spectrograms [36,46]. DNN, and in particular CNN, can also work directly on raw speech signal, as shown for 1D-CNNs. All these works demonstrated the feasibility of the task without, however, showing competitive performance with invasive approaches. On the contrary, transformer end-to-end architectures in [6,26,29,39] have started to show that voice analysis represents, with these architectures, a powerful non-invasive diagnostic approach. [27,31] showed that including different voice sources, such as sustained vowels and sentence readings, further improves the detection performance.

Still, all AI models work end-to-end on the raw data without providing almost any form of interpretability. To address this challenge, various AI research groups have increasingly focused on explainable AI (XAI) [32], and more recently, on C-XAI methodologies [38]. Concept-based XAI techniques can be divided into two main categories: *post-hoc* and *explainable-by-design* approaches. Post-hoc methods operate on models trained conventionally and aim to detect the presence of concepts within their learned representations. In contrast, explainable-by-design methods integrate concepts directly into the architecture of the neural model, encouraging the learning of effective concept representations during training. TCAV [23], ACE [12], and CaCE [13] are examples of the former. These methods identify concepts within the learned representation of the model and quantify their influence on the final prediction. For the latter, existing approaches include supervised methods such as CBM [25], CEM [48], and ProbCBM [24]; unsupervised methods such as SENN [1] and ProtoPNet [5]; and generative approaches such as Label-free CBM [33] and LaBo [47]. A comprehensive review of these techniques is provided in the work by [38]. Supervised explainable-by-design techniques proved to be the most effective in terms of improving the interpretability of the neural representation, while maintaining competitive performance. For instance, CBM and CEM models explicitly associate a node (CBM) or an embedding (CEM) to a specific concept. For these reasons, we adopted this approach in our work.

3 Method

This paper aims to create a concept-based model for detecting voice pathologies in an interpretable way. The first requirement of supervised concept-based models is the availability of a dataset annotated with concepts. Thus, the procedure followed in this paper consists in (i) extracting a set of annotated concepts from the textual files contained in the dataset with a Large Language Model (LLM) (see Sect. 3.1), and (ii) training a Concept Bottleneck Model and a Concept Embedding Model on the concepts extracted and feeding these concepts to

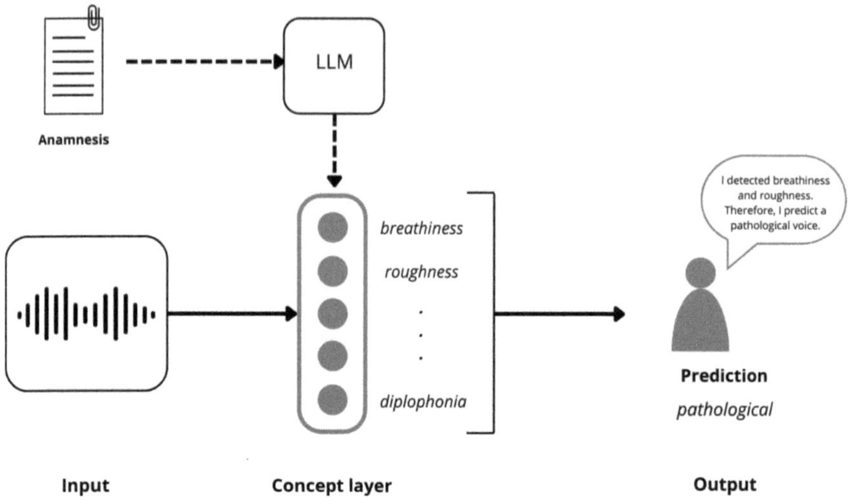

Fig. 1. Concept-based model framework. The upper part of the figure shows how an LLM can provide concept annotation during training. We depict this process with dashed lines, as it is only required during training. The bottom part represents how a model can learn to predict intermediate concepts to justify the final classification decision.

a binary classifier for detecting a voice pathology (see Sect. 3.2). The encoder layers of the models are derived from a pre-trained audio transformer architecture (HuBERT [16]), while the classification head changes depending on the solutions adopted (e.g., CBM and CEM). Figure 1 depicts the overall framework with the audio waveform and the anamnesis document serving as input data. During training, the first is used to extract the concept annotations by means of an LLM, while the second is given as input to an audio transformer to learn to output the concepts and the final predictions. At test time, the LLM and the anamnesis are not required anymore, since the audio model has now learned to predict the concepts.

3.1 Concept Annotation

The first step to train a concept-based model is to obtain a concept-annotated dataset. In our case, we utilize the IPV dataset [26], which presents, for most cases, a PDF or Word file containing a written anamnesis of the patient. These files do not have a standardized structure, as they were not designed for concept prediction: they are written by medical experts in a textual form. Thus, after an initial technical consultation with experts and through a deep analysis of the data, both automated and manual, we identified a set of 14 candidate concepts that were reported in most anamneses[1]. By "candidate concept", we mean a

[1] List of candidate concepts: *smoking*, *professional voice use*, *dysphonia*, *irregular mucosal wave*, *mucous*, *diplophonia*, *strain*, *roughness*, *breathiness*, *asthenicity*, *phonastenia*, *glottic hourglass configuration*, *dysodia*, *gender*.

concept that describes a particular characteristic of the patient, which may help distinguish between pathological and euphonic cases.

```
Extract the following concepts from the provided text, returning a complete JSON object. Each concept must have exactly one of the allowed values.
[
  "smoking": allowed values: "yes"/"no",
  "professional voice use": allowed values: "yes"/"no",
  "dysphonia": allowed values: "no"/"light"/"light-moderate"/"moderate"/"severe",
  "irregular mucous wave": allowed values: "yes"/"no",
  "mucous": allowed values: "pink"/"eutrophic"/"hyperemic"/"not present",
  "diplophonia": allowed values: "yes"/"no",
  "strain": allowed values: "yes"/"no",
  "roughness": allowed values: "yes"/"no",
  "breathiness": allowed values: "yes"/"no",
  "asthenicity": allowed values: "yes"/"no",
  "phonasthenia": allowed values: "yes"/"no",
  "glottic hourglass configuration": allowed values: "yes"/"no",
  "dysodia": allowed values: "yes"/"no",
  "sex": allowed values: "male"/"female"
]
If the concepts are not explicitly mentioned in the text, their value must be "no" - or "not present" only when the anamnesis explicitly include "not present" among the allowed values (such as "mucous").

Important: Concepts like asthenicity, phonasthenia, roughness, or strain must be marked as "yes" only when they are explicitly mentioned in the text.

Here is an example of the output format to provide and strictly follow:
{
  "smoking": (your answer),
  "professional voice use": (your answer),
  "dysphonia": (your answer),
  "irregular mucous wave": (your answer),
  "mucous": (your answer),
  "diplophonia": (your answer),
  "strain": (your answer),
  "roughness": (your answer),
  "breathiness": (your answer),
  "asthenicity": (your answer),
  "phonasthenia": (your answer),
  "glottic hourglass configuration": (your answer),
  "dysodia": (your answer),
  "sex": (your answer)
}
# Example 1:
...
# Example 2:
...
# Example 3:
...
# Example 4:
...
```

Listing 1.1. Example of prompt used to annotate concepts with the Gemini model. Following the anamnesis language the original prompt was in Italian but it has been translated here for the sake of readability. The four input/output examples used for few-shot learning are not reported for brevity.

To extract the concepts from each anamnesis file, we used an LLM, which is capable of interpreting natural language. This approach was particularly suitable, as a method based on structured data was not applicable. We applied a technique known as *few-shot prompting*, which involves including input-output examples within the prompt to better guide the model toward the desired output. In our case, we randomly selected four different files from the dataset as examples. We manually edited some of the original concept values to avoid repetition. By using different combinations of concept values, we aimed to cover every possible value of each concept, in order to improve the model's ability to recognize them. After partial editing, these examples were included in the prompt along with their corresponding manually annotated concepts. An example is shown in Listing 1.1.

We considered two distinct LLM models: `Mistral 7B-v0.1-hf` [19] and `Gemini-pro generative` [11]. Mistral is an open-source model that aims to find a compromise between performance and complexity, while Gemini is a powerful proprietary model developed by Google DeepMind, accessible only through API. In order to test the models' annotation capabilities and compare their results, we manually constructed a validation set: 69 files were selected from the original dataset, and each was humanly annotated with the corresponding concepts.

Since concept-based models such as CBM and CEM require binary concepts, we applied one-hot encoding to concepts with more than two possible values (e.g., *dysphonia: absent, light, moderate, severe*). As a result, the total number of concepts in the candidate set increased from 14 to 20. After technical consultation with medical experts, we decided to exclude some concepts (e.g., *mucous*) because they represented physical characteristics that could not be predicted through perceptual exams, but only via invasive procedures. Other concepts, such as *gender* or *phonasthenia*, are information directly obtainable from the patient and do not require prediction. Finally, with the guidance of the medical experts, the concept *dysphonia light-moderate* was merged with the concept *dysphonia moderate* since it was an unnecessary distinction. The final set (Table 1) consists of 9 predictable concepts and 5 patient-provided concepts. The integration of these two groups is discussed in the following section. Out of the 9 predictable concepts, 8 represent values within the GRBAS scale [41], a tool used by experts to evaluate the quality of voice. In this scale, "G" stands for the grade of dysphonia (represented by 4 concepts), "R" for roughness, "A" for asthenia, and "S" for strain.

3.2 Concept-Based Architecture

In order to create an interpretable voice disorder detector, we propose a concept-based architecture, which can be adapted, with minor modifications, for both CBM and CEM approaches. An overview of the proposed scheme is reported in Fig. 2. To obtain meaningful audio embeddings, we used HuBERT [16], an unsupervised pre-trained model specialized in speech representation, as a feature extractor. The use of a pre-trained model is particularly suitable given the limited size of our dataset.

Table 1. Concept selection for the final concept set.

Predictable	Patient-provided	Excluded
Dysphonia absent	Smoke	Irregular mucous wave
Dysphonia light	Professional use of voice	Mucous pink
Dysphonia moderate	Gender	Mucous hyperemic
Dysphonia severe	Phonasthenia	Mucous eutrophic
Diplophonia	Dysodia	Hourglass gottic configuration
Strain		
Roughness		
Breathiness		
Asthenicity		

In CBM models, the function $g(x)$, corresponding to the concept classifier, maps the input composed of d-dimensional space into the concept space, while $f(c)$, the task classifier, maps the concepts into the class space. In our case, we adapt the concept classifier to work on the audio embedding $e = h(x)$, where $x \in X \subset \mathcal{R}^{dt}$ is the input data represented as a sequence of tokens of dimension d and maximum length t, while the embeddings are represented as $e \in E \subseteq R^m$, where m is the dimension of the embedding representing each sample. On the other side, we still require concepts and tasks to be valid for the entire sequence, hence $c \in C \subseteq [0,1]^k$ and $y \in Y \subseteq [0,1]$.

It is important to note that the task classifier bases its prediction solely on concepts and never has access to the audio signal or its representations. In our CBM model, we add a classification head composed of a sequence of linear layers on top of the feature extractor. The final linear layer corresponds to the *bottleneck layer*, where each node is associated with a unique concept. We obtain the bottleneck simply by resizing this layer to match the number of concepts to predict. In our case, the bottleneck layer outputs 9 different logits, corresponding to the 9 concepts to predict, on which a sigmoid function is applied. Through a threshold (0.5), the concepts are binary classified as present or absent. The 9 predicted concepts $\hat{c} = g(x)$ are concatenated with the 5 user-provided concepts c" into a binary concept tensor $\bar{c} = [\hat{c}, c"]$ that is fed to the task classifier $\hat{y} = f(\bar{c})$. A second classification head, also consisting of linear layers, takes the concept tensor as input and produces the final class prediction. The model is then trained as a *joint bottleneck*, where the concept loss and the task loss are minimized at the same time using a combined loss:

$$\hat{f}, \hat{g} = \arg\min_{f,g} \sum_i \left[\mathcal{L}_Y(f(g(x^{(i)})), y^{(i)}) + \sum_j \lambda \mathcal{L}_{C_j}(\hat{c}; c^{(i)}) \right]$$

where $\mathcal{L}_Y$ represents the task loss, while $\mathcal{L}_{C_j}$ corresponds to the concept loss. The hyperparameter λ regulates the weight of the concept loss in the total loss computation.

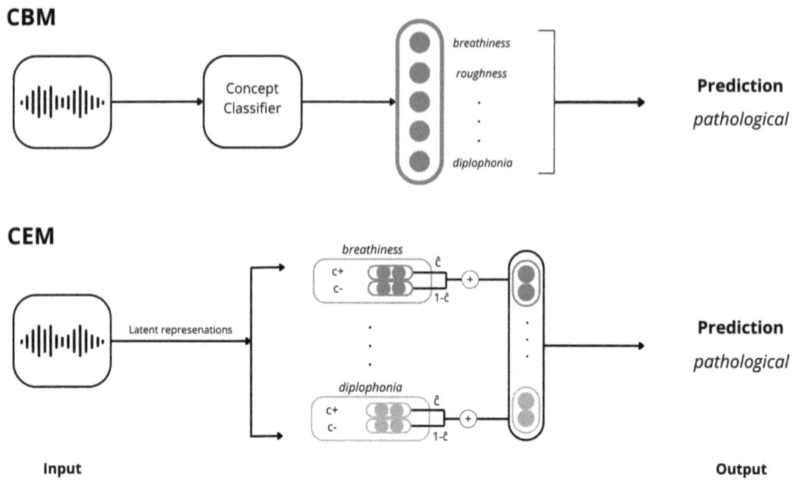

Fig. 2. CBM vs CEM architecture. CBM predicts a logit for each concept in the bottleneck layer. In contrast, CEM represents each concept with two distinct embeddings: one for the active state and one for the inactive state; these embeddings are then weighted by the probability of the concept being active $\hat{c}$ and inactive $1-\hat{c}$, respectively.

The structure of the CEM model is nearly identical to that of the CBM model. The bottleneck layer is replaced by an *embedding layer*, hence $\mathbf{c} = g_{CEM}(x)$, where $\mathbf{c} \in \mathbf{C} \subset \mathcal{R}^{kh}$, where h is the dimension of each concept embedding[2]. As shown in Fig. 2, instead of a direct one-to-one association between nodes and concepts, in this layer each concept is represented by two distinct embeddings, one corresponding to its active state and the other to its inactive state. The embedding layer also predicts the probability of each concept being active, over the concatenation of the positive and negative embeddings $\hat{c}_i = s[(\mathbf{c}_i^+, \mathbf{c}_i^-])$, which are predicted by means of a learned scoring function shared across concepts. The final classification head receives as input the concatenation of the concept embeddings $f(\mathbf{c})$, which are mapped into a shared latent space.

4 Experiments

We design our experiments to evaluate whether concept-based models (CBM, CEM) can match the performance of end-to-end models while offering greater interpretability in pathological voice classification from clinical recordings.

4.1 Dataset

The dataset used in the experiments is the Italian Pathological Voice (IPV). It consists of recordings, anamnesis, and exam results of 513 patients, collected

[2] CEM does also provide concept prediction $\hat{c}$ and condition the concept embedding through convex combination of the concept prediction with the positive and negative concept embeddings $\mathbf{c} = g(x) = \hat{c} \cdot \mathbf{c}^+ + (1 - \hat{c}) \cdot \mathbf{c}^-$.

from several private phoniatric and speech-therapy practices and hospitals in Italy. The dataset presents 170 euphonic cases and 340 dysphonic cases. For each patient, the dataset contains the recording of the reading of five phonetically balanced sentences derived from the Italian adaptation of the CAPE-V [22], and the recording of the sustained production of the vowel /a/. In addition to the AVQI exam results, which are not used in this paper, there are also the files containing the anamnesis of the patient, written directly by the doctor who performed the visit. Out of 513 cases, only 385 present a written anamnesis, out of which 134 are euphonic cases and 251 pathological cases. Since the dataset size is very limited, especially for large models as transformers, we performed 10-fold cross-validation to ensure robustness.

4.2 Experimental Details

Concept Annotation. We tested two distinct LLMs, the open-source `Mistral 7B-v0.1-hf` and the closed-source `Gemini-pro generative` models on the manually annotated test set. The experiments were conducted on the annotations of the original concept candidate set, composed of the 14 concepts, in order to test the capability of the LLMs to recognize all the selected concepts, both predictable and patient-provided. Given that a structured and coherent output was needed, the temperature of both models was set to 0.1. To better evaluate the models, we used both concept accuracy and the macro average F1 score. To facilitate the comparison, we also considered the total number of annotation errors.

Voice Pathologies Detection. The voice pathologies classification experiments were conducted only on cases that included a written anamnesis. We chose to use the recordings of the CAPE-V sentences, as this type of data contains more significant information. Each recording was padded to the maximum length of the dataset, as HuBERT requires inputs of equal length. All audio signals are resampled at 16 kHz. HuBERT model outputs a representation for each frame[3]. To obtain a unique representation, we applied max pooling over the model output. This technique was preferred to other methods, such as average pooling, as vocal characteristics tend to manifest as local peaks. In order to have a baseline comparison for the concept-base models, we also trained a conventional neural network, i.e., a HuBERT architecture with a classification head composed of sequential linear layers, with layer dimensions progressively decreasing: 1-layer [128], 2-layer [256,128], 3-layer [512,256,128]. We set the learning rate for HuBERT to 5e-5, while for the concept-based models, we used 5e-5 for the concept classifier and 5e-4 for the task classifier. For the CEM model, we employed an embedding size $h = 16$. We trained the models for 30 epochs, with early stopping criteria. We also applied a warm-up strategy: we froze the task loss for the first 2 epochs of training, leaving active only the concept loss.

[3] A frame is a fixed-length time interval over the audio signal, from which the model extracts a representation. Typically, the length of this interval is 20ms.

Table 2. Concept annotation. Results of the concept annotation performed by the two considered LLMs.

Model	Concept Acc	Concept F1 macro	Total Errors
Mistral 7B	0.9706	0.9670	42
Gemini-pro	**0.9865**	**0.9810**	**20**

By doing so, the model begins to learn the task after learning better concept representations.

We evaluate the models using concept accuracy, task accuracy, and task F1 score. Concept accuracy is crucial to assess whether the model correctly learned effective representations of concepts. To prioritize this aspect during training, we weighted the total loss as 0.9 (λ) for the concept loss and 0.1 for the task loss. The F1 score is important to evaluate if the model learned to distinguish between both classes, especially given the significant class imbalance in the original dataset.

5 Results

We first report the effectiveness of the concept annotations in order to ensure that the concept-based models would train on reliable data. We then analyze the performance of the CBM model and CEM model, comparing the results with those obtained by training a standard transformer model.

Concept Annotation. As shown in Table 2, both LLMs achieve satisfying results. It is important to note that some errors occur in concepts that were either vaguely described in the clinical reports or whose annotation heavily relied on interpretation. For instance, if the degree of dysphonia is not explicitly stated, the corresponding concept value must be inferred.

The Gemini model performs slightly better than Mistral in terms of accuracy and F1 score. The difference in performance increases if we consider the errors on the total number of concept predictions. Based on these considerations, Gemini was selected to perform the full annotation of the original dataset.

Table 3. Results of the concept-based model, compared to the conventional DNN and the Ideal CBM.

Model	Concept Accuracy	Task Accuracy	Task F1
HuBERT	-	**0.9133** (±0.0414)	**0.9085** (±0.0476)
CBM	0.8443 (±0.0346)	0.8776 (±0.0247)	0.8566 (±0.0175)
CEM	**0.8450** (±0.0205)	0.8730 (±0.0385)	0.8599 (±0.0168)
Ideal CBM	-	0.9052 (±0.0259)	0.8953 (±0.0309)

Voice Pathologies Prediction. As end-to-end baseline, the best-performing architecture overall is the 2-layer classification head, which achieves a Task Accuracy of 0.9133 and an F1 score of 0.9085, as reported in Table 3. We adopt this model as the baseline for the comparison with the concept-based models.

We trained the concept-based models using the annotations produced by the Gemini model. The concept accuracy was calculated on the 9 predicted concepts. To ensure that the identified concepts are effective in distinguishing the two classes, we trained a model (referred to as Ideal CBM), which receives the true concept values as input and predicts the corresponding class. In Table 3 we report the results of CBM and CEM models, the best-performing standard HuBERT model trained end-to-end for the voice pathologies detection task, and the Ideal CBM. It is worth noting that, with an ideal concept accuracy of 100.00% (IdealCBM), the performance of the CBM is very close to that of HuBERT, highlighting the effectiveness of the selected concepts for the classification task.

The actual concept accuracy achieved by CBM and CEM is approximately 84.50%. This can be attributed to the ambiguity of some annotations, which can cause erroneous predictions. Concept-based models achieve results comparable to those of the end-to-end approach in terms of both accuracy and F1 score, maintaining high classification effectiveness and introducing a significant level of interpretability. A pathological voice can be justified with a specific degree of dysphonia and by the presence of features such as *breathiness*, *roughness*, *diplophonia*, and *strain*. CBM slightly outperforms CEM in task accuracy despite having lower concept accuracy. Overall, however, the performance of the two models remains nearly identical.

6 Conclusion

In this paper, we proposed a concept-based approach to the voice disorders prediction task, in order to reach a high degree of interpretability, crucial in a delicate field as healthcare. We demonstrated the effectiveness of these models in recognizing both vocal concepts and pathological voices, achieving performance comparable to the conventional approach.

Future Work. A possible direction going forward could be considering not only the read sentences but also sustained vowels as input data, utilizing transformer models pre-trained for this kind of data [28,30]. An interesting direction for future development could also be the enhancement of the explanation interface. Concept predictions could be linked to a generative model (e.g., LLM) to produce a report-like document, including a description of the vocal analysis, suggested guidelines, and other clinically relevant information. Furthermore, the concept-based models employed in this paper could be evaluated on different datasets, such as AVFAD [18]. Concept annotations are required only during training, making this approach potentially applicable to different voice disorder datasets.

Disclosure of Interests. Authors have no competing interest.

References

1. Alvarez-Melis, D., Jaakkola, T.S.: Towards robust interpretability with self-explaining neural networks (2018). https://arxiv.org/abs/1806.07538
2. Attia, Z.I., et al.: Screening for cardiac contractile dysfunction using an artificial intelligence-enabled electrocardiogram. Nat. Med. **25**(1), 70–74 (2019)
3. Bhattacharyya, N.: The prevalence of voice problems among adults in the united states. The Laryngoscope (2014)
4. Brunner, E., Eberhard, K., Gugatschka, M.: Prevalence of benign vocal fold lesions: long-term results from a single European institution. J. Voice (2023)
5. Chen, C., Li, O., Tao, A., Barnett, A., Rudin, C., Su, J.K.: This looks like that: deep learning for interpretable image recognition. In: Advances in Neural Information Processing Systems (NeurIPS), vol. 32 (2019)
6. Ciravegna, G., et al.: Non-invasive ai-powered diagnostics: the case of voice-disorder detection-vision paper. In: Proceedings of the Workshops of the EDBT/ICDT 2024 Joint Conference, vol. 3651. CEUR (2024)
7. Cohen, S.M., Thomas, S., Roy, N., Kim, J., Courey, M.: Frequency and factors associated with use of videolaryngostroboscopy in voice disorder assessment. Laryngoscope **124**(9), 2118–2124 (2014). https://doi.org/10.1002/lary.24688. epub 2014 May 7
8. Cohen, S.M.: Self-reported impact of dysphonia in a primary care population: an epidemiological study. The Laryngoscope (2010)
9. Esteva, A., et al.: Dermatologist-level classification of skin cancer with deep neural networks. Nature (2017)
10. Fantini, M., et al.: The rapidly evolving scenario of acoustic voice analysis in otolaryngology. Cureus **16**(11) (2024)
11. Gemini Team: Gemini: A family of highly capable multimodal models (2025). https://arxiv.org/abs/2312.11805
12. Ghorbani, A., Wexler, J., Zou, J., Kim, B.: Towards automatic concept-based explanations (2019). https://arxiv.org/abs/1902.03129
13. Goyal, Y., Feder, A., Shalit, U., Kim, B.: Explaining classifiers with causal concept effect (CACE) (2020). https://arxiv.org/abs/1907.07165
14. Gulshan, V., et al.: Development and validation of a deep learning algorithm for detection of diabetic retinopathy in retinal fundus photographs. Jama **316**(22), 2402–2410 (2016)
15. Hamdan, A.L., Ghanem, A., Natout, T.E., Khalifee, E.: Diagnostic yield of office-based laryngeal biopsy in patients with leukoplakia; a case study with review of the literature. J. Voice **37**(2), 282–286 (2023). https://doi.org/10.1016/j.jvoice.2020.11.026. epub 2021 Jan 28
16. Hsu, W.N., Bolte, B., Tsai, Y.H.H., Lakhotia, K., Salakhutdinov, R., Mohamed, A.: Hubert: self-supervised speech representation learning by masked prediction of hidden units (2021). https://arxiv.org/abs/2106.07447
17. Islam, R., Abdel-Raheem, E., Tarique, M.: Voice pathology detection using convolutional neural networks with electroglottographic (EGG) and speech signals. Comput. Methods Programs Biomed. Update **2**, 100074 (2022). https://doi.org/10.1016/j.cmpbup.2022.100074, cC BY-NC-ND 4.0
18. Jesus, L.M., Belo, I., Machado, J., Hall, A.: The advanced voice function assessment databases (AVFAD): tools for voice clinicians and speech research. In: Fernandes, F.D.M. (ed.) Advances in Speech-language Pathology, chap. 14. IntechOpen, Rijeka (2017). https://doi.org/10.5772/intechopen.69643

19. Jiang, A.Q., et al.: Mistral 7b (2023). https://arxiv.org/abs/2310.06825
20. Kadiri, S.R., Alku, P.: Analysis and detection of pathological voice using glottal source features. IEEE J. Sel. Topics Signal Process. **14**(2), 367–379 (2020). https://doi.org/10.1109/JSTSP.2019.2957988
21. Karabayir, I., Goldman, S.M., Pappu, S., Akbilgic, O.: Gradient boosting for Parkinson's disease diagnosis from voice recordings. BMC Med. Inf. Decis. Making (2020)
22. Kempster, G., Gerratt, B., Verdolini Abbott, K., Barkmeier-Kraemer, J., Hillman, R.: Consensus auditory-perceptual evaluation of voice: development of a standardized clinical protocol. Am. J. Speech Lang. Pathol. **18**, 124–132 (2009). https://doi.org/10.1044/1058-0360(2008/08-0017)
23. Kim, B., et al.: Interpretability beyond feature attribution: quantitative testing with concept activation vectors (TCAV) (2018). https://arxiv.org/abs/1711.11279
24. Kim, E., Jung, D., Park, S., Kim, S., Yoon, S.: Probabilistic concept bottleneck models (2023). https://arxiv.org/abs/2306.01574
25. Koh, P.W., et al.: Concept bottleneck models. In: Proceedings of the 37th International Conference on Machine Learning (ICML). Proceedings of Machine Learning Research, vol. 119, pp. 5338–5352. PMLR (2020). https://proceedings.mlr.press/v119/koh20a.html
26. Koudounas, A., et al.: Voice disorder analysis: a transformer-based approach. In: Interspeech 2024, pp. 3040–3044. ISCA (2024). https://doi.org/10.21437/interspeech.2024-1122
27. Koudounas, A., et al.: MVP: multi-source voice pathology detection. In: Proceedings of the Interspeech 2025 (2025)
28. Koudounas, A., La Quatra, M., Siniscalchi, S.M., Baralis, E.: voc2vec: a foundation model for non-verbal vocalization. In: 2025 IEEE International Conference on Acoustics, Speech and Signal Processing (ICASSP), ICASSP 2025, pp. 1–5 (2025). https://doi.org/10.1109/ICASSP49660.2025.10890672
29. La Quatra, M., Koudounas, A., Salerno, V.M., Siniscalchi, S.M.: Exploring generative error correction for dysarthric speech recognition. In: Proceedings of the Interspeech 2025 (2025)
30. La Quatra, M., et al.: Benchmarking representations for speech, music, and acoustic events. In: 2024 IEEE International Conference on Acoustics, Speech, and Signal Processing Workshops (ICASSPW), pp. 505–509 (2024). https://doi.org/10.1109/ICASSPW62465.2024.10625960
31. Liu, Q., Ciravegna, G., Koudounas, A., Cerquitelli, T., Baralis, E., et al.: Multimodal fusion techniques to enhance voice disorder diagnoses. In: CEUR Workshop Proceedings, vol. 3946. CEUR (2025)
32. Mersha, M., Lam, K., Wood, J., AlShami, A.K., Kalita, J.: Explainable artificial intelligence: a survey of needs, techniques, applications, and future direction. Neurocomputing **599**, 128111 (2024). https://doi.org/10.1016/j.neucom.2024.128111
33. Oikarinen, T., Das, S., Nguyen, L.M., Weng, T.W.: Label-free concept bottleneck models. arXiv preprint arXiv:2304.06129 (2023)
34. Palaniappan, K., Lin, E.Y.T., Vogel, S.: Global regulatory frameworks for the use of artificial intelligence (AI) in the healthcare services sector. In: Healthcare, vol. 12, p. 562. MDPI (2024)
35. Pastor, E., Koudounas, A., Attanasio, G., Hovy, D., Baralis, E.: Explaining speech classification models via word-level audio segments and paralinguistic features. In: Proceedings of the 18th Conference of the European Chapter of the Association for Computational Linguistics (Volume 1: Long Papers), pp. 2221–2238 (2024)

36. Peng, X., Xu, H., Liu, J., et al.: Voice disorder classification using convolutional neural network based on deep transfer learning. Sci. Rep. **13**, 7264 (2023). https://doi.org/10.1038/s41598-023-34461-9
37. Pietruszewska, W., et al.: Comparative analysis of high-speed videolaryngoscopy images and sound data simultaneously acquired from rigid and flexible laryngoscope: a pilot study. Sci. Rep. **11**(1), 20480 (2021). https://doi.org/10.1038/s41598-021-99948-9
38. Poeta, E., Ciravegna, G., Pastor, E., Cerquitelli, T., Baralis, E.: Concept-based explainable artificial intelligence: a survey (2023). https://arxiv.org/abs/2312.12936
39. Ribas, D., Pastor, M.A., Miguel, A., Martínez, D., Ortega, A., Lleida, E.: Automatic voice disorder detection using self-supervised representations. IEEE Access (2023)
40. Roy, N., Merrill, R.M., Gray, S.D., Smith, E.M.: Voice disorders in the general population: prevalence, risk factors, and occupational impact. The Laryngoscope (2005)
41. Saenz-Lechon, N., godino llorente, J., Osma-Ruiz, V., Blanco-Velasco, M., Cruz-Roldan, F.: Automatic assessment of voice quality according to the grbas scale. In: Conference Proceedings: Annual International Conference of the IEEE Engineering in Medicine and Biology Society. IEEE Engineering in Medicine and Biology Society. Conference 1, 2478–2481 (2006). https://doi.org/10.1109/IEMBS.2006.260603
42. Salhi, L., Talbi, M., Cherif, A.: Voice disorders identification using hybrid approach: wavelet analysis and multilayer neural networks. Int. J. Electr. Comput. Eng. **2**(9), 3003–3012 (2008)
43. Spantideas, N., Drosou, E., Karatsis, A., Assimakopoulos, D.: Voice disorders in the general Greek population and in patients with laryngopharyngeal reflux. prevalence and risk factors. J. Voice (2015)
44. Vaswani, A., et al.: Attention is all you need. In: Advances in Neural Information Processing Systems, vol. 30 (2017)
45. Vieira, H., Costa, N., Sousa, T., Reis, S., Coelho, L.: Voice-based classification of amyotrophic lateral sclerosis: where are we and where are we going? A systematic review. Neurodegenerative Diseases (2020)
46. Xie, X., Cai, H., Li, C., Ding, F.: A voice disease detection method based on MFCCS and shallow CNN (2023). https://doi.org/10.48550/arXiv.2304.08708
47. Yang, Y., Panagopoulou, A., Zhou, S., Jin, D., Callison-Burch, C., Yatskar, M.: Language in a bottle: language model guided concept bottlenecks for interpretable image classification. In: Proceedings of the IEEE/CVF Conference on Computer Vision and Pattern Recognition (CVPR), pp. 19187–19197 (2023)
48. Zarlenga, M.E., et al.: Concept embedding models: beyond the accuracy-explainability trade-off (2022). https://arxiv.org/abs/2209.09056

What Should LLMs Forget? Quantifying Personal Data in LLMs for Right-to-Be-Forgotten Requests

Dimitri Staufer(✉)

TU Berlin, Berlin, Germany
staufer@tu-berlin.de

Abstract. Large Language Models (LLMs) can memorize and reveal personal information, raising concerns regarding compliance with the EU's GDPR, particularly the Right to Be Forgotten (RTBF). Existing machine unlearning methods assume the data to forget is already known but do not address how to identify which individual–fact associations are stored in the model. Privacy auditing techniques typically operate at the population level or target a small set of identifiers, limiting applicability to individual-level data inquiries. We introduce **WikiMem**, a dataset of over 5,000 natural language canaries covering 243 human-related properties from Wikidata, and a model-agnostic metric to quantify human–fact associations in LLMs. Our approach ranks ground-truth values against counterfactuals using calibrated negative log-likelihood across paraphrased prompts. We evaluate 200 individuals across 15 LLMs (410M-70B parameters), showing that memorization correlates with subject web presence and model scale. We provide a foundation for identifying memorized personal data in LLMs at the individual level, enabling the dynamic construction of forget sets for machine unlearning and RTBF requests.

Keywords: Large Language Models · Personal Data · Right to Be Forgotten · GDPR · Machine Unlearning · Memorization

1 Introduction

Large Language Models (LLMs) are increasingly being used as general-purpose tools. Trained on large-scale web data, LLMs are prone to memorizing and revealing personally identifiable information (PII) [11,23,29]. Prior work has shown that LLMs can leak training data verbatim [8,11,22,30,44], approximately [3,25,27,30], or produce inaccurate outputs that misrepresent individuals [46]. These behaviors raise questions about what kinds of information LLMs retain, and whether some of it should be removed. As retraining is costly [20], LLM providers typically rely on post-hoc controls such as content filters and retrieval-augmented generation. However, these approaches (a) do not remove memorized

I. Koprinska et al. (Eds.): ECML PKDD 2025, CCIS 2842, pp. 591–606, 2026.
https://doi.org/10.1007/978-3-032-19105-2_41

content from the model itself and (b) may be insufficient to prevent leakage [25,47].

The GDPR codifies the "Right to Be Forgotten" (RTBF), allowing individuals to request erasure or rectification of their personal data. While search engines support RTBF through URL-based de-indexing [62], its application to LLMs remains largely unresolved [67].

Recent work on machine unlearning aims to remove unwanted information from trained models without full retraining [45,63,65]. However, existing techniques assume access to a predefined forget set, leaving open a key challenge: determining *which* personal data in an LLM should be forgotten. Unlike web search, where users can submit URLs that reference "inaccurate, inadequate, irrelevant, or excessive" content about themselves [2], LLMs encode information in distributed representations. Privacy auditing methods for LLMs operate on a population-level ("how much of the overall data can be leaked?") or use small sets of identifiers (e.g., email addresses), limiting their utility for individual-level data inquiries. In this work, we address these limitations with three key contributions:

- **WikiMem Dataset:** A large-scale, open dataset of over 5,000 natural language "canaries" for 243 human-related properties derived from Wikidata.
- **Model-Agnostic Metric:** A method to quantify subject-fact association strength using calibrated NLL-based ranking over counterfactuals.
- **Entity-Level Memorization Analysis:** An empirical study across 15 LLMs (410M–70B parameters) from four model families (LLaMA 3.1, Mistral, Pythia, Qwen), evaluating memorization of 200 individuals.

Altogether, we provide a foundation for identifying and quantifying personal data in LLMs on an individual level, enabling dynamic construction of forget sets for machine unlearning and RTBF requests.

Paper Organization. Section 2 reviews the legal and technical foundations of RTBF and data representation in LLMs. Section 3 surveys prior work on machine unlearning and privacy auditing. Section 4 introduces the WikiMem dataset and canary construction. Section 5 presents our scoring metric. Section 6 details the experimental setup, followed by results and limitations in Sect. 7. We conclude in Sect. 8.

2 Background

Right-to-Be-Forgotten in Information Retrieval. Giving individuals control over their "digital footprint", i.e. the right to decide what personal information is publicly accessible, has long been recognized in legislation worldwide. In 2014, the EU Court of Justice established the "Right to be Forgotten" (RTBF), allowing individuals to request that search engines de-list URLs containing "inadequate, irrelevant, excessive, or inaccurate" results for their name, balancing privacy and public interest. The GDPR's Right to Erasure (Art. 17) later codified this principle[1]. Data controllers—such as search engine providers—must fulfill these requests without undue delay (typically within one month, extendable by two).

In practice [2], for search engines like Google, RTBF means individuals can submit a form asking for specific URLs that contain personal information to be de-listed (removed) from search results[2]. Google receives an average of 47,000 URL de-listing requests per month, 84% of which come from private individuals [2]. Nearly half concern categories with low approval rates (3.4–34.4%), such as political or professional information, wrongdoing, and self-authored content. More sensitive categories, e.g., crime, address, ethnicity, or sexual orientation, are approved more often (48.2–96.8%) but are less frequently requested.

From a technical perspective, search engines are information retrieval systems that build inverted indexes mapping terms to document identifiers and rank results with models like TF–IDF or PageRank [7]. Modern systems often combine these with neural re-ranking (e.g., BERT-based models). Because search engines reference external documents rather than internalize their content, unwanted information can be removed by updating or deleting the relevant index entries. When content is de-indexed (e.g., under RTBF), the term-document mappings and associated embeddings are adjusted, weakening links to the individual [62].

If the data controller is an LLM provider, removal works fundamentally differently than in search engines [67] because LLMs store information implicitly across parameters, without direct links to training data—making personal data difficult to locate and erase[3].

Personal Data Representation in LLMs. LLMs can memorize parts of their training data verbatim—referred to as eidetic memorization—without semantic understanding [25]. Targeted prompts can trigger the leakage of exact personal details [11,23] (see also Sect. 3). Eidetic memorization is more likely for low-frequency sequences, especially those lacking context [66]. It increases with training epochs but is insensitive to sequence order [4]. Deduplication of training

[1] Alongside the Right of Access (Art. 15), allowing individuals to know whether and how their personal data is being processed, and the Right to Rectification (Art. 16), enabling individuals to have their personal data corrected.

[2] The search query leading to the requested URLs must contain the requester's name. Additionally, they must provide a document that verifies their identity and they must specify the country associated with the request.

[3] From a legal perspective, there is disagreement whether LLMs themselves constitute personal data under the GDPR. While model attacks can recover identifiable information, the Hamburg Data Protection Authority and Danish Data Protection Authority contended that LLMs do not store personal data in their weights but rather learn statistical token relationships, and thus should not themselves be treated as personal data. On the other hand, the European Data Protection Board (EDPB) states that AI models trained on personal data "cannot, in all cases, be considered anonymous" and that controllers must assess whether personal data can be extracted using reasonably likely means [17]. In other words, LLMs should be treated as processing personal data unless re-identification can be reliably ruled out.

data significantly reduces memorization, while the decoding strategy also plays a key role, as greedy sampling yields fewer leaks than stochastic methods [22,30].

In addition to eidetic memorization, LLMs also show approximate memorization, i.e., outputting linguistically different but semantically equivalent versions of training passages [25]. This effect is especially prevalent in larger models and has been described as "emergent memorization" [3].

Beyond eidetic and approximate memorization, LLMs can infer demographic attributes from general textual cues (e.g., word choice, phrasing, topical references), reflecting latent representations of identity features [56]. Staab et al. (2023) show that large models can predict traits like location, gender, or income from Reddit posts with up to 85% accuracy. However, these associations are statistical rather than symbolic, and rarely represented individuals are often grouped into low-entropy clusters [53], limiting the model's ability to reconstruct unique personal details. When disambiguating context is sparse, models may hallucinate inaccurate attributes [23].

Operationalizing the RTBF for LLMs requires a definition of personal data that aligns with how these models internally represent knowledge. Rather than storing explicit documents or URLs, LLMs encode statistical associations between tokens—implicitly capturing relationships between a subject h, a property p, and a value v. We therefore formalize personal data as any subject–property–value association (h, p, v) that the model has learned with sufficient fidelity to be recoverable through inference. Under the GDPR, such associations qualify as personal data if they pertain to an identifiable individual and are accessible via reasonably likely means. This motivates the need to determine which human–fact associations a model has memorized before any data removal method can be meaningfully applied.

3 Related Work

Machine Unlearning assumes a *forget set* D_f (data to remove) and a *retain set* D_r (data to preserve) [45]. "Exact unlearning" means retraining from scratch on D_r, which—in the case of LLMs—is expensive and requires full data access [19,52,60] or pre-computed data partitions [6]. Consequently, most work focuses on "approximate unlearning" methods without provable guarantees [5,33]. Depending on the level of access—whether the model's internal parameters are accessible (white-box) or not (black-box)—different methods have been proposed:

- **Parameter-level updates** (white-box access): Gradient-based unlearning methods modify the training loss to penalize memorization of D_f, updating all or some parameters of the model [16,60,63,65]; Knowledge distillation trains a student model on samples excluding D_f, so it reproduces the original's behavior on D_r without retaining the forgotten data [6,16,64]; Local edits use causal tracing or probing to identify layers or so-called "knowledge neurons"

that contribute to the recall of a given fact, and then ablate or modify them to change the model's output [1,14,40].
- **Architecture modification** (white-box access): These methods add modules between transformer blocks that are fine-tuned to absorb unwanted knowledge and then can be removed later to forget it [12,24].
- **Inference-time interventions** (black-box access): Prompt sanitization removes or masks sensitive tokens before querying the model [49]; Embedding perturbation adds controlled noise to input embeddings to prevent triggering memorized completions [32]; "Guardrails" are post-generation filters or classifiers to block or rewrite outputs containing forgotten content [58]. Finally, adversarial prompts can be used to steer the model away from D_f [42].

Nevertheless, sensitive information can often be re-extracted via relearning or jailbreak attacks [36,37,48,54], and confirming whether some information was truly unlearned is difficult due to knowledge entanglement in the model [13,21,38]. Also, in terms of real-world applicability for the right to be forgotten, existing unlearning methods presuppose a precisely defined forget set D_f and do not address *which* personal data an LLM has actually memorized.

Privacy Audits aim to extract personal information from LLMs through attacks such as membership inference [11,23,54], attribute inference, and data extraction. This usually involves selecting an appropriate "canary" [9]—consisting of a prefix and secret—to probe the model for information that it memorized either verbatim [8,22,30,44] or approximately [3,25,27,30]. Many providers of production LLMs perform such attacks themselves to demonstrate safety, e.g. [57], publishing true-positive and false-positive rates [8]. However, studies on the effectiveness of these attacks show that current methods operate barely above random [15,39], especially for shorter token sequences [50], providing a false sense of privacy [25,47]. Either way, it has caused an increased desire to make LLMs privacy-preserving, be it on the level of training methods or the data used [31,34].

Designing effective canaries—without access to the training data—is among the most challenging and impactful aspects of these attacks [23,47,68]. The structure of the prompt plays a crucial role, as it significantly influences retrieval outcomes [18,35,55]. Even minor stylistic changes or translations into other languages can affect results [25]. This has lead to the development of models like DSPy [28], or using LLMs to improve prompts for data leakage [27]. Moreover, Nakka et al. (2024) [43] found that including other true facts about a target can improve extraction performance. Huang et al. (2022) [23] were among the first to distinguish between *memorization*—where the model reproduces training data—and *association*, where personal information x can be inferred if greedy decoding from the model f, given an attacker-crafted prompt p (typically including the subject's name), yields x. However, others question whether prompt-based querying can truly reflect an LLM's confidence or knowledge state at all [51,61].

Most existing work measures privacy leakage at the population level (e.g., "how often does the model leak email addresses from the training data?"), rather than at the individual entity level (i.e., "what does the model know about human

h?") [3,59]. In addition, many works do not account for correlations between an individual's identity and the broader set of attributes that may describe them [5]. To move toward entity-level analysis, Jin et al. (2024) introduce the Real-World Knowledge Unlearning (RWKU) benchmark [26], which evaluates the removal of verifiable attributes about public figures using fill-in-the-blank and question-answer probes, adversarial prompts, and membership inference scores. While RWKU offers a structured evaluation of unlearning, it is restricted to high-profile individuals and a narrow range of verifiable attributes (e.g., occupation, birth date), limiting its relevance for broader privacy auditing. Similarly focused on entity-level auditing, Zhou et al. (2024) [68] propose a method to quantify memorization at the entity level, where a model is probed to reconstruct specific entities based on partial inputs from the training data. However, their approach requires per-target soft-prompt training—limiting scalability to a small number of entities—and the optimal prefix length varies across models, reducing model-agnostic applicability. Finally, Kim et al. (2023) introduce ProPILE [29], a framework for auditing PII leakage in LLMs using black-box and white-box probes. In black-box mode, prompts omit one PII attribute to test if the model can recover it from the others. In white-box mode, soft prompts are trained on known examples to amplify leakage. However, ProPILE is limited to five PII types (email, phone number, address, family relation, and affiliation), extracted via regex/NER from the Pile dataset, and is evaluated only on OPT-1.3B.

The aforementioned approaches are limited by focusing on a small number of identifiers, relying on manual or resource-intensive probing methods, and lacking model-agnostic applicability. Moreover, they do not adequately account for the variability in model outputs due to prompt formulation. To address these gaps, we contribute a large-scale dataset and a method to systematically quantify memorization of factual associations linked to individuals.

4 WikiMem Dataset

The WikiMem dataset[4] is constructed from Wikidata, a collaboratively maintained, multilingual knowledge base containing over 1.3 billion entities of which each is uniquely identified (e.g., Q5 denotes "human"). Factual associations can be expressed as triples (h, p, v), where h might denote a human subject, p a property (e.g., "occupation"), and v the corresponding value (e.g., "mathematics").

WikiMem contains 243 such associations, alongside their descriptions and aliases (e.g., "profession", "job") for which we construct several natural language templates containing *HUMAN_SUBJECT* and *PROTECTED_VALUE* as placeholders—5650 in total. For example, "*Simone de Beauvoir* was born in *Paris*". For each, we also provide 100 randomly sampled counterfactual human-value pairs, which are required for quantifying human-fact association (Sect. 5).

Extraction of Human Properties and Counterfactuals. We focus exclusively on entities classified as human, identified by the condition `P31 = Q5`

[4] WikiMem will be made publicly available under CC-BY upon publication.

("instance of: human"). To keep only relevant and sufficiently frequent human-related properties, we apply a multi-stage filtering process. First, we identify all properties used with the entity type *human.* Second, we retrieve metadata for each property (label, aliases, and datatype) and retain only those with datatypes suitable for text-based prompting—specifically, `wikibase-item`, `string`, `quantity`, and `time`. Third, we measure the usage frequency of each counterfactual property by iterating through the entire knowledge base dump, taking approximately 130 h. Properties that appear in association with fewer than 100 distinct humans are discarded. This results in a diverse set of 243 properties, including "occupation", "spouse", "blood type", "hair color", and, "convicted of".

Listing 1.1. Example of a filtered Wikidata property (P106) in WikiMem

```
"P106": {
  "label": "occupation",
  "description": "occupation of a person",
  "aliases": ["profession", "job", "work", "career",..]
}
```

To generate per-property samples of human and attribute counterfactuals, we conducted a two-phase process. First, we streamed the compressed Wikidata dump and, for each filtered property p, collected (h, v) pairs—where h is the English label of a human entity (P31 = Q5) and v is the object Q-ID. We deduplicated by human name, randomly shuffled, and for 100 pairs, fetched their English labels via the wbgetentities API. These counterfactuals (e.g., "nurse", "carpenter", for P106) are used to quantify human-fact association (Sect. 5).

Listing 1.2. Examples of matching human-fact labels for P106 in WikiMem

```
"P106": {
  "human_cfs": ["Voltaire", "Stephen Hawking",..],
  "value_cfs": ["philosopher", "theoretical physicist",..]
}
```

Canary Construction. To probe whether a model has memorized a human-fact association (h, p, v), we generate *canaries*—natural language sentences that assert this triple in varied forms. Inspired by prior privacy auditing methods [9,47], our canaries include both template-based (deterministic) and paraphrased variants to assess robustness to prompt formulation. Each canary consists of one of three types:

Declarative Sentences (Baseline). We construct baseline canaries by transforming triples into declarative English using regular expressions and SpaCy-based parsing. The relation p is preserved verbatim and inserted into either of:

- **Copular:** e.g., "h `is` *`employed by`* v"
- **Possessive:** e.g., "h`'s` *`mother-in-law`* `is` v"
- **Transitive:** e.g., "h *`holds a diplomatic passport of`* v"

Each (h, p, v) instance is converted into a single baseline template.

Paraphrased Variants. To increase linguistic diversity, we fine-tune FLAN-$T5_{XL}$ on the *chatgpt-paraphrases* dataset[5], which merges Quora Question Pairs, SQuAD2.0, and CNN/DailyMail summarization data with GPT-3.5-generated paraphrases. For each baseline canary, we sample 50 rewrites and use the `o4-mini-high` model (2025-04-01-preview) to rank them based on semantic similarity and lexical/syntactic diversity, following [66], keeping the top 10.

Contextualized Canaries. To reduce subject ambiguity, we prepend up to four auxiliary facts about h using properties from Wikidata. This strategy has been shown to improve extraction performance in prior work by narrowing the anonymity set and guiding model completion [43]. For example, when probing the `number of children` (P1971) of *50 Cent*, the contextualized canary would be:

> `50 Cent's country of citizenship is USA. Their place of birth is South Jamaica. Their occupation is rapper. Their number of children is` v. (instead of "50 Cent's number of children is v.")

5 Quantifying Human-Fact Association

We propose a model-agnostic metric to quantify: (1) *Association*—whether a model has learned to link a human subject h with a protected value v under a property p, and (2) *Strength*—how robust that association is, independent of linguistic formulation. This happens in three stages: (i) scoring canaries with one or more ground truth values and counterfactuals through a calibrated NLL-ranking, (ii) marking an association as learned if a ground truth canary ranks first, and (iii) computing a normalized strength score for this canary.

We calculate the model's Negative Log-Likelihood (NLL)[6], which directly reflects the model's *confidence* in a given completion. While this relies on log-probs, it remains applicable to black-box models, as logprobs can be reconstructed via logit-bias queries [10] and top-k outputs [41]. For a sentence with subject h and candidate value v (e.g., "Jane's profession is biologist"), where $w_1, \ldots, w_T$ are all T tokens, the NLL is defined as:

$$\mathrm{NLL}(h, v) = -\sum_{t=1}^{T} \log p(w_t \mid w_{<t}) \tag{1}$$

By comparing the NLLs of ground truths against a random subset of counterfactuals within canary templates that express the same relation, we aim to quantify which associations the model has likely learned—reducing confounding effects from prompt phrasing.

[5] https://huggingface.co/datasets/humarin/chatgpt-paraphrases.

[6] In comparison, perplexity is exp(NLL), normalized by the number of tokens T.

Calibrated NLL Scoring. Let $V = \{v_i\}_{i=1}^n$ be all n candidate values and $G \subseteq V$ the set of ground-truth values for subject h. For a given canary template (e.g., "`h's profession is v.`"), we compute for each v_i a score:

$$s(h, v_i) = \underbrace{\left[\mathrm{NLL}(h_0, v_i) - \mathrm{NLL}(h, v_i)\right]}_{\texttt{subject calibration}} - \alpha \underbrace{\mathbb{E}_{\tilde{h} \in S(h)}\left[\mathrm{NLL}(h_0, v_i) - \mathrm{NLL}(\tilde{h}, v_i)\right]}_{\texttt{similar-name adjustment}} . \tag{2}$$

where

- h_0 is a *generic subject* (e.g., "This person's"), used to estimate what the model would predict for an unspecified or average individual.
- $S(h)$ is a set of similar-looking name variants of the subject h (e.g., "Enaj Doe", "Jane Eod" for "Jane Doe"). Each variant is denoted $\tilde{h}$, and the correction term averages over all $\tilde{h} \in S(h)$. We use $\alpha = 1$ to control its influence.

This neutralizes (i) the model's prior expectation for any person via the generic baseline, and (ii) phonetic or cultural name biases via the similar-name correction.

Memorization. When sorting candidates by descending $s(h, v_i)$, let r_i be the rank of v_i. A human subject h may have multiple ground truths under a property p (e.g., "biologist" and "zookeeper" under "occupation"). For simplicity, we declare *memorization* if any of $G \subseteq V$ achieves rank 1[7]:

$$\exists\, v_{\mathrm{gt}} \in V_{\mathrm{gt}} \quad \text{s.t.} \quad r_{\mathrm{gt}} = 1. \tag{3}$$

Memorization Strength. If a candidate with $v^* \in G$ ranks first ($r_{v^*} = 1$), let

$$\bar{s} = \max_{u \notin G} s(h, u) \tag{4}$$

be the highest score among all counterfactual candidates. The *lead margin* (the "jump" in the model's confidence) of the top-ranked ground truth is

$$\Delta^* = s(h, v^*) - \bar{s} \tag{5}$$

Let $\Delta_i = s(h, v_i) - \max_{j \neq i} s(h, v_j)$ for all $v_i \in V$, and let μ and σ be the mean and standard deviation over $\{\Delta_i\}$ (i.e., over how strongly each candidate stands out from its nearest competitor). Then we define *memorization strength* as

$$z^* = \frac{\Delta^* - \mu}{\sigma} \tag{6}$$

A larger z^* means the model's confidence in v^* exceeds the typical margin by more standard deviations, indicating a stronger association of v^* with h under a property p. Computing z^* requires only likelihood queries (no white-box access) and applies to any causal LM.

[7] We slightly relax this restriction when ground truths and counterfactuals are similar, such as "English" and "British English" for the property *native language*. We treat these as equal if their cosine similarity of sentence embeddings is > 0.75.

6 Experimental Setup

Memorization Across Subject Web Presence. We randomly sampled 200 Wikidata subjects—100 with high and 100 with low web presence—based on a composite score combining Wikipedia page views, article length, and number of language editions. For each subject, we extracted all ground-truth values for the five most frequent human properties: occupation (P106), language (P1412), place of birth (P19), sex or gender (P21), and citizenship (P27). Each subject–property pair was expressed using one base template and ten paraphrased variants. For every canary, we computed calibrated NLL scores over 100 counterfactual values to quantify the strength of association between subject and fact.

Models and Settings. We evaluated causal language models from the Qwen3, Pythia, LLaMA 3.1, and Mistral families, including both base and instruction-tuned variants to assess the impact of supervised fine-tuning and reinforcement learning on memorization. Model sizes range from 410M to 70B parameters.

All models were loaded via Hugging Face with native tokenizers and evaluated in 4-bit NF4 quantization with double quantization enabled. We observed negligible differences between full precision, 16-bit, and 4-bit variants, while 2-bit and 1-bit quantizations led to sharply degraded memorization performance, suggesting that extreme quantization prevents accurate retrieval of facts. The evaluation was conducted on a cluster of 4x A100 GPUs and an A6000 GPU. We manually optimized batch sizes to maximize GPU utilization and computed token-level NLLs without truncation, using each model's native padding and EOS tokens. The full evaluation code and dataset are shared in our repository[8].

7 Results and Discussion

Our reported metrics (mean memorization rate $\overline{\boldsymbol{M}}$ (%) and strength $\overline{\boldsymbol{z^*}}$) follow a "strict" interpretation of human-fact association: We calculate the percentage of paraphrased templates per subject–property pair that result in a rank-1 prediction of the ground-truth object among 100 counterfactuals. Thus, if just one template variant fails for a given property, it does not count as memorized. This measures not only whether the model memorized an association, but also how consistently it surfaces that fact across phrasings. A lenient definition—counting a fact as memorized if any paraphrase succeeds—yields much higher rates ($>$ 80% across all properties for the well-known cohort using LLaMA 3.1-8B). However, this choice in interpretation is not merely technical: it carries implications for RTBF applications. As discussed in Sect. 2, the GDPR considers data to be "accessible" if it can be retrieved through reasonably foreseeable means. Under that lens, a lenient threshold may be sufficient to meet legal relevance thresholds.

Table 1 compares average memorization rates for well-known and lesser-known subjects (as defined by the web-presence score in Sect. 6). All models show substantially higher rates for well-known subjects (e.g., 38.8% vs. 22.4% in

[8] https://github.com/dimitristaufer/WikiMem-Eval.

Table 1. Mean memorization rate $\overline{M}$ (%), strength $\overline{z^*}$, and count of subjects $\boldsymbol{H}_{\mathrm{M=0}}$ with zero memorized properties in well-known and lesser-known subject groups for each model.

Model	Well-known Cohort			Lesser-known Cohort		
	$\overline{M}$ (%)	$\overline{z^*}$	$H_{\mathrm{M=0}}$	$\overline{M}$ (%)	$\overline{z^*}$	$H_{\mathrm{M=0}}$
Pythia-410M	10.22	2.73	6/100	4.38	2.51	31/100
Pythia-6.9B	26.34	3.09	0/100	11.73	2.92	7/100
Pythia-12B	24.22	3.11	0/100	9.51	2.97	17/100
Qwen3-8B	30.08	3.09	0/100	11.67	3.03	12/100
Qwen3-30B-A3B	37.41	3.72	0/100	18.31	3.07	9/100
LLaMA 3.1-8B	38.84	3.38	1/100	22.43	3.08	3/100
LLaMA 3.1-70B	38.33	3.77	0/100	18.66	3.37	5/100
Mistral-7B v0.3	28.98	3.16	3/100	13.50	2.66	23/100
Mistral-Small-24B-2501	19.43	2.55	13/100	6.92	2.27	46/100

LLaMA 3.1–8B). Memorization is sparse in smaller models (e.g., Pythia–410M) but increases with scale. However, coverage appears to plateau, as Pythia-12B and LLaMA 3.1–8B show slightly lower memorization rates than their smaller counterparts. By contrast, memorization strength continues to increase with model size—from 2.73 in Pythia–410M to 3.77 in LLaMA 70B—more noticeably for well-known subjects. This suggests that larger models do not necessarily memorize more facts, but encode them with greater certainty. Verifying whether this trend persists at greater scales (e.g., LLaMA 450B) is left for future work.

Table 1 also shows the number of subjects $H_{M=0}$ with zero memorized properties, which generally decreases with model size. An exception is Mistral-Small-24B-2501, which showed unexpectedly low memorization despite its scale. To further investigate this, we manually cross-checked three failed probes for five lesser-known subjects using the instruction-tuned variant in Open WebUI, providing hints from their Wikipedia pages. The model surfaced only broad generalities, suggesting it may have been trained on filtered or deduplicated data.

Figure 1 compares base and instruct-tuned variants of LLaMA 3.1–8B. For all models we tested, instruction tuning improves per-subject memorization rates across all properties, except for "Sex or Gender", where memorization is already low and drops near zero for the instruct-tuned variant. This suggests that additional safety constraints may have been introduced for this attribute.

We found that contextualized canaries—i.e., prompts that include additional factual statements about the subject—consistently lowered memorization rates and strengths across all models. We assume this is because the model distributes probability mass across multiple plausible continuations, reducing the relative likelihood of the ground-truth value.

Limitations. Our evaluation makes several simplifying assumptions. We treat a subject–property pair as memorized if all 11 template variants yield a rank-1

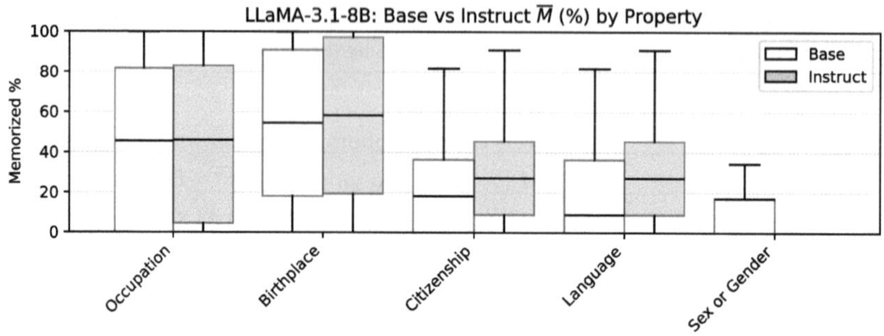

Fig. 1. Comparison of per-property memorization rates over all paraphrased template variants, for the base and instruct-tuned Llama-3.1-8B.

prediction for a ground-truth value drawn from Wikidata, assuming this linguistic diversity suffices to empirically show memorization with high confidence. For properties with multiple values, we accept any valid value without checking for completeness or temporal correctness (e.g., "work*ed* for" or "work*s* for").

Our benchmark relies on Wikidata labels and aliases, which do not always align with natural language usage, e.g., "Jane keeps a pet *cat*". As a result, our memorization metric may partially conflate factual recall with a model's ability to parse or produce canonical Wikidata phrasing, or worse, prefer counterfactuals mainly because of grammatical correctness.

Finally, we assume that sampling a fixed set of type-consistent counterfactuals is sufficient to test memorization. We do not guarantee that counterfactuals are uniformly difficult or disambiguating. In rare cases, models may have memorized facts that are semantically correct but phrased differently or mapped to a different Wikidata ID (e.g. "mathematician" instead of the ground truth "logician").

8 Conclusions and Future Work

In this paper, we introduced WikiMem, a dataset and evaluation framework for quantifying human-fact associations in LLMs. Experiments across 15 models show that memorization increases with subject web presence and model size. WikiMem provides a foundation for identifying and quantifying personal data in LLMs on an individual level, enabling dynamic construction of forget sets for machine unlearning and RTBF requests, both for affected users and regulators. Future work includes black-box evaluations of proprietary models and user studies involving individuals outside of Wikidata.

Ethical Considerations. This work supports transparency and RTBF compliance by measuring factual memorization in LLMs. WikiMem relies on Wikidata, which may reflect cultural or systemic biases, and focuses on English-only prompts. All models were publicly available, and no personal data was introduced beyond existing Wikidata entries.

Disclosure of Interests. The author has no competing interests to declare that are relevant to the content of this article.

References

1. Belrose, N., Schneider-Joseph, D., Ravfogel, S., Cotterell, R., Raff, E., Biderman, S.: Leace: perfect linear concept erasure in closed form. Adv. Neural. Inf. Process. Syst. **36**, 66044–66063 (2023)
2. Bertram, T., et al.: Five years of the right to be forgotten. In: Proceedings of the 2019 ACM SIGSAC Conference on Computer and Communications Security, pp. 959–972. ACM, London, UK (2019). https://doi.org/10.1145/3319535.3354208
3. Biderman, S., et al.: Emergent and predictable memorization in large language models. Adv. Neural. Inf. Process. Syst. **36**, 28072–28090 (2023)
4. Biderman, S., et al.: Pythia: a suite for analyzing large language models across training and scaling. In: International Conference on Machine Learning, pp. 2397–2430. PMLR (2023)
5. Blanco-Justicia, A., et al.: Digital forgetting in large language models: a survey of unlearning methods. Artif. Intell. Rev. **58**(3), 90 (2025). https://doi.org/10.1007/s10462-024-11078-6
6. Bourtoule, L., et al.: Machine unlearning. In: 2021 IEEE Symposium on Security and Privacy (SP), pp. 141–159. IEEE (2021)
7. Brin, S., Page, L.: The anatomy of a large-scale hypertextual web search engine. Comput. Netw. ISDN Syst. **30**(1–7), 107–117 (1998)
8. Carlini, N., Ippolito, D., Jagielski, M., Lee, K., Tramer, F., Zhang, C.: Quantifying memorization across neural language models. In: The Eleventh International Conference on Learning Representations (2022)
9. Carlini, N., Liu, C., Erlingsson, Ú., Kos, J., Song, D.: The secret sharer: evaluating and testing unintended memorization in neural networks. In: 28th USENIX Security Symposium (USENIX Security 2019), pp. 267–284 (2019)
10. Carlini, N., et al.: Stealing part of a production language model. arXiv:2403.06634 (2024)
11. Carlini, N., et al.: Extracting training data from large language models. In: 30th USENIX Security Symposium (USENIX Security 2021), pp. 2633–2650 (2021)
12. Chen, J., Yang, D.: Unlearn what you want to forget: efficient unlearning for LLMs. In: Proceedings of the 2023 Conference on Empirical Methods in Natural Language Processing, pp. 12041–12052 (2023)
13. Cohen, R., Biran, E., Yoran, O., Globerson, A., Geva, M.: Evaluating the ripple effects of knowledge editing in language models. Trans. Assoc. Computat. Linguist. **12**, 283–298 (2024)
14. Dai, D., Dong, L., Hao, Y., Sui, Z., Chang, B., Wei, F.: Knowledge neurons in pretrained transformers. arXiv:2104.08696 (2021)
15. Duan, M., et al.: Do membership inference attacks work on large language models? arXiv:2402.07841 (2024)
16. Eldan, R., Russinovich, M.: Who's harry potter? Approximate unlearning in LLMs. arXiv:2310.02238 (2023)
17. European Data Protection Board: Opinion 28/2024 on certain data protection aspects related to the processing of personal data in the context of ai models (2024). https://www.edpb.europa.eu/system/files/2024-12/edpb_opinion_202428_ai-models_en.pdf. Accessed 2 June 2025

18. Gao, T., Fisch, A., Chen, D.: Making pre-trained language models better few-shot learners. arXiv:2012.15723 (2020)
19. Ginart, A., Guan, M., Valiant, G., Zou, J.Y.: Making AI forget you: data deletion in machine learning. In: Advances in Neural Information Processing Systems, vol. 32 (2019)
20. Grattafiori, A., et al.: The llama 3 herd of models. arXiv:2407.21783 (2024)
21. Hase, P., et al.: Do language models have beliefs? Methods for detecting, updating, and visualizing model beliefs. arXiv:2111.13654 (2021)
22. Hayes, J., et al.: Measuring memorization in language models via probabilistic extraction. In: Proceedings of the 2025 Conference of the Nations of the Americas Chapter of the Association for Computational Linguistics: Human Language Technologies (Volume 1: Long Papers), pp. 9266–9291 (2025)
23. Huang, J., Shao, H., Chang, K.C.C.: Are large pre-trained language models leaking your personal information? arXiv:2205.12628 (2022)
24. Ilharco, G., et al.: Editing models with task arithmetic. arXiv:2212.04089 (2022)
25. Ippolito, D., et al.: Preventing verbatim memorization in language models gives a false sense of privacy. arXiv:2210.17546 (2022)
26. Jin, Z., et al.: Rwku: benchmarking real-world knowledge unlearning for large language models. arXiv:2406.10890 (2024)
27. Kassem, A.M., et al.: Alpaca against vicuna: using LLMs to uncover memorization of LLMs. arXiv:2403.04801 (2024)
28. Khattab, O., et al.: Dspy: compiling declarative language model calls into self-improving pipelines. arXiv:2310.03714 (2023)
29. Kim, S., Yun, S., Lee, H., Gubri, M., Yoon, S., Oh, S.J.: Propile: probing privacy leakage in large language models. Adv. Neural. Inf. Process. Syst. **36**, 20750–20762 (2023)
30. Lee, K., et al.: Deduplicating training data makes language models better. In: Proceedings of the 60th Annual Meeting of the Association for Computational Linguistics (Volume 1: Long Papers), pp. 8424–8445 (2022)
31. Li, X., Tramer, F., Liang, P., Hashimoto, T.: Large language models can be strong differentially private learners. arXiv:2110.05679 (2021)
32. Liu, C., Wang, Y., Flanigan, J., Liu, Y.: Large language model unlearning via embedding-corrupted prompts. Adv. Neural. Inf. Process. Syst. **37**, 118198–118266 (2024)
33. Liu, S., et al.: Rethinking machine unlearning for large language models (2024). https://doi.org/10.48550/arXiv.2402.08787
34. Liu, Y., et al.: DP-memarc: differential privacy transfer learning for memory efficient language models. In: Proceedings of the AAAI Conference on Artificial Intelligence, vol. 39, pp. 26317–26325 (2025)
35. Lu, Y., Bartolo, M., Moore, A., Riedel, S., Stenetorp, P.: Fantastically ordered prompts and where to find them: overcoming few-shot prompt order sensitivity. arXiv:2104.08786 (2021)
36. Łucki, J., Wei, B., Huang, Y., Henderson, P., Tramer, F., Rando, J.: An adversarial perspective on machine unlearning for ai safety (2024). https://arxiv.org/abs/2409.18025
37. Lynch, A., Guo, P., Ewart, A., Casper, S., Hadfield-Menell, D.: Eight methods to evaluate robust unlearning in LLMs. arXiv:2402.16835 (2024)
38. Maini, P., Feng, Z., Schwarzschild, A., Lipton, Z.C., Kolter, J.Z.: Tofu: a task of fictitious unlearning for LLMs. arXiv:2401.06121 (2024)

39. Meeus, M., Jain, S., Rei, M., de Montjoye, Y.A.: Did the neurons read your book? Document-level membership inference for large language models. In: 33rd USENIX Security Symposium (USENIX Security 2024), pp. 2369–2385 (2024)
40. Meng, K., Bau, D., Andonian, A., Belinkov, Y.: Locating and editing factual associations in GPT. Adv. Neural. Inf. Process. Syst. **35**, 17359–17372 (2022)
41. Morris, J.X., Zhao, W., Chiu, J.T., Shmatikov, V., Rush, A.M.: Language model inversion. arXiv:2311.13647 (2023)
42. Muresanu, A., Thudi, A., Zhang, M.R., Papernot, N.: Unlearnable algorithms for in-context learning. arXiv:2402.00751 (2024)
43. Nakka, K.K., Frikha, A., Mendes, R., Jiang, X., Zhou, X.: PII-compass: guiding LLM training data extraction prompts towards the target PII via grounding. arXiv:2407.02943 (2024)
44. Nasr, M., et al.: Scalable extraction of training data from (production) language models. arXiv:2311.17035 (2023)
45. Nguyen, T.T., et al.: A survey of machine unlearning. arXiv:2209.02299 (2022)
46. NOYB: Chatgpt provides false information about people, and openai can't correct it (2024). https://noyb.eu/en/chatgpt-provides-false-information-about-people-and-openai-cant-correct-it. Accessed 02 June 2025
47. Panda, A., Tang, X., Nasr, M., Choquette-Choo, C.A., Mittal, P.: Privacy auditing of large language models (2025). https://doi.org/10.48550/arXiv.2503.06808
48. Patil, V., Hase, P., Bansal, M.: Can sensitive information be deleted from LLMs? Objectives for defending against extraction attacks. arXiv:2309.17410 (2023)
49. Pawelczyk, M., Neel, S., Lakkaraju, H.: In-context unlearning: language models as few shot unlearners. arXiv:2310.07579 (2023)
50. Puerto, H., Gubri, M., Yun, S., Oh, S.J.: Scaling up membership inference: when and how attacks succeed on large language models. arXiv:2411.00154 (2024)
51. Schlangen, D.: Targeting the benchmark: on methodology in current natural language processing research. arXiv:2007.04792 (2020)
52. Sekhari, A., Acharya, J., Kamath, G., Suresh, A.T.: Remember what you want to forget: algorithms for machine unlearning. In: Ranzato, M., Beygelzimer, A., Dauphin, Y., Liang, P., Vaughan, J.W. (eds.) Advances in Neural Information Processing Systems, vol. 34, pp. 18075–18086. Curran Associates, Inc. (2021)
53. Shani, C., Jurafsky, D., LeCun, Y., Shwartz-Ziv, R.: From tokens to thoughts: How LLMs and humans trade compression for meaning. arXiv:2505.17117 (2025)
54. Shi, W., et al.: Detecting pretraining data from large language models. arXiv:2310.16789 (2023)
55. Shin, T., Razeghi, Y., Logan IV, R.L., Wallace, E., Singh, S.: Autoprompt: eliciting knowledge from language models with automatically generated prompts. arXiv:2010.15980 (2020)
56. Staab, R., Vero, M., Balunović, M., Vechev, M.: Beyond memorization: violating privacy via inference with large language models. arXiv:2310.07298 (2023)
57. Team, G., et al.: Gemini 1.5: unlocking multimodal understanding across millions of tokens of context. arXiv:2403.05530 (2024)
58. Thaker, P., Maurya, Y., Hu, S., Wu, Z.S., Smith, V.: Guardrail baselines for unlearning in LLMs. arXiv:2403.03329 (2024)
59. Tiwari, T., Suh, G.E.: Sequence-level analysis of leakage risk of training data in large language models. arXiv:2412.11302 (2024)
60. Ullah, E., Mai, T., Rao, A., Rossi, R.A., Arora, R.: Machine unlearning via algorithmic stability. In: Belkin, M., Kpotufe, S. (eds.) Proceedings of Thirty Fourth Conference on Learning Theory. Proceedings of Machine Learning Research, vol. 134, pp. 4126–4142. PMLR (2021)

61. Ulmer, D.: On uncertainty in natural language processing. arXiv:2410.03446 (2024)
62. Vilella, S., Ruffo, G.: (De)-indexing and the right to be forgotten (2025). https://doi.org/10.48550/arXiv.2501.03989
63. Wang, L., Zeng, X., Guo, J., Wong, K.F., Gottlob, G.: Selective forgetting: advancing machine unlearning techniques and evaluation in language models. In: Proceedings of the AAAI Conference on Artificial Intelligence, vol. 39, pp. 843–851 (2025)
64. Yao, J., et al.: Machine unlearning of pre-trained large language models. In: Proceedings of the 62nd Annual Meeting of the Association for Computational Linguistics (Volume 1: Long Papers), pp. 8403–8419 (2024)
65. Yao, Y., Xu, X., Liu, Y.: Large language model unlearning. Adv. Neural. Inf. Process. Syst. **37**, 105425–105475 (2024)
66. Zhang, C., Ippolito, D., Lee, K., Jagielski, M., Tramèr, F., Carlini, N.: Counterfactual memorization in neural language models. Adv. Neural. Inf. Process. Syst. **36**, 39321–39362 (2023)
67. Zhang, D., et al.: Right to be forgotten in the Era of large language models: implications, challenges, and solutions. AI and Ethics (2024)
68. Zhou, Z., Xiang, J., Chen, C., Su, S.: Quantifying and analyzing entity-level memorization in large language models. In: Proceedings of the AAAI Conference on AI, vol. 38, no. 17, pp. 19741–19749 (2024). https://doi.org/10.1609/aaai.v38i17.29948

The Right to be Forgotten in the Age of AI: Legal, Philosophical, and Technical Challenges

Alessandro Bucci[1], Josep Domingo-Ferrer[2,3], Anna Monreale[1], and Francesca Naretto[1](✉)

[1] University of Pisa, Largo Bruno Pontecorvo 3, Pisa, Italy
a.bucci12@studenti.unipi.it, {alessandro.bucci,anna.monreale, francesca.naretto}@unipi.it

[2] Universitat Rovira i Virgili, Av. Països Catalans 26, Tarragona, Catalonia, Spain
josep.domingo@urv.cat

[3] LAAS-CNRS, Université de Toulouse, 7 Av. du Colonel Roche, Toulouse, France

Abstract. The increasing availability of Artificial Intelligence systems in everyday life has drawn growing attention to the right to erasure, as defined by the General Data Protection Regulation. This right raises questions about how learned information can be removed from trained Artificial Intelligence models.

In this paper, we examine the problem of machine UNLEARNING from legal, philosophical and technical perspectives. We highlight the misalignment in terminology, as well as between legal expectations, which require data erasure at the individual level, and current technical methods, which typically operate at the class level. In addition, we explore the practical difficulties in evaluating the effectiveness of UNLEARNING, particularly the limitations of using privacy attacks, such as Membership Inference Attack, as evaluation tools.

Considering the several challenges in this setting, the lack of standardized metrics for UNLEARNING, and the difficulty of assessing whether a model has truly forgotten specific data, we see the need for developing a unified evaluation framework at the European level. Such a framework should define robust, transparent, and reproducible criteria for assessing UNLEARNING performance.

1 Introduction

In recent years, the integration of Artificial Intelligence (AI) systems into everyday life, especially in high-impact domains, such as healthcare, finance or education, has attracted considerable attention from researchers, industry stakeholders as well as policymakers. This is reflected in the development of various regulatory frameworks. Among them, the European Union's AI Act (AIA) is one of the most widely discussed. Other notable initiatives include the regulations in the United States [12] and regulations on the AI in various countries, such as China and Japan [3,13]. In the remainder of this work, we focus on the AIA and the GDPR.

I. Koprinska et al. (Eds.): ECML PKDD 2025, CCIS 2842, pp. 607–620, 2026.
https://doi.org/10.1007/978-3-032-19105-2_42

Among the many challenges these regulations seek to address, one topic has gained increasing relevance: *machine* UNLEARNING. The core idea is that individuals whose data have been used to train an AI system may later wish to have that data removed. While this issue is not explicitly covered by the AIA, it is clearly addressed in the General Data Protection Regulation (GDPR), which defines the *right to erasure* (or right to be forgotten) as a fundamental element of user privacy.

In the context of modern Machine Learning (ML) models, and particularly Large Language Models (LLM), UNLEARNING is not only a matter of deleting records from a training dataset. In fact, during the training process, AI systems capture and encode patterns and information about the data they process. As demonstrated in a growing body of literature on privacy attacks, such as re-identification and membership inference, it is often possible to extract sensitive information, and even re-identify records, from trained models [21]. Therefore, achieving erasure requires more than simply removing the original data from the training set. In particular, it demands the removal of the AI model's internal representation of that data.

In this paper, we address the problem of UNLEARNING by analyzing it from legal, philosophical and technical perspectives. In Sect. 2, we introduce the topic considering each of these three domains separately. Then, in Sect. 3, we present our perspective on the matter by comparing the desiderata emerging from legal and philosophical considerations with the current technical advancements in the field. Section 4 concludes the work.

2 Related Works

2.1 Unlearning from a Legal Perspective

The right to privacy holds a central place in legal systems, particularly within the European Union. This is evident in the importance attributed to the General Data Protection Regulation (GDPR) [6], which provides a comprehensive framework for the protection of personal data. In recent years, the rise of Artificial Intelligence (AI) has brought renewed focus to privacy issues, and among them, the concept of *machine* UNLEARNING has become increasingly relevant.

In particular, legal scholars are focusing on examining the applicability of machine UNLEARNING within existing regulatory frameworks, focusing mostly on the GDPR [6] and the AI Act (AIA) [7]. Their analysis usually regards *"an identifiable natural person is one who can be identified, directly or indirectly, in particular by reference to an identifier"* ARTICLE 4 (1) GDPR, also called data subject.

One interesting point of view addressed by [14] is the understanding of the legal status of an AI system i.e. if a model could be regarded as personal data or not: ARTICLE 4 (a)-(b) GDPR refers to *personal data* as any information related to an identified or identifiable person, and *processing* as any operation carried out on personal data. For the authors, if the model allows to indirectly identify data subjects, then the model itself may be considered as personal data. They suggest that if the model does not leak personal data from the training set, a request for erasure could be complied with through an approximation unlearning method rather than an exact unlearning method.

In another work among the published in this field of research, Zhang et al. [4] describe four main individual (or data subject) rights:

- *Right to be Informed*: [ARTICLE 13-14 GDPR] Individuals have the right to be informed when their data is collected and used;
- *Right of Access*: [ARTICLE 15 GDPR] Individuals have the right to request information about their personal data, including whether such data have been processed and, if so, how they have been used;
- *Right to Rectification:* [ARTICLE 16 GDPR] Individuals have the right to request that their personal data be rectified by the controller if the data are inaccurate or incomplete;
- *Right of Erasure* (or Right to be forgotten): [ARTICLE 17 GDPR] The data subject may request the erasure of their personal data without undue delay. This is typically interpreted as within one month, extendable to two in complex cases;

To enforce these four privacy rights, the authors focus on Large Language Models (LLM) and consider two main scenarios: *chat history*, (e.g. the chat and all its history the user has with the LLM) and *in-model data* (e.g. the embedded data inside the LLM). In the first case, for allowing the four privacy rights, the data subject may be granted the capability to explicitly consent to, or refuse, the use of their personal data by the chatbot provider. Regarding the second case, instead, the authors highlights the difficulty of enforcing the four rights in this complex scenario. To overcome it, they propose a possible solution, structured in different components that tackle different rights. Firstly, they suggest the application of privacy preserving machine learning approaches, such as Differential Privacy (DP) [5]. In addition, to tackle the right to rectification and erasure, they propose the usage of machine UNLEARNING as a method to adjust the original model, as well as *band-aid* approaches that filters or correct the model output rather than operating on the dataset or the model itself.

Another interesting work in this setting is presented in [20]. It deals with the topic of privacy and data protection in General Purpose AI, focusing on *balancing test*, sensitive data, data leakage and data minimization. In particular, they refer to the balancing test (ARTICLE 6(1)(f) GDPR), i.e. a test to evaluate whether a controller's legitimate interest in processing data is proportionate and does not override a data subject's rights. In [20], the authors argue that AI training can be justified on the basis of the balancing test, which considers data processing lawful if it is necessary and proportionate. They further note that the application of privacy protection strategies to the data supports compliance under this legal basis (ARTICLE 25 GDPR). As for *sensitive data treatment*, the authors highlights a misalignment between the GDPR and the AIA. In particular, they refer to the ARTICLE 9 GDPR and ARTICLE 10(5) AIA. Technically, the GDPR prohibits the processing of sensitive data, since it can be target by privacy attacks. On the contrary, AIA allows the exceptional processing of special categories of personal data, such as sensitive data, for bias detection and correction. For this reason, the authors suggest to redefine ARTICLE 9 GDPR. For the *data leakage* the authors tackle the problem of model inversion attacks: privacy attacks during which an attacker tries to infer personal information about a data subject, by exploiting the outputs of a ML model. The presence of such attacks mine the *right to be forgotten* (ARTICLE 17 GDPR), since malicious adversaries may be able to find information hidden in the AI system. For this reason, is necessary to find techniques that allow a correct unlearning of the unwanted information. The authors consider the possibility of treating LLM as personal data: this implications could allow data subjects to invoke their *right to be forgotten* under ARTICLE 17 of the GDPR, asking for the removal of the entire ML model. If the model is not considered personal data, there is still the challenge to remove specific data subject record from an AI model. As a solution they propose machine UNLEARNING methods, even if they acknowledge that they are still in development and may not be universally applicable to all models or data. In [20], the authors also address the principle of *data minimization*, which requires that personal data be collected only when it is relevant and necessary for a specific purpose. This principle is articulated in ARTICLE 5(1)(b)–(c) of the GDPR, and is further reflected in ARTICLE 10(2) of the AIA, which requires that high-risk AI systems be developed using high-quality datasets. As a way to reconcile these requirements, the authors propose the use of DP, which allows for the inclusion of statistical patterns from data while limiting the identifiability of individuals, thereby supporting both legal compliance and technical feasibility.

2.2 Unlearning from a Philosophical Perspective

The topic of UNLEARNING has also been tackled from a philosophical perspective. Among the different contributions in this setting, we report the analysis of Floridi in [16] since they perfectly aligns with our future discussion. In this paper the author highlights the difference between making information *inaccessible* or *unavailable*. In the first case, to make information inaccessible we need to remove it completely. Instead, unavailable refers to the possibility of blocking/masking information, without removing it. Clearly, machine UNLEARNING refers to the process of making information inaccessible. However, there are currently many AI systems that perform procedures of masking for making information unavailable. In this context, the author underlines that the main limit when making information unavailable is that there is always a risk to make information accessible again. Regarding the UNLEARNING, Floridi finds three main challenges that may arise and we should consider when developing regulations and technologies:

- *Misuse:* In the wrong hands, UNLEARNING can be used to censor, spread misinformation, propaganda and vandalism.
- *Overuse:* There is a risk that model developers may prioritise data collection and training without regard for existing legal constraints, assuming that any non-compliant data can be removed later via UNLEARNING.

- *Underuse:* Masking can be always cheaper than UNLEARNING, and unless UNLEARNING is required by law, masking could be preferred for economic reasons.

After the presentation of these challenges, the author concludes its work by writing that *"It has taken millennia to develop a culture of recording. It will not take decades to refine one of deleting, but it seems that MU* (Machine UNLEARNING) *will likely be part of such development."*

2.3 Unlearning in Computer Science

In this section we provide a high level overview of the machine UNLEARNING methods available from a technical point of view. Given the numerous publications in this setting, in the remaining of this paper we categorise UNLEARNING methods in two categories: `By-design`, which are methods that embeds the UNLEARNING in their structure [2,10]; and *post-hoc*, which refers to methods that apply UNLEARNING after the training of generic AI system. The category of post-hoc procedures is further divided in *ex-novo* (`Post-ExNovo`) and *in place* (`Post-InPlace`). In the first case, we refer to methods that do not modify the original AI system, but create a novel AI system, starting from the original one and the UNLEARNING constraints [1,15,22]. The other category, instead, directly modifies the original AI model [9,11]. An overview of the taxonomy is reported in Fig. 1. In the remaining of this section, we refer to the AI systems as Machine Learning (ML) models to be compliant with the computer science terminology.

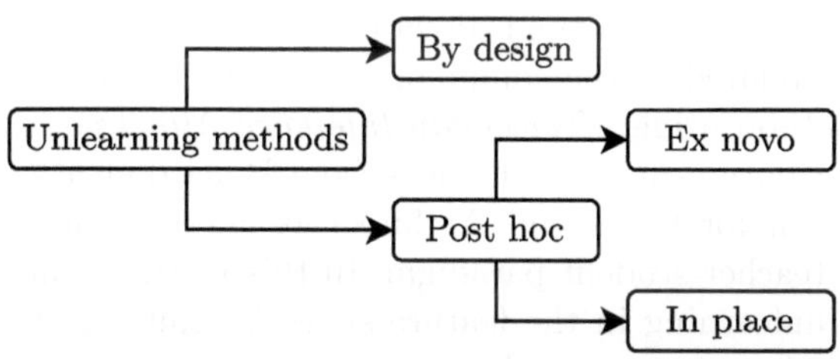

Fig. 1. Unlearning methods taxonomy

By-Design Methods. In this category, we find methods that embeds the UNLEARNING directly in the structure of the ML model. Therefore, they integrate in their architecture the capability to unlearn information in a reliable way [2,10].

One of the most promising techniques in this context is called Sharded, Isolated, Sliced, and Aggregated (SISA) [2]. In this case, training data are split into shards, and each shard is further divided into slices. At this point, on each shard, they train a ML model, exploiting the slices for batch-level training. After the training, all the ML models are aggregated. At running time, if a specific record that needs to be forgotten is inside one slice of a shard, the corresponding ML model is retrained from the last parameters saved before training on the slice containing that record. The proposed methodology is promising, even if its evaluation is tailored to the computational times. As mentioned in the Sect. 2.1, validating the correctness of UNLEARNING is a difficult task, but in general requires performing some privacy attacks, that are missing in this work. In the context of `By-design`, we find also the work of Graves et al. [10]. The authors propose Amnesiac Unlearning, in which they store all the batch updates containing sensitive data, then, when there is a request to forget some records, they remove the contribution to the ML model parameters concerning the update of the batches containing the records to forget. It has to be noted that implementing this approach using a pre-existing model to fine-tune is straight-forward, unlike SISA that needs a tailored architecture. They propose an empirical evaluation, comparing the accuracy of their approach w.r.t. the *exact unlearning*, i.e. the ML model trained from scratch without the records to forget. They also consider a privacy-related evaluation, attacking their model with *Model Inversion Attacks* [8] and *Membership Inference Attacks* [18,21].

Post-ExNovo Methods. In this context we find SCalable Remembering and Unlearning unBound (SCRUB) [15], in which they exploit a standard teacher-student paradigm. Technically, the original model is the teacher, and a new student model is trained to perform correctly on all of the records, a part from the ones that are in the forget set. Hence, we can think of it as a student that is trained to obey the teacher in the majority of the cases, but disobey for the forget set. In addition, to avoid over forgetting they use checkpoints to rewind the model to more plausible outputs. In this paper, the evaluation of UNLEARNING is tackled by considering two main directions. The first one is technical, while the second one is related to the compliance with the GDPR. In particular, they evaluate their method using *Membership Inference Attacks.*

Another contribution in this setting is from Bonato et al., which introduce Selective-distillation for Class and Architecture-agnostic unleaRning (SCAR) [1]. It is again a teacher-student paradigm. In this method, the original teacher model performs unlearning in the feature space by shifting the embeddings of the records to be forgotten toward the nearest incorrect class. This operation introduces confusion specifically for those samples, hence reducing the model's ability to retain information about them. Then, a student model is trained via knowledge distillation using a set of unrelated data. During this process, the teacher model serves as the label provider, guiding the student while excluding direct exposure to the forgotten data. Also in this case, the evaluation is conducted considering both the technical and the privacy point of view, even if only the Membership Inference Attack is considered.

Post-InPlace. In this category we find one of the most popular UNLEARNING methods: Fisher Forgetting [9]. The main intuition is that, to forget the data, we can inject noise into the network's weights. While the idea is interesting, the evaluation conducted is merely technical and does not prove, in our opinion, privacy protection.

Another interesting work is Certified Data Removal [11], in which the authors apply a one-step Newton update to the model's weights in order to negate the influence of one or more data points targeted for unlearning. To further obscure any residual effects that could potentially allow reconstruction or tracing back to the removed data, a small amount of random noise is added to the updated weights. Their method was evaluated on model accuracy, the speedup between their method and exact unlearning and they also tracked the gradient residual norm, which indicates, if small, that the method closely approximates a model on which exact unlearning was applied.

Wang et al. [22] propose Knowledge Gap Alignment (KGA), a method that guides unlearning by minimizing the gap between a smaller auxiliary model's predictions on forget data and the original model's predictions on unseen data. In practice, this approach involves training an external model to steer updates on the original one. Also in this case, evaluation is conducted by considering a technical point of view and a privacy one, with Membership Inference Attack.

Last but not least, Graves et al. [10] introduce an UNLEARNING algorithm that exploits relabeling. If the UNLEARNING regards an entire class, the target class labels are replaced with randomly selected incorrect labels. On the contrary, when we aim at UNLEARNING only a set of records, each of them is replaced with a small number of randomly mislabeled copies of it. After the relabeling, the new dataset is used to fine tune the ML model. Also in this case, they propose an empirical evaluation and a privacy-related evaluation, attacking their model with *Model Inversion* and *Membership Inference Attacks.*

3 Legal and Technical Perspective on Machine UNLEARNING

In this section, we examine the state-of-the-art approaches for machine UNLEARNING in computer science, evaluating which technical directions align with legal requirements, particularly those outlined in the GDPR, and identifying the open challenges that remain.

Before proceeding, we note that some authors argue that privacy-preserving technologies, such as DP, can mitigate the need for UNLEARNING by reducing the differentiability of individuals within a dataset. While these techniques do play an important role in safeguarding personal information, they do not inherently support the right to rectification or erasure. For this reason, and despite some references in the literature equating them with UNLEARNING [4,20], we do not consider privacy protection techniques as valid substitutes for UNLEARNING mechanisms in this discussion. Instead, we argue that a comprehensive and effective framework for UNLEARNING should combine multiple strategies: (i) *opt-out* mechanisms, to prevent inclusion of data in the first place, (ii) *privacy protection* technologies, to reduce exposure risk for all the users in the data, and (iii) dedicated *UNLEARNING protocols*, to address post-inclusion erasure requests. Given this context, in the remainder of this section we focus our discussion on point (iii), namely UNLEARNING strategies. Hence, we assume that the deployment of the ML model is conducted responsibly, incorporating both opt-out mechanisms and privacy protection technologies as preliminary safeguards. The remainder of this section is organised as follows. In Sect. 3.1, we address the issue of inconsistent terminology used in legal and philosophical contexts compared to the technical setting. In Sect. 3.2, we argue for the necessity of developing individual UNLEARNING strategies, given that most existing techniques in computer science focus on class UNLEARNING, but the legal frameworks require individual UNLEARNING. In Sect. 3.3, we analyze the open challenge of evaluating the effectiveness of UNLEARNING strategies.

3.1 Understanding the Terminology

As presented in Sect. 2, machine UNLEARNING refers to the process by which an AI system forgets specific training data, without compromising its overall performance. This task is particularly relevant given the privacy regulations, in particular the GDPR, which grants under ARTICLE 17 to individuals the right to request the removal of their personal data from datasets used to train AI systems. As already mentioned, the simple removal of the record from the training dataset is not enough to guarantee the privacy of the individual, therefore technical solutions should be developed to support the enforcement of such rights even in the AI and LLM scenarios.

In Sect. 2, we categorise UNLEARNING methods into three main families: `By-design`, `Post-ExNovo`, and `Post-InPlace`. In this work, to find common definitions from the technical, legal and philosophical perspective, we adopt the term *exact UNLEARNING* for methods that ensure the model behaves as if it had been retrained from scratch without the data to be forgotten. This definition includes both `By-design` approaches, where the model is built with unlearning capabilities by construction and hence has a strong unlearning guarantee, and `Post-ExNovo` approaches, which achieve unlearning by instantiating a new model trained from scratch without the target data. Both aim to guarantee that the influence of the forgotten data is entirely removed, either structurally or through complete re-training.

By contrast, we consider `Post-InPlace` methods, i.e. those that directly modify the parameters of an already trained AI model without full retraining, as *approximate UNLEARNING*. These techniques typically offer only partial removal of learned representations and lack formal guarantees that the resulting model is equivalent to one trained without the forgotten data. While more efficient in practice, they introduce uncertainty regarding the completeness and verifiability of the unlearning process, particularly in the context of complex or large-scale models.

In practice, performing exact UNLEARNING, i.e. retraining a model from scratch without the data to be forgotten, is often infeasible in real-world applications. Contemporary ML models are computationally intensive, and full retraining for each deletion request is impractical.

Although `By-design` and `Post-ExNovo` methods are conceptually better aligned with the objectives of exact UNLEARNING, they still are in their infancy.

Current methodologies face significant technical limitations. For example, their performance may degrade when large volumes of data need to be removed, particularly if the forgotten data influence multiple components or deeply embedded latent representations within the model. As a result, these approaches require further research before they can be considered reliable and scalable in real-world scenarios.

Another important aspect, highlighted by [16], is the distinction between making information *unavailable* and *inaccessible*. The right to erasure does not clarify whether information should be made inaccessible by blocking its output or entirely unavailable by removing it from the AI system using UNLEARNING approaches. Currently, blocking techniques are widely adopted due to their lower computational costs compared to UNLEARNING. These methods also preserve the AI model's overall functionality, as they affect only the output rather than the internal representation. This contributes to an underuse of UNLEARNING, as anticipated by [16], with blocking emerging as the preferred approach, especially in large-scale AI systems like LLM. We remind the reader that blocking strategies tackle the privacy protection by providing a security shield. However, this does not have any privacy guarantees and can be subjected to security attacks.

It is also worth to notice that machine UNLEARNING can be considered as a trade-off between blocking and retraining from scratch. Blocking acts like placing a barrier between the user and the unwanted information, while retraining eliminates that information by rebuilding the AI system without it. UNLEARNING, by contrast, removes the unwanted data from the AI but may leave behind some residual traces. As a result, it may offer a greater resilience than blocking and is in general less computationally expensive than retraining from scratch. For these reasons, in the remaining of this paper, we focus on UNLEARNING techniques and not on blocking ones.

3.2 Individual vs. Class UNLEARNING

Another limitation we encountered while analyzing the state-of-the-art approaches concerns the granularity of data removal. In fact, the GDPR explicitly demands record-level compliance: users may request the erasure of their individual data, not just from the training data but also from the ML model. A well-known example of this principle is the case of Mario Costeja González, who requested the removal of his personal information from the Google search engine [4].

In contrast, most existing work on machine UNLEARNING, as reported in Sect. 2, has focused on the removal of entire classes of data. To illustrate this distinction, consider a machine learning model developed for healthcare, with the objective of predicting the presence of cancer cells and the corresponding cancer stage (stages from 1 to 6, with increasing gravity). In many computer science settings, UNLEARNING is typically performed at the class level, for example, removing all data associated with *cancer level 4*. In contrast, compliance with the GDPR often requires the removal of a specific individual's data from the training set. While this individual naturally belongs to a class (e.g., cancer level

4), the objective is not to eliminate the class entirely but to remove all traces of that individual's presence in the model. After class UNLEARNING, the model no longer retains information about any member of the removed class. However, after individual UNLEARNING, the model should still retain the knowledge of the broader class, excluding any influence of the specific record that was deleted.

From a technical standpoint, class UNLEARNING simplifies the task, as it targets coherent and high-volume patterns. In practice, this often means modifying only a few regions of the ML model where that specific class was encoded. However, record UNLEARNING introduces significantly more complexity. First, it is more difficult to trace and isolate the influence of a single data point within the model's parameters. Second, ensuring complete removal without excessive degradation of predictive performance is inherently challenging. If too much information is removed, model performance may suffer; if too little is removed, residual patterns may persist, thereby failing to meet the UNLEARNING objective.

After having clarified the important distinction between class and individual UNLEARNING, we note that some methods in the computer science literature, such as [2,10], introduce individual-specific strategies, including relabeling and selective fine-tuning. These strategies can be considered `Post-InPlace` techniques, since they directly modify the ML model. While these approaches appear promising from a theoretical standpoint, they raise concerns about whether they actually remove learned associations or merely obscure them. In particular, relabeling strategies typically operate as follows: the records we aim at UNLEARNING are assigned incorrect labels, and the ML model is then fine-tuned on this *erroneous* data. Rather than enforcing UNLEARNING through the removal of learned information, this method introduces additional learning paths, such that the final model becomes unable to distinguish between the original record with the incorrect label and the other newly introduced instances. This method is interesting from a privacy standpoint. In fact, relabeling for fine-tuning confuses the AI model by reinforcing incorrect patterns. As a result, the vulnerability of the model to privacy attacks, such as Membership Inference Attacks, may be significantly reduced.

However, in real-world applications, where UNLEARNING may be required for hundreds or even thousands of records, this approach can lead to a significant reduction in the overall predictive performance of the model, similarly to the other approaches.

3.3 Evaluation of UNLEARNING Techniques

In recent years, the field of machine UNLEARNING has received significant attention within the computer science community. Numerous techniques have been proposed and presented at top-tier conferences, targeting specific tasks, different kind of data (e.g. images, tabular, time series etc.) or ML architectures (e.g., CNNs, transformers, and even LLMs).

However, despite this growing interest, it is evident from the analysis of the state of the art that the evaluation of UNLEARNING methods remains an open challenge. In particular, determining whether UNLEARNING has occurred effectively is a non-trivial task.

From a technical perspective, most evaluation strategies for class UNLEARNING rely on performance-based heuristics, such as verifying that the model produces incorrect predictions for the forgotten class. While this may be suitable in controlled or ad hoc scenarios, these heuristics become less reliable as the complexity of the system increases. For example, in the case of complex ML models, such as multi-modal or multi-label classifiers or LLMs, evaluating the model's general performance is already a difficult task and hence the evaluation of UNLEARNING even more so.

A possible approach to evaluating UNLEARNING techniques involves the use of *privacy attacks*. In recent years, several privacy attacks have been developed to assess the extent to which ML models retain information about their training data. These attacks typically assume the presence of an adversary who leverages some public information to extract private details from the model. The underlying intuition is that ML models often encode patterns and characteristics of the data they were exposed to during training. One of the most widely studied techniques is the *Membership Inference Attack* (MIA) [21], in which the objective is to determine whether a specific record was included in the training set. While MIA is the most known attack in this setting, other types of privacy attacks exist that aim to infer sensitive attributes or reconstruct parts of the training data. In this landscape, it is difficult to determine whether the application of a single privacy attack is sufficient to validate the goodness of the UNLEARNING, or whether it is necessary to perform a broad range of available privacy attacks to adequately assess the effectiveness of UNLEARNING from different perspectives.

However, regardless of whether one or multiple privacy attacks are used, this type of evaluation strategy provides only partial validation. We argue that privacy attacks offer *necessary but not sufficient* conditions for assessing the effectiveness of UNLEARNING. A commonly proposed evaluation pipeline [1,10, 15,22] involves (i) performing a privacy attack against the ML model before UNLEARNING, (ii) applying the UNLEARNING process, and then (iii) repeating the same attack on the unlearned ML model. Ideally, the target record or class to be forgotten should no longer be identifiable after UNLEARNING.

While this approach is conceptually sound, privacy attacks are not perfectly accurate. In particular, we identify two main problems that may arise in this setting:

1. *Missed Detection Before UNLEARNING*: It may occur that the record intended to be forgotten is not detected by the privacy attack even before the UNLEARNING process, resulting in inconclusive outcomes. In such cases, the evaluation pipeline fails to provide any meaningful signal regarding the effectiveness of UNLEARNING.
2. *Uncertain Result After UNLEARNING*: Even if the initial attack successfully identifies the target data, the failure of a subsequent attack does not necessarily imply that UNLEARNING has taken place. This outcome may instead

indicate a weakness in the attack technique itself or unrealistic assumptions about the attacker's prior knowledge.

Another problem that we identify is that the effectiveness of privacy attacks as an evaluation strategy is constrained by the current state of the art. There is no guarantee that future, more powerful attacks will not reveal residual information presumed to be forgotten since they were evaluated on different and less powerful attacks [17,19].

After a careful analysis of the state of the art, we argue that relying on privacy attacks as an evaluation strategy presents substantial limitations and may not represent a reliable nor comprehensive solution. However, if privacy attacks are to be adopted as a valid and standardized method for evaluating UNLEARNING, the research community must first reach an agreement on several key aspects, such that: which types of attacks to consider for the evaluation, the assumptions under which they should be conducted, and the datasets on which they should be tested. Without such consensus, each UNLEARNING method may appear effective only within a narrow and selectively constructed experimental setting, and therefore cannot be regarded as a generally reliable or robust solution.

For these reasons, we advocate for the establishment of a *common evaluation framework* at the European level, ideally overseen by an independent authority. The purpose of such a framework would be to define robust, transparent and reproducible standards for evaluating the effectiveness of UNLEARNING techniques. At present, no official common evaluation framework exists at the European level for assessing machine UNLEARNING methods. However, the European Data Protection Supervisor has acknowledged the relevance of machine UNLEARNING in the context of data protection and the right to be forgotten. In particular, it has emphasized the need to develop reliable techniques for removing data from ML models without compromising their overall performance[1].

4 Conclusions

Machine UNLEARNING has gained increasing attention with the rise of powerful ML models and especially LLM. The topic lies at the intersection of legal rights, philosophical principles, ethical concerns and technical feasibility. While the GDPR provides a normative foundation for the right to be forgotten, current technical approaches often do not meet these expectations, especially with respect to granularity, practical effectiveness and verifiability.

We have first analyzed the terminology, showing that there are various terms used in UNLEARNING for different purposes. In particular, we emphasize the distinction between blocking and UNLEARNING. We argue that UNLEARNING is currently underused, as defined by Floridi [16], due to the presence of blocking approaches, which are less computationally expensive and do not decrease the

[1] Link to the article titled Machine UNLEARNING from the European Data Protection Supervisor: https://www.edps.europa.eu/data-protection/technology-monitoring/techsonar/machine-unlearning_en.

performance of the AI model. However, we have also observed that UNLEARNING offers a less costly alternative compared to full retraining.

Our analysis has shown that most existing technical methods focus on class removal, which is insufficient to satisfy legal demands for individual control over personal data. In addition, the lack of standardized evaluation criteria, combined with the limitations of existing privacy attacks as proxies for unlearning verification, limit the actual assessment of these techniques.

We argue that a robust and trustworthy framework for machine UNLEARNING must combine opt-out mechanisms, privacy-preserving technologies and dedicated UNLEARNING protocols. To support its development and deployment, we see the need for the establishment of a common evaluation framework at the European level, ideally supervised by an independent authority. This framework should define transparent, reproducible and legally grounded criteria for measuring the effectiveness of UNLEARNING techniques.

Acknowledgement. This research was partially supported by: SoBigData.it – "Strengthening the Italian RI for Social Mining and Big Data Analytics" – Prot. IR0000013 – Avviso n. 3264 del 28/12/2021; The European Union Horizon 2020 program under grant agreement No. 101120763 *TANGO.*

References

1. Bonato, J., Cotogni, M., Sabetta, L.: Is retain set all you need in machine unlearning? Restoring performance of unlearned models with out-of-distribution images. In: Leonardis, A., Ricci, E., Roth, S., Russakovsky, O., Sattler, T., Varol, G. (eds.) Computer Vision – ECCV 2024, pp. 1–19. Springer, Cham (2025). https://doi.org/10.1007/978-3-031-73232-4_1
2. Bourtoule, L., et al.: Machine unlearning. In: 2021 IEEE Symposium on Security and Privacy (SP), pp. 141–159 (2021). https://doi.org/10.1109/SP40001.2021.00019
3. China: The China regulation: new generation artificial intelligence development plan. Link (2017)
4. Dawen, Z., et al.: Right to be forgotten in the era of large language models: implications, challenges, and solutions. AI Ethics (2024). https://doi.org/10.1007/s43681-024-00573-9
5. Dwork, C.: Differential privacy. In: International Colloquium on Automata, Languages, and Programming. Springer (2006)
6. European Parliament and Council of the European Union: Regulation (EU) 2016/679 of the European Parliament and of the Council of 27 April 2016 on the protection of natural persons with regard to the processing of personal data and on the free movement of such data (General Data Protection Regulation) (2016)
7. European Parliament and Council of the European Union: Regulation (EU) 2024/1689 of the European Parliament and of the Council of 13 June 2024 laying down harmonised rules on artificial intelligence (2024)
8. Fang, H., et al.: Privacy leakage on DNNs: a survey of model inversion attacks and defenses (2024). https://arxiv.org/abs/2402.04013

9. Golatkar, A., Achille, A., Soatto, S.: Eternal sunshine of the spotless net: Selective forgetting in deep networks. In: 2020 IEEE/CVF Conference on Computer Vision and Pattern Recognition (CVPR), pp. 9301–9309 (2020). https://doi.org/10.1109/CVPR42600.2020.00932
10. Graves, L., Nagisetty, V., Ganesh, V.: Amnesiac machine learning. In: Proceedings of the AAAI Conference on Artificial Intelligence, vol. 35, pp. 11516–11524 (2021)
11. Guo, C., Goldstein, T., Hannun, A., Van Der Maaten, L.: Certified data removal from machine learning models. In: III, H.D., Singh, A. (eds.) Proceedings of the 37th International Conference on Machine Learning. Proceedings of Machine Learning Research, vol. 119, pp. 3832–3842 (2020). https://doi.org/10.5555/3524938.3525297
12. Mökander, J., Juneja, P., Watson, D.S., Floridi, L.: The us algorithmic accountability act of 2022 vs. the EU artificial intelligence act: what can they learn from each other? Minds Mach. **32**, 751–758 (2022). https://doi.org/10.1007/s11023-022-09612-y
13. Japan: Japan: the development of artificial intelligence (2019). Link
14. Juliussen, B.A., Rui, J.P., Johansen, D.: Algorithms that forget: machine unlearning and the right to erasure. Comput. Law Secur. Rev. **51**, 105885 (2023). https://doi.org/10.1016/j.clsr.2023.105885
15. Kurmanji, M., Triantafillou, P., Hayes, J., Triantafillou, E.: Towards unbounded machine unlearning. Adv. Neural. Inf. Process. Syst. **36**, 1957–1987 (2023). https://doi.org/10.5555/3666122.3666217
16. Luciano, F.: Machine unlearning: its nature, scope, and importance for a "delete culture". Philos. Technol. **36**(2), 42 (2023). https://doi.org/10.1007/s13347-023-00644-5
17. Mariani, G., Monreale, A., Naretto, F.: Privacy risk assessment of individual psychometric profiles. In: Discovery Science - 24th International Conference, DS 2021. LNCS, vol. 12986, pp. 411–421. Springer, Cham (2021). https://doi.org/10.1007/978-3-030-88942-5_32
18. Monreale, A., et al.: Agnostic label-only membership inference attack. In: 17th International Conference on Network and System Security. Springer, Cham (2023). https://doi.org/10.1007/978-3-031-39828-5_14
19. Naretto, F., et al.: Evaluating the privacy exposure of interpretable global and local explainers. Trans. Data Priv. (2025)
20. Novelli, C., Casolari, F., Hacker, P., Spedicato, G., Floridi, L.: Generative ai in EU law: liability, privacy, intellectual property, and cybersecurity. Comput. Law Secur. Rev. **55**, 106066 (2024). https://doi.org/10.1016/j.clsr.2024.106066
21. Shokri, R., Stronati, M., Song, C., Shmatikov, V.: Membership inference attacks against machine learning models. In: 2017 IEEE Symposium on Security and Privacy (SP) (2017)
22. Wang, L., Chen, T., Yuan, W., Zeng, X., Wong, K.F., Yin, H.: KGA: a general machine unlearning framework based on knowledge gap alignment. In: Rogers, A., Boyd-Graber, J., Okazaki, N. (eds.) Proceedings of the 61st Annual Meeting of the Association for Computational Linguistics (Volume 1: Long Papers), pp. 13264–13276. Association for Computational Linguistics (2023). https://doi.org/10.18653/v1/2023.acl-long.740

Rotation- and Scale-Invariant Shape Extraction from Vessel Trajectories for Human-in-The-Loop Monitoring: A Case Study at the Ports of Brittany

Cristiano Landi[1,2](✉), Natalia Andrienko[3,4], and Gennady Andrienko[3,4]

[1] University of Pisa, Largo Bruno Pontecorvo 3, 56127 Pisa, PI, Italy
cristiano.landi@phd.unipi.it
[2] ISTI-CNR, Via Giuseppe Moruzzi 1, 56127 Pisa, PI, Italy
cristiano.landi@isti.cnr.it
[3] Fraunhofer Institute IAIS, 53757 Sankt Augustin, Germany
[4] City St George's, University of London, London EC1V 0HB, UK

Abstract. Maritime vessel monitoring is vital for ensuring navigational safety, protecting marine ecosystems, and enforcing regulations. This work presents a framework to support expert analysis and monitoring of vessel activities using AIS trajectory data. By extracting rotation- and scale-invariant shape signatures through a relative Hough transform, our system clusters and organizes subtrajectory patterns, enabling intuitive visual exploration. Experts interactively associate representative shapes with maritime events such as trawling or port visits, creating an event-to-shape map used for real-time detection in new trajectories. The framework efficiently captures geometric and motion dynamics, supports interpretable, trustworthy AI through human-in-the-loop validation, and facilitates labeled data creation to enhance future automated analysis. We demonstrate its effectiveness with a case study using real-world data of fishing vessels collected from the ports of Britannia, highlighting its potential for scalable, human-in-the-loop maritime surveillance.

Keywords: Vessel monitoring · Spatiotemporal data · Visual analytics · Interpretable Machine Learning · Trustworthy AI · Transparent Data Mining

1 Introduction

Efficient maritime vessel monitoring is critical for ensuring navigational safety, protecting marine environments, and supporting regulatory compliance [18]. A core element in this process is AIS (Automatic Identification System) data, which provides key information such as vessel identity, position, speed, and course. While numerous machine learning approaches have been proposed to process and analyze AIS data [15,24], a major challenge lies in the lack of clear, formal definitions for maritime events within this complex and heterogeneous data [2].

I. Koprinska et al. (Eds.): ECML PKDD 2025, CCIS 2842, pp. 621–631, 2026.
https://doi.org/10.1007/978-3-032-19105-2_43

Events such as entering or exiting a port, anchoring, or engaging in specific activities like trawling are commonly of interest, yet difficult to formally define in a consistent, machine-readable way [2]. Most machine learning approaches typically require large volumes of labeled data to detect such patterns reliably, yet labeled datasets in the maritime domain remain limited [23]. Recent approaches increasingly rely on deep learning methods [6,9,17,21], which can achieve good performance in identifying complex patterns. However, these models often function as black boxes, offering little insight into how decisions are made. This lack of interpretability becomes a serious limitation in settings where labeled ground truth is scarce or unavailable, as it prevents users from verifying or understanding the model's outputs. Human experts, by contrast, can frequently recognize these events by visually inspecting vessel trajectories on a map, drawing on contextual and domain knowledge. Yet relying on expert analysis for large-scale monitoring or labeling is not practical due to the significant time and cost involved. These challenges highlight the need for scalable approaches that combine the pattern recognition capabilities of automated systems with the contextual awareness of human expertise, ideally in a way that supports interpretability and minimal reliance on labeled data.

In this paper, we propose a framework to assist human experts in monitoring vessel activity near ports. The approach builds on two key observations. First, vessel activities can often be inferred from trajectory shapes [10] –for example, trawling typically involves slow movement with repeated turns, forming zigzags, loops, or shapes resembling the infinity symbol. Second, as shown in [12], applying the shapelet transform to trajectories captures both shape and movement dynamics. The framework builds on rotation- and scale-invariant trajectory representations extracted via a Hough transform [4,22], enabling robust comparison of subtrajectory shapes. Clustering groups similar shapes, while human-in-the-loop exploration allows experts to associate meaningful events with representative movement patterns. Finally, the framework uses these expert-validated shapes to detect and monitor events in new trajectories, supporting scalable, interactive maritime surveillance. Additionally, this interactive process also helps generate high-quality labeled data, which can support further machine learning applications.

The rest of the paper is organized as follows: Sect. 2 introduces the essential notation needed to understand the proposed framework; Sect. 3 presents the framework; Sect. 4 demonstrates its capabilities on a dataset of 71 fishing vessels[1] [1,19]. Finally, Sect. 5 concludes the paper and outlines future research directions.

2 Background

This section introduces the essential notation and definitions needed to understand the proposed framework. We define a trajectory as follows:

[1] Data extracted from https://zenodo.org/records/1167595.

Definition 1 (Trajectory). A *trajectory* X is a sequence of spatio-temporal points $X = \{(\mathbf{x}_1, t_1), \ldots, (\mathbf{x}_m, t_m)\} \in \mathbb{R}^{m\times 2}$ where the spatial vectors $\mathbf{x}_j = (\text{lat}_j, \text{long}_j)$ are sorted by increasing time t_j, i.e., $\forall 1 \leq j < m$ we have $t_j < t_{j+1}$.

For simplicity, we use a single symbol m to denote the lengths of the trajectories, even if a dataset can contain trajectories with a different number of observations. Similarly, we emphasize that there is no constraint on the sample rate, i.e., we can have a non-constant sample in the same trajectory. Furthermore, we define a *subtrajectory* as:

Definition 2 (Subtrajectory). Given a trajectory X of length m, a subtrajectory $\{\boldsymbol{s}_j, \ldots, \boldsymbol{s}_{j+l}\} \subset X$, of length $l \leq m$, is an ordered sequence of consecutive values such that $0 \leq j \leq m - l$. We denote such subtrajetory as $X_{j:j+l}$.

For simplicity, we define subtrajectories based on sliding windows over the number of observations. However, due to irregularities in such data, sliding windows based on time intervals [2] or traveled distance may be preferable.

Given a distance function d, we define the trajectory-to-subtrajectory distance vector $\boldsymbol{d}_{X,S}$ from trajectory X to subtrajectory S as:

$$\boldsymbol{d}_{X,S} = \left[d\big(shift(X_{j:j+l}), shift(S)\big)\right] \qquad \forall j \in [1, m-l] \tag{1}$$

where $shift(X) = \{\boldsymbol{x}_0 - \boldsymbol{x}_0, \ldots, \boldsymbol{x}_m - \boldsymbol{x}_0\}$. Additionally, as in [12,14], we define the best fitting of S in X as the minimum distance between X and S, i.e., $bestfit(X, S) = \min \boldsymbol{d}_{X,S}$.

Finally, we introduce the Hough Transform [4]. The Hough Transform is a feature extraction technique used in computer vision to detect geometric shapes by mapping points from Cartesian space into a parameter space. For line detection, each point in Cartesian space votes for all possible lines passing through it, typically parameterized in polar coordinates by (ρ, θ), where ρ is the perpendicular distance from the origin to the line, and θ is the angle of the line normal. Peaks in this accumulator space correspond to dominant linear structures. The voting process is governed by the equation $\rho = x\cos\theta + y\sin\theta$, which maps each point (x, y) into a sinusoidal curve in the (ρ, θ) space. The Hough accumulator is a 2D matrix of size $N_\rho \times N_\theta$, where N_ρ and N_θ are the number of discretized bins for ρ and θ, respectively. Although other computer vision trajectory analysis methods exist [7,11], this is the first application of the Hough Transform to this type of data. Unlike image-based approaches, our method applies the Hough Transform directly to point sets, allowing overlapping or repeated points to contribute proportionally more votes.

3 Framework

We introduce a framework for visually exploring vessel movements, composed of three phases: shape preparation, shape exploration, and vessel monitoring. The system integrates a rotation- and scale-invariant trajectory representation,

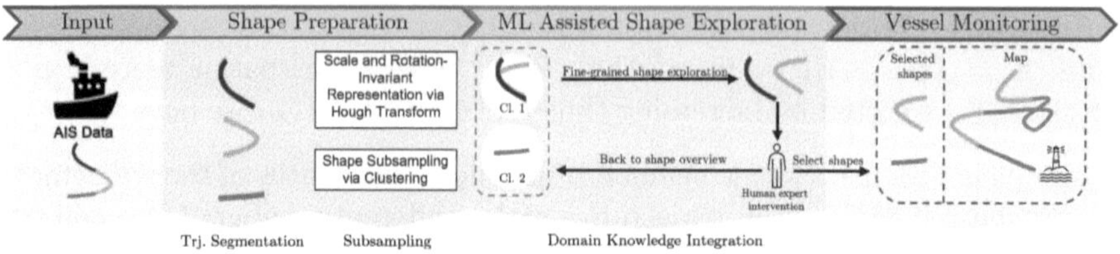

Fig. 1. Framework overview

a distance measure for variable-length comparisons, and multiple clustering algorithms, helping to organize shapes for user interaction.

These components are organized as shown in Fig. 1. The framework is composed of three phases: shape preparation, shape exploration, and vessel monitoring.

Shape Preparation. In this phase, the framework partitions the input trajectories and extracts a subsample of representative subtrajectories. Given a partitioning $p : X \rightarrow X_{0:l}, \ldots, X_{m-l:m}$ we compute the relative Hough accumulator. Partitioning can be performed using a fixed-length sliding window or via spatial tessellation, where trajectories are split according to spatial grids [5]. The choice of partitioning method is data-dependent and should be guided by insights into the underlying movement patterns. Inspired by [22], we extract the shape signature by summing the squared values in each column of the Hough accumulator. Each subtrajectory $X_{j:j+l}$ is then represented as a vector $X'_{j:j+l}$ of size N_θ. Fig. 2 illustrates this process: on the left is a visual representation of a movement pattern identifying trawling vessels; in the center, the Hough transform is shown, where each sinusoid corresponds to a point of the subtrajectory; on the right, the shape signature is obtained by summing the Hough accumulator vertically. The scale of the trajectory does not affect the shape signature, but rotation results in a shift along the θ axis. To account for this shift, we define the (dis)similarity between two shape signatures $X'_{j:j+l}$ and $X'_{h:h+l}$ as:

$$d_{Hough}(X'_{j:j+l}, X'_{h:h+l}) = \left| \sum_{i=0}^{\theta} X'_{j+i} - X'_{h+i} \right| \tag{2}$$

While [22] proposes using the magnitude of the Fourier Transform coefficients to handle rotation, our approach has lower computational complexity and avoids potential artifacts introduced by frequency domain analysis. Equation 2 takes the signed sums of the element-wise difference between the two shape signatures. This allows similar shapes with shifts in rotation or scale to yield a low distance, as differences tend to cancel out. Although such cancellation could theoretically occur for dissimilar shapes as well, our experimental evaluation showed this happening only in rare cases.

The shape preparation phase concludes by extracting a representative subsample of similar subtrajectories from different shapes. This is done by cluster-

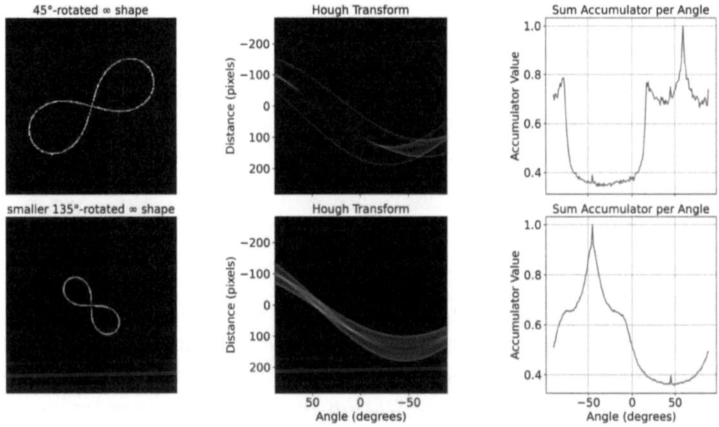

Fig. 2. Overview of shape signature extraction. Left: Example of a trawling vessel trajectory. Center: Hough transform of the subtrajectory, where each sinusoid corresponds to a trajectory point. Right: shape signature obtained by vertically summing the (squared) Hough accumulator.

ing shapes using the Hough-based shape signature, then sampling elements from each cluster[2].

Given a set of vessel trajectories, the framework splits each trajectory into segments using a partitioning function p. These segments are then transformed into rotation- and scale-invariant representations. A clustering algorithm groups similar shapes, and a sorting function organizes these clusters for user presentation.

Shape Exploration. The second phase integrates domain knowledge through a human-in-the-loop process.

Using the clusters from the previous phase, the expert selects relevant features and interesting shape clusters that align with specific movement patterns. Given the large shape set, the system filters the shapes within the chosen cluster and re-applies clustering based on the selected features, such as speed, acceleration, or trajectory complexity. The expert can iterate between shape-based and feature-based clustering, refining the selection to build a diverse set of shapes representing different vessel behaviors. To label events, the expert links each activity (e.g., trawling, entering port) to one or more representative shapes, creating the event-to-shape map E.

Vessel Monitoring. In the shape preparation phase, trajectory segments were extracted based purely on geometric differences. In the shape exploration phase, expert-defined features guided the selection and labeling of shapes, building the map E. In this final step, we use E to recognize events in new trajectories. This requires a similarity function that accounts for both geometric and kinematic

[2] Sampling methods depend on the clustering algorithm. For example, in k-means or k-medoids, the centroid or medoid of each cluster can serve as a representative.

aspects. We adopt the *bestfit* function, shown in [12], to match shapes while preserving motion dynamics. Depending on the selected shapes, we might need to handle invariance to rotation and scale, so we introduce a modified Euclidean distance. It is defined as a minimization problem over a rotation angle θ and a scale factor s, aligning two subtrajectories S_1 and S_2. The rotation angle is constrained to a bounded interval, e.g., $\theta \in [-\pi, \pi]$.

$$d(S_1, S_2) = \min_{\theta \in [-\pi,\pi],\ s>0} \|S_1 - s \cdot R(\theta) \cdot S_2\| \tag{3}$$

where $R(\theta)$ is the 2-dimensional rotation matrix. Although this enhanced distance is designed to be invariant to rotation and scale, using it in the shape preparation and exploration phases is computationally infeasible for a real dataset. The added cost of solving the minimization problem must now be considered in the overall complexity of the *bestfit* function, which is quadratic in the length of the input trajectories. Please note that the modified Euclidean distance can be avoided if, during the shape exploration phase, the expert selects representative shapes that already cover different orientations and scales. Thanks to the structure of the framework, the initial clustering based on rotation- and scale-invariant signatures groups such variation together, making it easier for the expert to include them in the event-to-shape map E.

Finally, the framework renders a geographic visualization showing the spatial distribution of detected events, allowing users to observe where specific vessel activities occur. This helps analysts interpret patterns, verify detections, and identify areas of interest or unusual behavior.

4 Case Study

In this case study, the framework processes real AIS data from 71 fishing vessels by first segmenting their trajectories into subtrajectories of approximately 10 km with a 3 km overlap[3], totaling 12520 subtrajectories.

For initial clustering of the shape representations, we tested OPTICS[4] [3,8] and HDBSCAN[5] [16]. OPTICS identified 1232 clusters, while HDBSCAN identified 983. The distance function used is the one described in Eq. 2. To better evaluate the similarity between the results of the two clustering algorithms, we used V-measure [20], which is the harmonic mean of homogeneity and completeness. Homogeneity measures whether each cluster contains only members of a single class, while completeness assesses whether all members of a given class are assigned to the same cluster; both measures range from 0 to 1, the higher the better. We obtained a V-measure of 0.846, suggesting that the two results are quite

[3] Dataset available at: https://zenodo.org/records/1167595 [19].

[4] We tested different values of the *eps* and *bic_eps* hyperparameters without significant shifts in the results. We selected the result obtained with default sklearn hyperparameters for further analysis.

[5] with a minimum cluster size of 5.

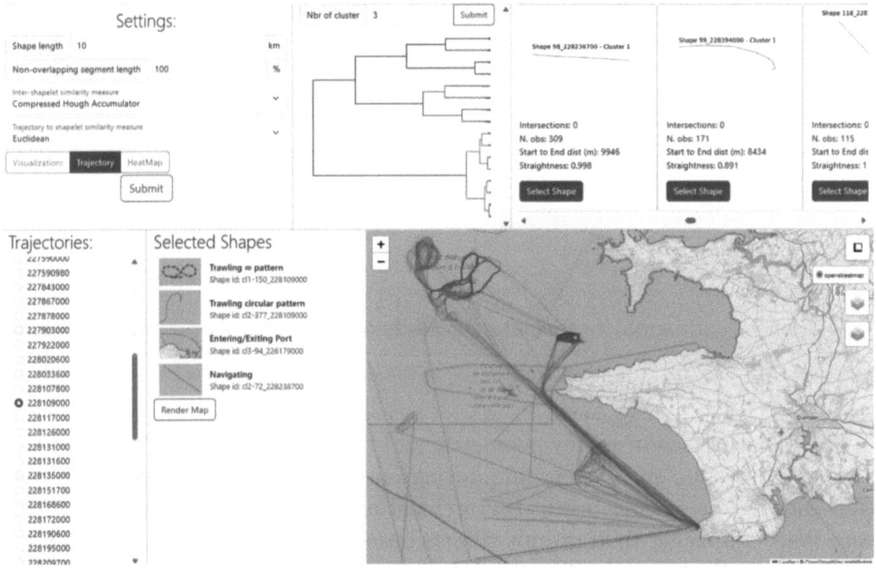

Fig. 3. Monitoring System

Table 1. Median values per cluster for the three selected features.

	Cluster 1	Cluster 2	Cluster 3	Cluster 4	Cluster 5	Cluster 6
SE (m)	3700	9819	6910	3463	1088	5128
I	0	0	0	0	1	12
Str	0.650	0.997	0.908	0.999	0.420	0.596

similar, i.e., OPTICS essentially refines the HDBSCAN clusters. OPTICS is chosen due to its data-driven approach that automatically determines the number of clusters based on density. This avoids the need to pre-specify cluster counts, which is important given the variability and complexity of vessel trajectories. The resulting clusters represent distinct movement patterns in the data.

To organize these shapes for presenting to an expert, we selected three features [13]: the distance between the start and end points of a subtrajectory (*SE*), straightness (*Str*), and the number of self-intersections (I). For a given (sub)trajectory X of length m, the features are computed as follows:

$$SE(X) = g(\boldsymbol{x}_1, \boldsymbol{x}_m) \qquad Str(X) = \frac{g(\boldsymbol{x}_{min}, \boldsymbol{x}_{max})}{\sum_{i=1}^{m} g(\boldsymbol{x}_i, \boldsymbol{x}_{i+1})} \qquad I(X) = nbr.\ int.\ lines \tag{4}$$

where $g(\cdot)$ compute the geodesic distance using the *WGS-84* ellipsoid and x_{min} and x_{max} represents the minimum and maximum coordinates of trajectory X.

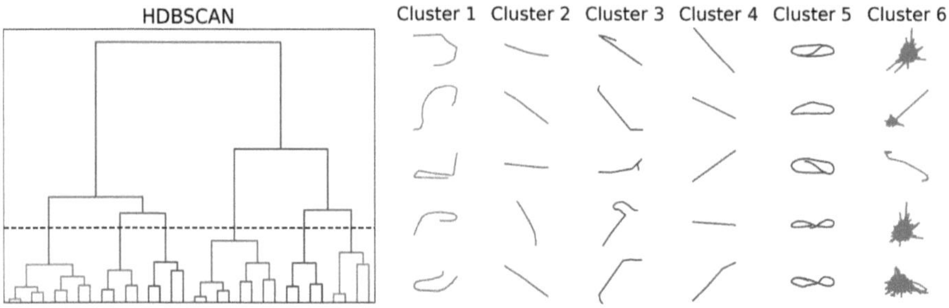

Fig. 4. (left) Dendrogram from hierarchical clustering. (right) Subsample of shapes from each cluster

These features capture key geometric and behavioral characteristics relevant to maritime events, such as circling during anchoring or straight-line movement when entering or exiting ports. Hierarchical agglomerative k-means clustering, using Ward's linkage, then groups shapes based on these features, and the dendrogram visualization (Fig. 3) offers the user an intuitive way to explore relationships among shape clusters at different levels of granularity. Figure 4 (left) shows the dendrogram from hierarchical clustering; the black dashed line marks the inter-cluster distance used to cut and obtain 6 clusters. Figure 4 (right) shows a subsample of shapes from each cluster, while Table 1 reports the median value per cluster for the three selected features. Clusters 2, 3, and 4 mainly consist of almost straight, non-intersecting lines and differ in how far the subtrajectory extends. Clusters 2 and 4 include straight trajectories with no return, typically representing transit. The key difference is the distance between the start and end points: cluster 2 has a median SE value of 9819 meters –close to the partitioning threshold–, while cluster 4 has a significantly lower median SE value of 3463 m. Cluster 3, in contrast, has lower SE and Str values, appearing almost straight (Str) but with more curvature (SE). Clusters 1 and 5 display curvilinear patterns, often linked to trawling. Cluster 1 features large, smooth curves with few or no intersections, suggesting wide-area movements. Cluster 5, in contrast, contains intersecting paths forming tight loops or figure-eight shapes, indicating more localized activity. Cluster 6 includes dense, intersecting trajectories typical of anchored vessels drifting slightly, forming compact, repetitive shapes. Since clusters can reflect overlapping behaviors and no single cluster maps cleanly to one activity, expert input and iterative, human-guided shape exploration are essential. The proposed user interface supports interactive selection of clusters and individual shapes, enabling domain experts to label movement patterns corresponding to maritime events of interest. This human-in-the-loop approach leverages expert knowledge to build an event-to-shape map, improving detection accuracy for subsequent monitoring.

Finally, once shapes are associated with events, the user can select specific vessel trajectories and visualize detected events on an interactive map, providing spatial context to the identified behaviors. Figure 3 illustrates the GUI in action, showing the clustering dendrogram, shape previews, and event mapping. While still under development, the tool offers a practical and extensible base for refining event detection and supporting real-world maritime monitoring.

5 Conclusion

We introduced a framework for expert analysis and monitoring of vessel activities by visually exploring movement patterns. Using rotation- and scale-invariant shape representations combined with interactive clustering, the system effectively identifies and labels key maritime events like trawling and port visits. Unlike traditional methods that depend heavily on labeled data or predefined rules, our approach leverages human expertise through intuitive visual interfaces, enabling flexible, scalable analysis with minimal prior assumptions. A demonstration with fishing vessel data shows its practical value for scalable, human-in-the-loop maritime surveillance. The initial setup may be time-consuming and costly, as it requires expert exploration to build the event-to-shape map. However, once created, the map can be reused for new data with only minor updates and can also support automatic decision systems with human oversight.

Since the framework doesn't rely on specific locations, we plan to test its adaptability across different ports. Future work includes organizing events into transition graphs to support higher-level behavioral analysis, integrating live AIS data for real-time monitoring, and expanding the approach to other domains such as air traffic control. We also aim to develop quantitative evaluation metrics and conduct user studies to assess system effectiveness, usability, and expert adoption in operational settings.

Acknowledgments. This work has been partially supported by the Italian Project Fondo Italiano per la Scienza FIS00001966 "MIMOSA", by the European Community Horizon 2020 programme under the funding schemes ERC-2018-ADG G.A. 834756 "XAI", by the European Commission under the NextGeneration EU programme – National Recovery and Resilience Plan Project: "SoBigData.it – Prot. IR0000013 – Av. n. 3264 del 28/12/2021, M4C2 - Investimento 1.3, Partenariato Esteso PE00000013 - "FAIR" - Spoke 1 "Human-centered AI", and *GreenDatAI* G.A. 101070416 and Crex-Data (grant no. 101092749), and by Federal Ministry of Education and Research of Germany and the state of North-Rhine Westphalia as part of the *Lamarr Institute for Machine Learning and Artificial Intelligence* (Lamarr22B).

Disclosure of Interests. The authors have no competing interests to declare that are relevant to the content of this article.

References

1. Andrienko, N.V., Andrienko, G.L.: Visual analytics of vessel movement. In: Guide to Maritime Informatics, pp. 149–170. Springer, Cham (2021). https://doi.org/10.1007/978-3-030-61852-0_5

2. Andrienko, N.V., Andrienko, G.L., Artikis, A., Mantenoglou, P., Rinzivillo, S.: Human-in-the-loop: visual analytics for building models recognizing behavioral patterns in time series. IEEE Comput. Graphics Appl. **44**(3), 14–29 (2024)
3. Ankerst, M., Breunig, M.M., Kriegel, H., Sander, J.: OPTICS: ordering points to identify the clustering structure. In: SIGMOD Conference, pp. 49–60. ACM Press (1999)
4. Ballard, D.H.: Generalizing the hough transform to detect arbitrary shapes. Pattern Recognit. **13**(2), 111–122 (1981)
5. Boots, B., Tiefelsdorf, M.: Global and local spatial autocorrelation in bounded regular tessellations. J. Geogr. Syst. **2**(4), 319–348 (2000)
6. Duan, H., Ma, F., Miao, L., Zhang, C.: A semi-supervised deep learning approach for vessel trajectory classification based on ais data. Ocean Coast. Manage. **218**, 106015 (2022). https://doi.org/10.1016/j.ocecoaman.2021.106015
7. Endo, Y., Toda, H., Nishida, K., Kawanobe, A.: Deep feature extraction from trajectories for transportation mode estimation. In: PAKDD (2). Lecture Notes in Computer Science, vol. 9652, pp. 54–66. Springer, Cham (2016). https://doi.org/10.1007/978-3-319-31750-2_5
8. Ester, M., Kriegel, H., Sander, J., Xu, X.: A density-based algorithm for discovering clusters in large spatial databases with noise. In: KDD. pp. 226–231. AAAI Press (1996)
9. Han, F., Liu, Y., Tian, H., Li, J., Tian, Y.: A comprehensive framework incorporating deep learning for analyzing fishing vessel activity using automatic identification system data. ICES J. Mar. Sci. **82**(2), fsae166 (2024). https://doi.org/10.1093/icesjms/fsae166
10. Kontopoulos, I., Chatzikokolakis, K., Tserpes, K., Zissis, D.: Classification of vessel activity in streaming data. In: DEBS, pp. 153–164. ACM (2020)
11. Kontopoulos, I., Makris, A., Tserpes, K.: Traclets: a trajectory representation and classification library. SoftwareX **21**, 101306 (2023)
12. Landi, C., Guidotti, R.: Shape-based methods in mobility data analysis: Effectiveness and limitations. GeoInformatica (2025), just Accepted
13. Landi, C., Guidotti, R., Nanni, M., Monreale, A.: The trajectory interval forest classifier for trajectory classification. In: SIGSPATIAL/GIS, pp. 67:1–67:4. ACM (2023)
14. Landi, C., Spinnato, F., Guidotti, R., Monreale, A., Nanni, M.: Geolet: an interpretable model for trajectory classification. In: IDA. Lecture Notes in Computer Science, vol. 13876, pp. 236–248. Springer (2023)
15. Liu, H., Chen, X., Wang, Y., Zhang, B., Chen, Y., Zhao, Y., Zhou, F.: Visualization and visual analysis of vessel trajectory data: a survey. Vis. Inf. **5**(4), 1–10 (2021)
16. McInnes, L., Healy, J., Astels, S.: Hdbscan: aierarchical density based clustering. J. Open Source Softw. **2**(11), 205 (2017)
17. Petry, L.M., Júnior, A.S., Bogorny, V., Brandoli, B., Matwin, S.: Challenges in vessel behavior and anomaly detection: from classical machine learning to deep learning. In: Canadian AI. Lecture Notes in Computer Science, vol. 12109, pp. 401–407. Springer, Cham (2020). https://doi.org/10.1007/978-3-030-47358-7_41
18. Pitsikalis, M., Artikis, A., Dreo, R., Ray, C., Camossi, E., Jousselme, A.: Composite event recognition for maritime monitoring. In: DEBS, pp. 163–174. ACM (2019)
19. Ray, C., Dréo, R., Camossi, E., Jousselme, A.L.: Heterogeneous integrated dataset for maritime intelligence, surveillance, and reconnaissance (2018). https://doi.org/10.5281/zenodo.1167595
20. Rosenberg, A., Hirschberg, J.: V-measure: a conditional entropy-based external cluster evaluation measure. In: EMNLP-CoNLL, pp. 410–420. ACL (2007)

21. Shahir, A.Y., Charalampous, T., Tayebi, M.A., Glässer, U., Wehn, H.: Triptracker: unsupervised learning of fishing vessel routine activity patterns. In: IEEE BigData, pp. 1928–1939. IEEE (2021)
22. Vlachos, M., Vagena, Z., Yu, P.S., Athitsos, V.: Rotation invariant indexing of shapes and line drawings. In: CIKM, pp. 131–138. ACM (2005)
23. Wang, S., Bao, Z., Culpepper, J.S., Cong, G.: A survey on trajectory data management, analytics, and learning. ACM Comput. Surv. **54**(2), 39:1–39:36 (2022)
24. Yang, Y., Liu, Y., Li, G., Zhang, Z., Liu, Y.: Harnessing the power of machine learning for ais data-driven maritime research: a comprehensive review. Transp. Res. Part E Logist. Transp. Rev. **183**, 103426 (2024)

Author Index

I. Koprinska et al. (Eds.): ECML PKDD 2025, CCIS 2842, pp. 633–635, 2026.
https://doi.org/10.1007/978-3-032-19105-2

MIX
Papier aus verantwortungsvollen Quellen
Paper from responsible sources
FSC® C105338
FSC
www.fsc.org

If you have any concerns about our products,
you can contact us on
ProductSafety@springernature.com

In case Publisher is established outside the EU,
the EU authorized representative is:
Springer Nature Customer Service Center GmbH
Europaplatz 3, 69115 Heidelberg, Germany

Printed by Libri Plureos GmbH
in Hamburg, Germany